ORGANIZAT[...]N[...] BEHAV[...]

A Management Approach

Harry R. Knudson

University of Washington

C. Patrick Fleenor

Seattle University

Winthrop Publishers, Inc.

Cambridge, Massachusetts

Library of Congress Cataloging in Publication Data

Main entry under title:

Organizational behavior.

Includes bibliographical references.
1. Organizational behavior — Addresses, essays,
lectures. 2. Organizational behavior — Case studies.
3. Industrial management — Addresses, essays, lectures.
4. Industrial management — Case studies. I. Knudson,
Harry R. II. Fleenor, C. Patrick
HD58.7.069   658.4   77-28387
ISBN 0-87626-623-5

Cover design by Karyl Klopp
Interior design by Richard Spencer

© 1978 by Winthrop Publishers, Inc.
    17 Dunster Street, Cambridge, Massachusetts 02138

10   9   8   7   6   5   4   3   2   1

to

Sallye, Sara, and Eric

and

Margaret, Wendy, Michelle, and Timothy

and to

our parents

CONTENTS

PART 2
COMMUNICATION IN ORGANIZATIONS / 73

PART 3
INDIVIDUAL MOTIVATION AND BEHAVIOR / 119

PART 4
GROUPS IN ORGANIZATIONS / 177

PART 5
LEADERSHIP / 219

READINGS

CASES

EXERCISES

PART 6
ORGANIZATIONAL RELATIONSHIPS
AND DECISION MAKING / 287

READINGS

PART 7

THE MANAGEMENT OF CONFLICT / 375

PART 8
CHANGE IN ORGANIZATIONS   /   415

PREFACE

Organizational Behavior: A Management Approach deals with the broad field of organizational behavior, with concentration on "people problems" in organizations from the viewpoint of the manager. This managerial viewpoint is extremely important and is a constant thread running through the book.

We have developed the book for the first course in subjects such as management and organization, organizational behavior, or human relations at whatever level it appears, and have presumed no previous study or knowledge of the area on the part of the students. Most of the materials are aimed at this level, although in some places there are more advanced materials building upon the basic concepts.

The book consists primarily of a variety of good, tested teaching materials so that the instructor faced with teaching the initial course wil have a highly useable, proven package covering the significant concepts and issues in the area.

Many books in the field of organizational behavior place a strong emphasis on the individual and examine the issues from a highly psychological, individual perspective. While this is important, we feel that an action-oriented, management approach is more appropriate for those who are or who aspire to be practicing managers. The difference in the two approaches is notable. There is quite a iontrast, for example, between understanding the impact of group dynamics on an individual and understanding the impact on a manager who must, somehow, *do something* with the informal groups in his organization. The difference between the two is the difference between simple understanding and understanding leading to action.

The book consists of a series of conceptual readings, cases, and experiential exercises. We have seen strong emphasis on experiential approaches lately, and while we think these have great merit, it seems to us that there is benefit to be derived from a balanced approach to the teaching of organizational behavior — covering some of the more traditional methodologies as well as the newer things — especially at a basic level. Our experience with the experiential approach — and we have a great deal of this — suggests that it may be less effective at the basic levels simply because students do not have enough meaningful experience with which to relate to classroom simulations. For this reason, experiential approaches tend to work much better with managers and older students than with younger students. However, there are some positive benefits to be gained by using experiential materials, and we have included an ample number of exercises in the book. The criteria for selection of the readings were: (1) The readings should be understandable to students without previous knowledge in the field. We purposely avoided readings heavily laden with jargon from the social sciences or with strongly research-oriented points of view. (2) The readings should be "classics" in the field — readings that have stood the test of time and are still valid. It did not concern us that an article had been published several years ago *if* it still made sense from a managerial point of view. (3) The articles should emphasize applications of theory rather than theory itself. Given our managerial emphasis we were most concerned with how the manager *uses* information. While we assumed that it will be some time before some readers will in fact be managers, we were interested in impressing upon them the action orientation of the manager and how managerial concepts actually can be put to use. (4) The readings should be relatively short. Given the fundamental level of the approach, we felt it inappropriate that the book should contain very lengthy articles. We were concerned with a relatively small number of very important basic concepts, and we wanted students to understand them properly. (5) The readings should be selected from a variety of sources so that the book would not have the flavor of any particular journal or publication.

The cases are, without exception, cases that have been widely used and proven very effective in classroom and management seminar situations. The cases are action oriented, and in almost every instance an action decision must be made.

Many of the same kinds of comments apply to the experiential exercises. We have focused upon action-oriented exercises in which the participants must take some actions and then live with the consequences of these actions. We have developed several simulations that are in a context meaningful to less experienced students, dealing with issues current for the students rather than issues which they may face several years from now as managers. In addition, several of the exercises require students to come in contact with real organizations.

In summary, we have provided in one volume a unique package of proven, effective teaching materials that is most appropriate for the initial course in organizational behavior.

We want to acknowledge the help and assistance of many organizations and individuals who have cooperated with us in this endeavor. Of major importance are those who granted permission for us to use materials that they had developed or that had appeared in their publications. These contributions are acknowledged individually on the first page of each selection in the book. The willingness of these organizations and individuals to share their materials made it possible for this book to make a significant contribution to teaching materials available in the field of organizational behavior.

A special note of appreciation goes to Bob Davis, of the Prentice-Hall/Winthrop field staff, who provided the impetus for the book. With his boundless enthusiasm and mixture of good and bad (mostly bad) jokes, he kept us stimulated, on track, and more or less on schedule.

Then there's Nona! We wish that we could accurately describe her participation in this project, but in order to retain the "G" rating the book has been given, we will simply say that she contributed greatly to design and organization as well as to the mechanics of getting the manuscript in final and acceptable form. Nona particularly inspired us on the several occasions when we believed the project to be under control. She assured us that, as usual, we were wrong.

Seattle, Washington   H.R.K.
                                                                             C.P.F.

PART I

CURRENT ISSUES AND PERSPECTIVES

The practicing manager has responsibilities extending beyond the immediate details of his or her task environment. Increasingly, to be successful, managers must be future oriented and develop sensitivity to changes in their surroundings.

In this first part, we introduce you to a few very important areas in which the manager must have knowledge: characteristics of workers, common barriers to managerial effectiveness, and some behavioral aspects of the ethical-legal environment. To perform effectively, the manager must know the organization and the environment within which the organization exists. While there are many dimensions of the organizational environment — competitors, suppliers, customers, government agencies, and the general economic situation — those aspects of management concerned with human behavior seem to be of primary importance to managers and are the focus of this book.

Within the organization, the manager must be aware and have knowledge of characteristics of workers and managers, the decision-making process, the patterns of communication, and the other institutional arrangements that facilitate or hinder the accomplishment of organizational and personal goals. Finally, the manager must know himself or herself. The more one knows about one's self, the easier it is to overcome biases and known weaknesses.

If you read the articles in this chapter carefully and reflect upon the questions we have asked, you have taken the first step toward being an effective manager: knowledge of the environment in which you operate.

"Adapting to the New Work Ethic" by Myers and Myers addresses an area of substantial concern and interest to sociologists, social psychologists, and managers, an apparently "new" attitude toward work. The reading relates some interesting research on personal values and lifestyles. As you read the article, try to frame in your own mind the conditions that might cause personal development to be arrested at one of the lower levels of psychological existence described by the authors. Might some jobs restrict progress in psychological growth? If so, should such jobs be restructured to allow potential for growth? Regardless of the answer, there will be significant costs — Can you think of some? If it is desirable for workers to "grow" on the job, what could a manager do to encourage an employee to move from one level to another?

In recent years managers and many behavioral scientists have been discussing a phenomenon that they call "blue collar blues." Blue collar blues are said to afflict production line workers, those stalwarts who often spend the work day performing endless repetitions of a few simple maneuvers. These workers' prospects are to spend another ten years, twenty years, or even more doing the same thing day after day. It is argued that workers afflicted by blue collar blues are, at best, indifferent toward the job, and at worst actually engage in sabotage just to relieve the monotony of work. Although the production worker may find enjoyment and fulfill his or her needs outside the job to a substantial degree, approximately a third of his or her waking hours may be spent doing something distasteful.

Although the preceding is greatly oversimplified, impressive empirical evidence exists that millions of workers in the industrialized countries suffer from what could be called blue collar blues. More recently, evidence has indicated that other groups of workers, including many office workers, suffer from the syndrome. In fact, the blues may strike any worker who feels that he or she is not encouraged to perform at high levels, whose job does not allow for personal growth, and whose task environment does not allow autonomy or creative thought. What kinds of similarities can you discern between clerical jobs and assembly line jobs? What is the effect of blue collar blues on the organization? What is the effect on society? In the face of a changed orientation toward work, what needs to be done? And who should do it? As you ponder these questions, keep in mind that, ultimately, the responsibility for implementation of new programs will lie with the managers of the next decade.

In "The Psychological Barriers to Management Effectiveness," Schaffer explores some common psychological factors that affect our ability to perform as managers. The way we perceive the world around us greatly affects the way we react to situations. Even when observing the same situation as another person we may interpret the situation quite differently. For example, when policemen interview witnesses to a crime, they often find that the witnesses' descriptions conflict. In most cases, none of the witnesses lie but report what they actually saw. The problem is that they saw different things! The reasons for the different reports are many and often very complicated but frequently rest in an individual psychological readiness to perceive things in a certain way.

Schaffer describes some of the more common psychological theories and concludes with recommendations for minimizing the effect of the most common barriers to effectiveness. Keep in mind that psychological barriers afflict everyone; so the manager may often be faced with the dual problem of diagnosing and attacking personal barriers, as well as barriers in his or her subordinates.

After finishing the article, you may find it helpful to write down the behavioral escapes you have used in the last week and the situations in which you used them. Some people keep a log for extended periods to catalog their use of escapes. You may wish to begin a log for yourself and maintain it for the remainder of the quarter or semester. What other barriers not listed in the article might apply to you or to other people?

In recent years, the rights of minority groups and the obligation of organizations to safeguard those rights have been matters of much discussion and publicity. Although almost half the work force in the United States is composed of women, there is no question that many members of this large minority have been discriminated against in employment practices. Many recent E.E.O. (Equal Employment Opportunity) law suits have demonstrated clearly that women often are not afforded the same opportunities or the same salaries as males with the equivalent education, experience, and skill levels. What are the causes for this apparently systematic discrimimation? In "The Executive Man and Woman: The Issue of Sexuality," Bradford, Sargent, and Sprague address what are considered to be some of the major causes of sex discrimination. Although the reading focuses upon the executive level of the organization, the effect is visible throughout many organizations, and the resulting problems are serious regardless of level.

You may be surprised to learn that much of the problem apparently lies in the early socialization process. Behavioral scientists have clearly documented that male and female children are treated differently in specific and systematic ways from the day of birth. For example, little boys are expected to be dominant, aggressive, and competitive, while little girls are expected to be submissive, polite, and noncompetitive. As we learn and accept the male or female role, we inherit the "blind spots" that come with the role.

As you read the article, reflect upon how your own sexuality influences your interaction with other people. The problem described by Bradford et al. is a serious one and cannot be solved at the institutional level alone. Individual managers and aspiring managers must be prepared to cope with the situation as it arises and as it concerns them.

ADAPTING TO THE NEW WORK ETHIC

M. Scott Myers and Susan S. Myers

Do you "see red" when a long-haired man walks into your office? Are there some "ungrateful wretches" in your organization who don't appreciate what the company is doing for them? What's wrong with people today who don't do what they're told to do? Whatever happened to company loyalty?

As organizational psychologists, we are finding supervisory problems to be symptoms of clashing or poorly understood value systems. A supervisor in a production department expressed it this way:

> People here aren't what they used to be. Several years ago most of our employees had WASP (White, Anglo-Saxon, Protestant) values. They were ambitious, conscientious, hard-working and honest, and you could count on them to get the job done. It was relatively easy to supervise this kind of person.
>
> We still have some of these, but now we're getting some different types who are difficult to supervise. Some are hippies who are bright enough, but their ideas are far-out, and they don't seem to care about pay, job security or recognition from their supervisor.
>
> At the other extreme is a troublemaker or free-loader type who isn't interested in the quantity or quality of work and is frequently absent or tardy. Some of them seem to look for opportunities to break the rules and will lie, cheat and steal. Many of these come from the ghetto.

This supervisor's lament is echoed by those who apply traditional supervisory methods to people of the new work ethic. The problem is not restricted to business organizations, but is encountered in all walks of life. Parents and teachers are sometimes distressed by the appearance and behavior of young people. Clergymen are finding more concern with the here-and-now than in the hereafter, and government officials are encountering increasing rebellion against bureaucratic constraints. Union leaders are losing control of their members, and athletic coaches are learning that Lombardi-like charisma and domination no longer assure obedience and commitment among athletes. Some managers see these problems as symptoms of illness in society. A board chairman of a billion-dollar corporation cited as a sign of deteriorating values the inability of small local art shop managers to hire and retain young people. Noting that the pay was adequate and the work not uninteresting, he suggested that perhaps exposure to a severe economic depression might help realign their values.

This article provides a framework

From *The Business Quarterly,* Winter 1973, pp. 48–58. Reprinted by permission of *The Business Quarterly* (School of Business Administration, The University of Western Ontario, London, Canada).

for understanding this problem, and defines some practical guidelines for organizational behavior, climate, and systems appropriate for people of today's values.

VALUES — OLD AND NEW

Based on 16 years of observation and research, Professor Graves[1] of Union College found that people seem to evolve through consecutive levels of "psychological existence" which are descriptive of personal values and life styles. Relatively independent of intelligence, a person's level of psychological existence can become arrested at a given level or it can move upward or downward depending on that person's cultural conditioning and his perception of the opportunities and constraints in his environment.

A diagrammatic version of Graves' framework is presented in Exhibit 1. The single-term label used at each stage of existence inadequately describes the syndrome it represents, but is used for convenience of discussion.

Level 1. The *reactive* level of existence is most commonly observed in newborn babies or in people psychologically arrested in, or regressed to, infancy. They are unaware of themselves or others as human beings, and simply react to hunger, thirst, urination, defecation, sex, and other periodic physiological stimuli. Few people remain at

[1]Clare W. Graves, "Levels of Existence: An Open System Theory of Values," *Journal of Humanistic Psychology*, Fall 1970 Vol. 10, No. 2, pp. 131–155.

Existential

High tolerance for ambiguity and people with differing values. Likes to do jobs in his own way without constraints of authority or bureaucracy. Goal oriented but toward a broader arena and longer time perspective.

Manipulative

Ambitious to achieve higher status and recognition. Strives to manipulate people and things. May achieve goals through gamesmanship, persuasion, bribery or official authority.

Egocentric

Rugged individualism. Selfish, thoughtless, unscrupulous, dishonest. Has not learned to function within the constraints imposed by society. Responds primarily to power.

Reactive

Not aware of self or others as individuals or human beings. Reacts to basic physiological needs. Mostly restricted to infants.

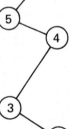

Sociocentric

High affiliation needs. Dislikes violence, conformity, materialism and manipulative management. Concerned with social issues and the dignity of man.

Conformist

Low tolerance for ambiguity and for people whose values differ from his own. Attracted to rigidly defined roles in accounting, engineering, military, and tends to perpetuate the status quo. Motivated by a cause, philosophy, or religion.

Tribalistic

Found mostly in primitive societies and ghettos. Lives in a world of magic, witchcraft and superstition. Strongly influenced by tradition and the power exerted by the boss, tribal chieftain, policeman, schoolteacher, politician, and other authority figures.

EXHIBIT 1 • Levels of Psychological Existence

this stage as they move toward adulthood; however, those at the threshold of subsistence in some of the larger cities of the Middle East seem to be little beyond this stage of existence. People at this level are generally not found on payrolls of organizations.

Level 2. Most people, as a matter of course, move out of the reactive existence to a *tribalistic* stage. Tribalism is characterized by concern with feelings of pain, temperature control, safety, and by tacit submission to an authority figure, whether he be a supervisor, policeman, government official, teacher, priest, parent, big brother or gang leader. Tribalism is commonly observed in primitive cultures where magic, witchcraft, ritual, and superstition prevail. For example, the Bantu who work in the coal, gold and diamond mines of South Africa are largely tribalistic. Man at this level is locked into the rigid traditions of his tribe, and he is dominated by the tribal chieftain or his substitute.

Level 3. *Egocentrism* is an overly assertive form of rugged individualism. This person's behavior reflects a philosophy which seems to say, "to hell with the rest of the world, I'm for myself." He, or she, is typically pre-moral — thus unscrupulous, selfish, aggressive, restless, impulsive and, in general, not psychologically inclined to live within the constraints imposed by society's moral precepts. To this person, might is right, and authoritarian management, preferably benevolent, seems necessary to keep him in line. Typical group techniques are not usually successful for this type of person, but structured participative management, properly administered, promises to be an effective

strategy for getting him out of this egocentric mode.

Both egocentrism and tribalism are found in U.S. ghettos — not as a function of ethnic determinants, but rather as a result of cultural disadvantage. Now that equal opportunity laws are accelerating the employment of minority people, egocentric and tribalistic behavior is more prevalent in organizations.

Level 4. Persons at the *conformity* level of existence have low tolerance for ambiguity, have difficulty in accepting people whose values differ from their own, and have a need to get others to accept their values. They usually subordinate themselves to a philosophy, cause, or religion, and tend to be attracted to vocations circumscribed by dogma or clearly defined rules. Though often perceived as docile, the conformist will assert or sacrifice himself in violence if his values are threatened. For example, in 1954, the normally law-abiding Archie Bunkers of Little Rock, Arkansas, erupted in violence against equal opportunity measures which violated the predominant value system of that region. Conformists prefer authoritarianism to autonomy, but will respond to participation if it is prescribed by an acceptable authority, and if it does not violate deep-seated values. They like specific job descriptions and procedures, and have little tolerance for supervisory indecision or weakness. People at this level have been the mainstay of the hourly work force since the beginning of the Industrial Revolution.

Level 5. The fifth level of psychological existence is characterized by *manipulative* or materialistic behavior. Persons at this level are typically products of the Horatio Alger, rags-to-riches philosophy — striving to achieve their goals through the manipulation of things and people within their environment. They thrive on gamesmanship, politics, competition, and entrepreneurial effort, measure their success in terms of materialistic gain and power, and are inclined to flaunt self-earned (as against hereditary) status symbols. Typical of level 5 persons are business managers, who define their goals and strategies in terms such as cash flow, return on investment, profits, share of the market and net sales billed, and their focus is generally on short-term targets such as the quarterly review or annual plan. They tend to perceive people as expense items rather than assets, to be manipulated as supplies and equipment.

Level 6. People at the sixth, or *sociocentric,* level of existence have high affiliation needs. Getting along is more important than getting ahead, and the approval of people they respect is valued over individual fame. At this level he may return to religiousness, not for its ritual or dogma, but rather for its spiritual attitude and concern with social issues. Many members of the original "hippie" cult were sociocentrics — their hirsute and dungareed appearance being a symbolic put-down of the organization-man appearance approved by the establishment. On the job the sociocentric responds well to participative management, but only on the condition that he and the others he values believe in his product or service. He tends to articulate his protests openly, but characteristically dislikes violence and would counter authoritarianism with passive resistance. Sociocentrics are frequently perceived as cop-outs by

4's and 5's, and their behavior is not generally rewarded in business organizations. As a result, persons at this level who do not ultimately capitulate by regressing to the organizationally accepted modes of manipulation and conformity, or adapt by evolving to the seventh level of psychological existence, may become organizational problems because of alchoholism, drug abuse, or other self-punitive behavior.

Level 7. The individual at the *existential* level of existence has high tolerance for ambiguity, and for persons whose values differ from his own. On the job his behavior might say, "O.K., I understand the job to be done — now leave me alone and let me do it my way." In some respects he is a blend of levels 5 and 6 in that he is goal-oriented toward organizational success (level 5) and concerned with the dignity of his fellowman (level 6). Like the level 5, he is concerned with organizational profits, the quarterly review, and the annual plan, but he is also concerned with the ten-year or fifty-year plan and the impact of the organization on its members, the community and the environment. Like the level 6, he is repelled by the use of violence. However, his outspoken intolerance of inflexible systems, restrictive policy, status symbols, and the arbitrary use of authority is threatening to most level 4 and 5 managers, and he may be expelled from the organization for reasons of nonconformity or insubordination.

Most people in today's organizations can be described in terms of levels 2 through 7. Though level 7 is not the ultimate level of development, models for higher levels are sufficiently scarce to make their definition difficult and, for the purpose of this paper, unnecessary.

MEASURING VALUES IN THE BUSINESS ORGANIZATION

Seeing in Graves' theory a possible explanation for many organizational problems, we chose this framework for analyzing the problem of disparate values in organizations. The first step was to develop and standardize a questionnaire* for measuring levels of psychological existence and for determining the extent to which the various levels are represented in the business organization. The Values for Working questionnaire consists of 18 job and employment-oriented types of items, such as systems and procedures, job descriptions, benefits, career development, and supervision. Each multiple choice item was developed and refined so that each of its six responses correlated most significantly with the factor it was intended to represent. For example, in

the item about Boss below (Table 1), these relationships are expressed as correlation coefficients.

IMPLICATIONS FOR MANAGEMENT

Data collected from salaried exempt persons comprise norms for making subgroup comparisons. Sources of potential conflict are revealed in Exhibit 2 which shows actual value profiles (not necessarily typical) of individuals in various levels and functions in industry.

For example, Profile A represents a conservative president (solid line) and one of his vice presidents (broken line), who left the company to become president of another organization. The vice president, with his greater need for independence, higher tolerance for people of differing values, and lower conformity needs, clashed with the more egocentric and highly conforming president who had little tolerance for people whose views differed from his own.

*M. Scott Myers and Susan S. Myers, "Values for Working." © 1973, Dallas, Texas.

The kind of boss I like is one who	Correlation Coefficients					
	T	E	C	M	S	X
a — calls the shots and isn't always changing his mind, and sees to it that everyone follows the rules.	20	-00	44	01	-17	-28
b — gives me access to the information I need and lets me do my job in my own way.	-28	-33	-27	-29	11	46
c — tells me exactly what to do and how to do it, and encourages me by doing it with me.	26	11	19	04	06	-12
d — doesn't ask questions as long as I get the job done.	13	15	01	28	-12	-24
e — gets us working together in close harmony by being more a friendly person than a boss.	01	12	-15	00	32	-13
f — is tough but allows me to be tough too.	06	33	17	19	-26	-13

TABLE 1

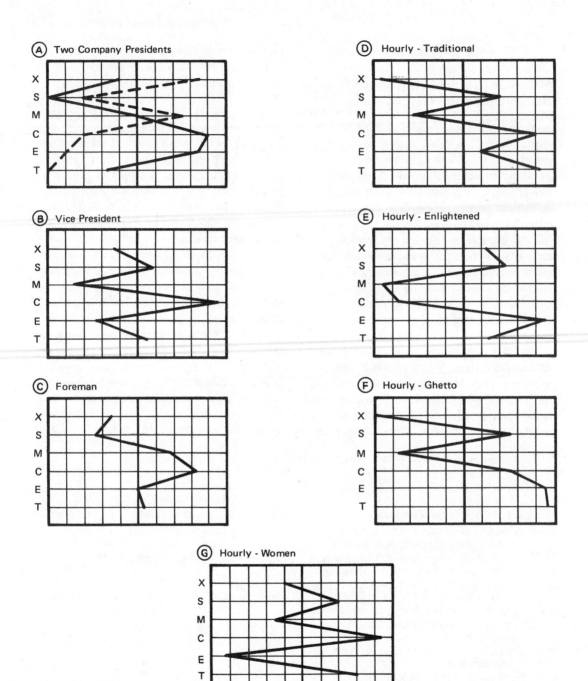

EXHIBIT 2 • *Value Profiles*

The profile of the new president offers better potential for the development of free thinking and inner-directed vice presidents than that of his former boss. The senior president's role, in practice, is similar to that of an over-protecting parent who has high expectations of his children, arbitrarily dispensing rewards and punishments, and developing dependency relationships. But the president is only perpetuating values which he was rewarded for possessing by his dynamic board chairman boss.

Knowing that the chairman dislikes yes-men, these high-level yes-men have learned how to protest in an acceptable fashion. For example, on one occasion the president pounded the table during a board meeting in exaggerated protest to the chairman's perceptive allegation that managerial dereliction was a cause of the unionization of a plant and that other union penetrations were imminent. The president asserted loudly that unionization of the one plant was caused by forces beyond the control of the company and that until the other plants were, in fact, unionized, such an accusation was only speculation. However, the board chairman's concern with unionization touched off a manipulative anti-union strategy far more costly than preventive measures would have been. But the table-pounding in the board room probably served to show the chairman that he was not surrounded by docile conformists.

In a young organization, independent, entrepreneurial types come to the top. But, as success is achieved, these early risk-takers become more conservative and intolerant of the very type of behavior that enabled them to succeed.

Ambitious managers on the way up have a choice of leaving the organization, asserting their initiative under a facade of conformity, or acquiescing to puppetry. Under this style of leadership, conformity-oriented managers are promoted.

Profile B in Exhibit 2 is a vice president in an organization that is beginning to show signs of hardening of the arteries. His higher conformity, sociocentric and tribalistic profile and lower manipulative, egocentric and existential scores are descriptive of a person who seeks to please the boss, perpetuate tradition and avoid rocking the boat. Frequently prefacing his directives to his subordinates with "Now what I believe Max (president) wants is . . ." or "Max is quite concerned (for example) with blocked growth opportunities in the company, therefore, we should be collecting data to shed light on this problem — just in case he asks for it;" he is more concerned with anticipating the boss's whims than he is with the real problem facing the organization. Sometimes a simple and innocent observation or question by the president is transformed and amplified by this conformist zealot into a high priority and arbitrary edict. Though it is the vice president's interpretations that are in error, it is the president's fault for having nurtured conformity behavior.

The foreman's high conformity and manipulative profile (C) is typical of the person who has been promoted from the ranks, and is ideal for evoking and perpetuating conformity behavior among the traditional hourly ranks (D). Though the high egocentric score of the traditional hourly reflects self-centered opportunism, it is strongly counterbalanced by high tribalistic, conformity and sociocentric scores. In other words, this person needs to protect his self-esteem by following a strong and respected leader, clearly defined rules, and group acceptance, rather than take the risk of striking out on his own.

The "enlightened hourly" employee (E) tends to be younger, better informed, concerned with social issues, idealistic, and somewhat anti-establishment in his views. Potentially this more enlightened person would not have the high egocentric score shown here. This regression to lower level values typically occurs when this type of person finds himself boxed in by inappropriate management, as would come from foreman C. Often restless and unwilling to adjust to automaton conformity, he has the ability to view life in perspective, and recoils at the thought of 30 years of monotony climaxed by retirement with a gold watch. Though their educational backgrounds range from college dropouts to little formal education, most enlightened hourlies have acquired much information (selectively assimilated) from television, travel, and social interaction. They respond best to a supervisor who respects them, asks for and uses their ideas, and gives them freedom to socialize and manage a job.

The foreman also encounters problems in dealing with the culturally disadvantaged from the ghetto (F), whose high egocentrism-tribalism combination often focuses their conforming and socializing activities toward peer group rebellion against the organization. Egocentrics are against the world in general and, if he's black, against "whitey" in particular. Hence, the white supervisor,

regardless of his qualifications, has little opportunity to succeed with black egocentrics. The black supervisor, on the other hand, can impose supervisory constraints in the language of the ghetto, avoiding allegations of racial discrimination. However, experience has shown that one level of black supervision is not enough — it is often perceived as tokenism or "Uncle-Tomism." But if at least two levels of black supervision exist in the organization (for example, foreman and superintendent), a new message comes through to the black egocentric that "this is my organization too, and I and my people can succeed here." If two or more levels of black supervision exist in the organization, the white supervisor can successfully supervise blacks, as long as blacks are also supervising whites. This principle is not restricted to black-white relationships, but applies wherever occupational discrimination occurs; for example, such as once existed between the English and French-speaking Canadians in the Province of Quebec, or between men and women in most organizations.

Profile G is typical for hourly paid women. Their highs in 2, 4, and 6, and lows in 3, 5, and 7, reflect their cultural conditioning to be friendly, loyal and obedient followers. Reinforced by tradition, women have been rewarded for performing support roles, both in the home and at the work place. Thus, they can be found in large numbers on assembly lines, behind typewriters, in libraries, at telephone switchboards, and at key-punch machines — but not in board rooms or offices — unless they are serving the coffee. It is interesting to note, however, the similarity between their profile (G) and that of the vice president in profile B . . .

LEVEL 4 AND 5 PROTOTYPES

Conservative or manipulative managers, who tend to dominate most organizations, typically engage in defensive strategies ranging from pretending a problem doesn't exist, through adopting more restrictive personnel selection criteria, to attempting to reshape the values of the "misfits" now on the work force.

A manager from a large manufacturing organization deplored the disappearance of what he referred to as the old-style, dynamic leaders — like Vince Lombardi. "What we need in our organization," he said, "is a lot of Vince Lombardis — leaders who will drive through and achieve organizational objectives" — not realizing that Lombardi's leadership, effective for coaching a football team in the '60's, may be inappropriate for today's business organization. In the first place, his style of leadership tends to overshadow the talent in the organization, creating little opportunity for the development of subordinates. For instance, none of the coaches that served under Lombardi succeeded in emulating his success as a result of his tutelage. Furthermore, there is room for only one Lombardi in an organization, as he calls all the shots; but a business organization has many interdependent functions to be managed through the cooperation of many able leaders. When the Lombardi-type person leaves, the organization tends to lose its effectiveness because of the dependency relationships fostered by his personality.

Lombardi's life style most closely fits the pattern of a level 4. For example, he was a faithful churchgoer, he dictated the life styles of his players, and reinforced his values by replaying a recording of an evangelistic West Point speech about love, honor, and duty by Douglas MacArthur, one of his heroes. Most level 4 people need heroes, just as they, in turn, need to be heroes and need to dominate people in their organization. This is not a criticism of Lombardi; his success as a football coach speaks for itself. But, it is a criticism of this style of leadership for organizations in which increasing numbers are above the 2, 3, and 4 levels of psychological existence.

Managers are not only culturally conditioned by the tradition of 5 and 4 style management, but they are also influenced by persons outside the organization whose values can affect the organization's status. Market analysts, for example, will respond positively to a layoff that will improve the cost-earnings ratio in a way that increases stock prices. Hence, short-range 4 and 5 thinking by analysts inspires and perpetuates 4 and 5 management strategies in organizations.

Of course, some of the level 4 and 5 influence may come more directly from the manager's wife and other members of his family. Women, long conditioned to conservative support roles or defensively skilled in manipulation, often exert subtle but significant influences on the life style of the manager. However, in many cases, the wives and children are also serving as bridges between industry and society, providing a counterbalancing influence to the organization by sensitizing managers to sociocentric and existential concepts.

GUIDELINES FOR COMPATIBILITY

In spite of their conditioned high regard for Lombardi-like leadership, managers are, with increasing frequency, finding themselves out of step with the people they supervise. Conformity behavior, once taken for granted, can no longer be expected. Not only are the managers out of step, but so are many of the systems which they use to achieve organizational goals. Since systems reflect the values of their designers and administrators, it is only natural to find people responding to systems as they do to the managers who create and administer them. Exhibit 3 (pp. 16–17) presents capsule descriptions of supervisory values, systems characteristics, and subordinate or systems user values.

The three left columns of Exhibit 3 show characteristic supervisory (S) attitudes toward subordinates at levels 2 through 7 as they relate to the supervisory functions of performance review, communication and career planning. Immediately beneath the supervisor's value statement at each level is shown a characteristic value statement for supervised employees (E) at that level.

The right side of Exhibit 3 contains descriptors and values relating to three personnel management systems — compensation, attitude survey, and job posting. At each level is a capsule descriptor of the system (S) as it might characteristically be conceived by a system designer at that level of psychological existence. Immediately beneath each descriptor is summarized an expectation of the system as it might characteristically be expressed by an employee (E) at that level.

This table identifies conditions of compatibility and conflict within the organization. For example, in considering the "communication" relationships, the level 7 supervisor's view (we discuss things informally, and I give them access to any information they want), is compatible with the needs of the 7's, 6's, and 5's he supervises:

7: I like to feel free to talk to anyone, and to get the information I want.

6: He's easy to talk to, and is interested in us personally.

5: If I'm to do a good job, I need to know everything my boss knows.

However, in reading further down the column it becomes apparent that the needs of the 4's, 3's and 2's are less compatible:

4: He should tell us what we're supposed to know to do our job properly.

3: The less I hear from my boss, the better.

2: He tells us what to do in a friendly way and lets us know he'll help us. The 4's and 2's want more structure, and the 3's need more structure than the 7 would naturally provide.

However, the actual situation in organizations is more serious than the partial incompatibility reflected in the above example. Managers are typically more 5 or 4 than 7 in their orientation and, consequently, encounter more conflict. For example, the level 5 supervisor's communication philosophy (I give them the information I think they need to get the job done.) is not easily compatible with any level except 4 (He should tell us what we're supposed to know to do our job properly.) This means that level 5, the most common type of leadership style, has little opportunity to succeed unless he surrounds himself with conformists. In the long run, he and the organization would, of course, be defeated by excessive conformity.

The same phenomenon exists regarding the compatibility of people and management systems. Compensation, attitude survey, and job posting systems designed in terms of level 7 concepts are compatible with 7, 6, and 5 values, but not with 4, 3, and 2 values. Since most systems are designed in terms of level 4 and 5 concepts, they tend to satisfy the 2, 3, and 4 levels and frustrate people at the 5, 6, and 7 levels. In other words, systems in most organizations are designed more for people at the conformist, egocentric and tribalistic level than they are for the entrepreneurial self-starters in 5, 6, and 7. This stems in part from the fact that the job of systems and procedures writer is more likely to attract level 4 conformists than any other level. Hence, as a counterbalancing influence, level 7 criteria must be applied to remove the unnecessary and inflexible constraints typically reflected in policy and procedure statements.

CONCLUSIONS

The new work ethic is not a new set of values; rather, it represents a shift in the source of influence. The seven levels of psychological existence described in this paper have long existed, but people in the middle ranges of manipulation and conformity have, until recently, been the unchallenged source of influence in business organizations and in most realms of society for at least the past 600 years.

Now, thought-leaders are beginning to come as well from the existential and sociocentric levels. Though they still represent a minority, their values are permeating our culture at an accelerating rate. In business organizations, for example, pressures are being felt on many fronts. Corporate managers are beginning to forego promotional transfers to stay in the community of their choice. Some employees are refusing overtime or to work on implements of war. Others pressure their management to cease trade with South Africa. Union members are more interested in meaningful work than fatter benefits. Thus, neither management nor labor is immune to the influence of 6 and 7 thinking.

New thought-leaders are also surfacing issues which precipitate social, civic and legislative action. It was largely level 5 interests that planned to host the 1976 Winter Olympics in Colorado, but it was apparently level 7 and 6 leadership (concerned with ecology and commercialism), coupled with level 4 conservatism, that defeated the effort at the polls. The 4's were probably always against exploitation of their area, but heretofore were not psychologically predisposed toward organizing opposition.

Women's liberation groups have initiated a number of reforms under level 7 leadership such as that of Aileen Hernandez. Their influence has reduced employment discrimination against women, changed abortion laws, opened vocational opportunities in restricted fields such as business, law, and medicine, and promises to secure legal implementation of the Equal Rights Amendment to the Constitution.

Though conformists still conform, they are beginning to emulate new models. For example, the mod look of

SUPERVISION · SYSTEMS

	Performance Review	Communication	Career Planning	Compensation	Attitude Survey	Job Posting
7 S	We work together in setting goals and reviewing progress.	We discuss things informally, and I give them access to any information they want.	Self-development is the key; people should have the opportunity to plan their own careers.	A smorgasbord approach which rewards merit and adapts to individual needs.	A democratic process involving all people in analyzing problems and suggesting improvements.	A system for maximizing organizational effectiveness by encouraging the natural flow of talent.
7 E	I like to have a major role in defining my goals and methods for achieving them.	I like to feel free to talk to anyone, and to get the information I want.	I am responsible for my own career, and require the opportunity to develop my capabilities.	A good system rewards merit and doesn't tie you to the organization.	Greater commitment and solidarity are achieved when people have a hand in solving problems.	Now that I know what the openings and requirements are, I can run my own maze.
6 S	I try to review their performance without hurting their feelings.	I want to be on good terms with them so they will feel they can discuss anything with me.	Every career should include the ingredients of social and civic responsibility.	Pay and benefits tailored to the needs of the people and their circumstances.	A vehicle for diagnosing and solving human problems.	A system providing opportunity for employees to find compatible work groups and supervisors.
6 E	He should use this occasion to get better acquainted with us.	He's easy to talk to and is interested in us personally.	Our careers should be oriented toward bettering relationships among all people.	Money should serve all people, and be more equitably distributed.	Working with others in analyzing survey results is a good way to improve human relations.	I like being able to find a job where the people and work don't clash with my values.
5 S	I find that the carrot and stick works best.	I give them the information I think they need to get the job done.	I keep track of their progress and specify developmental programs and assignments.	Distribution of money according to amount of responsibility and level of performance.	A management tool for taking the pulse of an organization.	A controlled competitive system to upgrade the best employees into company job openings.
5 E	I like to set my own goals and get recognition for achieving them.	If I'm to do a good job, I need to know everything my boss knows.	My career depends on my taking the initiative in finding opportunity for advancement.	Money is a measure of my success.	If what we learn from an attitude survey can make our employees more productive, I'm all for it.	It's one way to find advancement opportunities, but it helps to know the right people.

		Performance Review	Communication	Career Planning	Compensation	Attitude Survey	Job Posting
4	S	I define the goals and standards I expect them to follow.	I give them the information they should have, and keep our relations business-like.	I define their career paths and promotional opportunities and give them continuous guidance.	Compensation programs based on community and industry surveys and standard practice.	The systematic measurement of attitudes toward company goals, policies and practices.	The orderly, systematic and fair implementation of a promotion-from-within policy.
	E	We need to know the company goals and how we can support them.	He should tell us what we're supposed to know to do our job properly.	I will be promoted when I earn it through productiveness and loyalty.	Money is a reward for loyalty and hard work, and should not be subject to favoritism.	Management is asking for our help, and it is our duty to answer all questions as honestly as possible.	I will be given the job I bid on if I deserve it.
3	S	I make clear what he has to do if he wants to keep his job.	I tell them whatever I feel like telling them.	It's every man for himself—don't look to me for your breaks.	Manipulative, arbitrary and secretive use of money.	Rigged questions and whitewashed reports.	Posting of jobs that can't be filled more economically from the outside.
	E	I don't like anyone finding fault with me and telling me how to act.	The less I hear from my boss, the better.	I don't want anyone planning my life—I'll look after No. 1 myself.	I'll work for the highest bidder.	I don't want any part of a stool pigeon system that can be used against me.	It's no use trying—the cards are stacked against you.
2	S	I tell them how I think they did and how they can improve.	I explain company rules to them and talk with them about their problems.	They expect me to tell them what to do and to take care of them.	A fair and uniform system administered by the boss.	A way of letting employees know the company is interested in their ideas.	A way of increasing job security by filling job openings from within.
	E	I want him to tell me if I've done what he wanted me to do, and if I've let him down.	He tells us what to do in a friendly way and lets us know he'll help us.	What's most important is that I'll always have a steady job and a good boss.	I need steady pay to make ends meet.	My boss should know how we feel so he can help us.	I'll bid on a job if my supervisor tells me to.

S (Supervisor System)
E (Employee)

EXHIBIT 3 • Expectations and Needs by Value Level

the level 6 has become the conformity model of the level 4 in American society. People of other values adopt the new look, but for different reasons. Level 5's wear sideburns and variegated apparel when it is advantageous to do so, and level 7's may wear the new look simply because it suits their fancy. Level 3's wear anything that symbolizes independence, and 2's wear what their "tribal chieftains" expect them to wear.

Value conflicts that exist today are not resolved, of course, by simply adopting the mod clothing and language. They can be ameliorated only by learning to operate from a new source of influence. The level 4 or 5 manager tends to operate from influence derived from official authority and tradition. To succeed with the new work ethic, he must operate from a base of influence stemming from the competence of people at all levels of the organization. That is, he will be skilled in organizing manpower and material in such a way that human talent can find expression in solving problems and setting goals. He will know he is succeeding when the people stop fighting him, and show commitment in achieving job goals. Incidentally, when he reaches this level of competence, he will find that the person who has changed the most is himself — and he and the level 7's are now talking the same language.

THE PSYCHOLOGICAL BARRIERS TO MANAGEMENT EFFECTIVENESS

Robert H. Schaffer

psychological needs. In the case of managers, this universal mechanism often interferes seriously with the enterprise. The author describes how managers escape anxiety provoking situations through perceptual distortion and counterproductive behavior. The claim of "doing all I can" and denial of certain facts are examples of the first; busyness, the manager's "Linus blanket," and escapes into structure are examples of the second. An understanding of these forces can help management. The author lists the principles that underlie three strategic concepts: the use of multivariate strategies for change, imposition of work disciplines on the management job, and maintenance of tough achievement goals.

Everyone subtly molds his behavior for what appear to be rational goal-oriented reasons; actually, we are also satisfying

From *Business Horizons,* April 1971, pp. 17–25. Copyright 1971 by the Foundation for the School of Business at Indiana University. Reprinted by permission.

The body of literature on the relationship between psychological factors and the achievement of organization results is large and still growing; a minimum, however, has been written about the issue that is probably the most pervasive and most expensive and that holds the greatest potential for change. The reason so little has been written about it is that, like the atmosphere, it is all around us yet invisible to the unaided eye.

"It," in this case, refers to the countless ways all of us subtly mold our jobs and our behavior on the job for what we believe to be rational, goal-oriented reasons, when actually we are being impelled by the pressure to satisfy psychological needs of which we are largely unaware. Sometimes these invisible or camouflaged mechanisms actually help the business, but often they drain energy from the enterprise or interfere seriously with its work. This article will try to make this ubiquitous phenomenon more visible and to suggest its far-reaching implications for strategies of management.

THE DUALITY OF BEHAVIOR

All human behavior is a fascinating blend of the rational and the irrational, the conscious and the unconscious. On the one hand, people are logical machines that perceive reality, make measured evaluations and judgments, and then respond with behavior calculated to achieve explicit objectives. At the same time, we attempt to satisfy psychological needs and minimize anxiety by methods of which we are largely unaware. This is an unending 24-hour-a-day job: to avoid situations in which we feel anxious, threatened, or depressed, or appear to be incompetent, foolish, weak, and so forth. We steer toward situations (and try to manipulate the situations we are in) so that we feel accepted, respected, productive, and safe. The subtle (and usually unconscious) stratagems that we employ to succeed in this endeavor are known by the familiar term "defense mechanisms."

Rational goal-oriented behavior and unconscious defenses do not operate as two independent mechanisms. During a lifetime, the defensive reactions become built into everything we do. Yet we tend to see our behavior as logical and rational, and thus have difficulty in distinguishing that part which is shaped by our need to minimize anxiety. Thus while we share the same reality with others, we each tend to see that reality in our own terms.

For example, imagine that we are going to interview all the managers in a company, asking each two questions: "What is it that keeps your enterprise from achieving much more than it is currently achieving?" and "What will it take to get this enterprise moving more effectively?" Although responses will vary a great deal from person to person, we can predict one result with considerable certainty. Virtually no one will attribute the shortcomings of the enterprise to shortcomings in his own managerial competence or behavior. Similarly, few will suggest that improvement in his own effectiveness might be a key to accelerating the organization's performance.

This predictable finding (test it if you doubt it) illustrates one of the most common and most limiting perceptive defense mechanisms of managers — the *"doing all I can in these circumstances" illusion.* Most managers place a definite boundary around their own scope for initiative. Within that boundary they see themselves as doing all they possibly can. When the boss is stuck he can blame it on unmotivated, unqualified, or disloyal people; the people can blame it on their boss or various circumstances beyond their control. Needed improvements are always somebody else's job.

During the 1970–1971 recession many managers have been heard to rationalize almost every kind of disappointing performance in terms of the "state of the economy."

A team of managers in a large company was confronted with a demand for reduced costs. Although statistical evidence indicated that comparable companies were indeed performing at higher levels, most of these managers asserted that "their conditions were quite different," and that only by sacrificing quality or cutting maintenance could costs be reduced.

Thus, step by step, each manager whittles away huge areas of opportunity for initiative. We simply take them out of our line of vision. If they remain in sight, we have to confront each pathway of unexploited opportunity, and this could give rise to anxiety about our inability to respond. It is simpler to live in an environment that has been circumscribed so that it is controllable. Imagine how an enterprise would change if each of its managers perceived his current level of performance as not the ultimate of what could be achieved, but as the mere beginning of a constantly expanding level of achievement. But this will not happen easily. These distortions in perception are extremely important to the people who hold them and, more-

over, are completely believable to them and to almost everybody else.

Another form of defense by perception is *denial*. In the film "Never on Sunday" the heroine, Ilya, perceives the Greek tragedies as syrupy soap opera. While murder and mayhem occur before her eyes, she sees only love and happiness. This was a joke in the film, but similar behavior on the part of management is not uncommon. If the problem is too difficult to cope with, we may solve it by not seeing it.

Even though a possibly superior competitive product was already being market tested, managers of one company convinced themselves that their key customers, many of years' standing, would never be so disloyal as to leave them.

One company enjoyed an unusual spurt of growth and profits because of certain market conditions that were temporary in nature. In the resulting euphoria, however, all of its top management acted as if *they* had found the secret to a perpetual Christmas.

The head of a newly created, highly sophisticated central staff group assured his boss and his colleagues that the new function had been very well received throughout the organization. In fact he had aroused considerable suspicion and hostility and few people would trust him with sensitive information.

We are much more aware of the defense behavior of other people, though we may not diagnose it as such or understand what causes it. We are all well aware of the buck-passer, the responsibility escaper, and the corporate underachiever, the man with ability who somehow always seems unable or unwilling to deliver. We know there is nothing rational behind examples of behavior like these that we see every day of our working lives:

A bright and able vice-president of R&D has an assistant director who is regarded generally as rather incompetent. Yet, for some reason, the boss is quite pleased with his assistant and has just given him a raise.

This president, whenever a crisis looms or a severe problem arises, calls a series of meetings involving everybody who might have something to contribute, and many who do not. These meetings are animated and lengthy. Rarely do they result in clear agreement on actions to be taken. Often the crises are settled in ways completely unrelated to the meetings. Nevertheless, whenever an emergency arises, all the officers prepare for meetings that last well into the night.

Mr. X is a prototype "authoritarian" manager. He never invites his people to participate in decisions; he always issues orders; and he often addresses his people in a tough tone of voice. An acute observer would see that, despite his manner, he rarely is explicit and clear-cut in his demands. Thus, for all his toughness, they have a million ways to not do what he wants them to do.

Although written as humor, Parkinson's books come closer than much of the academic literature to capturing the mysterious ways in which men's hidden motivations lead organizations down pathways that are quite unrelated to where everyone says he wants to go.[1] But the fact is that so far most of what has been perceived and written about is the noticeable, or even the off-beat and bizarre.

Before focusing on the interference between rational and defensive behavior in management, the point should be made that defense mechanisms often produce considerable successful managerial behavior. The forces that drive the most successful, able, and hardworking managers ahead, that encourage them to take risks, that inspire them to innovate and perform in many other unusual ways often stem from needs of which they are unaware. This positive side contains many clues for management strategy, once we better understand the other side of the picture, the rich variety of disguised behavior that managers use to satisfy their own psychological needs which are nonproductive for the enterprise.

The phenomena described here do not represent any psychological breakthrough by the author; rather, the effects of some well-known and thoroughly described psychological principles will be illuminated, effects which (like the missing "Emperor's New Clothes" in the children's story) are obvious but unrecognized.[2]

DEFEAT WITHOUT TRYING: THE INVISIBLE BARRIERS

People try to minimize anxiety first by perceiving and interpreting the events around them, and then by acting in response to those perceptions, in ways that are most ego protective and reas-

---

[1]See, for example, C. Northcote Parkinson, *Parkinson's Law* (Boston: Houghton Mifflin Company, 1957).

[2]For more detail concerning these principles, see Chris Argyris, *Interpersonal Competence and Organizational Effectiveness* (Homewood, Ill.: Richard D. Irwin, Inc., 1962); Alan N. Schoonmaker, *Anxiety and the Executive* (New York: American Management Association, 1969), pp. 138–50; or the master himself, Sigmund Freud, "The Psychopathology of Everyday Life" in *The Basic Writings of Sigmund Freud* (New York: Random House, Inc., 1938).

suring. And both these mechanisms, perceptual and behavioral, can permit managers to achieve anxiety reducing results at the great expense of organization achievement results.

Distortions in Managerial Perception

Everybody wears colored glasses in order to see things in terms that are most fitting to our particular psychological needs and readiness.

Xenophobia describes a third form of defense by perceptive distortion. Man has a general tendency to differentiate between the good guys (with whom he identifies) and the bad guys. Thus the world is divided into heroes and villains, our team and their team, the "free" world vs. the Communists, and so on. There is the same tendency in enterprise to see our team — the idealized heroes — lined up against the villains. It takes many forms: production vs. sales, headquarters vs. the field, line vs. staff, one product line vs. another, and so forth.

During a major operations improvement effort in a large multiplant company, headquarters staff people complained that the managers in operations resisted new approaches to their jobs. Field people maintained, with equal vigor, that headquarters was presenting them with "academic" and impractical recommendations. These fervent accusations spared each group from focusing on its own need to change and improve.

In another company the president told a consultant, "We're just not getting enough good new products from R&D." The head of R&D told the consultant, "I can't set any directions for either our basic research or our product development because top management simply won't tell us where this company is supposed to be heading."

In a fast-moving, highly competitive industry, one company's marketers were convinced that their manufacturing division was incompetent because of increasing costs, poor quality, and poor service. The manufacturing people were equally convinced that unnecessary "catering to customer whims," and excessively large variety of sizes and custom options, and too many changes in instructions from production planning were undermining their ability to even hold their own, to say nothing of improve.

Of course, there is almost always some truth — often plenty of truth — to these allegations, which only makes it more difficult to see the psychological defense mechanisms at play. So long as one sees the major responsibility for change as resting with the other fellow, he need not feel a sense of responsibility for taking initiative. Thus management can blame the union and the union can blame management; planners can blame the operators for being "too focused on today" and the operators can blame the planners for being "too academic." This sort of distortion permits us to free ourselves, to a certain extent, of self-doubt. The nagging anxiety that might be aroused is masked as we get increasingly agitated about what the other fellow is not doing.

When Don Quixote dreams the impossible dream it is romantic, even inspiring. But when managers *dream the impossible dream* (another form of perceptual distortion) rather than come to grips with possible solutions, the enterprise suffers. This happens when a manager, to relieve his anxiety about a very tough goal, convinces himself that it is really beyond achievement. Once convinced, what more need he do? A variant of the impossible dream defense is to believe that the only way to reach an important goal is through some prior accomplishment which, at the moment, looks impossible. This too will relieve the manager of the pain and struggle of searching for approaches that might be within his power.

> For years this consumer products company suffered from impossibly difficult union relationships. Plant productivity, abysmally low, reflected this state of affairs. Management felt that improvement depended on a shift in relations between management and the union, and a thaw on the part of the union with regard to work restrictions. Such a thaw would undoubtedly have opened the pathway to greater productivity, but it was highly unlikely to occur. Since the managers firmly believed, however, that this was *the* key to performance improvement, they were free to overlook many programs of action that were feasible even in their current situation.

The preceding examples illustrate how we organize our perceptions of the world to reassure ourselves and minimize personal anxiety and uneasiness. While this may be useful to us in one way, it often closes off the great number of alternatives and possibilities for realistic action that are open to us.

Behavioral Escapes

There are many different ways in which managers, by their actions as well as their perceptions, can unwittingly minimize their anxiety at the price of accomplishing the very goals they seek. Probably the most common escape is through *busyness* — the manager's "Linus blanket." Almost all managers complain that they are too busy. They wish they had more time to think, to plan, and to view their jobs from a broader perspective. The assumption is that their busyness is a result of real job demands. The fact is, however, that many managers keep themselves comfortable by keeping busy. Quiet, unplanned time, empty desk tops, and silent telephones can provoke tremendous anxiety. Such pauses give them time to recognize many of their doubts about how things are going.

The large enterprise provides limitless opportunities for managers to keep busy. There are countless documents to be read and responses to be written (which will in turn generate new papers to be read); there are frequent meetings; telephone calls come in a random pattern. Any number of problems, emergencies, and crises cry out for management time. There are dependent subordinates who are happy to take up as much time as the executive cares to give, and company showmen who enjoy putting on presentations or meetings for anyone who will take the time to listen.

One of the greatest rationalizations of management is: "We've simply got to figure out how to get some time around here to do some thinking and planning." Considerable effort has been wasted in trying to redesign executive jobs, delegate routine tasks, shift the flow of paperwork, and so forth, in the hope that these steps will free the managers for the planning and thinking. The fact is that, for most managers, this "freedom" is often very uncomfortable.

> One director of a large manufacturing operation reorganized his job and his relationships with his associates so that they would carry more responsibility. Shortly thereafter, he went on a two-week vacation. When he returned, his in-basket contained only five or six items.

In the past, there would have been enough material upon his return to fill two brief cases and an entire week end at home. "To tell you the truth," he confided, "even though I designed this result myself, I can tell you that I feel damned uncomfortable and out of touch with things."

Managers are also able to keep themselves psychologically comfortable by *escapes into structure and system*. In order for large enterprises to work, human endeavor must be organized and institutionalized; there must be regular, understood procedures and routines. Thus every enterprise builds up its own pattern of operation at every level, which makes it possible for everybody to understand how things should be done. At the same time, in order to survive and thrive, the enterprise must be able to change directions and policies; a balance is needed between routine and change. The problem here is that familiar routines are comforting and reassuring, while abandoning or restructuring institutionalized behavior can be disquieting. Thus, particularly in relatively stable organizations, it becomes increasingly difficult to distinguish clearly between those institutionalized practices that serve a real function and those that are merely vestigial.

Certain regular meetings are held, not necessarily because there are purposes to be served but because that is when that committee has always met. Reports are produced, not because somebody needs information but because somebody else has the responsibility of producing those reports. The executive committee meets every Monday morning, and its agenda tends to be made up in the same way each week. The methods of running and meeting — including what people feel free to bring up — tend to remain the same. But what is it that the committee is trying to accomplish? What do they want to do over the next six months or a year? Could they best accomplish these results by meeting five times a week? Or once a month? What are the means by which they should attack their most important objectives? These are tough questions, and frequently it is more reassuring to simply carry on with the regular meetings in the regular way with the same faces.

Even those who protest most loudly about "too damn many meetings in this place" are often co-conspirators in maintaining the schedule. Why? Frequently because a three-hour meeting on the schedule "takes care of" that chunk of time. The manager no longer has to consider how best to use those hours in the face of competing possibilities.

Management literature universally stresses the need to "manage by objectives," to have clear, well-defined goals and a method for measuring progress towards them. Most managers, however, are very skillful at *escaping from commitment*, avoiding unequivocal acceptance of exceptionally difficult goals. All sorts of escape hatches are built into the establishment of goals to allow for "conditions beyond control" in case of short-falls (although most managers will not hesitate to take credit for achievement).

Financial vice-president: "Sure we can go for a new issue now, but if you think we can get $25 a share in this market you're crazy."

Manufacturing manager: "Sure you can cut our maintenance budget, but you'll just pay for it in down time and off-spec product."

School superintendent: "I agree it is important to measure and evaluate the results of educational programs. But the measures have to take into account some of the problems we have in this district that you don't find elsewhere."

How many progress reports have we read that say something like this: "While our achievements are up from last year, we feel that this is only a small fraction of what we should have been able to accomplish. We have therefore set our sights on . . ."

Our observations suggest that many managers become quite uncomfortable when they discover that their subordinates' view of a reasonable goal is significantly lower than their own. While the human relations literature, focusing on theories X and Y stresses the inhibiting effect of the boss on the subordinate,[3] the fact is that anticipation of a direct confrontation on the question of appropriate goals with one's subordinates can be traumatic to the boss. The manager wonders whether his people will rebel or, by one means or another, refuse to do the job or sabotage the goals. Will they be able to prove somehow that his goals are outrageous? Or might they quit?

To avoid these awful possibilities, managers frequently scale down the goal to a level that will be acceptable. They do not do this consciously, of course, and there are always enough "facts" to explain such a de-escalation even to themselves. Sometimes a manager who has been forced to give ground will harbor an underlying sense of irritation. He

may react by becoming overtly aggressive, hostile, or authoritarian, or engaging in other histrionics that reassure him as to his toughness.

The insidious nature of all these unconscious barriers to management effectiveness is best perhaps illustrated by cases in which managers, seeking to upgrade the effectiveness of the organization or overcome its problems, *adopt programs which are in themselves forms of escape.* When confronted with the consequences of inadequate performance, managers often prefer to see the fault clearly directed away from themselves. They also like to be able to look elsewhere for solutions, and are all too ready to believe that problems arise from faulty organization arrangements, the wrong management "style," inadequate information systems, lack of motivation on the part of others, or poor human relations or communications in the enterprise. They will carry out — or engage staff groups or consultants to carry out — all sorts of programs that are supposed to solve the problems. New management information systems will be installed. The enterprise will be reorganized. Managers will go off to examine their human relations.

These programs are often demanding, difficult, and time consuming. A manager deeply engrossed in them enjoys a number of self-defeating "benefits." He can comfort himself with the thought that he is vigorously attacking the issues. If he has brought in staff or consulting help, he can assure himself that experts are studying the situation.

---

[3]See, for example, Douglas McGregor, *The Human Side of Enterprises* (New York: McGraw-Hill Book Company, 1960).

This permits him to overlook the things that *he* might be able to do differently to achieve better performance.

> The president of one company could not bring himself to look his associates in the eye and reach agreement and commitment on some necessary tough performance goals. Instead, he went off with them to a human relations "confrontation" session in which many of his methods were subject to attack. After much open give-and-take, a variety of new ways of working were agreed upon. None of the discomfort of that meeting and the consequent shufflings around in company relationships and procedures, however, was as upsetting to him as forcing the issue on performance achievement would have been.

> Another company whose profits were slipping downward went through a whole series of company reorganizations, each one designed to produce the "right" structure to manage the company effectively.

THE UBIQUITOUS FORCES

The illustrations in this article suggest the profound and pervasive ways by which anxiety-minimizing behavior becomes imperceptibly blended into the life of the enterprise through either unconscious or partly conscious means. These illustrations are merely samplings from a catalog that could easily outweigh Sears Roebuck's. We have focused on the "problem" side, but we must not forget that unconscious anxiety-reducing drives also impel us to behavior which can be highly productive.

How can a grasp of these ubiquitous forces help the leaders of enterprise? Four important principles underlie three strategic concepts which I believe are of universal importance to everybody concerned with establishing appropriate goals for an enterprise and mobilizing resources to achieve them.

The Principles

Universality Every human being, by one means or another, employs unconscious or partly conscious devices to keep from feeling uncomfortable. Some of these devices may help us achieve goals that we and our associates say we want to achieve. Others, as we have seen, are obstacles. Some may have no effect whatever on the achievement of goals.

Necessity These forces are universal because they are essential to the maintenance of equilibrium. If one considers all of the real and imagined dangers to which man is exposed — including the fact that life is a temporary condition — it is obvious that worries and fears could easily overwhelm us. These defense mechanisms permit us to put worries out of our minds.

Individuality Early in life we begin developing ways of dealing with difficult and trying events. These early patterns affect later ones, and gradually each person develops his own unique pattern of responses and defenses. This pattern of defensive reactions is built into all our behavior and becomes a major part of what we think of as each person's personality.

Stability These patterns of reaction, gradually developing over a lifetime deep within the personality, tend to become fairly fixed in people by the time they reach adult life.

Any strategy of management based on ignoring or thwarting the reality of these defense mechanisms is bound to fail as is any based on the illusion that these fundamental patterns can be readily changed in an individual or a group. It seems to me that the major weakness of even the most creative work in human relations is its failure to come to terms with these facts. There seems to be a persistent belief that some universal ideal style for management can be defined (for example, Theory Y). But the facts suggest that while Theory Y may be great for some managers, others perform at their worst in ambiguous situations and at their best when they are told what to do.[4] Similarly, the belief that a brief human relations training program can produce insights that permit people to successfully change their fundamental work patterns flies in the face of too much data.

Similar weaknesses underlie many other one-variable attacks on management effectiveness.[5] When management tries to upgrade performance by reorganizing the company or a department, by introducing new management sciences approaches, or by increasing an R&D budget, it may be dealing with the manifest aspects of a problem while failing to come to grips with the latent aspects. Thus, hidden barriers continue to undermine the new system or the new organization as effectively as the old.

The Strategies

This leads to what I believe to be the three most important strategic implications for making the most of managerial

potential and minimizing the inhibiting effect of the escape mechanisms. These are the use of multivariate strategies for change, the imposition of work disciplines on the job of management, and the maintenance of tough achievement goals.

Multivariate Strategy of Change
Any major effort to change the productivity or effectiveness of an enterprise must be designed so that, as new managerial methods, systems, and approaches are introduced, there are simultaneous efforts to help managers develop, grow, and become confident in operating in new ways. In considering any major change, it is important to discover not only what the objective facts suggest, but also to determine the readiness for change in the enterprise. To design a change that goes beyond what people are able to deal with is to invite the mobilization of defenses against success of the new organization, method, or approach.

If change projects are designed to match both what is objectively needed and what people are ready to do, the project can not only accomplish its immediate purposes, but also provide managers with new skills as well as the reassurance and positive reinforcement necessary to create readiness for more ambitious steps. In this kind of framework, major change, instead of becoming a series of disruptive crises and battles, becomes an accelerating, self-sustaining process involving many

---

[4]For one good study on this subject, see John J. Morse and Jay W. Lorsch, "Beyond Theory Y," *Harvard Business Review* (May–June, 1970).
[5]For a cogent attack on "simplistic" models of organization change, see Leonard Sayles, "Whatever Happened to Management?" *Business Horizons* (April, 1970), pp. 25–34.

aspects of the organization's performance. Success at each level provides the
foundation for next steps. As the enterprise changes, its managers grow, and
as they grow they can handle more
change.

**Imposing Work Disciplines on
Management**   The production worker's
job, the clerical job, and the first-line
supervisory job can be defined in terms
of specific behavior and specific results.
The further up the line, the more difficult it becomes to describe precisely the
goals and the steps to achieve them.
Thus the more responsible the job, the
greater the opportunities for managers
to confuse their escape and defensive behavior with their result-producing behavior. To minimize this possibility, it is
necessary for management to attempt to
capture in writing as much of their jobs
as possible in terms of commitment to
definable (and quantifiable) goals; the
strategies and work plans to be employed in achieving them; the timing of
various steps; and the measures of progress along the way.

Each new decision area that management considers begins as ill-defined
ideas. Only as management strives to
shift more and more of the ambiguous
and ill-defined into the orbit of specific
control — where its work is defined,
measured, and recorded in writing —
can management protect itself from its
own subtle and insidious escape
mechanisms.

Maintaining Tough Goals   As the

real demands for achievement in an
organization diminish, the degree to
which escape mechanisms dissipate
energy increases geometrically. The
organizations in which people seem to
have the greatest morale and human relations problems, which have too many
meetings, and whose executives are
unavailable because they are so busy,
are those organizations whose members
have the lowest achievement goals (or, if
their goals are high, the easiest means
of escaping from failure to achieve the
goals).

One of the classic errors of modern
organization theory is the belief that in
such cases the morale and human relations problems must be solved as a prerequisite to improving productivity.
This view confuses cause and effect.
Where the real demands for management performance are high, where tremendous energy and concentration are
required, and where there may not be
enough people to get the job done, the
least energy is dissipated on off-target
escapes. High standards and high productivity may be the key variable here.

In trying to employ these three strategies, of course, the manager must
battle with his own escape desires, since
each of the three strategies requires him
to move into possibly uncomfortable
and anxiety provoking areas. But it can
be done on a gradual step-by-step basis
— if not alone, then with the help of
staff or outside consultants — and the
results are worth the fight.

THE EXECUTIVE MAN AND WOMAN: THE ISSUE OF SEXUALITY

David L. Bradford, Alice G. Sargent, and Melinda S. Sprague

When the issue of hiring women in management arises, a frequent response from male executives is joking about the sexual implications: "Won't that make field trips more interesting!" "No woman would be safe in this office with Bill here." Such comments enrage advocates of affirmative action, who see the issue as one of fairness and the opportunity for options other than housewife or secretary. We believe the problem of women in management is complex, encompassing far more than sexual interplay, but this joking reveals more than simple prejudice. Many of the difficulties men and women experience in their relationships at work revolve around sexuality.

Sexuality covers a wide area, and so initially we need to distinguish several ways sex influences managerial behavior. The first refers to the effect of *differential socialization* of males and females. This socialization covers a wide

area of which only a part relates to sexual behavior per se. A substantial body of research demonstrates that from birth boys and girls are consistently treated differently. The types of games, toys, and books given to boys, as well as the kind of behavior for which boys are rewarded and punished, teach boys different values, aspirations, and behavioral skills than girls. Boys are supported for being aggressive, assertive, analytical, and competitive, while girls are praised for being helpful, passive, deferential, and concerned with interpersonal relationships.

Teachers as well as parents support these differences. One example is the research by Serbin (1973), who found that elementary school teachers, both male and female, responded more often to questions raised by boys than girls, and gave the boys longer answers that were richer in content. Girls received more perfunctory answers often accompanied by a pat on the head or arm around the shoulder — as if support and not cognitive content were the important response. Little wonder that this differential training is excellent preparation for men to succeed in management while handicapping women who want to travel the same route.

By college the differences are learned well. Aries (in press) found in a mixed sex group of college students that men typically talked two-thirds of the time. When women did communicate, they directed their comments to men rather than to other women and were more concerned about acceptance and relationships while men were more attuned to authority and impressing each other.

A second way sex influences managerial behavior is through *stereotypes* of the other sex. Definite expectations exist regarding the values, interests, aptitudes, and abilities of a person just because the other happens to be male or female. Women, as well as men, often expect other women to be interested in fashion design, not finance, and in personnel, not line management. Managers assume that a married women will not want out-of-town job assignments while such consideration is not given to a married man.

Many times, expectations about competence levels differ solely on the basis of sex, so that the *same* output is often judged of lower quality when observers believe it to have been done by a woman rather than a man. Goldberg (1968) and Pheterson et al. (1971) found that females also have lower expectations of a woman's competence. In these studies women evaluated paintings and written reports as of lesser quality when they bore a female signature than when a male's. Clearly, these perceptions and expectations influence the type of job assignments male supervisors allocate, the performance level they expect, the way they assess tasks performed, and the candidates they consider when opportunities for advancement arise. Fear of failure may be a major concern for most men, but Horner's (1970) research on college students found that because women are punished for success by being ostracized by other women and rejected by men, they are ambivalent about success. In fact, in Horner's research college women and black men demonstrated a comparable conflict.

The third area deals with how *sexuality* per se influences how men and women work together. Sexuality here refers not just to sexual attraction and office affairs but to the various ways in which a male manager sees himself as a sexual male and responds to the sexuality of a female coworker — and the ways a female manager experiences her own sexuality in responding to males.

This article will focus on this third area of sexuality and discuss the following four aspects: (1) the way that men define and measure their masculinity and females their femininity, and the relation of these self-images to work success; (2) the sexual messages behind many male-female interactions; (3) the likelihood that introducing females to all levels of management will be disruptive to the way men commonly relate to other men; and (4) the matter of mutual attraction leading to sexual intercourse. Obviously these four aspects do not apply to all males or females in management, nor is each necessarily of the same intensity as one moves from first-level supervision to the executive suite. What we are suggesting is that sexuality in one form or other helps to explain why managers feel ambivalent about affirmative action for women, why many men and women have difficulty relating to each other in the office, and why women executives are handicapped in their search for success.

A. HOW SEXUALITY IS DEFINED

1. Masculinity and Work Success: The Compatible Equation

An important aspect of the sense of self-identity for both males and females is their masculinity and femininity. The charge of not being masculine is as devastating an attack for a man as questioning a woman's femininity is for a woman. How do males assert their sexuality? Teen-agers resort to fistfighting, playing "chicken" with cars, playing football, and competing against one another to see who can consume more beer or have more dates. While this may do for youth, an educated adult must find more discreet and indirect proofs.

For many men, work serves as the major vehicle defining their identity, including sexual identity. A job indicates not only a person's competence and worth but even who he is. When people meet socially, one of the first questions asked is, "What do you do?", for the answer is seen as telling a great deal about the individual. Being a plumber or a physicist, an executive or an engineer, is perceived as saying a lot about the individual's values, abilities, personality, and worth. Conversely, as Bakke's (1934) work of the Depression showed, being unemployed has a detrimental effect on a person's self-image and worth.

Status and pay of the job also bear an element of sexuality. The lumberjack and construction worker exemplify the rough masculinity of physical labor, but there is an aura of sexuality around success itself, as most clearly seen with famous individuals whose power and male sexuality are highly correlated. Not only does sexuality frequently contain elements of competition, dominance, and

power, but power often takes on sexual implications. Even some of the terms used for the former are borrowed from the latter. A person's program is said to have been "emasculated" by a certain decision, and the manager who fails is described as "impotent."

This equation of power with affirmation of masculine sexuality relates not only to the type of occupation, but also to specific task accomplishments on the job. Not infrequently a task dispute in a staff meeting takes on an overtone of interpersonal rivalry, often with a *macho* flavor. Logical arguments, the pros and cons of various positions, can mean more than just arriving at the best solution. Certainly there are other motives at work so that the "winner" feels more competent and valued by the organization, but we suggest he might also feel more masculine and reaffirmed as a man. Men once dueled physically, but now verbal wit and repartee have replaced the sword. In academic circles this has been perfected to an art, where logical arguments between colleagues are the forum for dominance.[1]

For men and for the women who admire them and help them stage these roles, there is congruence between sexuality and work performance. This refers not only to the compatibility between how boys are socialized (i.e., raised to be verbally aggressive, competitive, concerned with the task more than the relationship) and requirements of the workplace, but also to a similar congruence between work success and affirma-

---

[1]Another sign that verbal arguments can have a sexually competitive component is the behavior that not infrequently arises when an attractive female is in an otherwise all-male group. While she is not directly addressed, the men compete among themselves to see who is wittiest and sharpest.

tion of masculinity. Thus men strive to advance, build up their programs, and compete in meetings partially to obtain status and financial records that connote masculine success, but also to affirm their masculinity more directly. Even those who do not use success for sexual reassurance may feel threatened as males if they experience work failure.

This perception of the overlap between sexuality and professional success may help to explain some of the opposition to the advancement of women. To lose to a woman is inevitably more shattering to a male's self-image than to be bested by another male. Men often apply the term "castrating" to an aggressive or competent female, implying that her intentions are to lessen the masculinity of the male. But the same action or behavior may vary in its apparent impact depending on whether it comes from a male or female colleague. Behavior that is acceptable in a man is denigrated in a woman. A man may be assertive, but a woman is overly aggressive. A man may attack, but a woman castrates! Are there that many women who really try to destroy the masculinity of male coworkers? Or is the real issue that because so many men make the connection, often unconsciously, between their masculinity and job performance, any assertiveness or task success by women is experienced by the male as a threat at that level?

2. The Perceived Incompatibility of Femininity and Work Success

Task competence and sexuality interact for women as well, but for women an incompatibility exists between behaviors intrinsic to task success. Such traits include being passive, acting emotionally, being supportive, and relating well to others. Since high school, many women have felt a conflict between "being competent" and "being popular." These women must find validation of their sexuality elsewhere, since the charge of nonfemininity is a common response to any show of competence by a woman.

The options are not very satisfying for women who feel this dilemma. One alternative is to hold back from expressing competence or to express it through others. The latter ploy may mean saying things through a male, preferably the boss, so that he and others think it is his idea. When a woman does present an idea or suggestion, it is often in a deferential manner without the assurance or bluster that enables men to get their ideas accepted. Furthermore, when her idea is attacked, she is more likely to concede than to rebut: even when a woman can have ideas, she is not expected to defend them very staunchly. These evasions help some women to preserve their femininity, as traditionally defined, but at the cost of inhibiting competence.

The other extreme is forfeiting acceptance as a female to facilitate the more direct expression of ability. This is the stereotype of the "iron maiden" who is so determined to battle it out in the man's world that any warmth or softness is suppressed.[2]

These are extreme positions, whereas in actuality most females in the managerial world work out a solution some-

---

[2]Hennig (1974) reports that a not infrequent occurrence for the woman who has gone this route is, around age forty, to realize the personal cost and begin to express the warmth and softness so long suppressed.

where in between. Clearly this dilemma exists for women but not for men. The male executive, finding work and sexuality synergistic, does not have to spend time and energy working out a compromise. Furthermore, the very term "compromise" implies some concession whereby competence and/or sexual self-identity is lessened in the resolution.

B. MALE-FEMALE RELATIONSHIPS

The way males and females relate to one another at work has a sexual component in that the behavior of each is constantly influenced by the sex of the other. Most obviously this occurs when that person is viewed in terms of sexual attractiveness. One manager put it this way: "I don't know whether it's right for me to act this way, or whether it makes me a Male Chauvinist Pig, but the first time I meet a woman, I respond to her as a sexual object and only later as a person." We are not suggesting that all males or females have this same initial orientation, but even with those who don't, their interactions with the opposite sex have a sexual component even when sexual attraction is not involved.

In our culture certain ritualized ways of relating to the opposite sex have developed that have their roots in courtship behavior. For men, this may take the form of respectful deference to the "fair sex." Or it could include a protectiveness and solicitousness. To illustrate this point, imagine the following incident at a cocktail party. Three men have been discussing the state of the economy when a woman joins their group. They pull in their stomachs,

stand a little straighter, and shift the subject to some mild flirtatious bantering, compliments on her attire, or some solicitous query about the family. If the conversation moves back to business, it would not be unusual to see some competitive jostling among the men to determine who sounds more astute, and attempts to one-up the other. Approving comments from the female are welcomed, inane comments tolerated, but highly perceptive comments from her would certainly produce astonishment. It would be even more unsettling if she were to disagree with one of the males on a business issue, particularly if she were to correct him. If the male thus corrected replied defensively, the others would rush to her defense.

Yet this is a cocktail party. So what if the men are showing off a bit to the female present? What harm is there in some mild flirting? What is wrong with chivalry? And what does this scenario say about sexuality and women in management?

This interaction reinforces, in the minds of all of those involved, the woman's inferior position. She is expected to be naive and submissive, ignorant about business matters, unable to take care of herself and therefore in need of a man for protection. But if she is to be successful in the work world, she must learn how to operate in that more hostile environment. Passivity and deference will not get her far. One woman described it thusly:

"None of the behaviors I learned from watching my mother talk to my father are helpful at work. In fact, they are dysfunctional."

The type of relating described at the cocktail party reflects the typical courtship behavior that is part of the dating-relating game males and females have engaged in since puberty. The problem is that such interaction has permeated society. Being influenced and responding either consciously or unconsciously to the sexuality of the other is the primary way men and women have learned to relate to each other.[3]

1. Roles and Their Uses

The problem is that this set of attitudes and behavior cannot be confined to the date or cocktail party but carries over to the office. It is most clearly seen between the manager and *his* secretary. The mild flirtation, compliments on her new hair style, perfume, or dress, is part and parcel of the daily interaction.[4] As long as it is verbal, this interaction probably causes few problems and is the kind of friendly banter that makes interaction between the sexes enjoyable. But this mode of relating may not be limited to occasional kidding. It may underly much of the relationship between males and females on the management level.

This kind of relationship is not attributable solely to the male; the tendency exists in both directions. The female is aware that she is relating to males and acts accordingly. Thus men and women get locked into reciprocal roles that have a semisexual basis. While not the only ways that they interact, the following four role relationships are illustrative of the assertion that ways of relating developed on the outside carry over to the office in a manner that limits the potential of both parties by isolating the person and limiting the range of behavior rather than encouraging the full scope of self-expression.[5]

a. The "Macho" and the Seductress The primary mode of relating for these two roles is sexual. Actual seduction may not occur, but the nature of their interaction usually has a sexual flavor with elements of flirting and game playing. The man is concerned that women see and value him as a potent male and makes constant verbal efforts to emphasize this. He frequently attempts to assert his dominance over the woman by kidding with her about her attractiveness and then by putting her down for

---

[3]If this seems a bit farfetched to the reader, we would like to suggest the following exercise. The next time you observe a male and female interacting, change the sex of the woman so that "he" is using the same words, tone, gesture, and way of relating. It works just as well to change the man's sex instead. In either case, having the two be of the same sex produces a jarring effect. In both cases the sexuality will become apparent, for with the sex the "same," the interaction takes on a homosexual flavor.

[4]Note that a similar relationship between a female manager and her *male* secretary would not be deemed quite appropriate, because that contradicts rather than complements the organizational hierarchy for a male is usually dominant sexually. The quasi-sexual aspect of the boss-secretary relationship not infrequently develops between a person with a great deal of power and his personal assistant. A major politician, top executive, or company president may never think of having sexual intercourse with his personal secretary, but part of her devotion and loyalty is based on more than her job responsibilities.

[5]This analysis owes much to the thinking of Rosabeth Kanter (1974), who developed the concept of stereotypic roles women play in male-dominated settings. "Seductress," "Pet," and "Mother" are her terms.

her incompetence in some other area. The cost to the woman is that she is seen more as a sexual object than as a person who has business-related knowledge and competence. The satisfaction for both is that it reaffirms their sexuality.

The Seductress role is similar for the woman. In some cases she is actively seeking affirmation that she is sexually desirable and wants to have men respond to her as highly attractive. At times men place her in that role and respond to her as potentially available. Being Seductress, either through her own efforts or the expectations of men, gives her great power, for she confers potency on those men to whom she gives approval. This role has the advantage for the woman of affirming her femininity, but it inhibits direct expression of competence.

The presence of such a woman, particularly if there are only one or two females in the group, can be an energizer as the men compete for her approval, but such a situation rapidly becomes dysfunctional if there is a highly interdependent task which requires collaboration. In addition, the competence of the woman is not fully available, since her concern is to be valued as an attractive woman, not as a skilled colleague.

b. Chivalrous Knight and Helpless Maiden This is perhaps the most common set of roles, for they are highly engrained in our culture. Here the male sees himself as stronger and more competent than women and responsible for them. While politely tolerant of women, and respectful of them as women, he would not perceive a woman as having many task-related skills. Conse-

quently he would be less likely to challenge her or make the same demands on her that he would on males.

With this relationship the female, playing the role of Helpless Maiden, can use these stereotypes to manipulate the male for her own ends. Korda (1972) quotes just such a person.

> ... When it's a question of using my sex, I use it. I don't mean I sleep around — I don't. But if you have any kind of looks and you're not scared yourself you can get what you want. You listen to them, flirt a little, cry when things go wrong, and say, "Gee, I wish you could show me how to do this, you know so much more about this than I do." It's a snap. [p. 29]

Rather than truly being helpless and withdrawing from the competition, the Helpless Maiden in this case feigns ineptness and derives a sense of power because men serve her. Many men become furious at having become ensnared into this protective stance, for the woman is taking his stereotype, usually used to legitimize female subservience, and turning it against him for her own advantage. To add insult to injury, the very beliefs the men hold — that give Helpless Maiden her power — prevent men from directly confronting her and calling her on this game. To do so would be to treat her like a strong, competent person, i.e., another male. The damage to the Helpless Maiden is great, too. She may "overlearn" these behaviors and never get free of them, losing the opportunity to learn to take care of herself. This reinforces her dependency on a man, which limits her mobility as she fails to develop the direct assertiveness necessary for self-expression and success in the work world.

c. Protective Father and the Pet   A combination that crops up, particularly between an older man and younger woman, is a protective father-daughter relationship. This differs from the Knight-Maiden in that the Father tends to be more active in assuming a protective role and the woman's dependence is less likely to be a means of manipulation. The Pet functions almost as a cheerleader for the men she works with. If the Pet, or mascot, goes to lunch with a group of men, she laughs at their jokes, encourages them to talk about themselves and their ideas, but rarely contributes to the content herself.

Not infrequently the Pet and the Seductress get linked with high-status males, which increases the power of both. As in the case of the Seductress, this can validate the Pet's femininity, but at the cost of not being able to show competence directly. The two roles differ in that the Pet, like the overdeveloped but underaged teen-ager, is not perceived as sexually available.

d. Tough Warrior and Nurturant Mother   For many men, masculinity is defined in the "John Wayne" tradition of being tough and independent and suppressing all emotions. While functional at times for occupational success, this role definition is costly. This artificial self-sufficiency not only has personal costs, but can interfere with task success as well. Work requires collaboration as well as competition, interdependence as well as independence, and giving and receiving of support and help as well as giving and receiving of ideas.

The reciprocal of this role is that of the Nurturant Mother who serves as the confidante to whom others can bring

their problems and seek support. While they are not relating to her as a sexual object, they do not respond to her as a total person; rather they respond to one aspect of the female stereotype. At least, this role removes her from sexual competition, but as Kanter points out, it has three major costs: (1) she is valued because of the support and service she can provide to the males and not because of her individual abilities or actions — thus it tends to cut down on her tendency to take independent initiative around task areas; (2) she often is placed in the role of the "good, accepting mother," which inhibits the extent to which she can use her critical abilities; and (3) she becomes the specialist in emotional issues and shields men from accepting responsibility in their areas; this division of labor serves to further the stereotype that men are rational and logical while women are overly emotional.

We have given these four descriptions of male-female roles as examples of how each can be trapped when relating to the other. While they have been paired, each can exist without the counterpart. A man can play Chivalrous Knight even when none of the women are acting helpless. These roles are overlearned from a multitude of past situations, and so the mere fact of being the only woman present might encourage a woman's tendency to nurture others without any of the men turning to her for support. But it is also likely that a dominant style from one sex evokes the reciprocal in the other. It is difficult to be *Macho* to the Nurturant Mother but easy if the woman is playing Seductress.

Clearly not all interactions are of this type, for people of the opposite sex can relate to each other as individuals with a minimum of such role playing.[6] Furthermore, these ritualized ways of relating are less prevalent in the higher echelons of the organization. These four role types all limit expressions of competence in women and thus are dysfunctional for success. Males do not experience the reciprocal roles as much of a hindrance. Their roles are evoked only by the presence of women, but women executives almost always work with men and so their roles are more likely to emerge.

More and more women, and to some extent men, are attempting to break these role constraints, but change is slow. For example, it is hard for a woman to keep from being the protected child when her boss treats her as one. She may not be aware of the extent to which he shields her from assignments that are challenging and risky, but which are necessary if she is to develop and advance. Even if she is aware, how can she confront someone who is "only trying to help"?[7]

In the same way, men often feel confused about how to deal with women. While some females are attempting to change the norms governing interaction between the sexes, there is far from universal agreement by women about how they want to be treated. Males often feel confused about such simple issues as "Should I open the door, help her on with her coat, pick up the tab, or call

her Ms.?" Or issues of more substance: "Will she feel I'm patronizing her if I give her some advice about her career?" Relationships have become much more complex, with greater ambiguity about what is expected and what is correct. Like the white liberal who feels helpless when called a racist by a black, so many males feel constrained for fear of being labeled "sexist."

Ironically, the reason men often feel so uncertain about how to relate to women is that they are trapped in traditional sex roles themselves. They are shackled by the social mores of how gentlemen should relate to ladies: protecting them, taking care of them, being responsible for them. Men and women need the freedom to respond to each other as one individual to another.

C. MALE-MALE BONDING: THE INTERFERENCE OF WOMEN

When men are together, a bonding process develops that does not occur when women are present (Tiger, 1969). The mechanisms are many and varied. For some it can be a discussion of last weekend's football game, cars, or an offhand comment about the physical dimensions of a passing secretary. For others it can be comparing golf scores, or discussing politics and the stock market, or working together on a task. But whatever the subject, the style and tone are such that the message is clear: this is a

---

[6]The term "role playing" does not imply that the male or female is necessarily consciously "playing a role." As we have mentioned, roles can be so ingrained from countless encounters as to have become an integrated part of that individual's personality and behavioral style.

[7]One of our female colleagues made the point that she has been held back more by "friends" than by enemies. "With the latter you know where you stand, but with friends they are forever trying to protect you from situations where you might fail."

"man's world." The rapport is perpetuated only so long as the membership is totally male.

Why the change when a female appears? One reason is that these topics serve as one way to assert a traditional definition of masculinity. This form of bonding is based on the exclusion of women. What is shared are interests supposedly not held by women rather than what the members have in common as a result of working on the same project or being employed by the same company. What would happen if a woman in the group were equally knowledgeable and vocal about sports, cars, and politics? If the basis for bonding were solely common interests, then her contributions should be welcome. But isn't it likely that men would feel uncomfortable if a woman corrected them on Monday night's game, knew more about the racing specs of the Porsche, or had a lower handicap? The conversation would soon die out and men would lose the camaraderie that had existed before.

The points raised in the previous section give a clue to another reason why women interfere with the bonding that occurs in an all-male group. The introduction of a woman could activate male-female role relationships so that men would feel great consternation not only about how they should act, but also about what subjects and language are appropriate and inappropriate. The bantering among men often has a veiled competitive tone that attempts to score points without hurting feelings or causing retaliation. Many men feel uncomfortable treating women in a similar fashion or even demonstrating such behavior in front of them. It would be even more threatening if a woman were

attractive and fit the Seductress role. This could provoke a different kind of rivalry among the men that would undermine any sense of trust and solidarity among them.

Even when the female is not responded to as the Seductress, concerns about sexuality can interfere with other activities used by men for bonding. Frequently work goes on during lunch and over a drink after five. Not only is work conducted, but people become better acquainted, both crucial in facilitating later business interactions as well as the individual's career development. But men may be hesitant to involve women in such activities. Will luncheon meetings be seen by the woman and coworkers in the same light as if one were to go out with a male peer? Similarly, going out on the town while at conventions or on business trips may not be the same when women are present.

D. THE FEAR OF SEXUAL ENTANGLEMENTS

Sexual liaisons within the same organization, while not unknown, still tend to be negatively sanctioned. Data from the Sex Research Center at the University of Indiana suggest that at least three-fourths of the males in this country commit adultery, but it is not clear how this is spread throughout the management hierarchy. A recent study (Johnson, 1974) reported that only 20 percent of top executives acknowledge having sex outside of marriage. Of these, only one in four indicates involvement on a regular basis; and only 8.8 percent of those, or less than 2 percent of the total sample, reported an affair with a woman in the office. Most of these men go outside of their marriage between the tenth and twentieth years of marriage and are between the ages of thirty-five and forty-five. Regrettably, there are no comparable data on women.

Questions can be raised about whether this sample is representative and whether information were gathered under conditions where the executives would be completely candid. But whatever the actual incidence of office affairs, the fear of their occurrence is very high. Hence the need exists for greater understanding of some of the issues and feelings involved.

Many people with whom we have talked say that when women and men work together in a noncompetitive relationship, it is only a matter of time before sexual attraction starts to develop. It is doubtful that this occurs in all, or nearly all, cases, but one of the most consistent findings in social psychological research is that contact leads to liking, which in turn leads to more interaction. Two people who work together for some time learn to trust, rely on, and respect each other with a corresponding increase in liking.

Obviously this does not occur in all cases. Knowing another more fully may lead to discovering something we don't like, and working on a project can also be a source of strain and conflict. Also, knowing a man or woman as an equal may remove the mystique and could lead to a rich friendship without sexual involvement.

There are two reasons why it is likely that the incidence of sexual attraction will increase, in addition to the obvious fact that the presence of more women in management raises the number of potential pairs. One is the changing internal structure of contemporary organizations, and the other is the changing cultural norms. As organizations grow more complex with a wide distribution of offices, plants, and clients, travel will increase. The companies that send only males to the field, thus hindering the career opportunities of female executives, may become targets for affirmative action litigation. No longer are women working just eight to five; trips, evening meetings, and conferences set up conditions that make affairs easier to occur.

Societal norms about premarital and extramarital sexuality are changing. While such behavior is not sanctioned by organizations or society, there is greater tolerance for what was once considered highly deviant behavior. Although an affair may still bring great personal pain and can incur costs to job success and reputation, particularly for the female, it is not likely to be as shattering as in the past. Behavior at work cannot be isolated from societal trends, and changes in the culture are likely to be reflected in the office.

Sexual attraction and affairs obviously have their cost, but often overlooked are costs incurred when managers are overly concerned about preventing intimacy from developing. Such vigilance can prevent the emergence of normal relationships. The fear of getting emotionally involved can lead male and female executives to bend over backwards to avoid situations that might appear compromising, like having dinner together or working after hours, but that might increase their task performance. The female can be so worried about appearing seductive that she becomes totally asexual and inhibits all expressions of warmth and caring. The wife at home may be jealous of the female coworker who is able to display skills that the wife has had to submerge. In order to avoid such conflict, the husband may avoid contacts with the female office mate for fear this will cause difficulties at home.

E. WHERE DO WE GO FROM HERE?

The problems we have discussed are complex and deeply rooted in our culture. No easy solutions exist, but as men and women begin to work together to build adult relationships, a first step seems to be to acknowledge the various ways sexuality may be expressed in the office. With this awareness, executives can become sensitive to the possibilities of responses based on sexual stereotypes. They can be more attuned to how men respond to women differentially so that such personally limiting ways of relating can be avoided.

Until recently, consciousness raising has been seen as the domain of women and then of only a few. In several urban areas — Berkeley, Boston, and New York — parallel groups of men have developed to look at the constraints of the male sex role. Such activity has rarely been seen as the concern of organizations. Executives have taken the stance that, at best, participation in such groups is an aspect of personal growth that can be undertaken after hours but it is nothing that business should initiate.

If our analysis is correct, the constraints men and women feel in relating to each other have direct application to work effectiveness. The manager, to be effective, needs to explore to what extent he has been enslaved by sex-role stereotypes, how he feels constrained from arguing with and directly confronting women, how confined he is by traditional definitions of masculinity as seen in films and advertising. The ultimate goal is not one of women's liberation or men's liberation but of human liberation that permits personal development according to individual interests rather than societal sex-role constraints.

For the long run this requires a major shift in cultural mores, but one does not have to wait for societal norms to change before changing the climate in the office. The superior can be very influential in determining what behavior is valued and what is not. Clear signals that competence in women is desired can provide the needed reassurance to the female who is afraid that assertiveness will be seen as unfeminine or castrating. Discouraging the games that men and women play can prevent their continuation.

For such changes to be permanent there must be support throughout the organization. Management development seeks to train executives to better handle technical and administrative aspects of their jobs. Training on the issues we have discussed would be equally useful to increase their awareness of sexism and to develop their ability to more effectively relate to and work with members of the opposite sex.

It is neither possible nor even desirable for people to ignore the sex of one another. At this point in our cultural development it is more desirable to increase awareness so that one can understand how the sex of another is affecting one's behavior. The statement "I want to treat her like I would any other person" is often a veiled form of sexism, for it usually means "like I would any other male." Growing up male or female has had a major impact on the person and how he or she relates to others.

What we are suggesting is that in order for the male executive to understand a woman as an individual, he needs to be aware of how her being a woman has influenced her attitudes and behavior. Equally important, he needs to be aware of how being male has influenced his perceptions and responses to women. Likewise, the woman needs to be aware of how her stereotypes influence her behavior and limit her options in responding to the male executive. What is crucial is that the reality of sexuality as an issue be acknowledged so that men and women in organizations can begin to recognize and explore these issues.

F. SEXUAL ATTRACTION

Increased awareness of the roles that sexuality and sexism play in male-female interaction may help with many of the issues we have discussed but may be less useful in resolving the problem of sexual attraction. If history is any predictor of the future, there may be no simple answer. Troy was not the first, nor last, empire to be lost over sexuality. Each person has to work out his or her own resolution. Some resolve it by working hard to make sure feelings never develop. However, although such a solution prevents the problem from arising, it may have a hidden cost, for

to be so concerned and guarded against ever developing attractions can produce a greater than necessary distance and formality. After all, friendship and interpersonal liking are important facilitators in work, be they between the sexes or with the same sex.

Another resolution distinguishes between feelings and behavior. The former need not dictate the latter. People have much more control over their actions than over their emotions. When verbally attacked, it is difficult not to feel anger but easy to refrain from slugging back. So it is with sex. A person can have strong feelings of attraction, and these can continue to exist without leading either to an affair or to disruption of the work relationship.

When feelings of attraction do develop, should they be communicated? In our discussions with managers, no clear outcome emerges. In some situations, sharing of feelings appears to reduce some of the intensity and ambiguity so that individuals can continue to work together and even go out for lunch without fear that intentions will be misinterpreted. Open discussion also allows both people to decide how to deal with their attraction. The attraction then becomes a fact of life and people are free to turn to the task at hand.

For others, such a discussion is uncomfortable; they would much prefer not to acknowledge the attraction. There are no simple answers. What is important is that the issue of sexuality be recognized as a fact of organizational life.

Women in management have been described as a "problem" and an "issue" that must be faced. But equal employment may be the source of greater enrichment for the individual and for the total society as well as for the enlightened organization, and thus

any problems encountered may be well worth the price.

REFERENCES

1. ARIES, ELIZABETH, "Male-Female Communication in Small Groups," in Alice G. Sargent (ed.), *Beyond Sex Roles*, St. Paul, Minn.: West, in press.
2. BAKKE, E. W., *The Unemployed Man*, New York: Dutton, 1934.
3. GOLDBERG, P. A., "Are Women Prejudiced against Women?" *Trans-Action*, April 1968.
4. HENNIG, MARGARET, "Family Dynamics and the Successful Woman Executive," in Ruth B. Knudsin (ed.), *Women and Success: The Anatomy of Achievement*, New York: Morrow, 1974.
5. HORNER, MATINA, "Femininity and Successful Achievement: A Basic Inconsistency," in Judith Bardwick, Elizabeth Douvan, Matina Horner, and David Guttmann (eds.), *Feminine Personality and Conflict*, Belmont, Calif.: Brooks/Cole, 1970.
6. JOHNSON, HARRY J., *Executive Life Styles: A Life Extension Institute Report on Alcohol, Sex and Health*, New York: Crowell, 1974.
7. KANTER, ROSABETH MOSS, "Women in Organizations: Change Agent Skills," paper presented at the NTL Conference on New Technology in Organization Development, 1974, published in the conference proceedings.
8. KORDA, MICHAEL, *Male Chauvinism!* New York: Random House, 1972.
9. PHETERSON, G. I., S. B. KIESLER, and P. A. GOLDBERG, "Evaluation of the Performance of Women as a Function of Their Sex, Achievement, and Personal History," *Journal of Personality and Social Psychology*, vol. 19, no. 1, 1971.
10. SERBIN, LISA, unpublished doctoral dissertation, Department of Psychology, State University of New York at Stony Brook, 1973; presented at the American Psychological Association, Philadelphia, Spring 1973.
11. TIGER, LIONEL, *Men in Groups*, New York: Random House, 1969.

SEABROOK MANUFACTURING COMPANY

CASE 1

"All we need now is a strong man to complete the side show!" exclaimed Joe Larson, purchasing manager of the Seabrook Manufacturing Company, as he entered the office of Dale Wolff, personnel representative for the Purchasing Department.

"What do you mean, Joe?" asked Dale.

"You know that we have a lot of visitors and suppliers through here, and that old bag isn't doing much to doll up the area. These secretaries have a good deal to do with the impressions people get of our outfit, and they should be at least presentable! We spend thousands of dollars for carpeting and pictures and now this!"

"Whom are you talking about?"

"I don't know what her name is, but you know damn well whom I'm talking about! The Blimp! Take care of it, will you?"

The Purchasing Department of Seabrook Manufacturing Company occupied the major portion of the third floor of the headquarters building of the company. The main working force was located in a large open area at several rows of desks. Executives of the division, all of whom were under the control of Larson, were located in private offices that extended along the outer edge of the general working area.[1] The secretary for each executive was situated at a desk directly in front of the office of the executive for whom she worked, but was separated from the rest of the workers by a wide aisle. This aisle was the main passage used by visitors and personnel from other divisions of the company to get from the reception lobby to the executives' offices. The secretaries' desks were finished with a walnut stain as contrasted with the lighter-colored finishes used on other desks in the open area, and the space between secretaries' desks was significantly greater than the space between other desks on the floor. The office layout of the Purchasing Department is shown in Exhibit 1.

Mary Lampson, the secretary in question, had just been promoted to her new position as Jack Henderson's secretary and had moved to her new location while Larson had been away on a business trip. After his former secretary had submitted her resignation, Jack Henderson had selected Mary Lampson as his new secretary after reviewing the personnel files and talking with several individuals currently employed in the department whom Dale Wolff had rec-

[1]Dale Wolff reported directly to Joe Larson.

ommended as candidates for the position.

Mary Lampson was forty-eight years old, and had been with the Sea-brook Manufacturing Company for seventeen years, ten in the Purchasing Department. She had started work at Seabrook shortly after her husband died. Prior to her assignment as Henderson's secretary, she had performed secretarial duties for several units in the department, but had always been located in the open area with the general employees of the division. She had two grown sons who had completed college and had moved to other parts of the country, and one other son, twenty years old, who was a sophomore at Eastern State University. Her record at Seabrook was unblemished. She had

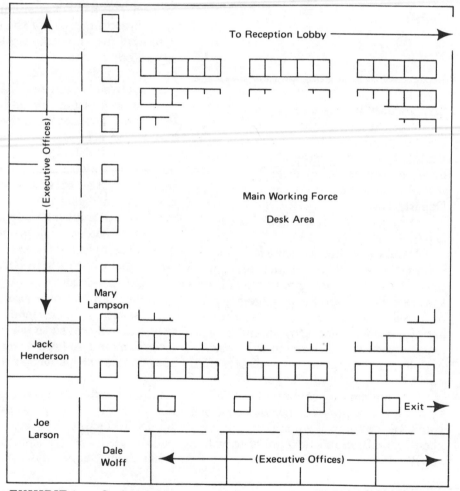

EXHIBIT 1 • *Seabrook Manufacturing Company — Purchasing Department Office Layout*

created favorable impressions wherever she had worked, and her former supervisors were unanimous in their praise of her abilities.

Mary Lampson was five feet four inches tall and weighed two hundred and twenty-five pounds. Although her weight had been a continuing problem for her, she was very pleased with her recent progress on a weight control program, and had lost sixty pounds in the last two years by following her doctor's orders very closely. She was enthusiastic about her new job, for she could use the increase in salary to help put her

youngest son through college, and, as she put it, "keep the creditors a little farther from my door."

While not knowing quite how to "take care of it," Dale Wolff decided that his first step should be to talk with Jack Henderson, Mary's boss.

After Wolff related his conversation with Larson, Jack Henderson replied: "What a hell of a way to run a railroad! You do what you want to, Dale, but things are in pretty miserable shape when looks are more important than ability. I'm certainly not going to mention this to Mary!"

UNITED MUTUAL INSURANCE COMPANY (A)

CASE 2

The United Mutual Insurance Company was organized in 1939 by Paul and James Taylor. Since its organization, these two men have maintained active, personal direction of the company. The company is located in Kansas City, Missouri, and writes all forms of auto-

mobile and general casualty insurance. At the present time, 1961, United Mutual is represented by more than 2,000 agents located in Wisconsin, Illinois, Iowa, Missouri, Kentucky and Colorado, and it has 32 field managers and 80 claims adjusters working out of 47 offices. The company has grown steadily since it was founded.

The home office of the United Mutual has about 425 employees of which approximately 75% are women. Due primarily to marriage and family obligations of many of the women, annual labor turnover is 25–30%. There has been a mild labor shortage in Kansas City the past few years which has made it difficult to obtain secretaries, typists, and file clerks. Of the 425 persons in the home office, about 100 are "supervisory employees." The term "supervisory employees" or "supervisors" in this company refers to those persons who do not have to punch time clocks and do not receive overtime pay. It includes both people who direct the work of others, and also some technical and professional people such as lawyers and underwriters. About 90 per cent of these "supervisors" are men. An organization chart of the persons primarily involved in this case is shown in Figure 1.

Employees of United Mutual were required to work an eight hour day with no authorized rest periods prior to 1955. By 1955 many companies had estab-lished policies granting coffee breaks of 10 to 15 minutes in the morning and afternoon, but such was not the case at United Mutual. According to Mr. G. B. Townsend, United Mutual did not have facilities to serve coffee even if coffee breaks were authorized. Mr. Townsend came to United Mutual in 1953 from another insurance company in Michigan. His responsibilities as head of the General Services Department are payroll, company budgets, and building maintenance. He became involved in the coffee

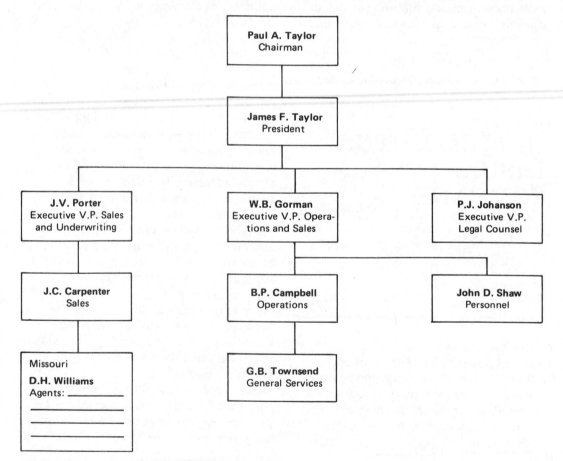

FIGURE 1 • *Partial Organization Chart of United Mutual Insurance Company, 1961* Source: Company records

problem almost as soon as he came to United Mutual because of his responsibility for payroll. (Should a clerk be "docked" for overstaying her unauthorized rest period?) and for general building services, which would include cafeteria service if it were installed. On matters pertaining to the coffee problem he worked directly with Mr. Gorman.

Mr. Townsend stated that when he came to United Mutual Company, officials were concerned about employees leaving their desks in the morning and afternoon for a half hour or more when time was not allowed for any break. Black's Drug Store was located one block from United Mutual, and it became more or less routine for many of the employees to drop by Black's twice a day for coffee. In fact, many supervisory employees started spending a good share of the morning patronizing their favorite coffee spot (Black's). Finally the word came to department heads from James Taylor to stop these morning and afternoon breaks immediately, but since the department heads were some of the greatest violators, little was done and Black's still remained a favorite morning and afternoon "hangout." Mr.

Townsend went on to state that things finally became so bad that some employees were actually going downtown, a distance of some six or seven blocks, for coffee and were gone as long as 3/4 of an hour to an hour.

Mr. W. P. Gorman, Vice President of Operations and Claims, who was responsible for home-office operations including the personnel function, decided that additional steps were needed to stop these unauthorized coffee breaks, and he proceeded to make plans for a cafeteria in the United Mutual Building. Plans were approved by James and Paul Taylor and other top executives. The cafeteria was installed in the basement of the building in September of 1955, in the location shown in Figure 2.

A cafeteria board was organized by Mr. Gorman, and after many meetings and long hours of discussion, members came to the conclusion that each day there would be two coffee breaks consisting of fifteen minutes each. The coffee breaks were to be regulated by the department heads, who were men in charge of separate functions such as claims, legal, and underwriting. In most cases they reported to a vice-president,

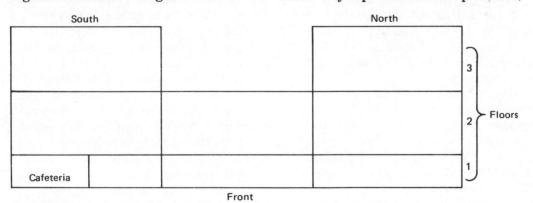

FIGURE 2 • *United Mutual Building 1955–1958*

but some were one level removed from him. It was their job to see that rules for the coffee hour were observed and that someone was always in the department to look after it during coffee break. Mr. Townsend was designated by the cafeteria board to make spot checks to see how the new plan worked. He reported that most employees took their allotted fifteen minutes and very few exceeded it. Productivity increased considerably, and, according to Mr. Townsend, morale was much higher. In fact he stated that the problem of coffee breaks was "about licked," but then early in 1956 many of the supervisory employees started taking advantage of the coffee breaks and overstayed their time in the cafeteria.

When the non-supervisory employees saw what was happening, they also started to take longer coffee breaks than were authorized. Before many months had passed most all of the employees were taking longer breaks than were allotted. When Mr. Townsend and Mr. Gorman questioned several of the supervisory employees as to why they spent so much time during the coffee breaks when they knew that only fifteen minutes were authorized, the standard reply was, "We were discussing business problems of United Mutual," or "We were having a meeting, so we actually were working."

It is probable that many overstayed coffee breaks actually were informal business meetings, because most of the supervisors were either Underwriters, Claims Adjusters, or Operations Supervisors, and daily meetings of some of these people were common to discuss their business problems. There was, of course, no way to prove which discussions were social and which were informal business meetings. One thing seemed sure. It was almost impossible to get non-supervisory employees to believe that supervisors were actually working during coffee hour; so Mr. Gorman told the supervisors that they had to keep within their 15 minutes in order to set an example for the rest of the employees. They failed to heed his word, and the coffee break continued to be violated. To add to the complication, too many employees were coming to the cafeteria at the same time which resulted in much congestion and waiting to get their coffee. Mr. Gorman decided that further action was necessary because many hours of production were lost each day by employees taking too much time during the scheduled coffee periods. At this time United Mutual did not have a personnel director or personnel department, and Mr. Townsend and Mr. Gorman more or less looked after personnel problems that arose. There was an employment manager, but he had no overall personnel responsibilities.

Top management knew it had a problem on its hands, and much discussion resulted concerning possible solutions to the coffee period. There was even some discussion about discontinuing the coffee hour and returning to the old schedule of no breaks whatsoever. James Porter, Executive Vice President in charge of sales and underwriting said, "Eliminate the coffee hour, just a waste of time." When one secretary was asked what she thought of the coffee hour, she replied, "Might as well not have a coffee hour; then I might lose some weight."

Of course the majority of the employees enjoyed their breaks during the day, and Mr. Gorman concluded that whether there was an "authorized" coffee break or not, employees were still going to take time out for these breaks. Something had to be done to get employees to observe the time limit on coffee hours. Mr. Gorman decided it would be useless to distribute an order instructing employees to obey the time limit of the coffee break as there wasn't any police action to back up the order. Department heads and supervisors were just as guilty as the rest, and surely the president and vice presidents could not watch everybody to see that the order was obeyed. Mr. Gorman, realizing that the supervisory employees were the greatest violators of the coffee break, decided that their coffee privileges

should be suspended for a trial period. On November 8, 1957, he issued to all supervisory employees the memorandum in Figure 3.

According to Mr. Townsend this memorandum met with great disapproval and some of the supervisory employees even threatened to quit United Mutual. Many of them brought their own thermos bottles of coffee and took time out anyway while others started going back to Black's Drug Store for their breaks. Two comments are typical.

Phil Adams, underwriter in charge of Baxter County: "It really hurt the morale of the company; I can't see how it did any good at all."

Mr. B. P. Campbell, Assistant Opera-

UNITED MUTUAL INSURANCE COMPANY
MEMORANDUM

To: Department Heads and Supervisors

From: W. P. Gorman

Subject: Rest Periods

Rest periods are used in business and industry for the purpose of giving needed relief to employees on continuous and confining types of activity. Here at United Mutual we have extended the courtesy to all home office employees. However, a recent study reveals that supervisory employees are the principal violators of our rest period rule.

Our major problem is a supervisory staff that is setting a bad example rather than a good one. To see how supervisory people can supervise themselves, it is suggested that:

a. Supervisory people refrain from using the cafeteria and second floor Coke room facilities for two weeks starting Monday, November 12.
b. Non-supervisory employees remind themselves that they have a fifteen-minute morning and afternoon coffee period. Necessary time commuting from and to your desk is recognized over and above the fifteen minutes.
c. Department heads reappraise the schedules now being followed by their own departments.

11/8/57
WG:mc

FIGURE 3 • *Memorandum by Mr. Gorman*

tions Manager: "It didn't do a darn bit of good."

Mr. Townsend stated that he thought the memorandum was bad because it clearly distinguished the non-supervisory from the supervisory employees.

After the specified two weeks, Mr. Gorman's executive memorandum expired, but the coffee break problem still remained. In an effort to keep the coffee break limited to fifteen minutes, Mr. Townsend started staying in the cafeteria during the complete coffee hour and watching for offenders who stayed over the time limit. He in turn reported the offenders to department heads who were supposed to take action necessary to insure that their employees obeyed the coffee period time limit. For the next few months employees observed the fifteen-minute coffee period very closely with few exceptions. Then the department heads again became lax, and non-supervisory, as well as supervisory, employees began exceeding the time limit on coffee periods.

Again Mr. Gorman and Mr. Townsend went into consultation, and this time they came up with the idea of installing bells in the cafeteria. These bells were then installed and were adjusted to ring every ten minutes. Considering that it took a few minutes for the employee to get from her/his office to the cafeteria, Mr. Gorman and Mr. Townsend felt that ten minutes in the cafeteria was the maximum time that could be allowed in order to still stay within the limits of the fifteen-minute coffee period. Schedules were set up by the department heads so that employees were supposed to arrive at the cafeteria when the bells rang and they would stay until the bells rang again, at which time they were supposed to leave. Mr. Townsend noted that the bells did keep some employees in the cafeteria for only ten minutes, but it was very difficult to synchronize the various groups. People were sifting in and out of the cafeteria all of the time and not according to the schedule for which the bells were adjusted. Also when one group was leaving the cafeteria, another group was scheduled to enter which added to the congestion. The general opinion among some employees was that the bells made them feel "like they were in prison cells" and could not get out until the bells rang. Others thought the bells very irritating and said it was impossible to enjoy the coffee period. It was soon evident that the bells were not solving the coffee period problem, but since no better solution was offered, the bells remained and employees continued to complain about them.

UNITED MUTUAL INSURANCE COMPANY (B)

CASE 3

Early in 1958 top management realized that United Mutual was expanding to the extent that there was definite need for a personnel director to handle the coffee break problem as well as the increasing number of other personnel problems existing within the home office. Therefore, in July of 1958 John Shaw was hired as Personnel Director of United Mutual. Mr. Shaw had sixteen years' experience in personnel work and was highly regarded in local personnel circles. Soon after his arrival at United Mutual the current personnel problems were explained to him, and of course one of these problems was the coffee breaks. Mr. Shaw soon found out for himself that employees were taking more than their allotted time during coffee periods. The president wanted something done to remedy the situation, and this problem was, therefore, given to Mr. Shaw, the new personnel director of United Mutual Insurance Company.

Mr. Shaw tackled the problem rapidly and directly. In his own words, "I made periodic checks with all of the department heads concerning the coffee hour and found out what their reactions were. I told the department heads to keep check on the employees under their jurisdiction and to try to keep the coffee break confined within the fifteen-minute period."

Mr. Shaw soon found out that the bells were ineffective and unpopular. He had them removed from the cafeteria. A few executives approached Mr. Shaw and suggested that the coffee periods be discontinued. Mr. Shaw countered with the following argument: "The labor shortage in our city is critical at the present time. We have 25 vacancies within the Company and yet you want me to discontinue the coffee periods and as a result perhaps lose more employees."

In December, 1958, top management asked Mr. Shaw to justify his stand that the coffee hour was necessary, and if he could justify it, to provide a remedy to the problem. Mr. Shaw gave the following reasons why the coffee periods should be continued:

1. "A coffee break helps new employees make friends with people in their own and other departments. United Mutual has a 25-to-30% labor turnover each year so you can see that several new employees are coming to the company every week.
2. "By having a coffee break there is a cross-pollination of ideas and this prevents stratification and cliques.
3. "A coffee break will give renewed vigor to the employees and this will result in greater productivity.
4. "The nature of detailed work and mental activity is so confining that people need a respite from their routines."

After much deliberation and consultation, Mr. Shaw arrived at a solution for the coffee break and submitted it to the top executives. They approved it, including his proposal that coffee be furnished free to employees. Free coffee was first given on March 23 by means of a routine announcement in the cafeteria. The remainder of Mr. Shaw's proposal was put into effect by a memordandum issued on March 31, 1959, by Mr. Shaw to all home office employees of United Mutual (see Figure 4).

The memorandum was well received

FIGURE 4 • *Memorandum to Employees*

To: All Home Office Department Heads and Employees
From: Personnel
Subject: Changes in Working, Lunch, and Rest Period Schedules

Effective May 4, the working schedule of the office will be as follows:

8:00 A.M. to 12:00 noon.
Forty minute lunch periods will be scheduled at five regular intervals.
Fifteen minute morning *rest periods* will be scheduled at five regular intervals.
The working day will end at 4:25 P.M.

This new working schedule reduces the work day by ten minutes and makes an over-all work week of 38.75 hours. We feel sure that employees will welcome this change since it will help to avoid further the evening traffic congestion, and will facilitate bus and trolley connections.

The morning rest periods will be scheduled from 9:30 A.M. through 10:25 A.M. Departments will be scheduled at ten minute intervals. *Fifteen minutes will be allowed for each employee, which includes travel time to and from the cafeteria.* It is important that employees adhere to the schedules listed below since the principal reason for staggering is to eliminate confusion and congestion and to improve service in the cafeteria. It will be the responsibility of department heads to make certain that employees follow the assigned schedules. Following is the morning rest period schedule for all departments.

All personnel on the third floor in the North Building including the following:

Departments	*Rest Period*
Claims Clerical	9:30–9:45
Legal and Workmen's Compensation	

All personnel on the second floor in the South Building including the following:

Departments	*Rest Period*
Illinois Bonds	9:45–10:00
Missouri Iowa	
Indexing and File Units	

All personnel on the first floor in the South Building including the following:

Departments	Rest Period
Kentucky Casualty	10:00–10:15
Personnel	
Colorado Automobile	
Audit and Engineering	
Fire Underwriting	
Indexing, Daily Report, Mail, Sewing	

All personnel on the third floor in the South Building including the following:

Departments	Rest Period
Accounting	10:15–10:30
Branch Audit	
Payroll	

All personnel on the first and second floors of the North Building including the following:

Departments	Rest Period
Agency and Advertising	10:25–10:40
Purchasing and Supply	
Baxter County Underwriting	
Baxter County Claims and Sales	
Mail and Printing	

Where stand-by telephone service is required, department heads will exercise discretion in keeping their operation staffed during the morning rest and lunch periods.

In keeping with national trend in offices, smoking will be permitted at the working desk by all employees. We know that employees will exercise discretion in respect to both safety requirements and office etiquette.

With the reduction of the work week by fifty minutes and the provision for the new smoking privilege, we feel that the afternoon rest period is unnecessary. The cafeteria will be closed after the last lunch group has been served.

3/31/59
JDS:rg

by most all of the employees. The work week was cut from 39 hours, 35 minutes, to 38 hours, 45 minutes, and the employees who smoked enjoyed the privilege that was given them. Mr. Shaw believed that everything would have turned out all right if United Mutual had not been remodeling and adding to its building at that time as shown in Figure 5.

As can be seen from the diagram, this construction meant that all employees from the North Building had to walk outside and around the center building in order to get to the cafeteria for the coffee period. Employees on the third

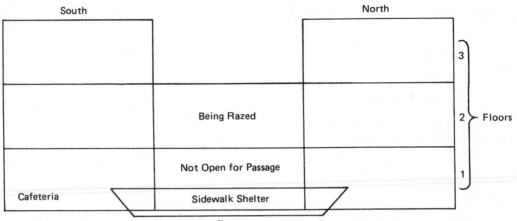

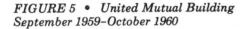

FIGURE 5 • *United Mutual Building*
September 1959–October 1960

floor took as long as six to seven minutes to reach the cafeteria, which caused their break to extend beyond the fifteen-minute limitation. In the ensuing months, department heads became slack in enforcing the memorandum issued by Mr. Shaw, and employees again started taking more time than was allotted to them. Most department heads had their departments split into two sections. One section was to go for their coffee and the other section was to wait until the first section returned. The only trouble was that the second section was not waiting for the first section to return before they left. The result was mass confusion in the cafeteria. Groups did not come on the regular schedule, and when they did come, they stayed over 15 minutes. Mr. Shaw conferred with all the

department heads and told them that if the practice of "long" coffee breaks continued in the future, there was a strong possibility of not having any coffee breaks at all.

One department head realized the seriousness of the problem and issued a memorandum to all his employees (see Figure 6). Each person received an individual copy.

Mr. Gorman upon reading Mr. Williams' memorandum suggested to Mr. Shaw that copies of this memorandum be distributed to all department heads and supervisors. Mr. Shaw followed Mr. Gorman's suggestion and attached copies of Mr. Williams' memorandum to a memo of his own, as shown in Figure 7.

FIGURE 6 • Memorandum to City Employees

To: City Sales Department Employees and Agents

From: Don H. Williams

OFFICE HOURS AND PRIVILEGES

There are times when an organization the size of ours must stop and take an inventory and endeavor to eliminate any unusual conditions that affect the services rendered to our agents and policyholders. This is one of those times, and this memorandum is something that I would like for you to read very carefully. I am sure after you have understood the problem, we will have your usual full cooperation.

Although most companies work on a so-called 40-hour week schedule, we formerly worked from 8:00 to 4:35 and granted a 10 minute rest period morning and afternoon to the employees. When the coffee hour was inaugurated, the present office hours were submitted to the employees and unanimously agreed upon. These office hours are now 8:00 to 4:25 with a 15-minute coffee period in the morning. Not including the deduction for the coffee hour, 8:00 to 4:25 amounts to 38 hours and 45 minutes per week instead of the usual 40 hours, but by deducting the 15-minute coffee period, it comes down to a net of 37 hours and 30 minutes. As you can see, this is much below the usual office hours and considerably below our operation of several years back, before the 40-hour week came into vogue.

COFFEE PERIOD

The coffee period is set to begin at 9:30 and close at 10:35 in order that ample time may be available to have the cafeteria cleared and set up for the lunch hours, which begin at 11:30. This warrants my requesting that each of you keep that period in mind and not go down to the cafeteria until 9:30 and clear it by 10:35, so that everything may work uniformly. The coffee period has been limited as outlined above to 15 minutes, but the company has been rather tolerant on this situation, until it was violated too much. We are requesting all employees to limit this coffee period to 15 minutes, and when you realize there are some 400 people in the building, I think you see what an extra 5 or 10 minutes for each person can amount to.

Unusual as it may seem, a lot of the newer and minor employees rather take the attitude that if someone else can do it, they may do it also. In order to set an example, we would suggest that you limit your coffee drinking time in the cafeteria to 15 minutes so that everybody can be back at their desks at the proper time. This, we feel sure, will enable us to get in more active performance of the job of properly servicing our agents and policyholders in a more expeditious manner.

There has been a Coca-Cola machine on the second floor of this building, which is being removed. We find it necessary to use that room for the Legal Library, and the move will be made the latter part of the week. Also, we find there has been considerable violation of the no rest period in the afternoon, which the employees get by a shorter work day and getting off earlier in the afternoon. In fact, in some cases, it would seem that we are giving two rest periods again instead of the one agreed upon.

With that thought in mind, I am asking the young ladies in the office not to consume Coca-Cola during the afternoon, because we surely want to keep them actively at their own work and let them perform their duties in the specified hours of their employment. Our building is to be equipped with air conditioning before warm weather comes as an additional comfort.

In summing it all up, it means just this: We want to limit the coffee period to 15 minutes per person so that everybody can get back to the job on time, and eliminate the Coca-Cola drinking at the desks for the very same reason. We believe the above suggestions fit into the whole program of our employment practices.

1/27/60
DHW:bb

FIGURE   7 • Memorandum   to   Accompany Figure 6

To: All Home Office Department Heads and Supervisors

Subject: Morning Coffee Period

From: John D. Shaw

This is a follow-up letter on the recent personal visit I had with all of you regarding the morning coffee period. The interest and cooperation that all of you displayed in correcting any abuses of this privilege is sincerely appreciated.

It has been decided not to issue a general letter to all employees. It is felt that this can be done more efficiently and effectively through department heads either as a personal visit with employees, through a department memorandum, or a talk with known violators.

A very fine example of a department memorandum by Don Williams is attached for your reading.

In summary, the following are points of violation that have been discussed:

1.   Over-staying the coffee period in excess of 15 minutes.
2.   Coming to the cafeteria prior to 9:30 A.M. and staying beyond the closing period — 10:35 A.M.
3.   Some employees are still taking an afternoon rest period which was eliminated March, 1959, when the work week was reduced by 50 minutes and smoking was permitted at the desk.

3/9/60
JDS:rg

UNITED MUTUAL INSURANCE COMPANY (C)

CASE 4

During the latter part of 1959, United Mutual's management decided that an opinion survey might help solve some of the personnel problems encountered by the company. In this survey approximately 60 employees complained about the coffee period. Many of them didn't drink coffee and wanted to know why coffee was free while the rest of the liquid refreshments were not. There were some complaints about not having an afternoon coffee break in addition to the morning break. Mr. Shaw conferred with the vice-president, Mr. Gorman, and they decided to offer free tea and cocoa as well as free coffee to employees, but the practice of only one coffee break each day would be continued. Mr. Shaw informed all department heads that the coffee break was still only fifteen minutes and in the mornings only, but that cocoa and tea were free to employees beginning June 1, 1960. He also mentioned that this free coffee, tea, and cocoa would cost United Mutual $400 a month, and in order for this coffee break to be continued, employees would have to restrict their coffee break to the time mentioned in the memorandum which was fifteen minutes.

In October of 1960, the building was finished and employees could walk through the building again to get to the cafeteria. A new middle section had been added to the building and considerably more space existed for all employees. Also an elevator was installed for the convenience of all employees.

The coffee break in the morning continued, and employees seemed to like the free coffee, tea, and cocoa. In fact, they liked it so much that most of them started taking second cups and overstaying their allotted fifteen minutes. In an effort to remind employees that the coffee break was still only fifteen minutes, Mr. Shaw had napkins printed, saying, "Coffee break is 15 minutes," and placed them in the cafeteria during coffee periods.

These napkins were placed on the tables in the cafeteria in January, 1961. The napkins were removed from the tables once or twice a week so that employees would not get a "routine feeling" about the napkins and would know that they were there for a purpose. The napkins served a very useful purpose as many of the employees did limit their coffee break to fifteen minutes, but there still were several (mostly supervisory employees) who continued to break the time limit on the coffee period.

In February 1961, the case interviewer began a study of the coffee problem at United Mutual. On his first random visit to coffee hour he made the following observations:

1. Although the coffee break wasn't scheduled to start until 9:30, approximately 35 persons were in the cafeteria prior to that time.
2. At 9:35 A.M. there were approximately 200 employees in the cafeteria when there should have been only 75 to 100. This resulted in much congestion, and when the 9:45 group came to coffee, there weren't enough clean cups due to the overflow at 9:30.
3. At 9:45 when the first group of employees was supposed to have left the cafeteria, there were still approximately 25% of them in there, mostly men.
4. On the basis of spot checks it appeared that about 90% of the female employees obeyed the fifteen minute coffee-break rule and the other 10% were just a few minutes over the limit. Spot checks of several supervisors showed that they spent anywhere from fifteen minutes to over an hour in the cafeteria. Typical examples are one supervisor who stayed in the cafeteria for twenty-two minutes and another who stayed approximately thirty minutes. One supervisor spent an hour and ten minutes in the cafeteria.
5. A check of two departments revealed that in each the second section left for coffee hour before the first section returned.

Mr. Shaw feels that a problem still exists at United Mutual concerning the coffee period. He commented, "Many people don't realize the cost to the company when employees exceed their authorized coffee break. I have found no sure way of solving the problem, but I do have some ideas that I may try in the future."

Two of his ideas are to install an automatic coffee vending machine on each floor of the building or to bring coffee to each desk by cart. The latter could be done once or twice a day, and the employee would drink the coffee at his desk while working. Another idea of Mr. Shaw's is to eliminate the free coffee, cocoa, and tea in the cafeteria. He feels that the second cup may not be so inviting if the employee is paying for it himself; and if the employees do not have that second cup, they might not spend so much time in the cafeteria. The current action which Mr. Shaw is taking is to revise the coffee-hour schedule in order to prevent congestion and achieve better control. Neither Mr. Gorman nor Mr. Shaw are sure what else should be done, if anything.

MISSILES, INCORPORATED

CASE 5

Rodney Daniels was employed in the purchasing department of Missiles, Inc., a large manufacturing company engaged in producing air defense systems for the United States government. He had worked for Missiles, Inc. for four years, was twenty-five years old, and single. When he was hired, he had had only a high school education. However, by working part-time and on the swing shift he had put himself through the local university and at the time of the case had a B.A. degree in business administration. Rodney Daniels was a veteran and a member of the army reserve. As a part of his army reserve training program he was required to attend military training sessions for a period of two weeks each year. In accordance with routine company policy, he was excused from his work to participate in such sessions.

About two weeks before Rodney Daniels was scheduled to leave for his current tour of reserve duty, the buying group in which he worked, along with several other buying groups of the purchasing department, was moved across town to new quarters. The security and control of classified material involved in the operations of these groups was a measure of concern in the new quarters, as the offices to which the groups had been moved had not been constructed with security considerations in mind. Because of the special circumstances involved, each group was responsible for establishing and maintaining its own security program.

As was true of many organizations involved in defense work, each employee of Missiles, Inc. was required to wear an identification badge at all times while on the job. This badge identified an employee by name and payroll number and also told by a code of colors and numbers an individual's division, whether he was a supervisor or an hourly employee, and his work group. Consequently it was fairly easy by examination of the badges of individual employees to determine which employees should or should not have access to restricted areas.

In determining the security system to be used in the new quarters, the management of Rodney Daniels' buying group established a physical arrangement of the work area as noted in Exhibit 1.

As each individual entered the area of the building in which the buying group was located he had to walk past a security guard, who would check his badge to determine if he should have access to the area. Each group was required to provide its own guards at the entrances to its area. Since Rodney Daniels' group had moved into the new offices, one of the secretaries located in front of the executives' offices had handled the security function at guard post "A." However, this particular girl was due to be transferred to a new assignment in the near future.

While away on his tour of reserve duty Rodney Daniels' injured his hand, with the result that his ability to write was temporarily impaired. When he returned from his military tour and made his injury known, his supervisor decided that until such time as his hand was better, it would be logical for him to serve as the security guard at post "A" to replace the girl who was leaving.

When he was informed of this decision Daniels was quite indignant. He viewed the proposed assignment as a definite downgrade, and made his views known to his supervisor. He felt that although he had injured his hand, he could still write well enough to perform his regular duties satisfactorily. He stated that all he really had to do was make adequate rough notes, which could then be given to a typist for final preparation. This practice was routine, and followed by all of his co-workers.

After discussing the situation with his immediate superior to no avail Daniels said that he would seek the advice of Pat Morgan, assistant in charge of personnel for the chief pur-

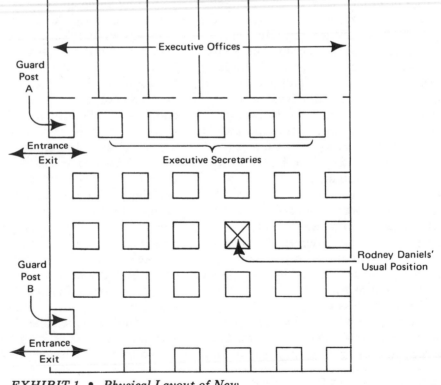

EXHIBIT 1 • Physical Layout of New Office

chasing agent. His supervisor encouraged him to do so. In subsequent conversations with Morgan, Daniels was again emphatic that he did not want the new position. He even suggested that as his injury had been sustained while on military duty, Missile, Inc. could, if it wished, extend his regular two-week leave of absence so that he could return to the military base where his injury had occurred and take advantage of government medical facilities until such time as his hand had healed satisfactorily. Morgan would not accept this suggestion, however, for he felt that Daniels' injury was not serious enough to warrant this type of action.

After several discussions with him, Morgan noted from comments that he had made that Daniels' apprehensions about accepting the temporary position as security guard seemed to be based on the following factors:

1. If he were assigned to guard post "A", even though continuing to do some of his regular buying duties, he would be the only man in a row of women employees who functioned as executive secretaries.

2. During his normal duties, Daniels customarily came into contact with individuals representing outside concerns which supplied various materials to Missiles, Inc. Many of these individuals were of high position in their respective organizations and Morgan noticed a definite apprehension on Daniels' part that these people, seeing Daniels in his new location, would naturally assume that he had been demoted.

3. Morgan also learned from these interviews that Daniels' family had a history of strong union membership and support and he felt that this played a factor in this reluctance to accept what seemed to Morgan, at least, to be a logical, reasonable, temporary assignment.

After having had three interviews with Daniels in two days, Morgan had not yet determined what action, if any, he should take.

SCANNING
THE ENVIRONMENT

INTRODUCTION

In this exercise, we want to give you an opportunity to look at the environment in which the manager functions. While there are many aspects of this environment (economic, political, and sociological, for example), we want to concentrate on the human factors in a manager's environment.

PROCEDURE

1. Find a manager whom you can interview. This manager could be managing one of several different kinds of organizations — hospital, furniture store, manufacturing organization, university, restaurant, etc.
2. Make an appointment for an interview of approximately thirty minutes duration. You may find it helpful to give the manager a copy of your interview questions in advance to give him/her an opportunity to think about them.
3. The interview should emphasize (a) current behavioral problems in the organization and (b) changes in the character and intensity of organizational behavioral problems in the past five years. The following questions might provide the basis for your interview.
   a. What are the three most serious problems (in the human area) you are now facing? List them in order of importance.
   b. What are the three most important things you do as a manager?
   c. What changes, if any, have you seen in the "work ethic" of your employees in the past four or five years? Over longer periods of time?
   d. What experiences, if any, has your organization had with the issue of sexuality?

There are many other questions which you will probably want to ask during the interview. Quickly review the readings for this section and write down any questions that arise from this activity. Add any other questions that you have. It is important that you determine what questions you will ask *before the interview,* although in the process of the interview you will undoubtedly think of others.

INTERVIEW RESULTS

Take good notes during the interview and be prepared to make a presentation to your group about the results of your interview. Your instructor may want you to prepare a written report on the interview.

Your instructor will give you specific instructions concerning the results of your interview.

EXERCISE 2

STANDARD MANUFACTURING COMPANY

INTRODUCTION

In this exercise, you will have an opportunity to become aware of some of the problems and situations faced by a manager. In attempting to deal with these situations, you should gain a greater appreciation of the scope of a manager's job as well as some indication of the way in which you might approach these kinds of issues.

PROCEDURE

Some general instructions are contained in the exercise. Your instructor probably will want to give you additional directions, and you should not proceed further until you have received these.

> You are Joe Sterling, president of the Standard Manufacturing Company of Springvale, Ohio. Your organization manufactures a line of special shipping containers used by various industrial firms to transport delicate products or instruments — usually communication, electronic, or research devices.
> The company concentrates on special packaging problems, and does not manufacture a standard line of shipping containers. Most of the containers require individual design, and you have on your staff an experienced packaging design engineer and an experienced packaging consultant to help solve the sometimes unique packaging problems of your customers. Most of the containers are manufactured from lightweight metals (although other materials may be used if required) and consist of the basic part of the container and whatever special braces are necessary to support a particular item so it can be shipped without damage. Standard has no part in the actual shipping process, but merely supplies the containers to its customers, who then handle all arrangements for shipping.
> You have owned and operated Standard Manufacturing Company for fifteen years. Before founding Standard, you had held several positions in the general field of shipping and packaging design since your graduation from the state university with a degree in mechanical engineering. From time to time you have attended numerous seminars and conferences concerning handling and packaging.

Although both you and Standard Manufacturing Company have been successful financially, the organization is not large, employing about ninety-five people, most of whom work in the factory. Average yearly sales have been about $2.65 million for the last three years. Exhibit 1 is a partial organization chart of the Standard Manufacturing Company.

At the present time you have just returned from a six-day trip to the East Coast, where you attended a materials handling seminar and visited several electronics firms in the Boston area who were potential customers. Now, your first opportunity since your return, you have just started to look over materials that have arrived during your absence. In forty-five minutes you have an appointment to meet with officials of the Kelly Corporation to discuss some special work you hope to do for them. You expect that this meeting will take the balance of the day. You have completed your preparations for the meeting.

Make notes regarding what actions, if any, you wish to take concerning the various situations, and rough out any letters, messages, and so on, that you might wish to send.

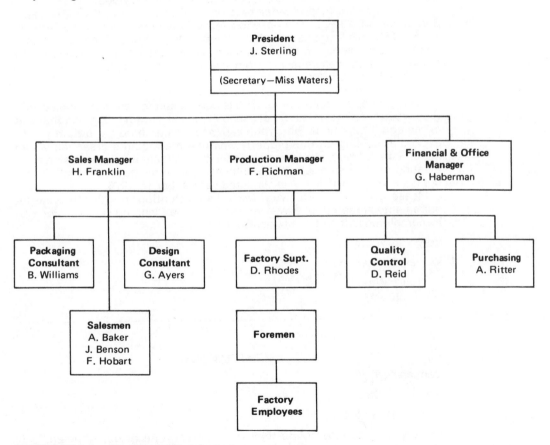

EXHIBIT 1 • Standard Manufacturing Company Partial Organization Chart

(1)   City of Springvale
                        Office of City Supervisor

January 2, 1978

Standard Manufacturing Company
114 Union Street
Springvale, Ohio

Attention: Mr. J. Sterling

Gentlemen:

I am writing with reference to the planting of a greenbelt surrounding your property at the above address. Please be advised that the city has received complaints that the greenbelt which you were to have provided for the industrial property at this address has not been provided.

In reviewing correspondence regarding this matter, I find a letter dated September 14, 1976, in response to a letter from your office dated September 6, 1976. This letter sets forth the applicable portions of the zoning ordinance — Ordinance No. 79. Inasmuch as no further correspondence or communication was received from you after your receipt of the above-mentioned letter, it was assumed that there was no further question regarding the requirements as set forth by the city.

Inasmuch as no apparent effort has been taken toward compliance with these requirements, it is felt necessary to call attention to the fact that one of the conditions upon which the variance was granted permitting you to expand a building on this property was that the required greenbelt would be furnished. This matter was discussed by the Planning Commission at its meeting of December 2, 1977, at which time the members reiterated their opinions as set forth in our letter dated September 14, 1976.

Please give this matter your immediate attention in order that the requirements agreed to between yourself and the Planning Commission can be completed at the earliest possible date.

Very truly yours,

Warren J. Wheeling

Warren J. Wheeling
City Supervisor

---

(2)   MEMORANDUM

January 3, 1978

To: J. Sterling

From: D. Rhodes

I am sorry to inform you that Mike Satters, one of our foremen, is in Springvale Hospital with an illness that has been tentatively identified as cancer. If this is true — we'll know for certain in about a week — his chances for survival are minimal. The men in the factory have taken up a collection to help Mrs. Satters and the kids and I told them that while I would have to clear it with you, I was sure that the company would match anything they contributed up to $500. Please advise if you have any disagreement with this.

---

(3)   MEMORANDUM

January 4, 1978

To: Joe Sterling

From: Harry Franklin

I am having a problem with Al Baker, one of our salesmen, concerning commissions. As you know, our policy in the past has been to pay commission only on those sales which a salesman develops and secures himself. Baker, however, did a lot of good work on the Justis Co. job, and even though they called on us and he wasn't in on it from the start, Baker feels he is entitled to his usual commission. If you recall, George Ayers was away while most of the design was worked out, and Baker did most of this. I am inclined to give him a commission — even though it is sizable ($3000) — but am reluctant to establish a precedent for other cases. Please let me know your feelings soon, as I have not given Baker a decision yet.

---

(4)   MEMORANDUM

January 6, 1978

To: Joe Sterling

From: Al Ritter

We have not been able to locate a satisfactory source of special gauge aluminum that can be delivered in time for the Evans Co. order to be completed. We can get it in time from Colonial Aluminum Distributors, but would have to pay a premium that will make most of our potential profit evaporate. We are scheduled to start production on the Evans order in two weeks. I think Colonial is trying to hold us up. Ever since we stopped buying from this company exclusively last year it has been hard to deal with. What do you advise?

---

(5)   MEMORANDUM

January 4, 1978

To: Joe Sterling

From: George Ayers

I should like your permission to attend a course in packaging design which will be offered by Eastern State University from January 26 to February 2. They are doing some fine work in this field which should have direct application for us. It is expensive — I estimate $750 for everything — but I think worth it. I realize that we have some big orders on the fire and that this will probably not be the most opportune time for me to be away, but even if we lose a sale or two, it will be worth it in the long run. Perhaps I could call on some customers on the way back.   Let me know as soon as possible, as they are trying to limit the class to twenty people, and I'm sure they will have no trouble filling it. Thank you.

---

(6)   Curtiss Packaging Company
                              6173 Dayton Lane
                              Bloomingdale, Illinois

January 3, 1978

Mr. Joseph Sterling, President
Standard Manufacturing Company
114 Union Street
Springvale, Ohio

Dear Joe:

As you know, we have been having a great deal of difficulty lately with our production operation. We have had several production managers in the past two years and none of them have proven satisfactory. It may seem presumptuous, Joe, but I would like your permission to contact Dennis Rhodes of your organization to see if I could entice him into coming with us. You have real strength in your production organization and Rhodes could have a great future with us, as well as solve our production problems.

Let me know what you think. I realize that my request may seem unusual, but I have been interested in Rhodes since I met him three years ago, and would like very much to have him on my team. Because of our friendship, however, I wouldn't want to do anything unless I had your permission.

Best personal regards.

Sincerely yours,

Harry Richards

Harry Richards
President

---

(7)   MEMORANDUM

January 4, 1978

To: Joe Sterling

From: Frank Richman

I hate to bother you with what may seem a small problem, but the parking situation has popped up again, and many people are quite irritated.

We now have space in the lot for about fifty cars. We have about seventy people who drive every day, and some days have as many as eighty cars. Before the city changed Union Street to "one-way" and prohibited parking, we were O.K. Now, we have twenty to thirty people a day who have parking problems. As you know, our "car pool" program has been strikingly unsuccessful.

We have to either increase the size of our parking facilities, which I realize would be expensive as we don't have any more land, or establish some system of priority for the parking lot. I think that at least all supervisory personnel ought to be assured a parking place. Will you give me your thinking as soon as possible? This problem must be resolved quickly.

---

(8)   Newman Electronics Company
                             108 Dexter Street
                             Cleveland, Ohio

January 3, 1978

Mr. Joseph Sterling, President
Standard Manufacturing Company
114 Union Street
Springvale, Ohio

Dear Mr. Sterling:

Please be advised that we are dissatisfied with the shipping containers which we recently ordered from your organization. At the time of their delivery we were concerned that our instruments would fit into the containers properly, and expressed our doubts to your Mr. Williams. He assured us that the containers had been manufactured especially for our particular instruments and that we had no cause for concern. With his assurance, we shipped the instruments. Breakage on this shipment was over 15 percent, which, as you know, is unreasonably high.

Our attorneys have advised us that as we did accept your containers and did not, in fact, insist that you examine them for adequacy before shipping our merchandise, we have no legal recourse. However, I wish you to know of our dissatisfaction, and that we feel you are solely responsible for the high loss on the shipment. We will not anticipate any future transactions with your organization.

Sincerely yours,

Walter Winston

Walter Winston
Vice President

---

(9)   MEMORANDUM

January 4, 1978

To: Joe Sterling

From: Harry Franklin

I have just received word from sources in the industry that Frank Hobart has been actively seeking a position with one of our competitors and has been engaged in this kind of activity while supposedly making calls for us. Please advise.

---

(10)   MEMORANDUM

January 2, 1978

To: Joe Sterling

From: Mary Waters

According to our salary administration plan, you should review the performance and salary level of all personnel over the rank of foreman during the next week. Please let me know if you wish me to schedule appointments and if you have any special instructions for those involved.

---

(11)   MEMORANDUM

January 5, 1978

To: Joe Sterling

From: Mary Waters

The Springvale city fire marshal called today to request permission to inspect our facilities as soon as possible. This is not the time for our regular inspection, and I am wondering if something unusual has precipitated his request.

---

(12)   MEMORANDUM

January 5, 1978

To: Joe Sterling

From: Grant Haberman

Based on our expected profit for the year I have done some preliminary figuring on the profit-sharing plan for Harry Franklin, Frank Richman, and myself. It looks like the checks will amount to approximately $5000 each. Do you have any special thoughts or ideas on this?

---

(13)   MEMORANDUM

January 5, 1978

To: Joe Sterling

From: Frank Richman

I have reason to believe that attempts will be made in the near future to unionize the factory workers. Several union organizers have been seen in town, and one unconfirmed report states that some of the men have been approached on company property re unionization. Please advise what action, if any, we should take.

---

(14)   MEMORANDUM

January 4, 1978

To: Joe Sterling

From: D. Rhodes

Oscar Hill will retire next week. As you know, he is our oldest employee in terms of service, having been here since the start of Standard. The boys in the factory plan to have a get-together for him. Will you say a few words? Do you have any special ideas? As far as I know, Oscar will be the first man at Standard to actually retire.

PART 2

COMMUNICATION IN ORGANIZATIONS

To the casual observer it often seems that most organizational problems are blamed upon "poor communication." While it is certainly not true that all problems stem from communication difficulties, many serious problems are in fact created by communication breakdown.

A communication network can be likened to the nervous system of the organization. Just as nerve endings in the body transmit information to the brain for processing, people in organizations transmit information to communication centers for processing. Any person in a supervisory role can be considered to be an information center. The supervisor must process incoming messages, retain and act upon those that are appropriate to his or her position, and transmit other messages to other parts of the organization. The manager must communicate effectively (and almost continually) with peers, subordinates, and superiors. Many managers must also communicate with clients.

How much time do managers spend communicating? A recent study of several hundred managers indicated that the average manager spends as much as 37.5 hours communicating per work week.[1] Does this mean the average manager spends too much time communicating and not enough time working? Probably not. Perhaps we should really conceptualize the manager as being a transmitter and receiver/processor of information. One of the key elements of any manager's job is to select relevant information, process it correctly and efficiently, and act upon it directly, or transmit it elsewhere for action.

---

[1]Klemmer, E.T. and Snyder, F.W., "Measurement of Time Spent Communicating," *Journal of Communication,* June 1972, pp. 142–152.

In the first reading, "Structuring Communication in a Working Group," Peter Mears relates what happened when lessons learned from some classic laboratory studies in communication were applied in a real organization. It is clear that the communication networks described in the laboratory studies exist in real organizations. It may help you to conceptualize the communication networks in organizations as being multidimensional, that is, extending both horizontally and vertically throughout the enterprise. A manager in a given organization will be a member of several different communication networks. The manager may be at the center of a wheel network composed of his or her own subordinates and, at the same time, be a peripheral member of a wheel network with his or her own boss at the center. The same manager may also be part of a circle network composed of peers.

Organization communications may be broadly considered to be either formal or informal. Formal communications follow the prescribed chain of command and are considered to be "official." Informal communications very often do not follow reporting channels but frequently play a key role in accomplishment of tasks.

It is important for the aspiring manager to know the effects of the various networks on the speed of information flow, the accuracy of problem solutions and the morale of the people within the networks. Although the shape of the communication network is not the sole determinant of those factors, there is no question that the shape does affect them.

In the second reading, "Vital Factors in Interpersonal Communication," Wayne Baty shifts the emphasis from organizational communication to interpersonal communication. Interpersonal communication may be viewed as the process shown in Figure 1.

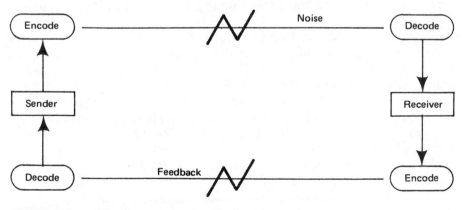

FIGURE 1 • *The Communication Process*

The person wishing to convey a message is called the sender. Before the message can actually be transmitted, the sender must encode it. During encoding the message is converted from the thought processes of the sender into a language, for example, words or mathematical symbols. The message is then ready to be transmitted through some communication channel, for example, face-to-face conversation, telephone, memo, letter, etc. When the message reaches the receiver, it must be decoded, that is, the receiver converts the symbols that constitute the message into meaning. It is important to realize that "noise" (distortion) may enter at any point in the process. The sender encodes the message in terms that make a great deal of sense to him or her. However the sender may have somehow misperceived the situation that he or she is trying to communicate. Thus the message may depart from objective reality at the very first step in the communication process. The channel itself may also create distortion, especially if the message is filtered through other parties. Finally, the message reaches the intended receiver. The receiver decodes the message by interpreting the meaning of the symbols. Unfortunately, quite often the receiver does not "receive" the message as intended by the sender. The way we encode and decode messages is affected by many things, including our past experiences, our expectations, and our desires. Professor Baty provides vivid examples of some of the common problems in interpersonal communication.

In "Active Listening," Rogers and Farson remind us that both parties in a communication exchange have obligations. It is of course vital that the sender of any communication take care to insure that the message transmitted will be clear and unambiguous and phrased in terms that the receiver can interpret. In two-way communication, there is the opportunity for the receiver to respond directly to the message and ask for clarification or for further interpretation. Rogers and Farson point out that, in a two-way exchange, it is important for both sender and receiver to engage in active listening.

As you will discover in reading the article, there are specific techniques that you can acquire to become a more active listener. We encourage you to use and practice these techniques with your friends, classmates, and fellow workers. Soon it will become almost a natural behavior for you and should greatly enhance your ability to communicate with other people. You will note and experience some of the problems associated with active listening as well. To be a good listener is sometimes psychologically threatening.

As teachers and consultants, the authors of this text can testify that it is difficult to overestimate the ability of people to misunderstand communications. In fact, one of us has a large poster in his office that reads:

I know you believe you understand what you think I said, but, I am not sure you realize that what you heard is not what I meant.

Yet, despite the problems and potential problems, communication skills can be learned. It is our observation that a distinguishing feature of most top-level executives is their ability to express themselves clearly both verbally and in writing. As a manager you will be spending most of your time communicating; thus, it is important for you to observe, study, and learn as much as possible about the communication process.

STRUCTURING COMMUNICATION IN A WORKING GROUP

Peter Mears

Theories of task-oriented group communication have been tested mostly in the laboratory. Here is their application to industrial management, with some surprising results.

An organization's effectiveness depends upon the performance of numerous small groups which function and interact within the overall organizational system. Because of this dependence, much emphasis has been placed on studies of sub-groups, their cultures, status, and group needs, in an attempt to determine the factors which are most likely to encourage group effectiveness. Since the activity of a small group depends to a great extent upon its information flow, the communications act has been studied as a means of influencing efficiency. Thus, research on communication networks has become increasingly important and promises better understanding of the functioning of organizations.

One major criticism of past work in communication networks has been directed at its lack of applicability to a business organization; experiments have been conducted primarily in nonorganizational environments with student subjects. This kind of experimentation has resulted in a number of constraints which must be recognized in applying or "forcing" such findings to a practical application in a real business setting. The purpose of this article is to overcome these constraints by briefly presenting the major research findings regarding communication networks, and then to apply these research findings to a business situation.

A communication network is the interaction required by a group to accomplish a task.

Working groups tend to be composed of four, five, or six people. Two people are not normally considered in a group; in a group of three there is a danger that two of the people will tend to "gang up" on the third person; and seven or more people in close proximity tend to split up into smaller, more manageable working units.

An organization may be composed of hundreds of such small working groups. This group idea is built into current management philosophy and is perhaps due to the notion that the managerial process involves the subdivision of brains as well as of labor. It is only natural for a business to try to increase the efficiency of these groups, and since the predominant activity of any group depends on the information flow, communication is one area in which the

From *Journal of Communication*, 24 (1): 71–79 (Winter 1974). Copyright 1974. Reprinted with permission.

group may be made more efficient.

Three major types of small-group communication networks are shown in Figure 1. These are the circle, wheel, and the chain networks. Each circle represents an individual in a working group, and the solid line connects the individual with the other members of the group he or she normally interacts with in performing a task.

Bavelas and Barrett performed some of the initial research on the effects of different communication networks. This work is summarized in Table 1. In the circle network an individual will normally converse with the person on his right or left, but not with any other members of the group. In the free circle group, all members converse frequently and equally with all other members of the group.

Appearances in these networks are deceptive. The wheel network on the left in Figure 1 is popularly referred to as an autocratic situation, and the wheel network on the right would be called a typical organizational setup. Both networks are the same; the only difference lies in the arrangement of the circles on the paper. The distinguishing characteristic of the wheel network is that the members do not normally communicate with one another. They interact with the hub of the wheel, the leader of the group.

The chain network has all the appearances of an organizational chain-of-command: A reports to B, who reports to C, and so on. In actual practice this network may appear within a working group whose members are all at the same organizational level or rank. The two end positions might be occupied by people who tend to be introverted and

Circle

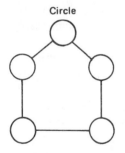

Free circle

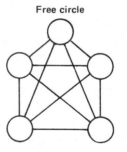

Wheel

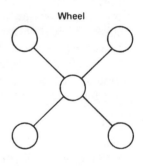

Chain

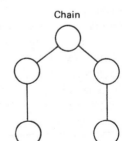

Wheel

Chain

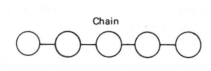

FIGURE 1 • Communication Networks

prefer normally to communicate with only one person. In the three middle positions, the normal interactions may be determined primarily by friendship.

This case study involves individuals interacting to solve a complex problem.

The individuals are Systems and Procedure personnel who represent specific divisions in a large aerospace firm. Each of the representatives is in charge of a small highly skilled, semi-technical work group which develops unique systems and procedures for each of the firm's respective divisions (see Figure 2). It is the function of the division representative from "A" to coordinate the systems and procedures among divisions for consistency. To do this, A sets up the working group of representatives whose communication structure is depicted in Figure 2. These division representatives communicate with each other in the interpretation and implementation of corporate directives as well as to obtain the cooperation of another representative to resolve an impending problem.

The solid lines depict both formal lines of authority and formal communication, while the dotted lines depict informal communication. This overlapping of the formal communication channel with an extensive network of informal communication channels occurs in many technical work groups. Mr. A, the formally delegated authority, may be well aware of these informal relationships as they pertain to the job, but interaction for the resolution of a common task is an accepted practice in management literature. In fact, the participative management approach may not only be viewed as an interaction between the subordinate and superior, but may also be viewed as encouraging subordinates to interact in the accomplishment of a task.

The communication of this systems and procedure group, as shown in Figure 2, was primarily a free circle network. Everyone in the group was free to utilize whatever channels of communication he desired, with the result that most of the group's time was spent in discussion, and very little work was accomplished. The morale of the group was very high; the only point of conflict

	Circle	Chain	Wheel
Speed	Slow	Fast	Fast
Accuracy	Poor	Good	Good
Organization	No stable form	Slowly emerging but stable organization	Almost immediate and stable organization
Emergence of leadership	None	Marked	Very pronounced
Morale	Very good	Poor	Very poor

TABLE 1 • Performance of the Circle, Chain, and Wheel Communication Networks

occurred when a member felt obligated to agree with something he opposed in order that group consensus could be achieved. This result is consistent with the findings of Festinger, who states that "pressures toward uniformity may exist within a group; these pressures act toward making members of a group agree concerning some issue, or conform with respect to some behavior pattern." (8)

Each person's advice was appreciated and carefully evaluated. Because the individual group member was able to make a contribution on a complex issue, his involvement was high and there was a feeling of pride in his accomplishments. This fact is consistent with the findings of Shaw, who discovered that "morale is higher with greater independence because independence permits the gratification of the culturally supported needs for autonomy, recognition and achievement." (19)

Bales (1), Etzioni (7), and Davis (6) point out that in most groups, in addition to a formal leader, an informal leader, more commonly called the social leader, tends to emerge. The social leader restores and maintains group unity and satisfaction. In the group I am describing, the Contract division representative filled that role. This result may not be consistent with the findings of Kahn and Katz when they say that "pride or involvement in the work group and productivity are interacting variables and that an increase in one tends to bring about an increase in the other." (12) This was only true to a very limited point: in the Systems and Procedure group, because of the lack of specific channels of communication, too much time was spent in discussion and useless debate.

After several months the division representatives accomplished almost nothing.

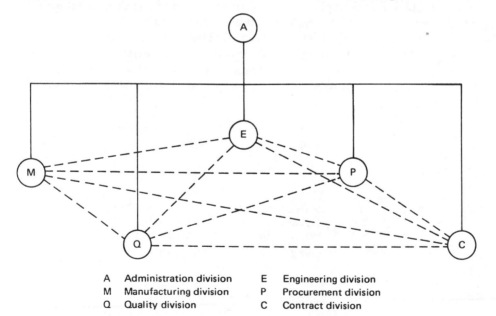

A   Administration division   E   Engineering division
M   Manufacturing division   P   Procurement division
Q   Quality division   C   Contract division

FIGURE 2 • The Initial Organization

Management stepped in and disbanded the meetings.

The group was reorganized by management as a wheel network. The new organization is shown in Figure 3. The change from an unrestricted network, the free circle, to a restricted network, the wheel, was essentially a change from a democratically-run group to an autocratically-run group. Under the free circle network, lengthy arguments and discussions sometimes extended well into the evenings after the formal group leader had left. Under the wheel network, in order to force all information to come through the wheel hub (the Administration representative), management issued a directive stating that any communication concerning procedures outside the individual's division was to be conducted only by the Administration division. This directive was ignored until one of the representatives was severely reprimanded for reaching an agreement with the Manufacturing representative without the concurrence of the Administration representative. After the reprimand, the group again became ineffective. Every representative lived up to the absolute letter of the directive. No opinion was voiced unless asked for, and then only the exact question asked would be answered.

Since only the representatives were competent to answer detailed questions about their divisions, information had to

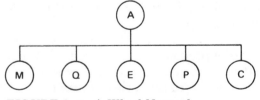

FIGURE 3 • A Wheel Network

be relayed by the Administration division to each representative. Since each representative would protect his own interest by commenting only on what affected him, the number of errors grew astronomically. The same job would be redone several times; if it did not exactly suit the divisional representative's interests, it would be vetoed. A virtual boycott of any new system developed.

For all practical purposes, the installation of a wheel (autocratic) network decreased output.

At first glance, this conclusion might seem inconsistent with the available literature. Bavelas and Barrett (2), Leavitt (15), and Guetzkow (11) quantitatively show the wheel as the fastest network for problem solution. Considering that their common conclusion was based on an experiment in which the participants had only to detect a missing symbol, their conclusion was justified. The actual solution of an industrial problem, however, may be very complex and quite often is based not purely on available facts but on a mixture of the facts available plus past experience on similar problems.

Mulder (17) indicates that the important element in group interactions may be the emergence of a decision structure. The decision structure determines the pattern of suggestion acceptance from one member to another. A change in the formal structure may disrupt the decision structure of the group, thus resulting in a loss of group efficiency.

When our group operated in a free circle network, what hurt efficiency was not the morale of the group, which was excellent, but the overabundance of communication channels available to each member. Shaw (19) would have stated that the saturation level of the individual was reached, that the total requirements placed on an individual in a network were excessive.

With the wheel network, the saturation level again accounted for the decrease in efficiency. The task was complex, and the individuals refused to accept the dictates of the central person without sufficient information. This forced the central person to handle more and more messages until he could do only one of two things: either state that he could not handle the job, or try to circumvent the group entirely by pointing out to management that the group was uncooperative. He took the second course.

Changing from democratic leadership to autocratic leadership had a disruptive effect on the group. People have a natural tendency to automatically develop a system for performing a task. Not having to think about how to go about doing a job reduces the uncertainty associated with the task; when people find themselves in a condition in which they again cannot automatically perform the required tasks, they center their attention on developing a system to accomplish the task. The wheel network demands an autocratic system, because its members cannot collectively interact, and the leader (hub) represents something that has introduced uncertainty. It is only natural that this uncertainty will be met with hostility by workers who are accustomed to a more participative system.

Cohen and Bennis (5) hold the same viewpoint, and Lawson (13) points out

that this knowledge holds a strong implication for training. If during a training period a group network is changed, then the individual's learning process will be disrupted; he will first concentrate on learning the new network and, after mastery, will then concentrate on the job.

After the disastrous effect of introducing a wheel network in the technical group, management recognized its error and carefully studied the interactions required by each group member. The Manufacturing division representative needed to communicate with Engineering and Quality division representatives. Analogously, since hardware under construction was ordered to Engineering specifications, problems with procured hardware should be discussed by Engineering and Procurement representatives. The addition of the Manufacturing representative would serve no useful purpose and would tend to slow the group down.

Each group member was requested to communicate only with the other members directly involved in the pertinent decision.

As a result of this new communication restriction, the "A" division was relieved of having to make all decisions (as under the wheel network), and the other divisions did not waste time when decisions did not concern them (as under the free circle network). Figure 4 shows the communication patterns in this revised group organization.

The new system, in the long run increased productivity and morale of the affected parties. But, just after the change in structure, there was a decrease in efficiency in the short run. The Contract members and the Procurement members had the lowest work load. Under the autocratic leadership their group morale had declined, and they had centered their attention on the problems internal to their own divisions. When the new network came into existence, they had to relearn the system, and it took several months for the members to obtain the satisfaction they had previously enjoyed under the free circle network. (In fact, they never fully reached the same high level of satisfaction.) Lawson (13) experienced the same conditions of disruptiveness, then increased efficiency and higher morale, when groups were changed from the more restrictive wheel to the freer circle.

In the business world, communication networks tend to be combinations of the prototypes depicted in Figure 1. Management should avoid getting too close to one of these extremes, or it may be forced to change the networks and create disruption and inefficiency in the work group.

Communication networks are not a theoretical abstraction from reality. The formal group is aware of the existence of the networks — informal as well as formal — and usually feels it must delegate the type of network in the interests of maximum efficiency. This may well be a desired practice, but network delegation must be done with respect to the complexity of the task, the desired morale, the desired efficiency, and the impact of the change. Omission of any of these factors from consideration will result in a network detrimental to the organization.

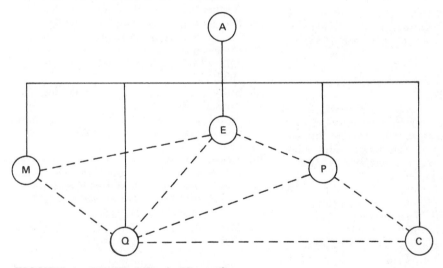

FIGURE 4 • *Modified Circle Network*

REFERENCES

1. BALES, ROBERT F. "In Conference." *Harvard Business Review,* March–April 1954, pp. 44–50.
2. BAVELAS, ALEX, and DERMOT BARRETT. "An Experimental Approach to Organizational Communication." *Personnel* 27 (March 1951), 366–71.
3. BELLO, FRANCIS. "The Information Theory." *Fortune* 48 (December 1953), 137.
4. BLAIR, ELENN MYERS, R. STEWART JONES, and RAYMOND H. SIMPSON. *Educational Psychology,* 3d ed. New York: The Macmillan Company, 1965.
5. COHEN, ARTHUR M., and WARREN G. BENNIS. "Continuity of Leadership in Communication Networks." *Human Relations,* 1959, pp. 359–65.
6. DAVIS, KEITH. *Human Relations at Work: The Dynamics of Organizational Behavior,* 3rd ed. New York: McGraw-Hill, 1967.
7. ETZIONI, AMITAI. "Dual Leadership in Complex Organizations." *American Sociological Review,* October 1965, pp. 688–98.
8. FESTINGER, LEON. "Informal Social Communication." *Psychological Review* 57 (1950), 271–82.
9. GUETZKOW, HAROLD. "Differentiation of Roles in Task-oriented Groups." *Group Dynamics: Research and Theory,* 2nd ed., edited by Doran Cartwright and Allen Zander. Evanston, Illinois: Row, Peterson & Company, 1960.
10. GUETZKOW, HAROLD, and WILLIAM R. DILL. "Factors in the Organizational Development of Task-oriented Groups." *Sociometry* 20 (1957), 175–204.
11. GUETZKOW, HAROLD, and HERBERT A. SIMON. "The Impact of Certain Communication Networks upon Organization and Performance in Task-oriented Groups. *Management Science* 1 (1955), 233–50.
12. KAHN, ROBERT L., and DANIEL KATZ. "Leadership Practices in Relation to Productivity and Morale." In *Group Dynamics: Research and Theory,* 2nd ed., edited by Doran Cartwright and Allen Zander. Evanston, Illinois: Row, Peterson & Company, 1960.
13. LAWSON, EDWIN D. "Changes in Communication Networks, Performance and Morale." *Human Relations,* May 1965, pp. 139–47.
14. LEAVITT, HAROLD J. "Small Groups in Large Organizations." *The Journal of Business* 28–29 (January 1955), 8–17.
15. LEAVITT, HAROLD J. "Some Effects of Certain Communication Patterns on Group Performance." *Journal of Abnormal Social Psychology,* 46 (1951), 38–50.
16. LYLE, JACK. "Communication, Group Atmosphere, Productivity, and Morale in Small Task-Groups." *Human Relations,* 1960, pp. 369–79.
17. MULDER, MAUK, *Group Structure, Motivation and Group Performance.* The Hague: Mouton & Co., 1963.
18. ROTHSCHILD, GERARD H., and MARVIN E. SHAW. "Some Effects of Prolonged Experiences in Communication Nets." *Journal of Applied Psychology,* October 1956, 281–86.
19. SHAW, MARVIN E. "Communication Networks." In *Advances in Experimental Social Psychology,* edited by Leonard Berkowitz. New York: Academic Press, 1964.
20. SHAW, MARVIN E. "Some Effects of Problem Complexity upon Problem Solution Efficiency in Different Communication Nets." *Journal of Experimental Psychology* 48 (1954), 211–17.
21. THAYER, LEE O. *Administrative Communication.* Homewood, Illinois: Richard D. Irwin, 1961.
22. "The Number One Problem." *Personnel Journal* 45 (April 1965), 237–38.

VITAL FACTORS IN INTERPERSONAL COMMUNICATION

Wayne Baty

The process of transmitting a message from one person to another (interpersonal communication) is often inefficient. To illustrate this point, students in a business communication class at Arizona State University were asked to examine the following drawing:

Then, they were given this problem: "Assume that you want another student to reproduce the drawing. You cannot demonstrate. You must write a set of instructions that will (if followed correctly) result in an accurate reproduction."

Students in one class tried to follow the instructions written by students in another class. Although 67 per cent of

the reproductions were reasonably accurate, here are some of the inaccurate results:

Some of the inaccuracies appeared to be the fault of those who *wrote* instructions; others, of those who *followed* instructions.

When a businessman *sends* a spoken or written message that appears in his mind as

it must be *received* in the other person's mind as

Otherwise, the results can be catastrophic.

Administrators in business and industry reportedly spend between 75 and 95 per cent of their time communicating (either sending or receiving messages).[1] They cannot afford the 33 per cent error experienced by these students.

So important is accuracy in transmitting ideas that Peter Drucker (well-known consultant and professor of management), says, ". . . ability to express

From *Arizona Business Bulletin*, 14 (4): 98–103 (April 1967) Reprinted by permission of College of Business Administration, Arizona State University.
[1]Lee O. Thayer, *Administrative Communication* (Homewood, Ill.: Richard D. Irwin, Inc., 1961), p. 3.

oneself is perhaps the most important of all skills a man can possess."[2] Yet, lack of this ability to express ideas is widespread. Personnel recruiters have difficulty in finding the right men for open positions. A recent survey of sales managers showed that they are looking primarily for recruits with a college background and high communication skills.[3] Another survey of marketing managers reported that ". . . the recruiters felt the greatest weakness in applicants did not stem from 'how to do it' courses, but from the inability of college students to express themselves clearly."[4] Regardless of whether communication is written or oral, some of the factors that result in failure can be attributed to the *sender;* others, to the *receiver;* and others, to either or both.

FACTORS THAT APPLY TO BOTH SENDERS AND RECEIVERS

Both sending and receiving are greatly influenced by (1) reputation, (2) rank, (3) metacommunications, and (4) grammar.

Reputation

What a businessman *says* or *writes* is strongly influenced by what he *is* and by what his listeners or readers *think him to be.* T. M. Higham, an industrial psychologist, says,

. . . if a person dislikes or mistrusts us, he is not likely to be receptive to what we have to say, and his version of our words is likely to be distorted by his personal opinions of us or his preconceived notions about our motives.[5]

The following incident illustrates how a receiver's evaluation of a sender's reputation can influence the message.[6] A cartoon "The Four Goals of Labor" was clipped from the CIO newspaper and photostated. A new legend was added at the bottom: "From the June 3 N.A.M. Newsletter." Twenty laborers were asked for their reactions to the goals stated. Four agreed with the statements. Two could not decide. Fourteen condemned them as "loaded," "patronizing," "paternalistic," and "makes you want to spit." No wonder the *Fortune* writer believes that "Only with trust can there be any real communication, and until that trust is achieved the techniques and gadgetry of communication are so much wasted effort."[7]

Implications for the Sender. To communicate effectively, be the right type of person — have a reputation for such qualities as integrity, industry, and efficiency. "You will not get any reception if you are not trusted."[8]

Implications for the Receiver. To understand effectively, try hard to concentrate on the message itself — resist

[2]Peter Drucker, "How to Be An Employee," *Fortune,* May, 1952, p. 126.

[3]"Communication Skills Outrank College Background in Sales Trainee Recruiting," *Marketing Insight,* February 20–24, 1967, p. 3.

[4]Robert E. Linneman and George L. Herpel, "On Marketing Curriculum: Does the Personnel Office Practice What the President Preaches?," *Collegiate News and Views,* Oct., 1966, p. 6.

[5]T. M. Higham, "Basic Psychological Factors in Communication," *Occupational Psychology,* Jan., 1957, p. 2

[6]"Is Anybody Listening," *Fortune,* Sept., 1950, p. 82.

[7]*Ibid.*

[8]Higham, *loc. cit.*

the temptation to vitiate a message just because the reputation of the sender is negative. A receiver can profitably keep in mind, also, that he could have been wrong in his evaluations of negative qualities in the sender.

Rank

One who can communicate effectively with others of his own rank may have difficulty in communicating with a superior or a subordinate. Schuyler Dean Hoslett accurately describes the problem:

> It is well known that the subordinate tends to tell his superior what the latter is interested in, not to disclose what he doesn't want to hear, and to cover up problems and mistakes which may reflect on the subordinate.[9]

Likewise, superiors often feel that they cannot confess to subordinates any problems or crises that reflect on themselves as superiors. Whether a sender is in the role of subordinate or superior, he runs the risk of revealing more than he thinks he should. Awareness of this risk may interfere with his ability to say what he means. When he is in the role of receiver, the same awareness may interfere with his ability to understand what another means. As a distracting factor in a communication, the influence of rank can be reduced if the following attitudes are cultivated: (1) willingness to expect and accept criticism, and (2) recognition that — even though communicating with a superior or to a subordinate — one is also communicating with a *person*.

Metacommunications

In a speech on the ASU campus in 1963, Dr. S. I. Hayakawa said, "With every communication goes an accompanying metacommunication."[10] That is, with every idea that is expressed in words goes an additional idea that is not expressed in words. The following incident involves a typical metacommunication:[11] A superintendent and his foreman were standing outside the latter's office. Upon hearing the girls in the office burst into loud laughter, the superintendent said, "The girls seem happy this morning the way they are talking and laughing." That was his *communication*. From this sentence, the foreman got one or more of the following messages: "Your secretaries are loafing on the job." "Your secretaries do not take their work seriously." "You are not exercising proper control." Later, the foreman reprimanded the girls and changed their working stations (at the expense of good morale).

At the end of a class hour, a student said to his teacher, "I'll have to be absent tomorrow. Will we be doing anything important?" The teacher replied, "Certainly. Everything we do is important." Along with his message, the student has conveyed this *metacommunication:* "From my experience in the class thus far, I note that some things are important and that others are triv-

[9]Schuyler Dean Hoslett, "Barriers to Communication," *Personnel*, Sept., 1951, p. 109.
[10]Dr. Hayakawa is author of *Language in Thought and Action* (New York: Harcourt, Brace & World, Inc., 1949).
[11]Burleigh B. Gardner and David G. Moore, *Human Relations in Industry* (Homewood, Ill.: Richard D. Irwin, Inc., 1955).

ial." The teacher was offended. What the student really wanted to know was whether a test would be given.

The sender needs to keep the following points in mind: (1) Metacommunications are always present. (2) Receivers may pay more attention to the metacommunication than to the communication itself. (3) Communications can be so presented that their accompanying metacommunications work *for* the sender, not *against* him.

The receiver needs to keep the following points in mind: (1) Try hard to concentrate on the idea that is put into words. (2) Remember that a negative metacommunication may have been accidental. (3) If the communication is oral, a receiver can easily verify whether he has understood the communication and whether a metacommunication has been properly interpreted.

Grammar

If one person is to understand another, both must have a basic knowledge of the language used. So essential is this knowledge that Peter Drucker says courses in English really are strictly vocational courses because they teach one to express himself.[12]

Among the common grammatical causes for misunderstandings are errors in the use of compound adjectives, participial phrases, modifiers, and superlatives. Although businessmen may have a better command of grammar than college freshmen, here are the results of a test given to 74 students at ASU. The students were asked for interpretations

of the following sentences:

1. We need six-foot soldiers for this assignment.

   (25.7 per cent incorrectly concluded that six soldiers were needed — that they were to be *foot* soldiers instead of any other type. 74.3 per cent correctly concluded that the soldiers needed were to be six feet tall.)

2. After helping with the balance sheet, George asked John to do the statement of profit and loss.

   (28.4 per cent incorrectly concluded that — if the sentence meant what it said — *John* was helping with the balance sheet. 71.6 per cent correctly concluded that *George* was helping with the balance sheet.)

3. She is the best typist.

   (17.6 per cent incorrectly concluded that two typists were being compared. 82.4 per cent correctly concluded that at least three typists were being compared.)

Such sentences are so common in business that both senders and receivers need to be familiar with the grammatical principles involved. A sender must be sure that his sentences are grammatically correct. (Errors can introduce distracting and uncomplimentary metacommunications; such as "Since he makes errors in English, he probably makes errors in judgment.")

If for any reason a sender recognizes that a sentence (even though grammatically correct) can be misunderstood, he should revise for clarity. A receiver must fight against being distracted by an error, he needs to know what the sentence means as written or spoken, he needs to use judgment sometimes to determine whether a literal interpretation is sensible, and he should be sure to ask for clarification when he is in doubt.

[12]Drucker, *op. cit.,* p. 127.

FACTORS THAT APPLY PRIMARILY TO SENDERS

Those who initiate communications frequently make errors in their selection of words, in failure to take the receiver's reaction into account, and in conveying messages at the proper time.

Words

Anyone who knows English is well aware that one word may have many different meanings. For example, the word "fast" has at least 14 different meanings. Of the 500 most commonly used words, there are over 14,000 different dictionary definitions.[13]

The young or immature person may sometimes yield to the temptation to use a big, unusual word for the sake of impressing others. He soon learns, however, that his message is either not understood or misunderstood. He may learn, too, that he did make an impression — a bad impression.

Even relatively common words are frequently misinterpreted. Carson reports about a questionnaire sent to field staff members of the Bureau of Old Age and Survivors Insurance.[14] About 20 per cent of the field staff had misunderstandings of instructional materials sent to them from headquarters. Link reports that of 69 articles from 13 representative employee papers, 37 were on a readability level too difficult for more than 67 per cent of the adult population.[15] (Some of the difficulty could have resulted from complicated sentences as well as words.)

Businessmen are encouraged to rely on the short, simple word; however, even these words can be misinterpreted.[16] [17] [18] A grocery clerk turned to her manager and said, "This fellow is demanding my money from the cash register." When the manager replied, "Let him have it," the robber shot both the manager and the clerk. To him, "Let him have it" meant "Shoot him." An engineer in a local firm instructed a subordinate to "Let the motor run continually." The subordinate erroneously let the motor run and run, without stopping at all (continuously). True, the subordinate did not follow instructions; but the engineer could have avoided the misunderstanding by choosing words that would be more readily understood; such as, "The motor is to run while the door is open; the motor is to remain stopped while the door is closed."

A sender's chances of doing his part in the communication process is im-

[13]William V. Haney, *Communication Patterns and Incidents* (Homewood, Ill.: Richard Irwin, Inc., 1960), p. 48.

[14]John Carson, "Weak Links in Chain of Command," *Public Opinion Quarterly*, Fall, 1945, pp. 346–349.

[15]Henry C. Link, "How to Get Listeners," *The Management Review*, February, 1951, pp. 62–63.

[16]Rudolph Flesch, *The Art of Readable Writing* (New York: Harper and Row Publishers, 1949).

[17]Robert Gunning, *The Technique of Clear Writing* (New York: McGraw-Hill Book Co., 1952).

[18]Donald R. Murphy, "Test Proves Short Words and Sentences Get Best Readership," *Printers Ink,* Jan. 10, 1947, pp. 61–62.

proved if he (1) relies mainly on the short, simple word, (2) uses them in the way his receiver would normally expect them to be used, and (3) restates in different words any ideas that he thinks might be misunderstood. In addition he needs to create an atmosphere of cordiality in which his receiver will not be reluctant to ask for clarification.

Receiver Reaction

Just as engineers are expected to plan before they build and writers are expected to outline before they write, communicators need to plan their messages before presenting them. If the receiver can be expected to be happy with the message that is about to be sent, the task is simple. Tell him the big idea that will make him happy; then, supply the details.

The problem of anticipating receiver reaction is especially important when the receiver is about to be sent some bad news. For example, assume a superior is planning to tell a subordinate that the latter's promotion will have to be delayed a year. Two ideas must be conveyed: (1) the fact of delay, and (2) the reasons for it. The *reasons* are very important. If they are thoroughly understood by the receiver, a noticeable loss in morale may be avoided. If they are not, the employee may either leave the firm or lose enthusiasm for his work. Since the reasons are so important, the sender must present his message in such

a way as to insure that the receiver actually listens while the reasons are being given.

If the sender should present the fact of delay first, the receiver may become emotionally involved or angered to such an extent that he will not listen to the reasons regardless of how good they may be. The chances of getting the reasons across are greatly improved if they are given first, if the reasons lead up to the denial.[19] [20] Kermit Rolland says, "If you can say *yes*, say it at once. If you must say *no*, take a little longer."[21]

Timing

A company on the West Coast was forced to reduce the pay of its employees. They had known for some time that the firm was in serious financial difficulties. However, when management sent a memorandum informing them of the reduction in pay, they ignored the memorandum because it was dated April 1! The memorandum would have been taken seriously at any other time.

Even though a sender can do his part of the communication task perfectly, his message may not be received if the timing is improper. If the receiver has just recently been jolted with an unexpected assignment, reprimanded, promoted, granted a vacation, or informed that his income tax form is being reviewed, he may have considerable difficulty in concentrating on any message he received.

---

[19]W. Wilkinson, J. H. Menning, and C. R. Anderson, *Writing for Business* (Homewood, Ill.: Richard D. Irwin, Inc., 1955), pp. 71–75.
[20]William C. Himstreet and Wayne Murlin Baty, *Business Communications* (second edition; Belmont, California: Wadsworth Publishing Co., 1964), Chapter 7.
[21]Kermit Rolland, "Letters Can Say No but Keep or Make Friends," *Printers Ink*, Oct. 7, 1949, p. 46.

FACTORS THAT APPLY PRIMARILY TO RECEIVERS

Even though a sender may do his job skillfully, communication may be ineffective if the receiver has difficulties with concentration, expectancy, and interest.

Concentration

Although one aspect of intelligence is the ability to hold important information in one's mind, another significant aspect is the ability to *exclude* everything except that which is being considered at the moment. This power to concentrate is to some extent innate, but it can also be developed through cultivation of good listening habits. Nichols lists six bad habits that prevent effective listening: (1) Faking attention, (2) listening so hard for the small details that major points are missed, (3) refusing to listen when the subject matter is difficult, (4) dismissing a subject prematurely as uninteresting, (5) criticizing delivery or physical appearance of the sender, and (6) yielding to distractions.[22]

Many people in group discussions pride themselves in being able to make a well polished contribution when their turn to speak comes (or when they can manage to cut in!). Yet, the contribution loses much of its impact when in the process of talking the speaker reveals that he was not listening to the preceding comments made by others; instead he was concentrating on how best to phrase his thoughts for maximum impact.

Rogers and Roethlisberger report an effective technique for forcing concentration in group discussions.[23] The members of a group are requested to follow these rules: "Each person can speak up for himself only *after* he has first restated the ideas and feelings of the previous speaker accurately and to that person's satisfaction." Although the technique is time consuming, its value in settling arguments is astonishing. When participants are forced to listen and understand, chances of genuine differences of opinion are greatly reduced.

Expectancy

Students in a class at ASU were being given some step-by-step instructions to draw a rectangular solid (but they had not been told what the finished drawing was to be). They had already received instructions that resulted in a drawing that looked like this:

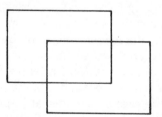

The next instruction was to make a line from A to B.

---

[22]Ralph G. Nichols and Leonard A. Stevens, *Are You Listening?* (New York: McGraw-Hill Book Company, Inc., 1957), pp. 104–113.
[23]Carl Rogers and F. J. Roethlisberger, "Barriers and Gateways to Communication," *Harvard Business Review*, July–Aug., 1952, pp. 46–52.

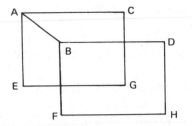

Before further instructions were given, a few students were observed to draw similar lines from C to D, E to F, and G to H. Because they had anticipated remaining instructions, they quit listening and continued drawing.

Those who are listening or reading must learn to resist the temptation to tune themselves out just as soon as they *think* they know what the remainder is to be. It may be vastly different from the expected.

Interest

If the receiver has no interest in a message, effective communication is unlikely. As an experiment to see how much distortion occurs in communication, Higham started rumors and then checked to see how much change had occurred after the rumors had been passed along to several people.[24] Typically, the rumors underwent considerable change as they went from one person to another. Then, he started a rumor about a test that a fellow faculty member was supposedly planning to give. This rumor had special interest to the students involved, for they were also taking the other teacher's class and their grades would be affected. Even though the rumor was passed through many students, there was almost no dis-

tortion. The differences in distortion were statistically significant. The receiver's problem is simplified if he is interested. If he is not, he should either get interested or strenuously resist the temptation to let his mind wander.

SUMMARY

Businessmen, employees, and students are frequently criticized for their lack of ability to communicate.

When two people fail in their efforts to communicate, either the sender or the receiver may be at fault. The sender may be so concerned with his own *reputation* or *rank* that he does not say or write exactly what he should. The receiver may be so concerned with the sender's reputation or rank that he inaccurately interprets the sender's perfectly prepared message. The sender sometimes transmits a *metacommunication* that gets more attention than the message itself. If either the sender or the receiver lacks a basic knowledge of *grammar*, serious misunderstandings may result.

The one who initiates a communication (the sender) makes a serious mistake if he chooses *words* that the receiver might not understand, or if he chooses words that can be readily misunderstood. If the sender does not anticipate a *receiver's reaction* and plan his message accordingly, the receiver may be so disappointed about one part of the message that he will not listen to the other parts. If a sender's *timing* is poor, the receiver may have difficulty in keeping his mind on the message.

---

[24]T. M. Higham, "The Experimental Study of the Transmission of Rumour," *British Journal of Psychology*, 1951, pp. 42–55.

The one who receives a communication makes a serious mistake if he attempts *concentration* on two ideas at once. He needs to exclude everything from his mind except the message he is now receiving. Because the receiver is in a state of *expectancy* (of knowing what he thinks the remaining message is to be), he may commit a serious error if he stops listening. Likewise, if he stops listening because of a lack in *interest*, he may miss a message that is vital to him and to the entire business.

The foregoing factors are not all-inclusive; others could be added. If interpersonal communication is to be effective, both senders and receivers must take such factors into consideration.

ACTIVE LISTENING

C. R. Rogers and R. E. Farson

THE MEANING OF ACTIVE LISTENING

One basic responsibility of the supervisor or executive is the development, adjustment, and integration of individual employees. He tries to develop employee potential, delegate responsibility, and achieve cooperation. To do so, he must have, among other abilities, the ability to listen intelligently and carefully to those with whom he works.

There are, however, many kinds of listening skills. The lawyer, for example, when questioning a witness, listens for contradictions, irrelevancies, errors, and weaknesses. But this is not the kind of listening skill we are concerned with in this booklet. The lawyer usually is not listening in order to help the witness adjust or cooperate or produce. On the other hand, we will be concerned with listening skills which *will help* employees gain a clearer understanding of their situations, take responsibility, and cooperate with each other.

Two Examples

The kind of listening we have in mind is called "active listening." It is called "active" because the listener has a very definite responsibility. He does not passively absorb the words which are spoken to him. He actively tries to grasp the facts and the feelings in what he hears, and he tries, by his listening, to help the speaker work out his own problems.

To get a fuller picture of what is

Reprinted by permission of the Industrial Relations Center of the University of Chicago.

meant by active listening, let us consider two different approaches to the same work problem.

Example No. 1

Foreman: Hey, Al, I don't get this production order. We can't handle this run today. What do they think we are?

Supervisor: But that's the order. So get it out as soon as you can. We're under terrific pressure this week.

Foreman: Don't they know we're behind schedule already because of that press breakdown?

Supervisor: Look, Kelly, I don't decide what goes on upstairs. I just have to see that the work gets out and that's what I'm gonna do.

Foreman: The guys aren't gonna like this.

Supervisor: That's something you'll have to work out with them, not me.

Example No. 2

Foreman: Hey, Ross, I don't get this production order. We can't handle this run today. What do they think we are?

Supervisor: Sounds like you're pretty sore about it, Kelly.

Foreman: I sure am. We were just about getting back to schedule after that press breakdown. Now this comes along.

Supervisor: As if you didn't have enough work to do, huh?

Foreman: Yeah. I don't know how I'm gonna tell the guys about this.

Supervisor: Hate to face 'em with it now, is that it?

Foreman: I really do. They're under a real strain today. Seems like everything we do around here is rush, rush.

Supervisor: I guess you feel like it's unfair to load anything more on them.

Foreman: Well, yeah. I know there must be plenty of pressure on everybody up the line, but — well, if that's the way it is . . . guess I'd better get the word to 'em.

There are obviously many differences between these two examples. The main one, however, is that Ross, the supervisor in the second example is using the active-listening approach. He is listening and responding in a way that makes it clear that he appreciates both the meaning and the feeling behind what Kelly is saying.

Active listening does not necessarily mean long sessions spent listening to grievances, personal or otherwise. It is simply a way of approaching those problems which arise out of the usual day-to-day events of any job.

To be effective, active listening must be firmly grounded in the basic attitudes of the user. We cannot employ it as a technique if our fundamental attitudes are in conflict with its basic concepts. If we try, our behavior will be empty and sterile and our associates will be quick to recognize this. Until we can demonstrate a spirit which genuinely respects the potential worth of the individual, which considers his rights and trusts his capacity for self-direction, we cannot begin to be effective listeners.

What We Achieve by Listening

Active listening is an important way to bring about changes in people. Despite the popular notion that listening is a passive approach, clinical and research evidence clearly shows that sensitive listening is a most effective agent for individual personality change and group development. Listening brings about changes in people's attitudes toward themselves and others, and also brings about changes in their basic values and personal philosophy. People who have been listened to in this new and special way become more emotionally mature, more open to their experiences, less defensive, more democratic, and less authoritarian.

When people are listened to sensitively, they tend to listen to themselves with more care and make clear exactly what they are feeling and thinking. Group members tend to listen more to each other, become less argumentative, more ready to incorporate other points of view. Because listening reduces the threat of having one's ideas criticized, the person is better able to see them for what they are, and is more likely to feel that his contributions are worthwhile.

Not the least important result of listening is the change that takes place within the listener himself. Besides the fact that listening provides more information than any other activity, it builds deep, positive relationships and tends to alter constructively the attitudes of the listener. Listening is a growth experience.

These, then, are some of the worthwhile results we can expect from active listening. But how do we go about this kind of listening? How do we become active listeners?

HOW TO LISTEN

Active listening aims to bring about changes in people. To achieve this end, it relies upon definite techniques —

things to do and things to avoid doing. Before discussing these techniques, however, we should first understand why they are effective. To do so, we must understand how the individual personality develops.

The Growth of the Individual

Through all of our lives, from early childhood on, we have learned to think of ourselves in certain, very definite ways. We have built up pictures of ourselves. Sometimes these self-pictures are pretty realistic but at other times they are not. For example, an overage, overweight lady may fancy herself a youthful, ravishing siren, or an awkward teenager regard himself as a star athlete.

All of us have experiences which fit the way we need to think about ourselves. These we accept. But it is much harder to accept experiences which don't fit. And sometimes, if it is very important for us to hang on to this self-picture, we don't accept or admit these experiences at all.

These self-pictures are not neccessarily attractive. A man, for example, may regard himself as incompetent and worthless. He may feel that he is doing his job poorly in spite of favorable appraisals by the company. As long as he has these feelings about himself he must deny any experiences which would seem not to fit this self-picture, in this case any that might indicate to him that he is competent. It is so necessary for him to maintain this self-picture that he is threatened by anything which would tend to change it. Thus, when the company raises his salary, it may seem to him only additional proof that he is a fraud. He must hold onto this self-picture, bad or good, it's the only thing he has by which he can identify himself.

This is why direct attempts to change this individual or change his self-picture are particularly threatening. He is forced to defend himself or to completely deny the experience. This denial of experience and defense of the self-picture tend to bring on rigidity of behavior and create difficulties in personal adjustment.

The active-listening approach, on the other hand, does not present a threat to the individual's self-picture. He does not have to defend it. He is able to explore it, see it for what it is, and make his own decision as to how realistic it is. And he is then in a position to change.

If I want to help a man reduce his defensiveness and become more adaptive, I must try to remove the threat of myself as his potential changer. As long as the atmosphere is threatening, there can be no effective communication. So I must create a climate which is neither critical, evaluative, nor moralizing. It must be an atmosphere of equality and freedom, permissiveness and understanding, acceptance and warmth. It is in this climate and this climate only that the individual feels safe enough to incorporate new experiences and new values into his concept of himself. Let's see how active listening helps to create this climate.

What to Avoid

When we encounter a person with a problem, our usual response is to try to change his way of looking at things — to get him to see his situation the way we see it, or would like him to see it. We plead, reason, scold, encourage, insult, prod — anything to bring about a change in the desired direction, that is, in the direction we want him to travel. What we seldom realize, however, is that, under these circumstances, we are usually responding to *our own* needs to see the world in certain ways. It is always difficult for us to tolerate and understand actions which are different from the ways in which *we* believe *we* should act. If, however, we can free ourselves from the need to influence and direct others in our own paths, we enable ourselves to listen with understanding, and thereby employ the most potent available agent of change.

One problem the listener faces is that of responding to demands for decisions, judgments, and evaluations. He is constantly called upon to agree or disagree with someone or something. Yet, as he well knows, the question or challenge frequently is a masked expression of feelings or needs which the speaker is far more anxious to communicate than he is to have the surface questions answered. Because he cannot speak these feelings openly, the speaker must disguise them to himself and to others in an acceptable form. To illustrate, let us examine some typical questions and the type of answers that might best elicit the feeling beneath it. (See Table 1.)

These responses recognize the questions but leave the way open for the employee to say what is really bothering him. They allow the listener to participate in the problem or situation without shouldering all responsibility for decision-making or actions. This is a process of thinking *with* people instead of *for* or *about* them.

Passing judgment, whether critical

or favorable, makes free expression difficult. Similarly, advice and information are almost seen as efforts to change a person and thus serve as barriers to his self-expression and the development of a creative relationship. Moreover, advice is seldom taken and information hardly ever utilized. The eager young trainee probably will not become patient just because he is advised that, "The road to success in business is a long, difficult one, and you must be patient." And it is no more helpful for him to learn that "only one out of a hundred trainees reach top management positions."

Interestingly, it is a difficult lesson to learn that positive *evaluations* are sometimes as blocking as negative ones. It is almost as destructive to the freedom of a relationship to tell a person that he is good or capable or right, as to tell him otherwise. To evaluate him positively may make it more difficult for him to tell of the faults that distress him or the ways in which he believes he is not competent.

Encouragement also may be seen as an attempt to motivate the speaker in certain directions or hold him off rather than as support. "I'm sure everything will work out O.K." is not a helpful response to the person who is deeply discouraged about a problem.

In other words, most of the techniques and devices common to human relationships are found to be of little use in establishing the type of relationship we are seeking here.

What to Do

Just what does active listening entail, then? Basically, it requires that we get inside the speaker, that we grasp, *from his point of view,* just what it is he is communicating to us. More than that, we must convey to the speaker that we are seeing things from his point of view. To listen actively, then, means that there are several things we must do.

Listen for Total Meaning.   Any message a person tries to get across usually has two components: the *content* of the message and the *feeling* or attitude underlying this content. Both are important, both give the message *meaning*. It is this total

Employee's Question	Listener's Answer
Just whose responsibility is the tool room?	Do you feel that someone is challenging your authority in there?
Don't you think younger able people should be promoted before senior but less able ones?	It seems to you they should, I take it.
What does the super expect us to do about those broken-down machines?	You're pretty disgusted with those machines, aren't you?
Don't you think I've improved over the last review period?	Sounds as if you feel like you've really picked up over these last few months.

TABLE 1

meaning of the message that we try to understand. For example, a machinist comes to his foreman and says, "I've finished that lathe set-up." This message has obvious content and perhaps calls upon the foreman for another work assignment. Suppose, on the other hand, that he says, "Well, I'm finally finished with that damned lathe set-up." The content is the same but the total meaning of the message has changed — and changed in an important way for both the foreman and the worker. Here sensitive listening can facilitate the relationship. Suppose the foreman were to respond by simply giving another work assignment. Would the employee feel that he had gotten his total message across? Would he feel free to talk to his foreman? Will he feel better about his job, more anxious to do good work on the next assignment?

Now, on the other hand, suppose the foreman were to respond with, "Glad to have it over with, huh?" or "Had a pretty rough time of it?" or "Guess you don't feel like doing anything like that again," or anything else that tells the worker that he heard and understands. It doesn't necessarily mean that the next work assignment need be changed or that he must spend an hour listening to the worker complain about the set-up problems he encountered. He may do a number of things differently in the light of the new information he has from the worker — but not necessarily. It's just that extra sensitivity on the part of the foreman which can transform an average working climate into a good one.

Respond to Feelings. In some instances the content is far less important than the feeling which underlies it. To catch the full flavor or meaning of the message one must respond particularly to the feeling component. If, for instance, our machinist had said "I'd like to melt this lathe down and make paper clips out of it," responding to content would be obviously absurd. But to respond to his disgust or anger in trying to work with his lathe recognizes the meaning of this message. There are various shadings of these components in the meaning of any message. Each time the listener must try to remain sensitive to the total meaning the message has to the speaker. What is he trying to tell me? What does this mean to him? How does he see this situation?

Note All Cues. Not all communication is verbal. The speaker's words alone don't tell us everything he is communicating. And hence, truly sensitive listening requires that we become aware of several kinds of communication besides verbal. The way in which a speaker hesitates in his speech can tell us much about his feelings. So too can the inflection of his voice. He may stress certain points loudly and clearly, and may mumble others. We should also note such things as the person's facial expressions, body posture, hand movements, eye movements, and breathing. All of these help to convey his total message.

What We Communicate by Listening

The first reaction of most people when they consider listening as a possible method for dealing with human beings is that listening cannot be sufficient in itself. Because it is passive, they feel, listening does not communicate anything to the speaker. Actually, nothing could be farther from the truth.

By consistently listening to a speaker you are conveying the idea that: "I'm interested in you as a person, and I think that what you feel is important. I respect your thoughts, and even if I don't agree with them, I know that they are valid for you. I feel sure that you have a contribution to make. I'm not trying to change you or evaluate you. I just want to understand you. I think you're worth listening to, and I want you to know that I'm the kind of a person you can talk to."

The subtle but most important aspect of this is that it is the *demonstration* of the message that works. While it is most difficult to convince someone that you respect him by *telling* him so, you are much more likely to get this message across by really *behaving* that way — by actually *having* and *demonstrating* respect for this person. Listening does this most effectively.

Like other behavior, listening behavior is contagious. This has implications for all communications problems, whether between two people, or within a large organization. To insure good communication between associates up and down the line, one must first take the responsibility for setting a pattern of listening. Just as one learns that anger is usually met with anger, argument with argument, and deception with deception, one can learn that listening can be met with listening. Every person who feels responsibility in a situation can set the tone of the interaction, and the important lesson in this is that any behavior exhibited by one person will eventually be responded to with similar behavior in the other person.

It is far more difficult to stimulate constructive behavior in another person but far more profitable. Listening is one of these constructive behaviors, but if one's attitude is to "wait out" the speaker rather than really listen to him, it will fail. The one who consistently listens with understanding, however, is the one who eventually is most likely to be listened to. If you really want to be heard and understood by another, you can develop him as a potential listener, ready for new ideas, provided you can first develop yourself in these ways and sincerely listen with understanding and respect.

Testing for Understanding

Because understanding another person is actually far more difficult than it at first seems, it is important to test constantly your ability to see the world in the way the speaker sees it. You can do this by reflecting in your own words what the speaker seems to mean by his words and actions. His response to this will tell you whether or not he feels understood. A good rule of thumb is to assume that one never really understands until he can communicate this understanding to the other's satisfaction.

Here is an experiment to test your skill in listening. The next time you become involved in a lively or controversial discussion with another person, stop for a moment and suggest that you adopt this ground rule for continued discussion: Before either participant in the discussion can make a point or express an opinion of his own, he must first restate aloud the previous point or position of the other person. This restatement must be accurate enough to satisfy the speaker before the listener can be allowed to speak for himself.

This is something you could try in your own discussion group. Have someone express himself on some topic of emotional concern to the group. Then, before another member expresses his own feelings and thought, he must rephrase the *meaning* expressed by the previous speaker to that individual's satisfaction. Note the changes in the emotional climate and the quality of the discussion when you try this.

PROBLEMS IN ACTIVE LISTENING

Active listening is not an easy skill to acquire. It demands practice. Perhaps more important, it may require changes in our own basic attitudes. These changes come slowly and sometimes with considerable difficulty. Let us look at some of the major problems in active listening and what can be done to overcome them.

The Personal Risk

To be effective at all in active listening, one must have a sincere interest in the speaker. We all live in glass houses as far as our attitudes are concerned. They always show through. And if we are only making a pretense of interest in the speaker, he will quickly pick this up, either consciously or unconsciously. And once he does, he will no longer express himself freely.

Active listening carries a strong element of personal risk. If we manage to accomplish what we are describing here — to sense deeply the feelings of another person, to understand the meaning his experiences have for him, to see the world as he sees it — we risk being changed ourselves. For example, if we permit ourselves to listen our way into the psychological life of a labor leader or agitator — to get the meaning which life has for him — we risk coming to see the world as he sees it. It is threatening to give up, even momentarily, what we believe and start thinking in someone else's terms. It takes a great deal of inner security and courage to be able to risk one's self in understanding another.

For the supervisor, the courage to take another's point of view generally means that he must see *himself* through another's eyes — he must be able to see himself as others see him. To do this may sometimes be unpleasant, but it is far more *difficult* than unpleasant. We are so accustomed to viewing ourselves in certain ways — to seeing and hearing only what we want to see and hear — that it is extremely difficult for a person to free himself from his needs to see things these ways.

Developing an attitude of sincere interest in the speaker is thus no easy task. It can be developed only by being willing to risk seeing the world from the speaker's point of view. If we have a number of such experiences, however, they will shape an attitude which will allow us to be truly genuine in our interest in the speaker.

Hostile Expressions

The listener will often hear negative, hostile expressions directed at himself. Such expressions are always hard to listen to. No one likes to hear hostile action or words. And it is not easy to get to the point where one is strong enough to permit these attacks without finding it necessary to defend himself or retaliate.

Because we all fear that people will crumble under the attack of genuine negative feelings, we tend to perpetuate an attitude of pseudopeace. It is as if we cannot tolerate conflict at all for fear of the damage it could do to us, to the situation, to the others involved. But of course the real damage is done to all these by the denial and suppression of negative feelings.

Out-Of-Place Expressions

There is also the problem of out-of-place expressions, expressions dealing with behavior which is not usually acceptable in our society. In the extreme forms that present themselves before psychotherapists, expressions of sexual perversity or homicidal fantasies are often found blocking to the listener because of their obvious threatening quality. At less extreme levels, we all find unnatural or inappropriate behavior difficult to handle. That is, anything from an "off-color" story told in mixed company, to seeing a man weep is likely to produce a problem situation.

In any face-to-face situation, we will find instances of this type which will momentarily, if not permanently, block any communication. In business and industry any expressions of weakness or incompetency will generally be regarded as unacceptable and therefore will block good two-way communication. For example, it is difficult to listen to a supervisor tell of his feelings of failure in being able to "take charge" of a situation in his department because *all* administrators are supposed to be able to "take charge."

Accepting Positive Feelings

It is both interesting and perplexing to note that negative or hostile feelings or expressions are much easier to deal with in any face-to-face relationship than are truly and deeply positive feelings. This is especially true for the business man because the culture expects him to be independent, bold, clever, and aggressive and manifest no feelings of warmth, gentleness, and intimacy. He therefore comes to regard these feelings as soft and inappropriate. But no matter how they are regarded, they remain a human need. The denial of these feelings in himself and his associates does not get the executive out of the problem of dealing with them. They simply become veiled and confused. If recognized they would work for the total effort; unrecognized, they work against it.

Emotional Danger Signals

The listener's own emotions are sometimes a barrier to active listening. When emotions are at their height, when listening is most necessary, it is most difficult to set aside one's own concerns and be understanding. Our emotions are often our own worst enemies when we try to become listeners. The more involved and invested we are in a particular situation or problem, the less we are likely to be willing or able to listen to the feelings and attitudes of others. That is, the more we find it necessary to respond to our own needs, the less we are able to respond to the needs of another. Let us look at some of the main danger signals that warn us that our emotions may be interfering with our listening.

Defensiveness. The points about which one is most vocal and dogmatic, the points which one is most anxious to impose on others — these are always the points one is trying to talk oneself into believing. So one danger signal becomes apparent when you find yourself stressing a point or trying to convince another. It is at these times that you are likely to be less secure and consequently less able to listen.

Resentment of Opposition. It is always easier to listen to an idea which is similar to one of your own than to an opposing view. Sometimes, in order to clear the air, it is helpful to pause for a moment when you feel your ideas and position being challenged, reflect on the situation, and express your concern to the speaker.

Clash of Personalities. Here again, our experience has consistently shown us that the genuine expression of feelings on the part of the listener will be more helpful in developing a sound relationship than the suppression of them. This is so whether the feelings be resentment, hostility, threat, or admiration. A basically honest relationship, whatever the nature of it, is the most productive of all. The other party becomes secure when he learns that the listener can express his feelings honestly and openly to him. We should keep this in mind when we begin to fear a clash of personalities in the listening relationship. Otherwise, fear of our own emotions will choke off full expression of feelings.

Listening to Ourselves

To listen to oneself is a prerequisite to listening to others. And it is often an effective means of dealing with the problems we have outlined above. When we are most aroused, excited, and demanding, we are least able to understand our own feelings and attitudes. Yet, in dealing with the problems of others, it becomes most important to be sure of one's own position, values, and needs.

The ability to recognize and understand the meaning which a particular episode has for you, with all the feelings which it stimulates in you, and the ability to express this meaning when you find it getting in the way of active listening, will clear the air and enable you once again to be free to listen. That is, if some person or situation touches off feelings within you which tend to block your attempts to listen with understanding, begin listening to yourself. It is much more helpful in developing effective relationships to avoid suppressing these feelings. Speak them out as clearly as you can, and try to enlist the other person as a listener to your feelings. A person's listening ability is limited by his ability to listen to himself.

ACTIVE LISTENING AND COMPANY GOALS

"How can listening improve production?"

"We're in business, and it's a rugged, fast, competitive affair. How are we going to find time to counsel our employees?"

"We have to concern ourselves with organizational problems first."

"We can't afford to spend all day listening when there's a job to be done."

"What's morale got to do with production?"

"Sometimes we have to sacrifice an individual for the good of the rest of the people in the company."

Those of us who are trying to advance the listening approach in industry hear these comments frequently. And because they are so honest and legitimate, they pose a real problem. Unfortunately, the answers are not so clear-cut as the questions.

Individual Importance

One answer is based on an assumption that is central to the listening approach. That assumption is: the kind of behavior which helps the individual will eventually be the best thing that could be done for the group. Or saying it another way: the things that are best for the individual are best for the company. This is a conviction of ours, based on our experience in psychology and education. The research evidence from industry is only beginning to come in. We find that putting the group first, at the expense of the individual, besides being an uncomfortable individual experience, does *not* unify the group. In fact, it tends to make the group less a group. The members become anxious and suspicious.

We are not at all sure in just what ways the group does benefit from a concern demonstrated for an individual, but we have several strong leads. One is that the group feels more secure when an individual member is being listened to and provided for with concern and sensitivity. And we assume that a secure group will ultimately be a better group. When each individual feels that

he need not fear exposing himself to the group, he is likely to contribute more freely and spontaneously. When the leader of a group responds to the individual, puts the individual first, the other members of the group will follow suit, and the group comes to act as a unit in recognizing and responding to the needs of a particular member. This positive, constructive action seems to be a much more satisfying experience for a group than the experience of dispensing with a member.

Listening and Production

As to whether or not listening or any other activity designed to better human relations in an industry actually raises production — whether morale has a definite relationship to production is not known for sure. There are some who frankly hold that there is no relationship to be expected between morale and production — that production often depends upon the social misfit, the eccentric, or the isolate. And there are some who simply choose to work in a climate of cooperation and harmony, in a high-morale group, quite aside from the question of increased production.

A report from the Survey Research Center[1] at the University of Michigan on research conducted at the Prudential Life Insurance Company lists seven findings relating to production and morale. First-line supervisors in high-production work groups were found to differ from those in low-production work groups in that they:

1. Are under less close supervision from their own supervisors.

[1] "Productivity, Supervision, and Employee Morale," *Human Relations,* Series 1, Report 1 (Ann Arbor, Mich.: Survey Research Center, University of Michigan).

2. Place less direct emphasis upon production as the goal.
3. Encourage employee participation in the making of decisions.
4. Are more employee-centered.
5. Spend more of their time in supervision and less in straight production work.
6. Have a greater feeling of confidence in their supervisory roles.
7. Feel that they know where they stand with the company.

After mentioning that other dimensions of morale, such as identification with the company, intrinsic job satisfaction with job status, were not found significantly related to productivity, the report goes on to suggest the following psychological interpretation:

> People are more effectively motivated when they are given some degree of freedom in the way in which they do their work than when every action is prescribed in advance. They do better when some degree of decision-making about their jobs is possible than when all decisions are made for them. They respond more adequately when they are treated as personalities than as cogs in a machine. In short if the ego motivations of self-determination, of self-expression, of a sense of personal worth can be tapped, the individual can be more effectively energized. The use of external sanctions, or pressuring for production may work to some degree, but not to the extent that the more internalized motives do. When the individual comes to identify himself with his job and with the work of his group, human resources are much more fully utilized in the production process.

The Survey Research Center has also conducted studies among workers in other industries. In discussing the results of these studies, Robert L. Kahn writes:

> In the studies of clerical workers, railroad workers, and workers in heavy industry, the supervisors with the better production records gave a larger proportion of their time to supervisory functions, especially to the interpersonal aspects of their jobs. The supervisors of the lower-producing sections were more likely to spend their time in tasks which the men themselves were performing, or in the paper-work aspects of their jobs.[2]

Maximum Creativeness

There may never be enough research evidence to satisfy everyone on this question. But speaking from a business point of view, in terms of the problems of developing resources for production, the maximum creativeness and productive effort of the human beings in the organization are the richest untapped source of power still existing. The difference between the maximum productive capacity of people and that output which industry is now realizing is immense. We simply suggest that this maximum capacity might be closer to realization if we sought to release the motivation that already exists within people rather than try to stimulate them externally.

This releasing of the individual is made possible first of all by sensitive listening, with respect and understanding. Listening is a beginning toward making the individual feel himself worthy of making contributions, and this could result in a very dynamic and productive organization. Competitive

---

[2]Robert L. Kahn, "The Human Factors Underlying Industrial Productivity," *Michigan Business Review*, November, 1952.

business is never too rugged or too busy to take time to procure the most efficient technological advances or to develop rich raw material resources. But these in comparison to the resources that are already within the people in the plant are paltry. This is industry's major procurement problem.

G. L. Clements, president of Jewel Tea Co., Inc., in talking about the collaborative approach to management says:

> We feel that this type of approach recognizes that there is a secret ballot going on at all times among the people in any business. They vote for or against their supervisors. A favorable vote for the supervisor shows up in the cooperation, teamwork, understanding, and production of the group. To win this secret ballot, each supervisor must share the problems of his group and work for them.[3]

The decision to spend time listening to his employees is a decision each supervisor or executive has to make for himself. Executives seldom have much to do with products or processes. They have to deal with people who must in turn deal with people who will deal with products or processes. The higher one goes up the line the more he will be concerned with human relations problems, simply because people are all he has to work with. The minute we take a man from his bench and make him a foreman he is removed from the basic production of goods and now must begin relating to individuals instead of nuts and bolts. People are different from things, and our foreman is called upon for a different line of skills completely. His new tasks call upon him to be a special kind of a person. The development of himself as a listener is a first step in becoming this special person.

---

[3] G. L. Clements, "Time for 'Democracy in Action' at the Executive Level," an address given before the A.M.A. Personnel Conference, February 28, 1951.

ACME AIRCRAFT CORPORATION

CASE 1

George Bruster took an engineering job with the Acme Aircraft Corporation soon after his graduation from State Engineering College. He was initially assigned the responsibility of supervising a group of engineers and engineering aides involved in conducting experimental test programs on various models of airplanes and airplane components.

Prior to his graduation, Bruster had spent several summers working for Acme Aircraft and had worked part-time for this organization for a period while attending school. At the time of his permanent employment he had held every position in the testing group other than that of crew chief. Because of his previous experience he was assigned the position of crew chief — an unusual assignment for a "new" engineer.

The average size of a testing crew was seven to ten individuals, of whom five were usually graduate engineers and the remainder engineering aides and technical assistants. The responsibilities of the crew chief included the over-all planning and coordinating of the test programs with which his group was involved. Approximately half of the crew chief's responsibilities were administrative rather than technical; and because of the nature of his responsibilities, the crew chief often was not the engineer on the crew who had the most experience or the greatest technical knowledge. Often older engineers, specialists in electronics or design, for example, would be working on crews headed by younger, less experienced engineers. This type of arrangement had rarely created friction in the past — especially as the older specialists were usually not interested in accepting responsibility for anything but their particular part of a testing series. In addition, crew membership was constantly changing as crews were disbanded and reformed as tests were completed and new tests undertaken.

Figure 1 is an example of the organization of a typical testing unit.

On November 1, about four months after he had taken the full time job with Acme, George Bruster's group was assigned the project of testing a new model component for an experimental aircraft which Acme was developing. It was only the second major assignment that George's group had had since he took over as crew chief. This particular test series was of prime importance, for the results of the tests would be instrumental in providing data upon which Acme would base its design proposal to government representatives. If the company could provide an acceptable design, it would be in a favorable position eventually to gain a large — and profitable — production contract.

The unit supervisor stressed the importance of this particular series of tests to George and informed him that the entire testing group was under considerable pressure from top management to get quick and accurate results. Top men from the model design and instrumentation groups had been assigned to the tests, as well as one of the best report writers in the coordinating group.

Because of scheduling problems regarding the test facilities available at the Bristol plant of Acme — the "home" office of the test group headed by Bruster — arrangements were made for the current series of tests to be conducted at the Culver City facilities of Acme. Culver City was located approximately 900 miles from Bristol; and while the Culver City operations were organized in the same manner as those at Bristol, the operations were run autonomously because of the physical distance between the two facilities. Thus, while Bruster and his crew would actually conduct the tests, they would be using the equipment and facilities of the Culver City operation.

George Bruster arrived at the Culver City test facility on November 7 to coordinate with the people there and make final test arrangements. After determining that the test was scheduled for December 1 and that his crew would receive the full cooperation of the local facility, he went to the data reduction group to arrange for the computer processing of data that would result from the test. The head of the data reduction unit, Gil Harmon, introduced George to the chief programmer, Dick Jones, with whom he was to work throughout the data reduction process.

George explained the importance of the test and showed Dick the type of in-

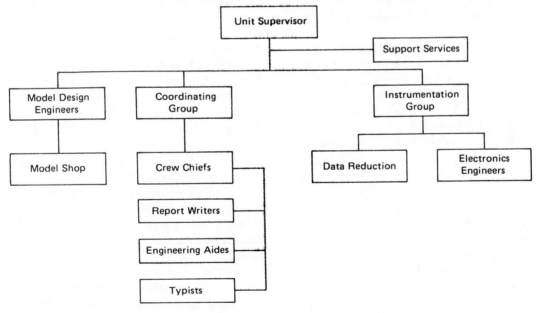

FIGURE 1 • Organization Chart of a
Testing Unit

formation that would be required as final data from the digital computers.

After studying the information for a few minutes, Dick said, "I'll have to write a new program in order to give you the information you want. None of our present standard programs are capable of handling this job."

"How long will it take to write a new program?" George asked. "Oh, I could probably have it finished by the fifth of December. That's the last day of your test, so it will be done in time to reduce your data."

"That won't do!" George exclaimed. "We must have data from day to day all during the test. This proposal is red hot, and we must analyze our data on a day-by-day basis. That's the only way we can be sure we are taking the right approach in our test program. Each day's testing will be dependent on the data from the day before."

"So, what do you think? Can you have your program finished by the first?"

"Well I dunno," mumbled Dick. "I might be able to finish by the first if there are no hitches in the program, but things seldom go that smoothly."

" But it is possible to finish by the first?" insisted George.

"It's possible, but I have other important programs to work on. Everything would have to work properly the first time."

"This project is so important it just has to be done on time. We don't have any choice but to plan it for the first of the month."

"Okay, I'll give it all the effort I can. With a little luck it will probably be ready for the first."

"Swell," concluded George. "I'll

count on it."

After concluding all pretest arrangements, George returned to Bristol. During the remainder of November he was in frequent telephone communication with Culver City. All preparations were progressing satisfactorily and Dick Jones assured George that the program would be finished by the last day of November.

On November 30 George and his crew arrived at Culver City. The test was to begin the next day.

George found everything in readiness for his test, except that the data program was not quite finished. He went to Dick Jones and asked what the holdup was.

"No holdup," Dick replied. "The program will be completed by the end of the day, and we can check it out on the computer first thing in the morning. If everything checks out okay, we will be able to run your data from the first day's testing sometime tomorrow night. So you'll have your data the next day, just as you requested."

"What happens if everything doesn't check out?" asked George.

"It'll take a little while to iron out any bugs that may show up. But it shouldn't hold us up much; a few hours maybe."

"Will you be able to work overtime on this if it becomes necessary?"

"I think so. We should be able to get your data for you one way or another, so don't worry. We'll let you know if we run into any major problems."

George was reassured and returned to his hotel satisfied that all was in readiness for the start of his test the following day.

The testing groups existed as staff units. As such, they conducted tests at the request of line and project groups who were in need of the particular information. It was the usual practice for the group requesting a test to send along a representative to make whatever decisions regarding the test program that might come under the jurisdiction of the line organization.

The requesting group for this test had sent along their senior project engineer, Richard Wallen, because of the importance of the test. Wallen was a fairly new supervisor but was well qualified technically. He was a "driver," worked his subordinates hard during rush programs such as this, and had a reputation of sometimes "rubbing people the wrong way" in order to achieve an immediate goal.

Wallen was directly responsible to the division general manager for the success of the program. One of his major concerns was whether or not the final data would be ready on a day-to-day basis. He asked George about it the night before the test.

George replied, "Dick Jones told me everything would be ready on time. The odds are real slim that anything would go wrong; and if something went wrong, it would only slow us down a couple of hours."

The following day the data from the first shift of testing was turned over to Jones for processing. However, the program did not check out properly and Jones was unable to give George his data the following day.

The same situation occurred the next two days of testing, with Jones unable to make his program work despite working several hours overtime

each day.

On the fourth day the results were no better. Three hours after the testing shift was completed Wallen and Bruster went to see Jones. When they found that Jones had gone home, Wallen "blew his top" and told George Bruster to telephone Jones at his home and demand to know why he wasn't at the office working on the programing problem.

A few minutes later Gil Harmon, head of the data reduction unit, received a worried phone call from Jones, who quoted George as saying "If you don't get down here and start working on this program, it may cost you your job!"

Harmon passed on this information to Conners Simpson, who was instrumentation supervisor at Culver City. Simpson was shocked and angered at the attitude the visiting group was taking toward one of his men. He immediately phoned Wallen and demanded an explanation. He told him in no uncertain terms to "lay off" his men and also told Wallen to follow the proper chain of command and notify him first next time there was a problem. In addition, Simpson stated that he "had no intention of letting Jones come down and work on your damn program. Jones has been working twelve hours a day for the past week and has several other problems to deal with also. Besides, it's too late to salvage much of the data."

Before he hung up the phone, Simpson told Wallen, "This thing has gone too far. I'm going to take it to the boss and get it ironed out first thing in the morning. I want you and your crew chief to meet me, Jones, and Harmon in the boss's office at eight o'clock tomorrow morning."

The meeting was held, but the test series was considered unsatisfactory by all involved. The group had failed to get the desired information, and additional tests would have to be rescheduled at considerable cost in time and money.

The meeting proved to be a unique experience for George Bruster. Wallen denied outright that he had told George to use the strong language in speaking to Jones that had upset everyone so badly.

George could only reply that he thought that such language was Wallen's intent. George subsequently left the meeting shaking his head unhappily and trying to understand how the whole affair had deteriorated into such a mess.

LESTER MANUFACTURING COMPANY

CASE 2

One February morning, George Healey, personnel director of the Lester Manufacturing Company, received a document entitled "The Trouble with Lester" from Mike Bossart, one of his assistants. It had been given to Bossart by Frank Baxter during the customary exit interview which had followed Baxter's voluntary resignation the day before. The document read as follows:

THE TROUBLE WITH LESTER

DEDICATED TO THE FRUSTRATED SOULS WHO SPEND THEIR WORKING HOURS IN THE SUFFOCATING JUNGLE OF THE ACCOUNTING DEPARTMENT

Without the Lester Company the economy of our city and the state would collapse. This statement, constantly reiterated is undoubtedly true. But even with Lester, unemployment in the state has reached one of the highest figures in the nation.

It follows that with the current changing product emphasis, Lester, like others in the field, will, in the future, be operating with less manpower. Thus, inevitable cutbacks and mounting unemployment will follow.

Lester could care less. They have their defense contracts. The Lester products, both military and commercial, are universally respected. The company will still reap financial profit.

But what will become of the state, and the people who live here? They have suffered, and are doomed to suffer more, from the weaknesses of an overbalanced economy. Nearsighted leadership, and moss-backed legislation have made it difficult to attract new industry. In contrast to other states which promote new industries with lease-free land, our state offers prohibitive taxes.

A remedy must be found.

In the meantime, Lester, without competition, floats like a fat shark in a pool of shellfish, taking all, giving nothing, and spitting out the bones.

No, the picture isn't that morbid. Actually, Lester is benevolent. They provide a huge payroll. They have a rewarding Suggestion System, which benefits the ingenious employee (as well as the company). Cash awards are made on everything from designing a labor-and-expense-saving casting to suggesting that Maintenance install bigger signs over the restrooms for nearsighted personnel. Suggestions concerning the value of specific employees, or where they should go, are not accepted.

Lester supports the Community Chest, and they have a personal Blood Bank. They also have a Credit Union, where an employee can obtain a loan at a reasonable interest rate. Payments are deducted from the second paycheck of every month. It is not advisable to borrow too much, however. It is difficult to take a $500 loan payment out of a $175 termination check and end up with any money.

The company protects its employees with insurance. The rumor that they were forced into it by the federal government is false.

The company has a pension (?) plan. However, unless you work for Lester for 120 years, don't expect to retire to the Bahamas on the money they give you. Better line yourself up with a part-time job as a Western Union boy.

Lester provides schools where the employee can better himself. The courses are related to the company and its business. Supervision urges that employees take advantage of this built-in education system, and attend as many classes as possible. The fact that you have taken some classes goes in your personnel folder, and will help you advance. I know a fellow who has been

with the company six years and has taken twenty-four classes. (That's an average of four a year.) He's an expediter — at the next to bottom grade.

The company stimulates leisure activities. It has hobby clubs and athletics.

In addition, different departments (for example, the Accounting Department) sponsor social functions for their employees. This promotes a feeling of "togetherness" in the section. There are dances, picnics, mixed overnight camping trips, and assorted orgies.

For the employee working in Accounting, the Accounting Dance is a social must. This gives the peon a chance to cultivate his supervisor. An interchange of dances is a good approach. What do you care if his wife is a foot taller than you and has halitosis? So she wants to lead? When dancing, try to Charleston in front of the Chief's table. In this way you may be able to strike up an acquaintance with him. This is especially true if you kick him in the mouth.

Bowling is the best of departmental athletics. The whole gang is down at the alley. You can joke, and kid, and drink beer with your supervisors. It's a hell of a lot of fun. But don't try to win, or you'll be permanent second shift. (This is comparable to being permanent K.P., or permanent latrine.) And for God's sake don't laugh if some superior falls down delivering the ball or gets a split.

Lester provides for sick leave. But if you work in Accounting, don't take it unless you have polio. If you break an arm, put it in a splint and come to work. If you have malaria so bad your clothes are soaked through, put on another change and come to work. Supervision stresses attendance, and if they don't like the color of your ties, a bad attendance record (missing over two days a year) is a ready-made excuse for stopping your progress.

What happens to the employee working in the Accounting Department at Lester?

Foremost, his individualism is crushed. The bigness of the company, and its socialistic structure make him small. It's no wonder that he loses incentive.

He must conform. The proper dress is a white shirt and tie (conservative), and preferably a business suit. To get ahead, you should keep your suit coat on, even though it may be a rather sticky 95°, and four stenos have fainted.

Be intense. Furrowing the brow, and scowling, indicates that you have a business-like attitude, and are serious about your job, and not that you have a bad case of hemorrhoids. And for gosh sakes don't laugh during working hours. Laughing conveys frivolity, and may give some supervisor the idea that you don't give a damn about your job. (A small chuckle is permitted at lunchtime.) Don't grin, and smile only at superiors.

When traveling to another area, walk briskly. Don't loiter. An efficiency expert may be watching. Carry a piece of paper. A paper gives the carrier an air of importance.

Being on good terms with your supervisor is essential at Lester. Cultivate him. Asking him questions about the job is one method. Chances are he won't know the answer, but he can direct you to some experienced employee who will. Asking questions shows that you're enthusiastic. That's the image you must create.

Discover your supervisor's interests. If he cuts out paper dolls, buy a pair of scissors.

Be cautious in talking with your supervisor, or, for that matter, any supervisor. The relationship is a delicate one. Never disagree, even though you know he's dead wrong, and a jerk besides. Contradicting the supervisor means that you are out of line, have a bad attitude, and are not pulling with the team.

Your supervisor can make or break you, depending on his whims, and whether or not he's had his coffee. Despite all the "hogwash" about a "scientific" personnel evaluation system, all individual progress at Lester is based on the personal relationship of the supervisor with those under him. The man who thinks he can succeed through merit alone is living in an "ivory tower."

If the supervisor likes you, and considers you "sharp" it's one step into the "Up" elevator. If he doesn't think you "fit in," or aren't aggressive, it's the basement.

Stock cover-up phrases are used by supervisors in the "P.E." interview to conceal personal feelings. Such mouthings as "You don't communicate well," "You don't write an effective memo," or "You don't show enough initiative" are typical.

Movement is vital in the Accounting Department. Many a good man has stayed at the same desk month after month, watching new hires pass him by, because a supervisor has taken a dislike to him. This man may be a good, conscientious employee, well qualified for a better job, but he won't get it. Eventually this man must go out the door. He isn't moving.

Once you are stopped, start reading the want-ads.

Security is a hollow word at Lester. Nobody uses it, unless they're talking of the market. Anybody who thinks he has it here, should be advised to see a psychiatrist. When the cutbacks come, they can strike anywhere, both bottom and top. They will get worse.

After reading the document with a great deal of interest, Healey reviewed the personnel record of Frank Baxter. This record is reproduced in part in Figure 1.

A few days after he had received the document Healey made the following comments concerning Frank Baxter. "I've really never talked with him, so these are just observations that I have. I became acquainted with him, originally, or rather I noticed him originally, because of his sloppy dress. He has a real talent for looking sloppy if you know what I mean. You know, the kind of guy who makes even the best clothes look unkempt. I really don't think he would comb his hair if he were paid for it. He's balding, about thirty-six or thirty-seven years old, single, and, rather surprisingly, a university graduate.

"He is very interested in sports —

Work History		Position	Salary
Hired in	3/16/63		
Transferred to Accounting	5/25/64	Clerk C	$169.60/week
Reclassification	4/22/65	Accountant C	176.60
Merit raise	4/6/66		180.40
Reclassification	7/13/66	Accountant B	194.60
Merit raise	1/25/67		197.60
Merit raise	8/23/67		204.40
Reclassification	9/19/68	Controller B	210.60
Resigned	2/2/71		217.80

Evaluations (from Personnel Evaluation reports)

W. Bostrom	4/15/63 to 2/15/64 — Group 4 to Group 3. Good steady worker. Improve accuracy factor.
R. Kast	7/20/64 to 7/18/68 — Rating 60 to 72. Hard worker, good job knowledge. Needs to attain self-confidence and aggressiveness.
B.A. Lootkens	2/69 to 9/69 — Comments same as above.
V.R. Cone	11/69 — Reliable and cooperative. Needs initiative.
J.R. Lockover	6/70 — Improve initiative, productivity, judgment. Shown some improvement over last P.E.

Merits (from Merit Increase Evaluation form)

M.R. Ballert	1/67 to 8/67 — Good improvement. "Above average."
H.A. Berg	12/68 — "Average."
B.A. Lootkens	3/69 — Show more initiative & drive. "Above Average." 9/59 — "Below Average" — not concentrating.
J.R. Lockover	3/70 — Room for considerable improvement in job performance. "Below Average."
H.E. Martin	9/70 — Improved over past 6 months. "Average."

Memo dated 3/2/70: J.R. Lockover, regarding job performance. Placed on 30-day probation. Remarks: Needs to improve — initiative, reliability, response to Company needs, productivity, and judgrnent. Has capability to do good work, but needs to apply himself and show interest.

FIGURE 1 • *Personnel Record of Frank Baxter*

really an authority on them. He's the kind of guy, for example, who can quote batting averages for years back, knows who is playing whom three years from now, and how many night games the Yankees played in 1958. He is also a participant in sports to some degree, and I've heard that he's been active in some of the company's recreational programs.

"He is a man who has frequently been suggested to me as someone who might fill vacancies of higher positions in the accounting department. But just as frequently I've said 'Not interested.'

"He's obviously quite well liked by his fellow employees. I've received many indications through the grapevine that they have been asking if something can't be done to get him moved up the ladder or some way worked out that he could progress faster than he had been. There is no indication at all that he had any difficulty in getting along with his people. Indeed, quite the opposite. It is strange, though, in noting the comments on his personnel evaluation reports and merit evaluation forms, that this matter of sloppy appearance never came up. Yet this was what first attracted my attention to him.

"I've done nothing about the document. The guy has some good points in there. There's a real message, I think. For example, his comments about 'conformity' may be quite pertinent. Some of the people I've talked with about the document have suggested that we get it reproduced and distribute it to all our supervisors. I'm not sure this is the right approach, though. I think we should try and gain what good we can from this incident, and I'm not sure that circulating it with wide distribution will let us realize any of the benefits that are here. You can get good ideas from this or anything like this, but I'm afraid that if we circulate the document those supervisors who weren't involved might treat it facetiously and tend to ride their fellow supervisors who had had contacts with Baxter. Maybe a better approach would be discuss it with the chief supervisors who were involved and see if there is, in fact, any good that we can get out of the situation. I'm really not sure what I should do. There's probably some element of 'sour grapes' involved in this but, on the other hand, Baxter does make some good points."

ACTIVE LISTENING

INTRODUCTION

Before beginning the exercise, review the reading, "Active Listening," by Rogers and Farson.

PROCEDURE

The class will divide into subgroups of three persons. One or two groups of four can be formed if the numbers do not come out evenly.

Each member of the subgroup will play three roles in turn: communicator, listener, and observer. The communicator will select a problem of concern to present to the listener. The problem should be a real one of significant concern to the communicator. Examples might include choosing between summer jobs, whether to change one's major, conflict between groups or individuals at work, interpersonal conflict with an acquaintance, etc.

The listener will be placed in the role of consultant or counselor (an important part of the manager's job). He or she will (a) *listen* to the problem, (b) try to *understand* the problem, and (c) offer suggestions for *resolving* the problem.

The third person in the group will act as observer and take notes regarding the process. The observer will watch for and describe behaviors of both communicator and listener that facilitate *or* block effective communication. For example, does the communicator appear open and honest in describing the problem? What makes you think so? Are the physical cues consistent with the verbal message? When the listener responds, is the communicator defensive? How can you tell?

Does the listener attempt to understand the problem before trying to solve it? Does he or she paraphrase? Are there signs of defensiveness? Use a form similar to the one shown in Figure 1 for your notes.

Each member of the subgroup should act in turn as communicator, listener, and observer.

The total group should be reassembled for discussion of the behaviors encountered that facilitated or hindered communication.

Other discussion might center around the demands of the three roles. Which of the three did you find most difficult? What different types of skills do the three roles require? Create a skills inventory using a form similar to that shown in Figure 2. How might the needed skills be learned?

Communicator   **Listener**

Facilitating   Blocking   Facilitating   Blocking
1.   1.   1.   1.
2.   2.   2.   2.
3.   3.   3.   3.
4.   4.   4.   4.

FIGURE 1 • Facilitating and Blocking Behaviors

Skills required for:

Communicator   Listener/Consultant   Observer
1.   1.   1.
2.   2.   2.
3.   3.   3.
4.   4.   4.

FIGURE 2 • Skills Inventory

ONE-WAY AND TWO-WAY COMMUNICATION

INTRODUCTION

Most communication in an organization can be described as being one-way or two-way in nature. In one-way communication the sender transmits a message with no provision for response from the receiver. The listener is left to his/her interpretation of the message. Listening to a radio or watching television are examples of one-way communication. In the college setting the large lecture section will rely upon one-way communication, as do staff newspapers and bulletin board notices.

Two-way communication implies interaction between sender and receiver. Examples of two-way communication include telephone conversations, seminars or discussion sessions, and the small staff meeting.

This exercise demonstrates some important differences between one-way and two-way communication.

PROCEDURE

A member of the class will be selected to be the communicator, while the rest of the class will be receivers. The communicator will be given a sheet of paper with a diagram on it. The communicator's task is to describe verbally the diagram to the receivers, while the receivers working individually attempt to reproduce the diagram described.

In the one-way communication mode, the communicator should move to the back of the room or turn his/her back to the receivers. Receivers are not allowed to respond to the sender in any way, and should maintain complete silence. The communicator may take as much time as he/she wishes to describe the figures, and should attempt to describe them as accurately as possible. After the description has been completed, the course instructor will ask a series of questions regarding listener reactions to the one-way communication.

The sender will then move to the front of the room and will describe another diagram, this time utilizing two-way communication. Receivers will be allowed to ask questions of the communicator. All interaction must be verbal: neither sender nor receiver can draw figures in the air or hold up drawings. The verbal interaction may continue until there are no more questions for the sender.

The course instructor will gather information on reactions to two-way communication, and the communicator will reproduce the "correct" figures on the board.

Discussion will follow regarding the effects of one-way and two-way communication on accuracy, frustration, confidence, and time.

PART 3

INDIVIDUAL MOTIVATION AND BEHAVIOR

The word *motivation* is derived from the Latin *movere,* "to move." Interest in motivation is not new, of course. The motivation of people has been a central concern of writers in many disciplines for over two millennia. Early Greek writings suggested hedonism as the concept underlying motivation. Hedonsim suggests that a person will engage in activity that maximizes pleasure. That sounds like everyone we know, right? Unfortunately, to be of value, a theory of motivation must do two things: explain *and* predict behavior.

Hedonism is insufficient as a predictor. For example, if a person is given a choice of activities, it would be difficult or impossible to predict the choice he or she will make. Human learning is so diverse and experience so broad that activities deemed pleasurable by many are greeted with indifference by others, or even as outright unpleasant. As a theory of work motivation, hedonism is of little use.

In the early part of this century, psychologists began elaborating upon the concept. E. L. Thorndike argued that those responses to a situation that result in pleasurable consequences will be reinforced and will be more likely repeated in the same type of situation. Those responses that result in unpleasant consequences become less probable.[1] Although his "law of effect" has been supported countless times in experiments, it does not explain why consequences are pleasurable (desirable) or unpleasurable.

Other scholars began introducing the concept of instinct, while yet others developed the notion of unconscious motivation. Although the two concepts are fundamentally different, the implica-

---

[1] E. L. Thorndike, *Animal Intelligence* (New York: The Macmillan Co., 1911).

tions for work motivation are similar. In either case, the individual would be unaware of at least some of his or her own motives. In the case of instinct, some drives would be innate, that is, genetically encoded in the individual, and he or she would be powerless to change or block those drives, even if aware of them. In the case of unconscious motivation, the individual would simply not be aware of those particular motives. Unconscious motivation was popularized from the work of Sigmund Freud. The instinctual view fell into disrepute for decades, and has only recently been revived in the work of ethologists. Ethologists suggest that at least some aspects of human behavior can be explained in terms of instinct.

In this book, our interest is in the managerial applications of current motivation theory.

In "Assumptions about Man, Leadership and Motivation," Coffey, Athos, and Raynolds point out the importance of our assumptions, as managers, about the basic nature of man. Does what we think about people in general affect an employee's level of motivation? Perhaps not immediately or directly, but it is clear that people respond to the way they are treated. A supervisor who treats subordinates as irresponsible children may soon find himself managing a group of irresponsible children!

In 1943, A. H. Maslow, a pioneering social psychologist, proposed a theory of motivation that laid the groundwork for many years to come in the field of work motivation. As you read about Maslow's hierarchy of needs, keep these questions in mind: How can I use this information as a manager? If a need hierarchy *does* exist (which is by no means clear), is it *this* hierarchy? Would everyone have the same hierarchy? Are satisfaction and motivation one and the same?

The next major theory addressed by Coffey et al. is that of Frederick Herzberg, another leading social psychologist. The impact of this theory on job design in organizations has been substantial. The concept of job enrichment was given impetus by Herzberg's work, and huge amounts of organizational resources have been committed to "enriching" jobs, especially those at the lowest organizational levels.

As with any theory, the questions to be asked are: Is it real? And does it work? From Herzberg's research and that of other scholars, it is clear that not everyone considers those things labeled by Herzberg as motivators to be motivators. Nor does everyone consider Herzberg's hygiene factors actually to be hygiene factors. Thus, the answer to the first question about reality is, "Not for everyone." That implies the answer to the second question, "Not always." That being the case, there must be other considerations. Can you list some?

In writing about "Human Motivation in the Smaller Enterprise,"

Sutermeister and Saxberg confronted the changing values we encountered in Part 1 of this text. If values toward work change, traditional approaches to motivation may become less effective. As an alternative, Sutermeister and Saxberg suggest "humanizing" the organization, which involves increased attention to employee needs and values, and indicates that the small firm has a decided advantage. Is that necessarily true? What benefits can be expected from the "humanizing" process? Can you think of any hidden or potential costs?

In "Change through Behavior Modification," Hersey and Blanchard propose a concept called the *effective cycle*. There is a tendency for people to respond with performance levels expected of them — if a trusting relationship is present. In other words, expectation of high performance must be coupled with tangible evidence that the superior has genuine confidence in the subordinate's ability and trust in his willingness to perform. One approach to affecting subordinate (or superior) behavior is called *behavior modification*. As you read the article, think of as many positive and negative reinforcers as possible. What kinds of reinforcers would work best on you?

Finally, there is a very important, unresolved issue in work motivation that deserves examination. Does an organization and its management have a responsibility to create an environment in which an individual can achieve self-actualization, or should the organization take a much more limited view of its responsibilities in this regard?

One competent and successful manager of a large organization had decided that it was not his organization's responsibility to provide opportunities for self-actualization. He was conversant with the current thinking about motivation but had decided that since the work in his organization was highly routine, highly automated, and did not give much opportunity for individual initiative or flexibility, his main responsibility as a manager was to run a very efficient plant with great concern for safety factors so that his employees could receive the most money possible in a safe and healthy working environment and satisfy their needs for status and achievement elsewhere. While he recognized the needs for nonfinancial rewards and the right of every individual to self-actualize, he assumed that this would occur outside the organization as there was no way to deal with these issues in his situation. He felt that work and the rest of life could be distinctly separated and that his responsibility as a manager was limited to only the work aspect of his employees' lives. What do you think?

ASSUMPTIONS ABOUT MAN, LEADERSHIP AND MOTIVATION

Robert E. Coffey, Anthony G. Athos
and Peter A. Raynolds

One important determinant of a leader's
behavior toward his followers is the
assumptions he makes about man, and
particularly how he assumes man to be
motivated. In this chapter we will explore some of the kinds of assumptions
leaders make about man and about
motivation.

Many factors influence a manager's
or a leader's style of behavior. Two
important ones are the nature of his
subordinates and the setting. . . . Another is the nature and condition of the
leader himself. His attitudes, values,
psychological defenses, knowledge, and
skills all of which have been developing
since birth, influence his feelings, assumptions, perceptions, and behavior.
Although exploring the nature of man in
depth is beyond the scope of this book,
it should be pointed out as a centrally
relevant factor in understanding the behavior of individuals.

Two other important influencing
factors are the leadership style of the
leader's superiors and the values of the
organization. It is as difficult for a
leader with a democratic style to survive well under an authoritarian
superior as it is for one with an authoritarian style to survive under a democratic superior. It is equally difficult for
a leader to survive well if his style is incongruent with the values of the larger
organization. Those leaders tend to be
promoted who best reflect the values of
their superiors or the organization and
whose leadership style is congruent
with those values. Thus, organizational
values and related leadership styles tend
to be self-perpetuating and mutually
reinforcing and to constitute pressure
for conformity on the individual.

Assumptions about Man

All of us, though we may not be aware
of it explicitly, have developed theories
about man, from observing the kinds of
responses we get from people in various
situations and from a complex variety of
learning and folklore. This section will
explore some of the kinds of assumptions sometimes made about man and
show the effect that they can have on
leadership style.

Keep in mind during the following
discussion that frequently we will be
talking about *generic* man, not any individual man. The difference is important.
Also keep in mind that we will use two
dichotomous sets of assumptions in
order to emphasize the differences between these sets. The conceptual utility

From *Behavior in Organizations: A Multidimensional View* by R. E. Coffey, A. G. Athos,
and P. A. Raynolds, 2nd edition, copyright 1975, pp. 209–221. Reprinted by permission of
Prentice-Hall, Inc., Englewood Cliffs, New Jersey.

of such emphasis is at the expense of the sliding scale of reality.

One set of assumptions about man fits strikingly with the *rational, economic concept of man* fostered by writers like Adam Smith and Frederick Taylor. This set of assumptions would include the following:

1. Most men by nature resist work and are inherently lazy. Therefore, they must be motivated by external incentives.

2. The objectives of most men are in conflict with the objectives of the organization, and men must therefore be directed, motivated, coerced, and controlled in order to insure their conformity to the organizational needs.

3. Most men are motivated mainly by economic incentives. Because the economic resources of a firm are under the control of the managers, the managers have a powerful tool for motivating and controlling the employees, who must passively accept their fate if they expect to achieve economic rewards.

4. Most men seek security and want to avoid responsibility; therefore they are willing to accept the direction of managers.

5. Behavior based on feelings is irrational, and because many men behave according to their feelings, they cannot be trusted to direct their own behavior. However, some men are able to check their feelings and behave rationally. Because the organization must insure that feelings do not interfere with rational and economic decision making, these latter men must direct and control the majority, whose behavior is based on their feelings as well as their minds.[1]

Do you agree with these assumptions? Although many readers will feel reluctant about accepting them as they are bluntly stated above, more than a few may believe they are close to being accurate.

If you accept them, the implications for the kind of leadership or management required in an organization are clear. For example, if it is assumed that people are by nature lazy, passive, uncooperative, resistant to change, irresponsible, uncreative, dull, and motivated only by money, it follows that managers should make all decisions about what employees will do, tell them how and when to do it, oversee them, and establish controls to insure that they do it as directed. In addition, the managers must motivate their subordinates to work by either rewarding or punishing them. In sum, the manager who makes these assumptions is likely to follow a highly authoritarian approach.

Unfortunately, he is likely to have problems. Most workers will find this kind of management unpalatable, and some will actively seek to resist and even sabotage it. Others will become passive and unproductive. Only a few will voluntarily and enthusiastically support their boss and the organization's objectives. But, as noted above, this is exactly what the assumptions anticipated, and thus they are self-fulfilling.

A second path open to managers accepting the kinds of assumptions mentioned is what has been termed "the soft approach." Following this approach, a manager may be permissive, try to satisfy his workers' demands, and

---

[1]This set of assumptions and the one following are similar to those set forth by Douglas McGregor and classified under the terms "Theory X" and "Theory Y" in his *The Human Side of Enterprise* (New York: McGraw-Hill Book Co., 1960). See also Edgar H. Schein, *Organizational Psychology* (Englewood Cliffs, N.J.: Prentice-Hall, Inc., 1965), Chapter 5.

work for harmony, expecting that if he can make the workers happy, they will be more productive. However, many managers fear that such an approach only enables workers to take advantage of the organization and to be unproductive as well as happy.

Although most of us know people who tend to substantiate many of the assumptions made above, there is some doubt whether the assumptions are true because of the *nature* of man or because of the way organizations have been designed and the subsequent impact such designs have upon men. For example, if work is designed so that it is unchallengingly simple and if controls are established so that no creativity is allowed, it is not surprising that many men find their work dull and, in turn, become dull themselves.[2]

Those doubting the rational, economic concept of man have developed quite a different set of assumptions, leading to a *social, self-actualizing concept of man*. Some of the assumptions of this view are:

1. Most men enjoy some kinds of work and will sometimes voluntarily exert mental and physical energy in performing the tasks.
2. Most men have other reasons than money for working, and these reasons are at least as important to them as is money.
3. Most men are capable of directing and controlling their own work in achieving organizational objectives to which they are committed.
4. Most men are willing to accept and

even will seek responsibility under certain conditions.
5. Most men are capable of demonstrating more of both creativity and intellectual ability than they do in many organizational settings.
6. Most men want, seek, and enjoy friendly, supportive relations with other people.[3]

It is clear that the two sets of assumptions have quite different implications for leadership. If it is assumed that man has the potential for development, the capacity for assuming responsibility, and the readiness to direct his own behavior toward organizational goals, it follows that the task of managers is to create opportunities for him to do so. The manager thus becomes a facilitator, supporter, and sympathizer rather than only a director and controller. Rather than establishing all organizational conditions and directing all work, the manager would arrange conditions only to the extent that they enable people to direct their own efforts in achieving organizational objectives.

One of the major differences between the two approaches is that those managers accepting the rational, economic concept of man place heavy or exclusive reliance upon *external control* of human behavior, whereas those accepting the social, self-actualizing view rely heavily on *self-control* and *self-direction*. Managers accepting the latter view are likely to have a democratic style, with an occasional touch of laissez faire, assuming that some of the other factors mentioned are neutral.

---

[2]For an elaboration of this thesis, see Chris Argyris, *Personality and Organization* (New York: Harper & Row, Publishers, 1957) and *Integrating the Individual and the Organization* (New York: John Wiley & Sons, Inc., 1964).
[3]These assumptions underly McGregor's "Theory Y."

Hierarchy of Human Needs

One assumption about man that fits the social, self-actualizing view of him is that he has a hierarchy of needs. This concept, developed by A. H. Maslow, is helpful in explaining both the variety and complexity of human motives.[4] It helps explain why one man may behave differently from another in a similar situation, and at the same time suggests something that all men have in common. Maslow assumes that all men have basic human needs, which he classifies as follows:

1. *Physiological Needs*. Food, shelter, rest, exercise, and protection from the elements.
2. *Safety Needs*. Protection against nature and against the threat of physical or psychological danger or deprivation.
3. *Love Needs*. Association, affection, and acceptance.
4. *Esteem Needs*. (a) One's own need for achievement, confidence, independence, freedom, and a feeling of adequacy; (b) one's need for recognition and appreciation from others.
5. *Self-Actualization Needs*. To fulfill one's potentialities, to become what one is capable of being.

Maslow assumes that these needs exist in the form of a hierarchy, that some of them are more basic than others, and that man seeks to satisfy the more basic ones before directing his behavior toward satisfying the others. Thus, Maslow assumes that most men seek first to satisfy their physiological needs, then their safety needs, then their love needs, next their esteem needs, and finally their self-actualization needs. It is assumed that lower-order needs must be satisfied at least to a degree for man even to survive. Although it appears that a majority of people seek to satisfy their needs in an order that approximates Maslow's hierarchy, there are clearly some variations and exceptions.

An important point in the hierarchy of needs theory is that a satisfied need ceases to motivate. This means that as man's physical needs are satisfied, his other needs begin to create tensions that cause him to seek to satisfy them. The physiological needs continue to exist, but they become less important in motivating behavior. So long as a man has enough to eat, he will devote his time and energy to behavior aimed at satisfying some other need. But should he become really hungry, he will begin to spend his time trying to obtain food — a basic physiological need.

The concept that a satisfied need ceases to motivate has limitations. It clearly applies to certain phyical and safety needs, but it seems clear that the needs for love, esteem, and self-actualization are close to insatiable and, therefore, continue to motivate behavior even after they have been in some degree satisfied. Most of the people in the United

---

[4]Abraham H. Maslow. *Motivation and Personality* (New York: Harper & Brothers, 1954). You will recall that Chapter 6 presented a view of man based upon his "internal frame of reference." This view, which states that a specific individual behaves so as to protect, maintain, and enhance his self-concept, is most useful for thinking about the people you associate with, listen to, and learn about. But for man in general, or for specific persons about whom you know little, it is useful to think in terms of a need-hierarchy view of behavior. You can use both views as you come to sense some of the specific needs of specific people and how these needs relate to their own unique self-concepts.

States have, to a quite large extent, satisfied their physiological and safety needs. If these needs, once satisfied, cease to motivate behavior, it becomes clear that the primarily economic incentives offered by most business organizations, which are designed to help people satisfy just these needs, do not appeal to the real or potential motivators of behavior — the needs for love, esteem, and self-actualization. Indeed, until the last two or three decades, little attention was devoted to helping people satisfy their higher-order needs.

The hierarchy of needs concept helps us to gain some insight into why man is complex, variable, and dynamic. He is complex because he has a variety of needs, and at any given time several of them may be motivating him all at once, even though one or a few may appear to dominate.

HUMAN NEEDS AND MOTIVATION

Man is variable. Each person has his own set of needs, and there is no conclusive evidence that men feel their needs in the neat order suggested above. Quite the contrary, as Maslow himself points out. The variety with which each man feels his own needs is a major contributing factor to the uniqueness of man. It helps explain, in part, why it is dangerous to assume that all men will respond the same way to given stimuli.

Man is also dynamic. The hierarchy of importance of his personal needs changes with time, partly because certain needs cease to motivate as they are satisfied. Take a man whose behavior is not much directed to achieving his work goals because he feels an overwhelming need for achieving love and affection. Let him fall in love, and you may find that he works a lot harder than he did before. The needs hierarchy is dynamic, and it is dangerous to assume that a person's behavior can't change.

Motivational Process[5]

Needs alone do not adequately explain behavior. In this section we will develop a more complete model of the motivational process, which can serve as a tool for analyzing specific situations. The model includes several variables that influence the behavior of specific individuals. Each variable needs to be assigned meaning when applied situationally.

Incentives. We start building our model with the assumption that each individual surveys his world to find opportunities to satisfy his various needs. We will use the term *incentive* to mean much the same as opportunities, goals, and rewards. Thus, individuals direct their behavior toward reaching perceived incentives. These may be either positive and attracting incentives or negative ones to be avoided.

We make a further assumption that individuals are sometimes unconscious of both some of their needs and some of the reasons for their behavior. Much remains unknown about men's unconscious needs, feelings, thoughts, and behavior, and although psychologists debate the

---

[5]This section draws on the work of Lyman W. Porter and Edward E. Lawler, III, *Managerial Attitudes and Performance* (Homewood, Ill.: Richard D. Irwin, Inc., 1968); Victor H. Vroom, *Work and Motivation* (New York: John Wiley & Sons, Inc., 1964); J. G. Hunt and J.W. Hill, "The New Look in Motivation Theory of Organizational Research," *Human Organization* (Summer, 1969), pp. 100–109.

relative importance of the unconscious, virtually none dispute its existence. Thus, it is essential that we remember that needs can only be inferred from behavior; they cannot be seen.

Incentives alone do not always stimulate behavior. Before an individual exerts the effort to reach an incentive, he makes, either consciously or unconsciously at least three evaluations. First, he evaluates how important the incentive is to him in terms of his own need priorities. Although one incentive may be important to one person, it may not be to another. Second, he estimates the probability of reaching the incentive. If he perceives the probability of achieving it as low, he may not be motivated to exert the effort toward reaching even a valued incentive. Third, he evaluates the cost in terms of effort and lost opportunity to satisfy other needs. An individual may perceive an incentive as desirable and obtainable, but if the perceived cost in effort is too great, he is unlikely to move toward it.

Incentives, or goals, . . . can be categorized as *manifest* and *latent,* as well as extrinsic and intrinsic. To review, manifest goals are the apparent ones sought, and usually are organizational goals. They are instrumental in reaching latent goals, which are directly satisfying to personal needs. Thus, the rewards for achieving manifest goals have extrinsic value, and those for the achievement of latent goals have intrinsic value. For example, Joe may work hard to finish an assigned task early, even though he does not find the work interesting, challenging, or satisfying. What he really hopes to achieve is promotion, which in turn would be instrumental in partially satisfying his need for status. Working

hard is behavior-directed toward finishing the task early (first manifest goal), which in turn he hopes will lead to a promotion (second manifest goal), which in turn will satisfy some of his status needs (latent goal). If Joe does not perceive a relationship between hard work and a promotion, he is unlikely to be motivated to finish the task early. Further, if he lacked high status needs, the promise of a promotion would hold little attraction.

Effect and Performance. If an individual decides that a perceived incentive is important, achievable, and "profitable," he is likely to exert effort toward reaching it. Effort combined with ability leads to performance, or accomplishment; thus, even if an individual exerts effort, he may not perform adequately if he lacks either innate or learned ability. The relationship between performance and effort is mutually dependent. Poor performance may induce more effort for awhile, depending on the perceived value and achievability of the incentive, but continued poor performance often leads to reduced or withdrawn effort. On the other hand, high performance easily achieved might reduce effort. You can see, therefore, that effort depends on performance, just as performance depends on effort.

Satisfaction. The motivational process continues during and after performance as the individual evaluates the rewards he does or does not receive. Satisfaction is a function of his expectations and how fully he actually achieves the rewards he has sought. The following formula describes the relationship:

$$\text{Satisfaction} = \frac{\text{Realization}}{\text{Expectations}} + \text{Equity}$$

If "one" represents a normal, or expected, degree of satisfaction, an individual will realize greater than normal satisfaction if he realizes more reward than he expected, and vice versa. How "just" or equitable an individual perceives his reward in relation to other "reference" people will also affect his satisfaction.

We might assume that an individual with satisfied needs will continue to exert effort to perform. This assumption might often be correct, but not always. Recall that needs are dynamic, and that satisfied needs cease to motivate. Thus, some individuals may achieve more than expected satisfaction, and, as a result, will diminish their effort to perform in the direction of the satisifying incentive. For some individuals, lack of satisfaction may increase the need to exert even more effort to perform. At this point the individual is beginning the motivation cycle at the starting point where he surveys and evaluates the opportunities to satisfy his needs.

Model of the Motivational Process. The model illustrated in Figure 1 does not enable us to predict the behavior of any individual. However, it does provide a description of some of the important determinants to consider in understanding what might engage the motives of a specific individual. In making such an analysis try to answer these questions:

1. What are the latent goals an individual seeks? (What important needs is he trying to satisfy?)
2. What is the relationship between manifest goals and his latent goals as you perceive it and as he perceives it? (How he perceives it determines his behavior.)
3. What expectations does the individual have for reaching his latent goals by reaching the manifest goals?
4. How does the individual evaluate the potential profitability (reward less cost in effort or lost opportunity) of the incentive?
5. How effectively does the individual perform, and what relationship does this have to ability, effort, and satisfaction?

The model and its underlying assumptions suggest that no layman, and probably no professional, is ever fully equipped to understand another person. Most of us are not qualified as psychoanalysts, and to fully understand behavior requires an understanding of the unconscious and goal conflicts. But this does not mean we can do nothing. We can learn more about listening, empathizing, and understanding another. We can learn to be more aware of and sensitive to ourselves and others by observ-

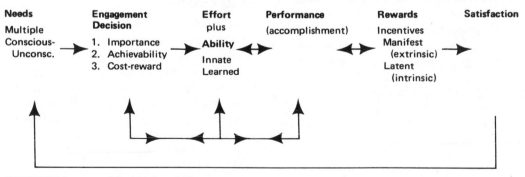

FIGURE 1 • *Motivational Process*

ing how each sees himself and his world. Such observation includes listening and looking for behavior patterns, including what people discuss, how they use their time, and what they appear to seek and avoid. An individual's talk and behavior give many cues about what he values, fears, and seeks.

Herzberg's Two-Factor Theory

Frederick Herzberg has developed a theory that has become popular with many managers. His two-factor theory is called the *hygiene-motivation theory.* He developed it first by researching a sample of accountants and engineers, but later extended his studies to various kinds and levels of people in organizations. He gave them these directions.[6]

> Think of a time when you felt exceptionally good or exceptionally bad about your job, either your present job or any other job you have had. This can be either the 'long-range' or the 'short-range' kind of situation, as I have just described it. Tell me what happened.

Herzberg divided the responses according to whether they represented good or bad feelings. He called the satisfiers "motivators" and the dissatisfiers "hygiene factors." He found that many of the motivators related to job content and job experiences, and that many of the dissatisfiers related to environmental conditions. Figure 2 shows some of the important factors in each category.

The concept of "dissatisfier" surprised some who thought of the items in that category as positive incentives for work. Herzberg reasoned that many people today consider less time, more money, and more security as "rights." If they are not in line with expectations, they cause dissatisfaction, but if they are in line, they are often taken for granted. In this respect they prevent dissatisfaction but do not induce positive motivation.

The logical application of Herzberg's findings and theory was *job enrichment.* Some possibilities for enriching a job include removing some of the controls while retaining accountability, increasing the accountability of individuals for their own work, providing a complete natural unit of work for the individual, introducing new and more difficult tasks not previously assigned, and providing opportunities for individuals to develop

---

[6]Frederick Herzberg, Bernard Mausner, and Barbara Block Snyderman, *The Motivation to Work,* 2nd ed. (New York: John Wiley & Sons, Inc., 1959), p. 141.

Dissatisfiers (Job environment)	Motivators (Job content)
Work rules	Challenging job
Lighting	Feeling of achievement
Coffee breaks	Responsibility
Titles	Growth
Seniority rights	Advancement
Wages	Enjoyment of work
Fringe benefits	Earned recognition

FIGURE 2

expertise. These steps all are intended to provide opportunities for satisfying what Maslow called the higher-level needs.

Many applications have been made of Herzberg's theory, and many successes have been reported. However, some failures have also been recorded and considerable criticism has been directed at the theory, much of it relating to methodology. The hygiene-motivation theory is relatively simple, which explains partially both its appeal and its weakness. Even though the theory is not without fault, it has had significant impact on management behavior and has helped advance our understanding of motivation and work.

Behavior Modification

Another applied approach to motivation is termed *behavior modification*. It is built on Edward L. Thorndike's "law of effect" and B. F. Skinner's "operant conditioning." The law of effect states that if behavior is reinforced it will tend to be repeated. Skinner is the best-known contemporary proponent of operant conditioning, which calls for positive reinforcement of desired behavior. Unlike those who take a more psychoanalytic approach, Skinner's followers do not concern themselves with subconscious or deep causes of behavior. Instead, they analyze the work environment to determine what causes an individual to behave as he does. They then use reinforcing techniques such as praise, recognition, and rewards along with systematic feedback that tells an individual how he is doing.

The kind of reinforcement and its timing are important aspects of behavior modification. Reinforcement can be positive or negative. Positive reinforcement strengthens the association between a response and its reward. A negative reinforcement can take the form of either withholding a positive reward or administering a "painful" punishment. Generally, research indicates that positive reinforcement is more effective than negative in achieving lasting change, although negative reinforcement may be effective in causing short-term termination of an undesirable behavior.

The closer positive reinforcement follows the desired behavior, the more likely it will be repeated. This can cause some problems in an organizational setting. For example, money has the potential for being an extrinsic reinforcer, but money is usually paid at regular intervals, which may occur too long after the behavior being reinforced. For this reason reinforcers such as praise and recognition are easier to administer.

Some reinforcers are intrinsic in nature. This means that the desired behavior produces directly related need satisfactions. For example, many people feel a keen sense of satisfaction when they complete a difficult task. This feeling can serve as reinforcement to tackle another task in order to get the same good feeling. On the other hand, extrinsic reinforcers, such as money, praise, and attention, are not a natural result of most desired behaviors, but they are satisfying to individuals and are effective reinforcers if associated with the desired behavior.

Although behavior modification has been practiced with good results in schools and mental institutions, it has not been given much attention in business until the past few years. Now, increasing numbers of companies are beginning to investigate this approach and to apply some of its techniques.[7] Although it is useful to know about behavior modification and to apply it when appropriate, it clearly is only a part of the total process of motivation. As with all management techniques, it is not a panacea.

Money as a Motivator

Money is a major incentive in our society. It has appeal as an incentive for managers because it is concrete and easily manipulable. However, money is also a complex incentive and for this reason is subject to being misused.

Money used to be considered the only important incentive under the assumption that people worked primarily for economic reasons. Researchers like Elton Mayo and Fritz Roethlisberger demonstrated in the famous Hawthorne studies that money is by no means the only incentive, and in some respects may not be most important.[8] They demonstrated the importance of recognition and affiliation as motivating incentives. Research studies subsequently showed that workers frequently mentioned money in about the middle of various incentives. Some people have subsequently concluded that money is not very important as an incentive. They are probably quite wrong.

Money is a multifaceted incentive, having both economic and psychological meaning. It is symbolic and instrumental in nature. In addition to providing for physical and safety needs, it may also help to satisfy the needs for power, status, esteem, and achievement. It can even be instrumental in partially satisfying social needs. Having sufficient money may enable someone to join a particular club or group. For achievement-oriented people it serves as a measurement of accomplishment.

Evidence indicates that money, in itself, does not usually serve as a motivator to work harder or better. However, in the absence of what is perceived by the recipient as adequate or fair compensation, money is a source of dissatisfaction. How a recipient compares in compensation with those he perceives as equals may be more important than the amount he receives. Money, then, is frequently related to levels of satisfaction, even though additional amounts normally do not lead to harder work.

Appropriate uses of money and other incentives as part of a motivational plan should be related to the needs of the workers, the motivational requirements of the job, the motives of the managers, and the organizational climate.[9] For example, whether or not a worker has high needs for achievement, power, or affiliation will likely make a difference in how he responds to incentives. Similarly, jobs vary in their motivational requirements. Assembly-

[7]"Where Skinner's Theories Work," *Business Week,* December 2, 1972, pp. 64–65.
[8]F. J. Roethlisberger and W.J. Dickson, *Management and the Worker* (Cambridge, Mass.: Harvard University Press, 1939).
[9]David C. McClelland, "Money as a Motivator: Some Research Insights," *The McKinsey Quarterly* (Fall,1967), pp. 10–21.

line jobs are hardly appropriate for people with high achievement needs, just as demanding jobs are not suitable for those with low achievement needs.

Assume you are in charge of a group of people who have high affiliation needs and enjoy being members of a group. If you assume that money motivates, and instigate a money incentive system that is meant to induce workers to produce more and socialize less, you may be introducing a dysfunctional element into the system. You might more appropriately try to develop a group incentive that would foster feelings of helping the group, thus increasing its cohesiveness.

A comprehensive discussion of money as an incentive is beyond our scope here. However, we want to emphasize the importance of careful situational analysis of a total system when attempting to design an incentive system.

SUMMARY

Concepts of generic man can help sharpen and deepen our understanding. But because concepts are abstractions of reality, there is some danger that they oversimplify the complex realities that truly characterize an individual man. The more we tend to accept one concept as explaining all there is to know about all men, the greater the danger is likely to be. Both the rational, economic view of man and the social,

self-actualizing view tend to highlight certain aspects of man's nature. The fact that research evidence and personal experience exists to support, at least partially, both of these views, as well as some others, only emphasizes that man is indeed a richly complex and fascinating (and sometimes frustrating) being.

The degree of satisfaction a man feels or the productivity he achieves depends on more than just the nature of his needs or his motivation. A man who is highly motivated to achieve a certain objective may lack the necessary skill, and thus experience feelings of dissatisfaction. Further, the very nature of the task may tend to stultify rather than satisfy his high motivation. Or he might find that he dislikes intensely the people with whom he is working, and even though highly motivated and able to do the work, may be both dissatisfied and ineffective. Thus we see that man's satisfaction, growth, and productivity are dependent upon a variety of psychological, social, and task factors — including both his ability and his social relationships.

Man is a highly complex, variable, and dynamic being. To understand him we do not need simple explanations or prescriptive formulas, but rather skills in sensitive observation, accurate diagnosis, and perceptive synthesis. These skills are neither easily nor cheaply achieved but must be acquired through practice.

HUMAN MOTIVATION IN THE SMALLER ENTERPRISE

Robert A. Sutermeister
and Borje O. Saxberg

Smaller businesses, employing from a few to several hundred people, have a built-in advantage over larger companies in their opportunities to motivate employees. We read and hear a great deal these days about "blue-collar blues," "white-collar blues," employee disaffection with their jobs and the dehumanization of individuals, particularly in large impersonal offices and plants.

CHANGES IN VALUES

There have been tremendous changes in values in the past ten years: values in society, values in individuals, and values in organizations. Some of the words associated with Benjamin Franklin and the Work Ethic sound quaint today: honesty, punctuality, uprightness, integrity, sobriety, frugality, diligence, self-reliance, and hard work. Today we hear more about people "doing their own thing," the importance of "here and now" and history dismissed as bunk because of its association with the past. We are confronted with an increasing demand for a promised equality and therefore the right to the same desserts. If one person does not have his share, he may well decide to "liberate" it from those who have more.

The values held by society affect the values of the organization and of individuals. Employees have been thinking more and more about the quality of life, the quality of work, and the enjoyment of leisure as a result of the affluence which characterizes our society and our economy. In the past some were satisfied to devote their entire lives to one organization with no thought of quitting, and gave only secondary concern to the family or to problems of society. Others, like professional men, devoted their lives to a single profession even if this required frequent changes of organizations, again with limited attention to family and society's problems. Today, more and more people view their work life as only one part of a broader life experience involving family, community, social responsibilities, and concern for political and economic issues. The organization is one part of a man's life; his job or profession is another, his concern for society another, and his commitment to an organization is increasingly influenced by wife and family. His wife's interest in her own career, or her desire to remain in one location to avoid switching schools for the children, may be important factors in a man's decision about his job.

From the *Journal of Small Business Management*, July 1973, pp. 7–12, copyright 1973 by the National Council for Small Business Management Development and the West Virginia University Bureau of Business Research. Reprinted by permission.

Society's changing values also have an impact on the values of organizations regardless of their size. Civil rights, environmental concerns, pollution control — what organization has not been affected by these developments in recent years and changed its values as a consequence? In Figure 1 are shown the relationships among changing values and how they exert pressure on the human resource management function in the organization.

Every firm must have a personnel function performed. Someone must decide how many employees are needed, where they are to be sought, how they are to be hired, paid, trained, rated and supervised. These are the traditional, vital personnel functions necessary to deal with the people dimension of the

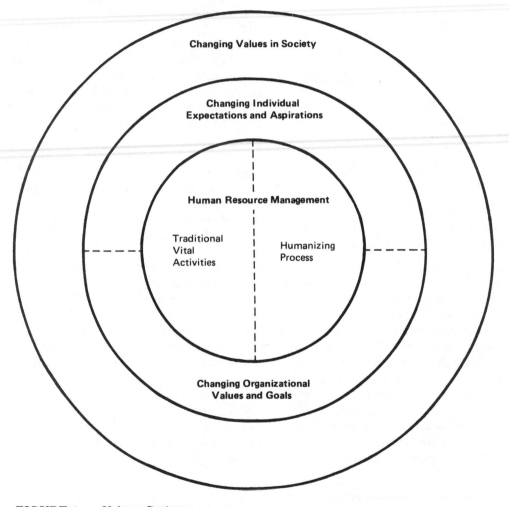

FIGURE 1 • Values: Society, Organization, Individual

organization. But in response to the rapidly changing values, it is a necessity to "humanize the organization." Some employees may have received high school and college education; some may be minorities in their first job experience; some may be women getting a new hearing for a fair share of job promotions. Each one is searching for satisfaction in life, but the routes to life satisfaction are many and varied and frequently changing.

HUMANIZING THE ORGANIZATION

Humanizing the organization means that the company will know its employees and what they are seeking in their jobs, and thus be able to support them in their search for life satisfaction. Here the smaller enterprise has a decided advantage — it can get to know its employees, their needs and their desires much more easily than a firm employing thousands. Attention to em-

ployee needs, the ability to motivate them, we believe will have a pay off in the form of increased productivity, and reduced turnover and absenteeism.

It is highly useful in this context to refer to Abraham Maslow's assumptions about the individual's need hierarchy.[1] In our society we can generalize for many situations that men have satisfied their needs beyond the level of social needs. To motivate them to further effort, they must be appealed to in terms of higher level needs or they will become frustrated and aggressively demand ever higher pay, or become apathetic. The need hierarchy is a useful way of thinking about motivation but not the only way.

We can here only briefly refer to Herzberg's suggestion that motivating forces can be divided into two categories.[2] We also need to refer to the most recent work of Lawler and Porter who suggest in their exploration of motivation that the individual is

[1]Maslow suggests that each individual has his needs organized in a series of levels — a hierarchy of importance. The basic level of needs refers to *physiological needs* for food, shelter, warmth, and so on. Only after these are somewhat satisfied does the next higher level of needs make itself felt: *safety needs* — concerns about physical hazards, knowledge about job procedures, and future developments affecting the job. And then in ascending order: *social needs* — love in an extended sense or human companionship and group acceptance; *egoistic needs* — need for recognition and esteem and a conviction of the worthwhileness of the present job; and finally the need for *self-actualization* — "man must do what he can do."

To this list of needs Maslow added the ultimate need of the individual for *meta-self-actualization* — where the individual is filled with a missionary zeal in which his commitment is beyond himself as he strives to make a contribution to mankind. Most importantly Maslow suggested that a *satisfied need does not motivate.* See Abraham Harold Maslow, *Motivation and Personality*, 2nd edition (New York: Harper and Row, 1967); idem, "A Theory of Metamotivation," *Psychology Today*, Vol. 2, No. 2, July 1968.

[2]These are environmental factors which contribute to removal of dissatisfaction and which he labels hygiene factors; and job content factors which contribute to satisfaction in the job and which he calls motivating factors. The hygiene factors are related to the job environment — benefits, working conditions, supervision, and so on. The motivators are related to aspects of the job itself and the individual's identification with it through participation in decision making, achievment, interest, recognition, and others. See Frederick Herzberg, Bernard Mausner, and Barbara Bloch Snyderman, *The Motivation to Work* (New York: Wiley and Sons, 1959).

strongly influenced by his expectations.[3] Where a reward is related to performance, the individual will experience satisfaction which may stimulate him to even better performance in the future. The reward refers clearly to many other things besides money.

In the context of the small businessman, frequently the founder-owner of the business, the *achievement motive* explored by McClelland and his associates is highly relevant.[4]

VARIOUS PATHS TO LIFE SATISFACTION

In Figure 2 are shown some of the needs which employees attempt to fill and some of the many paths they may choose in fulfilling these needs today. A person may seek his life satisfaction through job activities alone, through off-job activities alone, or through some combination of job activities and off-job activities. Looking at the JOB ACTIVITIES path he may desire a full time,

part time, temporary, or intermittent job. Can the organization adapt to those needs by being flexible in the jobs it offers? Can it provide a woman with child in school age a chance to work half a day; or can it utilize the concept of "sliding hours" by allowing her to come to work at 9:30 a.m. and work until 6:00 p.m. if such a schedule would match her home life demands? Or can it gain a full-time employee by permitting two individuals to handle a position jointly through schedules they agree on between themselves? Or if a woman wishes to work until she has children, drop out of the labor market for ten years or so, and then return to work — can the firm accommodate to those needs? The same questions hold for male employees who may wish to work for, say, four years, then take a leave for a year to assist in solving community problems or to go back to school to improve their educational background and then return to the company.[5]

Individuals choose different paths

---

[3]See Lyman W. Porter and Edward E. Lawler III, *Managerial Attitudes and Performance* (Homewood, Ill.: Irwin, 1968).

[4]He suggests that a society will have individuals who are characterized by different levels of need for achievement. There are high achievers and low achievers; the high achiever values achievement itself. Money may be an index to achievement but not an end in itself. Invariably he has found that businessmen and managers fall in the category of high achievers — thus an explanation for the question you may have why others who work for you have not accomplished what you have as an independent businessman. These individuals might fall in the category of low achievers; they have different motivation, different aspirations than those which you as a small businessman may have internalized in yourself. The challenge, as McClelland sees it, is for our society to continue to assure itself of a sufficient supply of high achievers to assure continued economic development for the nation. This represents a challenge for management in making sure that it recognizes those of its employees who as high achievers potentially may identify themselves with the company and the industry. If frustrated in this, they are likely to reduce their level of aspiration or seek their satisfaction outside work — thus be lost to the company and to the industry. This is even more probable in today's society for the leisure ethic and its new values compete with the work ethic. See David Clarence McClelland, *The Achieving Society* (Princeton: D. van Nostrand Company, 1961).

[5]Cf. News item of John Z. DeLorean's resignation from General Motors' top management to become president of the National Alliance of Businessmen, *Wall Street Journal*, April 19, 1973, p. 7.

toward their life satisfaction. Some may seek satisfaction of physiological needs only (IA), investing their time in return for a pay check, either having reached their limit or expecting their other needs to be fulfilled in off-job activities (II). Other individuals want more than pay. They may follow tracks A and B1 simul-taneously in seeking to satisfy needs but not minding their present routine work; again additional needs may be satisfied in off-job activities (II). Other individuals will be turned on only if they have work which is interesting and challenging to their abilities — tracks A and B2.

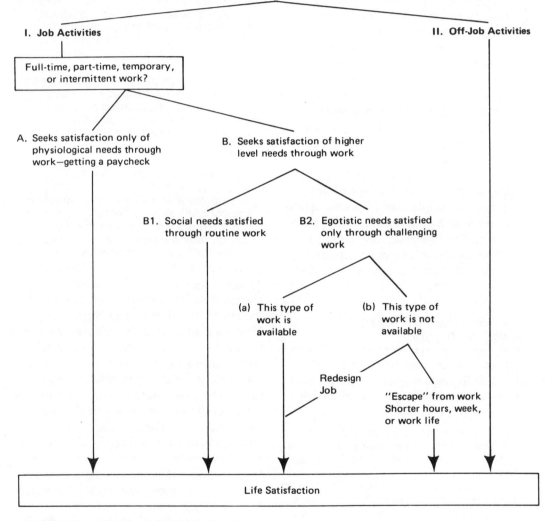

FIGURE 2 • *Needs of Individual and Paths to Life Satisfaction*

Management in the small firm should try to match individuals and their needs with the various jobs available. For individuals needing challenging work which may not be available, work should be redesigned so that it becomes challenging. Human motivation rests on a fit between the needs of the individual, whatever these may be, and the opportunities offered by the job.

In a situation where challenging work is not available and it is impossible to re-design jobs to make them meaningful, escape from work is a final alternative. This is represented in a shortening of the work day, a reduced work week such as a four-day week, or a reduced work life through early retirement. The United Automobile Workers are this year pressing for retirement after thirty years regardless of age. Having nothing to do represents for many retired people boredom and drudgery at its worst — and endless appointment with the television set. Chances for life satisfaction are much greater when the individual is involved, actively and productively.

SUGGESTIONS FOR MATCHING PEOPLE AND JOBS

What can the organization do to improve the fit between the employee and his job. Let us list steps taken already in some organizations:

1. Start with a philosophy of treating employees as job customers just as customers are treated as product customers.

2. Ascertain what each employee is seeking in his job experience — which track he wishes to follow in his search for life satisfaction.

3. Let the job applicant see the job for which he is being considered and even try it out; or, better yet, let him try several different jobs when possible and pick the one he likes best.

4. Introduce flexible hours and schedules to accommodate employees and their needs, as well as fluctuations in the work load of the company. Consider use of employees on a part-time, temporary, or intermittent work basis.

5. Match individuals with jobs. In some cases this may call for a redesign of jobs to make them more challenging. Provide expanded opportunities for participation corresponding to the qualifications of employees including planning and controlling (inspection). Job enlargement or job enrichment may be practical in your company — extending jobs to cover more varied and responsible activities, and through education, training, and rotation making an employee more competent in handling a variety of assignments. Volvo and Saab in Sweden have made efforts to eliminate the assembly line in producing automobiles and instead rely for the completion of assembly work on work groups within which the members decide how they will do what jobs, which jobs will be rotated and so on.

In summary, times are changing rapidly. As society's values have changed so have the expectations and values of individuals and organizations. To obtain and retain employees and to motivate them to effective and efficient performance represents a challenge to the management of the smaller enterprise. The goals of the company must be considered with the goals of the individual employees. The success in motivating them will be directly dependent on management's ability to humanize their organizations, to recognize and support employees' search for life satisfaction along whatever path they may be seeking. In short, if there is a fit between the employees' need and the job characteristics, the company will benefit from employee commitment, leading to high productivity and reduced turnover and absenteeism.

The small business organization represents a preferred place of employment for many who refuse or resist being cogs in a large bureaucratic organization. The opportunity is there for the small business manager to gain a committed and motivated work force by proper attention to individual employees and what each is seeking in his work experience.

THE MANAGEMENT OF CHANGE PART TWO: CHANGE THROUGH BEHAVIOR MODIFICATION

Paul Hersey and Kenneth H. Blanchard

Rensis Likert found that employee-centered supervisors who use general supervision tend to have higher producing sections than job-centered supervisors who use close supervision.[7] We underline the word "tend" because this seems to be high probability in our society, yet we also must realize there are exceptions to this tendency which are even evident in Likert's data. What Likert found was that a subordinate generally responds well to a superior's high expectations and genuine confidence in him and tries to justify his boss's expectations of him. His resulting high performance will reinforce his superior's high trust for him, for it is easy to trust and respect the man who meets or exceeds your expectations. This occurrence could be called the effective cycle.

Yet, since top management often promotes on the basis of short run output alone, managers tend to over-emphasize task accomplishment, placing extreme pressure on everyone to achieve high levels of productivity. This task-oriented leader behavior style, in some cases, does not allow much room for a trusting relationship with employees. Instead, subordinates are told what to do and how to do it. With little consideration, subordinates respond with

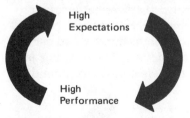

High Expectations

High Performance

FIGURE 1 • Effective Cycle

From *Training and Development Journal*, February 1972. Copyright 1972, by the American Society for Training and Development, Inc. Reprinted by special permission.
NOTE: Footnotes 1–6 appear in part 1 of this article, which is not reprinted in this text.
— ED.

minimal effort and resentment; low performance results in these instances. Reinforced by low expectations, it becomes a vicious cycle. Many other examples could be given which result in this all too common problem in organizations as shown in Figure 2.

These cycles are depicted as static but in reality they are very dynamic. The situation tends to get better or worse. For example, high expectations result in high performance, which reinforces the high expectations and produces even higher productivity. It almost becomes a spiral effect as illustrated in Figure 3.

In many cases, this spiraling effect is caused by an increase in leverage created through the use of what Frederick Herzberg calls "motivators."[8] In analyzing the data from his research, Herzberg concluded that man has two different categories of needs which are essentially independent of each other and affect behavior in different ways. He found that when people felt dissatisfied about their jobs, they were concerned about the environment in which they were working. On the other hand, when people felt good about their jobs, this had to do with the work itself. Herzberg called the first category of needs *hygiene factors* because they describe man's environment and serve the primary function of preventing job dissatisfaction. He called the second

category of needs *motivators* since they seemed to be effective in motivating people to superior performance.

Company policies and administration, supervision, working conditions, interpersonal relations, money, status and security may be thought of as hygiene factors. There are not an intrinsic part of a job, but are related to the conditions under which a job is performed. Herzberg relates his use of the word "hygiene" to its medical meaning (preventative and environmental). Hygiene factors produce no growth in worker output capacity; they only prevent losses in worker performance due to work restriction.

Satisfying factors that involve feelings of achievement, professional growth and recognition that one can experience in a job which offers challenge and scope are referred to as motivators. Herzberg used this term because these factors seem capable of having a positive effect on job satisfaction often resulting in an increase in one's total output capacity. In terms of the upward

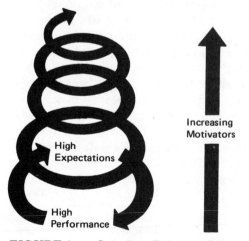

FIGURE 3 • *Spiraling Effect of Effective Cycle*

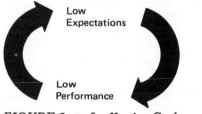

FIGURE 2 • *Ineffective Cycle*

spiraling effect, as people perform they are given more responsibility and opportunities for achievement and growth and development, which results in higher productivity and continued high expectations.

INEFFECTIVE CYCLE

This spiraling effect can also occur in a downward direction as shown in Figure 4. Low expectations result in low performance, which reinforces the low expectations and produces even lower productivity. It becomes a spiral effect like a whirlpool as shown in Figure 4.

If this downward spiraling continues long enough, the cycle may reach a point where it cannot be turned around in a short period of time because of the large reservoir of negative past experience which has built up in the organization. Much of the focus and energy is directed toward the perceived problems with hygiene factors rather than the work itself. This takes such form as hostility, undermining and slow-down in

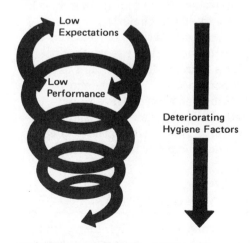

FIGURE 4 • Spiraling Effect of Ineffective Cycle

work performance. When this happens, even if a manager actually changes his behavior, the credibility gap based on long-term experience is such that the response is still distrust and skepticism rather than change.

STYLE CHANGE

One alternative that is sometimes necessary at this juncture is to bring in a new manager from the outside. The reason this has a higher probability of success is that the sum of the past experience of the people involved with the new manager is likened to a "clean slate," and thus different behaviors are on a much more believable basis. This was vividly illustrated by Robert H. Guest in a case analysis of organizational change.[9] He examined a large assembly plant of an automobile company, Plant Y, and contrasts the situation under two different leaders.

Under Mr. Stewart, plant manager, working relationships at Plant Y were dominated by hostility and mistrust. His high task style was characterized by a continual attempt to increase the driving forces pushing for productivity. As a result, the prevailing atmosphere was that of one emergency following on the heels of another, and the governing motivation for employee activity was fear — fear of being "chewed out" right on the assembly line, fear of being held responsible for happenings in which one had no clear authority, fear of losing one's job. Consequently, of the six plants in this division of the corporation, Plant Y had the poorest performance record, and it was getting worse.

Mr. Stewart was replaced by Mr. Cooley, who seemed like a truly effective leader. Three years later, dramatic changes had occurred. In various cost and performance measures used to rate the six plants, Plant Y was now truly the leader; and the atmosphere of interpersonal cooperation and personal satisfaction had improved impressively over the situation under Stewart. These changes, moreover, were effected through an insignificant number of dismissals and reassignments. Using a much higher relationships style, Cooley succeeded in "turning Plant Y around."

EXPECTATIONS CHANGE

On the surface, the big difference was style of leadership. Cooley was a good leader. Stewart wasn't. But Guest points out clearly in his analysis that leadership style was only one of two important factors. "The other was that while Stewart received daily orders from division headquarters to correct specific situations, Cooley was left alone. Cooley was allowed to lead; Stewart was told how to lead."[10] In other words, when productivity in Plant Y began to decline during changeover from wartime to peacetime operations, Stewart's superiors expected him to get productivity back on the upswing by taking control of the reins and they put tremendous pressure on him to do just that. Guest suggests that these expectations forced Stewart to operate in a very crisis-oriented, autocratic way. However, when Cooley was given charge as plant manager, a "hands off" policy was initiated by his superiors. The fact that the expectations of top management had changed enough to put a moratorium on random, troublesome outside stimuli from headquarters gave Cooley an op-

portunity to operate in a completely different style. One could raise the question, what might have happened if instead of hiring Cooley, top management had given Stewart this same kind of support and "free hand"? Could he have turned the plant around like Cooley did? Probably not. The ineffective cycle seemed to have been in a downward spiral far past the point where Stewart would have had a good opportunity to make significant change. But with the introduction of a new manager with whom the employees had no past experience, now-significant changes were possible.

While a new manager may be in a better position to initiate change in a situation which has been spiraling downward, he still does not have an easy task. Essentially, he has to break the ineffective cycle. There are at least two alternatives available to him. He can either fire the low performing personnel and hire people who he expects to perform well or respond to low performance with high expectations and trust.

The latter choice for the manager is difficult. In effect, the attempt is to change the expectations or behavior of his subordinates. It is especially difficult for a manager to have high expectations about people who have shown no indication that they deserve to be trusted. The key, then, is to change appropriately. This is where the concepts of behavior modification might be helpful.

BEHAVIOR MODIFICATION

In the normal work environment, managers feel that either close supervision and pressure (task-oriented behavior) or consideration and trust (relationship-oriented behavior) are the only ways to focus a subordinate on his task or change patterns of behavior. They use these methods even when they prove unsuccessful, because they are often unaware of better techniques. At one time, managers were too structured, rigid and punishing. Now there seems to be a swing to the overly trusting, unstructured manager. Both these strategies when inappropriate have created problems. Another alternative is behavior modification,[11] which can provide a strategy for shifting leadership style appropriately to stimulate changes in maturity. In order to illustrate the differences between these three strategies — task behavior, relationships behavior and behavior modifications — we can compare how a manager using each might handle a potential problem-worker.

Tony, a new employee right out of high school, is a very aggressive, competitive individual. During his first day on the job, he argues over tools with another young employee. Table 1 attempts to illustrate the possible reactions of a high task manager, a high relationships manager and a manager using behavior modification techniques.

Behavior modification (often referred to as operant conditioning or reinforcement theory) is based upon *observed* behavior and not internal psychological feelings or attitudes.[12] Its basic premise is that *behavior is controlled by its immediate consequences.* Any behavior will be made stronger or weaker by what happens immediately after it occurs. If what happens is positive, it tends to increase the frequency of that behavior occurring again. Positive rein-forcement is anything that is rewarding to the individual being reinforced. Reinforcement, therefore, depends on the individual. What is reinforcing to one person may not be reinforcing to another. Money might motivate some people to work harder, but to others money is not a high strength need; the challenge of the job might be the most rewarding incentive. Managers must look for unique differences in their people and recognize the dangers of generalizing.

POSITIVE REINFORCEMENT

In order for a desirable behavior to be obtained, the slightest positive behavior exhibited by the individual in that direction must be rewarded as soon as possible. This is called reinforcing positively successive approximations toward a goal. For example, when an individual's performance is low, one cannot expect drastic changes over night, regardless of changes in expectations or other incentives. Similar to the child learning some new behavior, we do not expect high levels of performance at the outset. So, as a parent or teacher, we would use *positive reinforcement* as the child's behavior approaches the desired level of performance. Therefore, the manager must be aware of any progress of his subordinate, so he is in a position to reinforce appropriately this change.

This is compatible with the concept of setting interim rather than final goals and then reinforcing appropriate progress toward the final goal as interim goals are accomplished. In this process, the role of a manager is not always setting goals for his followers. Instead, effectiveness may be increased

TABLE 1 • *Different Approaches Used in*
Dealing with a Disruptive Worker

	High Task Manager	**High Relationships Manager**	**Behavior Modification Manager**
Manager Reaction	"This worker is going to be a trouble-maker. This behavior must be stopped!"	"Oh dear, I hope I can get them interacting and happy."	"Feels Tony needs to learn to cope in positive ways to replace aggressive behavior!" Separates conflicting workers without hostility or comment.
Supervisor Subordinate Interaction	"Hey, you. Knock it off! We don't allow fighting around here," said with coldness or anger.	"How would you both like to give me a hand on a job over here."	Manager watches for any positive behavior he can immediately reinforce. Supervisor sets limits on some behavior and carefully ignores others.
Worker Reaction	Tony builds resentment and hostility. Next few days, behavior becomes more aggressive.	Tony finds he can get attention of supervisor by being disruptive because the supervisor wants to be "understanding." He causes trouble and watches supervisor's reaction. Supervisor pays more and more attention as his behavior gets worse. Disruptive behavior reinforced.	Tony finds the supervisor appreciates good things about him. Wants to gain his respect. Supervisor Strategy: 1. Watches for any occurrences of positive behavior to reinforce. 2. Decides which new behaviors Tony needs to learn first. 3. Plans strategy to get desired behavior. 4. Attempts to better understand Tony in an effort to use incentives appropriate for his need structure. 5. Uses the incentives to reinforce behavior Tony needs to learn. 6. Continues to evaluate to make sure incentives are still appropriate since these tend to change with time.

| Outcome | Tony feels disliked by supervisor. Self-image deteriorates as he attempts to defend ego from assaults. Becomes more hostile and aggressive or withdrawn. Avoids supervisor and learning tasks. | Aggressiveness remains. Becomes more obnoxious as other workers withdraw. Creates incidents to get attention and assigned to those jobs he wants. Does not learn. No friends. Low self-image covered by bravado. | Outcome in two or three weeks. Tony's work and acceptance by other members of his work group continue to improve. Builds new self-image on basis of new behavior he has learned. Hostile and aggressive behavior toward other employees stops. Begins to have a sense of accomplishment. Inner needs and feelings start to change. Aggressiveness used in constructive ways. Has friends and becomes a positive rather than a disruptive influence on his work group. |

by providing an environment where subordinates can play a role in setting their own goals. Research indicates that commitment increases when a person is involved in his own goal setting. If an individual is involved, he will tend to engage in much more goal-directed activity before he becomes frustrated and gives up. On the other hand, if the boss sets the goal for him, he is apt to give up more easily because he perceives these as his boss's goals and not as his own. Goals should be set high enough so a person has to stretch to reach them but low enough so that they can be attained.

So often final goals are set and the person is judged only in terms of success in relation to this terminal goal. Suppose, in our example, the manager had expected Tony to become a "perfect" employee overnight. Suppose after the first week Tony is better but still causing problems. The result is usually the manager reprimanding him (punishment) even though he has shown improvement. If this reprimanding continues to occur, there is a high probability that Tony may stop trying. His behavior, rather than improving, may become worse. An alternative for the manager is setting interim realistic goals which move in the direction of the final goals as they are attained. Then with a change in the desired direction, even though only moderate, positive reinforcement may be used rather than some form of punishment.

NEGATIVE REINFORCEMENT

While positive reinforcement tends to be more effective in working with people, experiencing some unpleasant consequences or *negative reinforcement* can sometimes strengthen a particular behavior. For example, suppose a manager reprimands Al, one of his subordinates, for sloppy work, rather than giving him his usual "praise." If Al becomes just anxious enough, finds out what he did wrong, then does it right and gets his boss's praise, the unpleasantness of the reprimand becomes a negative "reinforcer." In this case, the manager was not just trying to punish Al because he wanted to make him feel badly but was giving him negative feedback because he wanted him to do better. Al responded as he had hoped he would, giving the manager a chance to use positive reinforcement with him again.

A leader or manager has to be careful in using negative reinforcement or punishment because he does not always know what he is reinforcing in a person when he uses these methods. He might be reinforcing lying, manipulation or all kinds of undesirable behavior because the individuals involved may use these behaviors, rather than improved performance, to eliminate punishment or further negative reinforcement. Another possible reaction to punishment is that the individual may begin to use avoidance behaviors such as attempting to eliminate communications and interactions between himself and the person who makes him feel threatened.

EXTINCTION

Another way to respond to behavior besides positive or negative reinforcement is to not reinforce it at all. This is called *extinction* because it tends to get rid of a behavior. For example, suppose a worker is disruptive to get the attention of his supervisor. What would happen if

his supervisor paid no attention to him? After engaging in this behavior on several occasions without accomplishing anything, he soon would be trying other behaviors.

People do not tend to continue doing things that do not provide positive reinforcement. This is even true sometimes when they are behaving well. Parents often get into this situation when they tend to pay attention to their children only when they are behaving poorly. When children are behaving appropriately, adults may pay little or no attention to them, which in a sense could put that behavior on extinction. If a child wants attention from his parents (it is rewarding to him), he may be willing to endure what the parent thinks is punishment for that attention. In the long run the parents might be reinforcing the very behavior they don't want and extinguishing more appropriate behavior.

PSYCHOTHERAPY NOT APPROPRIATE

Behavior modification seems like a useful tool for practitioners since it can be applied, to some extent, in most environments. Therefore, it has relevance for most people interested in accomplishing goals through others. This was not the case with psychotherapy. This process was based upon the assumption that to change behavior one had to first start with the feelings and attitudes within an individual.

The problem with psychotherapy from a practitioner's viewpoint is that it is too expensive and is appropriate for use only by trained professionals. This is true because the emphasis in psychotherapy is on analyzing the reasons underlying behavior which often requires extensive probing into the early experiences in the life of an individual. Behavior modification, on the other hand, is not as complex since it concentrates on observed behavior using goals or rewards outside the individual to modify behavior.

NOTES AND REFERENCES

7. LIKERT, RENSIS, *New Patterns of Management*, McGraw-Hill, New York, 1961, p. 7.

8. HERZBERG, FREDERICK, BERNARD MAUSNER and BARBARA SNYDERMAN, *The Motivation to Work*, John Wiley, New York, 1959 and Herzberg, *Work and the Nature of Man*, World Publishing Co., New York, 1966.

9. GUEST, ROBERT H., *Organizational Change: The Effect of Successful Leadership*, Dorsey Press and Irwin Inc., Homewood, Ill., 1964.

10. PERROW, CHARLES, *Organizational Analysis: A Sociological View*, Wadsworth Publishing Co., Inc., Belmont, Calif., 1970, p. 12.

11. A discussion of behavior modification by Glema G. Holsinger in *Motivating the Reluctant Learner*, Motivity, Inc., Lexington, Mass., 1970, was very helpful in developing this section.

12. The most classic discussions of behavior modification or operant conditioning have been done by B. F. Skinner. See Skinner, *Science and Human Behavior*, Macmillan, New York, 1953, and *Analysis of Behavior*, McGraw-Hill, New York, 1961.

BEN REED

CASE 1

Shortly after Ben Reed, twenty-seven, graduated from the state university with a B.A. degree in psychology, he took a job as assistant office manager with the Acme Medical Association, a group health insurance organization. His salary was $8,500 per year. As assistant office manager, he was responsible for supervising approximately forty office employees who performed sorting, totaling, and recording operations concerning medical claims charged against Acme.

The office workers were situated at several rows of desks in a large open room. As assistant manager, Ben Reed had a desk in the same room but off to one side of the desks of the workers. His immediate supervisor, Charles Grayson, the office manager, had been with Acme for twenty years and had risen to his present position from a beginning job as a clerical assistant. During his career at Acme, he had watched the company grow and progress, and often referred to the increase in employees under his supervision with a great deal of pride.

According to Ben Reed, his work at Acme was not especially challenging. In describing his job he stated that his main duties were to check the time cards of the office workers each morning, to make sure that "everything was in order," and to answer questions concerning claims that might be brought to him. In addition, he did special statistical studies at the request of the controller's office or Grayson. These studies were infrequent, and during his first four months with Acme, Ben participated in only two such studies. He estimated that on the average he actually "worked" no more than one or two hours a day.

Partially because of some courses he had taken at the university, Ben Reed had some strong convictions concerning the supervision of the office employees. He was concerned about the situation at Acme for two reasons: the high turnover of office employees — which averaged about 48 percent per year and the apathy of many of the employees toward their work. He realized that he was new in the organization but nevertheless felt obligated to make some suggestions which he felt would improve the situation with regard to the office force. Grayson, his immediate superior, often did not agree with these suggestions.

For example, in order partially to utilize his unproductive time, Ben suggested that, as he had had several courses in physiology as a pre-med student before transferring to psychology, it might be helpful if he could spend an hour or two a week in instructing the of-

fice staff in some of the basic funda-
mentals of physiology. The nature of the
work was such that knowledge of the
various functions and systems of the
body would, he felt, be helpful in speeding up the sorting and processing of
claims that came in. Ben suggested to
Grayson that he would be happy to conduct these informal classes as a part of
his regular duties. Mr. Grayson, however, did not feel this was a good suggestion and did not permit Ben to go
through with his idea.

Ben also had a disagreement with
Grayson over the handling of the case of
D. Martin. Martin, a clerk-typist, approached Ben one day while Grayson
was out of the office to report feeling
sick. Ben made the necessary arrangements for Martin to have the rest of the
day off. When Grayson heard of this incident he was very upset. He told Ben
that he did not have the authority to
make these kinds of decisions and that
he, Grayson, would make all such decisions in the future. Although Ben felt
that, because of his position as assistant
office manager, because Grayson was
not in the office at the time the situation occurred, and because Martin was
obviously sick, he had made a good decision, he let the matter drop.

On December 10, Robert Colvin,
controller of Acme Medical Association,
called Ben into his office to discuss
plans for a new electronic data-
processing installation that the company was considering putting in to
speed up the processing of claims. He
spent about two and one-half hours with
Ben explaining the proposed system and
concluded the interview by stating that
he felt that as new people often had
good ideas for improvement, he would
welcome any thoughts that Ben might
have.

Ben was enthusiastic about Colvin's
approaching him, and spent several
hours that night at home working out a
plan that would permit the new process
to be installed in his area with a
minimum of difficulty. He submitted his
ideas to Colvin the next morning.

Colvin was very impressed with
Ben's ideas and immediately called a
meeting of several of the officials of
Acme, including Grayson, to review
Ben's plan. This meeting was held during the early afternoon of December 11.
About three o'clock that afternoon
Grayson entered the area in which the
workers' and Ben's desks were located,
approached Ben's desk, and slammed
down the folder containing Ben's plans,
exclaiming, "What in the hell is this?"
Before Ben could reply, Grayson com-
menced in a loud voice to lecture on the
necessity of going through channels
when submitting reports, ideas, and suggestions. His remarks attracted the attention of the office workers, most of
whom stopped work to watch the distur-
bance. Ben Reed interrupted Grayson to
suggest that they might continue their
discussion in Grayson's office, which
was glass-enclosed and out of earshot.
Grayson snatched the folder from Ben's
desk and stalked into his office, Ben
following.

The discussion in Grayson's office
consisted mainly of a continuation of
Grayson's diatribe. After Grayson had
concluded, Ben stated that he had not
been satisfied with his relationship with
Acme and intended to submit his resignation in the very near future. He then
left Grayson's office.

The next day, December 12, Grayson asked Ben to step into his office for a few minutes. He apologized to Ben for his conduct of the previous day, remarking that he had had several things on his mind which had upset him and that he certainly had full confidence in Ben's abilities. Ben accepted his apology, remarking that he might have flown off the handle a little bit himself. The meeting ended on a cordial note.

On December 13, Ben Reed submitted his resignation and subsequently left the Acme Company on December 24. At the time of his departure he did not have a new job.

THEORY Y OR UNVARNISHED CHARISMA?

CASE 2

During her course of study at the Business School Cherrie Nanninga, MBA '76, learned a great deal in class about modern theories of organizational direction and control. The concepts sounded good, but Cherrie wondered whether they really worked. Deciding to pursue some "real world" evidence on her own, she arranged to interview a San Francisco Bay Area retailer, Arthur Friedman, a man whose unusual management style had attracted consider-able attention. Results of the interview with Mr. Friedman and reactions to the Friedman approach from members of the Business School's organizational behavior faculty follow.

Six years ago Arthur Friedman had an outrageous brainstorm. He decided to make some major changes in the way he and his brother, Morris, ran their small business, *Friedman's,* a retail appliance store in Oakland. His scheme was to allow the company's 15 employees to set their own wages, determine their own hours, and take their vacations whenever they felt like it. Had he gone mad? His brother might have thought so, but he agreed to give it a try. Well, the result turned out to be even crazier than the idea. It worked.

Mr. Friedman, who is now 54, left Friedman's Appliances about a year ago, because "there didn't seem to be any more challenges there." To his knowledge, the store is still operating under the same system that he implemented originally. "I just can't imagine it running any differently," he comments.

A few months ago, Mr. Friedman opened another store in Oakland which deals exclusively in microwave ovens. He plans to run it exactly as he ran the other store. Besides selling ovens, the store also offers cooking classes for those who want to know how to use microwave ovens properly. These classes are not limited solely to those who buy ovens in his store. "That's against my philosophy," he says. Mr. Friedman describes more of his philosophy in the interview that follows.

Q: How did you come up with this revolutionary idea?

For a couple of years I had been teaching weekend seminars on various subjects such as communications, sensuality and hexing. These seminars were all built around a philosophy based upon a few principles — for example, "people will be whatever you want them to be: if you trust them, they will be trustworthy," and "we don't do anything we don't want to do." And then one day I realized that I wasn't really living my life that way. I was teaching the philosophy on the weekends, but I was living my life differently. So I gathered all the employees together and said, "From now on, you are going to be responsible for your own jobs, salaries and working conditions. I trust you completely, and I will give you whatever you ask for."

Q: What were the exact components of the plan?

It covered absolutely everything. There were no restrictions whatsoever. Hours, vacations, whether or not they did or did not want to do something — for instance, waiting on customers — were all included. In other words, if there was anything they didn't want to do all they had to say was, "Look, I don't want to do that," and it was cool.

Or if there was something they wanted to do, all they had to do was say so. As for their salaries, I refused to discuss them. They had only to go to the payroll clerk and say, "I want so much money for last week," and that's what they recieved. There was no discussion, no arguments, no "nos." Whatever someone wanted, they could have.

Even the cash drawer was open to everyone. I only asked them to put in a chit so I could balance the cash at the end of the day. But whatever they cared to put in was OK — be it $20 for a new tire or a case of beer. And I encouraged everyone to take more than they felt they had coming because I found that they never did. For instance, I'd say things like, "Inflation is terrible, and you haven't had a raise in a year. Don't you think you should have more money?"

"No, no," they'd say, "I'm getting along just fine."

Q: When you first decided to try this plan on your business, did you really think it would work, or did you have a few doubts?

If there had been any doubts, it would not have worked. I've had calls from businesspeople all over the country, and they all say the same things: "I want to run my business the way you run yours, but I want to make sure that my employees don't rip me off." Well, it's just not going to work that way. You have to have complete faith that people really are honest. If there's any doubt, they'll test you, and it'll fail. You have to convince them that there's nothing that they can ask for that you will not give them.

Q: Did anyone ever make any unreasonable demands of you?

There are no unreasonable demands

with this philosophy. If I start judging the things that are asked of me — *e.g.* this is reasonable, but this isn't — it won't work. I have to trust and believe that no one will ask for anything they don't feel they have coming.

It's also more than just laying down the rules. I have to make it safe for people to really ask for what they want. If they feel that I'm going to fire them or judge them wrongly, then again, it won't work.

Q: What was the initial reaction of your employees to your plan?

Stunned silence. Nobody said a word for a month, and I finally had to chase them down one by one. I'd tell them to name their own salary, and they'd say, "Well, all I want is what the other guys want." But I didn't let them off the hook; I made them name a figure. What I really did was transfer the responsibility from myself to them. If they were dissatisfied with what they were getting, they could no longer blame me. They had to say, "Look, he'll give me whatever I want," and they started believing that there was more to them than just a paycheck, that I appreciated what they were and what they did. They became proud to drive a *Friedman's* truck because I recognized them as people and not just workers.

Q: Did everyone eventually take an increase in pay?

No. Most of them said, "I only want what they get at Sears or other places." And I'd say, "But you're worth more. You're a better worker." My job was trying to get them to take more than they were willing to and that was extremely difficult. It sounds crazy, but it was difficult.

Q: Did anyone want to take a cut in pay because he wanted to work fewer hours or less hard than someone else?

Yes, we did have two servicemen who finally settled on different amounts of money. When I asked the one guy why he was taking less than the other, he replied, "Well, I don't want to work as hard as he does." Previously, when we were setting the salaries, they both received the same amount. But when they had a chance to look at their own efforts, they were able to decide how much they wanted to work and how much they wanted for it. You know, people are incredibly honest.

Q: Did anyone change his hours?

Not one. They all came to work at 8 a.m., and they all took the same vacations they'd always taken. And no one was ever out on sick leave. Yet they didn't even have to say that they were sick. If they wanted a day off, they could say, "Hey, I just want to goof off today." But they wouldn't do it. The more I'd tell them to take, the less they seemed to want to. For instance, sometimes I'd say, "Look, it's sunny today. Go swimming at Lake Temescal and enjoy yourself. You've been working too hard." And the response would be, "No, I've got too many calls to do."

Q: What about turnover — how did you handle new employees?

There wasn't any turnover. No one ever leaves. Occasionally, however, we'd need part-time help. So I'd call the employment service, and they'd send somebody out — often a guy from the ghetto who was used to people taking advantage of him. All the way over to the store he was probably saying. "Geez, I hope they give me $3 an hour, but

they'll probably only offer me $2.50."
When he finally walked in and asked
what we paid, I'd say, "Well, this store
works a bit differently than other
places, and we pay you whatever you
want." "Come on, really," he'd say,
"what do you guys pay?" "Quite seriously," I'd say, "we operate differently.
We want you to be satisfied working
here, so we'll give you whatever you ask
for." After finally convincing him, he'd
ask for $3 an hour and then give a day's
effort like he'd never given anyone before. So it costs another couple of bucks,
and I get twice the effort out of a person. I'm willing to take the chance that
he'll ask for $20 an hour. Nobody ever
does — they can't. Could you ask for
more than you feel you're worth? No
one can.

Q: *Were there any other interesting inci-*
dents that stand out in your mind?

Yes, I have a couple of really favorite stories. One of our servicemen is an
expert mechanic, but he would never
service his own truck. It seemed a
shame to pay garages for work that he
could do better. So one summer he
asked if it was all right if he used the
van to take the family camping. I told
him to go ahead and offered him a credit
card to use along the way. "Great," he
said, "I think I'll put new brakes in and
tune it up before I go." OK, brakes and
a tuneup are not a big deal — what do
they cost? But the incident indicates
that as soon as you're willing to give
someone what he wants, he'll give you
want you want. I didn't say that to get
him to tune up the truck. It just
happened.

Another of my favorites is about
Sam Robinson, the guy who does our

payroll. He came in one day, and he was
really down. A real drag to have in the
office. It was most unpleasant for both
of us — he didn't want to be there, and
I didn't want him around. So I said,
"Stan, apparently you're not in a good
mood today or you don't feel well. So go
take $50 out of the cash drawer and
have yourself a good time. Go do whatever you want." When I finally per-
suaded him to leave, he went to the
drawer, took out the $50 and put in a
chit. He walked out the back door, but
it wasn't two minutes he returned and
put the $50 back. "No," he said, "I've
got too much work to do." But he was
pleasant for the rest of the day. He realized that he was there because he
wanted to be there. Up to that time, he
was blaming me because he had to work
that day. But I got him to take responsibility for his life, and he recognized
that he was doing what he wanted to
do.

Q: *Are the workers unionized?*

Yes, I insist that they all join because the union has such excellent
health and welfare plans. But the union
never comes around. I just throw their
agreements in the wastebasket. Of
course, I would always tell the men,
"Look, take whatever you want, but
make sure it's at least union scale
so that I don't get in trouble." I
never argue with the union people,
and in a sense they feel like they're
out of a job.

Q: *Once your plan was well under way,*
did the morale improve noticeably?

Absolutely. And not only the morale
in the store, but also the morale in each
of the employee's homes. Their spouses
would call and say, "What have you

done with Ed?'' They just started treating their families the way I was treating them.

Q: Were your employees better able to understand your problems as an employer?

Yes, they all seemed to be saying the same thing: "We don't want to take advantage because we don't want to put him out of business.'' They all enjoyed working there, and they all wanted to stay. When I started seeing their viewpoint, they started seeing mine. We just stopped fighting each other.

Q: How were productivity and profits over the past six years?

Well, I don't know about all those fancy words, like cash flow and all that. All I know is that we did our thing, and 15 families have eaten well off the business. We've never been what I would call a very profit-oriented business. Net profit has increased each year, but that hasn't been the result of increased volume. Sales remain at about a million a year. Presumably, the increase in profits has resulted from greater productivity and efficiency. But, you know, I didn't implement this scheme to save money. It wouldn't work if it were for any ulterior motive.

You know, I like to play golf — I only work two or three days a week. And my brother plays tennis maybe four times a week. And those things are more important to us than making a hundred thousand a year. So what we're interested in is a living — a pleasurable living. I know I'm never going to end up rich anyway. But this is really the profitable way to do business, even if it doesn't seem that way on the surface. You get more productivity for less

money. For instance, one day I called one of our part-timers and asked him to work on a day that he was not scheduled to come in because we had a lot of deliveries. He said, "OK, I'll come in, but you have to give me time and a half.'' When I agreed, he changed his mind and said, "No, that's all right.'' It just never fails.

Q: Did your plan extend to your customers as well as your employees?

In a sense, yes. We had tried collection agencies, and it was very distasteful to me. I just don't like the idea of pressure. Trying to make someone do something they don't want to do is against my nature. When someone owes me some money because they choose not to pay for an appliance, I realize that they wouldn't owe me anything if I hadn't chosen to sell them that appliance and make a profit off of them. So I started sending people notes like, "If this bill isn't paid in two weeks we're going to cancel it.'' After that one went out for a while, we began mailing out notes such as, "For some reason which we cannot understand, you have decided not to pay us. This letter officially cancels the bill in question, and you are no longer under any obligation to pay us. We have decided not to give this bill to a collection agency, as our gain would be small compared to your loss. We would appreciate it, however, if you would take a moment to tell us why you made the decision not to pay us.'' Well, those two letters certainly did as much good as any collection agency. Besides, delinquent accounts are really a very small percentage of the total business. All they really do is keep the collection agencies in business.

Q: Do you plan on using the same system in your new store?

Oh yes, I couldn't possibly do anything any differently. It's just too enjoyable. Inasmuch as I don't know any of the answers, I may as well just do what I want to do.

Q: You mentioned that you've had a great many calls concerning your ideas. To your knowledge, has anyone actually implemented your system?

No. I've heard about a lot of almosts, though I have a friend who has a bakery in Berkeley, and he has told me that he lets his employees have whatever they want. "I tell them, of course, that we have to put aside a certain amount for taxes," he added. Well as soon as you make any restrictions, it's closer, but it's not the real thing.

A few months ago, someone called who has a farm equipment business somewhere in the Midwest. "I'm going to try your system," he said, "but I'm going to start with just my office staff." Well, what makes him think that his office staff is any more honest than his warehouse staff? His other employees would wonder why he didn't think as much of them as he did of the people in the office. Under those conditions, the system just won't work.

Often, when I tell people about the way I run a business, they are enthusiastic, but they ask what to do about the "bad apples." I can only answer that there are no bad apples in my barrel. People are what you expect them to be.

Q: Given the right attitude, do you think that this scheme could work for a much larger company? Is there a size limit?

I don't know. Everyone asks me

whether it would work for General Motors. I can only say that, heaven forbid if I should ever get to be in big business, there's no other way I would run my business. I tell other businessmen that there's no reason why they should do something my way. My message is — if indeed I have a message — I did it my way; you can do it your way. I give people the right to be what they want to be and I insist on that right for myself.

Q: At the Business School, we've often been told that what it takes to be successful in small business is an entrepreneurial ego. Would you buy that?

No. I'm not willing to buy anyone else's preconceived notions. What I do think you need to have, however, is commitment. A commitment to take in more money than you spend. If this is in the area of advice to people that may start small businesses, I have only one thing to say: If it seems like something you're going to enjoy doing, go ahead; if not, don't. Even if you do make a pile of bread, it's not going to be any fun. Look at those guys who started Victoria Station — such a classic in business now — they're having fun, *and* they're fantastically successful.

But that's just my viewpoint. There are a lot of people in the world who will be a lot richer than I, but I don't think there are any who will have more fun than I do. □

The term "theory Y," frequently referred to by members of the organizational behavior faculty, is a shorthand designation for a theory of human nature and human behavior advanced in 1960 by social scientist Douglas Mc-

Gregor in his book, *The Human Side of Enterprise.* McGregor labeled the principle theory Y to distinguish it from what he called theory X, the traditional underpinning for management direction and control. For readers not familiar with the McGregor theories, the assumptions of theories X and Y are described in the following excerpts from McGregor's book.

THEORY X ASSUMPTIONS

1. The average human being has an inherent dislike of work and will avoid it if he can.
2. Because of this human characteristic of dislike of work, most people must be coerced, controlled, directed, and threatened with punishment to get them to put forth adequate effort toward the achievement of organizational objectives.
3. The average human being prefers to be directed, wishes to avoid responsibility, has relatively little ambition, wants security above all.

THEORY Y ASSUMPTIONS

1. The expenditure of physical and mental effort in work is as natural as play or rest.
2. External control and the threat of punishment are not the only means for bringing about effort toward organizational objectives. Man will exercise self-direction and self-control in the service of objectives to which he is committed.
3. Commitment to objectives is a function of the rewards associated with their achievement.
4. The average human being leans, under proper conditions, not only to accept but to seek responsibility.
5. The capacity to exercise a relatively high degree of imagination, ingenuity, and creativity in the solution of organizational problems is widely, not narrowly, distributed in the population.

6. Under the conditions of modern industrial life, the intellectual potentialities of the average human being are only partially utilized.

In order to test the academic "validity" of an approach such as Mr. Friedman's, the *Alumni Bulletin* queried members of the Business School's organizational behavior faculty, among them David L. Bradford, Francine E. Gordon, Harold J. Leavitt, William G. Ouchi, Jerry I. Porras, and Eugene J. Webb.

As might be expected from any sample of an academic community, opinions differed considerably, with reactions running the gamut from skepticism to congratulations. Following is a sample:

Q: What do you think of Friedman's philosophy?

Bradford: I think he doesn't understand what he is doing. Let me pull out two quotes: "People will be whatever you want them to be;" and "We don't do anything we don't want to do." Those are contradictory because the second one says, in effect, nobody can force us to do anything; yet the first one says we are the product of a lot of social influences. Friedman is pretending he's doing the second, but in a very sophisticated, successful way, he's doing the first. It's clear that we do what we don't want to do all the time; that we are the result not only of our needs but of our expectations, social pressures, etc. If we pick up on the first quote — that people's expectations of us influence our behavior — then I think it's very true, and that would explain what is going on.

Gordon: Basically, I think Friedman's right. The only thing that he doesn't say, however, is that it depends on who the employees are. I suspect that there are people who would either exploit the system or would be uncomfortable with it. What usually happens in a work environment such as this is that the employees self-select — if it's not "right," those people leave.

Leavitt: I like his philosophy. However, I have another reaction to the implication at the beginning of the article that somehow this is terribly unusual. Although at this level, at this extreme, it is kind of unusual, it is, in fact, becoming commonplace in larger organizations. Since I've been watching — for the last 20 or 25 years — there have been some people who have had this philosophy and who have used it periodically. However, it is not, to my mind, a kind of bellwether of the future. It's going on in much larger companies on a much larger scale all over the country right now. Proctor and Gamble, and Alcoa, and half a dozen other companies have been playing games with it, using a kind of group-run production operation.

Ouchi: The strongest impression that I get about Mr. Friedman is not that he holds a particular philosophy, but rather that he has a very charismatic personal style. That is what he communicates. You could describe it as a philosophy, But that suggests that if others could learn his philosophy, they could elicit a similar response from people. But he's a unique type.

Porras: The general set of ideas — as an entity — are not revolutionary. The notion that "you establish your own pay, and you come in and tell my

accountant how much to pay you" — that is reasonably revolutionary. I don't know of any other organization that's doing it. The other parts — deciding what you want to do and what time you come in — that sort of thing is being done in other organizations.

I think Friedman's philosophy is coercive in the sense that it forces the individual to take responsibility for himself. Now, that's kind of consistent with the whole humanistic approach that says people can and should take control of their lives, that they should be responsible for their actions, and that if they're given this freedom, they will be responsible. Many of us have an orientation which values freedom of choice — that taking responsibility for your life is a good thing. But when you boil it down to realities, taking this responsibility also means bearing the consequences. And many people aren't willing to do that. That's to be expected because we've been socialized in organizations to not ever have the responsibility to make these types of choices. A good thing about Friedman is that somehow he was able to act consistently with his philosophy after he decided to implement it.

Q: Why do you think Friedman's system works?

Bradford: Friedman implies that people are basically good and if you leave them alone, they'll come up with the right answers. That's the theory of anarchy and it's the one theory which has never worked in practice. I think it would make more sense to see the employees' behavior as a result of a very intricate, complex set of social expectations and social pressures. And if you look at it that way, then what he's done is set up a very significant and very good reward system. He's given his people a lot of positive rewards — thinking well of them, freedom, pride, specialness. Friedman has made the company very different from others and, therefore, the employees have a lot going for them to make the system work. If they were to spoil it, if they were to kill the goose that lays the golden eggs, they would lose all that. In effect, Friedman is saying, "Look, I'll trust you and you get all these goodies as long as it works."

Gordon: There must be some awareness among the employees that they can put the owner out of business. You're talking about a guy with a relatively small budget. The employees are aware that they've got a good thing. How many times can you pick your vacation time, name your hours, and know that you can take extra money out of the till if you have a real need for it? And I suspect that most of these people are not in a very mobile job market. If they've looked for jobs elsewhere, they realize that they couldn't begin to approach the kind of working conditions they now have and thus want to do everything they can to perpetuate the system. That's why I think it would work here and not at GM, where there wouldn't be that sense of "if I exploit the system, I can put myself out of a job."

Ouchi: What Friedman is operating is clearly not a formal organization, in the sense that we normally think of it. It is more like a small tribe or a stake in the Mormon Church. It is a collection of people who feel a number of bonds holding them to each other. They each have

a great deal to gain by maintaining those bonds and a tremendous amount to lose by endangering them.

An alternative hypothesis is that perhaps he is a person who provides a great deal of emotional as well as financial security for his employees, the feeling that they are trusted, the feeling that he is going to be extremely tolerant of short-term problems they may have, of errors they may commit. Friedman gives them a tremendous sense of emotional, psychological security, of stability. Now these are not commodities that are in great supply these days.

Porras: I think that most people view the world in terms of being a "win-lose" situation. That's why we have labor unions. With his approach, Friedman has managed to change it into a "win-win" situation. Although large organizations might not be able to accomplish this in the same way, I think there's an important lesson they could learn. If we could move away from this "we-they" orientation between managers and workers, then I think both the organization and the employees would profit. Employees would be more productive workers, would be able to use more of their skills in the organization, and would feel better about themselves and the contribution they were making. And I'm not just talking about satisfaction, the whole happy workers' syndrome. We all accept that we can't always be happy. Therefore, to push for having a satisfied work force all the time is an unrealistic goal. I think what people really desire is the opportunity to be involved, to be alive in the system, to feel as though what they are contributing is important. It seems that Friedman is beginning to deal with this notion in his system. And that is something that larger organizations need to think about more deeply.

Webb: I guess in part it depends on what you mean by "works." Friedman says that 15 families have lived well off the business — something like that. He's made money, but he is not very profit-centered. If you mean "works" in the sense of him having a reasonable time and enjoyment and also keeping the wolf from the door, and we assume that these facts are true, then it's worked. Maybe he could have made more money on it, but he also would have had to pay the price of not operating in his style.

Q: What are the effective limitations of using an approach such as Friedman's?

Bradford: I think that this would work in a system in which social peer group pressure could be operative. Also, it's probably going to work when you have basic rapport between the management and the workers. If you have a history of animosity and conflict, then it may not work. People would then distrust you or else they would rationalize, saying, "Well, look, that SOB has ripped us off for five years and we are going to get our money now;" that would be an entirely different sense of equity. If people thought they'd been ripped off, then they might retaliate to gain that sense of equity.

Gordon: My gut feeling is that size is an issue. In Friedman's case, it was clear that he and his brother owned the store and their employees knew them personally. There was probably some sense of responsibility to individuals as well as to the company. What the size

limit cutoff is, I'm not sure. But I suspect that if you did something like this with GM, you would encounter the attitude that "it's a big company and if it gets ripped off, well, they can afford it." Whereas in a small company, you may bankrupt them.

I suspect that part of what's operating in Friedman's company is the attitude that what's good for the company is good for the employees. They want to stay with the organization and it's to their benefit to function in the most honest and growthful way. However, the assembly line workers at GM might feel "What the hell, if I take $40,000 a year salary, even though I may be only worth $20,000, what difference does it make?" It's a different kind of relationship. Somewhere in between Friedman's little store and GM there's a cutoff, but it would be difficult to ascertain just where that is.

I also think that if this sort of a system is to be used effectively, the employees must be aware of the part they play in the organization. But I don't think the kind of work the employees are doing or the amount of interaction among personnel represents important limitations.

Leavitt: One of the problems with this system is that it depends very much on the character of the person running the organization. Friedman points out that it is hard for other people to use the system in the same way that he's using it. He's made himself a very deep personal commitment. My guess is that it will die when he dies — and will be very difficult to transfer. On the other hand, that isn't to blame him. He isn't a theorist and he isn't trying to run a larger organization. He makes it very explicit that he's trying to live a good life, enjoy his work, and feel good about the way he's dealing with his people, and that's dandy. But it isn't a "system" in the sense that it isn't institutionalized. It focuses around him.

I don't think it has to be done personally, though. I think it can be done as part of the system, part of the culture — in larger organizations. But I think that the limitations of what he's doing are in part determined by his own personality and in part determined by the company size — by issues of that sort.

Most larger organizations that are using this sort of thing are moving cautiously, but clearly are going in this direction and clearly are getting results — results usually measured in peculiar ways, such as less labor unrest, less turnover, higher employee morale.

Friedman says he is doing this because he wants to have fun and a good life and because he thinks it is right. I think there's a certain amount of that in what a lot of other companies are doing, but I don't think that's the prime mover. The prime movers are the more traditional ones. They want to keep their businesses profitable. They want to keep them going — surviving and growing. These are simply mechanisms for doing that. It isn't a kind of great new face of man. It is a great new concern about how you keep an organization operating in 1976. It isn't morality, it isn't beauty, and it isn't motherhood. In Europe you have laws governing participation and we are moving in that direction, too. There's also social change, and people seem to be demanding other things of their work

than they used to. These are simply efforts to try and adapt the organization to meet those needs and to make it at least as productive, if not more productive, than it was before.

Ouchi: I'm sure it could work at General Motors, at General Electric, at General Instrument, at General Anything. I think the critical variables exist at the level of the society and culture. If GM were located in Italy rather than in the United States, then I think we would see it presently in a form much like Mr. Friedman's appliance shop. In fact, Fiat and Olivetti both have been studied by a number of Italian social scientists, and both of those organizations have many of the properties that you see in that appliance store. The reasons that I would attribute to the differences between those Italian companies and a typical American company have more to do with the social and economic organization of the society itself than with any factors that are peculiar to the industry or the firm.

Another critical variable is the sense of community, of belonging, of stability that Friedman provides. I have seen other businesses about the size of his and some larger that provide the same sense of security, of belonging, but where the expressed attitude of management is very instrumental or very authoritarian, rather than Friedman's kind of attitude. But what they all have in common is the property of offering stability, a sense of community. Maybe that's the thing that people see, that's the thing that generates such strong positive commitment from people. You can generate this commitment in a very large company — you see it in employees at Procter and Gamble, IBM,

Hewlett-Packard. In a sense, it almost doesn't matter what the philosophy is. What matters is that there is a philosophy, because to have a philosophy is to have a world view that brings order into a person's life and the feeling that here's a leader I can follow because he or she knows where they are going. I can't evaluate whether that's a good place to be going or not if I don't have my own philosophy, but at least I'd like to be attached to somebody who knows where they are going.

Porras: I think both size and ownership of the organization are important factors. Friedman owned the firm and it was small. People could identify with it, relate to it, not as some anonymous entity, but as a person. If they were ripping it off, they weren't just ripping off some unknown entity — they were ripping *him* off. Moreover, it was sufficiently small so that the employees realized that if they were ripping it off, they were endangering their fellow workers, the life of the system, in effect, themselves. They knew that if they really went hog wild, the place would go broke and they wouldn't have their jobs anymore. Now, in a large, anonymous organization, if people rip off that system, they don't believe that they are endangering themselves.

Another limitation is that not everyone really believes what Friedman believes — that people will come through if you give them a chance. That's what makes it difficult to implement this sort of orientation on a much wider scale. The problems are really compounded when you have a large organization. The managers have responsibilities to the stockholders and the risks are pretty high. And, if all the stockholders don't

have the same philosophy, can managers in all good conscience try to implement these kinds of ideas? Coordination is also a problem. Coordinating pay would be an administrative disaster. Coordinating work between groups, though, could be accomplished in the context of global tasks — "It's your job to produce cars. How you do it is up to you."

Webb: For one thing, what does the firm do? Friedman has a retail appliance store with 15 employees — not a very complicated venture. It isn't only the size of the firm that's important, but the complexity and the degree to which people have to be interrelated and how much the interrelationships of the different jobs are time-linked. When people come to work and how much time they spend at work is very important in an assembly operation, but may not be so important when the issue is whether to have two or three repairmen in a fixed period. Some kinds of operations really require very tight phasing of people. Friedman's doesn't. It's the kind of venture that's loose, giving him some flexibility in his operating procedures. He's also not trying to get the maximum out of his labor force.

Another thing, too, is the salary level. The question is what criteria you're going to operate under. Friedman is his own man, so he's got nobody hassling him on things like profits. He's got a venture that is loosely structured and doesn't have the problems of close coordination of his labor force. At first he says that everybody can decide their own pay. Later on he mentions the union situation. In effect, he's saying, "You can't take less than 'X' dollars (whatever the union scale is), but you can take up to what you think you're worth." So it isn't as cavalier a pay scale as he perceives it.

Q: Do you think this is really Theory Y management?

Bradford: It certainly is not. I don't know what you would label it — I don't think it really has a title. If he were to use a Theory Y management style, I think he could do something very similar. What I would do is call the employees together, tell them I think they are responsible, trustworthy people, and have *them* decide on what is fair pay, hours, and so forth. The way Friedman is doing it is very covert. It looks individualistic but it isn't, because everyone is comparing themselves with others. The individual is influenced by other people's expectations, but there is no way he can influence *their* expectations. It's not legitimate for the employees to talk to each other about the rules of the game. It is only legitimate for each person to act on his or her own. And it seems to me that a true Theory Y approach would set up conditions whereby individuals really can make the decision. Friedman acts as though his employees are making individual decisions. I'm suggesting that it is really a social decision — that the system he has set up is one where each individual can only work on his own. In a sense, Friedman's style is rather manipulative. It would be riskier for him to call the group together and say, "Let's publicly make all these decisions." But potentially, he could lose a lot more power if he were to use real Theory Y management practices.

Gordon: I would say that Friedman holds Theory Y assumptions. Theory Y has to do with people being motivated by something other than money. He's not using a group management approach — there's no doubt about that — but Theory Y has nothing to do with groups. There might be merit to encouraging the group to act as a group. I'm not sure. But I would not go so far as to say that if you don't use a group approach, it's bad. In some ways, Friedman is taking away group pressure.

Leavitt: The implication of the article is that here we have a rare and unusual example of Theory Y management because there ain't much Theory Y management around. And that's the part I don't think is true. There's a helluva lot of Theory Y management in the world and it's moving along very fast.

Friedman's approach is a little paternalistic. But the boundaries of the definition of Theory Y are difficult to determine. His style is in that direction. It is more of a humanistic management style — goofy, more self-determined by the people involved. And it is highly dependent on this particular guy, because if he goes away, it will go away. In a sense, the employees don't really self-determine beyond the boundaries of his control. It will probably only last one generation unless he does something to institutionalize it, and he doesn't seem to want to.

A lot of the other cases which are being carried out in larger systems are not nearly so personal. There are much more impersonal sets of rules and procedures governing the way the organization shall operate. Therefore, they have a much better chance of surviving through time. But they're still experimental in many cases, and I'm not sure that the world will move much more in this direction in 10 years than it is now. But I think it will.

Ouchi: Douglas McGregor expressed a series of assumptions which are labeled Theory Y assumptions about the basic nature of people. Someone who holds those beliefs may manage in style one, two, or three. But the ideas contained in Theory Y do not tell one how to manage or deal with people. They express a set of beliefs about what people are like. It appears from the interview that Friedman does indeed hold those beliefs. But I don't know the man. I wouldn't be willing to say that I thought I did without having met him, dealt with him. These kinds of things are subtle indeed, and it takes a great deal of care to understand what really is motivating somebody. But certainly what he says is consistent with the Theory Y set of assumptions about people.

Webb: This really isn't Theory Y. It's got a Theory Y assumption, but Theory Y is much more task-oriented, much more focused on what's involved in the enterprise to try to meet some things like profit goals.

Theory Y is not anarchistic, and on one level, Friedman's operation looks anarchistic. But it isn't at all obvious to me that it is. There is a structure. It is also coercive, because Friedman's either a very subtle Machiavellian or really naive. A lot of people are coercive by being nice and creating guilt. People respond to them on the basis of guilt. His employees may not want to do things that are not appropriate because those things would hurt Friedman — the giver of all good things, the old patriarchal figure. Friedman then becomes a benevolent despot.

Take Stan Robinson, for instance. He's down. "It's a drag to have him in the office," Friedman remarks, and he doesn't want him around. So he tells Stan in this very, what looks to be gracious, way to "get the hell outta here and take 50 bucks with you." He makes Stan feel guilty enough so that he then comes back and becomes, in Friedman's report, pleasant. "He was pleasant for the rest of the day. He realized he was there because he wanted to be there." That is Friedman's interpretation. Now, a hard-nosed interpretation is that Friedman is very, very slick. A very astute coerciveness — it's like the mother saying, "Eat the cake. I made it especially for you. You don't love your mother."

Q: What would happen if something were to disturb Friedman's system — for instance, if someone asked for $20 an hour?

Bradford: Friedman's employees are probably working consciously or unconsciously under an equity notion. The proof of the pudding would be, what would happen if somebody were to violate that notion? It would be an exciting experiment to send somebody who did take $20 an hour. My guess is that peer group pressure would be tremendous and that other employees would try to control the deviant. They would kid him, saying things like "here's the person who's going to kill our company." And then, if the person continued to get away with it, my guess is that everybody would raid the till — "If the ship is sinking, we may as well take what we can for ourselves." First, however, you would see a very strong social control mechanism.

Gordon: My gut feeling is that one of the first things that would happen would be that they would get angry. On the one hand, they would feel that they've got a nice thing going and here's someone who will put the guy out of business. At the same time, they might try to pressure the guy to lower his salary or leave. The only exception might be the guy who worked his tail off to the degree that the other employees would say, "Well, maybe he's worth it and I'm not willing to work that hard."

As for the boss, I suspect that his reaction would depend on the reaction of the employees. If everyone eventually came around and asked for $20 an hour, he probably couldn't afford it. Given Friedman's style, he might say, "If we do this, we'll all be out of jobs in a period of time, so do you want to reconsider?" I don't think he'd be willing to go out of business. He would probably fire the one guy and let everybody readjust their salaries accordingly, explaining why it wouldn't work — that economically, it wasn't feasible.

Porras: If someone were to ask for $20 an hour and do so for a period of time, and if we are to believe Friedman's philosophy, that person would eventually say to himself, "Hey, I don't really deserve $20 an hour. And the reason I was getting it was because I feel I've been screwed in the past" or "I didn't really believe that he'd do it — I was just testing him." There are a whole series of psychologically oriented explanations that somehow this person might have been trying to satisfy other needs. And when the person realized that the $20 an hour wasn't satisfying those needs, or when the needs were satisfied in other ways, he'd revert back to a realistic appraisal of his worth.

Webb: A good question here is what would happen if something happened to the economy to knock the demand out of retail appliances. Friedman says somewhere toward the end that he has a commitment to take in more money than he spends. What if, through no fault of his own, nor indeed through any fault of the way in which the employees are behaving, it turns out that he takes in less money than he spends? What happens on the down side? Would the style survive? I don't know.

CENTER CITY ENGINEERING DEPARTMENT

CASE 3

The Engineering Department of Center City employed approximately one thousand people, all of whom worked under the provisions of the civil service system. Of these employees, about one hundred worked in the Design Division. Parker Nolton, an associate engineer, had been employed in the Design Division for nineteen years and was known by virtually everyone in the division, if not in Center City itself. Nolton had held the position of associate engineer for seven years on a provisional basis only, for he had never been able to pass the required civil service examinations to gain permanent appointment to this grade, although he had taken them often. Many of his co-workers felt that his lack of formal engineering education prevented him from passing the examinations, but Nolton felt that his failures were the result of his tendency to "tighten up" when taking an examination. Off the job, Nolton was extremely active in civic affairs and city-sponsored recreational programs. During the past

year, for example, he had been president of the high school's parent-teachers association, captain of the bowling team sponsored by the Engineering Department in the Municipal Bowling League, and a member of the Managing Committee of the Center City Little League.

As Center City grew and the activities of the Engineering Department expanded to keep pace with this growth, younger men were hired into the department in relatively large numbers. Among those hired were Ralph Boyer and Doug Worth. Both of these young men were graduate engineers, and had accepted the positions with the Engineering Department after fulfilling their military obligations. Both had been officers in the Army Corps of Engineers. In order to give the new men opportunities to achieve permanent status in the civil service system, examinations were scheduled with greater frequency than they had been in the past. Nolton's performance on the examinations continued to be unsatisfactory. The new men, however, passed the exams for successively higher positions with flying colors. Ralph Boyer, in particular, experienced marked success in these examinations and advanced rapidly. Three years after his initial employment he was in charge of a design group within the Design Division. Parker Nolton, in the meantime, had been shifted from the position of a project engineer to that of the purchase order coordinator. The position of purchase order coordinator was more limited in scope than that of a project engineer, although the responsibilities of the position were great. He was still classified as an associate engineer, however.

Ralph Boyer continued his successful career and soon qualified for the position of senior engineer. A new administrative group that had been created to meet the problems that arose in the Design Division because of the expanding activities of the Engineering Department was placed under his direction. Doug Worth, too, was successful in his examinations and was shortly promoted to the grade of associate engineer and transferred into the administrative group headed by Ralph Boyer.

One of the functions under the new administrative group was that of purchase order coordination. This relationship required that Parker Nolton report to Ralph Boyer. Nolton, however, chose to ignore the new organizational structure and dealt directly with the chief engineer, an arrangement which received the latter's tacit approval. Nolton was given a semiprivate office and the services of a junior engineer to assist him in his activities. His assistant, John Palmer, soon requested a transfer on the grounds that he had nothing to do and that there was no need for anyone in this position. Nolton, on the other hand, always appeared to be extremely busy and was continually requesting additional manpower and assistance to help him with the coordination of purchase orders.

Some four months after the organizational changes noted above had taken place, the chief engineer left the company and his replacement, Stan Matson, was appointed from within the division. Matson was the logical successor to the position; his promotion came as no surprise and was well received by all the employees. His

appointment was shortly followed by the assignment of Ralph Boyer to a special position which took him completely out of the Design Division. Doug Worth was assigned to the position thus vacated, supervisor of the administrative group, and consequently inherited the supervision of Parker Nolton's activities. This assignment, initially made on a provisional basis, was soon made permanent when Worth passed the required examinations and was awarded the grade of senior engineer. Doug Worth had never worked closely with Parker Nolton but had been on cordial terms with him since his arrival in the Engineering Department. He had had contact with Nolton in several recreational activities in which they both had participated.

During the months which followed, Parker Nolton continued his direct reporting relationship with the chief engineer, now in the person of Stan Matson, and never consulted nor advised Doug Worth regarding the progress of his activities as purchase order coordinator. His former assistant, John Palmer, had been transferred and had been replaced by an engineering aide. Both the aide and Nolton appeared to be busy most of the time, and Nolton was still requesting through formal channels more manpower for his activities. When occasions arose which required Doug Worth to check on Nolton's activities, he was always forced to go to Nolton's office for information, for Nolton always claimed to be too busy to leave his own office. During the conversations which occurred when Worth visited Nolton, Nolton frequently gave the impression that he regarded Worth's activities and interest as superfluous. Several times he suggested that in future situations Worth just send the inquiring party directly to him if questions arose about his activities. He often made the comment that he knew everyone in the department and that it was often better to handle many situations informally rather than through channels.

Doug Worth was concerned with Nolton's attitude, for he did not feel that he could effectively carry out his responsibilities as supervisor of the administrative group if he did not know the current status of activities in all of the functions under his control. Consequently, he attempted to gain more cooperation from Nolton by approaching the subject at times when the two men were engaged in common off-hours recreational activities. Those attempts were uniformly unsuccessful. Nolton always quickly brought the conversation around to the standing of the bowling team, the progress of the P.T.A., or any other unrelated subject close at hand.

After several attempts to talk with Nolton in a friendly way off the job, Worth concluded that the situation as it currently stood was intolerable. While he realized he must do something, Worth felt he understood Nolton's attitude and reactions and was sympathetic toward the man. After all, Nolton had been in the department for years and had been relatively successful. He knew all the "ropes" and had many friends. Worth reflected that it must be a blow to a man like Nolton to have to report to young, relatively inexperienced men. Worth had faced similar problems during his military career, when he had had more experienced men many years his senior under his command. After much thought, he decided his best approach

would be to appeal to Nolton in a very direct manner for a greater degree of cooperation. Thus, Worth approached Nolton on the job and suggested that they have a talk in his private office where they would not be disturbed by all the activity in Nolton's office. Nolton protested that he could not take time away from his duties. Worth was firm, however, and Nolton reluctantly agreed to come to Worth's office, protesting all the way that he really could not spare the time.

During his opening remarks to what Worth had planned as a sympathetic discussion of the situation, Worth referred to "the normal relationship between a man and his superior." Nolton's reaction was violent. He stated that he didn't regard any young upstart as a "superior," especially his. He told Worth to run his own office and to let him run his. He concluded by saying, "If you haven't anything more to say I would like to get back to my office where important work is being neglected." Worth, realizing that nothing more could be accomplished in the atmosphere which prevailed, watched in silence as Nolton left.

Doug Worth subsequently reported his latest conversation with Nolton to Stan Matson, the chief engineer. He also related the events which had led to this conversation. In concluding his remarks, he stated that he could no longer take responsibility for Nolton's actions because Nolton would neither accept his guidance nor advise him of the state of his work. Matson's reply to this last statement was, "Yes, I know." This was the only comment Matson made during the interview, although he listened intently to Worth's analysis of the situation.

At the next meeting of the supervisory staff of which Worth was a member but Nolton was not, Worth proposed that Nolton be transferred to the position of Design Drafting Engineer — in effect a demotion. As Worth was explaining the reasons for his proposed action regarding Nolton, one of the other members of the supervisory staff interrupted to proclaim very heatedly that Nolton was "one of the pillars of the entire Engineering Department" and that he would be violently opposed to the demotion of "so fine a man." Following this interruption, a very heated, emotional discussion ensued concerning the desirability of demoting Nolton.

During this discussion Stan Matson remained silent; yet he reflected that he should probably take some action during the meeting regarding the Nolton situation.

EXERCISE 1

EMPIRE
COMMODITY CORPORATION

INTRODUCTION

Managers sometimes find themselves in situations in which they must deal with individuals who feel that they have not been treated fairly by the organization. They believe that the system is working to their detriment and want the manager to do something about it.

The manager may find this a difficult situation — especially if he or she is sympathetic with the position of the individual. However, even though a great deal of sympathy may be present, action to change the situation may be difficult. The organization may have consciously developed certain procedures and traditions over a long period of time, as in the Empire Commodity Corporation. In order for the manager to provide substantial relief in the situation, it may be necessary to challenge the entire system, perhaps at some personal risk.

The decision of what action, if any, to take often is difficult and depends on the outcome of the manager's analysis of a complex set of interrelated factors dealing with the individual, the organization, and the manager.

PROCEDURE

Your instructor will give you specific instructions for this exercise. Do not proceed further until you have received these instructions.

The Empire Commodity Corporation is involved in all phases of the agricultural industry except the actual operation of farms. The company buys and sells various grains on the open market for its own account and for the accounts of its customers, both in the United States and in foreign countries, and is a member of all the major commodity exchanges.

In addition, Empire owns and operates a series of grain-storage elevators located throughout the United States and manufactures special feeds for livestock and poultry. Although annual sales are over $75 million the company has only 3,500 employees. About 1,500 of these people are at the home office in Kansas City, Missouri; the rest are at Empire's branch offices located throughout the country. The staff of a typical branch office is small, consisting of one or two executives who keep in touch with local market conditions and advise the home office of prices and special "buy" or "sell" situations, and supporting clerical personnel. The largest branch office has 35 employees.

Most of the executives at both the branch offices and the home office are products of Empire's executive training program. Under this program promising college graduates are rotated through a series of jobs in various offices, plants, and grain-storage elevators for a period of about eighteen months. At the end of the training program, the personnel director, John Dorsey, talks with each trainee and they decide what division of the company offers the best opportunity for the trainee in the light of the company's needs and the trainee's interests and desires. As a trainee finishes each training assignment he is required to write a report covering his experiences on that particular job. These reports are then reviewed with the trainee by John Dorsey, so that the trainee can get maximum benefits from each assignment. In addition, reports on the trainee's performance are forwarded to Dorsey.

The company is very selective in choosing people for its training program. Each year company executives visit seventy to eighty colleges and universities in all parts of the United States looking for prospective trainees. While the number of trainees hired varies, usually about 25 new people are hired annually. In order to hire this number the company normally interviews 1,200 or 1,300 college seniors each year. From this number it offers jobs to about 40 people, of whom about 25 usually accept the job offer. As the president of Empire puts it, "We are looking for the Phi Beta Kappa who was captain of the football team, has an impressive string of extracurricular activities, and has worked his way through school." Company statistics have shown that a trainee usually had six or seven job offers in addition to that made by Empire. Thus, management has been very pleased about the high percentage of top-flight individuals who accept Empire's job offers.

The training program has been in operation for about forty-five years and is considered the best in the entire industry, both by Empire and by its competitors. About 90 percent of top and middle management are "graduates" of the training program.

Dorsey has been in charge of the Personnel Department and the training program for about ten years. He is well known throughout the company, and people customarily come to him if they have questions concerning any of the trainees or the training program itself.

This situation concerns Dorsey and Harry Clark, who works in the sample room in the home office. The first assignment for each new trainee is in the sample room, where samples of different kinds of grain are tested to determine their classification under standards and grades established by the federal government. For many trainees, the assignment in the sample room is their first contact with the agricultural industry, and the knowledge which they acquire concerning various kinds of grain, testing methods and procedures, and government standards is basic to their entire future with Empire.

Role for John Dorsey

Arnie Davidson, supervisor of the sample room, has just called you concerning a conversation he has had with Harry Clark, his assistant. According to Arnie, Harry is pretty mad because he has just found out that the starting pay for trainees is significantly higher than his own rate of pay. He feels that if he has to give the trainees the benefit of his experience so that they can go on to be successful, he should receive more money — especially since when it comes to doing work in the sample room, he and Arnie are the only ones who can do the difficult, exacting jobs. According to Arnie, Harry is "pretty sick of spending four years teaching a string of guys all he knows so they can move up — and not even getting as much money as they do." Arnie said that he had talked with Harry telling him how much the company depended upon the trainees for future management and that he was doing a real service for the company by helping the trainees as much as he could. Arnie told Harry that he had been doing this for thirty years and got a great deal of pride in seeing "his boys" succeed. He was gratified that many former trainees who were now top executives made it a point to stop in the sample room and say "Hello" occasionally.

According to Arnie, his attempts to smooth things over didn't seem too successful. Harry didn't say anything in direct reply to Arnie's comments, but asked if he could take some time to go to talk with you. Arnie suspected he was on his way to your office now.

After thanking Arnie for the information, you reflect on your imminent talk with Harry. This kind of thing is touchy at best, and while you realize that Arnie's comments to Harry were well intended, you wish that he had not said anything. This kind of situation had occurred before in other departments from time to time. Good people, many of whom had worked for the company for a long time and had cooperated very well with the training program, occasionally became distraught when they discovered how much the company had to pay to attract the kind of individuals it wanted in the training program. In many instances, the pay of a trainee was greater than that of the person doing the training. Precisely because this kind of problem had come up before, you have made it a point to advise each trainee not to discuss his salary with any of the people in the departments to which he would be assigned during his training program. Until now this seemed to have solved the problem, but evidently one of the trainees in the sample room must have divulged the amount of his salary to Harry.

As you await your secretary's announcement that Harry has arrived, you review what you know about him. Actually, you know quite a bit, for you customarily take each new trainee to the sample room and introduce him to Arnie and Harry; this is the first assignment for a trainee, and you want everything to go smoothly. Thus, you have had relatively frequent contact with Harry. You know, for example, that he is a local man, twenty-three years old, single, and has been with Empire for four years. After graduation from high school — he had had a good record — he spent two years in the navy and after his discharge started work in the sample room. He has a nice appearance, is alert, and has always been friendly and cooperative. Arnie's reports on his performance have been very good, and based on these, you have occasionally told Harry that he has been doing a good job. For the past two years, he has been taking evening classes in business administration at the local university and has been doing fairly well — mostly "C's" with an occasional "B." His current salary is about $250 less per month than the starting salary for trainees. You feel that this salary differential properly reflects the differences in ability of the people involved, although you recognize that you anticipate that a trainee would pay off in the future and that, right now, Harry was probably making a greater contribution to Empire than any particular trainee.

As you ponder the situation and what approach you should take, your secretary announces that Harry is waiting in the outer office to see you.

Role for Harry Clark

You're upset because one of the trainees in the sample room has just told you that the starting salary for trainees is a lot more than your monthly salary — about $250 a month more. You had suspected that trainees were pretty well paid, but this is ridiculous! You've been with Empire for four years, have done a good job — both Mr. Dorsey and Arnie, supervisor of the sample room, have often told you this — and look at your salary!

You wonder why you should pass on all the tricks of the trade to the trainees so they can rise to management positions. There's no percentage in beating your brains out to help them — and at low wages, at that, just so they can come back twenty years from now and say, "There's old Harry, he started me out in this business." That might be O.K. for Arnie, but he's only got a few years before retirement. You've got a whole career ahead of you. You're only twenty-three — younger than some of the trainees Empire hires!

And what's so great about trainees? Sure, some of them are Ivy Leaguers but then, you're a college man too, although you bet that you've had it harder. For the last two years you've been going to night school, and night school is no fun after a full day's work and a hurried dinner. And study time! If you had had as much time to study as they had had, your grades would be a lot better, although there was nothing wrong with "C's" and "B's" under the circumstances. And your two years in the navy ought to be worth something. Many of the trainees weren't veterans.

When you came to work for Empire, they told you that there was no limit to where you could go. They even spent a whole day orienting you to a "career with Empire." But it certainly seems like there is a limit! You're sort of a fall guy: you pass on all you know to someone else who gets the reward.

After talking with the trainee in the sample room, you were pretty angry and had told Arnie how you felt about things. His reply — that he got a great deal of pleasure and pride out of helping the trainees along — only made you more angry. You didn't want to hurt Arnie's feelings because he's a pretty good guy, so you merely asked if you could go to talk with John Dorsey, the personnel director.

At the present time, you are in Dorsey's outer office. His secretary has just gone in to announce that you are there. You want to find out just what kind of future you do have with Empire. As far as that goes, there's no reason you couldn't be a trainee yourself.

MOTIVATION
AT WORK

INTRODUCTION

In the reading "Assumptions about Man, Leadership and Motivation," Coffey, Athos, and Raynolds discuss Herzberg's two-factor theory of motivation. Herzberg found one set of factors that he called "motivators" that were very important in determining people's positive feelings about their jobs. Another set of factors, dissatisfiers, helped to prevent dissatisfaction if they were in line with people's expectations but did little to induce positive motivation. Herzberg's research showed the following:

Dissatisfiers (Job Environment)	Motivators (Job Content)
company policy and administration	challenging job
lighting	feeling of achievment
salary	growth
fringe benefits	responsibility
status	advancement
job security	enjoyment of work
supervision	earned recognition

In this exercise you will interview some people to determine what motivates them on their jobs — what causes satisfaction or dissatisfaction.

PROCEDURE

1. Interview at least three individuals who are currently employed. They can hold any kind of position in any kind of organization. If possible, attempt to interview individuals at different levels in their respective organizations. However, this is not a requirement.
2. In your interview, be certain to ask the following questions of each interviewee: (a) What are the things that give you the greatest feelings of satisfaction about your job? (b) How would you rank these in order of importance? (c) What are the things that give you the greatest feelings of dissatisfaction about your job? (d) How would you rank these in order of importance? In the course of your interviews you will probably ask many other questions about how your inter-

viewees feel about their jobs, but *be certain to ask these very specific questions*, and record the responses on forms similar to the one shown in Figure 1.

3. Another area to cover in your interviews is the importance of money as a motivator. Recall the statement from "Assumptions about Man, Leadership and Motivation":

> Evidence indicates that money, in itself, does not usually serve as a motivator to work harder or better. However, in the absence of what is perceived by the recipient as adequate or fair compensation, money is a source of dissatisfaction.

Ask your interviewees to rank money as compared with other motivators.

Interview #1

Person interviewed: _____

Type of job: _____

Level in organization: _____

Length of time in this job: _____

Length of time with this organization: _____

Approximate number of years working in any job: _____

Factors Causing Greatest Feelings of Dissatisfaction	Factors Causing Greatest Feelings of Satisfaction
1.	1.
2.	2.
3.	3.
4.	4.
5.	5.
6.	6.
7.	7.
8.	8.

Summarize feelings of interviewee about the importance of money as a motivator.

FIGURE 1 • *Recording Form*

4. After you have completed your interviews, form in groups of four to five persons and compare the results of your interviews. Compile a list of motivators and dissatisfiers as determined by your interviews. Discuss what trends, if any, are apparent. Can you rank the factors in each category in order of importance? That is, What are the most important motivators? Satisfiers?

   Discuss how the persons interviewed by members of your group feel about money as a motivator.

   Do the results of your interviews tend to support or refute the findings from Herzberg's research? How do you explain this?
5. Gather as a large group and discuss the results of the smaller group deliberations.

PART 4

GROUPS
IN
ORGANIZATIONS

Just as informal communication networks exist with the formal networks, there are informal organizations within the large formal organization. The formal organization is depicted in an organizational chart, with each box in the chart representing a specific position or department, and the lines connecting the boxes representing formal reporting relationships. However, the organization chart does not depict informal relationships, and the only groups represented in the chart are composed typically of single superiors and their subordinates. From experience as well as research, it is abundantly clear that many groups exist that in no way follow the profiles of the organization chart, yet operate on a continual basis.

In this section of the text you will discover that informal groups are inevitable. Such groups can have effects on organizational performance ranging from the very positive to the very negative.

A tremendous amount of research has been conducted with small groups. A recent bibliography listed over 5,000 articles and studies related to small groups,[1] and hundreds of studies have been conducted since then.

A good working definition of a group is "any number of people who (1) interact with one another, (2) are psychologically aware of one another, and (3) perceive themselves to be a group."[2] Therefore, many aggregations of people do not qualify as groups. For example, people on an airplane, in a movie theater, or on a city bus do not necessarily constitute groups.

---

[1]M. Knowles and H. Knowles, *Introduction to Group Dynamics,* rev. ed. (New York: Association Press, 1972).
[2]Edgar H. Schein, *Organizational Psychology* (Englewood Cliffs, N.J.: Prentice-Hall, Inc., 1965), p. 67.

In many ways, the small group acts as a "buffer" between the individual and the organization and serves as a very important identity point for its members. A person, when asked where he or she works, may respond "at Engulf and Devour Conglomerate," but Engulf and Devour *to that person* is usually a particular small group or set of groups in which he or she operates.

In the first reading of this section, "The Spontaneous Development of Informal Organization," E. Jackson Baur describes some background research in the behavior reflective of informal organization; he also describes the process by which groups develop. Surprising as it seems, it was well into this century before the behavior of informal groups was considered important by most practicing managers. The first studies of informal group behavior began in the late 1920s, but it was well into the 1930s before managers began to be concerned about the effect of group behavior on organization performance. The Baur article describes many of the important dimensions of group behavior, including the effect of group membership upon absenteeism and turnover and the apparent necessity of an informal social order.

The second reading, "Group Norms: Key to Building a Winning Team," by de la Porte, describes how group norms can have powerful effects on individual performance levels.

It is difficult for us to realize how greatly the groups to which we belong affect our behavior. This is perhaps because we are members of groups, literally from the instant of birth. Each of us is a member of many groups, and each of the groups affects our behavior to some degree. Since we are surrounded continually by groups, we tend not to appreciate or even to see the effect that a group has upon us. But even when strangers are formed into groups for purposes of psychological experimentation, the group effect can be a powerful influence upon the individual. Imagine the effect that groups of co-workers or close friends can have upon an individual.

There are also some structural factors that are important in shaping group behavior. The size of the group, the cohesiveness, and the physical distance between group members all have significant impact.

As a manager you will find yourself in charge of groups of subordinates; therefore, you should know in what ways the group can influence individual performance. De la Porte's article describes how the manager might develop profiles of group norms within his or her organization, and how he or she can use that information to improve task performance.

In "The Nature of Highly Effective Groups," Rensis Likert describes the effective work group and how it differs from less effective groups. Specific group behaviors that enhance performance or detract from it are described and analyzed.

Of course, for a group to be effective, members must be skilled in the technical aspect of the task. All the cohesion and positive thinking in the world will not overcome lack of skill. But given a modicum of skill and ability, group dynamics can make all the difference.

In this last reading, pay particular attention to the roles of the members and leaders. Two general sets of roles are required for the functioning of any group. Group task roles are related to the desired output or group "product." Group building and maintenance roles deal with the group's efforts to maintain itself as a group.

As you read the dimensions of the task and maintenance roles, try to think of specific examples for each that you have observed in the last week. What role behaviors do you feel are the most frequent in the typical group? Why? Are the group maintenance activities less important than the task activities? Why or why not?

Also consider two very different kinds of groups: for example, a volunteer community fund-raising committee and the board of directors of a corporation. Would you expect to see more maintenance behavior in one versus the other? Why or why not?

The inevitability of informal groups and the powerful effect of group membership on individual behavior provide excellent opportunity for the skilled manager to increase organizational performance. The readings of this chapter describe what the manager should look for, and how he or she can encourage and reward those behaviors that are useful to the organization and discourage those that are dysfunctional.

THE SPONTANEOUS DEVELOPMENT OF INFORMAL ORGANIZATION

E. Jackson Baur

We are all familiar with the office "grapevine" that transmits unofficial news, with the cliques that gather at the water cooler during coffee breaks or at lunch tables, and with "empire-building" by supervisors. These are all examples of the informal side of large organizations. Although administrators everywhere have been aware of these things for a long time, their significance to the organization has not always been apparent. The event that illuminated the importance of informal groups was the accidental discovery of the human factor in industry by social scientists who studied workers at the Western Electric Company in Chicago around 1930.

THE DISCOVERY OF HUMAN RELATIONS

A team of experts from Harvard University's Graduate School of Business Administration undertook to investigate the various environmental factors that affect the efficiency of industrial workers. They began their experiment by assigning six young women who assembled telephone relays to a separate room where they continued the same work, but under special supervisors and under conditions where their behavior could be observed and their individual work output measured. The experimenters first introduced rest pauses of differing duration and frequency; later, they varied the length of the working day and week. Throughout the two years of the experiment, the output of the girls followed a general upward trend, regardless of any particular change in rest pauses, or working hours. To the surprise of the investigators, productivity did not decline when they restored the original work schedule without breaks.

TWO UNANTICIPATED CHANGES

After testing and rejecting explanations for this phenomenon in terms of fatigue, monotony, and wage incentives, the experimenters concluded that the true explanation lay in two unanticipated changes: (1) the growth of cohesion and friendship among the six girls, and (2) the personal consideration and attention given them by their new supervisors. The girls themselves had been consulted and advised about the changes that were being made on the assumption that this would enlist their whole-hearted cooperation and minimize the effect of uncontrolled psychological factors. They had been set apart from the ordinary

Reprinted with permission from the quarterly journal of the American College of Hospital Administrators, *Hospital Administration* (now *Hospital and Health Services Administration*), Summer, 1963, pp. 45–58.

workers, observed by important visitors, and even interviewed in the superintendent's office. Their increasing productivity reflected gratifying changes in their social environment.

To learn more about the nature of these human factors within the plant, the Harvard social scientists designed another study for a group of workers. This time, however, they did not alter their working conditions or encourage them to cooperate. Instead, they merely observed and interviewed a dozen men who worked at wiring banks — parts of electrical equipment for telephone exchanges. The researchers simply wanted to find out what went on in such a group rather than to study the effects of experimental changes in working conditions.

The second study group was assigned to a special room where the facilities and procedures were identical with those of the department from which they were selected, except that a trained observer sat at a desk in the back of the room and kept a record of what occurred. An interviewer talked with the men occasionally and they were invited to talk to him privately about their work and what went on in the room whenever they felt like it. This objective study of the Bank Wiring Room uncovered some of the spontaneous relationships and informal activities that exert a strong influence on the attitudes and productivity of workers. Within this group researchers found friendship circles, leadership and distinctions of status, production standards different from those of management, techniques for disciplining, and ways of solving production problems without appealing to supervisors. In short, a complex informal system within the formal setting of the factory.

THE HUMAN RELATIONS MOVEMENT

The implications of this research for the personnel policies of management initiated what has been called the human relations movement in business administration that has affected a revolution in personnel practices. Subsequently, further research was done on informal groups in other organizations — military units in World War II, prisons, schools, hospitals — and in each case unplanned, personal relationships were found to exert a significant influence on the functioning of the larger system.

Studies of informal activities among employees, students, prisoners, and soldiers may give a false impression that cliques are peculiar to persons in the lower ranks who traditionally resist the demands of executives, supervisors and officers. Not so. Informal practices and groups are also found among executives and professional men. In the field of journalism, for instance, newspaper publishers have been found who have unannounced policies on the selection and treatment of news that conflicts with the official code of the publishers' association. Reporters get to know what these policies are from experience and the "grapevine." In one large city, physicians were found to be unified through a complex system of formal and informal ties controlled by an inner circle which selected men for admission to practice in the area and even determined their advancement within the profession.

In all enduring large organizations there is an informal aspect. However, it is not equally developed in all organizations; there are conditions that encourage or retard its growth. An informal system tends to flourish where large numbers of persons come together in the same place, as in factories, schools, and hospitals. There is more opportunity for close personal ties when the turnover of personnel is low. Perhaps informal associations achieve their fullest development among persons who are separated from their families, who room and board as well as work together, such as college students, sailors, soldiers, and prisoners. Informal contacts at work tend to increase when the job itself requires communication and cooperation between employees rather than separate tasks focused on materials or customers. For instance, a social scientist who studied the social structure of a bank found few informal bonds among tellers, but many among employees of departments that had no contacts with customers.

PERSONS WHO WORK TOGETHER, STAY TOGETHER

However, persons who work apart from one another may associate during "breaks" or after work if they are much alike and have similar problems. Private secretaries to the executives of a large corporation were found to spend much time together. Railroad men, although they are usually dispersed when at work, get together when they are off duty. Their irregular hours of work make it difficult for them to establish durable associations with men in occupations having routine working hours. Furthermore, those who pursue a craft with strong traditions and pride in their

work are inclined to recreate and socialize with others in the same trade. Printers in larger cities have formed a multitude of clubs for hobbies, sports, intellectual and political activity. Whenever persons in similar situations, and with the same status are confronted with comparable problems, they tend to find a collective solution to their individual needs.

For many persons, association with workmates on or off the job provides their most satisfying social activity. One study cited the case of an unemployed textile worker who carried her lunch to the mill every noon so she could continue to eat with the "girls." However, persons with a satisfying family life and congenial neighbors and relatives are less likely to form friendships with their workmates. This tendency was the explanation offered for the surprising discovery that British longshoremen preferred random work assignments to being assigned with the same men. A similar attitude was found among industrial workers with strong family ties who were recent migrants from rural areas. They may also have felt different from and rebuffed by the city-bred people among whom they worked.

LARGE AND SMALL INFORMAL GROUPS

The informal groups we have been considering consist of a few persons who know one another intimately — the kind of small group sociologists call "primary." Also important are large groups divided by differences of religion, nationality, race, socio-economic class, sex, or age that divide the personnel or organizations in ways highly significant to the employees but unrecognized in management's formal charts. The interactions of persons different in these easily recognizable ways, but who are not friends, are governed by stereotyped preconceptions. Since they treat one another in an impersonal, categorical way rather than as unique personalities, it is convenient to refer to these large divisions simply as categories. Categories may be temporary, or peculiar to one industry or a single establishment. A unionization drive may raise issues that for a short time divide workers into bitterly hostile factions. For instance, one study disclosed that the employees of a gypsum plant were divided between the below-ground miners and the above-ground mill workers, who although drawn from the same population, saw themselves as wholly different kinds of people.

PRIMARY GROUPS ARE ADJUSTIVE FOR INDIVIDUALS

Primary groups fulfill a number of significant functions for persons in large organizations. The newly hired worker often depends on the small, informal group to show him "the ropes," knowledge which supplements whatever formal training he may receive from his superior. News travels quickly via primary groups. They are the clandestine transmitters and receivers of information before it is officially released. After the news is released, they amend, amplify, and interpret it. Thus, each person gets a larger, more detailed, and meaningful — but possibly distorted and erroneous — picture of what is going on in the organization. In case of accidents or illness, members of a primary group

may help one another. When some of the most dexterous workers in the Bank Wiring Room at Western Electric completed what they felt was a normal day's work, they helped slower workers. Furthermore, if a member breaks a company rule, his primary group may "cover up" for him. The group often provides acceptable ways of compensating for personal deficiencies. The less competent interviewers in a state employment agency, one study revealed, used their lunch hour to cultivate friendships with their more able colleagues and thus compensated for their lower competitive position in the office.

Thus, the group protects its members from authoritative action. It provides a psychological buffer between the individual and the organization. In general, it functions as a haven from the impersonal, rationalized methods of large organizations. As such, it can be a positive aid for the adjustment of individual employees to the demands of the organization.

THE SUBCULTURE OF INFORMAL GROUPS

Informal groups are the source of many practices and customs. They generate new words, carry out ceremonies, invent games, exert discipline, and relate people to one another. In long established industries and services, informal groups create a unique way of life — what, in the language of the social scientist, is called a "subculture."

Perhaps the most colorful trait of any trade or profession is its jargon or special language. New words are coined to refer to tools and techniques — distinctions that are meaningful only to the practitioner. The argot includes words that express subtle and significant distinctions which can thereby be communicated with greater efficiency to those who share the language. However, new synonyms are often substituted for perfectly serviceable English words, which suggests that the jargon also serves the social function of secrecy and exclusiveness. It protects the in-group's monopoly of a given field of work and it distinguishes persons "in the know" from outsiders. It serves as a "pass" for mobile members of the trade.

Small groups tend to develop a set of rituals. Newcomers, for instance, must be initiated before they are fully accepted by members. The initiation may take the form of hazing or practical jokes which test the ability of the novice to "take it." Although these tests are rarely formalized, they have some of the same functions as initiation ceremonies of fraternal orders, and the ordeals of primitive adolescence rites. The group may also observe important events in the lives of its members, such as becoming a father or having a birthday. Such transition rituals confirm the acceptance of the individual who is honored as well as strengthens the bonds among all the members. Parties, on and off the job, and picnics or excursions add to the solidarity of the work group. Subsequent reports of these events take on the character of legends, especially if there is exaggeration in the retelling that emphasizes qualities valued or respected by the members.

ON THE LIGHTER SIDE

Work groups often develop habitual forms of play that fill time during "breaks," in the lunch hour, or after work. For example, the men at the copy desk of a morning newspaper that was studied always concluded their night's work with a gambling game invented by one of their group. The sport of corkball was invented by workers in one St. Louis brewery to while away time during the lunch hour.

The men of the Bank Wiring Room periodically engaged in a simple game of "binging" in which one man would strike another sharply on the upper arm thereby incurring the obligation to submit to a similar blow in return. The same technique was used when one member of the group incurred the displeasure of the others, except that the blow would be harder than usual. What started as play became a technique of control, along with the more familiar devices of razzing, name calling, and slighting. For example, one of the men was derisively called by the name of a famous race horse because he persisted in working faster than the others thought appropriate.

Restriction of output has been a chronic source of frustration to foremen and supervisors. Wherever several people are employed at the same job, they tend to develop a common understanding of what constitutes a fair day's work. Needless to say, it is invariably less than what their superiors think they could do. Although the men of the Bank Wiring Room were paid according to a group incentive plan, they adhered to a norm of 2,000 connections per day. Some consistently produced a little more and others a little less, but the coercive effect of their norm was apparent from the tendency of the overproducers to report less than they made and the underproducers to report more. One man who persisted in turning out *and reporting* more than the norm was subjected to ridicule and sarcasm. Not only was this "rate buster," to use the jargon, berated, but some of the other men who occasionally lagged below an acceptable rate were vilified as "chiselers." The punishment of both kinds of transgressors is evidence that the group abided by a real standard, and restriction of output was not simply an attempt to do as little work as possible.

INFORMAL STANDARDS AT WORK

Adherence to an informal standard of production served to protect the group from management's pressure to produce. It nullified the objective of the incentive payment plan. That it "worked" for the men is evident from the favorable attitude of their supervisors who felt that they were good, dependable workers with a satisfactory record of output and efficiency. It also reduced competition among the men in the group, thereby removing one source of internal tension. In sum, restriction of production contributed to group stability by minimizing internal dissension and providing protection from outside pressure.

Job trading was another practice contrary to the rules of the company that was engaged in by the employees under observation in the Bank Wiring Room. In spite of an explicit regulation prohibiting trading — on the apparent assumption that specialization is more efficient than versatility — wiremen frequently traded jobs with soldermen. Although trades were usually arranged among the men themselves, they occasionally requested permission of their

group chief, despite the fact that he was officially responsible for enforcing the very rule he helped violate. Without exception, all trades were made on the initiative of the wiremen and often reluctantly acceded to by the solderman. The significance of this sub rosa activity became apparent when it was noted that wiremen held a status in the group higher than that of soldermen. In light of the current trend in personnel practice away from over-specialization, we can surmise that informal trading was better practice than the company's official rules, at least in this particular situation.

THE INFORMAL SOCIAL ORDER

However, increased efficiency was certainly not the motive for trading or the reason it persisted. In addition to providing relief from the monotony of wiring, it appears to have fulfilled a need for expressing and acknowledging the superiority of wiremen over soldermen.

The status distinction between wiremen and soldermen was but one feature of the informal social order in the Bank Wiring Room. The men also divided themselves into two cliques, each including wiremen, soldermen, and inspectors. The clique of men who worked at benches near the front of the room were superior in status to the clique seated at the back of the room. Associations through play, trading, and helping one another tended to be confined to clique mates.

Rudimentary law and government, the researchers found, emerged through the acknowledged leadership of one member of the dominant clique who consistently took the initiative in emergencies. When disputants threatened to lose their tempers, he intervened and settled the quarrel. On one occasion, the group exhausted its supply of high-quality wire and the foremen would not distribute more until they had used up some that the men considered defective. At this juncture, the informal leader took matters into his own hands and obtained a supply of good wire through his connections in other departments.

From these illustrations, it is apparent that the informal work group, in a real sense, is a miniature society. It possesses in simple form all of the essential features of larger, more complex social systems. For example: (1) It has its own culture that includes a set of norms and values that fix standards of conduct for its members among themselves and with outsiders. (2) Its participants engage in a continuous process of communication and interaction facilitated by a specialized vocabulary and conventional patterns of action, ritual, and play elaborated far beyond the requirements of the job. (3) It has an internal social structure of roles and relationships divided by factional distinctions and graded into a hierarchy of ranks. (4) It is maintained by established techniques of social control that eliminate internal sources of tension by resolving conflicts and punishing offenders, and by protecting itself from threatening outside forces. (5) It possesses a conception of the whole organization and of its own place within this larger structure.

THE TYPICAL HISTORY OF AN INFORMAL GROUP

The informal group develops slowly and the very fact that its members have been together for some period of time makes a difference in their relations with one another and with newcomers. For this, and other reasons, we can distinguish a typical sequence of stages in the histories of informal groups.

It is obvious that a pre-condition for the emergence of a group is communication among the potential members. When people come into contact with one another and interact, the conditions are ripe for a group to take form. When they interact more frequently with one another than with others — and do this repeatedly for successive days and weeks — a rudimentary group has made its appearance.

The realization of common interests tends to knit informal groups together and marks the second stage of their development. The members may do the same kind of work or different — but coordinated — work in the same department; the linking element is a common interest in the product manufactured or the service performed. They may have similar problems or privileges. A significant effect of common interests is that they not only draw some people together but simultaneously separate them from others with divergent or conflicting interests. Common interests at one and the same time generate a sense of likeness and of difference. The consciousness of being different from others, or having higher or lower status, of being more or less privileged, strengthens the unity of the group. The *esprit de corps* among the girls in the Relay Assembly Test Room at Western Electric, for example, was attributed in large measure to their conception of themselves as a privileged group treated with consideration and solicitude not accorded ordinary assemblers.

TOWARD GROUP SOLIDARITY

Curiously, low status may also generate group solidarity. In one situation that was studied, the working conditions in the anodizing department of an aircraft plant were arduous and repulsive. Uncomfortable rubber clothing and masks were necessary to protect workers from the acid; the heat and non-porous clothing caused profuse sweating. In the plant, the department was generally referred to as the "tank hold," and the men who worked there as "those dirty tank men." Perhaps in part because of their despised status, they developed strong camaraderie.

As communication continues between a small group with common interests, they gradually begin to think alike and to understand one another. They agree on what constitutes a fair day's work. They coin words with a meaning unique to the group. Stories of past exploits give them a history. They introduce games, hold parties, and invent rituals. A whole complex of social activities is elaborated that goes far beyond the requirements of the job. In short, they act together, agree on how things are to be done, and decide what is and what is not important. They adhere to prescribed patterns of conduct and believe in the same values. The sociologist would say they exhibit "consensus" and possess a subculture.

Consensus can include acceptance of differences among themselves as well as likenesses. One among them becomes the leader, another his lieutenant, another the clown, and an eccentric one

perhaps the group's scapegoat. A status hierarchy becomes manifest in the consistency with which certain persons take initiative over others, and this crystallization of differentiated roles marks the third and most advanced stage of group development. With the roles and their inter-relations prescribed according to an established subculture, the group acquires a degree of stability and capacity for collective action that makes it appropriate to say it has a social structure.

If the group becomes larger, lays down rules, and chooses officers, it ceases to be an informal group and becomes a club or association. Some labor unions have originated in just this way. If the original group does not become formalized, it may split into factions and divide or dissolve altogether.

To summarize, the typical evolution of an informal group includes three definite stages, each distinguished by the emergence of interaction, common interests, and structure. Each stage is marked by the addition of new features until the group is fully developed and exhibits the essential qualities of a complete social system.

EFFECTS OF INFORMAL GROUPS ON THE ORGANIZATION

What are the effects of these informal groups on large organizations? As we have previously indicated, they do not necessarily conflict with the objectives of management, as is so often assumed. In fact, the findings of considerable social research suggest that informal groups are *essential for organizational stability*. Objectives studies of large organizations have shown that informal groups can strengthen employee morale, reduce absenteeism and turnover, promote harmony, and increase efficiency. These positive influences are stressed in this paper because they are often overlooked by administrators concerned over the informal group's possible negation of their attempts to effect good management.

The presence of small, spontaneous groups is one of the essential elements of morale in large organizations. Other ingredients include confidence in leadership, a reasonable expectation of continued employment, and opportunities for advancement. Morale depends upon solidarity with one's fellow workers or associates as well as upon a willingness to follow orders. Field studies of German soldiers at the close of World War II disclosed the power of primary groups to hold military units together despite fearful losses, frantic retreats, and broken communications. National Socialist political convictions contributed only slightly to the unity of the German army when compared with the solidarity motivated by dependence on primary groups for the satisfaction of fundamental personality needs. Soldiers, being cut off from families and friends, are more dependent on their comrades than workers, but the functions of primary groups in an enterprise or institution are similar if, less salient, than in an army.

MINIMIZING ABSENTEEISM AND TURNOVER

The value of informal groups in minimizing absenteeism and turnover was convincingly demonstrated by a comparison of two war-time aircraft plants in California. The causes of absences and resignations could be isolated because one plant had high and the other low turnover, yet both recruited employees from the same labor market. The firm with high turnover adhered to personnel policies that interfered with the development of spontaneous groups, while the other company made every effort to keep workers in their jobs, stabilize their relations, and create an environment favorable to the development of informal groups.

Efficiency is often increased by changes in the work assignments arranged among primary group members. They may divide work among themselves in order to increase the specialization of their tasks beyond what is prescribed in the job description. On the other hand, they may combine work by sharing and trading what is supposed to be done by separate persons. Perhaps the most common practice is the arrogation of supervisory functions, so abundantly evident in the earlier cited Bank Wiring Room, where the men set their own standard of production and developed techniques to enforce it.

Innovations in work techniques, it would seem, are accomplished more successfully when they are introduced to small groups who are given an opportunity to participate in the necessary planning for them rather than by simply telling workers to adopt new methods of doing their job. A study of operatives in a pajama factory demonstrated that the greater the amount of worker participation in adopting new techniques and adjusting rates of pay, the quicker they recovered a satisfactory level of efficiency, the lower was the rate of turnover, and the fewer expressions of hostility toward the company.

Evidence that informal groups are inevitable and that they can help attain management's objectives inescapably implies that the wisest course for administrators to follow is to encourage the development of constructive informal groups. A policy of discouraging spontaneous groups is futile and ignoring them is dangerous.

GROUP NORMS: KEY TO BUILDING A WINNING TEAM

P. C. André de la Porte

Corporate viability and success, management experts agree, rest on (among others) three essential human factors: commonness of purpose; adaptability to change in the business environment and operating conditions; and the qualitative excellence of each individual's work contribution. So far, so good, but attaining this state of effectiveness is not all that easy, chiefly because of the second factor — or absence of it. There seems always to be that hard wall of resistance to change.

Some ascribe this to general apathy in an increasingly impersonal world, others to waning senses of responsibility. Managers who give the problem deeper thought, however, are struck by the fact that traditional motivational and other approaches work well enough when the climate is receptive; they just fail to produce results when it is not — and that is most of the time in problem-ridden companies. Many personnel and top managers have long suspected this to be the crux of the problem. But no one seemed to have the answer.

Attitude surveys, for instance, do little more than point to the existence of a poor climate, without indicating what must be done to improve it. Other approaches, too, in most cases proved unsatisfactory.

This impasse persisted until the late 1960s, when research into group norms — a theory developed by the American organizational psychologist Dr. Saul Pilnick — began to be applied successfully to actual corporate problems. Simply put, group norms are man's attempt at resolving a potentially explosive conflict of interests. At stake are two universal, related phenomena; on one hand, our eternal quest for the company and recognition of our peers, those people we like to identify with, and on the other, the natural tendency toward exclusivity that established groups display. The solution: A "price" is set for admission and recognition, in the form of certain values and modes of behavior to be respected by group members at all times. These rules are formalized only rarely, when the group itself is or becomes formal, for example, in the by-laws of a club. More often, they are established informally, by group leaders or by tradition, and obeyed tacitly.

Norms are as varied and plentiful as there are groups. They come in three grades — positive, negative, neutral — as viewed from the standpoint of the group's ultimate aims — that is, they can support, obstruct, or have no effect on those aims. And members switch from one group's norms to another's with ease. For example, a soldier will casually use obscene language (his fellow-conscripts' norm) in the barracks, but when attending a meeting of his parent-teacher association, will put on his best behavior quite effortlessly.

THE SPECIAL NORMS OF A CORPORATE CLIMATE

How and why does all this relate to companies and their resistance-to-change problem? Systematic study of the phenomenon has verified the existence of a direct correlation between group norms and corporate profitability. Here are the elements behind this correlation:

- Man seeks to belong to peer groups wherever he congregates, including corporate surroundings. (The contrary would be surprising, since man spends about a third of his waking hours in this environment.)
- The tendency toward exclusivity exists even in open-ended situations, such as corporate ones, where people come and go. In fact, it does so there with a twist,

because the formation of groups is influenced by the fact that fellow-workers have been thrown together from the start in unnatural mixes. At a large cocktail party, say, groups will drift together and apart without constraint, but in a company, people with different backgrounds and views are forced to work together and form groups. The bigger the company and the wider the range in social (and other) attributes of individuals, the better the chances are that there will be numerous groups with tight-knit and defensive norms.

- When both formal and informal norms coexist, as they do in companies, the informal norms transcend the formal. This leads to what has been called "shadow organization," in which the apparent management structure is actually superseded in importance by the mesh of group-norm dictates.
- Individuals will go to extreme lengths to live up to their peers' expectations, even doing things that in other circumstances they recognize as going counter to their *own* best interests. They can persevere in this behavior, however, with the easy rationalization that "Everybody around here does it."
- Norms-imposed habits are lasting. Even when the original members of a group have disappeared and/or when the norms themselves have lost their original purpose, there will be strong norm remnants, unthinkingly respected by new members.
- Negative norms cannot be changed unless the norm-follower is made aware of their existence, because most — if not all — people respect and go along with norms quite unconsciously.

All these powerful forces can, and do, obstruct managers' best efforts to change given situations. Here is a simple illustration:

Most managers have heard at least once an employee righteously protest that the reason he failed to do something was that "It's not my department!'' Almost always, that employee is obeying a norm — unthinkingly, without bothering to question the norm's validity. This norm may originally have come about because some employee realized that there was no particular reward — if not downright criticism — for carrying out other departments' activities. He recounted the incident to his fellow-workers — his peer-group from 9 to 5 — and his conclusion may have been something to the effect that "there's no use breaking your back for *this* company. Just do what you're told and draw your salary." A new norm was born there and then, if his group agreed with the conclusion.

And, as we have pointed out, the norm will have a long life. This explains, for instance, why promising newcomers often turn out the same sort of performance as less-than-satisfactory department colleagues within a few weeks of their arrival. They've put membership in the group above management-approved performance. And the most frustrating aspect for a manager is that, however convincingly he talks to an employee, tries to make him see the light and mend his ways, and however much the employee seems to agree, there will be no change in his attitude, because the power of the group norms is stronger than that of any pep talk by his superior.

Still, this is not to say that there is no hope. Students of normative analysis have had successes — and lasting ones with this change-oriented technique. Here are some examples:

- Quality defects in a manufacturing company were reduced by 55 percent.
- The management committee of an international corporation found its decisions

being made twice as fast (and just as accurately), with a tangible improvement in participant commitment.
- Product breakage and pilferage in a retail chain was cut by 70 percent.
- Average productivity of sales calls in a food service company was boosted by 60 percent.
- A medium-size airline eradicated what it called the "bored ticket-puncher" mentality of its check-in hostesses.
- Absenteeism in a manufacturing plant was halved, and turnover considerably reduced.

Less easily measured than these, mostly profit-focused improvements, but of paramount importance nevertheless, are the gains in effectiveness, opportunity-catching mobility, and morale that the companies experienced by adopting normative system programs.

NORMATIVE ANALYSIS: IDENTIFYING THE NORMS

Bringing about change entails following three steps:

- Detecting norms and getting their followers to recognize their existence and influence.
- Scientifically measuring the norms and establishing the company's normative profile.
- Bringing about normative change.

To find out what norms exist within an organization, the investigators observe behavior patterns. This may or may not be combined with preliminary interviews; most people will tell of their behavior patterns if given a chance (though they are more likely to reveal them if an indirect approach is adopted, for example, if they are asked what other people do in certain circumstances).

From the start, identification of norms gives a strong push toward freeing members from behavior patterns that have until then been by and large beyond their control. People who have tacitly agreed to go along with negative norms will usually find, when these are brought to light, that they never wanted to behave according to them in the first place. And identifying the norm for them (or, better still, letting them identify it themselves) will also have the effect of suggesting alternative modes of behavior.

NORMATIVE ANALYSIS: THE NORMATIVE PROFILE

The formal identification of norms is followed by a process of charting them in order to arrive at the normative profile of the group under consideration. Corporate norms fall within one or another of ten norm clusters: (1) organizational pride; (2) performance; (3) profitability/cost effectiveness; (4) teamwork/communication; (5) planning; (6) supervision; (7) training and development; (8) innovation/change; (9) customer relations; and (10) honesty and security.

All norms have an ideal excellence point. The difference between that and their actual score on the profile is the normative gap (see Figure 1). Usually, a company will have a zig-zag profile, with certain norms more accentuated than others. The idea then, is to improve the mediocre norms, and keep the better-performing ones alive and healthy.

NORMATIVE ANALYSIS: THE CHANGE PROCESS

To perform this amelioration, we have worked out a systematic change process.

Flexible enough to authorize short-cuts in times of urgency, yet rigid enough that its users will not unwittingly skip one or more important phases, this system involves eight interrelated steps:

- Creating understanding and appreciation of the significance of norms, how they influence organizational effectiveness, and how they contribute to both the creation and the solution of key organizational problems. Group members are taught to think in normative terms and to identify and state norms. The process starts at the top of the company and permeates downward as each organizational level becomes involved in change.

- Establishing positive norm goals through cooperative action. A group can establish acceptable norm goals just as it would establish functional goals.

- Determining the excellence point of norms for the company concerned, and therefore the improvement distance to be covered.

- Establishing normative change priorities. The size of the normative gap is only one factor. More important is the relationship of the norm area to the effectiveness and profitability (or other problems) of the organization. This leads to weighting — and giving more urgent attention to — those norm clusters that have more direct impact than others on the given problem, even though the gap may be narrower than average.

- Developing systematic change strategies by examining and modifying ten specific (and crucial) areas, among which are management commitment to change; information, communication and feedback on and about results; recognition and reward of consistent employee behavior; and recruitment and selection of new employees. Inclusion of the last recognizes the fact that newcomers can introduce new negative norms, just as they can be trained to conform to positive norms.

- Implementing the change strategy. Here,

the essential point is to begin at the top of the organization and move downward, with the assurance of top management commitment, support, and modeling behavior.

- Providing follow-through and maintenance on a continuous basis. The emphasis here is on assigning responsibilities for change programs (often best accomplished by setting up a task force or change committee).
- Providing for continuous evaluation of the effectiveness of change strategies, and standing ready to modify plans, by reviewing change strategies, if and when they fall short of expectations.

One of the major built-in advantages of the normative change process is that it does not hurt anyone's feelings — no one is singled out. The existence of a negative norm, explained in terms of the norm concept, is freely admitted. The impersonal "we" of the group is substituted for the accusatory "you" and defensive "I." Moreover, since norm fol-

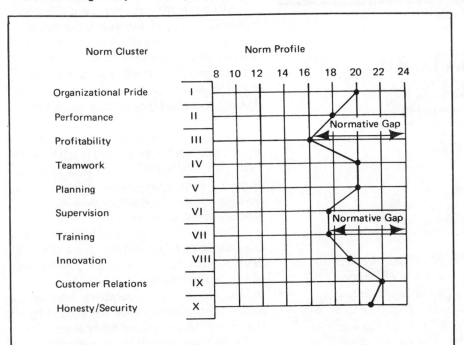

This (real) company's normative profile is characterized by a not unusual number of inconsistencies. Thus, a high level of organizational pride and good customer relations are more than offset by employees' lack of concern for profitability. What actually happened was that employees liked to work for this customer-oriented company, but placed customer desires so much in the forefront of their working priorities that they were eating into profits at a rate which stunned them when they discovered the underlying normative mechanism. The other gap relates to the low level of supervision and training, which left employees free to form close-knit, supervision-resenting groups, a common enough vicious circle.

FIGURE 1

lowers participate fully in the change process, bringing to light the negative effects of their own behavior and suggesting alternatives, the new course of action is enforced by the ex-offenders themselves — just as the old, negative norm was enforced by the group. Repeating the change process as often as negative norms are observed results in weaving a new norm fabric for the organization. Into it will go norms emphasizing teamwork, commonness of purpose, individual effort and achievement — norms will become part and parcel of the corporate makeup.

THE NATURE OF HIGHLY EFFECTIVE GROUPS

Rensis Likert

The form of organization which will make the greatest use of human capacity consists of highly effective work groups linked together in an overlapping pattern by other similarly effective groups. The highly effective work group is, consequently, an important component of the newer theory of management. It will be important to understand both its nature and its performance characteristics. We shall examine these, but first a few words about groups in general.

Although we have stressed the great potential power of the group for building effective organizations, it is important to emphasize that this does *not* say that all groups and all committees are highly effective or are committed to desirable goals. Groups as groups can vary from poor to excellent. They can have desirable values and goals, or their objectives can be most destructive. They can accomplish much that is good, or they can do great harm. There is nothing *implicitly* good or bad, weak or strong, about a group.

The nature of the group determines the character of its impact upon the development of its members. The values of the group, the stability of these values, the group atmosphere, and the nature of the conformity demanded by the group determine whether a group is likely to have a positive or negative impact upon the growth and behavior of its members. If the values of the group are seen by the society as having merit, if the group is stable in its adherence to these values, and if the atmosphere of the group is warm, supportive, and full of understanding, the group's influence on the development of its members will be positive. A hostile atmosphere and socially undesirable or unstable values produce a negative impact upon the members' growth and behavior.

Loyalty to a group produces presures toward conformity. A group may demand conformity to the idea of supporting, encouraging, and giving recognition for individual creativity, or it may value rigidity of behavior, with seriously narrowing and dwarfing consequences. This latter kind of pressure for comformity keeps the members from growing and robs the group of original ideas. Many writers have pointed to these deleterious effects of conformity. They often overlook the capacity of groups to stimulate individual creativeness by placing a high value on imaginative and original contributions by their members. As Pelz's findings . . . demonstrate, groups can contribute significantly to creativity by providing the stimulation of diverse points of view within a supportive atmosphere which encourages each individual member to pursue new and unorthodox concepts.

Some business executives are highly critical of groups — or committees — and the inability of committees to accomplish a great deal. Their criticisms are often well warranted. In many instances, committees are wasteful of time and unable to reach decisions. Sometimes the decisions, when reached, are mediocre. Moreover, some members of management at various hierarchical levels use committees as escape mechanisms — as a way to avoid the responsibility for a decision.

The surprising thing about committees is not that many or most are ineffective, but that they accomplish as much as they do when, relatively speaking, we know so little about how to use them. There has been a lack of systematic study of ways to make committees effective. Far more is known about time-and-motion study, cost accounting and similar aspects of management than is known about groups and group processes. Moreover, in spite of the demonstrated potentiality of groups, far less research is being devoted to learning the role of groups and group processes and how to make the most effective use of them in an organization than to most management practices. We know appreciably less about how to make groups and committees effective than we know about most matters of managing.

We do know that groups can be powerful. The newer theory takes this into account and tries to make constructive use of the group's potential strength for developing and mobilizing human resources.

The use of the term "group" may give the impression that groups have the capacity to behave in ways other than through the behavior of their members. Thus, such expressions appear as the "group's goals," "the group decides," or the "group motivates." In many instances, these expressions are used to avoid endless repetition of the words, "the members of the group." In other instances, something more is meant. Thus, in speaking of "group values," the intent is to refer to those values which have been established by the group through a group-decision process involving consensus. Once a decision has been reached by consensus, there are strong motivational forces, developed within each individual as a re-

sult of his membership in the group and
his relationship to the other members,
to be guided by that decision. In this
sense, the group has goals and values
and makes decisions. It has properties
which may not be present, as such, in
any one individual. A group may be
divided in opinion, for example, although this may not be true of any one
member. Dorwin Cartwright puts it this
way: "The relation between the individual members and the group is analo-
gous to the distinction made in mathematics between the properties of a set of
elements and the properties of the elements within a set. Every set is composed of elements, but sets have properties which are not identical with the
properties of the elements of the set."

THE HIGHLY EFFECTIVE WORK GROUP

Much of the discussion of groups . . .
will be in terms of an ideal organizational model which the work groups in
an organization can approach as they
develop skill in group processes. This
model group, of course, is always part of
a large organization. The description of
its nature and performance characteristics is based on evidence from a variety of sources. Particularly important
are the observational and experimental
studies of small groups such as those
conducted by the Research Center for
Group Dynamics (Cartwright & Zander,
1960; Hare et al., 1955; Institute for
Social Research, 1956; Institute for
Social Research, 1960; Thibaut & Kelly,
1959). Extensive use is made of data
from studies of large-scale organizations. . . . Another important source is
the material from the National Training

Laboratories (Foundation for Research
on Human Behavior, 1960d; National
Training Laboratories, 1953; National
Training Laboratories, 1960; Stock &
Thelen, 1958). The NTL has focused on
training in sensitivity to the reactions of
others and in skills to perform the
leadership and membership roles in
groups.

In addition to drawing upon the
above sources, the description of the
ideal model is derived from theory.
Some of the statements about the model
for which there is little or limited experimental or observational data have been
derived directly from the basic drive to
achieve and maintain a sense of importance and personal worth. At several
points . . . the author has gone appreciably beyond available specific research
findings. The author feels, however, that
the generalizations which are emerging
based on research in organizations and
on small groups, youth, and family life,
personality development, consumer behavior, human motivation, and related
fields lend strong support to the general
theory and the derivations contained in
this book.

It has been necessary to go beyond
the data in order to spell out at this
time in some detail the general pattern
of the more complex but more effective
form of organization being created by
the higher-producing managers. The
author hopes that the theory and model
proposed will stimulate a substantial
increase in basic and developmental research and that they will be tested and
sharpened by that research.

The body of knowledge about small
groups, while sufficiently large to make
possible this description of the ideal
model, is still relatively limited. Without

question, as the importance of the work group as the basic building block of organizations becomes recognized, there will be a great increase in the research on groups and our knowledge about them. The over-all pattern of the model described here will be improved and clarified by such research. Our understanding of how to develop and use groups effectively will also be greatly advanced.

The following description of the ideal model defines what we mean by *a highly effective group*. The definition involves reference to several different variables. Each of them can be thought of as a continuum, i.e., as a characteristic which can vary from low to high, from unfavorable to favorable. For example, a group can vary from one in which there is hostility among the members to one in which the attitudes are warm and friendly. The ideal model is at the favorable end of each variable.

THE NATURE OF HIGHLY EFFECTIVE WORK GROUPS

The highly effective group, as we shall define it, is always conceived as being a part of a larger organization. A substantial proportion of persons in a company are members of more than one work group, especially when both line and staff are considered. As a consequence, in such groups there are always linking functions to be performed and relationships to other groups to be maintained. Our highly effective group is not an isolated entity.

All the persons in a company also belong to groups and organizations outside of the company. For most persons, membership in several groups both within and outside the company is the rule rather than the exception. This means, of course, that no single group, even the highly effective work group, dominates the life of any member. Each member of the organization feels pressures from memberships in several different groups and is not influenced solely by loyalty to any one group.

Since the different groups to which a person belongs are apt to have somewhat different and often inconsistent goals and values, corresponding conflicts and pressures are created within him. To minimize these conflicts and tensions, the individual seeks to influence the values and goals of each of the different groups to which he belongs and which are important to him so as to minimize the inconsistencies and conflicts in values and goals. In striving for this reconciliation, he is likely to press for the acceptance of those values most important to him.

The properties and performance characteristics of the ideal highly effective group are as follows:

1. The members are skilled in all the various leadership and membership roles and functions required for interaction between leaders and members and between members and other members.

2. The group has been in existence sufficiently long to have developed a well-established, relaxed working relationship among all its members.

3. The members of the group are attracted to it and are loyal to its members, including the leader.

4. The members and leaders have a high degree of confidence and trust in each other.

5. The values and goals of the group

are a satisfactory integration and expression of the relevant values and needs of its members. They have helped shape these values and goals and are satisfied with them.

6. In so far as members of the group are performing linking functions, they endeavor to have the values and goals of the groups which they link in harmony, one with the other.

7. The more important a value seems to the group, the greater the likelihood that the individual member will accept it.

8. The members of the group are highly motivated to abide by the major values and to achieve the important goals of the group. Each member will do all that he reasonably can — and at times all in his power — to help the group achieve its central objectives. He expects every other member to do the same. This high motivation springs, in part, from the basic motive to achieve and maintain a sense of personal worth and importance. Being valued by a group whose values he shares, and deriving a sense of significance and importance from this relationship, leads each member to do his best. He is eager not to let the other members down. He strives hard to do what he believes is expected of him.

9. All the interaction, problem-solving, decision-making activities of the group occur in a supportive atmosphere. Suggestions, comments, ideas, information, criticisms are all offered with a helpful orientation. Similarly, these contributions are received in the same spirit. Respect is shown for the point of view of others both in the way contributions are made and in the way they are received.

There are real and important differences of opinion, but the focus is on arriving at sound solutions and not on exacerbating and aggravating the conflict. Ego forces deriving from the desire to achieve and maintain a sense of personal worth and importance are channeled into constructive efforts. Care is taken not to let these ego forces disrupt important group tasks, such as problem-solving. Thus, for example, a statement of the problem, a condition which any solution must meet, a suggested solution, or an item of relevant fact are all treated as from the group as a whole. Care is taken so that one statement of the problem is not John's and another Bill's. A suggested solution is not referred to as Tom's and another as Dick's. All the material contributed is treated as *ours:* "One of our proposed solutions is *A,* another is *B.*" In all situations involving actual or potential differences or conflict among the members of the group, procedures are used to separate the ego of each member from his contribution. In this way, ego forces do not stimulate conflict between members. Instead, they are channeled into supporting the activities and efforts of the group.

The group atmosphere is sufficiently supportive for the members to be able to accept readily any criticism which is offered and to make the most constructive use of it. The criticisms may deal with any relevant topic such as operational problems, decisions, supervisory problems, interpersonal relationships, or group processes, but whatever their content, the member feels sufficiently secure in the supportive atmosphere of the group to be able to accept, test, examine, and benefit from the criticism offered. Also, he is able to be frank and candid, irrespective of the content of the discussion: technical, managerial, factual, cognitive, or emotional. The supportive atmosphere of the group, with the feeling of security it provides, contributes to a cooperative relationship between the members. And this cooperation itself contributes to and reinforces the supportive atmosphere.

10. The superior of each work group exerts a major influence in establishing the tone and atmosphere of that work group by his leadership principles and practices. In the highly effective group, consequently, the leader adheres to those principles of leadership which create a supportive atmosphere in the group and a cooperative rather than a competitive relationship among the members. For example, he shares information fully with the group and creates an atmosphere where the members are stimulated to behave similarly.

11. The group is eager to help each member develop to his full potential. It sees, for example, that relevant technical knowledge and training in interpersonal and group skills are made available to each member.

12. Each member accepts willingly and without resentment the goals and expectations that he and his group establish for themselves. The anxieties, fears, and emotional stresses produced by direct pressure for high performance from a boss in a hierarchical situation is not present. Groups seem capable of setting high performance goals for the group as a whole and for each member. These goals are high enough to stimulate each member to do his best, but not so high as to create anxieties or fear of failure. In an effective group, each per-

son can exert sufficient influence on the decisions of the group to prevent the group from setting unattainable goals for any member while setting high goals for all. The goals are adapted to the member's capacity to perform.

13. The leader and the members believe that each group member can accomplish "the impossible." These expectations stretch each member to the maximum and accelerate his growth. When necessary, the group tempers the expectation level so that the member is not broken by a feeling of failure or rejection.

14. When necessary or advisable, other members of the group will give a member the help he needs to accomplish successfully the goals set for him. Mutual help is a characteristic of highly effective groups.

15. The supportive atmosphere of the highly effective group stimulates creativity. The group does not demand narrow conformity as do the work groups under authoritarian leaders. No one has to "yes the boss," nor is he rewarded for such an attempt. The group attaches high value to new, creative approaches and solutions to its problems and to the problems of the organization of which it is a part. The motivation to be creative is high when one's work group prizes creativity.

16. The group knows the value of "constructive" conformity and knows when to use it and for what purposes. Although it does not permit conformity to affect adversely the creative efforts of its members, it does expect conformity on mechanical and administrative matters to save the time of members and to facilitate the group's activities. The group agrees, for

example, on administrative forms and procedures, and once they have been established, it expects its members to abide by them until there is good reason to change them.

17. There is strong motivation on the part of each member to communicate fully and frankly to the group all the information which is relevant and of value to the group's activity. This stems directly from the member's desire to be valued by the group and to get the job done. The more important to the group a member feels an item of information to be, the greater is his motivation to communicate it.

18. There is high motivation in the group to use the communication process so that it best serves the interests and goals of the group. Every item which a member feels is important, but which for some reason is being ignored, will be repeated until it receives the attention that it deserves. Members strive also to avoid communicating unimportant information so as not to waste the group's time.

19. Just as there is high motivation to communicate, there is correspondingly strong motivation to receive communications. Each member is genuinely interested in any information on any relevant matter that any member of the group can provide. This information is welcomed and trusted as being honestly and sincerely given. Members do not look "behind" the information item and attempt to interpret it in ways opposite to its purported intent. This interest of group members in information items and the treatment of such items as valid reinforces the motivation to communicate.

20. In the highly effective group,

there are strong motivations to try to influence other members as well as to be receptive to influence by them. This applies to all the group's activities: technical matters, methods, organizational problems, interpersonal relationships, and group processes.

21. The group processes of the highly effective group enable the members to exert more influence on the leader and to communicate far more information to him, including suggestions as to what needs to be done and how he could do his job better, than is possible in a man-to-man relationship. By "tossing the ball" back and forth among its members, a group can communicate information to the leader which no single person on a man-to-man basis dare do. As a consequence, the boss receives all the information that the group possesses to help him perform his job effectively.

22. The ability of the members of a group to influence each other contributes to the flexibility and adaptability of the group. Ideas, goals, and attitudes do not become frozen if members are able to influence each other continuously.

Although the group is eager to examine any new ideas and methods which will help it do its job better and is willing to be influenced by its members, it is not easily shifted or swayed. Any change is undertaken only after rigorous examination of the evidence. This stability in the group's activities is due to the steadying influence of the common goals and values held by the group members.

23. In the highly effective group, individual members feel secure in making decisions which seem appropriate to

them because the goals and philosophy of operation are clearly understood by each member and provide him with a solid base for his decisions. This unleashes initiative and pushes decisions down while still maintaining a coordinated and directed effort.

24. The leader of a highly effective group is selected carefully. His leadership ability is so evident that he would probably emerge as a leader in any unstructured situation. To increase the likelihood that persons of high leadership competence are selected, the organization is likely to use peer nominations and related methods in selecting group leaders.

An important aspect of the highly effective group is its extensive use of the principle of supportive relationships. An examination of the above material reveals that virtually every statement involves an application of this principle.

LEADERSHIP FUNCTIONS

Several different characteristics of highly effective groups have been briefly examined. The role of the leader in these groups is, as we have suggested, particularly important. Certain leadership functions can be shared with group members; others can be performed only by the designated leader. In an organization, for example, the leader of a unit is the person who has primary responsibility for linking his work group to the rest of the organization. Other members of the group may help perform the linking function by serving as linking pins in overlapping groups other than that provided by the line organization, but the major linking is necessarily

through the line organization. The leader has full responsibility for the group's performance and for seeing that his group meets the demands and expectations placed upon it by the rest of the organization of which it is a part. Other members of the group may share this responsibility at times, but the leader can never avoid full responsibility for the adequate performance of his group.

Although the leader has full responsibility, he does not try to make all the decisions. He develops his group into a unit which, with his participation, makes better decisions than he can make alone. He helps the group develop efficient communication and influence processes which provide it with better information, more technical knowledge, more facts, and more experience for decision-making purposes than the leader alone can marshal.

Through group decision-making each member feels fully identified with each decision and highly motivated to execute it fully. The over-all performance of the group, as a consequence, is even better than the excellent quality of the decisions.

The leader knows that at times decisions must be made rapidly and cannot wait for group processes. He anticipates these emergencies and establishes procedures with his group for handling them so that action can be taken rapidly with group support.

The leader feels primarily responsible for establishing and maintaining at all times a thoroughly supportive atmosphere in the group. He encourages other members to share this responsibility, but never loses sight of the fact that as the leader of a work group which is part of a larger organization his behavior is likely to set the tone.

Although the leader accepts the responsibility associated with his role of leader of a group which is part of a larger organization, he seeks to minimize the influence of his hierarchical position. He is aware that trying to get results by "pulling rank" affects adversely the effectiveness of his group and his relationship to it. Thus, he endeavors to deemphasize status. He does this in a variety of ways that fit his personality and methods of leading, as for example by:

- Listening well and patiently
- Not being impatient with the progress being made by the group, particularly on difficult problems
- Accepting more blame than may be warranted for any failure or mistake
- Giving the group members ample opportunity to express their thoughts without being constrained by the leader pressing his own views
- Being careful never to impose a decision upon the group
- Putting his contributions often in the form of questions or stating them speculatively
- Arranging for others to help perform leadership functions which enhance their status

The leader strengthens the group and group processes by seeing that all problems *which involve the group* are dealt with by the group. He never handles such problems outside of the group nor with individual members of the group. While the leader is careful to see that all matters which involve and affect the whole group are handled by the whole group, he is equally alert not to undertake in a group-meeting agenda items or tasks which do not concern the group. Matters concerning one individual member and only that member are, of course, handled individually. Matters involving only a subgroup are handled by that subgroup. The total group is kept informed, however, of any subgroup action.

The leader fully reflects and effectively represents the views, goals, values, and decisions of his group in those other groups where he is performing the function of linking his group to the rest of the organization. He brings to the group of which he is the leader the views, goals, and decisions of those other groups. In this way, he provides a linkage whereby communication and the exercise of influence can be performed in both directions.

The leader has adequate competence to handle the technical problems faced by his group, or he sees that access to this technical knowledge is fully provided. This may involve bringing in, as needed, technical or resource persons. Or he may arrange to have technical training given to one or more members of his group so that the group can have available the necessary technical know-how when the group discusses a problem and arrives at a decision.

The leader is what might be called "group-centered," in a sense comparable with the "employee-centered" supervisor. . . . He endeavors to build and maintain in his group a keen sense of responsibility for achieving its own goals and meeting its obligations to the larger organization.

The leader helps to provide the group with the stimulation arising from a restless dissatisfaction. He discourages complacency and passive acceptance of the present. He helps the members to become aware of new possibilities, more important values, and more significant goals.

The leader is an important source of enthusiasm for the significance of the mission and goals of the group. He sees that the tasks of the group are important and significant and difficult enough to be challenging.

As an over-all guide to his leadership behavior, the leader understands and uses with sensitivity and skill the principle of supportive relationships.

Many of these leadership functions, such as the linking function, can be performed only by the designated leader. This makes clear the great importance of selecting competent persons for leadership positions.

Roles of Membership and Leadership

In the highly effective group, many functions are performed either by the leader or by the members, depending upon the situation or the requirements of the moment. The leader and members, as part of their roles in the group, establish and maintain an atmosphere and relationships which enable the communication, influence, decision-making, and similar processes of the group to be performed effectively. This means not only creating positive conditions, such as a supportive atmosphere, but also eliminating any negative or blocking factors. Thus, for example, groups sometimes have to deal with members who are insensitive, who are hostile, who talk too much, or who otherwise behave in ways adversely affecting the capacity of the group to function. In handling such a problem, the group makes the member aware of his deficiency, but does this in a sensitive and considerate manner and

in a way to assist the member to function more effectively in the group. The members of most ordinary groups stop listening to a member who expresses himself in a fuzzy or confused manner. In a highly effective group, the members feed back their reaction to the person involved with suggestions and assistance on how to make his contribution clear, important, and of the kind to which all will want to listen. Friendly assistance and coaching can help a member overcome excessive talking or help him to learn to think and express himself more clearly.

Benne and Sheats (1948) have prepared a description of the different roles played in well-functioning groups. These roles may at times be performed by one or more group members, at others times by the leader. The list, while prepared on the basis of roles in discussion and problem-solving groups, is useful in considering the functions to be performed in any work group which is part of a larger organization.

The following material is taken from the Benne and Sheats article (pp. 42–45) with slight modifications. Group roles are classified into two broad categories:

1. *Group task roles.* These roles are related to the task which the group is deciding to undertake or has undertaken. They are directly concerned with the group effort in the selection and definition of a common problem and in the solution of that problem.
2. *Group building and maintenance roles.* These roles concern the functioning of the group as a group. They deal with the group's efforts to strengthen, regulate, and perpetuate the group as a group.

Group Task Roles

The following analysis assumes that the task of the group is to select, define, and solve common problems. The roles are identified in relation to functions of facilitation and coordination of group problem-solving activities. Each member may, of course, enact more than one role in any given unit of participation and a wide range of roles in successive participations. Any or all of these roles may be performed, at times, by the group "leader" as well as by various members.

A. *Initiating-contributing:* suggesting or proposing to the group new ideas or a changed way of regarding the group problem or goal. The novelty proposed may take the form of suggestions of a new group goal or a new definition of the problem. It may take the form of a suggested solution or some way of handling a difficulty that the group has encountered. Or it may take the form of a proposed new procedure for the group, a new way of organizing the group for the task ahead.

B. *Information seeking:* asking for clarification of suggestions made in terms of their factual adequacy, for authoritative information and facts pertinent to the problems being discussed.

C. *Opinion seeking:* seeking information not primarily on the facts of the case, but for a clarification of the values pertinent to what the group is undertaking or of values involved in a suggestion made or in alternative suggestions.

D. *Information giving:* offering facts or generalizations which are "authoritative" or involve presenting an experience pertinent to the group problem.

E. *Opinion giving:* stating beliefs or opinions pertinent to a suggestion made or to alternative suggestions. The emphasis is on the proposal of what should become the group's view of pertinent values, not primarily upon relevant facts or information.

F. *Elaborating:* spelling out suggestions in terms of examples or developed meanings, offering a rationale for suggestions previously made, and trying to deduce how an idea or suggestion would work out if adopted by the group.

G. *Coordinating:* showing or clarifying the relationships among various ideas and suggestions, trying to pull ideas and suggestions together or trying to coordinate the activities of various members or sub-groups.

H. *Orienting:* defining the position of the group with respect to its goals by summarizing what has occurred, departures from agreed upon directions or goals are pointed to, or questions are raised about the direction the group discussion is taking.

I. *Evaluating:* subjecting the accomplishment of the group to some standard or set of standards of group functioning in the context of the group task. Thus, it may involve evaluating or questioning the "practicality," the "logic," or the "procedure" of a suggestion or of some unit of group discussion.

J. *Energizing:* prodding the group to action or decision, attempting to stimulate or arouse the group to "greater" activity or to activity of a "higher quality."

K. *Assisting on procedure:* expediting group movement by doing things for the group — performing routine tasks, e.g., distributing materials, or manipulating objects for the group, e.g., rearranging the seating or running the recording machine, etc.

L. *Recording:* writing down suggestions, making a record of group decisions, or writing down the product of discussion. The recorder role is the "group memory."

Group Building and Maintenance Roles

Here the analysis of member-functions is oriented to those activities which build group loyalty and increase the motivation and capacity of the group for candid and effective interaction and problem-solving. One or more members or the leader may perform each of these roles.

A. *Encouraging:* praising, showing interest in, agreeing with, and accepting the contributions of others; indicating warmth and solidarity in one's attitudes toward other group members, listening attentively and seriously to the contributions of group members, giving these contributions full and adequate consideration even though one may not fully agree with them; conveying to the others a feeling that — "that which you are about to say is of importance to me."

B. *Harmonizing:* mediating the differences between other members, attempting to reconcile disagreements, relieving tension in conflict situations through jesting or pouring oil on troubled waters, etc.

C. *Compromising:* operating from within a conflict in which one's ideas or position is involved. In this role one may offer a compromise by yielding status, admitting error, by disciplining oneself to maintain group harmony, or by "coming half-way" in moving along with the group.

D. *Gate-keeping and expediting:* attempting to keep communication channels open by encouraging or facilitating the participation of others or by proposing regulation of the flow of communication.

E. *Setting standards or ideals:* expressing standards for the group or applying standards in evaluating the quality of group processes.

F. *Observing:* keeping records of various aspects of group process and feeding such data with proposed interpretations into the group's evaluation of its own procedures. The contribution of the person performing this role is usually best received or most fittingly received by the group when this particular role has been performed by this person at the request of the group and when the report to the group avoids expressing value judgments, approval, or disapproval.

G. *Following:* going along with the group, more or less passively accepting the ideas of others, serving as an audience in group discussion and decision.

The *group task roles* all deal with the intellectual aspects of the group's work. These roles are performed by members of the group during the problem-solving process, which usually involves such steps as:

1. Defining the problem
2. Listing the conditions or criteria which any satisfactory solution to the problem should meet
3. Listing possible alternative solutions
4. Obtaining the facts which bear on each possible solution
5. Evaluating the suggested solutions in terms of the conditions which a satisfactory solution should meet
6. Eliminating undesirable solutions and selecting the most desirable solution

The *group building and maintenance roles* are, as the label suggests, concerned with the emotional life of the group. These roles deal with the group's attractiveness to its members, its warmth and supportiveness, its motivation and capacity to handle intellectual problems without bias and emotion, and its capacity to function as a "mature" group.

The membership roles proposed by Benne and Sheats, while they are not definitive or complete, nevertheless point to the many complex functions performed in groups and dealt with by leader and members. The members of a highly effective group handle these roles with sensitivity and skill, and they see that the emotional life of the group contributes to the performance of the group's tasks rather than interfering with them.[1]

[1]Although the Benne and Sheats list does not define each category unambiguously, it is useful in helping a group analyze and improve its processes. Another list has been prepared by Bales (1950) which has relatively precise definitions. The Bales list will be of interest to those who wish to do research on group processes or who wish to observe and analyze them systematically.

The highly effective group does not hesitate, for example, to look at and deal with friction between its members. By openly putting such problems on the table and sincerely examining them, they can be dealt with constructively. An effective group does not have values which frown upon criticism or which prevent bringing friction between members into the open. As a consequence, it does not put the lid on these emotional pressures, causing them to simmer below the surface and be a constant source of disruption to the performance of group tasks. The intellectual functions of any group can be performed without bias and disruption only when the internal emotional tensions and conflicts have been removed from the life of the group. Differences in ideas are stimulating and contribute to creativity, but emotional conflict immobilizes a group.

Group building and maintenance functions and group task functions are interdependent processes. In order to tackle difficult problems, to solve them creatively, and to achieve high performance, a group must be at a high level of group maintenance. Success in task processes, fortunately, also contributes to the maintenance of the group and to its emotional life, including its attraction to members and its supportive atmosphere.

In the midst of struggling with a very difficult task, a group occasionally may be faced with group maintenance problems. At such times, it may be necessary for the group to stop its intellectual activity and in one way or another to look at and deal with the disruptive emotional stresses. After this has been done, the group can then go forward with greater unity and will be more likely to solve its group task constructively.

The leader and the members in the highly effective group know that the building and maintenance of the group as well as the carrying out of tasks need to be done well. They are highly skilled in performing each of the different membership and leadership roles required. Each member feels responsible for assuming whatever role is necessary to keep the group operating in an efficient manner. In performing these required roles, the member may carry them out by himself or in cooperation with other group members. Each exercises initiative as called for by the situation. The group has a high capacity to mobilize fully all the skills and abilities of its members and focus these resources efficiently on the jobs to be done.

The larger the work group, the greater the difficulty in building it into a highly effective group. Seashore (1954) found that group cohesiveness, i.e., attraction of the members to the group, decreased steadily as work groups increased in size. This finding is supported also by other data (Indik, 1961; Revans, 1957).

To facilitate building work groups to high levels of effectiveness it will be desirable, consequently, to keep the groups as small as possible. This requirement, however, must be balanced against other demands on the organization, such as keeping the number of organizational levels to a minimum. This suggests the desirability of running tests and computing the relative efficiencies and cost of different-sized work groups. It is probable also that the optimum size for a group will vary with the kind of work the group is doing.

The highly effective group . . ., it will be recalled, is an "ideal model." It may sound completely unattainable. This does not appear to be the case. There is impressive evidence supporting the view that this ideal can be approximated, if not fully reached, in actual operations in any organization. This evidence is provided by the highest-producing managers and supervisors in American history and government. If the measurements of their work groups and the reports of their work-group members are at all accurate, some of these managers have built and are operating work groups strikingly similar to our ideal model.

We started by observing that groups can have constructive or destructive goals and can achieve these goals fully or partially, that there is nothing inherently good or bad about groups. If we reflect on the nature and functional characteristics of the highly effective group, however, some qualification of our initial comments may be warranted. In the highly effective group, the members can and do exercise substantial amounts of influence on the group's values and goals. As a consequence, these goals reflect the long-range as well as the short-range needs, desires, and values of its members. If we assume that the long-range desires and values will reflect, on the average, some of the more important long-range values and goals of the total society, we can draw some inferences about the highly effective group. These groups will, in terms of probability, reflect the constructive values and goals of their society. They are likely to be strong groups seeking "good" goals.

EX-POLICEMAN TELLS WHAT MAKES A "BAD COP"

by a former Denver policeman as told to Mort Stern, Denver Post

CASE 1

DENVER, Nov. 4. (A.P.) — What makes a policeman go sour? I can tell you. I was a Denver policeman until not so long ago. Then I quit so I could hold my head up.

Don't get me wrong. I'm not trying to shift the burden of responsibility for the burglaries, break-ins, safe jobs and that sort of thing. That is bad, very bad. But I will leave it to the big shots and the newspapers and the courts to say and do what needs to be said and done about that.

My concern is about the individual officer, the ordinary, hard-working, basically honest but awfully hard-pressed guy who is really suffering now.

Young fellows don't put on those blue uniforms to be crooks. There are a lot of reasons, but for most of the guys it adds up to the fact they thought it was an honorable, decent way of making a living.

Somewhere along the line a guy's disillusioned. Along the way the pressures mount up. Somewhere along the way he may decide to quit fighting them and make the conscious decisions to try to "beat" society instead.

But long before he gets to that point, almost as soon as he dons the uniform in fact, he is taking the first little steps down the road that does, for some, eventually lead to the penitentiary.

Let me back up a little. I want to talk about how you get to be a policeman, because this is where the trouble really starts.

Almost any able-bodied man can become a policeman in Denver. If he is within the age brackets, if he is a high-school graduate, if he has no criminal record, he is a cinch.

There isn't much to getting through the screening, and some bad ones do get through. There are the usual examinations and questionnaires. Then there is the interview. A few command officers ask questions. There is a representative of civil service and a psychiatrist present.

They ask the predictable questions and just about everybody gives the predictable answers: "Why do you want to become a policeman?" "I've always wanted to be a policeman. I want to help people." Five or ten minutes and it is over.

Five or ten minutes to spot the sadist, the psychopath — or the guy with an eye for an easy buck. I guess they weed some out. Some others they get at the Police Academy. But some get through.

Along with those few bad ones,

there are more good ones, and a lot of average, ordinary human beings who have this in common: They want to be policemen.

The job has (or had) some glamour for the young man who likes authority, who finds appeal in making a career of public service, who is extroverted or aggressive.

Before you knock those qualities, remember two things: First, they are the same qualities we admire in a business executive. Second, if it weren't for men with these qualities, you wouldn't have any police protection.

The Police Academy is point No. 2 in my bill of particulars. It is a fine thing, in a way. You meet the cream of the Police Department. Your expectations soar. You know you are going to make the grade and be a good officer. But how well are you really prepared?

There are six weeks at the academy — four weeks in my time. Six hectic weeks in which to learn all about the criminal laws you have sworn to enforce, to assimilate the rules of evidence, methods of arbitration, use of fire-arms, mob and riot control, first aid (including, if you please, some basic obstetrics), public relations and so on.

There is an intangible something else that is not on the formal agenda. You begin to learn that this is a fraternity into which you are not automatically accepted by your fellows. You have to earn your way in; you have to establish that you are "all right."

And even this early there is a slight sour note. You knew, of course, that you had to provide your own uniforms, your own hat, shoes, shirts, pistol and bullets out of your $393 a month.

You knew the city would generously

provide you with the cloth for two pair of trousers and a uniform blouse.

What you didn't know was that you don't just choose a tailor shop for price and get the job done.

You are sent to a place by the Police Department to get the tailoring done. You pay the price even though the work may be ill-fitting. It seems a little odd to you that it is always the same establishment. But it is a small point and you have other things on your mind.

So the rookie, full of pride and high spirit, his head full of partly learned information, is turned over to a more experienced man for breaking in. He is on "probation" for six months.

The rookie knows he is being watched by all the older hands around him. He is eager to be accepted. He accepts advice gratefully.

Then he gets little signs that he has been making a good impression. It may happen like this: The older man stops at a bar, comes out with some packages of cigarets. He does this several times. He explains that this is part of the job, getting cigarets free from proprietors to resell, and that as a part of the rookie's training it is his turn to "make the butts."

So he goes into a skid-road bar and stands uncomfortably at the end waiting for the bartender to acknowledge his presence and disdainfully toss him two packages of butts.

The feeling of pride slips away and a hint of shame takes hold. But he tells himself this is unusual, that he will say nothing that will upset his probation standing. In six months, after he gets his commission, he will be the upright officer he meant to be.

One thing leads to another for the

rookies. After six months they have been conditioned to accept free meals, a few packages of cigarettes, turkeys at Thanksgiving and liquor at Christmas from the respectable people in their district.

The rule book forbids all this. But it isn't enforced. It is winked at at all levels.

So the rookies say to themselves that this is O.K., that this is a far cry from stealing and they still can be good policemen. Besides, they are becoming accepted as "good guys" by their fellow officers.

This becomes more and more important as the young policeman begins to sense a hostility toward him in the community. This is fostered to a degree by some of the saltier old hands in the department. But the public plays its part.

Americans are funny. They have a resentment for authority. And the policeman is authority in person. The respectable person may soon forget that a policeman found his lost youngster in the park, but he remembers that a policeman gave him a traffic ticket.

The negative aspect of the job builds up. The majority of the people he comes in contact with during his working hours are thieves, con men, narcotics addicts and out and out nuts.

Off the job his associations narrow. Part of the time when he isn't working, he is sleeping. His waking, off-duty hours are such as to make him not much of a neighbor. And then he wants to spend as much time as he can with his family.

Sometimes, when he tries to mix with his neighbors, he senses a kind of strain. When he is introduced to someone, it is not likely to be, "This is John Jones, my friend," or "my neighbor"; it is more likely to be, "This is John Jones. He's a policeman."

And the other fellow, he takes it up, too. He is likely to tell you that he has always supported pay increases for policemen, that he likes policemen as a whole, but that there are just a few guys in uniform he hates.

No wonder the officer begins to think of himself as a member of the smallest minority group in the community. The idea gradually sinks into him that the only people who understand him, that he can be close to, are his fellow officers.

It is in this kind of atmosphere that you can find the young policeman trying to make the grade in the fraternity. But that is not the whole story.

A policeman lives with tensions, and with fears.

Part of the tensions come from the incredible monotony. He is cooped up with another man, day after day, doing routine things over and over. The excitement that most people think of as the constant occupation of policemen is so infrequent as to come as a relief.

Part of the tensions come from the manifold fears. I don't mean that these men are cowards. This is no place for cowards. But they are human beings. And fears work on all human beings.

Paramount is the physical fear that he will get hurt to the point where he can't go on working, or the fear that he will be killed. The fear for his family.

There is the fear that he will make a wrong decision in a crucial moment, a life-and-death decision. A man has been in a fight. Should he call the paddy wagon or the ambulance? A man aims a pistol at him. Should he try to talk to him or shoot him?

But the biggest fear he has is that he will show fear to some of his fellow officers. This is the reason he will rush heedlessly in on a cornered burglar or armed maniac if a couple of officers are present — something he wouldn't do if he were alone. He is tormented by his fears and he doesn't dare show them. He knows he has to present a cool, calm front to the public.

As a group, policemen have a very high rate of ulcers, heart attacks, suicides and divorces. These things torment him, too. Divorce is a big problem to policemen. A man can't be a policeman for eight hours and then just turn it off and go home and be a loving father and husband — particularly if he has just had somebody die in the back of his police car.

So once again, the pressure is on him to belong, to be accepted and welcomed into the only group that knows what is going on inside him.

If the influences aren't right, he can be hooked.

So he is at the stage where he wants to be one of the guys. And then this kind of thing may happen: One night his car is sent to check in a "Code 26" — a silent burglar alarm.

The officer and his partner go in to investigate. The burglar is gone. They call the proprietor. He comes down to look things, over. And maybe he says, "Boys, this is covered by insurance, so why don't you take a jacket for your wife, or a pair of shoes?" And maybe he does, maybe just because his partner does, and he says to himself, "What the hell, who has been hurt?"

Or maybe the proprietor didn't come down. But after they get back in the car

his partner pulls out four $10 bills and hands him two. "Burglar got careless," says the partner.

The young officer who isn't involved soon learns that this kind of thing goes on. He even may find himself checking on a burglary call, say to a drugstore, and see some officers there eyeing him peculiarly.

Maybe at this point the young officer feels the pressure to belong so strongly that he reaches over and picks up something, cigars perhaps. Then he is "in," and the others can do what they wish.

Mind you, not all officers will do this. Somewhere along the line all of them have to make a decision, and it is at that point where the stuff they are made of shows through. But the past experience of the handouts, the official indifference to them, and the pressures and tensions of the job don't make the decision any easier.

And neither he nor the department has had any advance warning, such as might come from thorough psychiatric screening, as to what his decision will be.

Some men may go this far and no farther. They might rationalize that they have not done anything that isn't really accepted by smart people in society.

This is no doubt where the hard-core guy, the one who is a thief already, steps in. A policeman is a trained observer and he is smart in back-alley psychology. This is especially true of the hard-core guy and he has been watching the young fellows come along.

When he and his cronies in a burglary ring spot a guy who may have what it takes to be one of them, they may approach him and try him out as a lookout. From then on it is just short steps to the actual participation in and planning of crimes.

Bear in mind that by this stage we have left all but a few policemen behind. But all of them figure in the story at one stage or another. And what has happened to a few could happen to others. I suppose that is the main point I am trying to make.

ADDENDUM

The following item appeared in the Tax Report column of the May 2, 1962, issue of *The Wall Street Journal:*

Denver police salaries would be raised out of a $2.7 million yearly hike in revenues from a proposed boost in the city's sales tax to 2% from 1%. The proposal comes before Denver voters June 5. Officers' low pay has been blamed in part for a recent scandal involving the arrest of 57 Denver policemen on burglary charges. A 2% retail sales tax is levied by the state.[1]

JAMISON FURNITURE COMPANY

CASE 2

Let me tell you about a situation I got involved in several years ago and that I still can't get completely out of my mind.

Shortly after I finished college I took a job with the Jamison Furniture Company. I had really never thought of a career in the furniture industry but when I graduated, jobs were pretty hard to get. I'd finished my education on the G.I. Bill and I was quite low on money. Consequently, when the Jamison people made me an offer at a pretty attractive salary for those times, I took it. Formally I was the assistant to Bill Blackwell, the plant manager, but actually I was a jack-of-all-trades who did just about anything that needed to be done. I worked on the books, helped with the production scheduling and shipping, and was responsible for what we vaguely called "personnel relations."

As you may know, the Jamison Furniture Company is located in a small town in Ohio. It manufactures a high-quality line of occasional furniture, dinette pieces, desks, and occasional tables and chairs. When I was with them they employed about 150-160 people and had sales of about $40,000 per week. Finished furniture was sold to a large number of independent furniture stores throughout the country. The company has been quite successful and I'd guess that at the present time their sales are four or five times what they were then.

Most of the people who worked at Jamison were relatively long-time employees. Most of the jobs didn't really require skilled labor and almost anyone with the proper attitude and a reasonable degree of intelligence and physical dexterity could be trained in time to do what had to be done. Nevertheless, as the company did produce a high quality line of furniture, it was important that the employees do their work well, especially in the staining and finishing operations. If a table or desk was improperly finished, for example, it had to be sold as a "second" and the company took a terrific beating on profit.

Well, the particular situation I referred to took place in the department which manufactured and finished occasional tables. The people involved were Bill Blackwell, the plant manager; Stu Thurston, foreman of the department; and Betty and Alice Sawyer, mother and daughter who worked for Stu. Betty, the mother, had worked for Jamison about twelve years before Stu came with the company. Alice Sawyer had worked for Jamison for about two years and had been in Stu's department during that time. Before I go any further, let me tell you that Stu had a reputation for being quite a ladies' man. Whether he was or not I never knew,

but I do know that he did take a lot of good-natured kidding about "liking the girls." The sixteen women who worked for Stu especially liked to kid him a lot about this and often told him that if they didn't need the money so badly they wouldn't take the risk of working for such a "ladies man."

When I went to work for Jamison everything seemed to be fine in Stu Thurston's department. Production was high, everyone was meeting their quotas and the women seemed to be happy. Stu kidded them a lot and they kidded him right back. In retrospect, I'd say at that time that Stu's department was one of the best I had ever seen.

After I'd been with Jamison about four or five months it became obvious that Stu Thurston and Alice Sawyer were getting pretty serious romantically, and about two months later they announced their engagement to the apparent joy of all in the department. I remember particularly well that Stu and Betty Sawyer did an awful lot of kidding about their forthcoming relationship as son-in-law and mother-in-law.

When Stu and Alice got married, everyone chipped in and bought them a nice wedding gift and went to the wedding in a group. I remember one of them saying, "This was the biggest thing that ever happened at the Jamison Furniture Company." It was clear that everyone was excited and enthusiastic about the wedding.

After their honeymoon both Stu and Alice returned to work and things pretty much returned to normal. Stu was his own genial self, kidding all the time and they in return continued to kid him right back. They had a big thing going about his being able to boss his wife and mother-in-law on the job but "Oh, how different it was when he was at home." As I said, things went along swell for a while, but after about four or five months there was some inkling that the newly married couple weren't getting along as well as they might. Six months from the day they were married Stu started divorce proceedings against Alice on the grounds of mental cruelty. Then things really started to happen.

At first, reaction was pretty well mixed concerning this sudden change of events. No one really knew what happened, but some people felt that Stu must have had sufficient reasons for his action, and attempted to keep things going as they had in the "good old days." The rest of them headed by Alice and Betty, wouldn't have anything at all to do with Stu unless they absolutely had to. For example, the day that it became known that Stu had started divorce proceedings they stopped speaking to him unless it was in direct reply to a question or comment that he made. When they did speak they merely answered, "Yes, sir," or "No, sir," as the occasion demanded, and not in a very friendly tone of voice.

As the date for the final divorce decree got closer, Betty Sawyer, in particular, got more and more riled up. She started saying some pretty nasty things about Stu and it wasn't too long before she had all the women so incensed that they weren't speaking to him either. It even got to the point where Betty led a delegation to see Bill Blackwell and demanded that Stu be fired for "things that were going on in the department." They maintained that Stu "just wasn't a good foreman" and should be fired immediately. Bill handled the thing as well

as he could, I guess. He tried to press for specifics, but when it became apparent that they were so emotionally wrought up that they weren't making any sense, he just tried to get them quieted down and out of his office and back to work. I remember his talking to me about it later. He said something like "I sure don't know what to do, but we've got a real one on our hands."

Things got worse. The atmosphere in Stu's department was pretty icy and it wasn't too long before many people weren't making their quotas and rejects were rising at an alarming rate.

Stu Thurston talked with me at length about the situation one day. I can't remember all of our conversation but I do recall his saying that what he did in his personal life was his own affair and that what happened on the job was business. He didn't see any reason for anyone to care about what he did on his own time. I do remember very distinctly how our conversation ended, however. Stu wanted me to fire both Alice and Betty. He said, "I don't care what you do — fire them — no matter what the reason, get rid of them." His face was very flushed and he was quivering as he spoke. There was no doubt in my mind that if he had had any kind of weapon with him at the time, he would have used it on either or both of the women.

Well, as you can see, we had a pretty bad situation on our hands. It got really bad for me personally the next day when Bill Blackwell came back from a visit to Stu's department and shouted at me, "You're in charge of personnel relations. Do whatever you have to do to get that mess cleaned up!"

WHITFIELD
MANUFACTURING COMPANY

INTRODUCTION

The Whitfield Manufacturing Company exercise is a good example of the impact that an informal group can have upon the behavior of an individual. In this production situation, a newly promoted employee very quickly establishes a rate of production considerably above standard. After some time on the new job and some interaction with his co-workers, some problems develop that require the manager's attention.

PROCEDURE

Your instructor will provide you with specific instructions for this exercise. Do not proceed further until you have received these instructions.

The Whitfield Manufacturing Company produces and distributes a line of fishing reels, poles, and miscellaneous fishing supplies, such as artificial baits and lures. The company has been in business for over eighty years and the Whitfield name is respected and accepted by sportsmen as a standard of quality and performance in sporting gear.

In the Machine Shop, gear wheels for fishing reels are manufactured on semi-automatic machines. Employees in the Machine Shop are paid on an incentive system. Each employee who meets "standard" — 800 gear wheels in an eight-hour day — receives a base rate of pay. For each acceptable unit over standard he produces, he receives an additional quarter of a cent. The base rate for gear wheel production has been established by the Methods Department after several time studies had been run, and has been unchanged for six months. Most of the employees producing gear wheels are experienced men, and although the job is relatively complex, they have little difficulty in exceeding standard and qualifying for incentive pay. Average production on the job since the current standard has been established has been about 1050 gear wheels per day.

This exercise concerns Walter Bradford, supervisor of the Machine Shop, and Warren Holt, one of the employees who manufactures gear wheels.

Role for Walter Bradford

You are concerned about the recent performance of Warren Holt, one of the men in your department who produces gear wheels. Holt has been with

Whitfield Manufacturing Company for a little over a year but was promoted to his present job in the Machine Shop only three months ago. Prior to his promotion he had been assigned to the Shipping Department, where he had been responsible for inspecting finished products to see that they were properly packaged before shipment to customers. He was promoted because of his enthusiasm, his ability to do good work, and his general alertness and attitude. His former rate of pay was $62 per month less than the base rate of pay for his current job.

Warren Holt has done well on his new job in the Machine Shop from the very first day, though he had not had much experience with machine operation. In fact, after two weeks, his production record was among the best in the shop, averaging 1350 to 1400 units per day.

Recently, however, his output has fallen off. For the past three weeks his production has averaged only about 1150 units per day. This still ranks high relative to the other workers, but you know that he is capable of producing at his "old" rate. You have noticed that lately he spends time "goofing off" while at his machine, takes frequent breaks, and in general is not working as hard as he has in the past.

When you first noticed that his output had dropped you assumed it was a temporary thing. At the end of the second week of low production, however, you mentioned it to him in a casual way. He replied, with a smile, that he "guessed he was just having a low period."

Now, at the end of the third week of low production, you have become very concerned. While Holt's output is still above standard, and, in fact, above that of most of the men, you know that he can do better if he attends to business. You hate to see one of your best producers working at less than capacity, especially since you feel that the standard for gear wheels is not "tight" and that all of the men could produce a lot more if they desired to do so.

You have just sent for Holt so that you can investigate the situation and are now awaiting his arrival in your office.

Role for Warren Holt

You have been working in the Machine Shop on your present job of producing gear wheels for three months. Prior to this, you had worked in the Shipping Department for a little over nine months. Your job there was to inspect finished products to see that they were properly packaged before being shipped to customers. You were pleased with your promotion to the Machine Shop even though the base rate of pay for your new job was only $62 a month more than in the shipping department. But the work in shipping was not especially challenging, and you didn't particularly like the rest of the men working there.

In the Machine Shop, lately at least, the guys were good to work with, and you could have a lot more fun. In addition, you controlled your own effort and "standard" was pretty easy to make. In your first two months you had no trouble at all in producing 1350 to 1400 units per day — more than the old-timers did — and you were proud of the fact that your output often was the highest in the shop. It didn't make much difference in take-home pay, as you would have to produce about 2000 units per day to make any real money, but it did feel good to be doing better than anyone else.

It puzzled you at first, though, that the more experienced men didn't produce more. You noticed that they didn't have to work very hard to meet "standard" and yet they produced only 1000 to 1100 units per day. The men were a little cool toward you at first, too. It seemed that the more you produced the less friendly they were.

Then one day during lunch, Gus, the man with the most experience on the job, took you aside and put you "straight," in a very direct although friendly manner. According to Gus, everyone could put out 1400 units or more a day if he wanted to. That was no great feat. But, if they all did that, it wouldn't be long before the standard was raised to 1200 or 1300 units a day and everyone would be working a lot harder for the same take-home pay. And under the incentive system, you couldn't make much more producing 1400 units a day instead of 1000 — only $2.00 a day. It was much better to work at a reasonable pace, have time to talk, and have an extra cigarette now and then. He advised you to think it over and implied that things might be a lot more friendly if you saw things his way.

You did think it over and finally agreed with Gus, although not without some reservations. It didn't seem quite right; but then, all the other guys were doing it, and the extra pay really didn't make much difference. You'd rather have the friendship of the men.

So, for the last three weeks you've been slowing down, averaging 1150 units a day. You still want to produce a little more than the rest of the men, just so you would be on the high side of the scale. And Gus had been right; the men were a lot more friendly now, talking with you more frequently, and in general being a lot more pleasant.

At the end of the second week of your self-imposed slow-down, Mr. Bradford, the Machine Shop supervisor, had spoken to you about your low production. But you had just laughed it off. This worried you a little, but he hadn't pressed the matter, so you had relaxed.

Until now, that is. You have just been told to report to Mr. Bradford's office, and are certain that he wants to talk about your recent rate of production. You are not sure what to say. He has been awfully nice to you since you started in the Machine Shop, and you'd like him to know that your slow-down has nothing to do with him personally. You would like to tell him what is going on, but you're not sure what effect this would have on you, your job, and the rest of the men. You don't really see what he could do, however, except raise a fuss. He couldn't make you work harder than you want to unless he arbitrarily raised the standard.

At the present time you are on your way to Mr. Bradford's office.

GROUP PROCESSES

INTRODUCTION

Like the person who couldn't see the forest for the trees, we take little notice of the groups around us, simply because there are so many.

In this exercise, you will be asked to conduct a field observation of informal groups to describe the behaviors observed.

Carefully review the articles by Baur and de la Porte before locating a group for study.

PROCEDURE

Locate and begin observing an informal group. At public gatherings you will be able to see small groups in the midst of the greater mass. Often the groups are of similar age and of the same sex. Good places to look are at movie theaters or music performances during intermission, at sporting events during half-time, or at classes at a university. The best arenas for observation are lobbies or near concession areas.

If you have a younger sister or brother, observe them as they interact with a group of their friends.

Observe the groups for the existence of what Baur terms "subculture." Describe:

1. any jargon or special language used by the groups
2. rituals, for example, "binging"
3. the physical setting — speculate on why groups form where they do
4. interaction, if any, among different groups

Also attempt to observe and describe some behavioral norms of the groups. Do the norms appear to be positive, negative, or neutral in de la Porte's terms?

Repeated observations of the same groups are desirable but may not be possible. Therefore, make an effort to observe at least two groups, at different times.

Prepare a written outline of the group processes observed for general class discussion, or for processing in small task groups.

Think about informal groups of which you are a member. Describe behavioral norms for these groups. Describe the "subcultures" of these groups. Compare and contrast "your" group(s) with those observed in this assignment.

PART 5

LEADERSHIP

What is a leader? That question has intrigued people for generations. The concept has been the focus of essays by philosophers and theologians, books by novelists, speeches by politicians, and stories by reporters. *Time* has devoted a cover story to leadership, while a popular book has devoted entire chapters to instructing the corporate climber in what to say, when to say it, and how to dress, all toward the end of becoming a corporate leader. Behavioral scientists have conducted ingenious experiments and observational studies in an attempt to understand leadership. And above it all is the complaint that, whatever leadership is, there isn't enough of it.

Through history there have been several well-defined approaches to leadership. In the murky past when our ancestors dragged their knuckles on the ground as they walked, leadership was probably a function of physical strength and aggressiveness. As civilized societies developed, and with them recorded history, leaders have generally been portrayed as well bred, educated, articulate, and physically imposing in stature and dress. The focus on attributes of the individual leader has come to be called the *trait approach.*

Although the trait approach has been largely discredited for good reasons, it has been demonstrated in studies that there are certain physical, intellectual, and personality traits that leaders appear to possess. For example, on average the leader tends to be taller and heavier in stature than the follower. The leader also tends to have an IQ slightly higher than that of the average follower. Personality tests have indicated that leaders tend to be dominating, sociable, and high in sense of responsibility.

Although these results make for interesting cocktail party conversation, they are of little use to the manager who must select and hire people for leadership positions. Even though the traits mentioned can be empirically verified, they are not useful for predicting successful leadership. If they were, it would be possible to hire leaders by the pound! We could simply weigh and measure all of our job candidates, administer IQ tests and personality tests, and then hire the candidate who scored highest in the various traits.

Perhaps the single greatest weakness of the trait approach to leadership is that it focuses upon one person: the leader. Is leadership a function of the activities of a single person? The answer of course is no. Leadership must be viewed as a process rather than as the attributes of a specific individual. Of course, individual attributes and personality traits *can* affect the leadership process. For example, each of us has a preferred leadership style that may be a function of our personality. But attributes of the followers also affect the leadership process, as do aspects of the situation.

The readings in this chapter will serve as your introduction to the complex world of leadership. Tannenbaum and Schmidt, in "How to Choose a Leadership Pattern," offer the aspiring manager some good advice. Leadership behavior can range from the very autocratic where the boss makes all the decisions to the very democratic where subordinates are included in the decision-making process. The article presents some key questions that the manager should answer before adopting a given leadership pattern. The authors point out forces in the manager, forces in the subordinates, and forces in the situation that make certain leadership styles more effective than others. Are there other forces you can name that might affect the success of leadership? How do you feel the forces listed in the reading affect you as a leader and as a follower? There is no single leadership pattern that is effective for all situations. But knowing something about the variables that affect the quality of leadership can allow us to select the appropriate leadership pattern.

Shetty's article, "Leadership and Organization Character," introduces another variable that has an impact on leadership: the character of the organization itself. Shetty argues that such things as the methods of production, the way the work itself is divided among people, how the work flow is coordinated, how structured or unstructured the task is, and how many layers of management or supervision there are in the organization help determine the appropriate style of leadership.

Imagine two very different organizations, for examplee, an automobile assembly plant and a medical research laboratory. Try to list as many differences in their organizational "characters" as you can. How might those differences require different leadership styles?

In "The Uses of Leadership Theory," James Owens offers some practical guidelines on the uses of current leadership theory. Pay particular attention to the discussion of his matrix of leadership styles. He points out the most important benefits and weaknesses of different leadership styles. As you contemplate the various benefits and drawbacks, ask yourself what kind of leadership style you prefer. Then consider under what conditions your preferred style would be most effective. It is important to realize that no single style of leadership is appropriate for all conditions. Note that each of the styles in the matrix has powerful potential for organizational effectiveness, *if* certain conditions are met. It is of course necessary for the individual manager to determine if the conditions are fulfilled.

The final reading, by House and Mitchell, deals with one of the newest approaches to leadership — the path-goal theory.

Path-goal theory acknowledges that leadership effectiveness depends on a number of things related to the situation in which leadership is required. The path-goal approach attempts to identify important dimensions of the leadership process and specify approaches suitable for different situations.

Even though each of us tends to have a preferred leadership style, it is important for the manager to be flexible in adopting different styles as appropriate. Unfortunately, this is not as easy as it sounds. Many people find it difficult to change styles; indeed, some people find it impossible. Even those who are flexible are not necessarily good leaders. After all, it is possible to be flexible — and wrong! Selecting the appropriate style depends upon the level of one's knowledge regarding leadership, as well as sensitivity to changing situations.

HOW TO CHOOSE A LEADERSHIP PATTERN

Robert Tannenbaum and
Warren H. Schmidt

- *"I put most problems into my group's hands and leave it to them to carry the ball from there. I serve merely as a catalyst, mirroring back the people's thoughts and feelings so that they can better understand them."*

- *"It's foolish to make decisions oneself on matters that affect people. I always talk things over with my subordinates, but I make it clear to them that I'm the one who has to have the final say."*

- *"Once I have decided on a course of action, I do my best to sell my ideas to my employees."*

- *"I'm being paid to lead. If I let a lot of other people make the decisions I should be making, then I'm not worth my salt."*

- *"I believe in getting things done. I can't waste time calling meetings. Someone has to call the shots around here, and I think it should be me."*

Each of these statements represents a point of view about "good leadership."

Considerable experience, factual data, and theoretical principles could be cited to support each statement, even though they seem to be inconsistent when placed together. Such contradictions point up the dilemma in which the modern manager frequently finds himself.

NEW PROBLEMS

The problem of how the modern manager can be "democratic" in his relations with subordinates and at the same time maintain the necessary authority and control in the organization for which he is responsible has come into focus increasingly in recent years.

Earlier in the century this problem was not so acutely felt. The successful executive was generally pictured as possessing intelligence, imagination, initiative, the capacity to make rapid (and generally wise) decisions, and the ability to inspire subordinates. People tended to think of the world as being divided into "leaders" and "followers."

New Focus

Gradually, however, from the social sciences emerged the concept of "group dynamics" with its focus on *members* of the group rather than solely on the leader. Research efforts of social scientists underscored the importance of employee involvement and participation in decision making. Evidence began to challenge the efficiency of highly directive leadership, and increasing attention was paid to problems of motivation and human relations.

Through training laboratories in group development that sprang up across the country, many of the newer notions of leadership began to exert an impact. These training laboratories were carefully designed to give people a first-hand experience in full participation and decision making. The designated "leaders" deliberately attempted to reduce their own power and to make group members as responsible as possible for setting their own goals and methods within the laboratory experience.

It was perhaps inevitable that some of the people who attended the training laboratories regarded this kind of leadership as being truly "democratic" and went home with the determination to build fully participative decision making into their own organizations. Whenever their bosses made a decision without convening a staff meeting, they tended to perceive this as authoritarian behavior. The true symbol of democratic leadership to some was the meeting — and the less directed from the top, the more democratic it was.

Some of the more enthusiastic alumni of these training laboratories began to get the habit of categorizing leader behavior as "democratic" or "authoritarian." The boss who made too many decisions himself was thought of as an authoritarian, and his directive behavior was often attributed solely to his personality.

New Need

The net result of the research findings and of the human relations training based upon them has been to call into question the stereotype of an effective leader. Consequently, the modern mana-

ger often finds himself in an uncomfortable state of mind.

Often he is not quite sure how to behave; there are times when he is torn between exerting "strong" leadership and "permissive" leadership. Sometimes new knowledge pushes him in one direction ("I should really get the group to help make this decision"), but at the same time his experience pushes him in another direction ("I really understand the problem better than the group and therefore I should make the decision"). He is not sure when a group decision is really appropriate or when holding a staff meeting serves merely as a device for avoiding his own decision-making responsibility.

The purpose of our article is to suggest a framework which managers may find useful in grappling with this dilemma. First, we shall look at the different patterns of leadership behavior that the manager can choose from in relating himself to his subordinates. Then, we shall turn to some of the questions suggested by this range of patterns. For instance, how important is it for a manager's subordinates to know what type of leadership he is using in a situation? What factors should he consider in deciding on a leadership pattern? What difference do his long-run objectives make as compared to his immediate objectives?

RANGE OF BEHAVIOR

Exhibit 1 presents the continuum or range of possible leadership behavior available to a manager. Each type of action is related to the degree of authority used by the boss and to the amount of freedom available to his subordinates in reaching decisions. The actions seen on the extreme left characterize the manager who maintains a high degree of control while those seen on the extreme right characterize the manager who releases a high degree of control. Neither extreme is absolute; authority and freedom are never without their limitations.

Now let us look more closely at each of the behavior points occurring along this continuum.

• *The manager makes the decision and announces it.*

In this case the boss identifies a problem, considers alternative solutions, chooses one of them, and then reports this decision to his subordinates for implementation. He may or may not give consideration to what he believes his subordinates will think or feel about his decision; in any case, he provides no opportunity for them to participate directly in the decision-making process. Coercion may or may not be used or implied.

• *The manager "sells" his decision.*

Here the manager, as before, takes responsibility for identifying the problem and arriving at a decision. However, rather than simply announcing it, he takes the additional step of persuading his subordinates to accept it. In doing so, he recognizes the possibility of some resistance among those who will be faced with the decision, and seeks to reduce this resistance by indicating, for example, what the employees have to gain from his decision.

• *The manager presents his ideas, invites questions.*

Here the boss who has arrived at a decision and who seeks acceptance of his ideas provides an opportunity for his subordinates to get a fuller explanation of his thinking and his intentions. After presenting the ideas, he invites questions so that his associates can better understand what he is trying to accomplish. This "give and take" also enables the manager and the subordinates to ex-

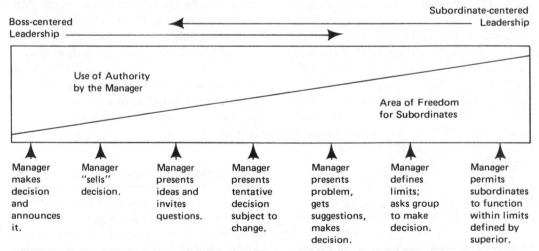

Boss-centered Leadership

Subordinate-centered Leadership

Use of Authority by the Manager

Area of Freedom for Subordinates

| Manager makes decision and announces it. | Manager "sells" decision. | Manager presents ideas and invites questions. | Manager presents tentative decision subject to change. | Manager presents problem, gets suggestions, makes decision. | Manager defines limits; asks group to make decision. | Manager permits subordinates to function within limits defined by superior. |

EXHIBIT 1 • Continuum of Leadership Behavior

plore more fully the implications of the decision.

• *The manager presents a tentative decision subject to change.*

This kind of behavior permits the subordinates to exert some influence on the decision. The initiative for identifying and diagnosing the problem remains with the boss. Before meeting with his staff, he has thought the problem through and arrived at a decision — but only a tentative one. Before finalizing it, he presents his proposed solution for the reaction of those who will be affected by it. He says in effect, "I'd like to hear what you have to say about this plan that I have developed. I'll appreciate your frank reactions, but will reserve for myself the final decision."

• *The manager presents the problem, gets suggestions, and then makes his decision.*

Up to this point the boss has come before the group with a solution of his own. Not so in this case. The subordinates now get the first chance to suggest solutions. The manager's initial role involves identifying the problem. He might, for example, say something of this sort: "We are faced with a number of complaints from newspapers and the general public on our service policy. What is wrong here? What ideas do you have for coming to grips with this problem?"

The function of the group becomes one of increasing the manager's repertory of possible solutions to the problem. The purpose is to capitalize on the knowledge and experience of those who

are on the "firing line." From the expanded list of alternatives developed by the manager and his subordinates, the manager then selects the solution that he regards as most promising.[1]

• *The manager defines the limits and requests the group to make a decision.*

At this point the manager passes to the group (possibly including himself as a member) the right to make decisions. Before doing so, however, he defines the problem to be solved and the boundaries within which the decision must be made.

An example might be the handling of a parking problem at a plant. The boss decides that this is something that should be worked on by the people involved, so he calls them together and points up the existence of the problem. Then he tells them:

"There is the open field just north of the main plant which has been designated for additional employee parking. We can build underground or surface multilevel facilities as long as the cost does not exceed $100,000. Within these limits we are free to work out whatever solution makes sense to us. After we decide on a specific plan, the company will spend the available money in whatever way we indicate."

• *The manager permits the group to make decisions within prescribed limits.*

This represents an extreme degree of group freedom only occasionally encountered in formal organizations, as, for instance, in many research groups. Here the team of managers or engineers undertakes the identification and diagnosis of the problem, develops alterna-

---

[1]For a fuller explanation of this approach, see Leo Moore, "Too Much Management, Too Little Change," *HBR* January-February 1956, p.41.

tive procedures for solving it, and decides on one or more of these alternative solutions. The only limits directly imposed on the group by the organization are those specified by the superior of the team's boss. If the boss participates in the decision-making process, he attempts to do so with no more authority than any other member of the group. He commits himself in advance to assist in implementing whatever decision the group makes.

Key Questions

As the continuum in Exhibit 1 demonstrates, there are a number of alternative ways in which a manager can relate himself to the group or individuals he is supervising. At the extreme left of the range, the emphasis is on the manager — on what *he* is interested in, how *he* sees things, how *he* feels about them. As we move toward the subordinate-centered end of the continuum, however, the focus is increasingly on the subordinates — on what *they* are interested in, how *they* look at things, how *they* feel about them.

When a business leadership is regarded in this way, a number of questions arise. Let us take four of special importance:

1. Can a boss ever relinquish his responsibility by delegating it to someone else?

Our view is that the manager must expect to be held responsible by his superior for the quality of the decisions made, even though operationally these decisions may have been made on a group basis. He should, therefore, be ready to accept whatever risk is involved whenever he delegates decision-making power to his subordinates. Dele-

gation is not a way of "passing the buck." Also, it should be emphasized that the amount of freedom the boss gives to his subordinates cannot be greater than the freedom which he himself has been given by his own superior.

2. Should the manager participate with his subordinates once he has delegated responsibility to them?

The manager should carefully think over this question and decide on his role prior to involving the subordinate group. He should ask if his presence will inhibit or facilitate the problem-solving process. There may be some instances when he should leave the group to let it solve the problem for itself. Typically, however, the boss has useful ideas to contribute, and should function as an additional member of the group. In the latter instance, it is important that he indicate clearly to the group that he sees himself in a *member* role rather than in an authority role.

3. How important is it for the group to recognize what kind of leadership behavior the boss is using?

It makes a great deal of difference. Many relationship problems between boss and subordinate occur because the boss fails to make clear how he plans to use his authority. If, for example, he actually intends to make a certain decision himself, but the subordinate group gets the impression that he has delegated this authority, considerable confusion and resentment are likely to follow. Problems may also occur when the boss uses a "democratic" facade to conceal the fact that he has already made a decision which he hopes the group will accept as its own. The attempt to "make them think it was their idea in the first place" is a risky one. We believe that it is highly important for the manager to be honest and clear in describing what authority he is keeping and what role he is asking his subordinates to assume in solving a particular problem.

4. Can you tell how "democratic" a manager is by the number of decisions his subordinates make?

The sheer *number* of decisions is not an accurate index of the amount of freedom that a subordinate group enjoys. More important is the *significance* of the decisions which the boss entrusts to his subordinates. Obviously a decision on how to arrange desks is of an entirely different order from a decision involving the introduction of new electronic data-processing equipment. Even though the widest possible limits are given in dealing with the first issue, the group will sense no particular degree of responsibility. For a boss to permit the group to decide equipment policy, even within rather narrow limits, would reflect a greater degree of confidence in them on his part.

Deciding How to Lead

Now let us turn from the types of leadership which are possible in a company situation to the question of what types are *practical* and *desirable*. What factors or forces should a manager consider in deciding how to manage? Three are of particular importance:

- Forces in the manager.
- Forces in the subordinates.
- Forces in the situation.

We should like briefly to describe these elements and indicate how they might influence a manager's action in a decision-making situation.[2] The strength of each of them will, of course, vary from instance to instance, but the manager who is sensitive to them can better assess the problems which face him and determine which mode of leadership behavior is most appropriate for him.

Forces in the Manager. The manager's behavior in any given instance will be influenced greatly by the many forces operating within his own personality. He will, of course, perceive his leadership problems in a unique way on the basis of his background, knowledge, and experience. Among the important internal forces affecting him will be the following:

1. His value system.

How strongly does he feel that individuals should have a share in making the decisions which affect them? Or, how convinced is he that the official who is paid to assume responsibility should personally carry the burden of decision making? The strength of his convictions on questions like these will tend to move the manager to one end or the other of the continuum shown in Exhibit 1. His behavior will also be influenced by the relative importance that he attaches to organizational efficiency, personal growth of subordinates, and company profits.[3]

---

[2]See also Robert Tannenbaum and Fred Massarik, "Participation by Subordinates in the Managerial Decision-Making Process," *Canadian Journal of Economics and Political Science,* August 1950, p. 413.

[3]See Chris Argyris, "Top Management Dilemma: Company Needs vs. Individual Development," *Personnel,* September 1955, pp. 123–134.

2. His confidence in his subordinates.

Managers differ greatly in the amount of trust they have in other people generally, and this carries over to the particular employees they supervise at a given time. In viewing his particular group of subordinates, the manager is likely to consider their knowledge and competence with respect to the problem. A central question he might ask himself is: "Who is best qualified to deal with this problem?" Often he may, justifiably or not, have more confidence in his own capabilities than in those of his subordinates.

3. His own leadership inclinations.

There are some managers who seem to function more comfortably and naturally as highly directive leaders. Resolving problems and issuing orders come easily to them. Other managers seem to operate more comfortably in a team role, where they are continually sharing many of their functions with their subordinates.

4. His feelings of security in an uncertain situation.

The manager who releases control over the decision-making process thereby reduces the predictability of the outcome. Some managers have a greater need than others for predictability and stability in their environment. This "tolerance for ambiguity" is being viewed increasingly by psychologists as a key variable in a person's manner of dealing with problems.

The manager brings these and other highly personal variables to each situation he faces. If he can see them as forces which, consciously or unconsciously, influence his behavior. he can better understand what makes him prefer to act in a given way. And understanding this, he can often make himself more effective.

Forces in the Subordinate.   Before deciding how to lead a certain group, the manager will also want to consider a number of forces affecting his subordinates' behavior. He will want to remember that each employee, like himself, is influenced by many personality variables. In addition, each subordinate has a set of expectations about how the boss should act in relation to him (the phrase "expected behavior" is one we hear more and more often these days at discussions of leadership and teaching). The better the manager understands these factors, the more accurately he can determine what kind of behavior on his part will enable his subordinates to act most effectively.

Generally speaking, the manager can permit his subordinates greater freedom if the following essential conditions exist:

- If the subordinates have relatively high needs for independence. (As we all know, people differ greatly in the amount of direction that they desire.)
- If the subordinates have a readiness to assume responsibility for decision making. (Some see additional responsibility as a tribute to their ability; others see it as "passing the buck.")
- If they have a relatively high tolerance for ambiguity. (Some employees prefer to have clear-cut directives given to them; others prefer a wider area of freedom.)
- If they are interested in the problem and feel that it is important.
- If they understand and identify with the goals of the organization.
- If they have the necessary knowledge

and experience to deal with the problem.
• If they have learned to expect to share in decision making. (Persons who have come to expect strong leadership and are then suddenly confronted with the request to share more fully in decision making are often upset by this new experience. On the other hand, persons who have enjoyed a considerable amount of freedom resent the boss who begins to make all the decisions himself.)

The manager will probably tend to make fuller use of his own authority if the above conditions do *not* exist; at times there may be no realistic alternative to running a "one-man show."

The restrictive effect of many of the forces will, of course, be greatly modified by the general feeling of confidence which subordinates have in the boss. Where they have learned to respect and trust him, he is free to vary his behavior. He will feel certain that he will not be perceived as an authoritarian boss on those occasions when he makes decisions by himself. Similarly, he will not be seen as using staff meetings to avoid his decision-making responsibility. In a climate of mutual confidence and respect, people tend to feel less threatened by deviations from normal practice, which in turn makes possible a higher degree of flexibility in the whole relationship.

Forces in the Situation. In addition to the forces which exist in the manager himself and in his subordinates, certain characteristics of the general situation will also affect the manager's behavior. Among the more critical environmental pressures that surround him are those which stem from the organization, the work group, the nature of the problem,

and the pressures of time. Let us look briefly at each of these:

1. Type of organization.

Like individuals, organizations have values and traditions which inevitably influence the behavior of the people who work in them. The manager who is a newcomer to a company quickly discovers that certain kinds of behavior are approved while others are not. He also discovers that to deviate radically from what is generally accepted is likely to create problems for him.

These values and traditions are communicated in numerous ways — through job descriptions, policy pronouncements, and public statements by top executives. Some organizations, for example, hold to the notion that the desirable executive is one who is dynamic, imaginative, decisive, and persuasive. Other organizations put more emphasis upon the importance of the executive's ability to work effectively with people — his human relations skills. The fact that his superiors have a defined concept of what the good executive should be will very likely push the manager toward one end or the other of the behavioral range.

In addition to the above, the amount of employee participation is influenced by such variables as the size of the working units, their geographical distribution, and the degree of inter- and intra-organizational security required to attain company goals. For example, the wide geographical dispersion of an organization may preclude a practical system of participative decision making, even though this would otherwise be desirable. Similarly, the size of the working units or the need for keeping plans confidential may make it necessary for the boss to exercise more control than would otherwise be the case. Factors like these may limit considerably the manager's ability to function flexibly on the continuum.

2. Group effectiveness.

Before turning decision-making responsibility over to a subordinate group, the boss should consider how effectively its members work together as a unit.

One of the relevant factors here is the experience the group has had in working together. It can generally be expected that a group which has functioned for some time will have developed habits of cooperation and thus be able to tackle a problem more effectively than a new group. It can also be expected that a group of people with similar backgrounds and interests will work more quickly and easily than people with dissimilar backgrounds, because the communication problems are likely to be less complex.

The degree of confidence that the members have in their ability to solve problems as a group is also a key consideration. Finally, such group variables as cohesiveness, permissiveness, mutual acceptance, and commonality of purpose will exert subtle but powerful influence on the group's functioning.

3. The problem itself.

The nature of the problem may determine what degree of authority should be delegated by the manager to his subordinates. Obviously he will ask himself whether they have the kind of knowledge which is needed. It is possible to do them a real disservice by assigning a problem that their experience does not equip them to handle.

Since the problems faced in larger or growing industries increasingly require knowledge of specialists from many different fields, it might be inferred that the more complex a problem, the more anxious a manager will be to get some assistance in solving it. However, this is not always the case. There will be times when the very complexity of the problem calls for one person to work it out. For example, if the manager has most of the background and factual data relevant to a given issue, it may be easier for him to think it through himself than to take the time to fill in his staff on all the pertinent background information.

The key question to ask, of course, is: "Have I heard the ideas of everyone who has the necessary knowledge to make a significant contribution to the solution of this problem?"

4. The pressure of time.

This is perhaps the most clearly felt pressure on the manager (in spite of the fact that it may sometimes be imagined). The more that he feels the need for an immediate decision, the more difficult it is to involve other people. In organizations which are in a constant state of "crisis" and "crash programming" one is likely to find managers personally using a high degree of authority with relatively little delegation to subordinates. When the time pressure is less intense, however, it becomes much more possible to bring subordinates in on the decision-making process.

These, then, are the principal forces that impinge on the manager in any given instance and that tend to determine his tactical behavior in relation to his subordinates. In each case his behavior ideally will be that which makes possible the most effective attainment of his immediate goal within the limits facing him.

Long-run Strategy

As the manager works with his organization on the problems that come up day by day, his choice of a leadership pattern is usually limited. He must take account of the forces just described and, within the restrictions they impose on him, do the best that he can. But as he looks ahead months or even years, he can shift his thinking from tactics to large-scale strategy. No longer need he be fettered by all of the forces mentioned, for he can view many of them as variables over which he has some control. He can, for example, gain new insights or skills for himself, supply training for individual subordinates, and provide participative experiences for his employee group.

In trying to bring about a change in these variables, however, he is faced with a challenging question: At which point along the continuum *should* he act?

Attaining Objectives. The answer depends largely on what he wants to accomplish. Let us suppose that he is interested in the same objectives that most modern managers seek to attain when they can shift their attention from the pressure of immediate assignments:

1. To raise the level of employee motivation.
2. To increase the readiness of subordinates to accept change.
3. To improve the quality of all managerial decisions.
4. To develop teamwork and morale.
5. To further the individual development of employees.

In recent years the manager has been deluged with a flow of advice on how best to achieve these longer-run objectives. It is little wonder that he is often both bewildered and annoyed. However, there are some guidelines which he can usefully follow in making a decision.

Most research and much of the experience of recent years give a strong factual basis to the theory that a fairly high degree of subordinate-centered behavior is associated with the accomplishment of the five purposes mentioned.[4] This does not mean that a manager should always leave all decisions to his assistants. To provide the individual or the group with greater freedom than they are ready for at any given time may very well tend to generate anxieties and therefore inhibit rather than facilitate the attainment of desired objectives. But this should not keep the manager from making a continuing effort to confront his subordinates with the challenge of freedom.

CONCLUSION

In summary, there are two implications in the basic thesis that we have been developing. The first is that the successful leader is one who is keenly aware of those forces which are most relevant to his behavior at any given time. He accurately understands himself, the individu-

---

[4]For example, see Warren H. Schmidt and Paul C. Buchanan, *Techniques that Produce Teamwork* (New London, Arthur C. Croft Publications, 1954); and Morris S. Viteles, *Motivation and Morale in Industry* (New York, W.W. Norton & Company, Inc., 1953).

als and group he is dealing with, and the company and broader social environment in which he operates. And certainly he is able to assess the present readiness for growth of his subordinates.

But this sensitivity or understanding is not enough, which brings us to the second implication. The successful leader is one who is able to behave appropriately in the light of these perceptions. If direction is in order, he is able to direct; if considerable participative freedom is called for, he is able to provide such freedom.

Thus, the successful manager of men can be primarily characterized neither as a strong leader nor as a permissive one. Rather, he is one who maintains a high batting average in accurately assessing the forces that determine what his most appropriate behavior at any given time should be and in actually being able to behave accordingly. Being both insightful and flexible, he is less likely to see the problems of leadership as a dilemma.

RETROSPECTIVE COMMENTARY

Since this HBR Classic was first published in 1958, there have been many changes in organizations and in the world that have affected leadership patterns. While the article's continued popularity attests to its essential validity, we believe it can be reconsidered and updated to reflect subsequent societal changes and new management concepts.

The reasons for the article's continued relevance can be summarized briefly:

- The article contains insights and perspectives which mesh well with, and help clarify, the experiences of managers, other leaders, and students of leadership. Thus it is useful to individuals in a wide variety of organizations — industrial, governmental, educational, religious, and community.

- The concept of leadership the article defines is reflected in a continuum of leadership behavior (see Exhibit I in original article). Rather than offering a choice between two styles of leadership, democratic or authoritarian, it sanctions a range of behavior.

- The concept does not dictate to managers but helps them to analyze their own behavior. The continuum permits them to review their behavior within a context of other alternatives, without any style being labeled right or wrong.

(We have sometimes wondered if we have, perhaps, made it too easy for anyone to justify his or her style of leadership. It may be a small step between being nonjudgmental and giving the impression that all behavior is equally valid and useful. The latter was not our intention. Indeed, the thrust of our endorsement was for the manager who is insightful in assessing relevant forces within himself, others, and the situation, and who can be flexible in responding to these forces.)

In recognizing that our article can be updated, we are acknowledging that organizations do not exist in a vacuum but are affected by changes that occur in society. Consider, for example, the implications for organizations of these recent social developments:

- The youth revolution that expresses distrust and even contempt for organizations identified with the establishment.

- The civil rights movement that demands all minority groups be given a greater opportunity for participation and influence in the organizational processes.

- The ecology and consumer movements that challenge the right of managers to make decisions without considering the interest of people outside the organization.

- The increasing national concern with the quality of working life and its relationship to worker productivity, participation, and satisfaction.

These and other societal changes make effective leadership in this decade a more challenging task, requiring even greater sensitivity and flexibility than was needed in the 1950's. Today's manager is more likely to deal with employees who resent being treated as subordinates, who may be highly critical of any organizational system, who expect to be consulted and to exert influence, and who often stand on the edge of alienation from the institution that needs their loyalty and commitment. In addition, he is frequently confronted by a highly turbulent, unpredictable environment.

In response to these social pressures, new concepts of management have emerged in organizations. Open-system theory, with its emphasis on subsystems' interdependency *and* on the interaction of an organization with its environment, has made a powerful impact on managers' approach to problems. Organization development has emerged as a new behavioral science approach to the improvement of individual, group, organizational, and interorganizational performance. New research has added to our understanding of motivation in the work situation. More and more executives have become concerned with social responsibility and have explored the feasibility of social audits. And a growing number of organizations, in Europe and in the United States, have conducted experiments in industrial democracy.

In light of these developments, we submit the following thoughts on how we would rewrite certain points in our original article.

The article described forces in the manager, subordinates, and the situation as givens, with the leadership pattern a resultant of these forces. We would now give more attention to the *interdependency* of these forces. For example, such interdependency occurs in: (a) the interplay between the manager's confidence in his subordinates, their readiness to assume responsibility, and the level of group effectiveness; and (b) the impact of the behavior of the manager on that of his subordinates, and vice versa.

In discussing the forces in the situation, we primarily identified organizational phenomena. We would now include forces lying outside the organization, and would explore the relevant interdependencies between the organization and its environment.

In the original article, we presented the size of the rectangle in Exhibit 1 as a given, with its boundaries already determined by external forces — in effect, a closed system. We would now recognize the possibility of the manager and/or his subordinates taking the initiative to change those boundaries through interaction with relevant external forces — both within their own organization and in the larger society.

The article portrayed the manager as the principal and almost unilateral actor. He initiated and determined group functions, assumed responsibility, and exercised control. Subordinates made inputs and assumed power only at the will of the manager. Although the manager might have taken into account forces outside himself, it was *he* who decided where to operate on the continuum — that is, whether to announce a decision instead of trying to sell his idea to his subordinates, whether to invite questions, to let subordinates decide an issue, and so on. While the manager has retained this clear prerogative in many organizations, it has been challenged in others. Even in situations where he has retained it, however, the balance in the relationship between manager and subordinates at any given time is arrived at by interaction — direct or indirect — between the two parties.

Although power and its use by the

manager played a role in our article, we now realize that our concern with cooperation and collaboration, common goals, commitment, trust, and mutual caring limited our vision with respect to the realities of power. We did not attempt to deal with unions, other forms of joint worker action, or with individual workers' expressions of resistance. Today, we would recognize much more clearly the power available to *all* parties, and the factors that underlie the interrelated decisions on whether to use it.

In the original article, we used the terms "manager" and "subordinate." We are now uncomfortable with "subordinate" because of its demeaning, dependency-laden connotations and prefer "nonmanager." The titles "manager" and "nonmanager" make the terminological difference functional rather than hierarchical.

We assumed fairly traditional organizational structures in our original article. Now we would alter our formulation to reflect newer organizational modes which are slowly emerging, such as industrial democracy, intentional

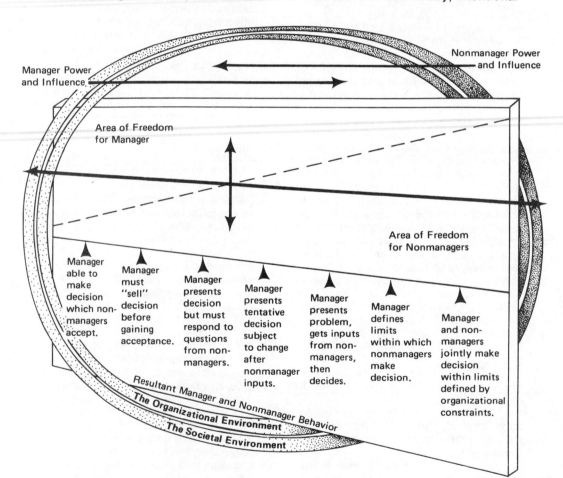

Manager Power and Influence

Nonmanager Power and Influence

Area of Freedom for Manager

Area of Freedom for Nonmanagers

Manager able to make decision which nonmanagers accept.

Manager must "sell" decision before gaining acceptance.

Manager presents decision but must respond to questions from nonmanagers.

Manager presents tentative decision subject to change after nonmanager inputs.

Manager presents problem, gets inputs from nonmanagers, then decides.

Manager defines limits within which nonmanagers make decision.

Manager and nonmanagers jointly make decision within limits defined by organizational constraints.

Resultant Manager and Nonmanager Behavior

The Organizational Environment

The Societal Environment

EXHIBIT 2 • Continuum of Manager-Nonmanager Behavior

communities, and "phenomenarchy."* These new modes are based on observations such as the following:

- Both managers and nonmanagers may be governing forces in their group's environment, contributing to the definition of the total area of freedom.
- A group can function without a manager, with managerial functions being shared by group members.
- A group, as a unit, can be delegated authority and can assume responsibility within a larger organizational context.

Our thoughts on the question of leadership have prompted us to design a new behavior continuum (see Exhibit 2) in which the total area of freedom shared by manager and nonmanagers is constantly redefined by interactions between them and the forces in the environment.

The arrows in the exhibit indicate the continual flow of interdependent influence among systems and people. The points on the continuum designate the types of manager and nonmanager behavior that become possible with any given amount of freedom available to each. The new continuum is both more complex and more dynamic than the 1958 version, reflecting the organizational and societal realities of 1973.

---

*For a description of phenomenarchy, see Will McWhinney, "Phenomenarchy: A Suggestion for Social Redesign," *Journal of Applied Behavioral Science,* May 1973.

LEADERSHIP AND ORGANIZATION CHARACTER

Y. K. Shetty

The evidence derived from social science research indicates that leadership does not consist of abstract personal qualities, as was once thought, but is a result of complex interaction between the manager and his employees in dynamic organizational situations. This variable — the organizational system — has a significant influence in shaping individual leadership styles.

Leadership styles can be portrayed on a scale depicting autocratic at the one end and free-reign on the other. In between these extremes, there is a *range* of leadership behavior which may fall anywhere on the continuum of the scale. At one extreme, the leader uses a high degree of authority and allows little freedom to his subordinates. At the other extreme he gives a high degree of freedom to his subordinates and maintains little control over their daily activities.

From *Personnel Administration*, July-August 1970, pp. 14–20. Reprinted by permission of the International Personnel Management Association, 1313 East 60th Street, Chicago, Illinois.

Certain leadership styles are more suitable or acceptable in particular organizational settings and for particular organizational structures. Structure, in turn, often depends on whether the organization is engaged in process production, unit production, mass production, or some balance of these activities.

The purpose of this paper is to explore some of the recent research on leadership behavior and organizational systems and point to a scheme for understanding how varying styles of leadership may develop in response to specific combinations of the manager, the employee and the organizational climate.

WHAT IS A LEADER?

The concept of leadership has run a varied course. The earliest attempt to explain the phenomenon of leadership was made by writers who have come to be known as "traitists." It was thought that a successful leader was one who had specific leadership traits. These traits were interpreted in terms of qualities such as physical and nervous energy, a sense of purpose and direction, enthusiasm, friendliness, affection, integrity, technical mastery, decisiveness, intelligence, teaching skill, and faith.[1] This approach assumed that leadership could be examined in isolation, without considering other factors. Research in this approach to leadership proved futile, since there was little agreement as to the universal traits required for leadership. Gouldner, after reviewing the empirical and conservatively interpreting evidence relating to "universal traits," concluded, "At this time there is no reliable evidence concerning the existence of universal leadership traits."[2]

The Leader and the Led

The inadequacies of explaining leadership by reference to traits invariably led others to posit that followers are an important variable in effective leadership. This theory emphasized that an effective leader is one who nearly always satisfied the personal needs of his followers. "The follower's persistent motivations, points of view, frames of reference or attitudes will have a hand in determining what he perceives and how he reacts to it. The psychological factors in the individual followers cannot be ignored in our search for a science of leadership."[3]

The follower-theory approach does not emphasize the qualities of the leader as the traitists do, but rather, those of the followers, such as their personal needs, whether present or remote.

The Leadership Situation

The situational approach to leadership is based on the notion that neither leader nor follower traits are the main determinant of who will succeed as a leader; rather, the situation or the environment is the relevant variable. Thus, a leader in one situation may not be a leader in another situation. In short, the leader's behavior is always responsive to the situation in which it occurs.

The situational approach is valuable because each organization is unique despite some structured similarities. It focuses attention not on the personality of the leader as such, but on the "personality" or culture of the organization as a whole. It is possible for almost anyone to become a leader, if circumstances allow him to perform functions dictated by the situation. An effective leader, according to situational theory, is one who understands the forces of the situation and effectively uses them.

The situational theorists do not completely abandon the search for significant variables, but they attempt to look for them in situations containing similar elements. "The qualities, characteristics and skills required in a leader are determined to a large extent by the demands of the situation in which he is to function as a leader."[4]

THE EMERGENCE OF LEADERSHIP STYLES

In spite of these "Trait," "Follower," and "Situational" theories, each focusing its own aspects, the common attitude, as Sanford points out, is to view leadership behavior as a complex phenomenon determined by all three of these variables. He further comments that to concentrate on any one of these facets represents an oversimplification of an intricate phenomenon.

The Case for Leadership Styles.

From various definitions of leadership (e.g., Gibb,[5] Bennis,[6] Tannenbaum,[7]) one can delineate several common elements which lead to an understanding of the real *functions* of leadership:

1. *Differentiation of function:* Without group activity the leader is deprived of the opportunity to coordinate the activities of the group, to produce group solidarity in the pursuit of a goal. The leadership function itself is a differentiated activity which arises out of group processes.
2. *The necessity of the group:* Leadership cannot exist without a group to be led.
3. *Objectives:* Leadership is directed toward the attainment of a specified goal or goals.
4. *The leader:* The leader interacts with the group, modifying goals and courses of action so that a unified group opinion results.

From these elements, it becomes clear that leadership is both a process and a function of three variables — the leader, the led, and the situation. Because leadership can be achieved through a variety of behaviors, the concept of types or styles of leadership emerges.

Three of these principal types are the familiar autocratic, democratic, and free-rein leader. Other terms are also used to describe different leadership styles, particularly the autocratic and democratic pattern. The literature on leadership shows that these styles can be characterized in various ways, but essentially they seem to come down to a dichotomy represented by [the distinctions shown in Table 1].[8]

Employee-Centered		Production-Centered
Considerate		Initiatory
Loose (General)		Close
Integrative	*as against*	Dominative
Persuasive		Arbitrary
Group-Centered		Leader-Centered
Participatory		Authoritarian

TABLE 1

Even though various concepts are used to characterize the two opposite styles, the characteristics within each style tend to correlate with one another; that is, the participatory leader is also likely to be employee-centered, persuasive, integrative, etc.

The Forces Behind Leadership Styles

Tannenbaum and others[9] suggest that there are three types of forces which are significant to the manager in shaping his leadership style: forces in the manager himself; forces in his subordinates; and forces in the general situation.

The forces within the manager involve (a) his value system, that is, the extent to which he thinks individuals *should* have a share in the decisions which affect them; (b) his confidence in his subordinates; (c) his own leadership inclination, that is, under what circumstances he feels most comfortable; and (d) his feelings of security in uncertain situations.

The forces within subordinates include (1) their needs for independence; (2) their tolerance for ambiguity; (3) their interest in a problem and its importance; (4) their degree of identification with the goals of the organization; (5) their knowledge and experience; and (6) their expectations that they should share in decision making.

The forces within the situation include (i) the type of organization including its culture, size of working units, geographical distribution and the degrees of inter- and intra-organizational interaction required to attain goals; (ii) group effectiveness; (iii) the nature and complexity of the task; and (iv) the amount of time available to make a decision or take action.

Even though Tannenbaum and others indirectly identify organization as a variable influencing leadership styles in their model, it is absorbed in the situation and given comparatively little analytical attention. This truncated perspective, for the most part, ignores the *crucial* role of technology and organization in shaping the leadership behavior.

In this paper, organizational system (technology and organization structure) is considered as an independent variable, separate from the situation. The situation is considered as a dynamic variable, which is of immediate concern to the leader. The attempt to give an independent status to organizational system or, to put it differently, to pay systematic attention to the role of organizational system in analyzing and studying leadership styles, is believed to be a distinctive feature of this paper.

ORGANIZATIONAL IMPACT ON LEADERSHIP STYLES

It is apparent from some of the recent research findings that both technology and organization structure have a strong influence on leadership patterns. Specifically, methods of production, division of work, work flow, certainty of tasks and structural attributes of the organization are interrelated and tend to shape leadership behavior.

Methods of Production

Production technology, as recently suggested by Woodward,[10] seem to limit the amount of discretion which subordinates can be given and the style of supervision used. She found that management structure varied with the type of technology, and that different technologies seem to have varying degrees of "management content."[11]

Some technologies are more management intensive than others.[12] Management content is substantially higher in "continuous-process" technology than in the "unit-production" technology. That is, fewer managers supervise more people in unit production than in mass-production or continuous process technologies. Since technology can dictate the supervisory ratio, it may, therefore, limit the amount of freedom which subordinates can be given.

Also, under unit production technology, relatively higher levels of skills may be necessary at the worker level; in terms of technical knowledge of the job, the methods, the tools, knowledge about operating errors, inspection skills and control. Under these conditions employees are more likely to perform effectively when they are given more freedom on the job. Research suggests that, compared to unskilled workers, skilled workers feel more involved in their jobs and are more eager for an opportunity to participate in making job related decisions.[13] Consequently, under these conditions the leader is *able* to exercise more democratic supervision.

Technology may determine the extent to which the job may be programmed (i.e., employee behaviors may be precisely specified). The kind of leadership required under low task structure is not the same as the kind of behavior required under high task structure.[14] It is meaningless to talk of permitting exercise of discretion to assembly line workers; the very nature of this technology requires that all the essential decisions be centrally programmed. Democratic supervision works best where the

nature of the job permits the employee to enjoy autonomy.

Division of Work

Ability to delegate is affected by the way in which work is divided among people — the greater the specialization and fragmentation, the less the delegation possible. Functional departmentation based on similarity and relatedness of activities is frequently appropriate for the earlier stages of a company's growth. But as organizations mature, other variations in departmentation may be tried.

The "integrated task team" is a recent form of grouping work, emphasizing a system's approach to work processing. All people who must coordinate their tasks to achieve a common goal are placed together under a common supervisor. This type of departmentation minimizes the problems of coordination and communication that are inevitable in a functionally grouped workforce. Under the integrated task team concept, people handle problems on a face-to-face basis with a minimum of bureaucratic friction among specialized functional areas.

The manner in which the work activities are organized will inevitably influence the style of leadership. People who work near one another and identify with the same group find it much easier to share the information they need to coordinate their jobs than do people who have infrequent contact with one another under a functional arrangement. The task team shares a relatively autonomous task. Each member of the group feels responsible for the entire organization. Under such circumstances competent internal coordination and group responsibility develops. It is far easier to exercise democratic supervision.

Work-flow

The amount of discretion given to subordinates seems to vary according to the work flow and type of specialization within the company. Parallel specialization occurs where work flow is organized so as to minimize the amount of coordination and interaction among individuals and departments. Interdependence specialization occurs where the activities of one individual or department are closely dependent on other individuals or departments.[15] Unit production technology often leads to parallel specialization while mass production technology leads to interdependent specialization.

Under unit-production, employees see themselves as responsible for a total product process and are able to see the total result of their efforts. For these reasons, under parallel specialization, a more democratic style of supervision may be appropriate.

Interdependent specialization is characterized by many more lateral relationships required to obtain effective coordination between specialized groups. Subordinates develop a "vested interest" in their own typical point of view or approach to problems and are unable to see the impact of their actions on others. Since only the personnel at the top (the managers) would be able to see the overall picture and integrate the efforts of different parts in order to achieve the overall organizational goals, they would tend to delegate less authority and rely on more autocratic methods of supervision.

Certainty of Task

Some studies show that leadership style may be related to the degree of certainty about the task in question. Fiedler[16] has assembled data from a variety of situations to relate leadership style to group effectiveness in performing tasks of varying certainty. He has found that where leaders have friendly relations with their groups but relatively few sanctions and rewards to offer, an uncertain task is best handled by a passive, permissive and considerate leadership style. On the other hand, under similar conditions with a highly structured, certain task, a more controlling and active leader is more effective.

These are just two examples of a number of possible situations involving different degrees of positional power and different types of leadership style which have been examined in Fiedler's work. It seems clear that different styles of leadership behavior lead to effective group performance in different conditions. Certainty of the group's task is one of the most important variables related to the effectiveness of a leadership style.

Organization Structure

"Tall" organizations are those that have several pyramidal levels of authority; "flat" structures have few. The tall organizations frequently lead to high supervisory ratios and therefore tend to encourage authoritarian supervision. With a relatively small number of subordinates, the supervisor is in a position to give detailed instructions and to exercise authoritarian control over each one. In a flat organization structure, with a relatively large number of subordinates, this type of supervision is often physically impossible. Since the supervisor frequently cannot make a decision on every problem, he tends to delegate more and appear more democratic.

The Sears, Roebuck Company study of tall vs. flat organizational structures concludes:

> Flatter, less complex structures, with a maximum of administrative decentralization, tend to create a potential for improved attitudes, more effective supervision, and greater individual responsibility and initiative among employees. Moreover, arrangements of this type encourage the development of individual expression and creativity which are so necessary to the personal satisfaction of employees and which are an essential ingredient of the democratic way of life.[17]

A NEW LEADERSHIP MODEL

The leadership style of a manager is a product of many forces: In the manager himself, in his subordinates, in the organizational system and in the dynamic situation which is of immediate concern. Leadership style seems to evolve through a complex and dynamic interaction between these four "subsystems" which can be depicted graphically as shown in the chart (Figure 1).

These forces, acting and interacting simultaneously, shape the pattern of leadership chosen by every manager. Every manager, at every level of the organization, needs to achieve an integration of these varying and complex pressures. Not only must he react to the many pressures and demands of environment, but he needs to understand those forces within himself, the individuals and groups he is dealing with and

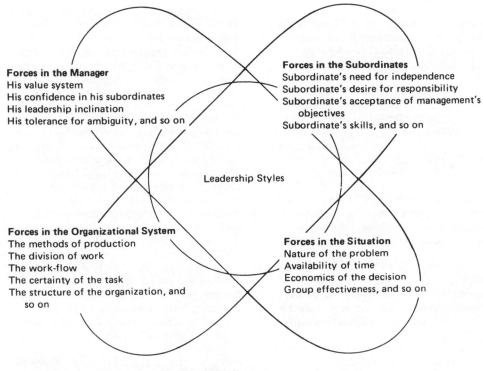

Forces in the Manager
His value system
His confidence in his subordinates
His leadership inclination
His tolerance for ambiguity, and so on

Forces in the Subordinates
Subordinate's need for independence
Subordinate's desire for responsibility
Subordinate's acceptance of management's
    objectives
Subordinate's skills, and so on

Leadership Styles

Forces in the Organizational System
The methods of production
The division of work
The work-flow
The certainty of the task
The structure of the organization, and
    so on

Forces in the Situation
Nature of the problem
Availability of time
Economics of the decision
Group effectiveness, and so on

FIGURE 1 • Interacting Forces Which
Shape the Manager's Leadership Style

the forces existing in the organization in order to *adjust* his style of leadership accordingly.

The successful manager is neither an autocrat, nor a complete democrat, rather one who integrates the forces operating in relation to the particular situation in question. The behavior of an effective leader under specific technological considerations may lead to failure under other technological situations.

The leadership appropriate in one organizational system may be irrelevant or even dysfunctional in another system.

Questions about leadership style should be answered in terms of what is most consistent with the *other* elements in the organization. For, in the long run, these system variables may be more useful for identifying and predicting the styles of leadership leading to optimal management in your organization.

REFERENCES

1. TEAD, ORDWAY, *The Art of Leadership* (New York: McGraw-Hill Book Company, Inc. 1935), p. 83.
2. GOULDER, ALVIN W., (ed.), *Studies in Leadership* (New York: Harper & Brothers, 1950), pp. 31–35.
3. SANFORD, FILLMORE H., "Leadership Identification Acceptance," in Harold Guetzkow, (ed.), *Groups, Leadership and Men* (Pittsburgh: Carnegie Press, 1951), p. 156.
4. STOGDILL, RALPH M., "Personal Factors Associated with Leadership: A Survey of the Literature," *Journal of Psychology*, January 1948, p. 63.
5. GIBB, CECIL A., "The Principles and Traits of Leadership," *Journal of Abnormal and Social Psychology*, July 1947, p. 267.
6. BENNIS, WARREN G., "Leadership Theory and Administrative Behavior: The Problem of Authority," *Administrative Science Quarterly*, December 1959, p. 261.
7. TANNENBAUM, ROBERT, and FRED MASSARIK, "Leadership: A Frame of Reference," in *Leadership and Organization* (eds.) Robert Tannenbaum, et al. (New York: McGraw-Hill Book Company, Inc., 1961), p. 24.
8. Adapted from BERELSON, BERNARD and GARY A. STEINER, *Human Behavior: An Inventory of Scientific Findings* (New York: Harcourt, Brace & World, Inc., 1964), p. 347.
9. TANNENBAUM, ROBERT and WARREN H. SCHMIDT, "How to Choose a Leadership Pattern," in *Leadership and Organization*, op. cit., pp. 67–79.
10. WOODWARD, JOAN, *Management and Technology* (London: Her Majesty's Stationery Office, 1958). Also, Woodward, Joan, *Industrial Organization: Theory and Practice* (New York: Oxford University Press, 1965).
11. The major categories of production methods are: *Unit production* — production of a single nonstandardized unit to customer order; one kind of item; *mass production* — standardized parts and products produced in large batches on assembly lines; *process production* — continuous flow of production, largely of liquids, gases and crystalline substances.
12. Management intensity is defined as the ratio of managers and supervisory staff to other personnel in the organization.
13. VOLLMER, HOWARD, *Employment Rights and the Employment Relationship* (Berkeley: University of California Press, 1960), Chapter 4.
14. This important variable is designated by Fiedler. For details see: FIEDLER, F. E., *A Contingency Model of Leadership Effectiveness*, Technical Report #10 (Urbana, Ill. Group Effectiveness Research Laboratory, University of Illinois, 1963). (Mimeograph).
15. SAYLES, LEONARD R., and GEORGE STRAUSS, *Human Behavior in Organiza-*

tions (Englewood Cliffs, N.J.: Prentice-Hall, Inc. 1966), p. 177.

16. FIEDLER, F. E., "Engineer the Job to Fit the Manager," *Harvard Business Review,*

September-October, 1965, pp. 115–122.

17. WORTHY, JAMES C., "Factors Influencing Employee Morale," *Harvard Business Review*, January 1950, pp. 169–179.

THE USES OF LEADERSHIP THEORY

James Owens

Carl L. was facing a crisis. A technician by background and now in his late thirties, he had recently become manager of a group of technicians and found himself in the midst of almost open rebellion. He knew the job well and was outstanding in his abilities to organize, handle detail, plan and control. His technicians were competent. But the group's morale had fallen to a point where all spirit and will seemed suctioned out of the group; the talent was there in abundance but simply not operating. What had gone wrong? And what should he do about it? His career depended on the answers.

Carl's managerial failure and variations of it are, unfortunately, common-place incidents within organizations, despite the personal tragedy and organizational nightmares involved.

What had gone wrong in Carl's group? Probably leadership, that still mysterious and only vaguely understood ingredient which must be created and sustained daily by a manager; with it, other managerial skills and resources come to life and work; without it, managerial skills and group talents become paralyzed — and work results grind to a halt.

This article aims (1) to present a practical framework, consisting of essential leadership theory, which can serve to facilitate a manager's understanding, analysis and evaluation of his personal leadership skills; and (2) to report on a composite managerial opinion about leadership practices, drawn from the author's work with many practicing managers over the past seven years, summarizing the insights of these managers themselves based on their years of practical experience.

Thus, my intent is to present a blend of research theory and practical managerial experience as, hopefully, a rich information-base for any manager seriously intent on improving his own managerial performance and career growth.

From *Michigan Business Review*, January 1973, published by the Graduate School of Business Administration, The University of Michigan. Reprinted by permission.

TRAIT THEORY VERSUS BEHAVIOR THEORY

The earliest studies of leadership hypothesized that what makes a leader (manager) effective is his personality, what he is as a person. Proponents of this "trait theory" searched for some set of built-in traits which successful leaders possess and ineffective leaders lack, such as "aggressiveness," "self-control," "independence," "friendliness," "religious orientation," "optimism," and many others. Decades of social science research, when finally tallied, added up disappointingly to very ambiguous results: effective leaders were found to be sometimes aggressive, self-disciplined, independent, friendly, religious, and optimistic — but often none or few of these things.

The mystery of leadership was not so easily or simplistically to be revealed and entered, definitively, into neat columns. Such research proved what most managers know intuitively, sometimes from bitter experience — such as Carl's — that effective leadership is one of the most complex phenomena in human relations and an ever-elusive riddle to those who must master it. (The obvious irony here is that the successful manager must master this phenomenon in practice, if not in theory and understanding, because — unlike social scientists — his very survival, as a career manager, depends on it!)

A "behavior theory" of leadership then came upon the scene: what makes a leader effective is (quite independently of his personality) simply what he does. Much less ambitious than trait theory, behavior theory tried to search out the right things that effective leaders do: such as how they communicate, give directions, motivate, delegate, plan, handle meetings, and so on. The value of the theory, to the extent it was valid, was its implication that "leaders need not be born to it but could be trained to do the right things," independently of their inner personality traits. Unfortunately, this approach, too, missed the essence of leadership and proved to be not only unambitious but too often degenerated into mechanical "techniques" and other superficial "gimmicks," which, on the job, emerged as robot-like counterfeits of genuine leadership — and thus failed.

The decades of work by both camps, however, were not wasted. It seems clear, today, that, on balance, there is truth — and valuable knowledge — to be gained from each theory.

THE USES OF TRAIT THEORY

Although trait theory advocates failed to build a comprehensive model of leadership, their work articulated and forced into sharp focus a practical truth: one's personality, what he fundamentally is as a person, is an ever-present and massive influence on how, and with what success, he functions as a manager.

The personality of a man is his inner life, including such inner elements as background, life history, beliefs, life experiences, attitudes, prejudices, self-image, fears, loves, hates, hopes and philosophy of life. In this sense, a man is like an iceberg: only a small fraction of what he is appears above the surface (his observable behavior, what he does); the rest is his inner life, the 7/8ths of the iceberg that lie, unobservable, below the surface.

However, the manager's inner personality causes — or "spills over" into — his behavior which, in turn, affects others with whom he works, eliciting from them either cooperative or resistance reactions. And, therein lies the manager's fate: cooperative reactions from his people spell success; resistance reactions, however irrational from the manager's viewpoint, usually assure his failure (as, probably, in the case of Carl above).

Any attempt to "formulize" this cause-effect process in the form of simple one-to-one correlations, such as trait "Z_1," causing invariably behavior "Z_2," causing invariably effect "Z_3," is doomed to failure — as the efforts of the trait-theorists proved. However, it is clear that there is an influential relationship between a manager's total personality and his success, as a manager, on the job. I have submitted this precise concept to several thousand practicing managers over the years and, based on their experience, virtually all acknowledge its validity. For example, most of these managers concluded that a manager who is naturally low in his ability to trust others, has little chance to succeed; despite his best efforts, he will be unable to delegate properly and thus becomes a "bottle-neck," as work piles up on his desk, and a source of frustration to people who want a chance to get involved and grow. Or, a manager whose personality requires a high degree of security in his life, is unable to take any risks, and thus fails because he decides and does nothing! Or, a manager who struggles within himself with a poor self-image and an inherent low level of self-confidence, avoids decisions and radiates, as a kind of "self-fulfilling pro-phecy," certain failure. Other examples include the effect on managerial success of personality characteristics like racial prejudice, intolerance for unfamiliar ideas, dislike or distrust of the young, respect for (or general cynicism about) other people because of their background, sex, intelligence, experience, or appearance, and so on.

The virtually unanimous opinion of these thousands of practical managers has been that any manager, who genuinely has ambitions for managerial growth and advancement, can achieve it only if he adds to his efforts a periodic evaluation of his total personality, especially his attitudes, and their effect on his people as well as the success (or failure) they produce for him. Such a manager, who is capable even of managing his own career, will find that most of his personality characteristics are assets; but, if he pursues the search objectively, he will find, too, that some are liabilities. These he must begin to change, if he can or wishes; and, if he cannot, then he must, as a mature person with mature judgment, assess himself carefully and find the kind of job that fits his personality.

In short, these managers believe — and I do too — that a manager can grow in his managerial career only if he grows as a total personality, which he is long before he begins to function as a manager. What a man is and brings to the office in the form of a total personality largely determines what and how he does and with what degree of success. What this means is that personal growth as a human being underlines and becomes, to a great extent, the real foundation upon which managerial and career growth can develop. Managerial success is not a peripheral set of "techniques"; it is a working-out of one's essential being in the form of action.

THE USES OF BEHAVIOR THEORY

What "behavior theory" has taught us, over the years, is that, within certain limits imposed by the inner personality of the individual, each person has the capability of cultivating habits of behavior (by act of will) which optimize his effects upon people. Many of us feel moody, but, by act of will, virtually never act moody. Constructive habits of courtesy, self-control, two-way communication, delegation and interest in the problems of others can be learned and practiced, by act of will.

The most important contribution of "behavior theory," however, is the development of a classification of leadership behaviors (styles) which provides a manager an analytical tool with which he can consciously and intelligently build a personally successful leadership style.

A MATRIX OF LEADERSHIP STYLES

Probably the most practical contribution of research to the day-to-day life of the manager is the analytic model of leadership styles — their description and properties. Virtually all of the managers to whom I have presented this classic model agree that it clarifies their options and serves well as a means for productive analysis and evaluation of their personal leadership styles as well as their relative success.

The exact form of the leadership matrix varies as do its details but the following version is standard. The brief descriptions of each style are, of course, stereotyped and over-simplified for purposes of clear identification and analysis. Also, they are defined in neutral language, avoiding, as much as possible, either favoring or disparaging overtones at this point. The five leadership styles, which comprise the matrix, are as follows:

1. The Autocratic Leader

The autocrat has authority, from some source such as his position, knowledge, strength, or power to reward and punish, and he uses this authority as his principal, or only method of getting things done. He is frankly authoritarian, knows what he wants done, and how, "tells" people what their work-assignments are, and demands unquestioning obedience. The autocrat ranges from "tough" to "paternalistic" depending on how much he stresses, as motivation, threat and punishment in the former case or rewards in the latter. The "tough" autocrat demands and gets compliance, "or else." The "paternalistic" autocrat demands and expects compliance but mainly on a "father-knows-best" — and often very personal — relationship, implying personal dependence, rewards, and security. The autocrat permits people little or no freedom.

2. The Bureaucratic Leader

Like the autocrat, the bureaucrat "tells" people what to do, and how, but the basis for his orders is almost exclusively the organization's policies, procedures, and rules. For the bureaucrat, these rules are absolute. He manages entirely "by the book," and no exceptions are permitted. He treats rules and administers their force upon people as a judge might treat and permit no departure or exception from — laws, including their every technicality. Like the autocrat, the bureaucrat permits people little or no freedom.

3. The Diplomatic Leader

The diplomat is an artist who, like the salesman, lives by the arts of personal persuasion. Although he has the same clear authority as the autocrat, the diplomat prefers to "sell" people and operate, as much as possible, by persuasion and broad-scale individual motivation of people. He will "revert," if necessary, to the autocratic style, but prefers to avoid this. Some term him a "sell-type" leader who uses a large variety and degree of persuasion-tactics, ranging from simple explanation of the reasons for an order to full-scale bargaining with people. He will usually relate his organizational goals to the personal individual needs and aspirations of his people. Such a leader retains his authority in that he knows and will insist on a particular course of action; but, he provides some — limited — freedom to his people in that he permits them to react, question, raise objections, discuss, and even argue their side of the issue.

4. The Participative Leader

The participative leader openly invites his people to participate or share, to a greater or lesser extent, in decisions, policy-making and operation methods. He is either a "democratic" or a "consultative" leader.

The "democratic" leader "joins" his group and makes it clear, in advance, that he will abide by the group's decision whether arrived at by consensus or majority vote. (This style is sometimes seen in the operations of research and development groups.)

The "consultative" leader consults his people and invites frank involvement, discussion, pro and con argument, and recommendations from the group, but makes it clear that he alone is accountable and reserves the final decision to himself.

In both forms of the participative style of leadership people are given a high degree of freedom — as they are, too, in the Free-Rein style.

5. The Free-Rein Leader

The "free-rein" leader (the analogy, of course, is to a horseman who has left the reins free) does not literally abandon all control. He sets a goal for his subordinate as well as clear parameters such as policies, deadlines, and budget and then drops the "reins" and sets his subordinate free to operate without further direction or control, unless the subordinate himself requests it.

THE "BEST" LEADERSHIP STYLE

Despite certain implications in the literature that there is a "best" and ideal leadership style, the managers I surveyed categorically reject this simple solution suggested by some social scientists. Their virtually unanimous view was that the "best" leadership style DEPENDS ON:

a. the individual personality of the manager himself ("Trait theory" revisited);
b. the individual followers, the kind of people they are and the kind of work they do;

c. and, the particular situation and circumstances on any given day or hour.

In short, no "cook-book" or formulized recipe for effective leadership "rang true" as realistic with these managers. The complexity and mystery of leadership does not permit simplistic approaches.

Only a manager, himself, examining, and exploring the varieties of leadership styles, their advantages and weaknesses, as well as the people and the situation with which he is dealing, can decide what is the "best" leadership style for him, and with them, and in this particular situation. It must be an act of individual judgment. A theoretical framework can assist, as can the opinions of thousands of managers, but the choice and practice of leadership style must always remain the act of judgment of the individual manager.

Some authors have coined the expression "tool-box approach" for this necessity that faces managers of choosing the "right style" at the "right time" in the "right situation" (as opposed to the easy and utopian formula of a single, predominant leadership style for all people and all situations).

A SUMMARY OF MANAGERS' VIEWS

Working closely over the years with many practicing managers, I have had the opportunity to learn much of what they learned about leadership — based, not on textbook abstractions, but realistically on years of hard experience. The essential results of this seven-year informal survey of these managers are organized below as telegraphic propositions expressed as either advantages or weaknesses of each classic leadership style. Each proposition is a kind of composite view representing a virtual consensus of the opinions of these managers. Naturally, they are general statements and, as such, allow for exceptions in individual cases. Even so, these propositions are experience-based insights of managers themselves and should be helpful to any manager seriously intent on evaluating and improving his own leadership.

I. The autocratic leadership style
    A. Advantages
        1. When appropriate, can increase efficiency, save time and get quick results, especially in a crisis or emergency situation.
        2. The paternalistic form of this style of leadership works well with employees who have a low tolerance for ambiguity, feel insecure with freedom and even minor decision-making requirements, and thrive under clear, detailed, and achievable directives.
        3. Chain of command and division of work (who is supposed to do what) are clear and fully understood by all.
    B. Weaknesses
        1. The apparent efficiency of one-way communication often becomes a false efficiency since one-way communication, without "feedback," typically leads to misunderstandings, communication breakdowns and costly errors.

2. The autocratic manager must really be an expert, not just think he is, because he receives little, if any, information and ideas from his people as inputs into his decision-making. He is really alone in his decision-making and this is generally dangerous in today's environment of technological and organizational complexity.

3. The critical weakness, however, of the autocratic style is its effect on people. Many managers pine for the good old days when the boss gave orders and people obeyed meekly and without question. These managers, however, agree that — like it or not — those days are gone forever. Today, most people resent authoritarian rule which excludes them from involvement and reduces them to machine-like cogs without human dignity or importance. They express their resentment in the form of massive resistance, low morale and low productivity (if not downright work stoppage or sabotage). This is especially true, today, with technical or educated people, youths entering the job market, and members of most minority groups.

II. The bureaucratic leadership style
   A. Advantages
      1. Insures consistency of policy and operations which can be critical in industries where legal parameters are common (banking, sales, etc.).
      2. Consistent application of personnel-related rules, for one and for all, contributes a sense of fairness and impartiality in the manager's many and complex dealings with people.
      3. People know where they stand. Most decisions concerning them are by known — and accepted — rule, predictable, objective (rather than by the whim or mood of a manager) — and there is security and a sense of fairness.
   B. Weaknesses
      1. Inflexibility in situations where exceptions to rules should be made or requested.
      2. Paralysis in situations not covered by rules or where rules are ambiguous (as is often the case: policies and rules represent legislation for the majority of situations but can never substitute for individual human judgment in a particular specific situation).
      3. The reaction of people working under a strongly bureaucratic manager is essentially the same as described above in the case of the autocratic manager: again, resentment, resistance, and low morale.

III. The diplomatic leadership style
   A. Advantages

1. People cooperate and work more enthusiastically if managers take even a few minutes — and respect people enough — to give them the simple reasons and explanations of the reasons that make a particular task important — rather than just a blind chore.

2. A manager's personal effort to explain to or persuade a subordinate is usually received as an important compliment and show of respect — and usually appreciated and responded to with a high degree of cooperation and effort.

3. This style of leadership is indispensable for the legions of so-called "staff" people (and even "line" people who realize the inadequacy of their real authority). They must achieve the results, for which they are accountable, "unfairly" deprived of the clear-cut authority required and, therefore, are utterly dependent on the skills of persuasion to get the help and cooperation needed.

B. Weaknesses

1. Some people interpret efforts to persuade them, rather than order them, as a sign of weakness and, thus lose respect for a manager. The basic weakness, however, of the diplomatic style is the same as the pitfall always facing those who use consistently the "tool-box" approach to leadership; namely, hypocrisy. Unless handled with judgment, skill and sincerity, the diplomatic style — as well as any "tool box" approach with people — quickly degenerates and "comes through" to people as insincerity, frank manipulation and exploitation — and is, thus, deeply resented and resisted. And, naturally, a complete failure.

2. Anyone employing the diplomatic style must be a skilled and competent salesman, who usually "wins" the "sale." A salesman routinely expects and invites objections — a manager who operates this way must be able to convince and "sell" people, or he will be forced to "revert" (hypocritically) to a frank autocratic order. The effect of this on people is both obvious and disastrous.

IV. The participative leadership style

A. Advantages

1. When people participate in and help formulate a decision, they support it (instead of fighting or ignoring it) and work hard to make it work, because it's their idea and, now, part of their life and their "ego."

2. The manager consistently receives the benefit of the best information, ideas, suggestions, and talent — and operating experience — of his

people. The rich information-source which they represent becomes his and a key input into his decison-making.

3. Group discussion, even though time-consuming, before a decision is made, can force critical information to the surface which, when considered, improves decision-making — or, in some cases, actually averts a disaster which would have occurred if key operating-level information were not made available.

4. This style of leadership permits and encourages people to develop, grow and rise in the organization (both in terms of responsibility they can assume and service they can contribute).

5. Most people work better, more enthusiastically and at a high level of motivation when they are given a reasonable degree of freedom to act and contribute. They enjoy a sense of personal importance, value and achievement, unlike human cogs in machine-like organizational systems.

6. Most importantly, as already implied above, the participative manager establishes a work-climate which easily unleashes the enormous power of people who are motivated by — and will strive hard for — goals which they help create and in the accomplish-

ment of which they gain deep personal satisfaction in the form of recognition, sense of accomplishment, sense of importance and personal value. In short, the participative manager has the critical factor of built-in personal motivation working for him.

B. Weaknesses

1. The participative style can take enormous amounts of time and, when used inappropriately, be simply inefficient.

2. Some managers "use" the democratic style as a way of avoiding (or abdicating) responsibility.

3. People resent the invitation to offer recommendations when such recommendations are consistently ignored and rejected. It follows that any manager, who must reject a recommendation, should quickly explain why such recommendations had to be rejected.

4. Use of the participative styles can easily, if not handled well, degenerate into a complete loss of managerial control.

V. The free-rein leadership style

A. Advantages

1. This style comprises the essence of full managerial delegation with its benefits of optimum utilization of time and resources.

2. Many people are motivated to full effort only if given this kind of free-rein.

B. Weaknesses

1. Very little managerial control and a high degree of risk.

2. This style can be a disaster if the manager does not know well the competence and integrity of his people and their ability to handle this kind of freedom.

CONCLUSION

Leadership is still an art despite the efforts of social science researchers to make it a science. The summaries, here, of essential leadership theory and managerial opinion (based on experience) are presented only as a help to (not a substitute for) the final individual judgment of the manager as he lives with his particular people in his particular situation.

Every such manager, however, must operate by some leadership style or styles and it is hoped that the ideas presented above will aid the manager in his analysis, evaluation and development of his own personal leadership style.

PATH-GOAL THEORY OF LEADERSHIP

Robert J. House and Terence R. Mitchell

An integrated body of conjecture by students of leadership, referred to as the "Path-Goal Theory of Leadership," is currently emerging. According to this theory, leaders are effective because of their impact on subordinates' motivation, ability to perform effectively, and satisfactions. The theory is called Path-Goal because its major concern is how the leader influences the subordinates' perceptions of their work goals, personal goals, and paths to goal attainment. The theory suggests that a leader's behavior is motivating or satisfying to the degree that the behavior increases subordinate goal attainment and clarifies the paths to these goals.

HISTORICAL FOUNDATIONS

The path-goal approach has its roots in a more general motivational theory called expectancy theory.[1] Briefly, expectancy theory states that an individual's attitudes (e.g., satisfaction with

From *Journal of Contemporary Business* (Autumn 1974): 81–97. Reprinted by permission.

supervision or job satisfaction) or behavior (e.g., leader behavior, or job effort) can be predicted from: (1) the degree to which the job, or behavior, is seen as leading to various outcomes (expectancy) and (2) the evaluation of these outcomes (valences). Thus, people are satisfied with their job if they think it leads to things that are highly valued, and they work hard if they believe that effort leads to things that are highly valued. This type of theoretical rationale can be used to predict a variety of phenomena related to leadership, such as why leaders behave the way they do, or how leader behavior influences subordinate motivation.[2]

This latter approach is the primary concern of this article. The implication for leadership is that subordinates are motivated by leader behavior to the extent that this behavior influences expectancies, e.g., goal paths, and valences, e.g., goal attractiveness.

Several writers have advanced specific hypotheses concerning how the leader affects the paths and the goals of subordinates.[3] These writers focused on two issues: (1) how the leader affects subordinates' expectations that effort will lead to effective performance and valued rewards: and (2) how this expectation affects motivation to work hard and perform well.

While the state of theorizing about leadership in terms of subordinates' paths and goals is in its infancy, we believe it is promising for two reasons. First, it suggests effects of leader behavior that have not yet been investigated but which appear to be fruitful areas of inquiry. And second, it suggests with some precision the situational factors on which the effects of

leader behavior are contingent.

The initial theoretical work by Evans asserts that leaders will be effective by making rewards available to subordinates and by making these rewards contingent on the subordinate's accomplishment of specific goals.[4] Evans argued that one of the strategic functions of the leader is to clarify for subordinates the kind of behavior that leads to goal accomplishment and valued rewards. This function might be referred to as path clarification. Evans also argued that the leader increases the rewards available to subordinates by being supportive toward subordinates, i.e., by being concerned about their status, welfare, and comfort. Leader supportiveness is in itself a reward that the leader has at his or her disposal, and the judicious use of this reward increases the motivation of subordinates.

Evans studied the relationship between the behavior of leaders and the subordinates' expectations that effort leads to rewards, and also studied the resulting impact on ratings of the subordinates' performance. He found that when subordinates viewed leaders as being supportive (considerate of their needs) and when these superiors provided directions and guidance to the subordinates, there was a positive relationship between leader behavior and subordinates' performance ratings.

However, leader behavior was only related to subordinates' performance when the leader's behavior also was related to the subordinates' expectations that their effort would result in desired rewards. Thus, Evans' findings suggest that the major impact of a leader on the performance of subordinates is clarifying the path to desired rewards and making such rewards contingent on effective performance.

Stimulated by this line of reasoning, House, and House and Dessler advanced a more complex theory of the effects of leader behavior on the motivation of subordinates.[5] The theory intends to explain the effects of four specific kinds of leader behavior on the following three subordinate attitudes or expectations: (1) the satisfaction of subordinates; (2) the subordinates' acceptance of the leader; and (3) the expectations of subordinates that effort will result in effective performance and that effective performance is the path to rewards. The four kinds of leader behavior included in the theory are: (1) directive leadership; (2) supportive leadership; (3) participative leadership; and (4) achievement-oriented leadership. Directive leadership is characterized by a leader who lets subordinates know what is expected of them, gives specific guidance as to what should be done and how it should be done, makes his or her part in the group understood, schedules work to be done, maintains definite standards of performance, and asks that group members follow standard rules and regulations. Supportive leadership is characterized by a friendly and approachable leader who shows concern for the status, well-being, and needs of subordinates. Such a leader does little things to make the work more pleasant, treats members as equals, and is friendly and approachable. Participative leadership is characterized by a leader who consults with subordinates, solicits their suggestions, and takes these suggestions seriously into consideration before making a decision. An achievement-oriented leader sets challenging goals, expects subordinates

to perform at their highest level, continuously seeks improvement in performance, *and* shows a high degree of confidence that the subordinates will assume responsibility, put forth effort, and accomplish challenging goals. This kind of leader constantly emphasizes excellence in performance and simultaneously displays confidence that subordinates will meet high standards of excellence.

A number of studies suggest that these different leadership styles can be shown by the same leader in various situations.[6] For example, a leader may show directiveness toward subordinates in some instances and be participative or supportive in other instances.[7] Thus, the traditional method of characterizing a leader as either highly participative and supportive *or* highly directive is invalid; rather, it can be concluded that leaders vary in the particular fashion employed for supervising their subordinates. Also, the theory, in its present stage, is a tentative explanation of the effects of leader behavior — it is incomplete because it does not explain other kinds of leader behavior and does not explain the effects of the leader on factors other than subordinate acceptance, satisfaction, and expectations. However, the theory is stated so that additional variables may be included in it as new knowledge is made available.

PATH-GOAL THEORY

General Propositions

The first proposition of path-goal theory is that leader behavior is acceptable and satisfying to subordinates to the extent that the subordinates see such behavior as either an immediate source of satisfaction or as instrumental to future satisfaction.

The second proposition of this theory is that the leader's behavior will be motivational, i.e., increase effort, to the extent that (1) such behavior makes satisfaction of subordinate's needs contingent on effective performance and (2) such behavior complements the environment of subordinates by providing the coaching, guidance, support, and rewards necessary for effective performance.

These two propositions suggest that the leader's strategic functions are to enhance subordinates' motivation to perform, satisfaction with the job, and acceptance of the leader. From previous research on expectancy theory of motivation, it can be inferred that the strategic functions of the leader consist of: (1) recognizing and/or arousing subordinates' needs for outcomes over which the leader has some control; (2) increasing personal payoffs to subordinates for work-goal attainment; (3) making the path to these payoffs easier to travel by coaching and direction; (4) helping

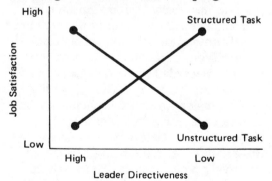

FIGURE 1 • *Hypothetical Relationship between Directive Leadership and Subordinate Satisfaction with Task Structure as a Contingency Factor*

subordinates clarify expectancies; (5) reducing frustrating barriers; and (6) increasing the opportunities for personal satisfacion contingent on effective performance.[8]

Stated less formally, the motivational functions of the leader consist of increasing the number and kinds of personal payoffs to subordinates for work-goal attainment and making paths to these payoffs easier to travel by clarifying the paths, reducing road blocks and pitfalls, and increasing the opportunities for personal satisfaction en route.

Contingency Factors

Two classes of situational variables are asserted to be contingency factors. A contingency factor is a variable which moderates the relationship between two other variables such as leader behavior and subordinate satisfaction. For example, we might suggest that the degree of structure in the task moderates the relationship between leaders' directive behavior and subordinates' job satisfaction. Figure 1 shows how such a relationship might look. Thus, subordinates are satisfied with directive behavior in an unstructured task and are satisfied with nondirective behavior in a structured task. Therefore, we say that the relationship between leader directiveness and subordinate satisfaction is contingent upon the structure of the task.

The two contingency variables are *(a)* personal characteristics of the subordinates and *(b)* the environmental pressures and demands with which subordinates must cope in order to accomplish the work goals and to satisfy their needs. While other situational factors also may operate to determine the effects of leader behavior, they are not presently known.

With respect to the first class of contingency factors, the characteristics of subordinates, path-goal theory asserts that leader behavior will be acceptable to subordinates to the extent that the subordinates see such behavior as either an immediate source of satisfaction or as instrumental to future satisfaction. Subordinates' characteristics are hypothesized to partially determine this perception. For example, Runyon and Mitchell[9] show that the subordinate's score on a measure called Locus of Control moderates the relationship between participative leadership style and subordinate satisfaction. The Locus-of-Control measure reflects the degree to which an individual sees the environment as systematically responding to his or her behavior. People who believe that what happens to them occurs because of their behavior are called internals; people who believe that what happens to them occurs because of luck or chance are called externals. Mitchell's findings suggest that internals are more satisfied with a participative leadership style and externals are more satisfied with a directive style.

A second characteristic of subordinates on which the effects of leader behavior are contingent is subordinates' perception of their own ability with respect to their assigned tasks. The higher the degree of perceived ability relative to task demands, the less the subordinate will view leader directiveness and coaching behavior as acceptable. Where the subordinate's perceived ability is high, such behavior is likely to have little positive effect on the motivation of the subordinate and to be perceived as

excessively close control. Thus, the acceptability of the leader's behavior is determined in part by the characteristics of the subordinates.

The second aspect of the situation, the environment of the subordinate, consists of those factors that are not within the control of the subordinate but which are important to need satisfaction or to ability to perform effectively. The theory asserts that effects of the leader's behavior on the psychological states of subordinates are contingent on other parts of the subordinates' environment that are relevant to subordinate motivation. Three broad classifications of contingency factors in the environment are: (1) The subordinates' tasks; (2) The formal authority system of the organization; and (3) The primary work group.

Assessment of the environmental conditions makes it possible to predict the kind and amount of influence that specific leader behaviors will have on the motivation of subordinates. Any of the three environmental factors could act upon the subordinate in any of three ways: first, to serve as stimuli that motivate and direct the subordinate to perform necessary task operations; second, to constrain variability in behavior. Constraints may help the subordinate by clarifying expectancies that effort leads to rewards or by preventing the subordinate from experiencing conflict and confusion. Constraints also may be counterproductive to the extent that they restrict initiative or prevent increases in effort from being associated positively with rewards. Third, environmental factors may serve as rewards for achieving desired performance; e.g., it is possible for the subordinate to receive the necessary cues to do the job and the needed rewards for satisfaction from sources other than the leader, e.g., co-workers in the primary work group. Thus, the effect of the leader on subordinates' motivation will be a function of how deficient the environment is with respect to motivational stimuli, constraints, or rewards.

With respect to the environment, path-goal theory asserts that when goals and paths to desired goals are apparent because of the routine nature of the task, clear group norms or objective controls of the formal authority systems, attempts by the leader to clarify paths and goals will be both redundant and seen by subordinates as imposing unnecessary, close control. Although such control may increase performance by preventing soldiering or malingering, it also will result in decreased satisfaction (see Figure 1). Also with respect to the work environment, the theory asserts that the more dissatisfying the task, the more the subordinates will resent leader behavior directed at increasing productivity or enforcing compliance to organizational rules and procedures.

Finally, with respect to environmental variables the theory states that leader behavior will be motivational to the extent that it helps subordinates cope with environmental uncertainties, threats from others, or sources of frustration. Such leader behavior is predicted to increase subordinates' satisfaction with the job context and to be motivational to the extent that it increases the subordinates' expectations that their effort will lead to valued rewards.

These propositions and specification of situational contingencies provide a heuristic framework on which to base future research. Hopefully, this will lead to a more fully developed, explicitly formal theory of leadership.

Figure 2 presents a summary of the theory. It is hoped that these propositions, while admittedly tentative, will provide managers with some insights concerning the effects of their own leader behavior and that of others.

EMPIRICAL SUPPORT

The theory has been tested in a limited number of studies which have generated considerable empirical support for our ideas and also suggest areas in which the theory requires revision. A brief review of these studies follows.

Leader Directiveness

Leader directiveness has a positive correlation with satisfaction and expectancies of subordinates who are engaged in ambiguous tasks and has a negative

Leader Behavior	and	Contingency Factors	Cause	Subordinate Attitudes and Behavior
1. Directive		1. Subordinate characteristics Authoritarianism Locus of control Ability	Personal perceptions Influence⟩	1. Job satisfaction Job → rewards
2. Supportive				2. Acceptance of leader Leader → rewards
3. Achievement-oriented		2. Environmental factors The task Formal authority system	Influence⟩ Motivational stimuli Constraints Rewards	3. Motivational behavior Effort → performance Performance → rewards
4. Participative		Primary work group		

FIGURE 2 • Summary of Path-Goal Relationships

correlation with satisfaction and expectancies of subordinates engaged in clear tasks. These findings were predicted by the theory and have been replicated in seven organizations. They suggest that when task demands are ambiguous or when the organization procedures, rules, and policies are not clear, a leader behaving in a directive manner complements the tasks and the organization by providing the necessary guidance and psychological structure for subordinates.[10] However, when task demands are clear to subordinates, leader directiveness is seen more as a hindrance.

However, other studies have failed to confirm these findings.[11] A study by Dessler[12] suggests a resolution to these conflicting findings — he found that for subordinates at the lower organizational levels of a manufacturing firm who were doing routine, repetitive, unambiguous tasks, directive leadership was preferred by closed-minded, dogmatic, authoritarian subordinates and nondirective leadership was preferred by nonauthoritarian, open-minded subordinates. However, for subordinates at higher organizational levels doing nonroutine ambiguous tasks, directive leadership was preferred for both authoritarian and nonauthoritarian subordinates. Thus, Dessler found that two contingency factors appear to operate simultaneously: subordinate task ambiguity and degree of subordinate authoritarianism. When measured in combination, the findings are as predicted by the theory; however, when the subordinate's personality is not taken into account, task ambiguity does not always operate as a contingency variable as predicted by the theory. House, Burrill, and Dessler recently found a similar interaction between subordinate's authoritarianism and task ambiguity in a second manufacturing firm, thus adding confidence in Dessler's original findings.[13]

Supportive Leadership

The theory hypothesizes that supportive leadership will have its most positive effect on subordinate satisfaction for subordinates who work on stressful, frustrating, or dissatisfying tasks. This hypothesis has been tested in ten samples of employees,[14] and in only one of these studies was the hypothesis disconfirmed.[15] Despite some inconsistency in research on supportive leadership, the evidence is sufficiently positive to suggest that managers should be alert to the critical need for supportive leadership under conditions where tasks are dissatisfying, frustrating, or stressful to subordinates.

Achievement-Oriented Leadership

The theory hypothesizes that achievement-oriented leadership will cause subordinates to strive for higher standards of performance and to have more confidence in the ability to meet challenging goals. A recent study by House, Valency, and Van der Krabben provides a partial test of this hypothesis among white-collar employees in service organizations.[16] For subordinates performing ambiguous, nonrepetitive tasks, they found a positive relationship between the amount of achievement orientation of the leader and subordinates' expectancy that their effort would result in effective performance. Stated less technically, for subordinates performing ambiguous, nonrepetitive tasks, the higher the achievement orientation of the leader, the more the subordinates were confident that their efforts would pay off in effective performance. For subordinates performing moderately unambiguous, repetitive tasks, there was no significant relationship between achievement-oriented leadership and subordinate expectancies that their effort would lead to effective performance. This finding held in four separate organizations.

Two plausible interpretations may be used to explain these data. First, people who select ambiguous, nonrepetitive tasks may be different in personality from those who select a repetitive job and may, therefore, be more responsive to an achievement-oriented leader. A second explanation is that achievement orientation only affects expectancies in ambiguous situations because there is more flexibility and autonomy in such tasks. Therefore, subordinates in such tasks are more likely to be able to change in response to such leadership style. Neither of the above interpretations has been tested to date; however, additional research is currently under way to investigate these relationships.

Participative Leadership

In theorizing about the effects of participative leadership it is necessary to ask about the specific characteristics of both the subordinates and their situation that would cause participative leadership to be viewed as satisfying and instrumental to effective performance.

Mitchell recently described at least four ways in which a participative leadership style would impact on subordinate attitudes and behavior as predicted by expectancy theory.[17] First, a participative climate should increase the clarity of organizational contingencies.

Through participation in decision-making, subordinates should learn what leads to what. From a path-goal viewpoint participation would lead to greater clarity of the paths to various goals. A second impact of participation would be that subordinates, hopefully, should select goals they highly value. If one participates in decisions about various goals, it makes sense that this individual would select goals he or she wants. Thus, participation would increase the correspondence between organization and subordinate goals. Third, we can see how participation would increase the control the individual has over what happens on the job. If our motivation is higher (based on the preceding two points), then having greater autonomy and ability to carry out our intentions should lead to increased effort and performance. Finally, under a participative system, pressure toward high performance should come from sources other than the leader or the organization. More specifically, when people participate in the decision process they become more ego-involved; the decisions made are in some part their own. Also, their peers know what is expected, and the social pressure has a greater impact. Thus, motivation to perform well stems from internal and social factors as well as formal external ones.

A number of investigations prior to the above formulation supported the idea that participation appears to be helpful,[18] and Mitchell presents a number of recent studies that support the above four points.[19] However, it is also true that we would expect the relationship between a participative style and subordinate behavior to be moderated by both the personality characteristics of the subordinate and the situational demands. Studies by Tannenbaum and Allport and Vroom have shown that subordinates who prefer autonomy and self-control respond more positively to participative leadership in terms of both satisfaction and performance than subordinates who do not have such preferences.[20] Also, the studies mentioned by Runyon[21] and Mitchell[22] showed that subordinates who were external in orientation were less satisfied with a participative style of leadership than were internal subordinates.

House also has reviewed these studies in an attempt to explain the ways in which the situation or environment moderates the relationship between participation and subordinate attitudes and behavior.[23] His analysis suggests that where participative leadership is positively related to satisfaction, regardless of the predispositions of subordinates, the tasks of the subjects appear to be ambiguous and ego-involving. In the studies in which the subjects' personalities or predispositions moderate the effect of participative leadership, the tasks of the subjects are inferred to be highly routine and/or nonego-involving.

House reasoned from this analysis that the task may have an overriding effect on the relationship between leader participation and subordinate responses, and that individual predispositions or personality characteristics of subordinates may have an effect only under some tasks. It was assumed that when task demands are ambiguous, subordinates will have a need to reduce the ambiguity. Further, it was assumed that when task demands are ambiguous, participative problem solving between

the leader and the subordinate will result in more effective decisions than when the task demands are unambiguous. Finally, it was assumed that when the subordinates are ego-involved in their tasks they are more likely to want to have a say in the decisions that affect them. Given these assumptions, the following hypotheses were formulated to account for the conflicting findings reviewed above:

1. When subjects are highly ego-involved in a decision or a task and the decision or task demands are ambiguous, participative leadership will have a positive effect on the satisfaction and motivation of the subordinate, *regardless* of the subordinate's predisposition toward self-control, authoritarianism, or need for independence.
2. When subordinates are not ego-involved in their tasks and when task demands are clear, subordinates who are not authoritarian and who have high needs for independence and self-control will respond favorably to leader participation and their opposite personality types will respond less favorably.

These hypotheses were derived on the basis of path-goal theorizing; i.e., the rationale guiding the analysis of prior studies was that both task characteristics and characteristics of subordinates interact to determine the effect of a specific kind of leader behavior on the satisfaction, expectancies, and performance of subordinates. To date, one major investigation has supported some of these predictions[24] in which personality variables, amount of participative leadership, task ambiguity, and job satisfaction were assessed for 324 employees of an industrial manufacturing organization. As expected, in nonrepetitive, ego-involving tasks, employees (regardless of their personality) were more satisfied under a participative style than a nonparticipative style. However, in repetitive tasks which were less ego-involving the amount of authoritarianism of subordinates moderated the relationship between leadership style and satisfaction. Specifically, low authoritarian subordinates were *more satisfied* under a participative style. These findings are exactly as the theory would predict; thus it has promise in reconciling a set of confusing and contradictory findings with respect to participative leadership.

SUMMARY AND CONCLUSIONS

We have attempted to describe what we believe is a useful theoretical framework for understanding the effect of leadership behavior on subordinate satisfaction and motivation. Most theorists today have moved away from the simplistic notions that all effective leaders have a certain set of personality traits or that the situation completely deter-

mines performance. Some researchers have presented rather complex attempts at matching certain types of leaders with certain types of situations, e.g., the articles written by Vroom and Fiedler in this issue. But, we believe that a path-goal approach goes one step further. It not only suggests what type of style may be most effective in a given situation — it also attempts to explain *why* it is most effective.

We are optimistic about the future outlook of leadership research. With the guidance of path-goal theorizing, future research is expected to unravel many confusing puzzles about the reasons for and effects of leader behavior that have, heretofore, not been solved. However, we add a word of caution: the theory, and the research on it, are relatively new to the literature of organizational behavior. Consequently, path-goal theory is offered more as a tool for direction research and stimulating insight than as a proven guide for managerial action.

REFERENCES

1. T. R. MITCHELL, "Expectancy Model of Job Satisfaction, Occupational Preference and Effort: A Theoretical, Methodological, and Empirical Appraisal," *Psychological Bulletin*, December 1974, pp. 1053–77.
2. D. M. NEBEKER and T. R. MITCHELL, "Leader Behavior: An Expectancy Theory Approach," *Organization Behavior and Human Performance* 11 (1974): 355–67.
3. M. G. EVANS, "The Effects of Supervisory Behavior on the Path-Goal Relationship," *Organization Behavior and Human Performance* 55 (1970): 277–98; T. H. HAMMER and H. T. DACHLER, "The

Process of Supervision in the Context of Motivation Theory," *Research Report No. 3* (University of Maryland, 1973); F. DANSEREAU, JR., J. CASHMAN, and G. GRAEN, "Instrumentality Theory and Equity Theory as Complementary Approaches in Predicting the Relationship of Leadership and Turnover among Managers," *Organization Behavior and Human Performance* 10 (1973): 184–200; R. J. HOUSE, "A Path-Goal Theory of Leader Effectiveness," *Administrative Science Quarterly* 16, no. 3 (September 1971): 321–38; T. R. MITCHELL, "Motivation and Participation: An Integration," *Academy of Management Journal* 16, no. 4 (1973): 160–79; G. GRAEN, F. DANSEREAU, JR., and T. MINAMI, "Dysfunctional Leadership Styles," *Organization Behavior and Human Per-*

formance 7 (1972): 216–36; G. GRAEN et al., "An Empirical Test of the Man-in-the-Middle Hypothesis among Executives in a Hierarchical Organization Employing a Unit Analysis," *Organization Behavior and Human Performance* 8 (1972): 262–85; R. J. HOUSE and G. DESSLER, "The Path-Goal Theory of Leadership: Some Post Hoc and A Priori Tests," in J. G. HUNT, ed., *Contingency Approach to Leadership* (Carbondale: Southern Illinois University Press, 1974).

4. M. G. EVANS, "Effects of Supervisory Behavior" and "Extensions of a Path-Goal Theory of Motivation," *Journal of Applied Psychology* 59 (1974): 172–78.

5. R. J. HOUSE, "A Path-Goal Theory"; R. J. HOUSE and G. DESSLER, "Path-Goal Theory of Leadership."

6. R. J. HOUSE and G. DESSLER, "Path-Goal Theory of Leadership"; R. M. STOGDILL, *Managers, Employees, Organization* (Ohio State University, Bureau of Business Research, 1965); R. J. HOUSE, A. VALENCY and R. VAN DER KRABBEN, "Some Tests and Extensions of the Path-Goal Theory of Leadership" (in preparation).

7. W. A. HILL and D. HUGHES, "Variations in Leader Behavior as a Function of Task Type," *Organization Behavior and Human Performance*, 1974.

8. K. E. RUNYON, "Some Interactions between Personality Variables and Management Styles," *Journal of Applied Psychology* 57, no. 3 (1973): 288–94; T. R. MITCHELL, C. R. SMYSER and S. E. WEED, "Locus of Control: Supervision and Work Satisfaction," *Academy of Management Journal* 18, no. 3 (1975): 623–30.

9. T. R. MITCHELL et al., "Locus of Control."

10. R. J. HOUSE, "A Path-Goal Theory"; R. J. HOUSE and G. DESSLER, "Path-Goal Theory of Leadership"; A. D. SZALAGYI and H. P. SIMS, "An Exploration of the Path-Goal Theory of Leadership in a Health Care Environment," *Academy of Management Journal* 17, no. 4 (1974); J. D. DERMER, "Supervisory Behavior and Budget Motivation" (Cambridge, Mass.: unpublished, M.I.T., Sloan School of Management, 1974); R. W. SMETANA, "The Relationship between Managerial Behavior and Subordinate Attitudes and Motivation: A Contribution to a Behavioral Theory of Leadership," Ph.D. diss., Wayne State University, 1974.

11. S. F. WEED, T. R. MITCHELL, and C. R. SMYSER, "A Test of House's Path-Goal Theory of Leadership in an Organizational Setting," paper presented at Western Psychological Association, 1974; J. D. DERMER and J. P. SEIGEL, "A Test of Path-Goal Theory: Disconfirming Evidence and a Critique," unpublished, University of Toronto, Faculty of Management Studies, 1973; R. S. SCHULER, "A Path-Goal Theory of Leadership: An Empirical Investigation," Ph.D. diss., Michigan State University, 1973; H. K. DOWNEY, J. E. SHERIDAN and J. W. SLOCUM, JR., "Analysis of Relationships among Leader Behavior, Subordinate Job Performance and Satisfaction: A Path-Goal Approach," unpublished mimeograph, 1974; J. E. STINSON and T. W. JOHNSON, "The Path-Goal Theory of Leadership: A Partial Test and Suggested Refinement," *Proceedings, 7th Annual Conference of the Midwest Academy of Management, April 1974*, pp. 18–36.

12. G. DESSLER, "An Investigation of the Path-Goal Theory of Leadership," Ph.D. diss., City University of New York, Bernard M. Baruch College, 1973.

13. R. J. HOUSE, D. BURRILL, and G. DESSLER, "Tests and Extensions of Path-Goal Theory of Leadership, I," unpublished, in process.

14. R. J. HOUSE, "A Path-Goal Theory"; R. J. HOUSE and G. DESSLER, "Path-Goal Theory of Leadership"; A. D. SZALAGYI and H. P. SIMS, "Exploration of Path-Goal"; J. E. STINSON and T. W. JOHNSON, *Proceedings;* R. S. SCHULER, "Path-Goal: Investigation"; H. K. DOWNEY, J. E. SHERIDAN and J. W. SLOCUM, JR., "Analysis of Relationships"; S. E. WEED, T. R. MITCHELL and C. R. SMYZER, "Test of House's Path-Goal."

15. A. D. SZALAGYI and H. P. SIMS, "Exploration of Path-Goal."

16. R. J. HOUSE, A. VALENCY and R. VAN

DER KRABBEN, "Tests and Extensions of Path-Goal Theory of Leadership, II," unpublished, in process.

17. T. R. MITCHELL, "Motivation and Participation."

18. H. TOSI, "A Reexamination of Personality as a Determinant of the Effects of Participation," *Personnel Psychology* 23 (1970): 91–99; J. SADLER, "Leadership Style, Confidence in Management and Job Satisfaction," *Journal of Applied Behavioral Sciences* 6 (1970): 3–19; K. N. WEXLEY, J. P. SINGH, and J. A. YUKL, "Subordinate Personality as a Moderator of the Effects of Participation in Three Types of Appraisal Interviews," *Journal of Applied Psychology* 83, no. 1 (1973): 54–59.

19. T. R. MITCHELL, "Motivation and Participation."

20. A. S. TANNENBAUM and F. H. ALLPORT, "Personality Structure and Group Structure: An Interpretive Study of Their Relationship through an Event-Structure Hypothesis," *Journal of Abnormal and Social Psychology* 53 (1956): 272–80; V. H. VROOM, "Some Personality Determinants of the Effects of Participation," *Journal of Abnormal and Social Psychology* 59 (1959): 322–27.

21. K. E. RUNYON, "Some Interactions between Personality Variables and Management Styles," *Journal of Applied Psychology* 57, no. 3 (1973): 288–94.

22. T. R. MITCHELL, C. R. SMYSER, and S. F. WEED, "Locus of Control."

23. R. J. HOUSE, "Notes on the Path-Goal Theory of Leadership" (University of Toronto, Faculty of Management Studies, May 1974).

24. R. S. SCHULER, "Leader Participation, Task Structure, and Subordinate Authoritarianism," unpublished mimeograph, Cleveland State University, 1974.

HILL ENTERPRISES

CASE 1

When Hill Enterprises was founded ten years ago, its total assets consisted of one automatic lathe, one contract worth $2200, and one employee. The employee was Robert Hill, president and sole owner, then twenty-nine years old. He had one objective in forming Hill Enterprises — that of retiring with a million dollars in his personal bank account at the age of forty.

According to Robert Hill, the reasons Hill Enterprises was able to survive the first difficult years were his considerable abilities as a machinist, which he had developed during the nine years he was employed in the machine shop of a large manufacturing company, his willingness to work long and hard hours, and his knack for raising money for working capital. During the early years, he would customarily spend his evenings working at the plant and his days visiting banks, insurance companies, and personal friends in an attempt to acquire sufficient funds to continue operations. For the most part he was successful, and though he often had the feeling he was a bit overextended financially, his business continued to grow and show profits.

Mr. Hill felt that another reason for his success was his ability to inspire the work force to work toward his personal goal of a million dollars. His typical comment in interviewing a prospective employee was: "If you work for me you will have to work hard, for I intend to retire with a million dollars by the time I am forty. This means overtime, long hard hours, and unswerving loyalty to Hill Enterprises. If you are willing to do this, I'll make sure that you will get your share of the profits."

Potential employees who were willing to accept these conditions found that Mr. Hill meant what he said. Loyalty to the common cause was based on the number of hours of overtime a man put in. This high amount of overtime had two effects. First, Hill Enterprises was able to give its employees approximately double the take-home pay they could receive from other companies, thus reinforcing the promises Mr. Hill had made concerning financial rewards to individual employees. Second, even though the company was constantly growing and the work force was increasing in size, the large amount of overtime kept the number of employees to a minimum so that Mr. Hill had continuing face-to-face contact with them and could maintain a personal relationship with each of the men.

As Hill Enterprises grew and progressed Robert Hill continued his earlier pattern of operations. He set a grueling pace, continuing to work long hours late into the night and spending a large share of his time during the day attempting to raise additional working capital and financial support. He often held important conferences at 5:00 A.M. in order that supervisory personnel would be free to handle their regular work during the "normal" working hours. Mr. Hill seemed to enjoy the pace and pressure and seemed especially to like his frequent contact with the employees. His office consisted of a single beat-up desk in one corner of the production area. Thus he was immediately available to all to help with any problem, whether it was a production problem or a personal one. Many employees availed themselves of his accessibility and while he was in the plant he seemed to be constantly talking with one employee or another, either in his "office" or on the production floor. Often he would report on the progress of his personal bank account to the men, a practice which they enjoyed tremendously, as Mr. Hill would very vividly recount his financial manipulations.

The employees of Hill Enterprises responded to the situation by working long hours in poor environmental surroundings and under the constant pressure of schedules and production deadlines. Hill Enterprises at this stage had set up operations in a deserted store building, and physical working conditions were considerably less attractive than those of competing organizations.

Under the constant pressures to meet schedules, tempers were often short. The accepted way to reduce individual tension was to "fly off the handle." It was the privilege of the president as well as of any employee, and it was a privilege that was often used. Robert Hill had the reputation of being able to deliver the best "dressing-down" of anyone in the organization, and it was not unusual for an employee to comment on the skill with which Mr. Hill had "chewed him out." This give-and-take was not all onesided, and employees regardless of their position felt free to talk back to Mr. Hill or the other supervisors and often did. And because this was the accepted way to decrease tension and to achieve action, the incident over which an outburst occurred was immediately forgotten. The employees seemed to enjoy their existence with Hill Enterprises and underneath the tension and pressure each employee felt that he was capable, and that he was contributing to the goals of the company.

But some nine years after the start of Hill Enterprises, as Robert Hill had often feared, his intricate financial dealings caught up with him. His considerably expanded enterprises were without adequate working capital and he was forced to bring in a new partner, Donald Robbins, who was willing to invest sufficient funds to keep the company going.

One faction of the work force thought that the arrival of Robbins was just another of Mr. Hill's seemingly endless manipulations for capital. The other faction believed that his arrival was the harbinger of the end of Hill Enterprises as they had known it. They sensed that it would be only a matter of time until Mr. Hill would lose control of the internal workings of his organization and that the high wages and overtime pay would be cut.

The immediate influence of the arrival of Robbins upon the operations of Hill Enterprises was negligible. Operations continued at the same hectic pace, and Mr. Hill's personal activities did not appear to be appreciably different. He maintained his old "office" and was still available to help out on any particular problems that arose. However, as time passed, it became more and more obvious to the employees that Robbins demanded a great deal of Mr. Hill's time. Although he retained his desk in the corner of the shop for awhile, Mr. Hill soon set up new headquarters in the more plush surroundings of a new building that had been constructed adjacent to the shop facilities to house the sales and office activities of Hill Enterprises. Because of his new location and the demands made upon him by his new partner, Mr. Hill was unable to spend as much time with the men in the shop as before. In addition, Robbins' apparent aloofness to the workings and problems of the production shop and its employees created resentment.

The employees noticed that shortly after Mr. Hill had moved his office, the time-honored method of "blowing off steam" as a prelude to constructive effort on a problem became more and more ineffectual. Mr. Hill was no longer around to arbitrate really serious disagreements and his customary "O.K., now that we've got that out of our system, let's get to work," was absent. While blowing off steam was still an accepted practice, an element of bitterness seemed to be apparent in such outbursts that occurred. This bitterness and a sense of resentment toward Robbins permeated the atmosphere of the shop, with the result that many employees adopted a fatalistic attitude both toward the future of Hill Enterprises and their own personal future.

In this atmosphere a second major organizational change occurred. A new man with the title of "Works Manager" arrived to fill the vacuum created by Mr. Hill's forced attention to matters other than production. This man, Rod Bellows, was the son-in-law of Donald Robbins, the new partner. He was thirty-five years old, a graduate of Eastern State College, and had had ten years' experience as an industrial engineer with a large chemical company. He was hired by Hill Enterprises on the insistence of Donald Robbins, who felt that the production activities were inefficient and excessively costly. His appearance on the scene came as a surprise to the shop and production employees.

During his first few days with the company, employees often saw Bellows and Robbins in the production area. The men appeared to be conversing in earnest, and often pointed and gestured toward machines or individuals. Bellows continually took notes on a large clipboard which he carried with him. During this period, none of the employees was spoken to by either of the two men. The men in the shop had not had official indication of Bellows' duties, responsibilities, or position in the company. They knew only by rumor that he was the new works manager.

Bellows made the following comments about his responsibilities at Hill Enterprises shortly after his arrival: "This Company has a tremendous potential and an unlimited future. Robert Hill is a dynamic individual with great skills. He has certainly been successful to date. Mr. Robbins and I, I think, will complement these skills and make the company even more successful. Mr. Robbins has the ability and experience to do some long-range planning and get our financial affairs in order, and I have the responsibility and ability to make our production activities more effective. A major part of the problem as I see it is that we use our time inefficiently in production. We don't have any effective scheduling procedures of channels or responsibility and authority, with the result that the men spend a lot of time bickering with each other and conversing about things with which they should not really be concerned. Their job is to get out the production. Our job is to organize the production activities in such a way that this can be done at least cost. The whole basis for the situation is that in the past Hill Enterprises has been small enough to be controlled effectively by one man. Now, however, we are no longer really a small firm and we cannot continue to operate like one. I have some ideas and some techniques which I plan to initiate that I think will increase the effectiveness and efficiency of our production operations by 50 percent in very short order."

At the beginning of his third week as works manager, Bellows issued a series of changes in procedures to the production employees. Without exception these changes were made without consulting any of the men in the shop. All of them were issued in typewritten memos, a new practice which many of the employees felt was unnecessary and undesirable because of the effectiveness with which they felt the existing informal channels of communications had been used. The extent of the changes requested by Bellows was significant, ranging from changes in production scheduling techniques to changes in working conditions for individual employees. One employee estimated that to carry out those written orders, hundreds of additional man-hours "which were just not available" would be required.

Bellows' personal contacts with individual employees were limited and consisted mostly of quick and forceful answers to any questions or problems that might be brought to his attention. Many of his decisions seemed to indicate a lack of awareness of the capacity of the tools used in the production processes. For example, because of his insistence on machine speedups for certain operations, several expensive tools were ruined and valuable production time was lost. After having received several memos from Bellows which they considered unreasonable, one small group of employees had christened him with the nickname "The Fool." As the number of written memos coming from Bellows office increased, the resentment toward these memos became more apparent, and a strong adverse reaction to his presence was evident on the part of the production employees.

Some four months after Bellows' arrival, cooperation between the "old-timers" — both the supervisors and the workers — hit a new high. Unfortunately, this "cooperation" was used to undermine any and all changes that the new works manager attempted to put into effect. As new orders and procedures originated from Bellows' office, the employees carried out the orders to the letter of the law because, in many cases, they afforded a justified means of wasting time and reducing production. Bellows gave no indication that he was aware of this situation.

Bellows also attempted to establish formal channels of communication within the production operations, for he felt that much needless discussion and confusion was in existence under the present system. He issued several organization charts which described the "approved" way in which communication was to be effected within the organization. These charts were uniformly ignored by the employees, who continued to rely on the previously accepted informal channels of action. It even became an unwritten policy that all information channeled to Bellows under the new system was censored and reviewed by the person or persons to be affected before it was sent to Bellows.

Yet in this new atmosphere the old loyalties to Robert Hill did not fade entirely. The office manager, the plant superintendent, and several foremen attempted to get his ear from time to time to inform him that things were not running smoothly. Mr. Hill was always surprised by such comments, and he attempted to reassure the men by making remarks such as "It will take some time for us to get to know each other well, but I'm sure that everything will be straightened out in a little while." In addition, he made several trips to the production area, talking with the men individually and asking them to give Bellows a chance, as it was important for the success of Hill Enterprises.

Morale seemed to improve for a short while until Bellows issued a statement stating that no one in the plant was to bother the president with plant problems without consulting with him first. Shortly after this statement was issued by Bellows, Robert Hill again made several trips to the production area, talking to individual workers, and attempting to explain that other problems prevented his spending as much time in the shop as he previously had. In several instances, he started to report on the status of his personal bank account. Noting that this was not too well received, however, he discontinued this practice.

As time passed, the situation continued to deteriorate. Many of Bellows' acts and orders seemed to be in direct contradiction to Mr. Hill's former policies and procedures. The individuals affected were confused as to which procedures to follow. Attempts to have Bellows clarify his orders either left the questioner more confused than before or were greeted with a curt, "We don't have time to discuss that. It is perfectly clear. Just read the memo." Within a few months, many of the personnel talked of leaving to look for other employment and a few did. Nine months after Bellows had taken the position of works manager approximately 25 percent of the production force had taken new jobs. The morale among those remaining was poor and a significant increase in product rejects was experienced. But during the same period both Robbins and Bellows felt that important advances had been made in "cleaning up" production activities and that the company was "looking better all the time."

CONVERSATION WITH A SUPERVISOR (A)

CASE 2

At the close of an executive development session conducted by the author, one of the participants expressed an interest in relating a "case" in which he was personally involved. An appointment was made, and the following conversation took place.

Supervisor: I've taken the time to look up some information on Frank, the guy I'd mentioned to you. He's not stupid — in fact, he has a B.A. degree from Northern University. Prior to working for us, he had several jobs as a salesman, which may have contributed to his major problem now, drinking.

Researcher: Drinking?

Supervisor: Yes. He is sixty-three years old, and he's been with the company nineteen years. He is a wino. Ninety-three percent of the time he is drunk — but you can't tell. He has been a drunk for so long that you can't even tell when he's been drinking any more. He doesn't stagger or look drunk, and it's not obvious that he is. But if you work with him at all, you know it; you can smell the liquor, for one thing.

He doesn't get in any trouble because he is under no direct supervision. He works on second shift, and we don't see him except for a few minutes at the start of his shift. But there's no supervisor on that shift. In fact, if there is one, he's it. He's the leadman.

Researcher: Leadman?

Supervisor: Informal leader. Not formally recognized as supervision on the chart, but the guy in charge of the workers. Usually, a leadman works directly under a supervisor, but not in this case.

One of the basic problems here is that we can't prove that he drinks on the job. He has never been seen to take a drink. We've run checks, even using the security guards on occasion, but no one has ever been able to find his bottle. But we know he drinks! He's as drunk at the end of the shift as he is at the beginning.

Researcher: And this affects his work?

Supervisor: His work is satisfactory, but not for a leadman. He works — he's there at least — but not of the caliber of a leadman. He does not lead at all. He has fallen asleep many times, but has never been caught by a supervisor. His people have seen it, though.

The men under him and others he works with don't like him at all, because they are unable to communicate with him or talk with him. He is very aloof from the rest of the people — very quiet. The people who work for him really hate his guts.

With a year and a half to work before he retires, it creates a problem as to whether to fire him right now or let him stay until he is sixty-five.

Researcher: You'd like to fire him?

Supervisor: Sure, but another major problem is with the union. Under the union deal — he's a member — in which they do the bargaining with the company, it is almost impossible to fire him without building up a big case. And you won't find that here *(tapping the employee's personnel file).* Otherwise, I'd fire him in a minute.

The main fault lies with the supervisors. Frank should have been fired years ago. But they just kept passing him on to the next guy and he became progressively worse, until now he is a confirmed alchoholic.

Look at this garbage in his folder. *(Supervisor reads the following from employee's evaluation reports in personnel folder.)* "Frank is very cooperative and has good attendance." "Very dependable, works well with assigned personnel and respected by personnel of associated departments." "Very dependable, cooperative and a good attitude." "Very good attendance and prompt handling of problems is appreciated."

Supervisors are worse then employees. They mother this guy along for nineteen years and his folder doesn't even mention the problem — that he's such a lush that he's no good to us.

Researcher: Have you taken any steps to . . . . ?"

Supervisor: I've put several memos in his folder about his drinking since he's worked for me. This doesn't win any popularity contests for me, either, I'll tell you, but you have to do this kind of thing.

The big boss agrees with me. We say fire him. But M.J., the personnel director, doesn't think so. He's the soft-hearted type. One of his supervisors should have taken the bull by the horns and had enough courage to have done something about him.

If he were fired now, he would still keep his vested rights in the pension plan. When he reaches sixty-five, he'll still be able to collect all he has vested in the plan.

Researcher: Would this be the same as full retirement?

Supervisor: No, but he'd get along. I fired the guy who was Frank's last supervisor. He also had about nineteen years with the company, but he was a poor supervisor. This guy had worked for Frank years ago, and I guess he figured he was obligated to him. But he didn't belong to the union, and was easy to fire. Whom can a supervisor complain to?

Too many supervisors are soft-hearted. If a person is not doing his job they find some reason to feel sorry for him, especially if they have been friends on the job.

It's awfully hard to let a man go on working as he has been — drinking, not doing his job for nineteen years — and let him get away with it, then all of a sudden in one week crack down and fire him.

Researcher: You said he was unsatisfactory as a leadman. Would he be a satisfactory employee if he didn't have lead responsibilities?

Supervisor: He might possibly be demoted and moved to first shift. There he would be under direct supervision, and they could watch him in an effort to build up a strong case against him. But this is not the answer. The damage has already been done. He is too old. What actually is happening is that he is retired at full pay.

Ninety-nine percent of the trouble is when supervisors let themselves become fond of their people and feel obligated not to let them go when they aren't doing a good job. What should have been done is to have watched him and kept a record of any rules broken — anything not done right — and by now we'd have a good case against him. But nobody kept that kind of record on him *(leafing through personnel folder).* Except for the fact that he has always been forgetful about punching in. He has even been suspended for this several times.

A good supervisor has to be mean — a real tyrant. A good supervisor is just that. He has to know where to draw the line, just as a professor in school can't become attached to the pupils or he might just as well not be a teacher.

CONVERSATION WITH A SUPERVISOR (B)

CASE 3

Several months after the information in Part A of this case had been obtained, Martin Johnson, the personnel director referred to in Part A, volunteered the following information.

"Say, I thought you might be interested to know what happened in that situation you talked about with Dave Blackwell [the supervisor in Part A] last summer.

"After a lot of consideration, we put Frank on the first shift and watched him pretty carefully. We found nothing at all to substantiate that he was a booze hound so we gave up on it. He was always there and he always did his job. We had no indication at all that he wasn't performing as he should be. Incidentally, Dave is still convinced he is a drunk. Now Frank's back on the second shift and on his old job and seems to be doing fine. We did make some changes, however, that provide for more supervision on the second shift by staggering

the hours of some of our day-shift supervisors, so at least a part of the night-shift time is covered.

"The interesting thing about this, though, is that we did find out how the whole thing came about. It was a woman. A gal by the name of Elma, who has been with us for a long time. Now we want to get rid of her. I knew her in the other division before the reorganization and she's been nothing but a troublemaker. She has good job knowledge, but then she ought to have because she's been with the company so long. We inherited her with the reorganization a few years back. She came with the function and there's nothing that we could do about it. But she's always been a troublemaker. She has a sense of pride of the worst type, if you know what I mean. She competes by cutting others down. For example, she is always calling the head of the plant security at home complaining about things that have happened to her — or that she thinks have happened to her. The 'Joe Smith is always swearing at me' kind of thing. She also tells the head of security of things that other people are doing that she considers bad. He's talked with me about her several times. Unfortunately, she's the shop steward, which of necessity requires that we handle her case with a great deal of discretion. Dave is now trying to 'surplus'[1] her but I'm afraid that could turn into a long-drawn-out affair.

"She got rid of the former shop steward by getting the Union officers and members aroused. The chap who was steward before she took the position was a former production worker who had lost an arm in an accident on the job. It was sort of understood that he would always have a job with the company, and he could work effectively in this particular section with his physical handicap. He was the kind of guy who was oriented toward the top. He wanted to be a focal point and have things funneled through him. As a result of this, he was very useful to the supervisors in the section because in a sense he could do part of their jobs for them. He was interested in the company and its welfare and provided a good informal channel of communication for information which the supervisors might not have been able to get by themselves.

"Well, Elma didn't like this at all. She got a lot of people in the section excited about the fact that the union steward was only interested in management and management problems and took management's side in all situations. It was almost a case of inciting to riot, and it wasn't too long before she had a lot of the people thinking that a new steward would be in the best interests of the employees. At the next election, she was chosen steward. Her timing on this maneuver was excellent. She really played it like an old-line politician.

"Well, I certainly won't fight Dave's attempts to try and get her 'surplused.' But this is going to be a hard thing to do. She's in a category that would be very difficult to get declared 'unessential to operations' and even if we did, with her seniority it would be hard to get her moved out of the area entirely, as she would have first call on similar jobs that might open up.

"I think there are some better ways to handle this situation. Maybe we can use the same type of tactics on Elma that she herself uses. For example, we've got a lot of new people in that section. One chap has had a great number of personal problems in the recent past. He's had ten or twelve garnishments on his wages as the result of his recent divorce. During the proceedings he acted as his own lawyer, and you can imagine what kind of settlement he got. His wife has since remarried. Well, the upshot of this whole thing is that we've stuck by this man and tried to do all that we could for him during his period of personal trouble. As a result, I think that he has a feeling of real appreciation for us and for the way he's been treated. I think our best bet to get rid of Elma would be to plant some ideas in this guy's head. He's pretty well liked among the other workers and if we could get him to raise some questions, such as 'Shouldn't the job of steward really be held by somebody on the first shift?' 'Shouldn't the job be rotated?' 'Shouldn't some of the newer people get a chance at the job?' etc., maybe we could get the same kind of end result that Elma got before. At least get her out of the steward's position if not out altogether.

"I favor this approach and think we could work it successfully, but it would take some planning on our part. I think it's either something like this or live with the situation in the hope that she'll voluntarily ask for a transfer."

HARKNESS COMPANY

INTRODUCTION

In the Harkness Company exercise, you are placed in the position of general manager of the company involved in the construction and sale of housing units. In this position you have the opportunity to exhibit leadership in a wide variety of situations. As you do so, think about some of the concepts and observations about leadership contained in the readings above, and see how your personal style of leadership relates to these concepts.

PROCEDURE

Some general instructions are contained in the exercise. Your instructor probably will want to give you additional directions, and you should not proceed further until you have received these.

You are Jack Harkness, general manager of the Harkness Company, an organization in Ft. Lauderdale, Florida, which is engaged in the construction and sale of housing units for the residential and commercial markets. Your activities cover the southeastern part of the United States. Sales have been approximately $5,000,000 per year for the last four years.

On some of your projects you construct parts of the building, primarily roofs, in your local plant and ship these completed parts to the job sites, where they are put into place. On other jobs, you do all your work right on the site. Often you will be only one of several construction firms working on a particular job, especially if it is a large project.

You are thirty-eight years old, a graduate of M.I.T., and have been active in the construction industry for twelve years. For six of these years, you operated the Harkness Company as an independent organization, building it from the ground up. Six years ago, you sold the company to Consolidated Construction, Inc., a New York firm that through various divisions and affiliates engages in construction activities on a national basis. Since then you have operated Harkness as a division of Consolidated Construction, Inc. You report directly to Larry Owens, southeastern regional manager for Consolidated, whose base is in Miami. A partial organization chart for Consolidated Construction, Inc., and the Harkness Company is shown in Exhibit 1.

Although sales have been good the last few years, the market has been difficult and, like many of your competitors, you are caught in the "profit squeeze" that has plagued the entire industry. Costs have been going up, while customers have been reluctant to pay higher prices. Harkness has just about been breaking even financially for the past four years.

It is May 2, 1977, and you have just returned from a ten-day trip to Atlanta, where you have been trying to close a deal for the construction of several large warehouses. If completed, the deal could be instrumental in Harkness' having a successful financial year. Your secretary, Miss Watson, has just brought you the material which has arrived during your absence and which she feels deserves your attention. She has also reminded you that you are scheduled to meet with officials of a local bank at nine o'clock, just forty-five minutes from now, to discuss financing possibilities for the Atlanta jobs. You have completed your preparations for this meeting.

Make notes regarding what actions, if any, you wish to take concerning

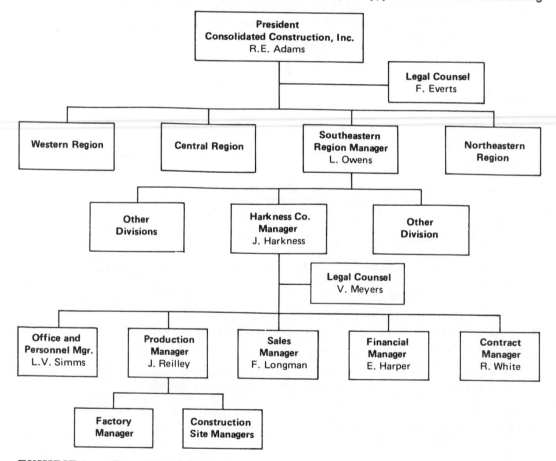

EXHIBIT 1 • *Consolidated Construction, Inc.-Harkness Company — Partial Organization Chart*

the various situations, and rough out any letters, messages, and so on, you might wish to send.

---

(1)
Harkness Company
Customer Reaction Report

April 28, 1977

Project Name: Andrews Apartments, Miami
Completion Date: March 1, 1977   Job No. 467
Source of reaction: Architect, Stanley Whitmeyer
Reaction obtained by: Longman

Comments: We were supposed to have 13 ft. of coverage for these roof joists, but when we brought them out we only had 12' 11" — or they were approximately 1" to ¾" short. Gaps to ¼" to ½" occurred on top of the vault where the butt joints of the lumber came together. There were several spots where this was supposedly corrected by stapling the top skin on: however, some of the staples were coming through the underside. The edges of the vaults were very ragged and there had to be considerable trimming. A 2 x 6 cap on the wall below had been painted — in fact, the entire job had been painted due to the delay in getting our material up. The men walked all over the 2 x 6 instead of tacking a board or something on top, and thus we ruined the paint and again aggravated the owner. All in all, Whitmeyer indicated that he had done three jobs with us and each one resulted in problems.

---

(2)
Consolidated Construction, Inc.

April 24, 1977

Interoffice memo:
From: Larry Owens
To: Jack Harkness
Re: Confidential

As you know, we have had several lengthy discussions concerning the Harkness Division and I should like to take this opportunity to put down in writing some of the points which I made, mostly to remind you that many of us feel that the situation is quite serious. I make these comments in all sincerity and as a friend, Jack, and trust that you will receive them in this light.

Quite bluntly, many people are concerned that our investment at Harkness has been steadily increasing without a corresponding increase in profitability. This fact, coupled with the apparent lack of control concerning overhead expenses which have also been steadily rising, has, as I have told you, caused some of our people to question the competence of the Harkness management. This is serious, as I'm sure you are very aware, and requires our undivided attention. I say "our," for I consider myself to be a part of the Harkness management team.

In essence, Jack, my superiors have informed me that they will be watching quite closely everything that Harkness does in the future, although they do have confidence in the basic soundness of the Harkness organization and do not, to my knowledge, anticipate any immediate personnel or organizational changes. However, in light of the above, I feel that you and I should work more closely regarding this situation, and I am asking you to suggest ways in which I can participate in at least the more significant decisions that are made. I realize that this may be distasteful to you, for you have been used to operating with a great deal of independence. Nonetheless, the recent criticisms of my superiors lead me to believe that this is our only alternative.

I should be pleased to have your thinking regarding how we might work out a system whereby, I could be more closely attuned to your activities. I feel that we should do anything and everything necessary to restore the confidence of my superiors in the Harkness Division.

---

(3)   TELEGRAM

May 1, 1977

Jack Harkness
Harkness Company
Ft. Lauderdale, Florida

Material shipped to Williams job site not accepted because of late delivery. Williams says we responsible for removal his premises. Bad weather could damage although material now temporarily covered. Please advise.

Hall — Site Manager

---

(4)   HARKNESS COMPANY

May 1, 1977

Memorandum
To: Jack Harkness
From: L.V. Simms

As you know, our union contract comes up for renewal on June 1. I have not been able to ascertain the precise nature of demands for this year, but if we are to avoid a strike such as we suffered last year, I think we should get together immediately to determine our position. Please advise.

---

(5)   HARKNESS COMPANY

April 26, 1977

Memorandum:
To: Jack Harkness
From: E.E. Harper

In accordance with Consolidated's accounting procedure, I have determined that an adjustment in the depreciation rates on our fixed assets is necessary and plan to increase our depreciation charge by $5350.00 beginning this month. This should put us in line with general accounting procedures, but, of course, will result in an increase in our overhead.

---

(6)   HARKNESS COMPANY
                             Customer Reaction Report

April 27, 1977

Project Name: Raymond Center Bowling Alley, Miami
Completion Date: February 17, 1977   Job No. 434
Source of reaction: Owner, Mr. Knoll
Reaction obtained by: Longman

Comments: As far as he was concerned everything has gone along just fine. He was well pleased with the appearance, workmanship, and installation of our job, and had absolutely no bad comments.

---

(7)   Consolidated Construction, Inc.

April 24, 1977

Interoffice memo:
To: Southeastern Region Manager
         Southeastern Region Division Managers
From: R.E. Adams

Gentlemen:
   Because there are problems between our operations and authorities which need to be resolved, I should like to have each of you set aside May 14 for a meeting to discuss these problems. The meeting will probably be held in New York or Philadelphia and details will follow.

---

(8)   Consolidated Construction, Inc.

April 25, 1977

Interoffice memo
To: Jack Harkness
From: Larry Owens

   I am becoming increasingly concerned over the problem that has developed at Top-Line Plumbing Supply Warehouse, particularly because I do not think I have been kept fully informed of developments in this field. I have just seen a letter from Mr. Warren Bert of Top-Line, addressed to Fred Everts, outlining the current situation. Obviously this story that one of our roofs caved in is going to get around the New York office and will certainly not be helpful to Harkness or to the administration of the Southeastern Region.

Again emphasizing that I do not know too much of the detail, I would urge you to be as prompt as possible in handling anything that is reasonable in connection with this and likewise to keep Fred and me fully advised.

There is also a lesson to be learned here which we long ago learned, and that is to be very careful in selecting our suppliers of material and to cast our lot with those who have a "tried and true" approved system of grading and grade-marking lumber.

In reviewing this just once more, I feel a little bit at a loss to understand whose responsibility it is to provide proper repair of this roof as other contractors were also involved. Can you clarify this for me?

---

(9)

George M. Lyman
Attorney-at-Law
Tallahassee, Florida

April 21, 1977

Mr. J.R. Harkness
Harkness Company
Ft. Lauderdale, Florida

Re: Family Motel — Tallahassee

Dear Sir:

Please be advised that I represent Mr. G.L. Bronson, who is presently constructing the Family Motel in Tallahassee.

He has informed me that the roof system that your engineers designed and installed on the one-story portion of their motel is defective, which fact you have been advised. We insist that you take immediate action toward correcting the defect as we have a crew of carpenters standing by who are anxious to start framing and do work preliminary to plastering. It is impossible for them to proceed at this time until the roof has been repaired, and therefore we are holding you responsible for the loss of time occasioned by this defective design and workmanship on your part.

Your man has been at the scene and informed us he would return with the crew to correct the defects immediately. This has not been done and we are losing valuable time as a result. I might also add that this will have a great deal to do with the order on the two-story unit which we are considering placing with your organization.

Please send your crew up here at once to take action on this matter, which you will admit is certainly not the fault of the owner.

Very truly yours,

George M. Lyman

George M. Lyman

---

(10)   HARKNESS COMPANY

April 23, 1977

Memorandum
To: Jack Harkness
From: R.A. Whitney
Re: Family Motel — Tallahassee

As you know, we have had considerable difficulty re: collecting for Family Motel job. They maintain that because of our defective work on the roof other contractors have been slowed down, time has been lost, etc., for which they plan to hold us responsible.

Jim Reilley and I looked at the job on April 18 and found that our work is good and that other contractors have caused the problem. They asked us to send a crew out to correct the defects, but we said we could not do that, as we were not responsible.

As they owe us $11,460.00, I talked with Ed Myers in your absence, and we have today sent out a standard Notice of Lien in this amount. I suspect we have not heard the last from the Family Motel.

---

(11)   Consolidated Construction, Inc.

April 23, 1977

Interoffice Memo
To: Jack Harkness
From: R.E. Adams

Dear Jack:

I hope that Frank and you had an excellent flight on your return, as a rest was certainly needed, particularly in light of the rough time I gave you folks while in New York last month.

I think it was well that we had an opportunity to air some of our differences and to come to a better understanding about the over-all expansion in the house-production program. My only regret is that we did not have another day to crystallize the many events. I want you to know that I had a discussion with Larry Owens about some of the things which we hashed over in our bull session at the Windsor Hotel. Out of this I think will come a stronger relationship, and you can be assured that I will be working as strong as ever on behalf of the proposed expansion. At my earliest opportunity I want to sit down and outline some of the more important points as I see them in regard to the over-all program. Costs and profit margin are primary among these. It would be ridiculous, of course, to expect you or anyone else to accept all of my viewpoints, but, as you have certainly found out, I am the kind of person who believes in fighting for what I believe is right until such time as someone else has convinced me otherwise.

May I assure you that I am on your team so long as what we are attempting to do makes sales sense from the over-all Company viewpoint.

With kindest personal regards to you and your family, I am

Very sincerely yours,

R.E. Adams

cc: Larry Owens

---

(12)   HARKNESS COMPANY

May 1, 1977

Memorandum
To: Jack Harkness
From: V.A. Myers

The attached copy of a letter from our neighbor, Mr. Davidson, to Mayor Warner is for your review. He is pressing the noise problem, and we should plan our strategy. Conceivably, the matter could end up in court, and we certainly want to prevent that. What do you suggest? I have done nothing yet.

Incidentally, I trust you didn't make the comments Mr. Davidson attributes to you in the letter.

April 28, 1977

To: Mayor George Warner & Members of the City Council
        Ft. Lauderdale City Hall
        Ft. Lauderdale, Florida

From: W.A. Davidson
        32 W. 64th Avenue
        Ft. Lauderdale, Florida

Re: Ft. Lauderdale Noise Ordinance

Gentlemen:
I would like to say that my family and I, along with our many neighbors, who are residents of Ft. Lauderdale in the area surrounding the Harkness factory, are very grateful for the recent passage of a Noise Ordinance. Some improvement has been noted as compared with the noise situation which prevailed at this time last year in the vicinity of the mill.

However, it is far from peaceful yet, and I feel this is important. Harkness has as yet taken no action to correct a very objectionable and constant source of noise which emanates from its blower system. (This blower takes sawdust and waste from the various machines to an elevated hopper which shakes, rattles, and vibrates along with the constant whine of the blower motor and fan.)

I am sure the Honorable Mayor and members of the City Council will recall that Harkness, through the voice of its lawyer, publicly stated before a Council Meeting held during the winter months, that as soon as favorable weather conditions permitted, they would take measures to reduce the sound caused by its blower. To be more precise, Harkness stated that three coats of sound-absorbent material would be sprayed over the blower structure as soon as a few dry days could be predicted.

Recently, I personally spoke to Mr. Jack Harkness, president of the Harkness Company, and asked him when he planned to subdue the noise coming from his blower. He replied, in no uncertain terms, that he has no intention of doing anything to improve the blower situation.

At the same meeting at which the Harkness lawyer promised correction of the blower, it was stated that the doors of the factory would be kept closed. This has not been the general rule, and on some days the noise is intolerable.

When the doors are closed, the sounds of dropping lumber, hammering, and the strident whine of the saws and other machines are considerably muffled. These sounds are still audible with the doors closed at a distance of approximately 200 feet. However, with the doors shut, it is much quieter. This is one improvement that would not cost Harkness any money.

I feel that my neighbors and I have been very patient in this matter. We assumed that Harkness would live up to its word.

It is requested that the Mayor and City Council take this matter up with Harkness.

W.A. Davidson

---

(13)   Consolidated Construction, Inc.

April 27, 1977

Interoffice Memo
To: Jack Harkness
From: George Mayer, Accounting Manager
           Southeastern Region
Re: Accounting Systems

At your request I have reviewed portions of your accounting system. This has consisted of random investigation in selected areas, and cannot in any sense be considered an audit. Repeated postponements by your Accounting Department in making records available and in keeping appointments set to discuss various aspects made further study impractical.

General Condition of Accounting

There has been substantial improvement in the records in recent months; however, in my opinion, the records are completely lacking in professional quality. There is an excessive incidence of cross-outs, erasures, corrected figures, and voided checks, despite the fact that many of the worst sheets have been copied over (which is a grievous offense to any auditor!).

The labor distribution is on the worst type of scratch sheet, entries are disorganized, crowded, and confused, which results in lost time and error. This is reflected in the numerous corrections and revisions made in job costing.

The entire approach to accounting seems to be to cram out checks, reports, etc., because operations always run behind, and to worry about essential internal checks afterward, which is then too late.

In my opinion accounting management at your division requires closest revaluation.

(14)   George M. Lyman
                              Attorney-at-Law
                             Tallahassee, Florida

April 30, 1977

Harkness Company
Ft. Lauderdale, Florida

Attention: Mr. J.R. Harkness

Gentlemen:

We are in receipt of your letter of April 23, 1977, and the enclosed copy of the Notice of Lien.

As you may know, I am a partner in the Family Motel and as such, I am very much concerned over the lien, of course. I believe you people are very much aware of the fact that there was an error in the construction and installation of the roof units. That is the reason you have not been paid prior to this date.

Because of the defective roof, other contractors lost time, blocks were cracked and plaster has cracked in some places because of it. A Mr. Reilley and another man from your organization were up here and talked to the fore-man, Tom Samuelson, but they left before Mr. Bronson, the owner, was able to talk with them. Although Mr. Bronson has been in the motel business over a considerable number of years, he is in no position to talk with you and your staff out of the presence of the construction foreman, Mr. Samuelson.

Most certainly, a meeting should be arranged between Mr. Reilley and other members of the organization and Mr. Bronson and Mr. Samuelson. We have facts and figures to go over with them, because in our estimation there is no question that an adjustment is due as a result of your defective workmanship.

A meeting here in Tallahassee would be logical because the defects are apparent on the building, and you should see them personally. If you would be so kind as to call Mr. Bronson, I am sure an appointment can be arranged to accommodate everyone. The sooner this meeting can be arranged, the sooner you will get the money you are entitled to.

Very truly yours,

George M. Lyman

cc: Family Motel
      Tallahassee, Florida

EXERCISE 2

ADDINGTON TIMBER COMPANY

INTRODUCTION

This exercise gives us a good opportunity to observe two very different leadership styles. In addition, we have an opportunity to examine the leadership style of the manager who must deal with some conflict arising because of the difference in leadership behavior of two subordinate managers.

PROCEDURE

Your instructor will provide you with specific instructions for the exercise. Do not proceed further until you have received these instructions.

The Addington Timber Company is a large, nationally known producer of lumber and plywood products. Addington's operations are vertically integrated and range from the growing of timber and maintenance of tree farms through all processes of manufacture to the final step, in some instances, of application of decorative finishes to lumber and plywood paneling for homes and offices.

The Williams Falls branch of Addington Timber Company, located in Williams Falls, Oregon, is concerned with the harvesting of trees and the concurrent reseeding processes. The Williams Falls branch employs about fifty men who operate the heavy machinery used in forestry operations, run hand power-tools, such as chain saws, and often use just plain muscle in carrying out their duties. The men are divided into crews of five to six men each. During the season when logging is permitted, the men live at the place where logging operations are underway, often 50 to 60 miles from the town of Williams Falls, until such time as operations are completed. Logging camps are established which provide sleeping, eating, and limited recreational facilities for the men. Often, when operations are particularly heavy, the men will spend several weeks at a time in the woods.

The management of the Williams Falls branch that stays with the loggers on the site consists of an operations manager, Jack Evans, two foremen, Dick Fredericks and Bob Ross, each of whom supervises five teams of loggers, and the maintenance and safety foreman, who is responsible for keeping the equipment in operating condition and seeing that safety regulations are followed. Other management personnel, including Phil Salmon, Branch Manager, are located at branch headquarters in the town of Williams Falls.

Jack Evans, thirty-eight years old, operations manager, has been with the Addington Timber Company for fifteen years. He has a fine record with the company and is considered by his supervisors to have a bright future, as he has a solid foundation in logging operations. As one indication of his potential, two years ago he was selected to attend a company-sponsored management seminar at the state university. Most of the men chosen to attend this seminar are considered to have the ability to advance into higher management positions. Jack Evans seems to be well liked by all his men.

Bob Ross is a recent graduate of the forestry college, and has been with Addington for only two years — all of which has been at the Williams Falls branch in the position of foreman. He does not have an imposing personality, and at first the men attempted to take advantage of him. However, after his first three months on the job the men came to respect his knowledge and supervisory ability, and what Jack Evans thought might become a difficult situation had worked itself out. Currently, the men on Ross's crews seem to respect and like him. Ross was added to the branch when logging operations expanded. Previously, Dick Fredericks had been the only foreman.

Dick Fredericks is an old-timer with Addington. He had started in the woods when he was only thirteen years old, and now, at the age of fifty-three, could claim forty years of experience — which he often did. Fredericks tended to supervise with an iron hand and, in the opinion of some of his men, often made arbitrary decisions, especially when new techniques were concerned. Often the men felt that he did not completely understand some of the newer developments. Fredericks frequently stated that he had earned his job as foreman with his fists when he had been only nineteen, and no one yet had been able to take it away — although anyone who thought he could was welcome to try.

Jack Evans felt that Fredericks was a good man although he tended to be inflexible. Evans felt that Fredericks would probably continue in his present job until retirement, although there were slight possibilities for promotion. This feeling was based on the assumption that Fredericks would continue to be acceptable to the men as foreman. From time to time, especially since the arrival of Bob Ross, the men in Fredericks' crews had complained that they were not being treated fairly by Fredericks.

Role for Jack Evans, Operations Manager

You have just made your daily radiophone report to Phil Salmon, branch manager. As you were about to complete your conversation, he mentioned that you had better have a talk with Dick Fredericks, as some of the men were evidently displeased with his recent activities. When pressed for specifics, Salmon replied that he wasn't sure what the specifics were, but that the grapevine had reported that Fredericks had recently made some arbitrary decisions contrary to the suggestions of his men which had resulted in excessive time spent on some operations. He stressed that he did not have the details but that Fredericks had evidently refused to accept some pretty good suggestions from one of his crews about how to handle a particular job.

You told Salmon that you wished that you had more information, but that you would talk with Fredericks. And, as operations were closing down for the day, you had sent one of the men to ask Dick Fredericks if he would see you before dinner. You are now waiting in your office for him to arrive.

As you wait, you have been speculating on several things. First is the unique characteristic of the grapevine which has managed to communicate information effectively some 50 miles from the logging site to Williams Falls while at the same time it has been unable to relay the same information about 2 miles to your office.

Second, you have been reflecting on Dick Fredericks. You and he have gotten along well, although he still has a tendency to "run his own show" and ignore you whenever possible. When you first started at Williams Falls, this tendency was quite pronounced and you had to let Dick know in very certain terms that you were boss. You still have to emphasize this occasionally, although you have had no real problem in this regard. You like to give your men as much leeway as possible in performing their operations. You consider Dick to be a good foreman, although somewhat of a "diamond in the rough."

You're not quite sure what this current situation is about, if anything. Several times in the past some of Dick's men have come to talk with you about his unwillingness to accept suggestions and ideas from them. You felt you had been able to convince them that all foremen didn't operate in the same manner and that while you appreciated their position, Dick Fredericks was a good foreman with a wealth of experience, even though he had his shortcomings. You had tried not to make a big issue of these things but had encouraged the men to talk with you again if they desired. None of them had come back a second time. You had not mentioned these visits to Dick Fredericks, as you felt them to be part of the normal griping to be expected on any job.

You attributed such visits to two things. The first was that with the arrival of Bob Ross on the job the men had had an opportunity to compare the two foremen. Dick was very much the boss and made all the decisions, whereas Bob was just the opposite, encouraging the men to make suggestions and take an active part in decision making. And the men themselves were changing. At one time loggers were pretty rough-and-ready individuals, and a stern, hard-headed approach seemed to be a foreman's only way to keep them in line. Recently, however, loggers in general were better educated, more serious, and steadier, with the majority being family men.

After you had completed the management course at the state university a few years ago, the difference in the approaches of your two foremen had become quite obvious to you. You felt that under current conditions the approach exemplified by Bob Ross would be more successful. You had attempted informally to point out some of these differences to Dick, but without a great deal of success — at least in terms of action. Dick was intelligent and realized that his methods were sometimes inadequate, but, as he put it, he knew what he knew, and generally it worked O.K. He admitted that he didn't know a lot of new stuff that the younger men did and that he didn't have much faith in some of the new techniques, but all in all he felt that he was a pretty good foreman. You had had to agree, for in many situations, especially those involving physical danger, Dick was about the best man you had. You knew that he prided himself on his crews' excellent safety record and often undertook some of the more risky jobs himself, even though doing so was not part of his responsibilities and was in some instances contrary to established safety procedures.

Realizing that Dick will arrive shortly, you turn your thoughts to what you will say to him. Somehow, you have to get him to change his philosophy of managing people.

Role for Dick Fredericks

You have just finished up for the day and are now on your way to the office of Jack Evans, operations manager. A few minutes ago one of the men had told you that Evans wanted to see you before dinner.

You're not sure what it's about, but you hope that it won't take long. You've got a headache and would like to rest for awhile before dinner if you can. You hope that it's not going to be another one of those fatherly talks about "human relations." Ever since Jack went to that course at the university a few years ago, he has been talking to you about human relations — whatever that is. For one thing, you're almost old enough to be Jack's father, and for another, as far as you can see, human relations is mostly being "buddy-buddy" with the men. While this might work in an office, you're sure it won't work in the woods. You've been in the woods for forty years now and know the dangers involved better than anyone else. Why, from the first day that you won your foreman's job in a fight with Ed Nomanski — rest his soul — you've had only two serious accidents on your crews. You don't build that kind of a record by being a "buddy." The boss has got to be the boss on the job or there's no telling what will happen. He has to decide what can or can't be done, and keep the men in line. The new foreman, Bob Ross, is a "buddy" and it doesn't work so well for him.

Just the other day one of your crews had tried to talk you into doing some new things that could have resulted in an accident. Sure, the new procedures had been approved by the safety man, but he didn't know what he was talking about. You had insisted on doing it your way, and while it may have taken a bit longer, no one had gotten hurt. You just didn't trust a lot of these new ideas, and had seen many cases in the past where some new technique had resulted in a pretty risky situation. As you had told Jack Evans before, you knew what you knew, and it had worked O.K. for forty years.

Well, whatever it was that Jack had on his mind, you hoped that it wouldn't take long.

PART 6

ORGANIZATION RELATIONSHIPS AND DECISION MAKING

In many ways the concept of organization structure is difficult to grasp. When we refer to organization structure we are not talking about a group of buildings or the way offices are arranged within buildings. Structure refers to the established patterns of relationships among the components or parts (people) of the organization. Formal structure is frequently defined in terms of the patterns of formal relationships and duties. Organization charts and job descriptions are both used in describing aspects of the formal organization. Employee guide books, formal rules, work procedures, and operating policies are also reflections of the formal structure in that they are attempts to guide employee behavior. Other aspects of structure include the span of control, that is, the number of people reporting to a given supervisor, the number of levels of management, the degree to which decision making is centralized, and the range of skill levels among workers. The formal organization, in a sense, is a blueprint for the way activities are to be accomplished.

Structure is not a static or unchanging dimension. In a recent three-year period, at least two-thirds of the 100 largest industrial companies in the United States reported major organization realignments. Many companies go through a major restructuring about every two years. The reasons for changes in structure are many, ranging all the way from a whim of top-level management to a change in technology or environmental circumstances that render the old structure ineffective.

Obviously, formal organization structure is not independent of the behavior of people within the enterprise. It has been demonstrated that many structural variables such as span of control, levels of authority, and degree of centralization in decision making can have significant effect on such worker attitudes as job satisfaction. And reactions of people can cause changes in structure. For example, large scale resistance to formal rules can result in abolition or modification of the rules.

In the first reading, Stanley Young describes the "Organization as a Total System." In his view the organization can be described as a set of flows, involving information, people, material and behavior. Young's model is only one of many described by scholars in recent years. For the manager, perhaps the major benefit of the systems view is the explicit requirement that variables *outside* the unit in question be considered in decisions affecting structure.

In the next article, "An Introduction to Organization Design," Michael B. McCaskey describes interesting research results related to the design of organizations. He makes it clear that there is no "one best way" to structure an organization. Different structures appear to be required for various environmental conditions.

Jay Galbraith then discusses "Matrix Organization Designs: How to Combine Functional and Project Forms." Matrix and project forms of management have shown much promise in several industries, particularly those utilizing sophisticated technologies. The aerospace industry has pioneered and continues to use project organization extensively.

The remaining two articles in this section focus on the decision making process.

The decision process involves at least five steps: (1) *Definition of the problem.* In the managerial setting, few problems are really clearcut, and the visible signs of the problem may really be only symptoms of a deeper problem. It is critical in this first step to identify the real problem, otherwise the manager may implement an elaborate and expensive program to solve a nonexistent problem. (2) *Data gathering.* Decision making requires the gathering of data that might have a bearing on the problem. Usually, decisions must be made on the basis of incomplete information, but as much data should be gathered as possible. (3) *Organization and analysis.* Particularly if one is working with a large amount of data, the information must be organized for comparison and analysis. (4) *Generation of alternatives.* Once the data are analyzed, alternative solutions to the problem should be generated. Of course, the options should be workable and within cost and other constraints that may exist. It is rare for a real-life problem to have only one solution, so it is important that as large a number of workable solutions be generated as possible. (5) *Alternative analysis and choice.* The alternatives must be judged by some set of criteria, such as cost, amount of risk involved, permanence of the solution, timing, or acceptability of the solution to other people. Testing alternatives against criteria often allows quick elimination of unacceptable options, thus focusing on a few better alternatives. Finally, one alternative is chosen for implementation.

It is important to note that choice of alternatives is *not* decision making, but the last step in the decision process. The picture of the silver-maned executive making lightning-like decisions is a romantic and unfortunate myth. Decisions are usually only as good as the analytical process underlying them, and today's organizations can ill afford managers who do not do their homework.

In the reading, "The Decision-Making Grid: A Model of Decision-Making Styles," Hall et al. are concerned with the effect of individual styles of decision making in the group setting. Many decisions in organizations are made by groups, and the authors discuss group decision making in terms of two dimensions: commitment for successful implementation and concern for decision adequacy. A decision-making grid is presented and various decision approaches are plotted on the grid and discussed. As you look at the grid, determine which approach is most appealing to you personally. The authors of the article argue that one of the styles is most effective, but is that true? Can you think of specific instances or conditions where the other styles might be more effective?

In "The Management of Decision Making within the Firm: Three Strategies for Three Types of Decision Making," Delbecq discusses the decision process in terms of appropriate group structure, the roles played by individuals within the group, the meeting process itself, the emotional environment, and the norms of the group. The types of decisions considered are routine decision, creative decision, and negotiated decisions where individuals and groups are in opposition. It will be extremely useful for you to know the most desirable conditions for each type of decision. Although the manager may have little control over problems that require decisions, he or she has direct, perhaps complete, control over the conditions surrounding the decision process itself. The more you know about conditions supportive of quality decision making, the better your decisions will be.

ORGANIZATION AS A TOTAL SYSTEM

Stanley D. Young

Increasingly, organizations are being considered from a systems point of view in both a descriptive and normative context.[1] Ashby's work would exemplify some of the descriptive work. Systems Development Corporation, Strategic Air Command, and Lockheed are effectively using the systems concept to redesign major phases of organizations in an operational and normative sense.[2] Many companies have expended similar efforts to certain subsystems such as steel-rolling mills and oil refineries.[3]

What appears to be occurring is that our conception of the organization is changing from one of structure to one of process. Rather than visualize the organization in its traditional structural, bureaucratic, and hierarchical motif, with a fixed set of authority relationships much like the scaffolding of a building, we are beginning to view organization as a set of flows, informa-

tion, men, material, and behavior. Time and change are the critical aspects. This change in construct will become more pronounced in the future because (and this is an assertion which I will not attempt to defend) I believe the systems approach is more productive. If we consider organization from a normative point of view, there is another reason for this trend which is of more immediate concern and is the working hypothesis of this paper. Only when the organization is designed (Organizational Planning) from a systems orientation will it be able to take full advantage of the new and emerging managerial technologies which include quantitative methods, the computer, information sciences, and the behavioral sciences. Although I will not attempt to prove this proposition in the rigorous sense, the balance of this analysis will be directed toward demonstrating how this might be accomplished.

However, before taking up this thesis, let us note the problems which currently exist that hinder the effective utilization of managerial technology. The problem relates to the absence of a construct as to how the new technology is to be used in an integrated and systematic manner; or consider it as the absence of a meaningful gestalt or whole into which such a technology would logically fit. What does exist might be categorized as a tool chest or "bits and pieces" state.

For example, let us suppose that a personnel manager has what he believes is a problem — excessive absenteeism.

From *Proceedings of the 9th Annual Midwest Management Conference*, Southern Illinois University Business Research Bureau, Carbondale, Illinois, 1966, pp. 20–31. Reprinted with the permission of the author and publisher. Dr. Young is Professor of Management at the University of Massachusetts.

Given the external and internal environment of the firm, the organizational constraints he has as a manager, and a set of behavioral information and managerial tools, how does he reduce the absenteeism rate? He knows something about psychology — perception, cognition, learning, and motivation theory — social psychology, attitude formation, and resistance to change. From sociology he recalls group theory; he can calculate the median, mean, and mode, run a correlation, and find a derivative. In other words, he is a qualified MBA student. Specifically, what should he do to reduce the absenteeism rate? The students and practitioners are given a tool chest filled with bits and pieces: a little math, a little psychology, a little sociology, and the manager is then admonished to build a better house. How is the application of the technology to be integrated so that the manager can be relatively assured that he is achieving a desired result? What is missing is the bridge or discipline between tools and organizational results. That those of a more traditional bent remain somewhat skeptical of the newer managerial technology is understandable.

Although one can raise many serious questions as to the reality, validity, predictability, and effectiveness of the classical principles approach, nevertheless, it can be said that it roughly holds together as a whole or single unit, and its parts are related in a logical fashion. Starting with the concept of private property and the delegation of authority, the organizational chart is drawn; authority is allocated; a division of labor is specified; the functions of management are outlined; and planning, organizing, and staffing are conducted. A

certain internal logic is present, not unlike the economist's model of perfect competition. The parts are related to each other in a particular manner. Viewed as a single construct, a traditional model is understandable and operational to students and practitioners alike.

The same cannot be said for the newer managerial technology. The General Management or Organization Theorist's domain is the whole. One is concerned with the problem of organization space, or the distance between subfunctions, subprocesses, tools, and techniques — the interface problems. To those who are concerned with the whole, the "bits and pieces" approach of the new technology is disconcerting. Where and how do all these parts fit together and what is the relationship between one piece and another? Sprinkling behavioral and quantitative courses about a business curriculum is of questionable effectiveness and has not, I believe, changed the basic manner in which organizations are managed. Therefore, as far as the newer technologies are concerned, a gestalt or general model has been missing which will integrate all the bits and pieces meaningfully. I am suggesting that the systems approach will provide this model.

Another problem which has emerged requiring the organization to be designed as a total system, is that all too frequently the organizational context into which the newer technologies are placed tend to be inappropriate. We are attaching sophisticated techniques to a primitive vehicle, the bureaucratic structure. Organizations should be designed around the technology; technology should not be forced to fit an existing

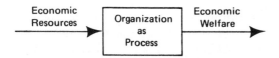

FIGURE 1 • *Organization as a System*

structure. Thus, some corporations, to be fashionable, have created operations research departments which, in fact, have been given little or nothing to do. One case was reported in which the primary duty of the OR official was to solve the school math problems of the Corporate President's daughter.

In the history of innovation one frequently finds that when a new device is invented, it is attached to the existing model. For example, when the gasoline motor was first invented, it was connected to a buggy. However, as additional innovations occurred, the vehicle itself eventually had to be modified. If advantage was to be taken of additional improvements, obviously one could not unite a 300 horsepower motor to a light shay with wooden wheels and axles. If innovation follows its normal course, we can expect the new managerial techniques to force a modification in the traditional organizational arrangements. This, indeed, has been taking place. The exploitation of the computer, particu-

larly when utilized in an on-line capacity, has led to a weakening or abolishment of the traditional divisional or departmental lines of authority. Improvements in the control and measurement of operations have the same consequences.

The hypothesis that a more sophisticated managerial technology can be fully utilized only when the organization has been designed as a total system, will be examined in accordance with the following model.

In this presentation, my approach will be analytical, or a successive breakdown of the whole into increasingly smaller parts.

ORGANIZATION AS A TOTAL SYSTEM

In Figure 1, the business organization is presented in its most simplified form. The basic input is economic resources, the organization is the process, and the output is economic welfare. Other organizations can be represented by changing inputs-outputs. For example, a hospital has a human input (sick patient) and a human output (healthy patient).

In Figure 2, the control or feedback mechanism is added to the organization

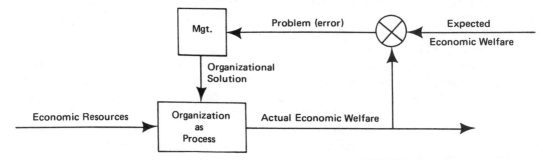

FIGURE 2 • *Organization with Control Unit*

which is represented by management. Or, in terms of control theory, the management segment constitutes the basic control element of the organization. Thus, given a certain welfare objective or expected welfare output (a profit increment), actual welfare is measured against expected welfare. If a difference exists, then a problem is indicated. This information is sent to the management segment which formulates a solution that becomes an input in the organization process. This feedback device will operate until the actual and expected welfares are approximately equal.

In Figure 3, the control unit is further broken down into a series of parts in order to provide an adaptive capability for the organization.[4] Given a change in certain environmental inputs, one initially has an input analyzer which indicates the nature of such changes. This is an information gathering or sensory device; and somewhat analogously, market research might be so categorized in terms of sensitizing the organization to some of the external variables as accounting functions for the internal changes. One also has a display

device or identifier which indicates the state of the organization or any of its subprocesses at any given time. Hence, if the subprocess was a production plant, the identifier at a given time might indicate the productive capacity, current running capacity, order backlog, inventory conditions, orders in process, production lines in operation, and machine breakdown. Such information is fed to a decision-making unit along with the information from the environment. We assume that a set of rules has been programmed. One of these rules will be selected, given a particular environmental input, and given the state of the process at some given point of time in order to achieve a certain output.

For example, if the initial input is a large order with a required completion date, the rule may be to go to overtime. This information is called a control signal and is sent to the control unit. The control unit is that element which actually changes the input before it enters the system or the process itself. The order could have been put into a queue. Such information is simultaneously sent to the identifier. Therefore, at any given

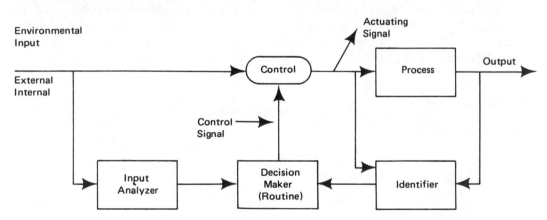

FIGURE 3 • *Organization as an Adaptive System*

time, the identifier tells us what inputs have entered the process, the state of the process, and its outputs.

Because the control signal and the control unit are frequently confused, the difference between the two should be noted. The example that is usually given is that of driving an automobile. If one wants to stop an automobile by pressing on the brake pedal, information is relayed to the brakes of the car. It is not the brake pedal that stops the car, but the brakes which constitute the control unit. Similarly, in a man-to-man system, the control signal and the control unit might appear as in Figure 4.

Let us suppose that the total employee population is the basic system and we want a higher work output. Further assume that we know exactly what the relationship is between need satisfaction input and expected work output. Given the figure for expected work output, the decision-maker will increase or decrease the amount of need satisfaction (for example, money) by a control signal to the financial department where need satisfaction is stored in the form of money. This department would release funds until the expected work output was achieved. The control element constitutes the reservoir and release of funds, not the decision to in-

crease work output, its relay to the employee, or even the decision to pay more. In other words, money may be to the employee what brakes are to an automobile.

For our particular purposes, those subparts of the organizational control mechanism, input analyzer, and so on, give the process an adaptive capability: the ability to adapt to changing inputs in order to maintain a desired or expected output.

In Figure 5, the organization is further broken down into a series of major subprocesses: marketing, production, and so on, each with its own adaptor. The adaptor consists of an input analyzer, decision rules, identifier, and control for each subprocess. Moreover, it is assumed that each of these subprocesses can be identified and separated from other subprocesses. A super adaptor applies a series of decision rules for subdecision makers to assure appropriate adjustment between processes. It is further assumed that each subsystem's adaptor has this same capability concerning sub-subprocesses. Consequently, the production system may have such subsystems as purchasing, inventory control, and maintenance. The inputs and outputs of these subsystems would have to be controlled appropri-

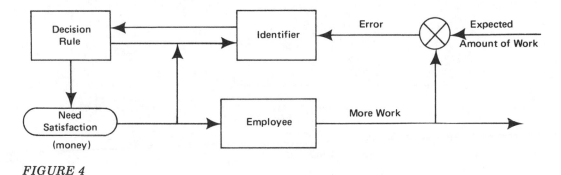

FIGURE 4

ately with the proper decision rules.

In Figure 6, a learning capability in the form of a designer is added to the adaptive system. A learning capability can be thought of as the ability of the system to redesign itself or learn from past mistakes in order to improve system performance. However, although the environmental state of the system and the application of what is thought to be the correct rule is given, the expected output may still not be produced. This indicates design problems.

The designer would receive information as to system performance. Then, in order to increase welfare output, he would attempt to improve the adaptive mechanism by formulating more effective decision rules for the decision-making routine; by improving the identi-

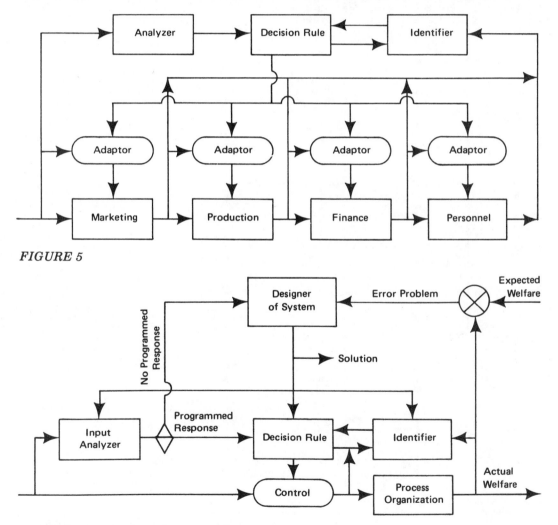

FIGURE 5

FIGURE 6 • *Adaptive System with Learning Capability*

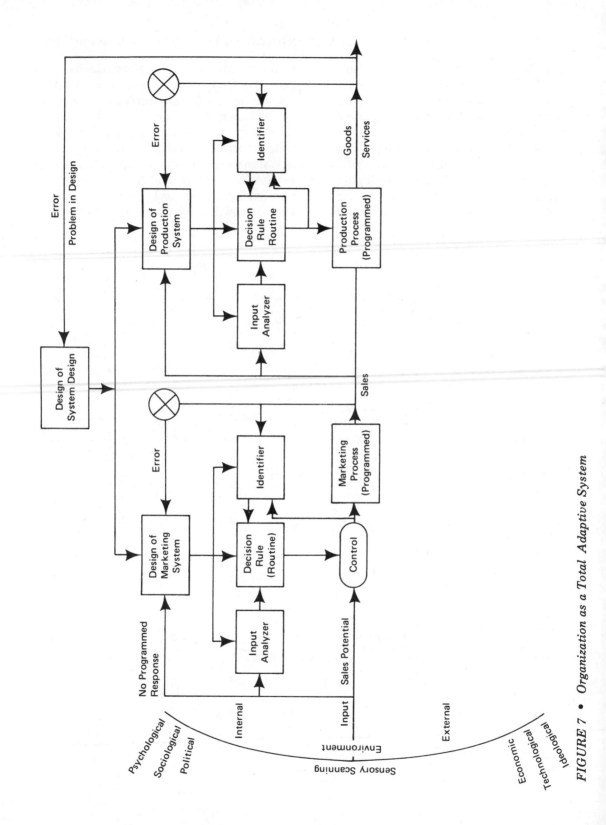

FIGURE 7 • *Organization as a Total Adaptive System*

fier in terms of more and better information; by achieving a more rapid response in information from the input analyzer; by improving the sensory devices; and by improving the control mechanism.

In Figure 7, we now see the total system in some detail. We have our environmental inputs on the left, both external and internal: psychological, sociological, etc. Two basic subsystems are shown, marketing and production, in which the marketing output becomes a production input. Each of these subsystems has its own adaptor and, although not shown, a coordinating adaptor to integrate the two. Further, each subsystem has its own design capability. The only new feature of the schematic is the box at the top, "Design of System Design." This particular function would integrate the work of subdesigners. For example, if the organization is viewed as an aircraft, design coordination is required for such areas as weight and structures, air frame, power, and information systems. Moreover, this function would advise as to design technique and strategy, and ideally, one might be able to reach a stage in which the actual design of subsystems could be programmed and routinized.

Thus, in looking at Figure 7, we see, in some detail, the organization as a total system that is self-regulating and self-learning and at least partially closed; a system in which the environment can be detailed and in which subsystems are integrated. Further, the adaptor provides for appropriate internal adjustments between subsystems. In other words, the organization, without too much difficulty, can be considered as a total system. All of its essential elements can be incorporated into a design. Also, with an appropriate index, one could detail the subsystems: each subsystem could be broken down into its sub-subsystems, etc. The indexing of the system's subparts schematic to assure appropriate usage is not an insurmountable problem. For example, it is estimated that the blueprints for a new aircraft may finally weigh two or three tons — more than the aircraft itself!

SYSTEM DESIGN

In Figure 8, we can briefly go through the design process which further analyzes the function of the designer. Given a statement of the problem or the type of system with which one is concerned, the next and key step is the construction of a model of the system. Such a model (which I believe should be essentially stochastic in nature) would stipulate the output, or mission, of the system and the inputs, of which there are three: (1) the input upon which the process is to operate or that input which enters the system, (2) environmental inputs which affect the process, and (3) instrumental or control inputs which modify the operation of the process or the process itself. (This last set of inputs concerns the technology of processing the load inputs.)

For example, in a marketing subsystem, if the initial input is a potential customer, he has to be processed through the subsystem so that a sale is secured. The system's logic relates to the set of decision rules or, given certain inputs, the state of the system and a certain control capability, such as the extent of advertising, what particular decision rule should be utilized to achieve some expected output? Information requirements relate to the classification, amount, and timing of information for the system to operate as expected. Concerning the environmental variables, it is necessary to know what information about which variables should be gathered and how often, how much, and how soon this information has to reach the decision rule.

At the outset, it would be a highly worthwhile investment to construct a fairly complete stochastic model of the proposed system in which output is the dependent variable and environmental and instrumental inputs are the independent variables. For example, one might be concerned with a personnel selection subsystem in which the output is a certain number of qualified employees. The environmental inputs might include

labor demand for certain occupations, amount of unemployment, and the number of graduates. The instrumental variables might include the recruiting budget, the number of recruiters, and the training program.

What is being suggested is that it is more efficient to construct one model to which various decision rules can be applied than to construct a new model every time a new decision rule is formulated. With the latter approach, one would always be reconstructing the model when there is a change in tools.

Assuming the model can be constructed, the research and development begins. One can experiment and try different decision rules and different hardware specifications, which lead to the

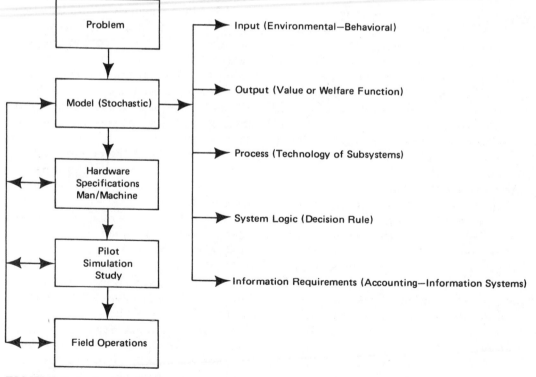

FIGURE 8 • System Design

next two steps in the design process. Given a new rule on a pilot basis, one can apply it to actual hardware. Naturally, one has to be sure that the data from pilot studies are meaningful in terms of the total system with which one is concerned. Experimentation is costly and uncertain, but there is little doubt that the payoff is greater than using an intuitive approach.

If it is successful, the new rule can be applied and data can be fed back regularly to the designer so that he can continually improve and refine his initial model. Although one may begin with a relatively unrefined model, with successive experimentation and field experience, hard data will constantly flow back to the designer. This will enable him to improve his model in terms of the nature of variables, the preciseness of the parameters, and predictability.

As for hardware specifications, apart from the consideration of costs, one is concerned with providing components that will execute the operations as specified. In Figure 8, the hardware problem how to convert what is essentially a paper model into something that approaches operating reality is of particular concern. (It seems to me that this is the area of greatest deficiency as far as the state of the arts is concerned.) We can construct reasonably good stochastic or econometric models, which can be used to simulate different decision rules, but the conversion of those models into operating reality with appropriate hardware is a different matter.

In operating context, the stochastic model or identifier becomes an information panel for a decision or rule-maker. In terms of hardware, what is needed are information collection or sensory devices which survey the environment and send such data to a central location so that the values of the variables of the model can be displayed. An example of this is the control room in a public utility in which the operator continually watches the changing values of significant variables. Only with such a display can appropriate action be taken. However, wiring such a system is a particularly difficult task.

For example, I am a member of a team that has been given the responsibility of designing a metropolitan poverty program as a total system. The primary inputs are poverty families and the output is supposed to be self-sufficient economic units. Although there exists some technical assurance that a stochastic model can be constructed, we have not been able to reach this design step because we are at the very primitive stage of inventing a sensory mechanism that will give us some running idea of the nature of our changing inputs. In this instance the changing inputs are the changing mix of the characteristics of our poverty family inputs. This program appears in Figure 9.

Another area that requires additional work is the control element, which actually modifies the operation of the system. In a man-to-man system, we do not have sufficient information about which variables to vary and the degree of variation necessary to achieve the desired human behavior. The crude reward and punishment system that we have all too often gives us dysfunctional results. Presumably, in the design process, when serious deficiencies arise, research and development should be directed to those areas.

MANAGERIAL TECHNOLOGY AS UTILIZED IN SYSTEM DESIGN

Although this view of an organization as a total adaptive system and the design process has been brief, perhaps it has been sufficient to indicate how one can take advantage of the newer managerial techniques in the use of the system analysis.[5] It is necessary to know where and how these techniques fit in terms of the system presented. As for the behavioral sciences, our environmental inputs or variables are behavioral in nature. To build a model, and eventually a display panel, such knowledge is essential. In the decision box we would utilize our various decision rules such as Linear Programming, Game Theory, Dynamic Programming, and PERT.

Because system design requires

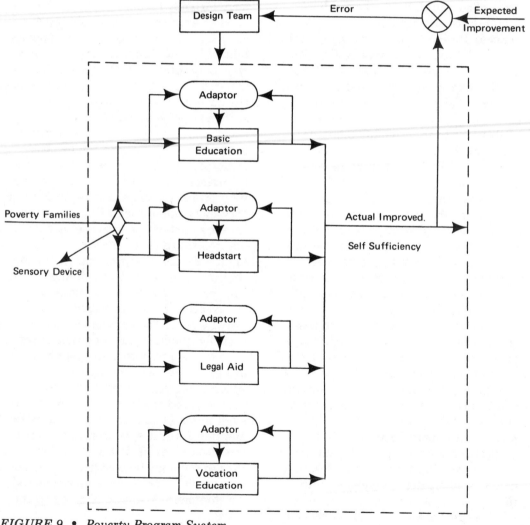

FIGURE 9 • *Poverty Program System*

eventual concern with a total subsystem such as marketing, we will probably become increasingly concerned with the problem of combining various decision rules. For example, Gerald Thompson has indicated that we must combine appropriate decision rules to achieve the most satisfactory system output. We must know under what conditions it is advisable to move from Linear Programming to rule of thumb and then back to Linear Programming. There is an over-concern with single decision rule, and we must learn how to use different combinations of rules under a variety of operating conditions. As Professor Thompson has noted, "We need to develop heuristics about using heuristics. That is, an executive program that would accept a problem and then decide which of a list of heuristics (decision rules) should be employed to give its solution."[6]

The information sciences relate to the input analyzer, collection, manipulation, and relay of information. Here we have all of our data, collection, and processing problems. The control element relates to the relatively new area of control theory; specifically, the direction of human effort. Finally, in designing a specific subsystem, such as personnel or marketing, we should have some knowledge with regard to the technology of these systems. For example, we should be able to use employment tests correctly in the selection process.

In designing an organization as a total system, it would appear that we would have to be familiar with and capable of using, a wide array of reasonably sophisticated managerial techniques and knowledge. The understanding and use of managerial techniques is an integral part of the design process. This is a counter-distinction to the bureaucratic structure, which merely attaches such techniques to the system with little purpose or place.

DESIGN CRITERIA

Design criteria are rules which are utilized to evaluate the acceptability of designs. Given a number of designs, we must determine which one is the best. Although there are numerous rules, the most widely used are measurability, feasibility, optimality, reliability, and stability. We will consider only the first three. Measurability is the system's ability to evaluate its performance. If its performance cannot be measured, a system's desirability or undesirability cannot be established and its particular excellences or deficiencies cannot be known. When models are measurable, the superior system can be inferred from the specific measuring devices used in each. In the model which I have suggested, the identifier as a display panel is the primary measuring mechanism since we would know the actual inputs, process, outputs, and decision rules. If the model is not working as expected, the errors would be fed to the designer on a more or less continual basis so that the system could be redesigned for more effective results.

One of the most serious weaknesses of the bureaucratic design as a management system is that it lacks measurability. When the bureaucratic system is redesigned from a product to a functional arrangement or when the line of command is lengthened by the introduction of additional levels of managers, no measuring devices exist, either in the previous or subsequent design, that will indicate what improvements, if any, have occurred.

Feasibility relates to the question of whether or not the model will operate as planned. A model must be realistic; it must be capable of being installed, of achieving expected payoff, and of performing its task requirements within the environment of the system. If a particular quantitative decision-making tool is suggested, we must be reasonably certain that it can be employed in an operational context.

The use of pilot studies or experimental models relates to the question of feasibility. Given any managerial device, we want to know whether it will increase organizational payoff when it is utilized, whether stockholders, employees, and consumers will be better off than before. Organizations are normative systems. All too often, the student and practitioner are exposed to quantitative manipulations and behavioral research that is interesting, but either no directions are provided as to how these findings are to be incorporated into the operations of the firm, or no measuring devices are suggested that will actually establish the quantity of welfare that the research results will actually produce. Frequently, we are highly impressed with the elegance and sophistication of the research and the virtuosity of the analyst, and then discover that the extent of research usefulness is limited.

The end purpose of the manager, as it is viewed in this analysis, is to design subsystems which will actually increase human well-being. The manager is not, per se, a mathematician, statistician, sociologist, or psychologist. However, he must rely on these disciplines in much the same way as the engineer has to rely on physics.

This does not mean that continuous research is unnecessary in these disciplines, but it does mean that such research will not automatically lead to improvements. It is only when the designer is able to incorporate findings into an operating reality that he can achieve the full value of the research.

A corollary to the feasibility criterion relates to balance between parts of the system. All parts of the system must not only be integrated, but also mutually consistent. We would not put a primitive input analyzer into practice and follow this with a complex regression analysis in the identifier. The final system output would be no more productive than the least productive part of the system. Each part acts as a constraint on all other parts. Consequently, the identifier can never be any better than the input analyzer, and so on.

The absence of integration and/or balance is self-defeating. For example, we frequently find information systems personnel providing voluminous data; that is, the input analyzer is well developed. However, the rest of the system may be missing — there is no identifier, set of decision rules, etc. In other instances, we may have an analysis of the usc of a single decision rule, as linear programming, but nothing else.

As long as we find this "bits and pieces" type of analysis, managers will always revert, out of necessity, to the most primitive part of the total system because this part represents the primary constraint. In such a context, increasing sophistication will not meet the criterion of feasibility. Even if it is used, no increment in organizational payoff will result.

For example, in the design of the poverty program system previously mentioned, the staff's initial impulse was to design an econometric model of the program, including exogenous variables. We immediately ran into the constraints of the rest of the system and realized that until we had a relatively effective input analyzer, a set of decision rules, and a control element, we could not move to the sophisticated model we wanted. In other words, when we design a total system, we are generally forced to start with a fairly elementary model. Then, when all the parts are developed, we can progress to a more complex system.

It seems to me that we are overly concerned with the optimality criterion in the "management sciences," while we tend to ignore such other criteria as measurability and feasibility on the assumption that, if one has an optimal solution, there is little else that has to be done. But unless all criteria are considered, we will not get the hoped-for results. To have a solution that is optimum but not feasible is meaningless. Obviously, a solution has to be measurable, feasible, and reliable before we can consider its optimality. For the most part, operating managers stress the feasibility criterion. At the outset, they want something that will work and actually function at this stage. They are not overly concerned with optimality. In dealing with a complex system, I am not sure of what constitutes an optimal solution. Engineers, for example, have told me that they really don't know what an optimal aircraft would be like.

Russel Ackoff has said, "One of the things Operations Research has learned about putting results to work is having considerable effect on its methods. This means the team must either translate elegant solutions into approximations that are easy to use, or side-step the elegance and move directly to a quick and dirty decision rule. Operations Research is learning that an approximation that is used may be a great deal better than an exact solution that is not."[7] Because design methodology imposes a specific discipline on the designer, we can be assured that new techniques will be effectively utilized.

SOME IMPLICATIONS

While this has been a rather broad treatment of the organization as a total system, nevertheless, certain implications can be inferred. First, on a normative basis, organizations should be viewed as a total system if we are to increase organizational output. Different organizations, corporations, universities, poverty programs, and so on, can be so categorized.

Further, although this is by and large an article of faith, some empirical evidence does exist; certainly in the area of complex weapons systems. If organizations are viewed as a total system, better results will be obtained. We are in the initial stages of this development and, at this time, we can only block out the basic characteristics of total systems. I am quite convinced, for example, that the poverty program on the local metropolitan operating level can only be designed as a total system.

Second, I have attempted to demonstrate that the systems approach is a highly conducive vehicle for the incorporation of current managerial technologies, unlike the bureaucratic structure. Irrespective of the developing managerial concepts, the bureaucratic structure itself represents such a serious constraint that only minimal advantages would occur.

Third, when viewed in this context, the essential role of the manager is that of designer of organizational or behavioral systems, just as the engineer is the designer of machine systems. The design of a large complex system will, however, necessitate a team effort of mathematicians, psychologists, and information specialists. But, as in the case of large machine systems, system specialists will be required to integrate the team effort. There is little reason why efforts cannot be organized to design a marketing system in the same fashion as the F-111 aircraft was designed.

If we were to speculate about the future, eventually the organization might be divided into two basic divisions, planning and operations. The computer, behavioral scientists, information specialists, and quantitative personnel would comprise the planning unit. This planning division would be comparable to the engineering division currently found in organizations. The organization of the poverty program, for instance, is divided between planning and control on the one hand, and operations on the other. Planning has the primary responsibility of total system design. This unit is an interdisciplinary team under the direction of a systems specialist. This is in contrast to the typical operations research arrangement in which a line manager may use operations research for assistance if he has a problem. In the poverty program, the manager is viewed as the operator of the system developed by the team.

Similarly, if the organization is to fully utilize the systems approach, the first step would be to establish a design team with planning responsibility. Also there is no reason why a particular team has to be concerned entirely with one subsystem, such as marketing or personnel. Once the development work has been done regarding one subsystem, the team should have the capability of designing any other subsystem. In the poverty program, the same team is dealing with headstart, legal aid, health, and manpower training subsystems.

There are educational implications suggested by this analysis; namely, a division of business education into two relatively distinct areas. One would represent the traditional bureaucratic approach and contain the basic principles, material and functional areas. The other would stress the organization as a total system (the alternative to principles), and would be the basic course upon which the newer management technologies (as exemplified by such courses as statistics) would be systematically built and integrated. At the University of Massachusetts, we have moved in this direction on the graduate level.

Thus, rather than offer behavioral and quantitative courses in a curriculum with little rhyme or reason, the new technologies can be integrated in the systems fabric. This is a rational program for the student because he now knows why and where the parts fit, why he has to be able to construct a stochastic model, and so forth.

In all probability, the two basic approaches — bureaucratic and systems —

will exist side by side in the curriculum over a number of years. Gradually, however, one would expect the bureaucratic material to be phased out in order to reflect changes in the real world. In form, organizations may continue as bureaucratic structures; in substance, they will take on systems orientation with a continual integration of operations and elimination of authority boundaries.

My final observation concerns the ultimate development in systems. It is hoped that, in the long run, the systems approach will result in a more "human use of human beings" in an organizational setting which the father of cybernetics, Norbert Wiener, suggested.[8] The ultimate goal of the designer of man systems is to increase the human welfare of the organization's membership. This will occur because the nature of the design process is to continually create a system that most closely fits the basic material of the system — man himself. I certainly concur with Chris Argyris'

comments upon the nonhuman characteristics of bureaucracy.[9]

The ideal organization or system would be a cybernetic one — a self-regulating mechanism in which individuals adjusted and adapted to their environment because they were self-motivated to do so. Such an organization would have the characteristics of the purely competitive economic mode. Yet, if we are to reach such an ideal state, such systems will have to be invented. To observe that the traditional bureaucratic structure has serious drawbacks, or that principles of management are not very vigorous, is not enough. If the present hierarchical scheme is deficient, then only a better one will rectify the situation. There is little question that we are at last in a position to invent better social systems. I have attempted to demonstrate, when we view the organization as a total system, we have taken the first step in this forward direction.

REFERENCES

1. For example, see JOSEPH LITTERER, *Analysis of Organizations*, New York: Wiley, 1965; CLAUDE MACMILLAN and RICHARD GONZALEZ, *Systems Analysis*, Homewood, Ill.: Irwin, 1965, Chaps. 11-4. ROSS ASHBY, *An Introduction to Cybernetics*, New York: Wiley, 1958, Chaps. 10-14; McDONOUGH and GARRETT, *Management Systems*, Homewood, Ill.: Irwin, 1964; RICHARD JOHNSON, FREMONT KAST, and JAMES ROSEZWEIG, *The Theory and Management of Systems*, New York: McGraw-Hill, 1963; STAFFORD BEER, *Cybernetics and Management*, London, English Universities Press, 1959.

2. For example, see DONALD G. MALCOLM, ALAN ROWE, and LARIMER MCCONNELL, *Management Control Systems*, New York: Wiley, 1960.

3. See CORNELIUS LEONDES, *Computer Control Systems Technology*, New York: McGraw-Hill, 1961, Chaps. 15-20.

4. For a review of adaptive systems, see EL. MISHKIN and LUDWIG BRAUN, JR., *Adaptive Control Systems*, New York: McGraw-Hill, 1961, and J. H. WESTCOTT, *An Exposition of Adaptive Control*, New York: Macmillan, 1962.

5. For a more complete review, see HARRY H. GOODE and ROBERT MACHOL, *System Engineering*, New York: McGraw-Hill, 1957.

6. GERALD L. THOMPSON, "Some Approaches to the Solution of Large Scale Combinatorial Problems," Pittsburgh: Carnegie Institute of Technology, working paper, p. 25.

7. RUSSELL L. ACKOFF, "The Development of Operations Research as a Science," in *Scientific Decision Making in Business*, Abe Shuchman, ed., New York: Holt, 1963, pp. 59–60.

8. See NORBERT WIENER, *The Human Use of Human Beings*, New York: Doubleday, 2d ed. rev., 1954.

9. CHRIS ARGYRIS, *Personality and Organization*, New York: Harper, 1957.

AN INTRODUCTION TO ORGANIZATIONAL DESIGN

Michael B. McCaskey

How does a manager choose among organizational design alternatives? How does he, for example, decide how precisely to define duties and roles? Should decision-making be centralized or decentralized? What type of people should he recruit to work on a particular task force? Organization design tries to identify the organizational structures and processes that appropriately "fit" the type of people in the organization and the type of task the organization faces.

Organizational design determines what the structures and processes of an organization will be. The features of an organization that can be designed include: division into sections and units, number of levels, location of decision-making authority, distribution of and access to information, physical layout of buildings, types of people recruited, what behaviors are rewarded, and so on. In the process of designing an organization, managers invent, develop, and analyze alternative forms for combining these elements. And the form must reflect the limits and capabilities of humans and the characteristics and nature of the task environment.[1]

Designing a human social organization is extremely complicated. An organization is a system of interrelated parts so that the design of one subsystem or of one procedure has ramifications for other parts of the system. Furthermore, the criteria by which a system design is to be evaluated (economic performance, survival capability, social responsibility, and the personal growth of organizational members) cannot be maximized simultaneously: the design of a human social organization can never be perfect or final. In short, the design of organizational arrangements is intended to devise a complex set of trade-offs in a field of changing people, environment, and values.

Minor adjustments in organizational design are always being made during the life of an organization, but the times for major concentration on organization design are early in the life of an organization, most likely after the basic identity and strategy have been largely worked out; when significantly expanding or changing the organization's mission; or when reorganizing.

Who designs the organization, organizational units, and task forces? Since organizational design concerns the arrangement of people and the division of tasks, a designer or planner has to have some influence or control over these variables. This task is most often handled by middle-level managers and up. However, the charter to design could be broadened to give organizational members at all levels more of a say in organizational design matters.

KEY CONCEPTS AND QUESTIONS

In approaching an organization design problem, some of the important questions to be answered are:

1. How uncertain is the task environment in which the organization operates?
2. In what ways should the organization be mechanistic and in what ways organic?
3. How should the sub-tasks be divided and how should the organization be differentiated? Should subsystems be organized by the *functions* people perform, by the *products* or services the company provides, or should some other form such as a matrix organization be used?
4. What kind of people are (or can be recruited to become) members of the organization? Under what conditions do they work and learn best?
5. How are activities to be coordinated and integrated? What mechanisms will be used, involving what costs?

Research and theory provide some findings that can be used as design guidelines, and we turn to consider them now.

Mechanistic Patterns of Organizing

Tom Burns' and G. M. Stalker's 1961 study[2] of electronics firms and firms contemplating entering the electronics industry in Scotland and England contributed the important design principle of distinguishing between mechanistic and organic patterns of organizing.

Mechanistic organizational units are the traditional pyramidal pattern of organizing. In a mechanistic organizational unit, roles and procedures are precisely defined. Communication is channelized, and time spans and goal orientations are similar within the unit. The objective is to work toward machine-like efficiency. To that end the task is broken into parts that are joined together at the end of the work process. Authority, influence, and information are arranged by levels, each higher level having successively more authority, more influence, and more information. Decision-making is centralized at the top and it is the top levels that make appreciative judgments[3] to determine what is important in the environment. Top levels also determine the channels whereby the lower echelons will gather and process information.

Thus the social organization is designed as a likeness of a machine. People are conceived of as parts performing specific tasks. As employees leave, other parts can be slipped into their places. Someone at the top is the designer, defining what parts will be and how they will all fit together.

Under what conditions is this pattern of organization appropriate? When the organizational unit is performing a task that is stable, well-defined, and likely to be programmable, or when members of the organization prefer well-defined situations, feel more secure when the day has a routine to it, and tend to want others to supply direction, the mechanistic pattern is applicable. Organization design findings show that, to the extent these conditions hold, a mechanistic form of organizing is more likely to result in high performance.

The mechanistic form is efficient and predictable. For people with a low tolerance for ambiguity it provides a stable and secure work setting. However, the mechanistic form is less flexible: once a direction and procedures have been set, it is hard to change them. Furthermore, mechanistic forms also entail the danger of stultifying their members with jobs that are too simple, with little responsibility, and no sense of worthwhile accomplishment.

Organic Patterns of Organizing

In contrast to mechanistic units, organic organizational units are based on a more biological metaphor for constructing social organizations. The objective in designing an organic unit is to leave the system maximally open to the environment in order to make the most of new opportunities. The demands of the task environment are ambiguously defined and changing, so people have multiple roles which are continually redefined in interaction with others. All levels make appreciations and there are few predetermined information channels. Decision-making is more decentralized, with authority and influence flowing to the person who has the greatest expertise to deal with the problem at hand. An organic organizational unit is relatively heterogeneous, containing a wider variety of time spans, goal orientations,

and ways of thinking. The boundaries between the system and the environment are deliberately permeable, and the environment exerts more influence over the activities of the system than is true for the mechanistic unit.

An organic form is useful in the face of an uncertain task or one that is not well enough understood to be programmed. The organic form is also appropriate for people who like the disorder of an ambiguous setting, for people who prefer variety, change, and adventure and who grow restless when they fall into the same routine day after day. The organic form is flexible and responds quickly to unexpected opportunities. However, the organic form is often wasteful of resources. Not having precisely defined authority, control, and information hierarchies, times can be wasted in search activities that duplicate the efforts of other members. Furthermore, the stress of uncertainty and the continual threat of power struggles can be exhausting.

Making the Choice

The choice of the most suitable form of organization is *contingent* upon the task and the people involved. There is no one form of organization that will work best in all situations, in all cultures, with every type of person. Organization design scholars using a contingency theory approach emphasize the need to specify the particular conditions under which a given form is most appropriate.

Note, too, that the same organizational unit can change its position on the organic/mechanistic continuum over time. The unit might start out being very mechanistically organized. But as the environment or staff change, the unit might move toward the organic end of the continuum. In fact, if the unit does not change its structures and processes to meet changed conditions, it is likely to suffer lower performance.

Even more important, one organization is likely to contain both organic units and mechanistic units at the same time. Burns and Stalker[4] characterized whole organizations as mechanistic or organic; but Paul Lawrence and Jay Lorsch[5] found that these descriptions more accurately described units of an organization. They researched and elaborated on a major contribution to organization design in the concept of differentiation and integration (D&I).

DIFFERENTIATION

Differentiation, the creation or emergence of differences in the organization, can take place in several ways: vertically — into levels; horizontally — into sections, department, divisions, and so on; division of labor — into occupational roles; and patterns of thinking — differences between units in members' goals, time, and interpersonal orientations.

By differentiating, the organization gains the advantages of both economies of scale and people becoming experts in particular areas like production, accounting, contracting, and so on.

Lawrence and Lorsch found horizontal differentiation and the differentiation of patterns of thinking to be the most important types of differentiation for organizational design. The organization segments the environment into parts so that organizational units interact with different subenvironments. While marketing interacts with the media, ad agencies, legal departments, competi-

tors' advertising, and the other elements that make up the marketing subenvironment, production is dealing with the machines, labor market, scheduling, cost consciousness, and safety regulations that pertain to their subenvironment. Furthermore, the structure and setting for each unit must supply the appropriate training and support for different job demands. Scientists, for example, need a milieu that will supply specialized information as well as support in projects that may take years to complete.

An important question in organization design, therefore, is how differentiated should the organization be? How should the environment be segmented and what activities should be grouped together? To what extent should the units differ in structures and procedures, types of people, and patterns of thinking?

Research indicates that business organizations in newer and more uncertain industries, like aerospace and electronics, need to be more highly differentiated because they face a greater range of subenvironments. As James Thompson[6] argues, organizations try to shield their technical core from the uncertainties of the environment. The subenvironment of the core technology unit, then, will be relatively stable and call for more mechanistic patterns of organizing. The units having uncertain subenvironments (often the R&D subenvironment) will need to be more organically organized. Looking at the organization as a whole, the differences between the units will be significant because the range of unit organizational patterns extends from the mechanistic end to the organic end of the continuum.

Conversely, research indicates that organizations in older, more established and more certain industries need to be less differentiated. They face a narrow range of subenvironments near the certainty end of the spectrum, and will probably pursue the efficiency given by more mechanistic patterns of organizing. An organization in a relatively stable and certain environment benefits from having uniform rules and procedures, vocabulary, and patterns of thinking throughout the organization. The problem of integration for these organizations, therefore, is less demanding.

INTEGRATION

At the same time the organization is differentiated to work more effectively on tasks, some activities of organizational units must be coordinated and brought together, or integrated. The manager/designer must resist differentiating the organization too radically — the greater the differences between the units, the harder it is for them to coordinate activities with each other. If all the units have similar goals, values, and time horizons, messages and meanings are more likely to be clear. But when an organization is highly differentiated, people have to spend more effort translating and appreciating the frameworks of people in different units. Most people habitually think in their own terms and it takes increased effort to move into another's frame of reference. The chances for misunderstandings increase in a highly differentiated organization.

The greater the differentiation, the heavier the burden on information processing and upon decision-making in the organization. This shows up in the array of techniques for coordinating the activities of a firm:

1. the use of rules and procedures along with the hierarchy of authority;
2. if two units are crucial and have trouble integrating, the appointment of a liaison;[7]
3. the building of a new unit into the work flow to serve as an integrating department.

This list of coordinating mechanisms shows progressively more elaborate ways to achieve integration. With greater differentiation, an organization has to spend more effort integrating and use the more expensive devices.

So in addition to asking how much the organization should differentiate to meet environment and people requirements, another question must simultaneously be raised. How much differentiation, at that cost, can the organization successfully integrate? How should people be grouped to provide the best working conditions for individuals *and* to secure the most advantageous work flow for the whole organization? A manager/designer works for the best practical answer to these questions. Many times he may decide to stop short of differentiating to perfectly meet task environment demands because his staff would find it too great a strain or because it would be too costly. Research findings show that in uncertain environments, the most successful organizations are the most highly differentiated *and* the most integrated. The difficult design decision of how to differentiate and how to integrate is often framed as the choice between produce or functional organization,[8] or some newer form like a matrix organization.

THE RESEARCH STUDIES

Table 1 summarizes a selection of research findings important for organization design theory. The studies were conducted mainly, although not entirely, with business firms. A wide range of methodologies has been used including historical study methods, an intensive case study of one division, a questionnaire survey of managers in different organizations, surveying and interviewing the top managers of all the business organizations in a given geographical area, and so on. All of the studies support a contingency approach to organizational design. Researchers found that explaining their data required them to specify the conditions upon which the use of a particular organization form was contingent.

In spite of different methods and vocabularies, certain patterns and continuities run through the findings. The design principle of distinguishing between mechanistic and organic forms is supported by the studies. Peter Blau's and Richard Schoenherr's[10] findings based on all instances (53) of one type of government agency lends support to the Lawrence and Lorsch[11] findings based on a selected sample of ten business firms. Both studies found that environmental diversity is related to greater differentiation in the organization. Blau and Schoenherr[12] found that differentiation raises the requirements for managerial manpower, and this is similar to Lawrence and Lorsch's[13] finding that greater differentiation requires more elaborate integrative devices. Furthermore, Jay Galbraith's[14] research provides something of an explanatory picture. His findings suggest that the need for more managerial manpower and more elaborate integrative mechanisms is related to the need for the organization to process more information.

Robert Duncan's[15] findings that an organizational unit appears to change its structure over time simply reinforces managers' feelings that organization charts are often incorrect and out-of-date. This is a promising area of research for developing a more accurate picture of how and when changes in organization structure occur.

As the studies indicate, substantial progress has been made. However, some important questions remain to be answered.

WORK YET TO BE DONE

Our knowledge of organizational design is still growing. Some of the important subjects which need further research are:

1. We need a better understanding of the *dynamics* of an organization developing a good fit to its environment and its members. The processes that span organization and environment, such as planning and selecting, recruiting and socializing new members, need to be researched. In addition to learning more about the enduring structural patterns, we also need to learn about the ways in which organization and environment adjust to one another.

2. We must consider the assertion of power in the interaction of organizations and their environments. How do organizations seek to make the environment more favorable to their operations? How does the environment coerce or influence the organization to meet its demands? What are the consequences of

Researchers	Types of Organizations Studied	Selected Findings
Burns and Stalker (1961)	20 firms in U.K. including a rayon manufacturer, an engineering firm, several companies in electronics and others contemplating entry into electronics.	"Mechanistic" management system suited to an enterprise operating under relatively stable conditions; "organic" required for conditions of change.
Chandler (1962)	Historical studies of DuPont, General Motors, Standard Oil of New Jersey, and Sears Roebuck, supplemented by brief reviews of over 70 other large American business companies.	By trial and error a new structural form (decentralized, multidivisional form) developed to fit changed environmental conditions.
Woodward (1965)	100 English manufacturing firms.	Patterns in management practice associated with how complex and how predictable production technology is.
Lawrence and Lorsch (1967)	10 U.S. companies in plastics, consumer food, and standardized container industries.	1) High performing organizations are differentiated to meet environmental demands; diverse and uncertain environments require greater differentiation of the organization. 2) Differentiation and integration are antagonistic states; the more differentiated an organization is, the more elaborate the integrative devices must be. 3) Additional support for above findings.
Galbraith (1970)	Case study of the Boeing Aircraft Division.	Structural changes to deal with greater task environment uncertainty related to the need to process more information.
Blau and Schoenherr (1971)	The 53 state employment security offices of the U.S. and territories.	1) Increasing size generates structural differentiation in organizations along various dimensions at decelerating rates. 2) Structural differentiation in organizations raises requirements for managerial manpower. 3) Horizontal, vertical, and occupational differentiation are positively related to environmental diversity.
Duncan (1971)	22 decision-making units in 3 manufacturing organizations and in 3 R&D organizations.	Structural profile used to make nonroutine decisions differs from that used to make routine decisions; suggests the same unit uses different organizing patterns over time.
Morse and Young (1973)	235 managers from 8 business organizations.	Individuals working on certain tasks preferred controlling authority relations and had a low tolerance for ambiguity; individuals working on uncertain tasks sought independence and autonomy and were high in tolerance for ambiguity.

TABLE 1 • Empirical Research Findings on Organizational Design

one element gaining sizeable amounts of control over the other? We need to learn about the processes which mediate this contest for control and influence.

3. Up until now researchers have mainly relied upon the criterion of economic performance to assess good fit. Clearly, using economic criteria alone is too limited. How can we judge goodness of fit in terms of people outcomes? Moreover, what about the people who are content to follow orders from the organization? Some argue that we cannot be normative on this value question. If a person is satisfied to be passive and dependent on the job, who can insist that he take more control over his own work life? My view is that a democracy can hardly afford a work system which mainly trains people to be docile, to follow orders, and above all to be loyal to the organization. But others emphasize that many prefer following orders, and this is where the issue is joined.

4. A related issue is the possible conflict between efficiency and human needs. Some elements of organization design concern social engineering to devise the most efficient organization to accomplish a task. Other elements of organization design are concerned with the full growth and development of individuals. It is too optimistic to assume that efficiently designed organizations will always or even usually be conducive to human intercourse. Mammoth operations built to meet economies of scale considerations teach us that efficiently engineered operations can be inhumane. If we had better non-economic measures of outcomes, maybe we could more accurately assess the design tradeoffs. As it stands now, much of organization design emphasizes an engineering approach, neglecting human growth aspects. Another challenge: How can we design organizations to meet both people and engineering concerns?

5. We also need to learn more about how facilities design supports or detracts from the intent of an organization design. How does the physical layout influence the pattern of social interaction? How does the visual display of information affect decision-making? At what distance for what types of activities does physical separation of people or units greatly strain the organization's ability to integrate? How can facilities be designed so that physical spaces can be rearranged to fit changes in organizing patterns? Robert Propst,[16] Fritz Steele,[17] and Thomas Allen[18] have begun work on some of these questions.

SUMMARY

A convenient guideline for reviewing what we know about designing organizations is the continuum from mechanistic to organic patterns of organizing. Most suited to stable, certain environments and a staff that prefers stability, the mechanistic form is the traditional hierarchical pyramid that is controlled from the top and programs activities tightly. Most suited to an unstable, uncertain environment and people tolerant of ambiguity, the organic pattern of organizing is more collegial and stresses flexibility in rules, decision-making authority, procedures, and so on. Of course, there are more than these two types of organizing patterns. They should be considered the ends of a continuum of types of organizing patterns.

An organization is likely to contain both organically and mechanistically organized units. How widely the units should range on the mechanistic/organic continuum is part of the question of differentiation. How great should the differences be between units in terms of structures, types of people, and patterns of thinking? Overall, organizations in mature and stable industries contain units that face more or less well-defined and certain subenvironments. Therefore, to meet environmental demands, the units should generally be more mechanistically organized and the organization as a whole will be less differentiated.

On the other hand, organizations in dynamic new industries must have some units organically organized to deal with an uncertain subenvironment. At the same time it should devise more mechanistic units (for example, production and accounting) to face more stable subenvironments. To cover that range of subenvironments, the manager/organization designer creates or allows to develop greater differences between the units. In addition, the organization tends to create more job roles (occupational differentiation) and more levels (vertical differentiation) in response to environmental diversity. The organiza-

tion, therefore, becomes more highly differentiated.

The opposite tendency from differentiation is the need to integrate, to coordinate the activities of different parts of the organization. The greater the differentiation, the harder it is to integrate. The choice of a particular integrating mechanism, such as a liaison in addition to rules, signals the manager/designer's decision to expend a certain amount of effort to coordinate activities. Concurrent with designing the extent of differentiation in an organization, a manager must consider what effort at what cost will be needed to integrate those differences. The greater the differentiation, the more elaborate and costly are the mechanisms needed for integration.

Organizational design choices are tradeoffs between good fit to the task environment and people characteristics, to monetary and human costs, and to short-term and long-term consequences. Such a design is never perfect or complete. Organizational design seeks to build knowledge about and provide guidelines for designing more efficient and more human organizations.

REFERENCES

1. HERBERT A. SIMON, *The New Science of Management Decision* (New York: Harper and Brothers, 1960), pp. 2, 43.
2. TOM BURNS and G. M. STALKER, *The Management of Innovation* (London: Tavistock, 1961.)
3. GEOFFREY VICKERS, *The Art of Judgment* (New York: Basic Books, 1965).
4. BURNS and STALKER, *loc. cit.*
5. PAUL R. LAWRENCE and JAY W. LORSCH, *Organization and Environment* (Boston:

Graduate School of Business Administration, Harvard University, 1967).
6. JAMES D. THOMPSON, *Organizations in Action* (New York: McGraw-Hill, 1967).
7. PAUL R. LAWRENCE and JAY W. LORSCH, "New Management Job: The Integrator," *Harvard Business Review* (November-December 1967), pp, 142–151.
8. ARTHUR H. WALKER and JAY W. LORSCH, "Organizational Choice: Product Versus Function," *Harvard Business Review* (November-December 1968), pp. 129–138; and JAY R. GALBRAITH, *Designing Complex Organizations* (Reading, Mass.: Addison Wesley, 1973).

9. DONALD RALPH KINGDON, *Matrix Organization: Managing Information Technologies* (London: Tavistock, 1973).

10. PETER M. BLAU and RICHARD A. SCHOENHERR, *The Structure of Organizations* (New York: Basic Books, 1971).

11. JAY W. LORSCH and PAUL R. LAWRENCE (eds.), *Studies in Organization Design* (Homewood, Ill.: Irwin-Dorsey, 1970).

12. BLAU and SCHOWENHERR, *loc. cit.*

13. LAWRENCE and LORSCH, *Studies in Organization Design, loc. cit.*

14. GALBRAITH, *loc. cit.*

15. ROBERT B. DUNCAN, *The Effects of Perceived Environmental Uncertainty on Organizational Decision Unit Structure: A Cybernetic Model,* Ph.D. dissertation, Yale University, 1971).

16. ROBERT PROPST, *The Office: A Facility Based on Change* (New York: Taplinger Publishing Co., 1968).

17. FRED I. STEELE "Physical settings and organizational development," in H. HORNSTEIN et al. (eds.), *Social Intervention: A Behavioral Science Approach* (New York: The Free Press, 1971).

18. THOMAS J. ALLEN, "Communication networks in R&D laboratories," *R&D Management, 1,* 1, (1970) Oxford, England, pp. 14–21.

MATRIX ORGANIZATION DESIGNS: HOW TO COMBINE FUNCTIONAL AND PROJECT FORMS

Jay R. Galbraith

Each era of management evolves new forms of organization as new problems are encountered. Earlier generations of managers invented the centralized functional forms, the line-staff form, and the decentralized produce division structure as a response to increasing size and complexity of tasks. The current generation of management has developed two new forms as a response to high technology. The first is the free-form conglomerate; the other is the matrix organization, which was developed primarily in the aerospace industry.

The matrix organization grows out of the organizational choice between project and functional forms, although it is not limited to those bases of the authority structure.[1] Research in the behavioral sciences now permits a detailing of the choices among the alternate intermediate forms between the project and functional extremes. Detailing such a choice is necessary since many businessmen see their organizations facing situations in the 1970s that are similar to those faced by the aerospace firms in the 1960s. As a result, a great many unanswered questions arise concerning the use of the matrix organization. For ex-

From *Business Horizons,* February, pp. 29–40. Copyright 1971 by the Foundation for the School of Business at Indiana University. Reprinted by permission.

ample, what are the various kinds of matrix designs, what is the difference between the designs, how do they work, and how do I choose a design that is appropriate for my organization?

The problem of designing organizations arises from the choices available among alternative bases of the authority structure. The most common alternatives are to group together activities which bear on a common product, common customer, common geographic area, common business function (marketing, engineering, manufacturing, and so on), or common process (forging, stamping, machining, and so on). Each of these bases has various costs and economies associated with it. For example, the functional structure facilitates the acquisition of specialized inputs. It permits the hiring of an electromechanical and an electronics engineer rather than two electrical engineers. It minimizes the number necessary by pooling specialized resources and time sharing them across products or projects. It provides career paths for specialists. Therefore, the organization can hire, utilize, and retain specialists.

These capabilities are necessary if the organization is going to develop high technology products. However, the tasks that the organization must perform require varying amounts of the specialized resources applied in varying sequences. The problem of simultaneously completing all tasks on time, with appropriate quality and while fully utilizing all specialist resources, is all but impossible in the functional structure. It requires either fantastic amounts of information or long lead times for task completion.

The product or project form of or-ganization has exactly the opposite set of benefits and costs. It facilitates coordination among specialties to achieve on-time completion and to meet budget targets. It allows a quick reaction capability to tackle problems that develop in one specialty, thereby reducing the impact on other specialties. However, if the organization has two projects, each requiring one half-time electronics engineer and one half-time electromechanical engineer, the pure project organization must either hire two electrical engineers — and reduce specialization — or hire four engineers (two electronics and two electromechanical) — and incur duplication costs. In addition, no one is responsible for long-run technical development of the specialties. Thus, each form of organization has its own set of advantages and disadvantages. A similar analysis could be applied to geographically or client-based structures.

The problem is that when one basis of organization is chosen, the benefits of the others are surrendered. If the functional structure is adopted, the technologies are developed but the projects fall behind schedule. If the project organization is chosen, there is better cost and schedule performance but the technologies are not developed as well. In the past, managers made a judgment as to whether technical development or schedule completion was more important and chose the appropriate form.

However, in the 1960s with a space race and missile gap, the aerospace firms were faced with a situation where both technical performance and coordination were important. The result was the matrix design, which attempts to achieve the benefits of both forms. However, the matrix carries some costs of its own. A study of the development of a matrix design is contained in the history of The Standard Products Co., a hypothetical company that has changed its form of organization from a functional structure to a matrix.

A COMPANY CHANGES FORMS

The Standard Products Co. has competed effectively for a number of years by offering a varied line of products that were sold to other organizations. Standard produced and sold its products through a functional organization like the one represented in Figure 1. A moderate number of changes in the product line and production processes were made each year. Therefore, a major management problem was to coordinate the flow of work from engineering through marketing. The coordination was achieved through several integrating mechanisms:

Rules and Procedures One of the ways to constrain behavior in order to achieve an integrated pattern is to specify rules and procedures. If all personnel follow the rules, the resultant behavior is integrated without having to maintain ongoing communication. Rules are used for the most predictable and repetitive activities.

Planning Processes For less repetitive activities, Standard does not specify the procedure to be used but specifies a goal or target to be achieved, and lets the individual choose the procedure appropriate to the goal. Therefore, processes are undertaken to elaborate schedules and budgets. The usefulness of plans and rules is that they reduce the need for ongoing communication between specialized subunits.

Hierarchical Referral When situations are encountered for which there are no rules or when problems cause the goals to be exceeded, these situations are referred upward in the hierarchy for resolution. This is the standard management-by-exception principle. This resolves the nonroutine and unpredictable events that all organizations encounter.

Direct Contact In order to prevent top executives from becoming overloaded with problems, as many problems as possible are resolved by the affected managers at low levels by informal contacts. These remove small problems from the upward referral process.

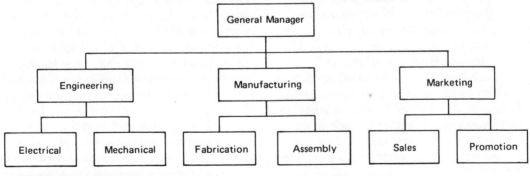

FIGURE 1 • Standard's Functional Organization

Liaison Departments   In some cases, where there is a large volume of contacts between two departments, a liaison department evolves to handle the transactions. This typically occurs between engineering and manufacturing in order to handle engineering changes and design problems.[2]

The Standard Products Co. utilized these mechanisms to integrate the functionally organized specialties. They were effective in the sense that Standard could respond to changes in the market with new products on a timely basis, the new products were completed on schedule and within budget, and the executives had sufficient time to devote to long-range planning.

Matrix Begins Evolution

A few years ago, a significant change occurred in the market for one of Standard's major product lines. A competitor came out with a new design utilizing an entirely new raw material. The initial success caused Standard to react by developing one of their own incorporating the new material. They hired some specialists in the area and began their normal new product introduction activities. However, this time the product began to fall behind schedule, and it appeared that the product would arrive on the market at a time later than planned. In response, the general manager called a meeting to analyze the situation.

Task Force   After a briefing, it was obvious to the general manager and the directors of the three functions what was happening. Standard's lack of experience with the new material had caused them to underestimate the number and kinds of problems. The uncertainty led to a deterioration in useful-

ness of plans and schedules. The problems affected all functions, which meant that informal contacts and liaison processes were cumbersome; therefore, the majority of problems were referred upward. This led to overloads on the directors of the functions and the general manager, which in turn added to the delays. Thus, the new situation required more decision making and more information processing than the current organization could provide.

The directors of engineering and manufacturing suggested that the cause of the problem was an overly ambitious schedule. More time should have been allowed for the new product; if realistic schedules were set, the current coordination processes would be adequate. They proposed that the schedules be adjusted by adding three to six months to the current due dates, which would allow more time to make the necessary decisions.

The director of marketing objected, reporting that the company would lose a good percentage of the market if the introduction was delayed. A number of big customers were waiting for Standard's version of the new product, and a delay would cost the company some of these customers. The general manager agreed with the marketing director. He proposed that they should not change the schedule to fit their current coordination processes, but that they should introduce some new coordination mechanisms to meet the scheduled due dates.

The group agreed with the general manager's position and began to search for alternative solutions. One of the solution requirements suggested was to reduce the distance between the sources of information and the points of decision.

At this point the manufacturing director cautioned them about decentralizing decisions. He reminded them of previous experiences when decisions were made at low levels of the engineering organization. The data the decision makers had were current but they were also local in scope; severe problems in the manufacturing process resulted. When these decisions were centralized, the global perspective prevented these problems from developing. Therefore, they had to increase decision-making power at lower levels without losing the inputs of all affected units. The alternative that met both requirements was a group with representation from all the major departments to enter into joint decisions.

The group was appointed and named the "new product task force." It was to last as long as cross-functional problems occurred on the new product introduction. The group was to meet and solve joint problems within the budget limits set by the general manager and the directors; problems requiring more budget went to the top management group. The purpose was to make as many decisions as possible at low levels with the people most knowledgeable. This should reduce the delays and yet ensure that all the information inputs were considered.

The task force consisted of nine people; three, one from each function, were full time, and the others were part time. They met at least every other day to discuss and resolve joint problems. Several difficulties caused them to shift membership. First, the engineering representatives were too high in the organization and, therefore, not knowledgeable about the technical alternatives and consequences. They were replaced with lower level people. The opposite occurred with respect to the manufacturing representatives. Quite often they did not have either information or the authority to commit the production organization to joint decisions made by the task force. They were replaced by higher level people. Eventually, the group had both the information and the authority to make good group decisions. The result was effective coordination: coordination $= f$ (authority $\times$ information).

Creation of the task force was the correct solution. Decision delays were reduced, and collective action was achieved by the joint decisions. Their product arrived on time, and the task force members returned to their regular duties.

Teams   No sooner had the product been introduced than salesmen began to bring back stories about new competitors. One was introducing a second-generation design based on improvements in the raw material. Since the customers were excited by its potential and the technical people thought it was feasible, Standard started a second-generation redesign across all its product lines. This time, they set up the task force structure in advance and committed themselves to an ambitious schedule.

Again the general manager became concerned. This time the product was not falling behind schedule, but in order to meet target dates the top management was drawn into day-to-day decisions on a continual basis. This was leaving very little time to think about the third-generation product line. Already Standard had to respond twice to changes initiated by others. It was time for a thorough strategy formulation. Indeed, the more rapid the change in technology and markets, the greater the amount of strategic decision making that is necessary. However, these are the same changes that pull top management into day-to-day decisions. The general manager again called a meeting to discuss and resolve the problem.

The solution requirements to the problem were the same as before. They had to find a way to push a greater number of decisions down to lower levels. At the same time, they had to guarantee that all interdependent subunits would be considered in the decision so that coordination would be maintained. The result was a more extensive use of joint decision making and shared reponsibility.

The joint decision making was to take place through a team structure. The teams consisted of representatives of all functions and were formed around major product lines. There were two levels of teams, one at lower levels and another at the middle-management level. Each level had defined discretionary limits; problems that the lower level could not solve were referred to the middle-level team. If the middle level could not solve the problem, it went to top management. A greater number of day-to-day operating problems were thereby solved at lower levels of the hierarchy, freeing top management for long-range decisions.

The teams, unlike the task force, were permanent. New products were regarded as a fact of life, and the teams met on a continual basis to solve recurring interfunctional problems. Task forces were still used to solve temporary problems. In fact, all the coordination mechanisms of rules, plans, upward referral, direct contact, liaison men, and task forces were used, in addition to the teams.

Product Managers   The team structure achieved interfunctional coordination and permitted top management to step out of day-to-day decision making. However, the teams were not uniformly effective. Standard's strategy required the addition of highly skilled, highly educated technical people to continue to innovate and compete in the high technology industry. Sometimes these specialists would dominate a team because of their superior technical knowledge. That is, the team could not distinguish between providing technical information and supplying managerial judgment after all the facts were identified. In addition, the specialists' personalities were different from the personalities of the other team members, which made the problem of conflict resolution much more difficult.[3]

Reports of these problems began to reach the general manager, who realized that a great number of decisions of consequence were being made at lower and middle levels of management. He also knew that they should be made with a general manager's perspective. This depends on having the necessary information and a reasonable balance of power among the joint decision makers. Now the technical people were upsetting the power balance because the others could not challenge them on technical matters. As a result, the general manager chose three technically qualified men and made them product managers in charge of the three major product lines.[4] They were to act as chairmen of the product team meetings and generally facilitate the interfunctional decision making.

Since these men had no formal authority, they had to resort to their technical competence and their interpersonal skills in order to be effective. The fact that they reported to the general manager gave them some additional power. These men were successful in bringing the global, general manager perspective lower in the organization to improve the joint decision-making process.

The need for this role was necessitated by the increasing differences in attitudes and goals among the technical, production, and marketing team participants. These differences are necessary for successful subtask performance but interfere with team collaboration. The product manager allows collaboration without reducing these necessary differences. The cost is the additional overhead for the product management salaries.

Product Management Departments   Standard Products was now successfully following a strategy of new product innovation and introduction. It was leading the industry in changes in technology and products. As the number of new products increased, so did the amount of decision making around product considerations. The frequent needs for trade-offs across engineering, production, and marketing lines increased the influence of the product managers. It was not that the functional managers lost influence; rather, it was the increase in decisions relating to products.

The increase in the influence of the product managers was revealed in several ways. First, their salaries became substantial. Second, they began to have a greater voice in the budgeting process, starting with approval of functional budgets relating to their products. The next change was an accumulation of staff around the products, which became product departments with considerable influence.

At Standard this came about with the increase in new product introductions. A lack of information developed concerning product costs and revenues for addition, deletion, modification, and pricing decisions. The general manager instituted a new information system that reported costs and revenues by product as well as by function. This gave product managers the need for a staff and a basis for more effective interfunctional collaboration.

In establishing the product departments, the general manager resisted requests from the product managers to reorganize around product divisions. While he agreed with their analysis that better coordination was needed across functions and for more effective product decision making, he was unwilling to take the chance that this move might reduce specialization in the technical areas or perhaps lose the economies of scale in production. He felt that a modification of the information system to report on a product and a functional basis along with a product staff group would provide the means for more coordination. He still needed the effective technical group to drive the innovative process. The general manager also maintained a climate where collaboration across product lines and functions was encouraged and rewarded.

The Matrix Completed

By now Standard Products was a high technology company; its products were undergoing constant change. The uncertainty brought about by the new technology and the new products required an enormous amount of decision making to plan-replan all the schedules, budgets, designs, and so on. As a result, the number of decisions and the number of consequential decisions made at low levels increased considerably. This brought on two concerns for the general manager and top management.

The first was the old concern for the quality of decisions made at low levels of the organization. The product managers helped solve this at middle and top levels, but their influence did not reach low into the organization where a considerable number of decisions were made jointly. They were not always made in the best interest of the firm as a whole. The product managers again recommended a move to product divisions to give these low-level decisions the proper product orientation.

The director of engineering objected, using the second problem to back up his objection. He said the move to product divisions would reduce the influence of the technical people at a time when they were having morale and turnover problems with these employees. The increase in joint decisions at low levels meant that these technical people were spending a lot of time in meetings. Their technical input was not always needed, and they preferred to work on technical problems, not product problems. Their dissatisfaction would only be aggravated by a change to product divisions.

The top management group recognized both of these problems. They needed more product orientation at low levels, and they needed to improve the morale of the technical people whose inputs were needed for product innova-tions. Their solution involved the creation of a new role — that of subproduct manager.[5] The subproduct manager would be chosen from the functional organization and would represent the product line within the function. He would report to both the functional manager and the product manager, thereby creating a dual authority structure. The addition of a reporting relation on the product side increases the amount of product influence at lower levels.

The addition of the subproduct manager was intended to solve the morale problem also. Because he would participate in the product team meetings, the technical people did not need to be present. The subproduct manager would participate on the teams but would call on the technical experts within his department as they were needed. This permitted the functional department to be represented by the subproduct manager, and the technical people to concentrate on strictly technical matters.

Standard Products has now moved to a pure matrix organization as indicated in Figure 2. The pure matrix organization is distinguished from the previous cross-functional forms by two features. *First*, the pure matrix has a dual authority relationship somewhere in the organization. *Second*, there is a power balance between the product management and functional sides. While equal power is an unachievable razor's edge, a reasonable balance can be obtained through enforced collaboration on budgets, salaries, dual information and reporting systems, and dual authority relations. Such a balance is required because the problems that the organization faces are uncertain and must be solved on their own merits — not on any predetermined power structure.

Thus over a period of time, the Standard Products Co. has changed from a functional organization to a pure matrix organization using dual authority relationships, product management departments, product teams at several levels, and temporary task forces. These additional decision-making mechanisms were added to cope with the change in products and technologies. The changes caused a good deal of uncertainty concerning resource allocations, budgets, and schedules. In the process of task execution, more was learned about the problem causing a need for rescheduling and rebudgeting. This required the pro-

cessing of information and the making of decisions.

In order to increase its capacity to make product-relevant decisions, Standard lowered the level at which decisions were made. Coordination was achieved by making joint decisions across functions. Product managers and subproduct managers were added to bring a general manager's perspective to bear on the joint decision-making processes. In addition, the information and reporting system was changed in order to provide reports by function and by product. Combined, these measures allowed Standard to achieve the high levels of technical sophistication necessary to innovate products and simultaneously to get these products to the

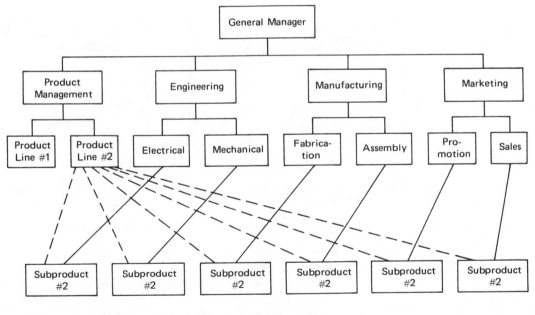

— — — — Technical authority over the product

——————— Formal authority over the product (in product organization, these relationships may be reversed)

FIGURE 2 • *Standard's Pure Matrix Organization*

market quickly to maintain competitive position.

HOW DO I CHOOSE A DESIGN?

Not all organizations need a pure matrix organization with a dual authority relationship. Many, however, can benefit from some cross-functional forms to relieve top decision makers from day-to-day operations. If this is so, how does one choose the degree to which his organization should pursue these lateral forms? To begin to answer this question, let us first lay out the alternatives, then list the choice determining factors.

The choice, shown in Figure 3, is indicated by the wide range of alternatives between a pure functional organi-

zation and a pure product organization with the matrix being halfway between. The Standard Products Co. could have evolved into a matrix from a product organization by adding functional teams and managers. Thus there is a continuum of organization designs between the functional and product forms. The design is specified by the choice among the authority structure; integrating mechanisms such as task forces, teams, and so on; and by the formal information system. The way these are combined is illustrated in Figure 3. These design variables help regulate the relative distribution of influence between the product and functional considerations in the firm's operations.

The remaining factors determining influence are such things as roles in bud-

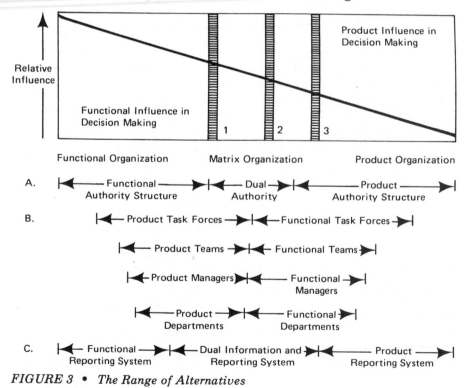

FIGURE 3 • The Range of Alternatives

get approvals, design changes, location and size of offices, salary, and so on. Thus there is a choice of integrating devices, authority structure, information system, and influence distribution. The factors that determine choice are diversity of the product line, the rate of change of the product line, interdependencies among subunits, level of technology, presence of economies of scale, and organization size.

Product Lines

The greater the diversity among product lines and the greater the rate of change of products in the line, the greater the pressure to move toward product structures.[6] When product lines become diverse, it becomes difficult for general managers and functional managers to maintain knowledge in all areas; the amount of information they must handle exceeds their capacity to absorb it. Similarly, the faster the rate of new product introduction, the more unfamiliar are the tasks being performed.

Managers are, therefore, less able to make precise estimates concerning resource allocations, schedules, and priorities. During the process of new product introduction, these same decisions are made repeatedly. The decisions concern trade-offs among engineering, manufacturing, and marketing. This means there must be greater product influence in the decision process. The effect of diversity and change is to create a force to locate the organization farther to the right in Figure 3.

Interdependence

The functional division of labor in organizations creates interdependencies among the specialized subunits. That is,

a problem of action in one unit has a direct impact on the goal accomplishment of the other units. Organizations usually devise mechanisms that uncouple the subunits, such as in-process inventory and order backlogs. The degree to which inventories and backlogs develop is a function of how tight the schedule is. If there is a little slack in the schedule, then the functional departments can resolve their own problems. However, if rapid response to market changes is a basis of competition, then schedules are squeezed and activities run in parallel rather than series.[7] This means that problems in one unit directly affect another. The effect is a greater number of joint decisions involving engineering, manufacturing, and production. A greater need for product influence in these decisions arises due to the tight schedule. Thus the tighter the schedule, the greater the force to move to the right in Figure 3.

Although the tightness of the schedule is the most obvious source of interdependence, tight couplings can arise from reliability requirements and other design specifications. If the specifications require a more precise fit and operation of parts, then the groups designing and manufacturing the parts must also "fit and operate" more closely. This requires more coordination in the form of communication and decision making.

Level of Technology

If tight schedules and new products were the only forces operating, every organization would be organized around product lines. The level of technology or degree to which new technology is being used is a counteracting force. The use of new technologies requires expertise in the technical specialties in engineering, in production engineering, in manufacturing, and market research in marketing. Some of the expertise may be purchased outside the organization.

However, if the expertise is critical to competitive effectiveness, the organization must acquire it internally. If the organization is to make effective use of the expertise, the functional form of organization is superior, as described earlier in the article. Therefore the greater the need for expertise, the greater the force to move to the left in Figure 3.

Economics of Scale and Size

The other factor favoring a functional form is the degree to which expensive equipment in manufacturing, test facilities in engineering, and warehousing facilities in marketing are used in producing and selling the product. (Warehousing introduces another dimension of organization structure, for example, geographical divisions. For our purposes, we will be concerned only with product and function dimensions.) It is usually more expensive to buy small facilities for product divisions than a few large ones for functional departments. The greater the economies of scale, the greater the force to move to the left in Figure 3. Mixed structures are always possible. That is, the capital intensive fabrication operation can organize along functional process lines, and the labor intensive assembly operation can organize along product lines.

The size of the organization is important in that it modifies the effect of expertise and economies of scale. That is, the greater the size of the organization, the smaller the costs of lost

specialization and lost economies of scale when the product form is adopted. Thus while size by itself has little effect on organization structure, it does moderate the effects of the previously mentioned factors.

The Choice

While research on organizations has not achieved a sophistication that would allow us to compute the results of the above factors and locate a point in Figure 3, we can still make our subjective weightings. In addition, we can locate our present position and make changes in the appropriate directions as product lines, schedules, technologies, and size change during the normal course of business. The framework provides some basis for planning the organization along with planning the strategy and resource allocations.

If the organization's present structure is on the left side of the figure, many of the symptoms occurring in the Standard Products example signal a need for change. To what degree are communication overloads occurring? Are top executives being drawn into day-to-day decisions to the detriment of strategy development? How long does it take to get top level decisions made in order to continue work on new products? If the answers to these questions indicate an overload, then some movement toward a matrix is appropriate. Probably a sequence of moves until the bottlenecks disappear is the best strategy; this will allow for the proper attitudinal and behavioral changes to keep pace.

If the organization is product organized, then movements to the left toward a matrix are more subtle. They must be triggered by monitoring the respective technological environments.

An example from the aerospace industry may help. In the late fifties and early sixties the environment was characterized by the space race and missile gap. In this environment, technical performance and technology development were primary, and most firms adopted organizations characterized by the dotted line at "1" in Figure 3. The functional departments had the greatest influence on the decision-making process. During the McNamara era, they moved to point "2." The environment shifted to incentive contracts, PERT-cost systems, and increased importance of cost and schedule considerations.

Currently, the shift has continued toward point "3." Now the environment is characterized by tight budgets, a cost overrun on the C-5 project, and Proxmire hearings in the Senate. The result is greater influence by the project managers. All these have taken place in response to the changing character of the market. A few firms recently moved back toward point "2" in response to

the decreasing size of some firms. The reduction in defense spending has resulted in cutbacks in projects and employment. In order to maintain technical capabilities with reduced size, these firms have formed functional departments under functional managers with line responsibility. These changes show how changes in need for expertise, goals, and size affect the organization design choice.

Many organizations are experiencing pressures that force them to consider various forms of matrix designs. The most common pressure is increased volume of new products. Organizations facing this situation must either adopt some form of matrix organization, change to product forms of organization, or increase the time between start and introduction of the new product process.

For most organizations, the matrix design is the most effective alternative. Managers must be aware of the different kinds of matrix designs and develop some basis for choosing among them.

REFERENCES

1. See JOHN F. MEE, "Matrix Organization," *Business Horizons* (Summer, 1964), p.70.
2. For a more detailed explanation, see JAY R. GALBRAITH, *Organization Design* (Reading, Mass.: Addison-Wesley Publishing Co., Inc., 1971).
3. See PAUL R. LAWRENCE and JAY LORSCH, "Differentiation and Integration in Complex Organizations," *Administrative Science Quarterly*, June, 1967.
4. PAUL R. LAWRENCE and JAY LORSCH, "New Management Job: the Integration," *Harvard Business Review*, November-December, 1967.
5. JAY LORSCH, "Matrix Organization and Technical Innovations" in JAY GALBRAITH, ed., *Matrix Organizations: Organization Design for High Technology* (Cambridge, Mass.: The M.I.T. Press, 1971).
6. For product line diversity, see ALFRED CHANDLER, *Strategy and Structure* (Cambridge, Mass.: The M.I.T. Press, 1962); for product change rate, see TOM BURNS and G.M. STALKER, *Management and Innovation* (London: Tavistock Publications, 1958).
7. For a case study of this effect, see JAY GALBRAITH, "Environmental and Technological Determinants of Organization Design" in JAY LORSCH and PAUL R. LAWRENCE, eds., *Studies in Organization Design* (Homewood, Ill.: Richard D. Irwin, Inc., 1970).

THE DECISION-MAKING GRID: A MODEL OF DECISION-MAKING STYLES

Jay Hall, Vincent O'Leary,
and Martha Williams

The success of the group decision-making process depends on the combined capacities of those engaged in decision making to work together with satisfaction and creativity. Too often decisions are made on the basis of fire-fighting methods, "rules of thumb," and gut-level intuition, rather than on the basis of any sound systematic procedures. The fact that decisions reached in the traditional manner frequently fail to accomplish the desired goals is reflected, for example, in continuing conflict between labor and management. Groups of decision makers find themselves making the same "bread and butter" decisions over and over again. Improperly solved dilemmas continue to pop up persistently until appropriate solutions have been found.

The paradox of decision making is that, despite the fact that groups generally tend to produce more adequate decisions than individuals working alone,[1] most executives are at a loss regarding the effective employment of groups in reaching decisions. This occurs even though individuals do most of their living, learning, working, and deciding within a group setting.

The confusion, frustration, and waste of time which may characterize an unsystematic attempt at group problem solving frequently result in the stronger members' adopting a "give me the ball — no strings attached" attitude which foreshadows the disintegration of the group. Rather than reflecting the resources in the group in such a way as to insure successful implementation, decisions are frequently imposed on the responsible groups. Time loss and confusion are avoided. Individual needs for action are met. But the decisions thus made must eventually be made again, resulting in more loss of time, additional confusion, and administrative impotence.

Failure to employ a systematic approach is not necessarily the fault of today's decision makers, however, for little theoretical information concerning decision making has been available to them from researchers in the field. A theory of decision making — individual or group — has proven to be a particularly slippery and elusive item for social scientists, despite forty years of research. By and large, investigators have had to content themselves with discovering and identifying facets of the decision-making process which seem to result in a decision of one quality or another. Consequently, decision makers who must daily confront realistic problems have been left to play business games, construct probability tables, and either "pass the buck" or monopolize the responsibility for decision making in their organizations.

A CONCEPTUAL FRAMEWORK

The purpose of this discussion, therefore, is to provide a conceptual framework from which a theory of decision making might be built. In keeping with the assumption that one must first be able to understand what is happening before one can undertake experimentation, this discussion will attempt to make sense out of the group decision-making dilemma through the use of a conceptual model called *The Decision-Making Grid* so that individual styles of decision-making behavior in a group context may be analyzed, and the consequences associated with particular styles may be explored.

Following are some typical approaches to decision making:

> Frankly speaking, too many chefs spoil the broth. If a man wants good decisions and action, then he shouldn't let himself get bogged down by "what the group thinks." All they'll do is run around in circles. Groups waste time looking at every irrelevant issue they think of and wind up with a decision which is a poor compromise. Facts are facts; and no amount of discussion is going to change that. When it comes to making decisions, turn me loose — no strings attached.

> Groups make me uncomfortable! I've seen some people get stepped on every time they open their mouths and I've known others who get so carried away with the group that they lose their own identities. I think most decisions have either already been made by the experts or can be made by following precedent. Personally, I can't see going out on a limb in front of a bunch of people and embarrassing myself. It's better to just "mark time" till the furor dies down and then throw in with the fellows who know what they're doing.

> Getting along with the people you work with is a lost art. The easiest thing in the world is to be critical of others and disagree with any idea you didn't think of first. It takes work and a certain amount of self-sacrifice to really understand other people, but in the long run things run smoother and everybody is happier if they all try to do this. I don't feel comfortable with decisions which everyone can't be happy with.

> No man is an island. Everybody would like to have his own way in making decisions, but the world doesn't work that way. You've got to work with other people and get the best decision you can with as much agreement as you can. You can't ever expect everybody to agree, but as long as enough support a position you're all right. It's a funny thing, but a good majority is just about always right.

> It seems to me that the more people share the responsibility for reaching a decision, the better it will be. There are a lot of resources floating around that you never know about unless you can get everybody involved in the decision. Disagreement occurs, sure, but it usually turns out to be valid and everybody wasn't aware of all the issues. I think it's sounder if a decision reflects the best thinking of everybody and not just my own. A decision without support is like a Cadillac without any gas; looks good, but can't go anywhere.

Each of the above statements reflects an individual's feelings about how "good" decisions can best be obtained. Each reflects a fairly common approach to decision making which all of us have encountered or used at one time or another. In practice, each differs from the other; but they all have some basic similarities in that they each represent behavior stemming from some "concerns" individuals have in working on decisions. The concerns people bring with them to the group decision-making situation often determine how well the group will be able to work in reaching decisions.

In an earlier discussion of decision making, it was suggested that one of the main factors contributing to the group decision-making dilemma was the difficulty in deciding how to tackle a given problem. It was further suggested that this difficulty reflected the inability of parties to the decision to arrive at a common understanding of the decision issues; that is, difficulties in group decision making may stem primarily from the failure to find and adopt a shared frame of reference for viewing the group's task.[2]

Assuming that the principal means of attaining a shared frame of reference is the interchange of information and opinions, the quality of the interaction of individuals becomes important. For a group to succeed in finding such a shared viewpoint, the individual members must be able to relate to one another in such a way as to create conditions under which people can be candid and open without fear of reprisal and under which everyone feels equally responsible.

The decision-making styles employed by the group members are important determinants of the extent to which people can relate to one another in this manner. More often than not, however, individuals are unaware of either the style they employ or its consequences for the group process. An instrument designed to delineate types of individual decision-making behavior in the group and the way in which these types affect the group process is the *Decision-Making Grid.*

A TEACHING MODEL

Rationale for the Grid

A grid format as a means of integrating fairly abstract kinds of information into meaningful conceptual tools has proven to be an effective teaching instrument in a number of settings.[3] Blake and Mouton,[4] for example, adapted many of the seemingly disparate theories and practices of management into the *Managerial Grid*, thus providing both a sound model for understanding managerial behavior and a vehicle for communicating otherwise nebulous concepts to managers in the field. The success obtained with the *Managerial Grid* suggests that a conceptual model employing a grid format might also lend a much-needed structure to the area of group decision making.

Basic Grid Dimensions

The *Decision-Making Grid* is constructed in such a way as to reflect the relationships between two basic dimensions. The two dimensions chosen for investigation are:

• The concern for decision adequacy experienced by the individual decision maker.
• The concern for commitment of others to the decision which individuals experience when working on a joint decision-making task.

Research in group decision making,[5] while not focusing directly on these two areas of concern to decision makers, has indicated that the degree of concern for either dimension — as reflected in the way members work on the task — is closely related to the effectiveness of the decision-making group. As stated earlier, the various concerns which individual members bring with them to the group session have been demonstrated to affect significantly the manner in which all parties to the decision are able to work together. Therefore, concerns bearing directly on decision-making behavior per se would seem to provide meaningful material for an investigation of group decision-making effectiveness through an analysis of the individual behavior of members in the group.

Orienting the Grid

The concern for decision-making adequacy and the concern for commitment are conceived in the Grid format as being independent of one another. A concern for one does not necessarily indicate a concern for the other. It is possible, therefore, for an individual to have a concern for adequacy without a concern for commitment, and it is possible for him to experience concern for commitment without having a concern for adequacy.

These two dimensions, because of their assumed independence, might be thought of as being at right angles to one another as shown in Figure 1. The horizontal axis of the Grid represents the concern for decision adequacy among those engaged in decision making. The vertical axis represents the concern for commitment of others which individuals experience in working toward decisions.

Each axis has been scaled from 1 to 9 in order to reflect the degree of a par-

ticular concern which individuals possess. Thus, for purposes of discussing the degree of concern for either dimension which is characteristic of a person, the value 1 denotes minimal "concern for" while the value 9 denotes maximal "concern for." By placing the two concerns at right angles to one another, decision-making styles can be evaluated from the standpoint of the relationship between concern for decision adequacy and concern for commitment which a given style represents.

THREE CONFLICT APPROACHES

Conflict "Theories"

Three approaches to decision making rest on the assumption that the concern for decision adequacy and the concern for commitment are mutually exclusive. They are seen as being in conflict. It is not deemed possible to experience concern for both simultaneously. Two of these individual "theories" view the two concerns as being so different that they embrace one to the exclusion of the other entirely. The third approach results in suppressing both concerns in order to make continued membership in the group tolerable.

Self-Sufficient Decision Making
The 9/1 position, at the lower right-hand corner of the Grid represents decision making which is characterized by a maximum concern for adequacy of the decision and minimal concern for commitment. This style is based on the assumption that the group is an inappropriate place for decision making and that discussion among several individuals can only result in losing sight of the relevant issues. The 9/1 decision

maker feels most confident with his own assessment of a problem. The facts — as he sees them — dictate the solution. He does not allow himself to become involved with others' thoughts or attitudes, but rather pushes for a solution to the problem which seems "best" to him. Whatever the circumstances, he conducts himself as if final responsibility for the decision were his alone and feels it is incumbent upon him either to "lead" the group to the correct solution or to make the decision and impose it on the group.

The success of the person who employs the 9/1 approach to decision making, in terms of getting his decisions incorporated in the group solution, is directly related to the amount of power he posesses. To the extent the 9/1 individual possesses either formal or informal power over the group, his decisions will tend to be incorporated in the final group product. Thus, a powerful 9/1 may usurp the power of the group and control the quality of its output. The powerless 9/1, however, frequently meets with open opposition from the

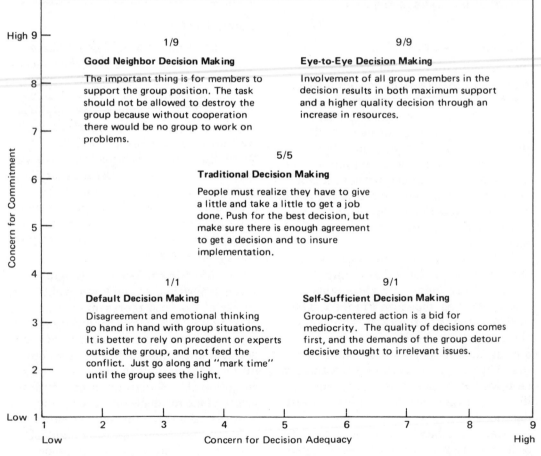

FIGURE 1 • The Decision-Making Grid

group — since it is not immobilized by an imbalance of power — and he may be rejected if he persists in selling his point of view. While the powerful 9/1 may also be rejected on a covert level, the powerless 9/1 can easily receive the type of open rebuffs reported in studies of opinion deviates.[6] This may result in the powerless 9/1's withdrawing from active participation in the group and assuming a more passive role, thus, in effect, reducing the size of the group.

Good Neighbor Decision Making
The good neighbor "theory" of decision making, as represented in the 1/9 or upper left-hand corner of the Grid, reflects a preoccupation with maintaining harmony and understanding among group members. The concern for commitment is high and overrides a concern for decision adequacy. The 1/9 decision maker feels that the group must be maintained in the face of task requirements and that the way to accomplish this is to work for agreement among members. Good neighbor decision making proceeds on the basis of an ostensible assumption of mutuality and trust among members, fair play, and peaceful co-existence. In reality, however, it occurs because of an innate feeling of *distrust*; directed primarily at one's self. The 1/9 decision maker trusts neither his own opinions nor his ability to deal effectively with conflict. Therefore, the primary responsibility of the 1/9 decision maker becomes one of minimizing conflict and promoting the general welfare within the group. The 1/9 individual is sensitized to discordant notes in the group's activity and is more concerned with fostering an atmosphere of co-operation than in pursuing conflict-laden issues, however relevant they might be

to the decision.

The 1/9 decision-making style may take the form of conformity behavior in the group. The individual may have such an aversion to disagreement and conflict that he tends to discredit his own opinions and, rather than open up touchy areas, may shift his judgments so that his ideas correspond with the rest of the group. Asch[7] has described this type of conformity behavior and attributed it to a "distortment of judgment" resulting from social pressures. Should the 1/9 individual's attempt at smoothing over troubled waters fail, he is likely to adopt a more passive role and go along with the group even though he disagrees.

Default Decision Making   Decision making by default, as depicted in the lower left-hand or 1/1 corner of the Grid, is not viewed as a "natural" phenomenon as are 9/1 and 1/9 styles of behavior. Rather, a 1/1 behavior is seen as a reaction to some potential or actual occurrence in the group which forces an individual to assume a passive, non-participating role. People commonly adopt 1/1 behavior because they are not interested in the discussion at hand. Still others become 1/1 in order to protect themselves. The person who feels inadequate or perceives others in the group as threatening frequently will assume the role of a "silent member," for example. Whatever the case, the individual may assume such a role only when he has suppressed his natural concern for either adequacy or commitment and when he sees such suppression as being in his own best interests. Thus, the powerless 9/1 described earlier may well fall back on a protective facade of 1/1 decision making. Similarly, the 1/9 individual may retreat to a less frustrating role of passivity when he is ineffective in his peacemaking attempts. Default decision making, like 1/9, may also take the form of conformity. Unlike the unconscious conformity via distorted judgments which characterizes 1/9 behavior, however, 1/1 conformity falls into a second category, identified by Asch:[8] conformity purposely adopted in order to avoid "seeming different."

Default decision making reflects an abdication of responsibility and concern for either adequacy or commitment. Thus, the 9/1 who assumes the 1/1 style is abdicating his concern for decision adequacy. The 1/9 who moves to the 1/1 position has suppressed his concern for commitment. Each has had to sacrifice but a single concern. While it may be possible to forego a decision-making style based on but one concern in assuming a 1/1 orientation, it seems unlikely that an individual whose decision-making style reflects a concern for both adequacy and commitment could comfortably suppress both concerns in coping with frustration in the group.

THREE MIXED APPROACHES

Mixed "Theories"

While the three "theories" discussed so far represent conflict or suppression orientations to the concerns for adequacy and commitment, there are several mixed approaches which reflect the notion that these concerns, though opposed to each other, may be considered simultaneously. These mixed "theories"

employ the 9/1, 1/9, or 1/1 positions in combinations.

Traditional Decision Making   In the center of the *Decision-Making Grid* is found the 5/5 or traditional decision-making style. This approach to decision making proceeds on the assumption that, while concerns for adequacy and commitment are both necessary, they exist in opposition to one another. The 5/5 individual believes that the more one concern is emphasized the less the other can be. Basically, the 5/5 decision/maker is more concerned with the adequacy of a decision; but, in view of his awareness that some commitment is necessary, he is willing to compromise decision-adequacy to a degree in order to insure "enough" commitment. Usually, "enough" commitment is defined as support from a majority of those participating in the decision making. This type of decision making is the more common style currently found at both the cultural and individual levels and reflects an attempt to employ the democratic process.[9]

The 5/5 individual is willing to confer with the group members on decision, share some of his power with them, and modify his position to reflect at least some of their views. He does this, however, more out of a perceived necessity for insuring action than out of an assumption that he or the decision can profit from the exchange of information. Traditional decision making is motivated primarily by the desire for an adequate decision, but it operates on the implicit notion that the majority is usually right. Thus, a great deal of 5/5 energy is expended in mustering a majority block of support, rather than in focusing on the basic issues as in 9/1 decision making.

The Bargaining Pendulum
Bargaining, as a special type of decision-making behavior, may be viewed as an attempt to insure incorporation of those elements of particular importance to the individual in the final decision. The motivation for bargaining behavior is that of a primary concern for decision adequacy, as defined by the individual, coupled with his awareness of resistance on the part of other group members. In order to get his own set of judgments accepted, the bargainer "trades out" with other group members on an "I'll support your two points if you'll support my three" basis. The bargainer is unconcerned with adequacy on the traded points. He is also unconcerned with the commitment as such and simply employs a bargaining strategy in an attempt to satisfy his concern for decision adequacy. Thus, the bargaining pendulum may be viewed as swinging from 9/1 (on "own" points) to 1/9 (on "traded" points) and back to 9/1 as long as necessary.

Needless to say, the bargaining pendulum style of decision making is not based on the notion that both commitment and adequacy are necessary, but on the expediency of reducing resistance by pledging support. Bargaining is frequently employed by groups in conflict such as labor and management or UN members and seems to represent a more extreme form of 5/5 traditional decision making.

The 9/1 Boomerang Effect Another style which seems to represent a combination of concerns is the 9/1 boomerang or the "I told you so" ploy. In this style

of decision-making behavior, the individual has withdrawn from a 9/1 position in the face of conflict to a 1/1 "marking time" attitude. The 1/1 phase of boomerang behavior is characterized by passivity and a form of self-contained hostility on the part of the individual. Should events fail to support the position taken by the individual, he might well continue to behave in a passive and hostile way; but should he be proven correct, he bounces back to a 9/1 orientation and reminds the group of its treatment of him — thus completing the boomerang swing.

Thus, groups which mistakenly feel that they have "convinced" a member that his position is wrong may be creating the conditions for 9/1 boomerang effect. The powerless 9/1 described earlier frequently employs this tactic in decision making when rejected by the group.

The Benign 9/1 On the surface benign 9/1 behavior closely resembles 1/1 decision making in appearance. The individual who employs benign 9/1 in working with others to reach decisions actually is primarily concerned with the adequacy of the decision as he sees it. He is unwilling to become involved in the group activity, however, unless he feels the group is prepared to adopt his ideas. His participation is contingent upon invitation from the group since this assures him that the group is aware of his presence and of its own reliance on him.

Once such an invitation is offered, the benign 9/1 individual abandons any semblance of 1/1 behavior and proceeds to "tell" the group of the solution to its problem. By waiting until he is asked, the benign 9/1 musters additional power for his position in that he can then remind the group "You asked me, remember!" In this way, otherwise powerless 9/1 individuals are often able to place the group at a disadvantage and force acceptance of their ideas.

Relevance and the 1/1 Seesaw
Probably the most commonly used mixed "theory" of decision making is the 1/1 seesaw. All of us have employed this style of behavior at one time or another, often unconsciously. Under this style, the individual adopts a polite detachment from group discussion during periods in which he is disinterested in the discussion content. Should the discussion turn in a direction which holds more relevance for his area of interests, however, he enters in vigorously with whichever style is characteristic of him. Thus, relevance is viewed as a weighting factor in this style and acts to counterbalance 1/1 withdrawal. The less relevant the discussion, the more 1/1 the behavior; the more relevant the discussion, the less 1/1 behavior becomes. The individual seesaws up and down in his interaction with the group, with the result that he may unintentionally undermine the group's motivation and contribute to a breakdown of group cohesion.[10]

By orienting the concern for decision adequacy and the concern for commitment dimensions at right angles to one another, it has been possible to delineate several styles of decision making which are commonly encountered when individuals join ranks for the purpose of reaching a group decision. In addition to three "pure" styles represented in the Grid, five "mixed" approaches have also been discussed. The individual theories of decision making which have been touched on thus far reflect a strong orientation toward the incompatibility of *concerns for decision adequacy* and *concerns for commitment*. It may be this orientation which is responsible for the general lack of a systematic approach which currently characterizes group decision-making activity.

Integrating Adequacy and Commitment

Realistically, if a decision-making group is to be effective, its members must have concern for the adequacy of the decision they reach. The notion that such a concern is basically incompatible with a concern for commitment may simply reflect the fact that most individuals do not possess either the theoretical orientation or the skills necessary for creating conditions under which the concerns can be satisfied simultaneously. Traditional 5/5 decision making would seem to represent an intuitive attempt at the integration of adequacy and commitment concerns, but once again it occurs as a result of the assumed incompatibility of the two.

A quite different orientation is represented in the assumption that a *concern for commitment is a concern for adequacy.* This is the assumption underlying the remaining anchor position on the Grid. It is an assumption based on research in decision making which indicates that task groups in which there is a high level of participation and involvement produce better decisions than groups not characterized by both task orientation and shared participation.

THE INTEGRATED APPROACH

Eye-to-eye Decision Making

This style, represented by the 9/9 position, is based on the assumption that better decisions can be reached if all available resources in the group are utilized. The utilization of resources, in turn, is viewed as possible only when all members are involved and contributing to the group task. Thus, eye-to-eye decision making represents a maximum concern for an adequate decision, on the one hand, as it is facilitated by a maximum concern for commitment, on the other.

The individual who employs 9/9 decision-making behavior has a learned tolerance for conflict because he considers conflict as symptomatic of an incomplete understanding of the issues on someone's part. He believes that a frank, yet constructive, facing up to and resolution of conflict is necessary if an understanding of issues — and hence, an adequate decision — is to be obtained. He shares individual power with other members, not in an attempt to win support as under 5/5 decision making, but because he recognizes the fact that to do otherwise tends to stifle creativity and suppress the expression of "different" ideas and opinions. The 9/9 decision maker considers a high degree — if not total — agreement among group members as definitely possible, in fact as necessary, for obtaining decisions of superior quality. Succinctly, the 9/9 individual views the group as a productive place for decision making.

A disciplined knowledge of human relations and an awareness of the by-products of particular kinds of interpersonal relationships are much greater under 9/9 decision making than under any of the other styles. Thus, the 9/9 decision maker employs an approach to conflicts, to the expression of feelings and opinions of members, to the use of power, and to the utilization of resources in the group which reflects a systematic use of the scientific method. In contrast to other styles of decision making, eye-to-eye decision making reflects a style based on conscious experimentation and study.

By-Products of This Style   Probably the three factors which most seriously impair the satisfaction and creativity of members in decision-making groups are:

1. Time-loss resulting from endless discussion of points not germane to the decision.
2. Lack of assurance that a decision once reached will be implemented.
3. Inability of the group to profit by its experience in future work sessions.

Self-sufficient decision making represents a style designed to deal with the first of the factors. Time-loss is generally reduced under 9/1 conditions, but assurance of implementation and a foundation for future decisions are sorely lacking under this style.

1/9 good neighbor decision making, on the other hand, usually results in an increased assurance that the decisions reached will be carried out because of the high commitment level among members. But time is lost in gaining commitment and the constant shifting of ideas which characterizes the 1/9 approach provides a shaky learning foundation at best for decision action in subsequent sessions.

Because of the "manipulative" character of 5/5 traditional decision making in trying to reach majority agreement, time is misused, assurance of implementation is qualified, and the foundations for continued work are too pragmatic under this approach to be of real utility. The 1/1 individual, in reaching decisions by default, neither saves time, insures implementation, nor learns anything from his efforts. In short, none of these styles can be said to deal effectively with all three disruptive factors of the decision-making situation.

9/9 eye-to-eye decision making, if it is actually to reflect that orientation, must necessarily deal with each of the three factors. Time-loss, implementation, and the generalization of learning are all problems for the decision-making group; and 9/9 decision making operates on the premise that problems must be confronted directly and dealt with constructively, rather than left to themselves.

While more time may be spent in working through procedures initially, in the long run time is saved since once the problem of "How do we do this?" is solved, it remains solved for the majority of decisions which will confront the group. Whereas the 9/1 spends little time in discussion and, consequently, feels that he has saved time, he will continue to spend time on the same problem over and over.[11] He saves time in discussion but loses it in repeated arguments. Rather than accumulating experience he confronts the same experience time and again. In addition to his obvious problems of gaining commitment, the self-sufficient decision maker may generate so much intragroup conflict that an adequate decision is unlikely to be obtained.[12] Conversely, eye-to-eye decision making may be characterized as saving time over the long haul because it avoids the duplication of effort characteristic of the other styles.

Implementation is seldom a problem in the 9/9[13] group, for the high level of commitment which accompanies decisions made on the basis of an integration of adequacy and commitment concerns insures a concomitantly high level of responsibility for success on the part of each member. People tend to support what they help create.

Perhaps in no other area does the 9/9 approach to decision making differ as greatly as it does from other styles as in learning from experience. Since the 9/9 style occurs on the basis of conscious experimentation with an evaluation of techniques for decision making on the parts of group members, individuals are acutely sensitive to what the results of their experimentation have been. Consequently, the group devotes time to criticizing its own performance in an attempt to identify those elements of process which facilitate group performance and those factors which hinder it. On the basis of such an evaluation, plans for continuing group activity can be made which insure utilization of tested procedures and lay the foundation for an improvement of skills.

Choosing a Style[14] The fact that eye-to-eye decision making is a result of systematic learning on the part of group members may pose a practical barrier to the individual's adopting a 9/9 style of decision making, for opportunities for such learning are limited by the individual's own initiative. Frequently individuals who employ other styles are just not interested in modifying their behavior in the 9/9 direction because of their perception of the 9/9 style.

For example, the 9/1 self-sufficient decision maker tends to view 9/9 as if it were 1/9 behavior because of its strong commitment component. He rejects it as being an unsatisfactory way of meeting his concern for adequacy. Conversely, the 1/9 good neighbor decision maker tends to see the strong adequacy component in 9/9 decision making as representing 9/1 behavior. He resists moving down the 9/1 path, and as a consequence, may also reject the 9/9 position.

Unlike the 9/1 and 1/9 decision makers, the 5/5 traditional decision maker does not view 9/9 as a style which focuses on concerns in which he has no interest, but rather he sees it as the style he is already employing. As far as the traditional decision maker is concerned, 9/9 is 5/5. For this reason — and this is important in terms of inducing change — the 5/5 person does not reject 9/9 but neither does he see any reason to change his present style.

Since the 1/1 default decision maker is concerned for neither adequacy nor commitment, 9/9 decision making represents the embodiment of all he is attempting to escape. For this reason it might be predicted that he may well reject the 9/9 style for himself more violently than either the 9/1 or 1/9 individuals. On the other hand, the heightened involvement and assumption of responsibility which characterize 9/9 behavior might lead him to support such behavior in others so that he might become even less conspicuous in the ongoing activity. Thus, the 1/1 person will remain passive with no desire to adopt 9/9 behavior but will not condemn others' attempts at change.

USES OF COMMUNICATION

Sharing Frames of Reference

In addition to affecting the group in terms of the degree of adequacy or commitment which it facilitates, the choice of a decision-making style may also be evaluated in terms of how well it aids in the creation of conditions for sharing frames of reference. The characteristic use of communications and power and the degree of sensitivity to the feelings of others associated with each style of decision-making behavior outlined in the Grid provide some insight into the efficacy of these styles in creating such conditions.

Communication under the 9/1 self-sufficient style is unilateral; that is, it flows from the 9/1 decision maker to his listeners, with little opportunity for an interchange. The 9/1's frame of reference is not explored but is merely repeated time and again until it is either completely accepted or completely rejected. If the self-sufficient decision maker has power, objections to his point of view are immediately cut off and his frame of reference is imposed on the group. Coerced compliance, of course, does not denote acceptance.

The "something for everybody" flow of communications and use of power which characterize 1/9 good neighbor decision making results in a confused array of issues and feelings which frequently provide little in the way of a useful frame of reference for decisions. While the 1/9 frame of reference may well be "shared," it often cannot be verbalized by the group members and, therefore, has little utility in helping the group move toward a decisive statement of the problem which precedes solution. Members of 1/9 groups have a tremendous sense of sharing, but they share they know not what. The general lack of structure and systematic orientation which results from this approach obscures the group's learning about its decision-making activity and frustrates the attempt to improve as a result of the experience.

The frame of reference which results from an interaction of 5/5 traditional decision makers usually reflects the views of the majority of the group and is shared to that extent. Those members who constitute the minority vote often fail to share the viewpoint, however, and despite the fact that the majority expects support and understanding from them, they are unable and reluctant to conform. Communication is used to "convince" others of the frame of reference and closely resembles the 9/1 use of communication. Power, on the other hand, is characteristically used in support of the sanctity of the "democratic process" and minority members are made to feel that they are obligated to yield to the majority position.

The frames of reference which result from both 1/1 and 9/9 behavior need little comment. Default 1/1 decision-making behavior minimizes the likelihood of any frame of reference being generated by the total group, and usually results in "borrowing" a viewpoint from someone else without bothering to test its appropriateness. In effect, 1/1 behavior creates conditions in the group for what Durkheim has labeled *Pluralistic Ignorance*; that is, conditions under which the viewpoints of the more articulate members are perceived as representative of the total group opinion cause individuals to adopt a "go along" attitude rather than to risk exposure. Eye-to-eye 9/9 decision makers, on the other hand, seem to represent those individuals who, when working in groups, are most adroit at creating the conditions for sharing frames of reference because of the open flow of communications, the equalization of power, and the assumption of responsibility by the total group.

VALUE OF THE GRID

Summary

An understanding of the *Decision-Making Grid* may be helpful for understanding the current state of group decision making. Through its analysis of the relationships of concerns for decision adequacy and concerns for commitment, it sheds some light on many of the day-to-day behaviors encountered in decision-making groups. In addition, it highlights some of the reasons for the inability of group members to work together with satisfaction and creativity.

While a number of "pure" and "mixed" theories of decision-making behavior have been discussed, the greatest emphasis has been placed on the 9/9 eye-to-eye decision-making style since most individuals are familiar with the other Grid styles. Eye-to-eye decision making represents a style which is based on theories and data from the behavioral sciences and, as such, presents a more novel method of approaching group decision making. It is suggested that, in terms of decision adequacy, commitment, and efficient use of group resources in establishing a common frame of reference, the 9/9 approach is more effective than any of the other styles discussed.

Eye-to-eye decision making is not noted for the ease with which it may be employed. The learning involved is tedious and of a different nature than that usually undertaken by people. But programs are currently in operation in industry and government which facilitate the acquisition of 9/9 skills.[15] For example, training techniques and instruments for improving interpersonal relations and adaptations of group dynamics principles are being employed in a number of training programs across the nation with members of state and federal parole boards. A test[16] designed to afford self-evaluation of individual decision-making styles within a Grid framework is currently being used effectively with this group of decision makers.

Individuals can learn 9/9 decision-making behavior if they are motivated by the desire for a more systematic approach to decision making and wish to increase their own contributions to the groups in which they are members. More fundamental than the learning of behavior, however, is the adoption of a philosophy; for 9/9 is a state of mind.

Normally, treatment of 9/9-*ism* has focused on the issue of "what constitutes 9/9 behavior?" But the answer to this question lies in experimentation, and any attempt to spell out the A-B-C's of eye-to-eye decision making seems premature. Therefore, it seems that the first step in obtaining the benefits of a 9/9 approach to decision making is one of discarding old assumptions regarding the relationship of decision adequacy and commitment and personally experimenting with the orientation or philosophy that *concern for commitment is a concern for adequacy*. By and large, one learns by doing and, at the same time, influences others to modify their own behavior. Thus, 9/9 decision making affects not only the individual who practices it, but those with whom he works as well.

REFERENCES

The National Parole Institutes are administered by the National Council on Crime and Delinquency and co-sponsored by its Advisory Council on Parole, the United States Parole Board, the Interstate Compact Administrators Association for the Council of State Governments, and the Association of Paroling Authorities. The program is supported by a grant from the President's Committee on Delinquency and Youth Crime under P.L. 84-274.

1. H. H. KELLEY and J. W. THIBAUT, "Experimental Studies of Group Problem Solving and Process," in G. LINDZEY, ed., *Handbook of Social Pschology*, Vol. I (Cambridge, Mass.: Addison-Wesley, 1954); I. LORGE, D. FOX, J. DAVITZ, and M. BRENNER, "A survey of studies contrasting the quality of group performance and individual performance, 1920-1957," *Psychological Bulletin*, IV (1958), 337-372.

2. J. HALL and V. O'LEARY, "Frames of Reference in Decision Making," National Parole Institutes, unpublished paper.

3. A. W. HALPIN and D. B. CROFT, "The Organizational Climate of Schools," research project under a grant from the United States Office of Education, Department of Health, Education, and Welfare, 1962; G. A. POWNALL, "An Analysis of the Role of the Parole Supervision Officer," doctoral dissertation, University of Illinois, 1963.

4. R. R. BLAKE and JANE S. MOUTON, *The Managerial Grid* (Houston, Texas: Gulf Publishing Co., 1964).

5. H. H. KELLEY and J. W. THIBAUT, *op. cit.*; I. LORGE, *et al.*, *op. cit.*; D. BARNLUND, "A Comparative Study of Individual, Majority, and Group Judgment," *Journal of Abnormal Social Psychology*, LVIII (1959), 55-60.

6. S. SCHACHTER, "Deviation, Rejection, and Communication," *Journal of Abnormal Social Psychology*, XLVI (1951), 190-207.

7. S. E. ASCH, "Effects of Group Pressures upon the Modification and Distortion of Judgments," in G. E. SWANSON, T. M. NEWCOMB, and E. L. HARTLEY, eds., *Readings in Social Psychology* (2nd ed.; New York: Holt & Co., 1952).

8. S. E. ASCH, *ibid.*

9. The majority vote has become a self-reinforcing practice as evidenced by the frequent use and teaching of Robert's Rules of Order and parliamentary procedure. Because of its utility with large assemblages, it has become the required decision-making technique in most formal groups, ranging from the legislature to stockholders' groups to ad hoc committees. One notable exception to the general rule of "majority will" is the requirement of a unanimous decision on the part of jurors for criminal cases. With many civil cases the majority vote is still sufficient. Hall, Mouton, and Blake, in a study now in progress, have found that untrained decision-making groups — as opposed to trained groups — composed of either business executives or neuropsychiatric patients resort to a majority vote technique almost immediately in dealing with the experimental task.

10. D. ROSENTHAL and C. COFFER, "The Effect on Group Performance of an Indifferent and Neglectful Attitude Shown by one Group Member," *Journal of Experimental Psychology*, XXXVIII (1948), 568 – 577.

11. A certain amount of psychological rigidity is indicated on the part of the 9/1 decision maker by virtue of the relationship of 9/1-*ism* to certain personality attributes. Robert Shaw, in an unpublished master's thesis at the University of Texas, has obtained significant correlations between 9/1 scores on the Decision-Making Grid Test and (1) dogmatism, (2) anxiety, (3) inflexibility, and (4) intolerance. In addition, negative correlations between 9/1 scores and intellectual efficiency, as measured by the *California Psychological Inventory*, were obtained in the same study.

12. R. EXLINE and R. ZILLER, "Status Congruency and Interpersonal Conflict in Decision-Making Groups," *Human Relations*, XII (1959), 147–162.

13. M. A. WALLACH, N. KOGAN, and D. J. BEM, "Diffusion of Responsibility and Level of Risk Taking of Groups," *Journal of Abnormal Social Psychology*, LXVII (1964), 263–274.

14. The generalizations contained in the following section stem from research on the "relativity of judgment" phenomenon and the distortion effects of egocentric attitudes·on the perception and judgment of attitude statements: Results indicate that individuals tend to displace attitudes and philosophies away from their own as a result of "lowered thresholds of rejection and raised thresholds of acceptance" which come into play during the comparison process. Thus, succinctly, individuals become hypercritical of beliefs and, by inference, of behaviors not in complete agreement with their own. For a further discussion of this phenomenon see: C. I. HOVLAND and M. SHERIF, "Judgmental Phenomena and Scale of Attitude Measurement: Item Displacement in Thurstone Scales," *Journal of Abnormal Social Psychology*, XLVII (1952), 822–832; and M. SHERIF and C. I. HOVLAND, *Social Judgment: Assimilation and Contrast Effects in Communication and Attitude Change* (New Haven and London, Conn.: Yale University Press, 1961).

15. See *Proceedings: Human Relations Training Laboratory*, Laboratory in Management Development Seventh Annual Session, The University of Texas, Austin, Texas, 1961; *Proceedings: Patient's Training Laboratory*, V. A. Hospital, Houston, Texas, 1961–1964; R. BLAKE and JANE S. MOUTON, "Developing Revolution in Management Practice," *American Society of Training Directors Journal*, XVI (1962), 29–50; R. BLAKE and JANE S. MOUTON, *Group Dynamics: Key to Decision Making* (Houston, Texas, Gulf Publishing Co., 1961).

16. J. HALL and MARTHA WILLIAMS, *The Decision-Making Grid: An Analysis of Individual Behavior in the Decision-Making Group*, instrument developed for The National Parole Institutes, 1963.

THE MANAGEMENT OF DECISION MAKING WITHIN THE FIRM: THREE STRATEGIES FOR THREE TYPES OF DECISION MAKING

André L. Delbecq

Recent theory concerned with group problem-solving suggests that different types of decision making require different group structures and processes. The administrator who "manages" the decision-making process must, therefore, organize the executive team in different ways as he deals with the variety of decision-making situations within the firm.

Every practicing administrator is well aware of these qualitative differences in the problem-solving situations which he and his management team face. Further, even without conscious effort on his part, the management group will often change its pattern of communication and individual managers will adjust their roles, as the management team faces different tasks. Research evidence shows that over time, problem-solving groups tend to adjust their behavior in keeping with changes in the nature of group problem-solving.[1]

On the other hand, the process of adjustment to new decision-making situations is often slow, usually incomplete, and occasionally nonexistent. Managers develop expectations about appropriate behavior in decision-making meetings with their superiors, so that their behavior falls into a pattern with limited variability which may be appropriate for some types of decision making, but highly inappropriate for other decision-making situations.[2] However, if the manager is highly sensitive to differences in the decision-making tasks faced by the management team, and can verbally redefine both his own and his subordinates' roles in a fashion congruent with the new decision-making situation, research indicates that the management group can much more readily change its behavior as the result of such role redefinition in order to adjust to a new decision-making situation.[3]

From *Academy of Management Journal*, December 1967, pp. 329–339. Reprinted by permission of the author and the *Academy of Management Journal*.

[1] Harold Guetzkow and Herbert A. Simon, "The Impact of Certain Communication Nets Upon Organization and Performance in Task Oriented Groups," *Management Science,* 1 (1955), 233–250; Rocco Carzo, Jr., "Organization Structure and Group Effectiveness," *Administrative Science Quarterly* (March, 1963), pp. 393–425.

[2] Leonard Berkowitz, "Sharing Leadership in Small, Decision-Making Groups," *Journal of Abnormal and Social Psychology* (1953), pp. 231–238: Andre L. Delbecq, "Managerial Leadership Styles in Problem-Solving Conferences," *Academy of Management Journal*, VII, No. 4 (Dec., 1964), 255–268.

[3] Andre L. Delbecq, "Managerial Leadership Styles in Problem-Solving Conferences: Research Findings on Role Flexibility," *Academy of Management Journal*, VIII, No. 1 (March, 1965), 32–43.

The purpose of this article is to set forth three decision-making strategies, each of which is tailored to a different type of problem-solving situation encountered within the firm. Further, each strategy will be examined to determine the degree to which it differs from the logic of classical organization models. It is hoped that this examination of the three different strategies will fulfill the following purposes:

1. The administrator will become more sensitive to the kind of group structure and process which each of the three problem-solving tasks demands,
2. The problems of implementing the strategies within a traditional formal organization culture will be clearer, and
3. The implications for the redesign of traditional formal organization models to facilitate greater flexibility for problem-solving can be suggested.

THE RELEVANCE OF "TASK" FOR GROUP STRUCTURE

Since the body of this article proposes that managers should reorganize group structure and process as they face different types of decision tasks, a word about the relevance of task as a variable around which to construct "organization" is appropriate. It is axiomatic to say that individual behavior is goal directed,[4] and that group behavior is purposeful or goal directed as well.[5] The task of a group is normally thought of, however, only in terms of the stated goal of the group's activity. Thus, there are familiar typologies of groups based on stated goals. For example, Wolman classifies groups as being Instrumental Groups (which individuals join for the satisfaction of "to take" needs, e.g., business associations), Mutual Acceptance Groups (in which "give" and "take" motives are important, e.g., friendship relations), and Vectorial Groups (which people join for the purpose of serving a lofty goal.)[6]

Another typology dealing with organizations as macro-groups is that of Scott and Blau who speak of Mutual Benefit Associations (where the prime beneficiary is the membership), Business Concerns (where the owner is the prime beneficiary), Service Organizations (where the client group is the prime beneficiary), and Commonweal Organizations (where the prime beneficiary is the public at large.)[7]

What is not immediately apparent in each of these descriptive typologies is that task, as a variable, affects several dimensions of the system (regardless of whether one is referring to a small group or a large organization) including:

1. *Group Structure:* In terms of the relationship between the individual members,
2. *Group Roles:* In terms of the behavior required of individual group members which are necessary to facilitate task accomplishment,

---

[4]Harold J. Leavitt and Ronald A. H. Mueller, *Managerial Psychology* (Chicago: University of Chicago Press, 1964). pp.8–9.

[5]Robert T. Golembiewski, *The Small Group* (Chicago: University of Chicago Press, 1962), p.181.

[6]Benjamin Wolman, "Instrumental, Mutual Acceptance and Vectorial Groups," Paper read at the Annual Meeting of the American Sociological Association, August 1953.

[7]Peter M. Blau and W. Richard Scott, *Organizations, A Comparative Approach* (San Francisco: Chandler Publishing Company, 1962).

3. *Group Process:* In terms of the manner of proceeding toward goal accomplishment,
4. *Group Style:* In terms of the social-emotional tone of interpersonal relationships (e.g., the amount of stress on individual members, the congeniality of interpersonal relations, the perceived consequences of individual and group success or failure,
5. *Group Norms:* Relative to each of the preceding four dimensions.

Thus, in treating task as merely the end goal, many of the theoretical as well as the practical implications of the group's or organization's tasks are not made explicit. For example, when mutual benefit organizations are compared with business concerns, one would expect the former to be characterized by greater dispersion of power (structure), broader membership participation in goal setting (roles and process), greater emotional support of individual members (style), and stronger egalitarianism (norms).

In a similar fashion, the problem-solving "task" faced by a particular managerial team, within a particular organization, at a particular point of time, likewise must affect the structure, roles, process, style, and norms of the management team if the group is to optimally organize itself to deal with its task.[8]

STRATEGIES FOR GROUP PROBLEM SOLVING

Against this background, we can now proceed directly to classify decision situations as found in groups and organizations and to specify group strategies implied in behaviorally oriented group and organization studies appropriate for dealing with each of the situations.[9]

Strategy One: Routine Decision Making

The first decision situation with which we will deal is the routine decision-making situation. In Simon's terminology, this is the "programmed" decision-situation; in Thompson's terminology, the "computational" decision.[10] Here, the organization or group agrees upon the desired goal, and technologies exist to achieve the goal. In such a situation, the following strategy can be specified as consistent with behavioral models:

1. *Group Structure:* The group is composed of specialists, with a coordinator (leader).
2. *Group Roles:* Behavior is characterized by independent effort, with each specialist contributing expertise relative to his own specialty, including the coordinator (leader) who specializes in coordination across task phases.
3. *Group Process:* At the beginning of the

---

[8]W.C. Schutz, "Some Theoretical Considerations for Group Behavior," *Symposium on Techniques for the Measurement of Group Performance* (Washington, D.C.: U. S. Government Research and Development Board, 1952), pp. 27–36.

[9]The reader should be clearly forewarned that each of the strategies is the author's own conceptualization. While an extensive review of the literature, both theoretical and empirical, underlies each strategy, it is not meant to be implied that the strategy represents a model about which scholars universally agree. Rather, the strategies represent the theoretical position of the author which is consistent with much of the literature, but is admittedly open to question and refinement.

[10]J. Thompson and Arthur Tuden, "Strategies, Structures and Processes of Organizational Decision," *Comparative Studies in Administration,* ed. Thompson, et al (Pittsburgh, Pa.: University of Pittsburgh Press, 1959), pp. 198–199; H. Simon, *The New Science of Management Decisions* (New York: Harper Brothers, 1960), Chapters 2, 3.

planning period, specialists, with the coordinator, specify the productivity objectives. Subsequently, excepting occasional joint meetings to review progress, coordination of specialist endeavors is generally obtained by means of dyadic (two-person) communication between individual specialists and their coordinator, or through horizontal communication between specialists.

4. *Group Style.* Relatively high stress is characteristic. Stress is achieved through quality and quantity commitments and time constraints, agreed upon in joint consultation at the beginning of the planning period. Responsibility is decentralized within areas of specialization, but coordination is centralized in the coordinator.

5. *Group Norms:* Norms are characterized by professionalism (high sense of individual responsibility and craftsmanship); commitment to shared team objectives relative to quantity and quality of output; economy and efficiency.

The above strategy evidences both similarity and dissimilarity when compared with classical organizational models. It is similar in that there is a clear division of labor, functional and structural specialization (specialization in work, and between work and coordination), and centralized coordination.

On the other hand, this "optimal" model is dissimilar in several significant ways. To begin with, responsibility is obtained primarily through team commitments to group objectives, dealing with both the quantity and quality of the output. This commitment, elicited through joint discussion between the specialists and the coordinator at the beginning of the planning period, places

responsibility on both the team members and the coordinator, rather than locating responsibility solely in the coordinator.

Control is obtained in two ways. First, the coordinator provides the feedback mechanism for the team by monitoring the progress of individual specialists to assure conformity to shared productivity and time objectives. Situations where actual performance deviated from prior commitments are brought to the shared attention of the team, which institutes appropriate correction measures. Thus, discipline rests upon joint commitments rather than upon superordinate sanctions.[11] Second, because motivation is task-intrinsic, specialists are "normatively" expected to be "self-controlled" through professional, reference-group standards. Authority is likewise decentralized, based upon specialist expertise and shared norms.

Since responsibility, authority, and discipline are shared within the management team, there is less status disparity between the coordinator and the specialist than is the case between supervisor and subordinates in traditional organization models. Indeed, coordination is seen as a type of specialization, rather than as a function of superior personal attributes, or positional status. As a consequence, there is a propensity for fluid changes in group personnel; different task experts bring to bear their differentiated competences at different points of time as the group encounters various

---

[11]For a treatment of the manner in which group norms control individual behavior, see André L. Delbecq and Fremont A. Shull, "Norms, A Feature of Symbolic Culture: A Major Linkage Between the Individual. The Small Group and Administrative Organization," *The Making of Decisions*, ed. W.J. Gore and J.W. Dyson (N.Y.: The Free Press of Glencoe, 1964), pp. 213–242.

phases of decision making in the completion of a project. Further, the role of the coordinator may shift between the specialists on occasions, as the coordination requirements demand different admixtures of skills at various phases of project management.

Admittedly, the strategy assumes high quality personnel in terms of both task skills and interpersonal skills. Further, it requires a degree of autonomy for both individual specialists and each specialist team, an autonomy which must be predicated on personal and organizational maturity. It also assumes that the objectives of the organization and each group can be integrated into a meaningful, internally consistent ends-means chain, where, at each level and between each area, objectives can be translated in terms of appropriate technologies.

Nonetheless, although a "pure" strategy (best approximated in project management, matrix management, or task-force groups), movement towards such a model for structuring groups dealing with "routine" tasks appears capable of avoiding many of the dysfunctions of classical organizational models, while captivating the advantages of division of labor, specialization, centralized coordination, and task-intrinsic motivation.

Strategy Two: Creative Decision Making

The second decision situation with which we will deal is the creative decision-making situation. Here we are talking about decision making which in Simon's terminology is "heuristic" and in Thompson's terminology is "judgmental."[12] The central element in the decision making is the lack of an agreed-upon method of dealing with the problem; this lack of certitude may relate to incomplete knowledge of causation, or lack of an appropriate solution strategy. In such a situation the following strategy can be specified as consistent with behavioral models.[13]

1. *Group Structure:* The group is composed of heterogeneous, generally competent personnel, who bring to bear on the problem diverse frames of reference, representing channels to each relevant body of knowledge (including contact with outside resource personnel who offer expertise not encompassed by the organization), with a leader who facilitates creative (heuristic) processes.
2. *Group Roles:* Behavior is characterized by each individual, exploring with the entire group all ideas (no matter how intuitively and roughly formed) which bear on the problem.
3. *Group Processes:* The problem-solving process is characterized by:
   a. spontaneous communication between members (not focused in the leader)

---

[12]Herbert A. Simon and Allen Newell, "Heuristic Problem Solving: The Next Advance in Operations Research," *Operations Research Journal* (Jan.–Feb., 1958); Thompson and Tuden, *op. cit.*

[13]Particularly useful models dealing with individual and group creativity can be found in William E. Scott, "The Creative Individual," *Journal of Management* (Sept., 1965); Larry Cummings, "Organizational Climates for Creativity," *Journal of the Academy of Management* (Sept., 1965); Victor A. Thompson, "Bureaucracy and Innovation," *Administrative Science Quarterly* (June, 1965); Gary Steiner, The Creative Organization (Chicago: University of Chicago Press, 1965); and Norman R. F. Maier, *Problem-Solving Discussions and Conferences* (New York: McGraw–Hill, 1963).

b. full participation from each member
c. separation of idea generation from idea evaluation
d. separation of problem definition from generation of solution strategies
e. shifting of roles, so that interaction which mediates problem solving (particularly search activities and clarification by means of constant questioning directed both to individual members and the whole group) is not the sole responsibility of the leader
f. suspension of judgment and avoidance of early concern with solutions, so that emphasis is on analysis and exploration, rather than on early solution commitment.

4. *Group Style:* The social-emotional tone of the group is characterized by:
a. a relaxed, nonstressful environment
b. ego-supportive interaction, where open give-and-take between members is at the same time courteous
c. behavior which is motivated by interest in the problem, rather than concern with short-run payoff
d. absence of penalties attached to any espoused idea or position.

5. *Group Norms:*
a. are supportive of originality, and unusual ideas, and allow for eccentricity
b. seek behavior which separates source from content in evaluating information and ideas
c. stress a nonauthoritarian view, with a relativistic view of life and independence of judgment
d. support humor and undisciplined

exploration of viewpoints
e. seek openness in communication, where mature, self-confident individuals offer "crude" ideas to the group for mutual exploration without threat to the individual for "exposing" himself
f. deliberately avoid credence to short-run results, or short-run decisiveness
g. seek consensus, but accept majority rule when consensus is unobtainable.[14]

Obviously, the above prescription for a strategy to deal with creativity does not easily complement classical organization theory. Structural differentiation and status inequality (other than achieved status within the group) are deemphasized. The decisive, energetic, action-oriented executive is a normative misfit. Decisions evolve quite outside the expected frame of references of the "pure" task specialist. Communication is dispersed, rather than focused in a superior or even a coordinator. Motivation is totally task-intrinsic, the pleasure being much more in the exploration than in an immediately useful outcome. Indeed, the very personnel who thrive by excellent application and execution of complex technologies in the first strategy, find the optimal decision rules for the second strategy unnatural, unrealistic, idealistic, and slow.

[14]In development of the above model, we have consciously avoided the issue of "nominal" groups (where members work without verbal interaction in generating solution strategies) vs. "interacting" groups. While preliminary evidence favors "nominal" groups in generating ideas, the question as to the appropriateness of the nominal group strategy for the total decision process (i.e., evaluation as well as idea generation) remains in question.

Further, the experimental tasks used in the studies may be different in kind from organizational decision making. In any event, the above model seems quite adaptable to separation into nominal and interacting processes at various phases, using modifications which do not vitiate the general tenor of the model. For a discussion of nominal vs. interacting groups, see Alan H. Leader, "Creativity in Management." Paper read at the Midwest Division of the Academy of Management, April 8, 1967; P. W. Taylor, P. C. Berry, and C. H. Block. "Does Group Participation When Using Brainstorming Facilitate or Inhibit Creative Thinking?" *Administrative Science Quarterly, III* (1958), 23–47.

Nonetheless, although all members of any organization will not find both of the strategies equally comfortable, it can be expected that most organizational members can approximate the strategy given appropriate role definitions. The point, here, is that the group structure and process which is called for to facilitate creativity is intrinsically different from our first strategy. While the first strategy called for an internally consistent team of complementary specialists who are "action" oriented, the second strategy calls for a heterogeneous collection of generalists (or at least generically wise specialists not restricted to the boundaries of their own specialized frame of reference, and even, not necessarily of the immediate group or organization) who are deliberately and diagnostically patient in remaining problem-centered. The membership, roles, processes, style, and norms of strategy two are more natural to the scientific community (or a small sub-set thereof) than to the practicing executive. The general implications, however, must await the exposition of the third strategy.

Strategy Three: Negotiated Decision Making

The third decision situation with which we will deal is the negotiated decision-making strategy. In this instance, we are concerned with a strategy for dealing with opposing factions which, because of differences in norms, values, or vested interests, stand in opposition to each other, concerning either ends or means, or both.[15] Organization theory has never given much attention to groups in conflict, since several elements of classical models precluded such open conflict. One element was, of course, the existence of monocratic authority. At some level in the hierarchical system, authority to "decide" was to be found. Parties representing various opinions might be given a hearing, but ultimately Manager X was to make the decision. Another element in classical thought which precluded open conflict was the conviction, however utopian, that conflict was merely symptomatic of inadequate analysis. Adequate problem solving would surely show that the conflict was artificial and that an integrative decision could be reached. Thus, the study of mechanisms for negotiation between groups in conflict was left to the student of political science and social conflict and was excluded from organizational models.

Nonetheless, the realities of conflict have been ubiquitous. Present models encourage the sublimation of conflict, veiling it in portended rationality. As one wag expressed the matter. "If people don't agree with me, it isn't that I am wrong, or that they are right, but merely that I haven't been clear." In spite of Trojan efforts at "clear communication," the elimination of all conflict through analysis is, indeed, a utopian desire. There have been, and will be, instances where the organization finds itself encompassing two "camps," each supported by acceptable values and logic, and each committed to a different

---

[15]In this respect, we assume a position different from that of Thompson and Tuden in their earlier model who posit that "compromise" decision making is predicted on disagreement about ends. Thompson and Tuden, *op cit.*

course of action, relative to either means, ends, or both. The question remains, then, as to what would be an appropriate strategy in those cases where "analysis" cannot provide an acceptable solution to both parties since the disparate opinion or positions are based on assumptions and premises not subject to total decision integration.

The following strategy can be specified:

1. *Group Structure:* The group is composed of proportional representation of each faction (but with the minority never represented by less than two persons), with an impartial formal chairman.[16]
2. *Group Roles:* Each individual sees himself as a representative of his faction, seeking to articulate and protect dominant concerns of the group he represents, while at the same time negotiating for an acceptable compromise solution.
3. *Group Processes:* The problem-solving process is characterized by:
   a. orderly communication mediated by the chairman, providing opportunity for each faction to speak, but avoidance of factional domination
   b. formalized procedures providing for an orderly handling of disputation
   c. formalized voting procedure
   d. possession of veto power by each faction
   e. analytical approaches to seeking compromise, rather than mere reliance on power attempts.
4. *Group Style:* Group style is characterized by:
   a. frankness and candor in presenting opposing viewpoints
   b. acceptance of due process in seeking resolution to conflicts
   c. openness to rethinking, and to mediation attempts

d. avoidance of emotional hostility and aggression.
5. *Group Norms:* Group norms are characterized by:
   a. desire on the part of all factions to reach agreement
   b. the perception of conflict and disagreement as healthy and natural, rather than pathological
   c. acceptance of individual freedom and group freedom to disagree
   d. openness to new analytical approaches in seeking acceptable compromise
   e. acceptance of the necessity of partial agreement as an acceptable, legitimate, and realistic basis for decision making.

There is, obviously, no parallel in either structure or norms to the above strategy in classical organizational models. The acceptance of open conflict; provision for due process between conflicting groups; openness to compromise; evolution of policy and objectives through negotiation; and "representative groups" while found in the "underworld" in most organizations, are outside the general organizational model. Indeed, managers involved in "negotiations," either in the personnel (labor relations) or marketing (customer relations) areas, find it difficult to articulate the legitimacy of many of their decisions except through rationalizations.

CONCLUSIONS AND IMPLICATIONS

Both the propensities for groups to change the nature of their interaction as they change task, and/or task phases, and the prescriptions for group strategies dealing with differentiated deci-

---

[16]The justification for the minority never being represented by less than two persons is that it is difficult for one person to represent his group across the boundary and that a minority of one is easy prey for a majority of two members, let alone more than two.

sion situations (as set forth above) indicate that the structure and processes of groups must be related to changes in the characteristics of the decision-making tasks. (Whether one agrees with each proposition in each of the decision strategy models set forth in this article or not, the fact that each of the decision-making situations is endemically different is difficult to refute.)

On the other hand, formal organizations as conceived in present organizational models are presumably structured in terms of the predominant type of task encountered by the system. (Thus, the "bureaucratic" model is based on facilitating "routine" decision making; the labor union council is structured to deal with negotiated decision making; etc.) Since task is, in the most pertinent sense, what members of the organization subjectively define it to be as they respond to the situation in which they find themselves, the internal features of a decision group within the organization will generally be conditioned by the predominant structured roles created to deal with the "typical" decisions encountered in day-to-day organizational tasks. As a result, role expectations and behaviors conditioned in the central organizational system (the formal organization) may inhibit the decision task

performance in the subsystem (the decision-making committee, conference, or task force).

Since there are several types of decisions to be made within complex organizations, with each general type calling for a different group structure and process, a major role of the manager in such a system is the evoking of appropriate changes in behaviors on the part of the managerial team as it moves across task types by means of role redefinition. This assumes that the manager can classify decision tasks according to the models presented here, or some other conceptual scheme, and that the managerial team can respond with congruent role flexibility. Earlier pilot research by the author indicates that such flexibility seems to be within the capacities of a large portion of the population, given appropriate role redefinition by the superior.[17]

In a real sense, then, management of the decision-making process is management of the structure and functioning of decision groups, so that these decision-making processes become congruent with changes in the nature of the decision-making task being undertaken at a particular point of time within the organization.

---

[17]André L. Delbecq (March, 1965). We agree that some individuals will find it impossible to assume flexible roles due to their particular developmental history which results in a fixated behavior pattern. We also agree that some roles will be more natural than others for individuals due to their developmental history. We disagree, however, with the notion that the normal population cannot assume at least functionally relevant roles in accordance with the various strategies, a point which appears to be the position of some theorists. A more conservative viewpoint than ours is assumed by Abraham Zaleznic in *Human Dilemmas of Leadership* (New York: Harper & Row, 1965).

NATIONAL LUMBER COMPANY

CASE 1

Frank Jensen was general manager of the Fabricated Components Division of the National Lumber Company. Located in Trenton, New Jersey, the Fabricated Components Division manufactured and sold a line of prefabricated components such as walls, floors, and roofing systems to building contractors on the Eastern seaboard. By utilizing the products of the Fabricated Components Division contractors could, under certain circumstances, achieve great economy in construction of their projects

The Fabricated Components Division was significantly different from the other operations of the National Lumber Company. National Lumber Company manufactured and sold a wide range of lumber products from a series of plants and wholesaling points throughout the United States. The National Lumber Company was a large, successful organization which had been in business for over 75 years. The Fabricated Components Division had been started on an

experimental basis, as the management of the National Lumber Company felt that prefabricated components offered real promise in the construction industry, and it wished to be aware of the problems and opportunities in the field. By establishing this division, management felt that valuable experience and insights could be gained and that the National Lumber Company would be in a good position to capitalize on the expected boom in components.

A large modern plant, more than adequate for the expected level of immediate operations, was erected in Trenton. Mr. Jensen, who had a great deal of experience in the fabricated components business as manager of one of the small independent organizations which were engaged in this type of activity, was hired for the purpose of supervising the construction of the plant and for heading the operations of Fabricated Components Division after the plant was completed. He was considered to be a very capable administrator by executives of National Lumber Company.

During the first year of operation many diverse things had to be done: building an organization to both manufacture and sell the products, staffing the office force, working at production and control difficulties, and establishing a market for what was basically a new, relatively untested concept in the building industry. Many problems were encountered, but at the end of the first year the Fabricated Components Division had shown a profit of $12,000 on sales of $400,000 and an investment of $250,000.

The second year was, according to

Mr. Jensen, a continuation of the "shakedown period." Changes in both the product and the organization were made, additional capital was invested in the plant, and advertising and selling expenditures were increased. The product line seemed to be gaining the approval of many contractors, although competition with the more traditional methods of construction was severe. At the end of the second year the operating statements showed a net loss of $4,000 on sales of $350,000 and a net investment of $300,000.

The third and fourth years of the life of Fabricated Components Division were, in Mr. Jensen's words, "a madhouse." Several new products were introduced, the plant was again expanded, advertising expenditures were increased still more, and a great number of people were added to the organization to handle the increased volume of business. Sales for the third year totaled almost $1 million. However, a net loss of $63,000 was realized. Mr. Jensen stated:

> It was mass confusion and things just got away from us. We had too many things to do and too many people involved. When we lived through the third year without going under, we expected things to go very well from then on, but we had unexpected problems with some of our people quitting. We also lost a lot of money on a big government order, partly because we didn't have good enough control of our operations. During the fourth year of operations we lost $80,000 on the big job and over-all $127,000. But I felt that we were learning through our mistakes and that we still had great potential in this part of the business. We had pretty well perfected our manufacturing operations in Trenton, had added some new equipment and had our organizational problems pretty well worked out.

> I was concerned about the increasing pressure I was subjected to from National Lumber, however. Naturally, I didn't expect top management to be overjoyed by our performance. When we started, both they and I knew that we would have some difficult times, but neither of us expected our financial picture to be quite so bleak. Although we were doing some very good work and were by far the most outstanding outfit in this part of the business, we did not seem to be able to make any money.

Pressures from above increased greatly during the fifth year. At one time or another Mr. Jensen was called on by literally every member of the top management of National Lumber, including the chairman of the board of directors. According to Mr. Jensen, these visits were relatively pleasant, but unproductive and prevented him from attending to what he considered at that time to be the most important part of his job — getting sufficient sales so that the large plant could be operated on a profitable basis. Mr. Jensen stated:

> We were like Grand Central Station! I couldn't get anything done, and the constant stream of top-level visitors was upsetting to our plant and office people. They knew that we hadn't yet proved ourselves financially, and all the top brass made them nervous.

> Some of our visitors were quite candid. One man told me he had no faith in the basic ideas of our organization and that he stopped by just "to see the rathole we're pouring all our money down." And when I found out many of our visitors were charging the expenses of their visits to our operations and we were getting billed for them through interdivisional charges, I really got pretty angry.

> But the main thing was that we got little realistic advice or help from these people. Several suggested we "do better," but didn't tell us how we might.

There were several things that I felt they could have done — but I got nowhere. Everyone had a gloomy attitude except me. I knew what our capabilities were and had great hopes. I didn't feel that many people understood the differences between running an old established business such as National Lumber and a new, struggling business such as the Fabricated Components Division.

During the fifth year Mr. Jensen was under considerable pressure from his immediate superior, Avery Randell, Eastern Regional Manager for the parent company. Mr. Randell sent Mr. Jensen a "confidential memo" about every other week in which he commented upon events that had occurred or decisions that Mr. Jensen had made that did not meet with his approval. Mr. Jensen regularly ignored these memos. He kept them locked in his desk — to which only he had a key — as he did not want their contents known to his subordinates for fear of the effect upon their morale. Mr. Randell also frequently asked Mr. Jensen to have lunch in New York, where Mr. Randell's office was located, so that he could keep in closer touch with the activities at Fabricated Components Division. Often Mr. Jensen would decline these invitations, but he did have lunch with Mr. Randell in New York City about every two weeks. In an effort to satisfy Randell's demands for information, Mr. Jensen started to send him a weekly report on the activities of Fabricated Components Division. The information that went into this report was carefully screened by Mr. Jensen so that nothing that would upset Randell or increase his demands on Jensen's time was included. According to Jensen, "The sole purpose of these reports was to keep him off my back."

Mr. Jensen made the following comments about his relationship with Mr. Randell:

Avery's O.K., but he's quite nervous about our operations. His division almost runs itself. His people are experienced and well trained, and he really doesn't have too much to do. He plays golf a lot and cruises on his boat for long weekends, while I'm at the plant seven days a week and most evenings. He doesn't know much about what we're trying to do and this makes him uncomfortable. We're a thorn in his side and the only "disreputable" part of his division financially. He inherited us because we're geographically close to him, but he doesn't have much sympathy for or understanding of what we're trying to do and the problems we face. I keep telling him that I'll take all the blame for our operations, but with all the attention we're getting from top management he's very much interested in taking part of many of our decisions — even though he doesn't know what is going on and is technically incompetent to assist in managing Fabricated Components Division. Personally, I like him and enjoy his company. Our meetings are very pleasant and we go to some very nice places for lunch. Avery does give us some kinds of help, too. For example, we've had some minor legal problems which he has gotten off our hands. But, in general, he is more of a hindrance than a help. He doesn't know enough about our operation to really help us, and the things he could do, he doesn't. I've wanted to hire another salesman for a long time, but I can't get Avery to approve it. It would cost us about $1,500 a month, but we need more sales and a good man would pay for himself in no time. But Avery's so upset about our losses that he won't let me hire anyone else without his approval, and he won't give it. I would guess that I spend 30% of my time either dealing with Avery or worrying about our relationship. I've told him that if I answered all of his memos, I wouldn't have time for anything else. He's been a real problem for me, and it keeps me from doing the really important things. I'd like to hire some kid to do all of that kind of thing so I would have time to run the business.

About two months before the end of the fifth year of operations, a meeting of top management of the National Lumber Company was held in New York to decide the future of Fabricated Components Division. Mr. Jensen was not asked to attend this meeting, which irritated him considerably. He was asked to submit his plans for the next year's operations, as well as several alternative plans and a capital and expense budget for the coming year. He spent a great deal of time preparing this information and submitted alternative plans ranging from considerable expansion of operations to shutting down of the plant completely and going out of business. In the letter submitting this information, he requested that he be permitted to attend the meeting. He received no reply to this request.

Two weeks after the meeting had been held Mr. Jensen had not been informed of what decision, if any, had been made. As he had had no information to the contrary, he assumed that operations for the next year would continue about as they had in the past. About three weeks after the meeting, Mr. Jensen began to hear rumors that the Fabricated Components Division would be shut down at the end of the year. These rumors came from sources both within and outside the company. On hearing these rumors, Mr. Jensen called Mr. Randell who told him that, "Things are still undecided, but don't spend any more money than you have

to." Mr. Jensen then called the chairman of the board of directors who informed him that the company had decided to shut down the Fabricated Components Division and go out of that part of the business. Shortly thereafter, Mr. Jensen received a letter from the president of National Lumber Company confirming this information. Mr. Jensen then began making plans for closing down the Fabricatred Components Division. He felt that a poor decision had been made, but that it would be useless to attempt to have the decision reversed.

During these last few weeks of operation Mr. Jensen was faced with several unique problems:

He was not sure what, if anything, to tell his employees — or what the timing should be. He was not greatly concerned about the fifty men in the plant, for they were skilled workers who could easily find other employment without suffering financial losses. He was especially concerned about the future of the production manager, the sales manager, and the office manager, all of whom had been with him since the start of Fabricated Components Division. Because none of these people had been with the National Lumber Company for very long, they would get little severence pay and though capable people, could well be faced with a period of unemployment until they found other jobs. He wanted to give these people adequate time to find new positions, yet felt that if the news was out, efficiency would drop considerably and the Fabricated Components Division would have an even greater loss than anticipated for its fifth — and last — year of operation.

Mr. Jensen also faced another kind

of problem. He still had great faith in the kind of thing that the Fabricated Components Division was doing and had often considered the advantages of operating his own company in this field. When he had learned that the Fabricated Components Division was to be shut down, he had quietly explored the possibilities of buying the business and had found that he could arrange adequate financing without too much difficulty. Much of the equipment was specialized and not readily saleable. He didn't know of anyone — other than himself — who might want to buy the Fabricated Components Division and felt that he could get everything that he needed to operate with at a reasonable price. Thus, if the Fabricated Components Division showed a great loss for the year, this might discourage any other prospective buyers, as well as increase National Lumber Company's desire to get out of an unprofitable venture for any kind of recovered investment, thus driving down the price he might have to pay.

Along these same lines, Mr. Jensen was undecided about what action, if any, should be taken regarding several large sales that were in the closing stages. It would be quite easy to defer action on these sales until after he had purchased the operations and thus start on his own with a considerable order file. If the sales were closed now, the customers would probably revert to conventional construction techniques when they learned that Fabricated Components Division was not going to be in business. Or it was possible that these orders would be farmed out to small independents by National Lumber Company before Mr. Jensen could get operating on his own.

In reflecting upon the history of the Fabricated Components Division Mr. Jensen observed that this was an excellent example of a good idea that had been defeated because of lack of support and meddling on the part of top management. "They bought the idea of the Fabricated Components Division in theory but refused, or were literally unable, to recognize the kinds of problems that would arise. When these problems did arise — and almost any new operation faces the same kinds of problems — they wouldn't leave me alone long enough to solve them. Certainly, I must take a great share of the blame for our poor record, but I sincerely believe that if we hadn't had so many visitors and so much attention from top management, we would have had a respectable, if not spectacular, financial success."

Avery Randell made the following comments regarding the Fabricated Components Division:

> Frank Jensen is a very capable man, but we never really got him to operate as part of the company. He ran the Fabricated Components Division as if it were an independent organization and never really accepted or respected our advice. This past year in particular we had the very definite feeling that Frank wanted no part of us, even though several of our top management people went considerably out of their way to help him. Frank has not yet learned how to live in a relatively large organization and, because of his inability to accommodate the organization, creates a lot of problems for himself and detracts considerably from his excellent technical skills. He probably knows more about prefabricated components than anyone in the country, but, because of his inability to adjust to the organization, he has been an unsuccessful manager for us.

WOOD LABORATORIES, INCORPORATED

CASE 2

Wood Laboratories, Inc. had been in the research and development business for more than twenty-five years. In its earliest period the company had specialized in R & D work for electrical and electronic equipment. Within the past ten years, however, it had primarily been engaged in the developing, manufacturing, and marketing of electronics equipment — and it had accomplished these objectives with a great deal of success. At one time the gross income of the laboratory had hit an all-time high of $3,300,000.

Not only was it successful in research and manufacturing; but it was also successful in an auxiliary phase — a by-product, so to speak — i.e., writing, publishing, and selling texts and manuals for technicians in the electronics field. This publishing and bookselling phase of the enterprise had developed into a $300,000 gross business annually. The increasing demand for these books was brought about by greater emphasis on service and repair of television sets, computers, sorting machines, and other electronically controlled devices. The willingness of management to enter what was at that time an untried field for the company was a source of pride to the president.

Mr. W. W. Benson, president and owner of the major portion of shares of stock of the company, proudly pointed to this $300,000 annually. In this connection he had been heard to say: "The meat and petroleum industries are noted for taking what at one time were wasteful, throwaway by-products and developing these into useful items which were marketed and which added greatly to their annual sales and to our standard of living. I saw no reason why we couldn't apply this approach to our own company. The labs have to employ draftsmen and technical writers anyway in order to prepare drawings normally used in our work and in developing sets of clear instructions. There is always a wide audience elsewhere interested in the same material — amateur electronic hobbyists, for example. Since we are doing this drafting and technical writing anyway as a normal course of our work, we can sell this material as a by-product in the form of published manuals and guides to the ever-increasing outside audience of electrical and electronic technicians."

Mr. B, as he was known to plant employees, was sixty-two years old. He had no heirs, and he had from time to time talked of retiring in favor of "new blood" at the top. He was regarded by associates in the industrial laboratory field as a man who was open-minded to new and better ideas by which to further the progress of the company. Mr. B was the "big wheel" — the board of directors did not carry much weight in the organization. However, he prided himself on his ability to delegate a good deal to his department heads — some of whom "had grown up" with the company, and with whom he had good rapport.

In speeches before professional management groups he spelled out his managerial concepts as follows:

"I believe in finding people with potential and, when I find them, delegate more and more responsibility to them. ... Give 'em their head and let them go full steam to the utmost limits of their capabilities and capacities. Sure I watch 'em and sometimes, as the situation dictates, I step in and make final decisions. Most of the time, though, my top staff is on their own and they make their own decisions. I'm always ready to accept ideas — even more, I tell 'em to go ahead and try the ideas out after they've thought them through and have presented plans of action to carry out their ideas. After all, we are a research and development outfit and I firmly believe we'll grow and prosper only through trying new ideas — not fearing failures — and applying what works. We are then able to market new or improved products, in which we can take pride, and which are meeting our society's needs."

Gene Price, chief of the Accounting Department, who had been with the firm since its inception, had for several years approached the president about once every six months with the idea that the company should expand beyond its present publishing boundaries; specifically, he suggested that the company should publish for sale a monthly magazine in the field of electronics. These discussions between Price and Mr. Benson were cordial and thorough. Mr. Benson never divulged to others the contents of these conversations with Price. The latter felt concern about his inability to sell this particular idea to Mr. B. When thinking about this situation and about his future prospects with the laboratories, he reflected:

"I know this magazine will go over ... all the research I did proves it ... libraries ... book stores ... research institutes ... all told me we'd make a killing on this item ... that dotard ... what's wrong with him in his old age ... can't see a good thing ... talks all this stuff about new ideas ... take the ball and run with it ... paying you guys for ideas and getting 'em across ... he's gonna die or retire soon ... gotta keep impressing him ... that Mack, he's in there plugging all the time ... gotta run things by himself ... this is my baby and I'm gonna put it across ... lots of changes when Benson goes ... after 25 years I'm gonna be in running for top honors ..."

Wally Mack, chief of Planning and Promotion, who had also been with the company since its establishment, learned through the grapevine of Price's visits with the "old man"; and when he thought about his own future his thoughts ran in this vein:

"That bastard Gene ... always skirtin' the end ... glad I told him off about that magazine pitch of his ... he shoulda come to me ... we're organized to push these ideas through ... his damn idea ain't so good nohow ... same old publishing pitch ... gotta diversify more ... need new ideas in new fields ... Gene is gonna hang himself on this one and I'm gonna help pull the string ... he's a lone wolf ... always butterin' up B with

his figures and cost breakdowns . . .
new accounting systems . . . he oughta
be glad with where he is in this outfit
. . . how you gonna plan and promote
with Price around? . . ."

Price had been spreading the idea of the
monthly magazine to other department
heads and to middle management — doing it informally but without interfering
with the official business at hand. Mack,
on the other hand, had been active in
cornering middle management and in
branding the magazine idea as a "screw-
ball" one the company could do without.

Mr. Benson was in the habit of
dropping in once or twice a week to the
general cafeteria to lunch informally
with the rank-and-file employees. On one
such occasion he chanced to overhear
the following conversation which came
from behind a column:

"Sorry I'm late, that Gene Price
interrupted my dictation . . . he was
bending my boss' ear trying to get him
to support the idea about our getting
into the magazine publishing field. . . ."

"That Mr. Price is really pushing
his idea, Gladys. He was down talking
to my boss yesterday about the same
thing . . . said something about the need
of employee-stockholders getting behind
this idea . . . that it meant additional income and prosperity for the company.
Boy, he was going at it hammer and
tongs, showing my boss figures and
whatnot. . . ."

"Come on, let's eat. I gotta get back
on time. Mr. Mack is keeping everyone
on the straight and narrow . . . seems to
be so upset lately . . . been a bear
around the office . . . keeps muttering
about going to see Mr. B and asking
him who in hell is running Planning and
Promotion Department."

"I own a few shares of stock in this
company . . . I'm gonna speak with Mr.
Price . . . find out more about what his
idea means to the benefit of this company."

"This is what I like about lunch
time . . . you find out so many things
about what's going on around here.

"SHHHH! There's Mr. B now!"

Benson postponed conferences with
Price and Mack, feeling that things
would smooth over. One day, however, a
copy of the company's monthly newspaper appeared on his desk with the
headline colmn: "MORE EMPLOYMENT
AND MORE OPORTUNITY FOR
ADVANCEMENT IF WE ENTER THE
MAGAZINE PUBLISHING BUSINESS."
The article coincided very much with
the idea Price had advanced several
times. Mary Simmons, the editor of the
newspaper, worked in the Administrative and Services Department. She was
generally considered to be a person of
good judgment: thus, her news copy had
neither been reviewed nor censored because of her fine record and the popularity which the monthly newspaper enjoyed under her editorship. The material
under the above heading was completely
presented in terms of "suggestions."

Mr. Benson read it and immediately
called Mary Simmons into his office.

"Now, Mary, I called you in to talk
with you about the article you wrote on
the magazine publishing business.
Frankly, Mary, I'm disappointed. I
didn't think you'd get into an issue involving top-level policy decision. I . . ."

"Mr. B, I . . ."

"Please call me Mr. Benson!"

"Mr. BENSON, I've been running
our newspaper for some time now with
some success. Neither you nor anyone

else in top management has ever questioned anything appearing in the paper before this. If you want my work edited, I ought to know about it beforehand."

"I merely want to know why you latched on to Mr. Price's idea."

"Mr. Price's idea! As far as I'm concerned the suggestion I made in the newspaper about our getting into the magazine publishing business is one I've been toying with for some time. I've never talked with Mr. Price or anyone else, for that matter, about it . . . Seemed to me to be in line with your policy about the need for greater diversification for continued growth of our organization."

"Mary, you mean to tell me that you haven't talked with Price or at least that you haven't heard that he's been pushing — pushing very hard I might add — the same idea that you headlined? It seems very un —."

"I don't care what it seems, Mr. Benson! Mr. Price did not pressure me into publishing this article. It's as I said: the whole thing seemed to come about spontaneously."

"Well, Mary, the fact remains that Mr. Price had this original idea some time ago and that he has been researching it for about a year. The headline in the newspaper, at this time, is extremely coincidental. I'll let you know more about this. Good afternoon, Mary."

"Good afternoon, Mr. Benson, I'd appreciate knowing about any change in policy or procedures concerning the publication of the paper."

The next day Mary received a one-month termination notice. The letter stated that the company had come to regard the monthly newspaper as a kind of luxury, that costs must be watched closely in the industrial laboratories field because of the increased competition, and that there would no longer be any need for a newspaper or an editor.

POINTE S.A.-HOLLAND

CASE 3

"If I am going to stay with the company there are four conditions that they will have to meet," said Alain Dubois, early in 1970. "First, I will insist that I'll be appointed a member of the new executive committee. Second, the president will have to agree to leave the sales force alone, he cannot continue to work with them as he has in the past. Third, we will have to discharge some people regardless of who their friends are in the company. We simply cannot afford to have anything but the most competent people with us now. And finally, I must have the authority to hire the kind of people that I need, both in terms of quality and numbers."

Alain Dubois, 33 years old, was the marketing director of the Pointe-Holland Company, a wholly-owned subsidiary in Holland of a large parent company with headquarters in France. The Pointe-Holland company manufactured and distributed a line of household and food products throughout Europe and was widely known and recognized because of its extensive advertising campaigns. While company headquarters were in France the parent company had wholly-owned subsidiaries in other European countries, each of which was organized as a separate company with separate presidents and administrative staff.

Each president was responsible for the operation of his organization and each subsidiary was run as a separate profit center. While there were some centralized direction from Pointe headquarters in France each subsidiary had wide latitude in determining the nature and extent of its activity, especially insofar as promotion and advertising of individual products or product lines were concerned. It was important for each subsidiary to have this freedom and flexibility to accommodate national characteristics and demands.

Alain Dubois had been director of marketing of Pointe-Holland for two years. He was responsible for all sales promotion, product development, advertising and sales management activities. He reported directly to the president of Pointe-Holland and had reporting to him all people in the organization involved with marketing activities.

Prior to joining Pointe-Holland, Alain Dubois had been an executive with an advertising agency in France, primarily responsible for preparation of advertising campaigns for organizations active in marketing consumer products. He was widely recognized in Holland for his knowledge of marketing and was considered to be one of the "bright young men" in the field.

Just prior to joining Pointe-Holland he had attended two executive management programs in the U.S. and, as a result of these programs and his own study and experience, was a leader in Europe in utilizing some of the newer concepts of marketing and management. In fact, his expertise in applying new concepts was one of the primary reasons why he was highly sought after by the Pointe headquarters in France for his current job.

In describing the background of this current situation Alain Dubois stated, "I was really put into Pointe-Holland by headquarters in France to see if something could not be done with our operations here. Up until the time I came we had been losing a great deal of money each year. We are still losing money, but the amount of loss has decreased substantially and according to my plan we should break even next year and each year after that make a small profit. My relationship with the president of Pointe-Holland is unique. He is a very fine individual and he and I get along very well on a social level. However, he is not up-to-date in his methods of management or in his knowledge and understanding of current marketing technique. In fact, while I report to him I really make most major decisions in the Branded-Good Division for the company in Holland, and most of what happens is done at my initiative. The president is still a figure-head but I really go ahead and do what is necessary without much regard for his opinions or feelings. I have been able to do that because I have had the support of the main office in France. I continue to have this support but some things have happened recently which make me concerned about being able to continue to make the progress that we have made here in Holland for the last two years."

One of the things that was of concern to Alain Dubois was the formation of the new executive committee. An executive committee had been formed recently to make and review major policy decisions. The two members of this committee were the president of Pointe-Holland and the vice-president for administration. Alain Dubois was not a member of this committee and thought that he should be. When asked what changes in his status would result if he were appointed a member, he replied that in effect he would be independent of the president's authority. As a member of the executive committee he would be on equal status with the president and consequently would not be subject to his control in any way.

A second issue that had been troubling Alain Dubois recently had been the president's actions with regard to some of the sales managers. The president of Pointe-Holland had had a long career as a salesman and still has very close personal relationships with many of the sales managers who had been with the company for some time. Often, perhaps every two months, the president and a few of his friends who were sales managers would meet to discuss the sales situation. Alain Dubois did not attend these meetings. According to Alain Dubois the meetings were primarily gossip sessions at which much information was exchanged, but information that had little basis in fact: For example, he described these meetings as one in which the sales managers would

report rumors from the trade, would predict how they thought people were going to react based on information
acquired during their sales activities,
etc. Usually the meetings were held at
rather elaborate restaurants and hotels.
As the sales force reported directly to
Alain Dubois he thought that these
meetings were not helpful to the overall
selling effort and that they should be
discontinued. He stated that he objected
to the meetings on two counts; first,
that they diluted his authority over the
sales managers and, secondly, that the
kind of information discussed and the
results of the meetings were not at all
useful to the selling effort.

Alain Dubois reported that the president had a very traditional concept of
authority and would occasionally walk
through the offices talking to the more
junior marketing people (e.g. Product
Managers), much in the way that a general might review an army. But Alain
Dubois felt that the president had no
real understanding of what marketing
people were now required to do. The
efforts of the salesmen of Pointe-
Holland could affect perhaps 40% of the
potential market. Many of the products
were sold directly to large chains of
retail outlets and the selling was done at
the headquarter's level rather than in
the traditional fashion of a salesman
calling on an individual customer.

Alain Dubois was especially concerned, too, about one sales manager in
particular, the general sales manager,
who he felt was not competent to handle
his job. This manager was a long-
standing friend of the president and this
made the matter more difficult for Alain
Dubois. He stated that: "I have no personal reasons for wanting to discharge

this man. My reasons are entirely professional. He is just not competent to
operate in the way that we have to operate now. For example, I am attempting
to promote the product manager concept
in which we have a great deal of flexibility in our approach for each product
depending on the situation. Unfortunately, the manager in question is very
traditional in his approach and cannot
adapt to this new thinking. He knows
my feelings about this but the support
from the president on a friendship basis
undercuts my efforts to initiate some
new concepts and ideas. If we were a
very large organization it might be possible to by-pass this man, but we do not
have enough personnel to let us do this.
Each of our people have to be a good
producer and, in my judgment, this particular sales manager just is not adequate. Many of the people who report to
him are more qualified than he and this,
of course, causes a problem of morale."

Another matter concerning Alain
Dubois was that he did not have as
complete freedom as he would like in
hiring new people. For example, he
thought that several additions to the
marketing staff were very necessary,
but he had not been able to secure the
authority to hire additional personnel
without discussing his reasons in great
detail with the president of Pointe-
Holland.

In summing up the current situation
Alain Dubois stated: "My relationship
with the president of Pointe-Holland has
been fine as long as I have been able to
ignore him. But with these new developments, especially the formation of the
executive committee, I am going to
have to get my status clarified.

"I am going to see the people of

France again very soon, but rather than discuss this matter only with the top management of the parent corporation I think that all of us should discuss it at the same time. So I plan to ask the president in France to arrange a meeting between him, the president, Holland, and myself for later this month. I will prepare a written statement of my position and give it to each man before the meeting so that each of them will know exactly how I feel. I hope that this can be resolved for I'd like to continue the work that I have started. But I feel very strongly that I must have the freedom and the authority to do what I think is right.

"Of course, I realize that there are different ways of satisfying the conditions I have established for my own involvement, but I feel very strongly that I must have complete freedom in each of the areas I mentioned. For example, if they would agree to appoint me a member of the executive committee but not give me freedom to hire the people I need, this would not be satisfactory. Or if they would give me the authority to hire but not appoint me to the executive committee that would not be satisfactory. In effect, I have to have all four of the conditions satisfied before I feel I can continue to make a contribution at Pointe-Holland."

EXERCISE 1

ADMINISTRATIVE
DECISION MAKING

INTRODUCTION

Managers are often involved in making decisions that directly affect
the people working for them. These are often difficult decisions, for
the manager may be faced with making a trade-off between the quality
of the decision from the point of view of the total organization and the
quality of the decision from the point of view of the individuals
involved.

In this exercise you will have the opportunity to engage in the process of making such a decision.

PROCEDURE

In addition to the following instructions, your instructor may have
some special directions for you.

1. Read the following information concerning Erik Toy, Sissel, and
   Tom.
2. Working individually, develop a list of criteria that you will use in
   making the decision to promote Tom or Sissel. You should consider *organizational criteria, personal criteria* from the point of view
   of Tom and/or Sissel, and *personal criteria* from *your viewpoint* as
   Eric Toy.
3. In groups of four or five people, develop one set of criteria per
   group.
4. Rank these criteria in order of importance.
5. Using these criteria, determine who you will promote. *Do not reveal
   this decision* until requested to do so by your instructor.
6. In the total group, discuss the criteria and priorities that were developed in each of the smaller groups. See if you can determine
   from the criteria developed by each group which person that group
   promoted.
7. Think about how the promotion decision might be communicated
   to the person not promoted.

This exercise is an adaptation of the exercise, "Administrative Decision Making," that
appears in *Management: An Experiential Approach* by H. R. Knudson, Robert T. Woodworth, and Cecil Bell. The original exercise was developed and copyrighted by Professor
Robert T. Woodworth. Adapted and reprinted in part by permission.

8. Select one person to play each of the roles of Erik Toy, Tom, and/or Sissel.

   Role play the situation in which Erik Toy informs either Tom or Sissel that he/she has not been selected for promotion.

9. Discuss the role play.

You are Erik Toy, the manager of a highly regarded budget division of one plant in a multiplant organization. The work of your office involves all aspects of the budgeting process for your plant, including the budget preparation, its dissemination, the development of control procedures, the monitoring of budget performance, and recommendations for changes in the budgeting process.

These activities involve the processing of a large amount of data and the preparation of detailed reports which are then sent to different divisions within the plant and to the headquarters office. While some of the work is routine, much of it requires technical expertise and some of it requires high personal skills to handle conflict situations with other organizational units over budget allocations and the control of expenditures.

You have just returned from a meeting at the home office of the various heads of the budgeting departments in the company. At that meeting you were given the assignment by your boss to choose one person to fill a vacancy caused by the death of the head of the budget office in a smaller plant. The vice president in charge of budgeting for the corporation has asked that you recommend a person from your office because of some of the excellent results that your division has produced, both in developing new budget techniques and in getting them successfully implemented within the plant.

While your initial reaction was one of pleasure (because the assignment to pick a person for the vacancy reflected credit on your organization), you are now having some second thoughts about what this responsibility might entail — you must think not only of the person being promoted but also of the effect which his leaving may have on your organization. As you consider the people in your organization, the possible candidates can be very quickly reduced to two — Sissel and Tom — each of whom heads up one of the two main sections in your department.

Sissel is a twenty-nine-year-old college graduate with a master's degree in accounting who has been with the organization for 4 years. While she is fairly young for the responsibility required in her present assignment, she has done an outstanding job. One of her characteristics is her ability to get people to work with her and for her. She does an excellent job of planning the work and delegating it. She has also been one of the people who has been instrumental in getting often recalcitrant department heads in other parts of the organization to go along with new and different budgeting ideas. The fact that she is attractive has opened doors for her, and her ability to work with other people in the organization has meant that the number of enemies that a budget department normally accumulates has been reduced significantly.

While Sissel is single, she has mentioned several times that she is very career-minded and plans to keep on working whether or not she marries.

As you further mull over the situation, you also remember the recent meeting in which the word was passed to all executives in the organization to pay special attention to assure that women got an equal opportunity as far as promotion opportunities were concerned.

On the other hand, Tom has also done an outstanding job. He has worked for the department for 15 years and is now forty-five years of age. He has an undergraduate degree in mathematics and philosophy. His progress in the organization has been slow and steady, but for the last 6 years he has been a very effective head of the other section in the department. As you look back on the work that he has done, you see that almost all the creative innovations in the budgeting processes in your plant have come as a result of his suggestions. He is not only creative, but technically is extremely sound. He has been able to devise a number of very effective yet simple procedures to carry out his plans.

You feel that there is probably no one who works harder in the organization than he does. He is often at work an hour before everybody else, leaves an hour or so after everybody else, and it is not surprising to find out on a Monday morning that he has been in on the weekends.

When he is in the office, he is all business and expects the people working for him to be the same. As a result he seems somewhat abrupt in his contact with employees working for him and with other people in the organization. He is married, has two children, and has talked with you before indicating that if an opportunity for promotion came up he would certainly like to have a shot at it. The workers in his section tend to respond to his "lead-horse" style of management by working hard themselves. Sometimes there are some conflicts due to missed communication signals, but overall the output of his group has been of extremely high quality.

All in all, as you start looking at the information that you have, the decision does not seem to be an easy one. Some of the organizational criteria that you feel are important are the following:

1. Effects on the people involved directly with the decision — Sissel and Tom.
2. Effects on the immediate work groups concerned with these people. What would be the effect of the promotion of either of these two people within the budgeting department? Would the department think a good decision had been made? Would they continue to function effectively? Also, what about the new budget group into which the person selected would go? How would either of these people fit into that organization at the smaller plant?
3. What would be the overall effects on the organization?
4. What would be the effects on *you* as a manager if you lost the services of either of these individuals? Should you recommend someone less qualified in order to preserve these people for your own operation?
5. The new job would require both technical and personal skills. Which ones would be especially important? As you consider Sissel and Tom, which one of them would best fit these criteria? What are the reasons that your division has been tapped to recommend somebody for this promotion? Was it the fact that new budgeting procedures had been developed and actually implemented within the plant? As you think back on this, Tom had been more involved in creating new ideas, and Sissel had been more involved in the process of getting them implemented.

Beyond just the development and listing of these criteria, you know you have the tougher job of prioritizing these characteristics in trying to determine which were the most important as far as the organization is concerned and which are most important to you personally.

Also there is the nagging recognition that whatever decision you make you would have to tell the person not promoted that he or she had not been promoted. It would be nice if the organization had enough flexibility so that you could give the one not promoted a raise or some other sort of reward. However, you know that the circumstances under which the organization is operating would not permit this kind of action.

You are aware of the following information regarding the small plant to which the person you select would go to head up its budget department. Located about 50 miles away, it has about forty people in the department — about half as many employees as are in your department. The department has had problems in the past getting new budgeting ideas developed and implemented, and as a result the plant it serves is one of the plants with a somewhat obsolete budgeting system. The plant manager has given assurances to you that he is very interested in getting someone to modernize his budget system and that he would give that person his full support. However, you know from many talks with the former budgeting manager of that plant that there are many line managers there who see no reason to change the present budgeting procedures and who would resist any changes.

You are now in the process of trying to systematically look at the forces involved and the criteria which you will use to make your decision.

As you think about these, you cannot help but consider the question, "How will it affect me personally if the person I choose is a success?" What will happen to *my* reputation if the person I choose fails? How will *my* performance be affected when I lose one of my two top people? Which one can I afford to more easily lose? In general, I have less technical skill than Tom does and probably on balance I'm not as good a leader as Sissel has shown herself to be. I have counted on these strengths in the past and used them to build what I think is an exceptionally fine and smooth running department. At the moment I see no one else in my department who could easily replace either one of them. However, I do remember a comment from Sissel saying that one or two of her people were showing great promise and developing quickly.

EXERCISE 2

ROBERTS' APPAREL SHOP

INTRODUCTION

The Roberts' Apparel Shop exercise provides the opportunity to look at both a variety of relationships that exist within an organization and a decision-making situation. As is often the case, some outside influence — in this case, complaints of the customers — brings the situation to the attention of the manager.

PROCEDURE

Your instructor will give you specific instructions for this exercise. Do not proceed further until you have received these instructions.

Roberts' Apparel Shop is a woman's shop located in an exclusive shopping district in San Francisco. Roberts carries the most fashionable line of clothes and accessories and caters to the discriminating woman who can afford to keep up with the latest styles.

According to Sally Copeland, manager, the success of Roberts is based upon its ability to forecast fashion trends, the skill of its buyers in purchasing the most attractive models and styles each year in the currently popular fabrics, and, most important, upon the high quality of service given to Roberts' customers by sales personnel. All the sales personnel are discreet, fashion-conscious women, most of whom have had a great deal of experience in selling high-quality women's clothing. In addition, Roberts is very liberal with regard to letting customers take merchandise "on approval," encourages shopping by telephone, and, in general, caters to the desires of its clientele.

An informal practice has developed among the sales personnel at Roberts under which each saleswoman develops and retains "her" special customers. Under the system, saleswomen attempt to wait on the same customers each time they come into the shop. The customers seem to appreciate this personalized attention, and the sales personnel favor this practice, for each is paid a commission on all the sales she makes. By developing friendships with regular customers, the saleswoman is in a position to know and understand their tastes and desires and consequently can suggest items and show merchandise which she thinks might be of interest. Often these suggestions result in additional sales and commissions. In most instances customers are not aware that they "belong" to a particular saleswoman and consider it coincidental that they are often served by the same person — if they consider it at all.

Recently, however, this practice has not been working too well — especially in the Sportswear Department. Customers have complained to Copeland that they couldn't get service even when some of the sales personnel in the department were obviously not busy. When they did get the attention of a clerk they were told that "Miss ——— [the customer's "regular" salesperson] will be with you in a moment." As the "moments" were often considerably longer, several customers preferred not to wait and left the shop. Some had complained to Copeland.

Copeland assumed that the number of complaints that she had received represented only a small part of the dissatisfied customers and made special efforts to alleviate the situation. For example, she attempted to spend more time than usual in the Sportswear Department. If it appeared that a customer was not getting prompt, courteous service, she would start to wait on the customer herself, but as soon as possible transfer the transaction to any of the four saleswomen who might be available — regardless of who felt she had "rights" to the customer. The saleswoman who actually completed such a sale received the commission for it.

In addition, Copeland had a talk with each of the women pointing out the need to provide all customers with fast, efficient service.

Neither of these actions had proven successful, however, and Copeland has called a meeting of the sales personnel of the Sportswear Department to discuss the situation. It is now one-half hour before regular opening time, and the four saleswomen are in the Sportswear Department awaiting Copeland's arrival.

Role for Sally Copeland, Manager

You have called a meeting of the four women who work in the Sportswear Department to see if the problem of customer service cannot be resolved. Although you have tried to ease the situation and have talked with each of the women individually, you are still getting complaints from customers. Because your customers are a select group and can easily transfer their loyalties to other shops in the immediate area, you do not wish to alienate them. In addition, Roberts has a reputation for providing the best of service.

You are aware of the practice that has become established of each saleswoman attempting to build her own clientele and, within reason, do not disapprove of it. The additional sales which result benefit the store. But the practice has some undesirable aspects, too, aside from the one which is currently plaguing you: a customer may not get prompt attention because "her" saleswoman is busy. Occasionally disagreements arise when the women cannot decide among themselves who has claim to a particular customer. Sometimes a "new" customer will be greeted by two or three saleswomen, each competing for the customer's favor and sometimes the women — especially Ann Leighton, who has been in the Sportswear Department the longest — take on presumptuous airs because they have a steady group of customers.

You don't really care how the problem is resolved, but you are greatly concerned about the complaints you have been receiving regarding the Sportswear Department and want to take some action to remedy the situation there as well as to prevent it from spreading to other departments in the store.

One solution, of course, would be to unilaterally dispense with the established, although not formally sanctioned, practice and insist that no saleswoman has the "right" to any customer. An even more drastic action would be to dispense with the commission system entirely, although you realize that this would have significant ramifications. You have asked the women to meet with you before the store opens this morning and you are now on your way to the Sportswear Department where the four women — Ann Leighton, Margaret Swanson, Charlene Olson, and Betty Bryant — should be waiting.

Ann Leighton has been in the department for six years and customarily has more sales than the others. Margaret Swanson has been in Sportswear for over three years and seems to be a good worker. She and Ann Leighton are close friends. Charlene Olson has been in Sportswear for two years and with Roberts for six years. Prior to working in Sportswear, she was in Millinery, where she had a good record. Since coming to the Sportswear Department, however, you have been disappointed in her sales and have spoken to her about it from time to time. Betty Bryant has been working only six months, is usually bright and cheerful, and seems to be doing O.K.

Role for Ann Leighton

You have been working in the Sportswear Department for six years and are pleased with the current system of waiting on customers. You have developed a large group of your own customers and, as a result, have done very well on commissions. You make it a point to suggest tactfully to each customer that you'll be glad to help her the next time she comes in. Your sales are always greater than those of the other clerks.

Sometimes, if you have been particularly busy, you don't rush to wait on a new customer, as you are pretty well satisfied with your current level of sales.

If you have two or three of "your" customers in the department at the same time, you attempt to serve them all. If it becomes too busy, however, you have worked out a system with Margaret Swanson, your best friend, whereby she will take over one of your customers if she is not busy and credit the sale to you. You do the same for her as the need arises. Margaret's group of customers is not as large as your own and occasionally you will permanently "give" her one of your customers.

You like Betty Bryant, who has been working in Sportswear for only six months, but you are not particularly fond of Charlene Olson. After two years in the department she still keeps talking about "the way they did things in Millinery." You had an argument with her soon after she transferred to Sportswear about "rights" to a customer — she had been waiting on the customer in Millinery and you had been waiting on her in Sportswear — and you still feel some bitterness over this, even though you won the customer.

When Sally Copeland talked with you about the customers' complaints, you assured her that it was only a temporary thing that would soon blow over. You hope it has, for you like the present system very much. You'd hate to have to compete for a customer every time she shopped in the Sportswear Department.

Sally Copeland has asked all the sales personnel to meet with her this morning before the store opens, and you are now in the Sportswear Department with the rest of the women awaiting her arrival.

Role for Margaret Swanson

You have been working in the Sportswear Department for a little over three years and like your job very much. While you've never been able to better the sales record of Ann Leighton, your closest friend on the job, you've done all right and are certainly doing much better than when you worked in a department store on straight salary. And as time goes on, you've been building up a nice list of customers of your own so you expect that things will get even better. Occasionally Ann will even "give" you one of her customers.

You're not quite certain why all the fuss about customer complaints has arisen. Sally Copeland has mentioned it to you, but you don't see anything to get excited about. The only time you've seen customers waiting, you've been busy putting stock back in order or doing something else that was necessary. You feel that, by and large, everyone does the best she can.

If you get too busy with your own special customers, you and Ann have a system where she will help you out and credit the sale to you. You do the same for her if the occasion arises.

If the other two people in the department, Charlene Olson and Betty Bryant, could work out such a system, things would probably be O.K. Of course, Betty has been here only six months and is still learning, but Charlene is experienced and should be able to figure out a little system like that.

Sally Copeland has asked all of you to meet with her this morning before the store opens, and you are now in the Sportswear Department with the rest of the women awaiting her arrival.

Role for Charlene Olson

You've been in the Sportswear Department for two years and with Roberts for six. Prior to working in Sportswear, you had spent four years in the Millinery Department. Things were certainly better over there, where you didn't have so much of this fighting for customers on the one hand and neglecting them on the other. The women in Millinery had their "own" customers, too, but they weren't so fanatic about it. The customer was "yours" only if she specifically asked for you each time she came in. And a customer would never be left waiting in Millinery under any circumstances.

When you first came to Sportswear, you tried to use this system but it hadn't gone over. Ann Leighton, in particular, was opposed to it, and you and she had gotten into a nasty argument or two about which customers belonged to whom. You don't like to work in this kind of atmosphere so you haven't pressed the issue, although you are sure that your sales record would be better if everyone had an equal chance at all customers. Sure, if a customer specifically asked for you it was okay and you've tried to build your own clientele on this basis; but the idea that a customer always "belongs" to a special salesperson — whether the customer knows it or not — is silly.

For a while you had thought about quitting your job, but about six months ago Betty Bryant came to work in the Sportswear Department and you and she have been getting along quite well. At least you now have someone besides Ann and Margaret Swanson to talk with.

When Sally Copeland spoke with you about the customers' complaints, you had agreed that it was a serious problem. You didn't tell her this, but you feel that the root of the problem lies with Ann and Margaret. They even have a system of exchanging customers if one of them gets too busy to handle her "regular" group.

Sally Copeland has asked all of you to meet with her this morning before the store opens, and you are now in the Sportswear Department with the rest of the women awaiting her arrival.

Role for Betty Bryant

You have been working in the Sportswear Department at Roberts for only six months. You like your job very much and particularly Charlene Olson, one of the other saleswomen who has been very nice to you. You have noticed that she isn't too friendly with Ann Leighton and Margaret Swanson, the other people in the department, however. Nor do they seem to be especially friendly toward her.

You are aware that Margaret and Ann have a group of what they call "their customers," and you have learned not to wait on these customers when either Margaret or Ann is around. One day you waited on a customer that "belonged" to Ann. She told you later that the woman had been "her" customer and that you should develop your own customers and let hers alone.

As you were very new at the time, you did not make an issue of it, but her attitude did bother you. Roberts was known throughout the city for customer service and you wanted to do your share in upholding this reputation.

Sally Copeland has spoken to you recently about complaints she has received concerning slow service to customers. You agreed that this is a bad situation and have tried to do whatever you could to speed up service. You want everything to go as smoothly as possible, and hope that Copeland is not displeased with you.

Copeland has asked all of you to meet with her this morning before the store opens, and you are now in the Sportswear Department with the rest of the women awaiting her arrival.

PART 7

THE MANAGEMENT OF CONFLICT

The term *conflict* has acquired varied meanings as a result of its uses in many different disciplines. It may be used to refer to disputes varying from a bloody skirmish in a war to the personal choice of a television program. This chapter is concerned with organizational conflict, and uses the term in reference to all types of opposition or antagonistic interaction. Conflict in the organization can usually be viewed as either antagonistic interaction or antagonistic psychological relations. The interactions are overt and vary from subtle forms of interference to direct struggle, while the psychological relations are seen in incongruent goals, differing value systems, and personality clashes.

Conflict appears to be an inherent property of the human condition. Our personal experience with conflict is helpful in understanding the pervasiveness of conflict and the importance of successfully managing it. Just as an individual's career may be influenced greatly by his or her ability to manage conflict, the success of an organization is influenced by its conflict management capabilities.

Until recently, conflict in the organization was always viewed as being negative or harmful. Throughout our society conflict is treated as something to be repressed and eliminated quickly when it does develop. As parents we attempt to maintain harmony (or at least quiet) in the home and discourage most forms of conflict. All of the major institutions in our society view conflict negatively. Thus it is no surprise that the first reaction of many managers is to find means of preventing and resolving organizational conflict.

However, conflict is not always dysfunctional. A certain degree of conflict can increase production and performance. Conflict can also lead to innovation and greater understanding. It can reduce boredom and even be considered a necessary evil in pursuit of personal goals. Conflict can also be a very positive force in the organization as a stimulus for change. If an organization is inflexible in the face of a changing environment, its very survival is threatened. And it should be remembered that our economic system is based upon the controlled conflict that we call competition.

There are many sources of conflict, but within the organization there appear to be at least three major sources: (1) *Bureaucratic conflict.* This type of conflict arises from a desire for autonomy on the part of individuals or subunits. Taken beyond some moderate point, this desire for autonomy directly conflicts with the organization's need for coordination of activities. (2) *System conflict.* This type of conflict arises from a divergence of subunit goals. Departments in a single firm often have goals that conflict at least to some degree. A common example involves sales and credit departments. Restrictive credit policies interfere with sales departments' goals of increased sales. While sales are of obvious importance, so is the goal of keeping bad debts at a respectable level. In this type of conflict both units will of course insist that they were acting in the best interest of the organization. (3) *Bargaining conflicts.* This very common type of conflict is caused by competition for scarce resources. Organizations have limited resources, e.g., budget dollars and staff services, that must be allocated to individuals and groups within the organization.

In the first reading, "Management of Differences," Schmidt and Tannenbaum take a diagnostic view of conflict management. The authors recommend that the management of differences be approached by the problem-solving method and point out that conflict rarely occurs spontaneously. That is, most conflict takes time to develop, and the effective manager must learn the steps in the conflict episode and their visible symptoms. Of particular importance is the inventory of approaches for dealing with disputes. There are actually a number of possibilities for dealing with conflict, each of which has some advantages and disadvantages. As you read about the various techniques, generate examples in your own mind of situations in which each approach would tend to be effective or ineffective.

Edgar Schein's article, "Intergroup Problems in Organizations," has become a classic in the literature of conflict. Schein describes conflict at the level of the group rather than that of the individual and illustrates what happens both within each competing group and between the competing groups. As you read the descriptions, ask yourself what benefits and drawbacks for the manager exist in such behavior. In other words, what opportunities do those behaviors present for increased organizational effectiveness?

There is also a description of what happens to the winning group and its members and what happens to the losing group and its members. The reading concludes with some methods for reducing or preventing intergroup conflict.

The manager must know what causes conflict, what its symptoms are, and how to deal with it. It must be emphasized that dealing with conflict can include directing it in a way that will help accomplish organizational goals. It should not be assumed that conflict is always undesirable.

MANAGEMENT OF DIFFERENCES

Warren H. Schmidt
and Robert Tannenbaum

— *How to diagnose an issue and its causes.*
— *How to decide on the best course of action.*

The manager often experiences his most uncomfortable moments when he has to deal with differences among people. Because of these differences, he must often face disagreements, arguments, and even open conflict. To add to his discomfort, he frequently finds himself torn by two opposing desires. On the one hand, he wants to unleash the individuality of his subordinates in order to tap their full potential and to achieve novel and creative approaches to problems. On the other hand, he is eager to develop a harmonious, smooth-working team to carry out his organization's objectives. The manager's lot is further troubled by the fact that when differences do occur, strong feelings are frequently aroused, objectivity flies out the window, egos are threatened, and personal relationships are placed in jeopardy.

TOWARD EFFECTIVE MANAGEMENT

Because the presence of differences can complicate the manager's job in so many ways, it is of utmost importance that he understand them fully and that he learn to handle them effectively. It is the purpose of this article to assist the manager to manage more effectively by increasing his understanding of differences among the people he works with, and by improving his ability to deal with others.

A large part of what follows will focus, for simplicity of exposition, on the differences which occur among a manager's individual subordinates. However, we would like to suggest that the principles, concepts, methods, and dynamics which we discuss throughout much of the article apply to intergroup, to interorganizational, and to international differences as well.

Our basic thesis is that a manager's ability to deal effectively with differences depends on:

- His ability to diagnose and to understand differences.
- His awareness of, and ability to select appropriately from, a variety of behaviors.[1]

From *Harvard Business Review*, 38 (6): 107–115 (November-December 1960). Copyright 1960 by the President and Fellows of Harvard College; all rights reserved. Reprinted by permission.
[1] For insightful treatments of the causes and consequences of conflict, and the alternative means of dealing with it — as well as with other expressions of difference — see Lewis A. Coser, *The Function of Social Conflict* (London, Routledge and Kegan Paul, Ltd., 1956); and Raymond W. Mack and Richard C. Snyder, "The Analysis of Social Conflict — Toward an Overview and Synthesis," *Conflict Resolution*, June 1957, pp. 212–248.

His awareness of, and ability to deal with, his own feelings — particularly those which might reduce his social sensitivity (diagnostic insight) and his action flexibility (ability to act appropriately).[2]

There are two basic assumptions underlying our approach to this problem. Let us examine them before going any further:

1. *Differences among people should not be regarded as inherently "good" or "bad."* Sometimes differences result in important benefits to the organization; and sometimes they are disruptive, reducing the over-all effectiveness of individuals and organizations.

2. *There is no one "right" way to deal with differences.* Under varying circumstances, it may be most beneficial to avoid differences, to repress them, to sharpen them into clearly defined conflict, or to utilize them for enriched problem solving. The manager who consistently "pours oil on troubled waters" may not be the most effective manager. Nor is the manager necessarily successful who emphasizes individuality and differences so strongly that cooperation and teamwork are simply afterthoughts. We feel, rather, that the effective manager is one who is able to use a *variety* of approaches to differences and who chooses any specific approach on the basis of an insightful diagnosis and understanding of the factors with which he is faced at that time.

DIAGNOSING DISAGREEMENTS

When a manager's subordinates become involved in a heated disagreement, they do not tend to proceed in a systematic manner to resolve their difference. The issues often remain unclear to them, and they may talk *at* rather than *to* one another. If a manager is to be helpful in such a situation, he should ask three important diagnostic questions:

1. What is the nature of the difference among the persons?
2. What factors may underlie this difference?
3. To what stage has the interpersonal difference evolved?

Nature of the Difference

Now, looking at the first of these three important questions, the nature of the difference will vary depending on the kind of issue on which people disagree. And there are four basic kinds of issues to look for:

- **Facts** Sometimes the disagreement occurs because individuals have different definitions of a problem, are aware of different pieces of relevant information, accept or reject different information as factual, or have differing impressions of their respective power and authority.
- **Goals** Sometimes the disagreement is about what should be accomplished — the desirable objectives of a department, division, section, or of a specific position within the organization.
- **Methods** Sometimes individuals differ about the procedures, strategies, or tactics which would most likely achieve a mutually desired goal.
- **Values** Sometimes the disagreement is over ethics — the way power should be exercised, or moral considerations, or assumptions about justice, fairness, and

---

[2]For definitions and discussions of social sensitivity and action flexibility see Robert Tannenbaum and Fred Massarik, "Leadership: A Frame of Reference," *Management Science*, Vol. 4, No. 1, October 1957; and Robert Tannenbaum and Warren H. Schmidt, "How to Choose a Leadership Pattern," *HBR* March-April 1958, p. 95.

so on. Such differences may affect the choice of either goals or methods.

Arguments are prolonged and confusion is increased when the contending parties are not sure of the nature of the issue over which they disagree. By discovering the source of the disagreement, the manager will be in a better position to determine how he can utilize and direct the dispute for both the short- and long-range good of the organization. As we will indicate later, there are certain steps which are appropriate when the differences are about facts, other steps which are appropriate when the differences are over goals, and still other steps which are applicable when differences are over methods or values.

Underlying Factors

When people are faced with a difference, it is not enough that their manager be concerned with what the difference is about. The second major diagnostic question he should ask is *why* the difference exists. As we try to discover useful answers to this, it is helpful to think in terms of:

- Whether the disputants had access to the same information.
- Whether the disputants perceive the common information differently.
- Whether each disputant is significantly influenced by his role in the organization.

These questions involve informational, perceptual, and role factors. Thus:

Informational factors   exert their influence when the various points of view have developed on the basis of different sets of facts. The ancient legend of the blind men and the elephant dramatizes this point as vividly as any modern illustration. Because each of the men had contact with a different part of the elephant, each disagreed violently about the nature of the animal. In the same way, when two persons receive limited information about a complex problem, they may well disagree as to the nature of that problem when they come together to solve it.

Perceptual factors   exert their influence when the persons have different images of the same stimulus. Each will attend to, and select from the information available, those items which he deems important. Each will interpret the information in a somewhat different manner. Each brings to the data a different set of life experiences which cause him to view the information through a highly personal kind of filter. The picture which he gets, therefore, is unique to him. Thus it is not surprising that the same basic "facts" may produce distinctive perceptual pictures in the minds of different individuals.

Role factors   exert their influence because each of the individuals occupies a certain position and status in society or in the organization. The fact that he occupies such a position or status may put certain constraints on him if the discussion is related to his role.

The concepts we have been discussing can be best illustrated by a concrete case. Such a case is presented in detail in Exhibit 1.

Stage of Evolution

Important conflicts among people ordinarily do not erupt suddenly. They pass through various stages, and the way in

The Facts

There is a disagreement over whether a company should introduce automated record keeping to replace its present manual system. The company's expert on office methods favors immediate introduction of such a system. The head of accounting is opposed to it. Some of the bases of disagreement and possible reasons for this disagreement are represented below.

Nature of the Difference

	Over facts	Over methods	Over goals	Over values
Expert on office methods	"Automation will save the company money."	"The new system should be installed fully and at once."	"We want a system that gives us accurate data rapidly — whenever we want it."	"We must be modern and efficient."
Head of accounting department	"The new system will be more expensive to install and operate."	"Let us move slower — one step at a time."	"We need most a flexible accounting system to meet our changing needs — managed by accountants who can solve unexpected and complex problems."	"We must consider the welfare of workers who have served the company so loyally for many years."

Reasons for the Difference

	Explanation of position of methods expert	Explanation of position of head accountant
Informational (Exposure to different information)	He has studied articles about seemingly comparable companies describing the savings brought about by automation. Representatives of machine companies have presented him with estimates of savings over a 10-year period.	He has heard about the "hidden costs" in automation. He has priced the kind of equipment he believes will be necessary and has estimated its depreciation. This estimated cost is much higher than the salaries of possible replaced workers.
Perceptual (Different interpretation of the same data because of differing backgrounds, experience, and so forth)	He regards the representatives of the machine company as being alert, businesslike, and knowledgeable about the best accounting procedures. He feels that their analysis of the company's needs is dependable and to be trusted.	He sees the representatives of the machine company as salesmen. Their goal is to sell machines, and their report and analysis must be read with great caution and suspicion.
Role (Pressure to take a certain stand because of status or position)	He believes that the company looks to him as the expert responsible for keeping its systems up-to-date and maximally efficient.	He feels responsible for the morale and security of his team in the accounting office. He must defend their loyalty and efficiency if it is ever doubted.

EXHIBIT 1 • Hypothetical Situation Illustrating a Difference

which the energy of the disputing parties can be effectively directed by the manager depends to some extent on the stage of the dispute when he enters the picture.

One way of diagnosing a dispute — the third major question — is to identify it as being at one of these five stages in its development:

Stage #1 — The Phase of Anticipation. A manager learns that his company is about to install new, automated equipment which will reduce the number and change the nature of jobs in a given department. He can anticipate that when this information is released, there will be differences of opinion as to the desirability of this change, the way in which it should be introduced, and the way in which the consequences of its introduction should be handled.

Stage #2 — The Phase of Conscious, But Unexpressed, Difference. Word leaks out about the proposed new equipment. Small clusters of people who trust one another begin discussing it. They have no definite basis for the information, but tensions begin to build up within the organization. There is a feeling of impending dispute and trouble.

Stage #3 — The Phase of Discussion. Information is presented about the plans to install new equipment. Questions are asked to secure more information, to inquire about the intentions of management, to test the firmness of the decision that has been made. During the discussion, the differing opinions of individuals begin to emerge openly. They are implied by the questions which are asked, and by the language which is used.

Stage #4 — The Phase of Open Dispute. The union steward meets with the foreman to present arguments for a change in plans. The foreman counters these arguments by presenting the reasons that led management to decide to install the equipment. The differences which have heretofore been expressed only indirectly and tentatively now sharpen into more clearly defined points of view.

Stage #5 — The Phase of Open Conflict. Individuals have firmly committed themselves to a particular position on the issue; the dispute has become clearly defined. The outcome can only be described in terms of win, lose, or compromise. Each disputant attempts not only to increase the effectiveness of his argument and his power in the situation, but also to undermine the influence of those who oppose him.

The power of the manager to intervene successfully will differ at each of these stages. He is likely to have the most influence if he enters the picture at stage #1; the least influence if he enters at stage #5. This range of possible behavior and action changes as the conflict passes through the various stages. For this reason, it is important for the manager not only to assess the nature of the given dispute and the forces affecting the individuals involved, but also to assess the stage to which the dispute has evolved.

SELECTING AN APPROACH

After the manager has diagnosed a given dispute (or a potential one) between subordinates, he is next confronted by the problem of taking action.

And here there are two additional questions that it will be helpful for him to consider:

1. What courses of action are available?
2. What must be kept in mind in selecting the best one?

Assuming, first, a situation in which the manager has time to anticipate and plan for an impending dispute, we suggest that the general approaches typically available to him are (a) avoidance, (b) repression, (c) sharpening into conflict, and (d) transformation into problem solving. In deciding which to use, the manager's primary concern should be to select the alternative that will yield optimum benefits to the organization.

Avoidance of Differences

It is possible for a manager to avoid the occurrence of many differences among his subordinates. He can, for example, staff his organization with people who are in substantial agreement. Some organizations select and promote individuals whose experiences are similar, who have had similar training, and who come from a similar level of society. Because of such common backgrounds, these individuals tend to see things similarly, to have common interests and objectives, and to approach problems in much the same way. A staff thus developed tends to be a very secure one: the reactions of one's fellows are both readily predictable and congenial to one's own way of thinking and doing.

The manager may also avoid differences among his subordinates by controlling certain of their interpersonal contacts. He can, for example, assign two potentially explosive individuals to different groups or physical locations or

he can choose not to raise a particularly divisive issue because it is "too hot to handle." But let us take a closer look:

When is this alternative appropriate? Some organizations depend heavily on certain kinds of conformity and agreement among their employees in order to get the work done. Political parties and religious denominational groups are perhaps extreme examples of this. If an individual holds a different point of view on a rather fundamental issue, he may become a destructive force within the organization. This approach may be especially important if he is dealing with somewhat fragile and insecure individuals. Some persons are so threatened by conflict that their ability to function effectively suffers when they operate in a climate of differences.

What are the difficulties and dangers in this approach? The manager who uses this approach consistently runs the risk of reducing the total creativity of his staff. Someone has said, "When everyone in the room thinks the same thing, no one is thinking very much." In an atmosphere in which differences are avoided, new ideas not only appear less frequently, but old ideas also are unlikely to go unexamined and untested. There is genuine danger of the organization's slipping unknowingly into a rut of complacency.

Repression of Differences

Sometimes a manager is aware that certain differences exist among members of his staff, but he feels that the open expression of these differences would create unproductive dissension and reduce the total creativity of the group. He may, therefore, decide to keep these differences under cover. He may do this by continually emphasizing loyalty, cooperation, teamwork, and other similar values within the group. In such a climate, it is unlikely that subordinates will express disagreements and risk conflict.

The manager may also try to make sure that the potentially conflicting parties come together only under circumstances which are highly controlled — circumstances in which open discussion of latent differences is clearly inappropriate. Or he may develop an atmosphere of repression by consistently rewarding agreement and cooperation and by punishing (in one way or another) those who disrupt the harmony of the organization by expressing nonconformist ideas. But once again:

When is this alternative appropriate? It is most useful when the latent differences are not relevant to the organization's task. It is to be expected that individuals will differ on many things — religion, politics, their loyalty to cities or states, baseball teams, and so forth. There may be no need to reach agreement on some of these differences in order to work together effectively on the job. It may also be appropriate to repress conflict when adequate time is not available to resolve the potential differences among the individuals involved. This might be particularly true if the manager's concern is to achieve a short-run objective and the potential disagreement is over a long-run issue. The wounds of disagreement should not be opened up if there is insufficient time to bind them.

What are the difficulties and dangers in this approach? Repression almost always costs something. If, indeed, the differences are important to the persons involved, their feelings may come to be expressed indirectly, in ways that could reduce productivity. Every manager has witnessed situations in which ideas are resisted, not on the basis of their merit, but on the basis of who advocated them. Or he has seen strong criticism arising over mistakes made by a particularly disliked individual.

Much has been said and written about "hidden agenda." People may discuss one subject, but the *way* they discuss it and the positions they take with respect to it may actually be determined by factors lying beneath the surface of the discussion. Hidden agenda are likely to abound in an atmosphere of repression.

When strong feelings are involved in unexpressed differences, the blocking of these feelings creates frustration and hostility which may be misdirected toward "safe" targets. Differences, and the feelings generated by them, do not ordinarily disappear by being ignored. They fester beneath the surface and emerge at inopportune moments to create problems for the manager and his organization.

Differences into Conflicts

When this approach is used, the manager not only recognizes the fact that differences exist, but attempts to create an arena in which the conflicting parties can "fight it out." However, like the promoter of an athletic contest, he will want to be sure that the differing persons understand the issue over which they differ, the rules and procedures by which they can discuss their differences, and the kinds of roles and responsibilities which each is expected to bear in mind during the struggle. Again:

When is this alternative appropriate? A simple answer is: "when it is clarifying and educational." Many an individual will not pause to examine the assumptions he holds or the positions he advocates until he is called on to clarify and support them by someone who holds contrary views. In the same way, the power realities within an organization can come into sharper focus and be more commonly recognized through conflict.

For example, the manager of production and the manager of engineering may develop quite different impressions of how the board of directors feels about the relative importance of their respective units. Each is sure that the board is most impressed with the caliber of the staff, output, and operational efficiency of his department. When a dispute arises over which group is to get priority space in a new building, top management may permit both departments to exert all the influence they can on the board. During the struggle, the two managers may each gain a more realistic assessment of, and respect for, the power of the other.

Another valuable thing learned is the cost of conflict itself. Almost invariably at the end of a long dispute, there is a strong resolve that "this shall not happen again," as the individuals reflect on the financial costs, tensions, embarrassments, uneasiness, and wasted time and energy it caused.

What are the difficulties and dangers in this approach? Conflict can be very costly. It not only saps the energy of those involved, but also may irreparably destroy their future effectiveness. In the heat of conflict, words are sometimes spoken which leave lifelong scars on people or forever cloud their relationship.

Because the risks involved in conflict are so great and the potential costs so high, the manager will want to consider carefully the following questions before he uses this approach:

1. What does he hope to accomplish?
2. What are the possible outcomes of the conflict?
3. What steps should be taken to keep the conflict within organizational bounds and in perspective?
4. What can be done after the conflict to strengthen the bonds between disputants, so that the conflict will be of minimum destructiveness to them and to their ongoing relationship?

Making Differences Creative

"Two heads are better than one" because the two heads often represent a richer set of experiences and because they can bring to bear on the problem a greater variety of insights. If the differences are seen as enriching, rather than as in opposition to each other, the "two heads" will indeed be likely to come up with a better solution than either one alone. For example, had the six blind men who came into contact with different parts of the same elephant pooled their information, they would have arrived at a more accurate description of the animal. In the same way, many problems can be seen clearly, wholly, and in perspective only if the individuals who see different aspects can come together and pool their information. Here, too, let us take a more specific look:

When is this alternative appropriate?   When it comes to choosing courses of action for a given problem, differences among the individuals in an organization can help to increase the range and variety of alternatives suggested.

The channeling of differences into a problem-solving context may also help to deal with some of the feelings which often accompany disagreement — frustration, resentment, and hostility. By providing an open and accepted approach, the manager helps to prevent undercurrents of feelings which could break out at inopportune moments. He also helps to channel the energy generated by feelings into creative, rather than into destructive, activities. Whereas conflict tends to cause individuals to seek ways of weakening and undermining those who differ with them, the problem-solving approach leads individuals to welcome differences as being potentially enriching to one's own goals, ideas, and methods.

What are the difficulties and dangers in this approach?   To utilize differences requires time. Often it is easier for a single individual (rather than two or more persons) to make a decision. Also, when a rapid decision is required, it may be easier and more practical to ignore one side of an argument in order to move into action. Finally, unless a problem-solving situation is planned with some care, there is always the risk of generating conflict which will be frustrating to all parties concerned.

ENRICHED PROBLEM SOLVING

Let us assume that the course of action decided on is the one just discussed —

turning the difference into creative problem solving. Let us further assume, now, that the manager enters the picture when his subordinates are already involved in conflict. What are the things he can do if he wishes to transform this conflict into a problem-solving situation?

He can welcome the existence of differences within the organization.

The manager can indicate that from the discussion of differences can come a greater variety of solutions to problems and a more adequate testing of proposed methods. By making clear his view that all parties contribute to the solution of problems by sharing their differences, he reduces the implication that there will be an ultimate "winner" and "loser."

He can listen with understanding rather than evaluation.

There is abundant evidence that conflicts tend to be prolonged and to become increasingly frustrating because the conflicting parties do not really listen to one another. Each attempts to impose his own views and to "tune out" or distort what the other person has to say.

The manager may expect that when he enters the picture, the individuals will try to persuade him to take a stand on the issue involved. While each adversary is presenting his "case" to the manager, he will be watching for cues which indicate where the manager stands on the issue. It is therefore important that the manager make every effort to understand both positions as fully as possible, recognizing and supporting the seriousness of purpose of each where appropriate, and to withhold judgment until all available facts are in.

In the process of listening for understanding, the manager will also set a good example for the conflicting parties. By adopting such a listening-understanding attitude himself, and by helping the disputants to understand each other more fully, he can make a most useful contribution toward transforming potential conflict into creative problem solving.

He can clarify the nature of the conflict.

In the heat of an argument, each participant may primarily focus on either facts, specific methods, goals, or values. Frustration and anger can occur when one individual talks about facts while another is eager to discuss methods. The manager, having carefully listened to the discussion, can clarify the nature of the issues so that the discussion can become more productive.

He can recognize and accept the feelings of the individuals involved.

Irrational feelings are generated in a controversy, even though the participants do not always recognize this fact. Each wants to believe that he is examining the problem "objectively." The manager, recognizing and accepting feelings such as fear, jealousy, anger, or anxiety, may make it possible for the participants squarely to face their true feelings. The effective manager does not take a critical attitude toward these feelings by, in effect, saying, "You have no right to feel angry!" Rather, he tries sincerely to communicate his sympathetic feelings.

Ordinarily, we do no real service to people by encouraging a repression of their feelings or by criticizing them for experiencing fear, anger, and so forth. Such criticism — whether implied or expressed openly — may block the search for new ways out of the controversy. There is considerable evidence that when a person feels threatened or under attack, he tends to become more rigid and therefore more defensive about positions to which he has committed himself.

He can indicate who will make the decision being discussed.

Sometimes heated disputes go on with respect to issues over which one or more of the persons involved has no control. When people have differing notions about the formal authority available to each, a clarification by the manager of the authority relationships can go far toward placing the discussion in clearer perspective.

He can suggest procedures and ground rules for resolving the differences.

If the disagreement is over *facts*, the manager may assist the disputants in validating existing data and in seeking additional data which will more clearly illuminate the issues under dispute.

If the disagreement is over *methods*, the manager may first want to remind the parties that they have common objectives, and that their disagreement is over means rather than ends. He may suggest that before examining in detail each of their proposed methods for achieving the goals, they might together establish a set of criteria to be used in evaluating whatever procedures are proposed. He may also want to suggest that some time be spent in trying to generate additional alternatives reflecting new approaches. Then after these alternatives have been worked out, he may encourage the parties to evaluate them with the aid of the criteria which these persons have developed together.

If the disagreement is over *goals* or goal priorities, he may suggest that the parties take time to describe as clearly as possible the conflicting goals which are being sought. Sometimes arguments persist simply because the parties have not taken the trouble to clarify for themselves and for each other exactly what they do desire. Once these goals are clearly stated, the issues can be dealt with more realistically.

If the disagreement is over *values,* the manager may suggest that these values be described in operational terms. Discussions of abstractions often tend to be fruitless because the same words and concepts mean different things to different people. To help individuals become more fully aware of the limitations to which their actions are subject, the question, "What do you think you can do about this situation?" usually leads to a more productive discussion than the question, "What do you believe in?" Because value systems are so closely related to a person's self concept, the manager may want to give particular attention to protecting the egos involved. He may make clear that an individual's entire ethical system is not being scrutinized, but only those values which are pertinent to the particular instance.

He can give primary attention to maintaining relationships between the disputing parties.

Sometimes, during the course of a heated dispute, so much attention is paid to the issue under discussion that nothing is done to maintain and strengthen the relationship between the disputing parties. It is not surprising, therefore, that disputes tend to disrupt ongoing relationships. Through oversight or deliberate action, important functions are neglected which sustain or further develop human relationships — for example, the functions of encouraging, supporting, reducing tension, and expressing common feelings. If a conflict is to be transformed into a problem-saving situation, these functions need to be performed by someone — either by the manager or, through his continuing encouragement, by the parties themselves.

He can create appropriate vehicles for communication among the disputing parties.

One of the ways to bring the differences into a problem-solving context is to ensure that the disputants can come together easily. If they can discuss their differences *before* their positions become crystalized, the chances of their learning from each other and arriving at mutually agreeable positions are increased. Having easy access to one another is also a way of reducing the likelihood that each will develop unreal stereotypes of the other.

Misunderstanding mounts as communication becomes more difficult. One of the values of regular staff meetings, therefore, is that such meetings, properly conducted, can provide a continuing opportunity for persons to exchange ideas and feelings.

If the manager wishes his subordinates to deal with their differences in a problem-solving framework, he will want to ask himself, "In what kind of setting will the parties to this dispute be best able to discuss their differences with a minimum of interference and threat?" He will exclude from such a setting any individuals whose presence will embarrass the disputants if the latter "back down" from previously held points of view. It will be a setting which reflects as much informality and psychological comfort as possible.

He can suggest procedures which facilitate problem solving.

One of the key needs in a dispute is to separate an idea from the person who first proposes it. This increases the chance of examining the idea critically and objectively without implying criticism of the person. Techniques like brainstorming, for example, are designed to free people from the necessity to defend their ideas during an exploration period. Another facilitating action is outlining an orderly set of procedures (e.g., examining objectives, obtaining relevant data) for the disputants to follow as they seek a constructive resolution of their difference.

MANAGERIAL OBJECTIVITY

Thus far we have tended to make the unrealistic assumption that the manager is able to maintain his own objectivity in the face of a difference among his subordinates. Obviously, this does not easily happen because his feelings also tend to become involved. It is, in fact, not unusual for people to react to differences more on the basis of their own feelings than on the basis of some rational approach to the problem at hand.

A manager may be deeply concerned about the disruptive effects of a disagreement. He may be troubled about how the persistence of a dispute will affect him personally or his position in the organization. He may worry about the danger of coming under personal attack, or of incurring the anger and hostility of important subordinates or a superior. He may become anxious as another person expresses deep feelings, without really understanding why.

While sometimes personal feelings of this kind are at the conscious level, often they are unrecognized by the manager himself because they lie in the area of the unconscious. This, then, highlights the importance of the manager's own self-awareness. While we do not intend to deal with this topic here, it might be well to note some "alerting signals" to which the manager might pay attention when he confronts a difference.

Certain kinds of behavior may indicate that the manager's handling of differences is strongly influenced by his personal needs and feelings rather than by the objective interests of the organization — as, for example:

- A persistent tendency to surround himself with yes men.
- Emphasizing loyalty and cooperation in a way that makes disagreement seem equivalent to disloyalty and rebellion.
- A persistent tendency to "pour oil on troubled waters" whenever differences arise.
- Glossing over serious differences in order to maintain an appearance of harmony and teamwork.
- Accepting ambiguous resolutions of differences which permit conflicting parties to arrive at dissimilar interpretations.
- Exploiting differences to strengthen his personal position of influence through the weakening of the position of others.

Any of these kinds of behavior could, as we have already suggested, be appropriate in certain situations and actually serve the general interest of the organization. If, however, they represent rather consistent patterns on the part of the manager, then it may be worth his while to examine more closely the reasons for his actions.

There are times in the lives of most of us when our personal needs are the strongest determinants of our behavior. Fortunately, most organizations can tolerate a limited amount of such self-oriented behavior on the part of their managers. The danger occurs if an individual believes that his actions are solely motivated by the "good of the organization" when, in fact, he is operating on the basis of other kinds of personal motivation without being aware of it.

The manager who is more fully aware of his own feelings and inclinations is in a better position to diagnose a situation accurately and to choose rationally the kind of behavior which is in the best interests of the organization.

INTERGROUP PROBLEMS IN ORGANIZATIONS

Edgar H. Schein

The first major problem of groups in organizations is how to make them effective in fulfilling both organizational goals and the needs of their members.

CONCLUSION

This article began with the assumption that many managers are uncertain and uneasy when differences arise. Because their own emotions and the feelings of others quickly become involved, they often deal with differences in a haphazard or inappropriate manner. We have attempted to suggest some more systematic ways to view differences and to deal with them. We believe that if a manager can approach a difference with less fear and with greater awareness of the potential richness that lies in it, he will better understand the basic nature and causes of the difference. And having done this, he will be in a better position to discover and implement more realistic alternatives for dealing with it.

The second major problem is how to establish conditions *between groups* which will enhance the productivity of each without destroying intergroup relations and coordination. This problem exists because as groups become more committed to their own goals and norms, they are likely to become competitive with one another and seek to undermine their rivals' activities, thereby becoming a liability to the organization as a whole. The over-all problem, then, is how to establish high-productive, *collaborative* intergroup relations.

SOME CONSEQUENCES OF INTERGROUP COMPETITION

The consequences of intergroup competition were first studied systematically by

Sherif in an ingeniously designed setting. He organized a boys' camp in such a way that two groups would form and would become competitive. Sherif then studied the effects of the competition and tried various devices for reestablishing collaborative relationships between the groups.[1] Since his original experiments, there have been many replications with adult groups; the phenomena are so constant that it has been possible to make a demonstration exercise out of the experiment.[2] The effects can be described in terms of the following categories:

A. What happens *within* each competing group?
1. Each group becomes more closely knit and elicits greater loyalty from its members; members close ranks and bury some of their internal differences.
2. Group climate changes from informal, casual, playful to work- and task-oriented; concern for members' psychological needs declines while concern for task accomplishment increases.
3. Leadership patterns tend to change from more democratic toward more autocratic; the group becomes more willing to tolerate autocratic leadership.
4. Each group becomes more highly structured and organized.
5. Each group demands more loyalty and conformity from its members in order to be able to present a "solid front."
B. What happens *between* the competing groups?
1. Each group begins to see the other groups as the enemy, rather than merely a neutral object.
2. Each group begins to experience distortions of perception — it tends to perceive only the best parts of itself, denying its weaknesses, and tends to per-

ceive only the worst parts of the other group, denying its strengths; each group is likely to develop a negative stereotype of the other ("they don't play fair like we do").
3. Hostility toward the other group increases while interaction and communication with the other group decrease; thus it becomes easier to maintain negative stereotypes and more difficult to correct perceptual distortions.
4. If the groups are forced into interaction — for example, if they are forced to listen to representatives plead their own and the others' cause in reference to some task — each group is likely to listen more closely to their own representative and not to listen to the representative of the other group, except to find fault with his presentation; in other words, group members tend to listen only for that which supports their own position and stereotype.

Thus far, I have listed some consequences of the competition itself, without reference to the consequences if one group actually wins out over the other. Before listing those effects, I would like to draw attention to the generality of the above reactions. Whether one is talking about sports teams, or interfraternity competition, or labor-management disputes, or interdepartmental competition as between sales and production in an industrial organization, or about international relations and the competition between the Soviet Union and the United States, the same phenomena tend to occur. If you will give just a little thought to competing groups of which you have been a member, you will begin to recognize most of the psychological responses described. I

[1] M. Sherif, O. J. Harvey, B. J. White, W. R. Hood, and Carolyn Sherif, *Intergroup Conflict and Cooperation: The Robbers Cave Experiment* (Norman, Okla.: University Book Exchange, 1961).
[2] R. R. Blake and Jane S. Mouton, "Reactions to Intergroup Competition under Win-Lose Conditions," *Management Science* 7 (1961): 420–41.

want to stress that these responses can be very useful to the group in making it more effective and highly motivated in task accomplishment. However, the same factors which improve *intragroup* effectiveness may have negative consequences for *intergroup* effectiveness. For example, as we have seen in labor-management or international disputes, if the groups perceive themselves as competitors, they find it more difficult to resolve their differences.

Let us look at the consequences of winning and losing, as in a situation where several groups are bidding to have their proposal accepted for a contract or as a solution to some problem. Many intra-organizational situations become win-or-lose affairs, hence it is of particular importance to examine their consequences.

C. What happens to the *winner*?
1. Winner retains its cohesion and may become even more cohesive.
2. Winner tends to release tension, lose its fighting spirit, become complacent, casual, and playful (the "fat and happy" state).
3. Winner tends toward high intragroup cooperation and concern for members' needs, and low concern for work and task accomplishment.
4. Winner tends to be complacent and to feel that winning has confirmed the positive stereotype of itself and the negative stereotype of the "enemy" group; there is little basis for reevaluating perceptions, or reexamining group operations in order to learn how to improve them.
D. What happens to the *loser*?
1. If the situation permits because of some ambiguity in the decision (say, if judges have rendered it or if the game was close), there is a strong tendency for the loser to deny or distort the reality of losing; instead, the loser will find psychological escapes

like "the judges were biased," "the judges didn't really understand our solution," "the rules of the game were not clearly explained to us," "if luck had not been against us at the one key point, we would have won," and so on.
2. If loss is accepted, the losing group tends to splinter, unresolved conflicts come to the surface, fights break out, all in the effort to find the cause for the loss.
3. Loser is more tense, ready to work harder, and desperate to find someone or something to blame — the leader, itself, the judges who decided against them, the rules of the game (the "lean and hungry" state).
4. Loser tends toward low intragroup cooperation, low concern for members' needs, and high concern for recouping by working harder.
5. Loser tends to learn a lot about itself as a group because positive stereotype of itself and negative stereotype of the other group are upset by the loss, forcing a reevaluation of perceptions; as a consequence, loser is likely to reorganize and become more cohesive and effective, once the loss has been accepted realistically.

The net effect of the win-lose situation is often that the loser is not convinced that he lost, and that intergroup tension is higher than before the competition began.

REDUCING THE NEGATIVE CONSEQUENCES OF INTERGROUP COMPETITION

The gains of intergroup competition may under some conditions outweigh the negative consequences. It may be desirable to have work groups pitted against one another or to have departments become cohesive loyal units, even if interdepartmental coordination suffers. Other times, however, the negative consequences outweigh the gains, and management seeks ways of reducing intergroup tension. Many of the ideas to be mentioned about how this might be accomplished also come from the basic researches of Sherif and Blake; they have been tested and found to be successful. As we will see, the problems derive not so much from being unable to think of ways for reducing intergroup conflict as from being *unable to implement some of the most effective ways.*

The fundamental problem of intergroup competition is the conflict of goals and the breakdown of interaction and communication between the groups; this breakdown in turn permits and stimulates perceptual distortion and mutual negative stereotyping. The basic strategy of reducing conflict, therefore, is to find goals upon which groups can agree and to reestablish valid communication between the groups. The tactics to employ in implementing this strategy can be any combination of the following:

Locating a Common Enemy For example, the competing teams of each league can compose an all-star team to play the other league, or conflicts between sales and production can be reduced if both can harness their efforts to helping their company successfully compete against another company. The conflict here is merely shifted to a higher level.

Inventing a Negotiation Strategy

which **Brings Subgroups of the Competing Groups into Interaction with Each Other** The isolated group representative cannot abandon his group position but a subgroup which is given some power can not only permit itself to be influenced by its counterpart negotiation team, but will have the strength to influence the remainder of the group.

Locating a Superordinate Goal Such a goal can be a brand new task which requires the cooperative effort of the previously competing groups or can be a task like analyzing and reducing the intergroup conflict itself. For example, the previously competing sales and production departments can be given the task of developing a new product line that will be both cheap to produce and in great customer demand; or, with the help of an outside consultant, the competing groups can be invited to examine their own behavior and reevaluate the gains and losses from competition.

Reducing Intergroup Competition through Laboratory Training Methods

The last procedure mentioned above has been tried by a number of psychologists, notably Blake, with considerable success.[3] Assuming the organization recognizes that it has a problem, and assuming it is ready to expose this problem to an outside consultant, the laboratory approach to reducing conflict might proceed as follows: (1) The competing groups are both brought into a training setting and the goals are stated to be an exploration of mutual perceptions and

---

[3] R. R. Blake, and Jane S. Mouton, "Headquarters — field team training for organizational improvements," *Journal of the American Society of Training Directors* 16 (1962).

mutual relations. (2) Each group is then invited to discuss its perceptions of and attitudes toward itself and the other group. (3) In the presence of both groups, representatives publicly share the perceptions of self and other which the groups have generated, while the groups are obligated to remain silent (the objective is simply to report to the other group as accurately as possible the images that each group has developed in private). (4) Before any exchange has taken place, the groups return to private sessions to digest and analyze what they have heard; there is a great likelihood that the representative reports have revealed great discrepancies to each group between its self-image and the image that the other group holds of it; the private session is partly devoted to an analysis of the reasons for the discrepancies, which forces each group to review its actual behavior toward the other group and the possible consequences of that behavior, regardless of its intentions. (5) In public session, again working through representatives, each group shares with the other what discrepancies they have uncovered and their analysis of the possible reasons for them, with the focus on the actual behavior exhibited. (6) Following this mutual exposure, a more open exploration is then permitted between the two groups on the *now-shared goal* of identifying further reasons for perceptual distortions.

Interspersed with these steps are short lectures and reading assignments on the psychology of intergroup conflict, the bases for perceptual distortion, psy-chological defense mechanisms, and so on. The goal is to bring the psychological dynamics of the situation into conscious awareness and to refocus the groups on the common goal of exploring jointly the problem they share. In order to do this, they must have valid data about each other, which is provided through the artifice of the representative reports.

The Blake model described above deals with the entire group. Various other approaches have been tried which start with numbers. For example, groups A and B can be divided into pairs composed of an A and B member. Each pair can be given the assignment of developing a joint product which uses the best ideas from the A product and the B product. Or, in each pair, members may be asked to argue for the product of the opposing group. It has been shown in a number of experiments that one way of changing attitudes is to ask a person to play the role of an advocate of the new attitude to be learned.[4] The very act of arguing for another product, even if it is purely an exercise, exposes the person to some of its virtues which he had previously denied. A practical application of these points might be to have some members of the sales department spend time in the production department and be asked to represent the production point of view to some third party, or to have some production people join sales teams to learn the sales point of view.

Most of the approaches cited depend on a recognition of some problem by the organization and a willingness on the

---

[4]I. L. Janis and B. T. King, "The Influence of Role Playing on Opinion Change," *Journal of Abnormal and Social Psychology* 69 (1954): 211–218.

part of the competing groups to participate in some training effort to reduce negative consequences. The reality, however, is that most organizations neither recognize the problem nor are willing to invest time and energy in resolving it. Some of the unwillingness also arises from each competing group's recognition that in becoming more cooperative it may lose some of its own identity and integrity as a group. Rather than risk this, the group may prefer to continue the competition. This may well be the reason why, in international relations, nations refuse to engage in what seem like perfectly simple ways of resolving their differences. They resist partly in order to protect their integrity. Consequently, the *implementation* of strategies and tactics for reducing the negative consequences of intergroup competition is often a greater problem than the development of such strategies and tactics.

PREVENTING INTERGROUP CONFLICT

Because of the great difficulties of reducing intergroup conflict once it has developed, it may be desirable to prevent its occurrence in the first place. How can this be done? Paradoxically, a strategy of prevention must bring into question the fundamental premise upon which organization through division of labor rests. Once it has been decided by a superordinate authority to divide up functions among different departments or groups, a bias has already been introduced toward intergroup competition; for in doing its own job well, each group must to some degree compete for scarce resources and rewards from the superordinate authority. The very concept of division of labor implies a reduction of

communication and interaction between groups, thus making it possible for perceptual distortions to occur.

The organization planner who wishes to avoid intergroup competition need not abandon the concept of division of labor, but he should follow some of the steps listed in creating and handling his different functional groups.

1. Relatively greater emphasis given to *total organizational effectiveness* and the role of departments in contributing to it; departments measured and rewarded on the basis of their *contribution* to the total effort rather than their individual effectiveness.
2. *High interaction* and *frequent communication* stimulated between groups to work on problems of intergroup coordination and help; organizational *rewards given partly on the basis of help* which groups give to each other.
3. Frequent *rotation of members* among groups or departments to stimulate high degree of mutual understanding and empathy for one another's problems.
4. *Avoidance of any win-lose situation;* groups never put into the position of competing for some organizational reward; emphasis always placed on pooling resources to maximize organizational effectiveness; rewards shared equally with all the groups or departments.

Most managers find the last of the above points particularly difficult to accept because of the strong belief that performance can be improved by pitting people or groups against one another in a competitive situation. This may indeed be true in the short run, and in some cases may work in the long run, but the negative consequences we have described are undeniably a product of a competitive win-lose situation. Consequently, if a manager wishes to prevent such consequences, he must face the possibility that he may have to abandon competitive relationships altogether and seek to substitute intergroup collaboration toward organizational goals. Implementing such a preventive strategy is often more difficult, partly because most people are inexperienced in stimulating and managing collaborative relationships. Yet it is clear from observing organizations such as those using the Scanlon Plan not only that it is possible to establish collaborative relationships, even between labor and management, but also that where this has been done, organizational and group effectiveness have been as high or higher than under competitive conditions.

THE PROBLEM OF INTEGRATION IN PERSPECTIVE

I have discussed two basic issues in this chapter, both dealing with psychological groups: (1) the development of groups within organizations which can fulfill both the needs of the organization and the psychological needs of its members; and (2) the problems of intergroup competition and conflict. To achieve maximum integration, the organization should be able to create conditions that will facilitate a balance between organizational goals and member needs and minimize disintegrative competition between the subunits of the total organization.

Groups are highly complex sets of relationships. There are no easy generalizations about the conditions under which they will be effective, but with suitable training, many kinds of groups can become more effective than they have been. Consequently, group-dynamics training by laboratory methods may be a more promising approach to effectiveness than attempting

a priori to determine the right membership, type of leadership, and organization. All the factors must be taken into account, with training perhaps weighted more heavily than it has been, though the training itself must be carefully undertaken.

The creation of psychologically meaningful and effective groups does not solve all of the organization's problems if such groups compete and conflict with each other. We examined some of the consequences of competition under win-lose conditions and outlined two basic approaches for dealing with the problem: (1) reducing conflict by increasing communication and locating superordinate goals, and (2) preventing conflict by establishing from the outset organizational conditions which stimulate collaboration rather than competition.

The prevention of intergroup conflict is especially crucial if the groups involved are highly interdependent. The greater the interdependence, the greater the potential loss to the total organization of negative stereotyping, withholding of information, efforts to make the other group look bad in the eyes of the superior, and so on.

It is important to recognize that the preventive strategy does not imply absence of disagreement and artificial "sweetness and light" within or between groups. Conflict and disagreement at the level of the group or organizational *task* is not only desirable but essential for the achievement of the best solutions to problems. What is harmful is *interpersonal* or *intergroup* conflict in which the task is not as important as gaining advantage over the other person or group. The negative consequences we described, such as mutual negative stereotyping, fall into this latter category and undermine rather than aid overall task performance. And it is these kinds of conflicts which can be reduced by establishing collaborative relationships. Interestingly enough, observations of cases would suggest that task-relevant conflict which improves over-all effectiveness is greater under collaborative conditions because groups and members trust each other enough to be frank and open in sharing information and opinions. In the competitive situation, each group is committed to hiding its special resources from the other groups, thus preventing effective integration of all resources in the organization.

ASPEN COUNTY HIGH SCHOOL

CASE 1

The following is part of a conversation between the Superintendent of Schools and Mr. Don Mason, Aspen County High School Principal, that took place at the regular Wednesday meeting of the Aspen County School District Board of Trustees during the last week of March.

Superintendent: Don, it seems like every time you come to our meeting you've got your hand out for more money. Last month it was money for new band uniforms. Before that you were trying to tell us the athletic teams needed another $2,000 worth of equipment. Now you hit us with this across-the-board raise for your faculty. You know we're working on a very limited budget and we have other demands that must be met, too.

Don Mason: Of course, it costs money to run a school district. I can understand your problems. But remember, the only way we're going to be able to offer good instruction to this community is by having well-qualified teachers on the staff. And good teachers cost money! Besides, remember you promised us last year when we asked for a raise that we'd get it this year, and . . . .

Superintendent: Now, just a minute Don. We never promised you that you'd get a raise this year. We simply said that it was impossible to give you a raise *last* year because Western Steel had closed down as a result of the strike and the district's income was decreased substantially.

At that time we thought that Western Steel would soon be operating at full

This case was developed and prepared by Professor Sherman Tingey, School of Business, Arizona State University. Reprinted by permission.

steam and that we would have the funds available for a raise *this year*. As everyone knows only too well, Western still is only operating at about one-third capacity. This means that their payroll is only about one third. Quite a few people have moved from the area to get jobs. Business income is low and some of the shops have closed their doors permanently. We just don't have the money in the General Fund and we probably couldn't pass a special bond issue at this late date anyway.

Aspen County School District was a unified district comprised of four elementary schools, two junior high schools, and one high school. The district served the entire population of the county. The major source of income for this small western community was Western Steel. Strikes and slowdowns at Western Steel often had resulted in extreme fluctuations in the population and the financial well-being of the community. As a result of these problems and others, the superintendent and the Board experienced frequent discord with the teachers and administrators on financial matters.

At 8:30 a.m. the following Monday, the thirty-seven faculty members and administrators of Aspen High School held their weekly faculty meeting. The meeting was called to order by the vice-principal of the high school, Bob Lane.

Bob Lane (Vice-Principal): We have a lot of business to cover in our meeting this morning, but first I think it is appropriate that we hear from Don. As most of you know by now, Don went to bat for the faculty against the Board for a salary increase and he wants to bring this item up first so that everyone will understand exactly how things are progressing.

Don Mason (Principal): I met with the Board last Thursday and asked about that raise they had promised us. They gave the same old excuse of no funds. It looks like we're going to have a tough battle on our hands if we expect to get an across-the-board raise this year. Since their major objection appears to be lack of funds, the Teachers' Welfare Committee has been working over the weekend on possible ways that the funds can be obtained. They have worked up a couple of alternatives that can be presented. The most attractive one involves not receiving your three summer month's checks in one lump sum in June as some of you have been doing. Phil, why don't you explain just how that is going to work?

Phil, the chairman of the Teachers' Welfare Committee, then explained to the group that approximately one half of the teachers had been exercising the option to receive their three summer checks in a lump sum at the beginning of the summer. If receipt of these checks could be postponed until after June 30, the expense would appear in the next fiscal year. This could be a permanent postponement. If only 75 percent of those now exercising this option were willing to forego this advantage, enough funds would be created to finance the desired salary increases. A hand vote of those who were willing to give up this option indicated that 16 of the 18 teachers involved would probably be able to rearrange their financial affairs to support the proposal.

Don Mason: Thanks very much for

your support. I'll present this proposal to the Board this Thursday and see if we can't work something out. Bob and I were talking just yesterday and we both expressed the opinion that we have an excellent staff here at the high school and we think that you deserve a raise in the salary schedule. Besides, Bob and I are on a schedule, too, and we'd benefit from a raise the same as you would. Both "X" County and "Y" County received schedule increases this year and our county is falling behind.

The meeting was turned over to Bob who conducted the remaining business. That same afternoon a group of teachers were discussing the situation in the teachers' lounge after school.

Teacher A: I heard Bill [an English teacher] say that he was going to investigate the possibility of a position at Sacramento if it looked like we weren't going to get a raise this year. Do you think we'll get the raise?

Teacher B: Naw, we probably won't. But I wouldn't leave because of that alone. Money isn't everything. I think the kind of work environment we have here is worth something. Not very often will you find a school where both the principal and vice-principal will stand behind their teachers and support them 100 percent. I think that's one of the reasons Don and Bob are so well liked by the teachers.

Teacher C: I'll agree with that! I'll never forget that incident with Bob Lane when I first came here. You remember that he asked me to be the Lettermen's Club Advisor? None of the coaches wanted the job because it takes a lot of time and the kids are pretty

rough to handle. Well, anyway, when he introduced me to the Club members, he said that the administration would stand behind me in whatever I wanted to do as long as I thought it was for the best benefit of the Club.

Later, when I told the Club members that the initiation had to be toned down considerably because of the danger of seriously hurting someone, they stormed right into Bob Lane's office complaining. They figured that since they had to go through all that rough stuff to be initiated, it was only fair for them to "get revenge" against the new members. Boy, it really made me feel good when I found out Bob had told them, "If that's the way your advisor wants it, then that's the way it's going to be." It surely made my job a lot easier from then on.

Teacher A: Do you remember that problem I had in the Boys' Cooking Class right at the first of the year?

Teacher B: No, what was that?

Teacher A: Well, it really wasn't a problem. I was nervous since this was my first teaching job. We were supposed to be making cookies. Two boys were laughing and goofing around and somehow they broke a bottle of milk. I was so upset that I sent them to the office. Really it was just an accident, but Don gave the boys a talking to anyway and told them not to goof off in class. I realized afterward that sending them to the office was too strong of a discipline measure, but I was surely glad that Don stuck up for me anyway.

Teacher D: I really think a lot of Don and Bob. Remember last fall when I was teaching that adult evening class in bookkeeping? Dayle [another teacher] and I had gone out for a little deer hunting after school one afternoon. We shot a three-point near the top of Hogback Mountain and it took us a lot longer than we expected to get that deer out. The class I was teaching was supposed to meet at 7:00 and we didn't get back to town until about 7:30. When Don phoned my home about 7:20 and found out that I was still out deer hunting, he said, "I'll tell the students to go ahead and work on their own. He's probably shot a big one and is having difficulty getting it out."

When I got to class 40 minutes late all my students were still there waiting for a deer hunting story. After class I met Don in the hall and he asked just one question: "Did you get your deer?"

The following Thursday at the Board of Trustees' meeting, Principal Don Mason presented the proposal of the Teachers' Welfare Committee in an effort to show the board members where they could get the funds for a salary increase. After considerable discussion of the proposal, the Board said they would take it into consideration but still didn't feel a salary increase would be forthcoming.

At this point in the meeting, the Board revealed to Don Mason that during the week they had decided to set his salary for the next year at $12,000. They emphasized that he would be receiving $900 increase in addition to the regular yearly increment of $400. They also emphasized that they expected a lot more cooperation from him in the future.

Mason expressed his thanks for the raise but also expressed his opinion that the teachers should also receive a salary schedule increase. He then rose to leave. As he was leaving he heard one member of the Board whisper, "Boy, talk about ungrateful!"

At the next Board meeting, Mason had arranged for members of the Teachers' Welfare Committee to meet before the Board in an effort to convince the board members of the necessity of a salary schedule raise and that the means for the raise were accessible. After the presentation by the committee, the Board said they would consider this information and requested time to verify the data the committee was using. They also expressed their opinion that there was little hope of obtaining raises this year.

Three days later, all the teachers at the high school received notification of a special faculty meeting to be held immediately after school for the purpose of discussing recent events in the negotiations of salary increases.

As some of the teachers met in the hall on the way to the meeting, Teacher G was asked if he knew what was going on. He replied, "I don't know for sure, but Bob Lane said it was 'something big' and for everyone to be sure to attend."

Teacher H: Maybe we're going to get our raise after all!

Teacher G: Not a chance! You know as well as I do the Board isn't going to let Don tell them what they should do. Something else must be in the air.

As Bob Lane, the vice-principal, called the meeting to order, some of the teachers were commenting on the absence of Principal Don Mason.

Bob Lane: I think everyone is here now. We've called this special meeting because we think that you should know exactly what has been going on during the past few days. Apparently Don has pushed the Board a little too hard for salary increases for the teachers. The night before last one of the board members called me at my home around 9:00 and asked me if I could come over to his house. When I arrived, three of the board members were there to greet me. They asked how I liked my job as an administrator in the high school and I told them I really enjoyed my work here. Then they asked me if I would like to be principal of the high school next year with a nice increase in salary. [Several oh's and ah's were heard in the group.] All I could think of was: What about Don? I asked them if Don had quit and they said, "No, but we aren't going to offer him a contract for next year." [Looks of astonishment and surprise appeared on many faces as a few teachers leaned over and whispered to each other.]

When I asked them why they weren't offering Don a contract, they said it was personal and they didn't want to discuss it with anyone. Well, I didn't hesitate to tell them if they didn't offer Don a contract for next year, they needn't offer me one either because I wouldn't sign it. Now I think this is information that you should know. I think Don finds himself in this position because of his efforts to help you teachers. If there is any way that you can support Don in his fight, I certainly think you should, and I know that he would welcome your help.

At this point Bob Lane left the room and Teacher P, the president of

the High School Teachers' Association, took over the meeting. The room was filled with loud talk and excitement.

Teacher P: May I have your attention, please! I know that this is quite an unexpected turn of events. It surprised me as much as it did you when Bob explained the situation to me about an hour ago. But you haven't heard the whole story yet. Don met with the Board in a special meeting that was called at Don's request last evening. He specifically requested reasons for his dismissal, but the Board said they did not have to give any reasons for their actions.

Contracts will be offered on the first of May — that's about ten days away. What can we do to help Don?

Teacher D: (jumping up excitedly): Well, I'll tell you one thing! If they fire Don they can find a replacement for me too. I don't want to work for a Board that can fire someone without any reason other than disagreeing with them.

Teacher E: I have no ties here. The main reason I stay is because I like to teach under Don and Bob. If they go, I'll go too, and I'd like to see the rest of you do the same.

The faculty meeting continued for another hour. It was determined by secret ballot that approximately 90 percent of the faculty would be able and willing to support Principal Mason in the following manner: If Don Mason was not offered a contract, the teachers would not sign their contracts. It was also decided that this information should be conveyed to the Board immediately.

On May 1, the teachers received their contracts in sealed envelopes. Also in each mailbox was a mimeographed note saying Don Mason had not received a contract. All contracts were to be returned to the Board of Trustees by May 15.

During the next two weeks the following appeared in the local newspaper:

Dear Editor:

I read in *The Daily Times* this evening that Mr. Don Mason has requested four times a statement from the school board as to why his contract was not renewed as principal of the Aspen High School.

I do not know much about civil law, but I do know of a moral law that reads: "Do unto others as you wish them to do unto you." Any person who has been employed in a school system whether principal or teacher for a period of years is definitely entitled, as a matter of courtesy, to be given an explanation as to why his contract is not renewed.

I feel this very unjust to the man and the teachers as a whole. No teacher can feel secure under an administration of this caliber. I think the public should demand an explanation. Any innocent member of the school board who sits back and lets this go on is as guilty as the rest.

Sincerely,
A parent

The following letter was signed by approximately one fourth of the 650 students at Aspen High School.

Dear Editor:

What is the school board trying to do by dismissing Mr. Mason without giving any reasons? We feel that Mr. Mason has done an excellent job of building up our high school.

We have been told that better than 90 percent of our teachers have refused to sign their contracts for the coming year. This would result in drastic conditions for our school system. If this happens our school could possibly become a nonaccredited school. This could pose many problems for the seniors planning to attend college.

Parents! Are we the only ones concerned about these problems?

A citizens committee had been formed to investigate the current school "crisis." This committee had requested the investigating services of Dr. Williams, an executive from the State Education Association. A special meeting was held at which Dr. Williams reported his initial findings to the Citizens Committee. The newspaper printed the following as part of the report of that meeting:

It was stated during the meeting that there has been a complete breakdown of the communications between teachers, administrators, and school board members, thus creating a crisis in the education system. There has been unwillingness on the part of the school board, it was said, to discuss the situations as they arise with the persons involved. In addition. . . .

Dr. Williams stated that he had checked with attorneys on such a problem and he was now certain that a school board has the right to refuse to give new contracts to teachers without having to give an explanation of the refusal. However, to prevent the type of breakdown that now exists here, that person should be called in and an explanation given as to the cause for action.

Five days prior to May 15, the date the contracts had to be returned to the Board, the local paper printed the following in its editorial column:

This week appears to be the week of decision, for the contracts are supposed to be returned to the school board within five days. The Board is apparently counting upon most of the good teachers signing up by the deadline.

Thinking on the basis of the present situation and eliminating what is already "water under the bridge," there seem to be three things that could happen: (1) the school board could reverse its deci-

sion regarding the principal, or (2) the teachers could decide they want their jobs even more than they want victory in this strange fight, or (3) the board and the teachers could remain adamant and the board could attempt to recruit as many new teachers as needed.

THE PRODUCTION DEPARTMENT

CASE 2

KCDE-TV is one of two television stations in Tuttle, a city of 100,000 population, with a metropolitan area of 175,000.

KCDE-TV (and radio) for some time had serious morale problems, especially in the television production department. KCDE employed 85 people in six departments: general office; data processing; news; engineering; radio; and television production. The television production group formed the single largest department, about 20 people. The functional areas of the production department are: announcing; directing; switching; camera operating; and video-

tape operating. See Exhibit 1 for description of these functions.

As is the case with many small to medium-sized stations, KCDE was looked upon as a training ground by many members of both management and staff. This was a reason offered by management on occasion for not granting a raise to an employee. It was suggested to the employee that if he wished to remain at KCDE he had better accept his present wage as the maximum for the foreseeable future. He then would find it necessary to move on to a bigger city if he expected to be paid more for the same job. The turnover, especially in the radio and production departments, was high.

Each employee negotiated his own salary with management since there was no union representation. There were no published salary ranges, but staff members knew that approximate ranges in 1970 were as follows:

Announcers	$850–950/mo.
Directors	850–925
Switchers	775–825
Video Tape Operators	750–825
Cameramen	700–750

The salaries were based on a 48-hour, six day week. Much conversation among the crew members centered around what they all agreed was a low pay scale. As one of the crew members put it regularly in conversation: "No where else can you work a six-day week, a night shift, and virtually every holiday for such lousy money."

Benefits were another sore point. The company made group insurance available, but there was no retirement program. Though providing paid vacations, the company paid the vacationing employee for two 40-hour weeks. The two-week paycheck then was less by sixteen hours of overtime what the employee was accustomed to.

Working conditions with regard to physical comfort and safety were adequate and about average for the industry.

It was a common feeling among the crew members that they were being "used" to one degree or another by management. The men knew that many general office workers for the city's major private employers and the state government were making more money than they, working better hours and shorter weeks. Adding salt to the wound was the feeling that the television job required infinitely more creative ability than the general office worker needed or had. At the same time, most felt their jobs were intrinsically interesting, and far more challenging than office or administrative work.

Great animosity was directed toward the assistant general manager of the station. His previous post was chief engineer of the station, where he was

---

Announcers are responsible for performing live commercials and programs, and for providing audio recordings for locally produced slide, film and video tape commercials. Since the work load is variable, they typically have other duties, e.g., writing commercial copy, or reading news for the radio station.

The director is ostensibly the most creative member of the crew. He is responsible for the "on-air" presentation. He either recommends a set for a commercial or program, or approves an idea presented by some other member of the crew. During the actual broadcast or recording session, the director is in charge of all activities.

The switcher, sometimes referred to as the technical director, performs the physical operations at the control board required to put various video sources on the air, and to mix the sources at the director's command. He also is responsible for loading slides and film on the various projectors.

The video-tape operator loads and "cues" video tapes on the video tape machines for the playback of commercials and programs on the air. He also sets-up the machines for the recording of commercials and programs. The video tape machines are extremely complicated and quite difficult to operate, requiring a practiced touch for trouble-free operation.

The cameramen operate the large studio cameras moving them on the director's cue and selecting the shots the director asks for. The cameramen do the actual construction of the sets, and do most of the lighting, sometimes under the direct supervision of the director.

An additional member of the operating crew is an engineer, who is not a member of the production department. He is expected to provide technical advice to the director. His primary responsibility however, is the maintenance of the expensive, complicated electronic gear.

EXHIBIT 1

tagged with the nickname "Overkill" by some members of the engineering department. This name was inspired by his tendency to over-react to situations. On one occasion he had fired an employee for smoking in the television control room. Though parts of the studio and control areas were posted against smoking, members of the staff looked upon this regulation as trivial. Care was taken not to smoke only when the assistant general manager was in the immediate area.

More than once, "Overkill" threatened to have a vital piece of equipment removed, ". . . unless you guys take better care of it." The threats were obviously hollow, since the station couldn't operate without the equipment. He had been heard to refer to the operating crew and the engineering department, or various members as "coolies."

The leader of the production department itself was not spared the crew's wrath. Every member of the crew looked upon Gary Brown, the production supervisor, as, as one of the switchers put it, "a miserable, two-timing s.o.b." More than one of the men had had the experience of making a request for a raise, only to find some weeks later that the production supervisor had "forgotten to take it up," or to be counseled that "this just isn't the right time to ask." It had been observed by everyone in the production staff that Gary often delivered different versions of a story to upper management than he gave to his subordinates. It was generally felt that he always sided with management, especially "Overkill," rather than backing his subordinates.

The general manager of the station, Gordon Frederick, was a retired military officer and an ex-mayor of the city. He was active in political causes and was out of town frequently, leaving the day-to-day operation of the station to the assistant general manager. Most of the staff members looked upon Frederick as being a slightly befuddled autocrat since he conducted regular "inspections" when in the building, and indulged a fetish for small detail, such as seeing that the flags were removed from the flagpole in front of the building promptly at sunset. He was responsible for, and for the most part the author of, a booklet of company rules and regulations called the Blue Book. In the Blue Book were voluminous descriptions of each job title within the organization, and page upon page of rules pertaining to coffee breaks, use of company telephones, and virtually every other activity within the building.

The Blue Book was treated with varying degrees of contempt by most staff members, and with utter contempt by the production department. Those who had been in the military service insisted parts of the Blue Book text were lifted wholesale from military manuals. It was felt that the book's only value was to management, in that some obscure regulation could be used to chastise an employee, while other rules were totally ignored. For example, the Blue Book stated that the company had a policy against members of the same family being employed. However, Overkill's son Steve worked as a full-time cameraman, one of the director's wives worked in the office, and the husband of the TV Program director served as a technician.

The Blue Book also contained rules for communication between departments, the management feeling being that the rank and file of one department should not communicate directly with their counterparts in other departments in matters of operations. For example, if a newsman became upset at a cameraman, director, or any other member of the production staff in connection with a newscast, he was to inform the news director, who would then take the matter up with the production supervisor. This rule was totally ignored.

Though the Blue Book delineated a very rigid chain of command, it was fairly common for orders to the production crew to come from "Overkill," the program director or Brown, the production supervisor. On occasion, in the case of an equipment failure or similar emergency, these orders would conflict, resulting in confusion until the three decided upon a common plan.

Job security was felt to be nonexistent. Many of the workers felt directly threatened by "Overkill" and verbally expressed their fear of his capricious behavior.

Seemingly arbitrary changes of shift upset some of the men. In early Spring of 1970, one of the directors was moved to the position of video tape operator. Though his salary was left at its old level, this move involved a real loss of prestige. No explanation was given to members of the crew. A cameraman was promoted directly to the position of director, by-passing several switchers. Again, there was no explanation.

Sabotage, in the name of "games," became quite common among the operating crew. It was not too unusual for a film projector to be mis-threaded, causing the film to be be torn to ribbons when the projector was started, result-

ing in program down-time. Program sets would occasionally topple over during a video taping session, or microphones would refuse to work. One favorite trick was the tripping of master light breakers for the control room areas. Another was pounding on the wall of an area where an announceer was on the air. One of the more ingenious acts involved the wiring of a prop telephone on the tv news set. The phone was then rung during a newscast, causing the newsman to "break up." Though members of management never appeared to suspect sabotage, its occurrence was by no means rare.

Also in the Spring of 1970, Ron E., an announcer, came to work for KCDE radio. The television and radio control areas were adjacent to one another, and some of the announcers worked both radio and television. There was a great deal of social contact between employees of both sides.

At the end of his first pay period, Ron became tremendously upset. His check totaled about $50 less for the two week period than he thought it would be. According to Ron, the radio station manager had hired him at $900 a month, but his first check was paid at the rate of $800 a month. Ron promptly complained to his supervisor, and the matter was taken to the general manager. He informed Ron that the radio station manager did not have the authority to hire an announcer at such a salary as Ron had been promised. There was no offer to compromise on the salary. Frederick offered to pay Ron's moving expenses back to the city he had left just weeks before. Ron's answer was; "And what the hell am I supposed to do for a job if I do return?" Feeling he had no choice, Ron accepted the lower salary.

In May, about a month after the salary episode, Ron began questioning other employees about the possibility of unionizing the station. His idea was met with great enthusiasm by the members of the production department. More than one of them indicated that though they did not like unions, they liked the management of KCDE even less. The few holdouts expressed fear for their jobs, but no one expressed any pro-management thoughts.

Several meetings were held with union representatives and the union formally notified Mr. Frederick of their intention to organize the production department. This action was met with disbelief on the part of Frederick, fol-lowed soon by a meeting to stress to employees that "the door is always open, and you know we're interested in your problems." Union "horror" stories soon followed, accompanied by a frigid atmosphere and veiled threats by both sides. Rumor generation reached very high levels.

In early August, Ron E. was fired for "inattention to duties." He filed an unfair labor practices suit against the station management with the National Labor Relations Board. The filing of the suit served to freeze the unionization proceedings until the suit was resolved.

In the meantime, Frederick, Brown and "Overkill" turned to a well known management consulting firm for help in analysis of the organizational and personnel problems.

EXERCISE 1

OPERATION EXURBIA

INTRODUCTION

Operation Exurbia is designed to give you an opportunity to participate in a complex situation involving a great deal of interaction among
competing teams, each striving to accomplish a specific objective. In
the process of interaction, you will have an opportunity to experience:

1. Leadership patterns
2. Group decision making
3. Group behavior under varying conditions
4. Interaction patterns among competing groups

In addition, you will have the opportunity to analyze your individual behavior as a member of a group engaged in a complex task.

PROCEDURE

Read the following material concerning Operation Exurbia. After you
have finished doing this, your instructor will give you some specific
directions and information about the objectives of your team and the
resources you have available to you to achieve these resources.

As of this time, the city of Exurbia, Ohio, is growing in many ways — its
population is increasing, its geographic limits are expanding, and there is
an increase in manufacturing and trading activity. On the north side of the
city, there is a tract of land which remains undeveloped, even though the
area surrounding it has been developed with homes, businesses, and certain recreational facilities.

Ten years ago, Mr. Raymond Sherman, owner of this tract, divided it
into twenty sections, and offered these for sale. There was an immediate
demand, and all twenty sections were sold within 2 years. While there were
some buyers who later resold their sections, the ownership of the various
sections as of this time is held by five business firms:

The Blue Manufacturing Company, a growing firm producing automotive
parts

The Highway Developers Corporation, a real estate firm which buys and
sells land

White Home Developers, Inc., a construction company which buys land, constructs residential homes and sells them to the public

Shopping Centers, Inc., a company which constructs a cluster of stores in a shopping center, and then either rents or sells them to a retail business

Orange Investors Corp., a company which invests funds of wealthy individuals in agriculture, industry or industrial real estate

Each of these companies is interested in the former Sherman Estate. They not only own property there now, but they wish to buy and/or sell such property, in order to improve their positions.

Each group begins the exercise with a statement of its present position, its goals or objectives, deeds to each piece of land owned, and, in some cases, specified amounts of money. This information will be provided by the instructor. From this point on, each group must depend on its own resources in attempting to accomplish its stated objectives. A unique feature of Operation Exurbia is that each group must "live with" decisions which it has made and base future considerations upon past actions.

The following ground rules should be fully understood before beginning the exercise.

1. All plots are equal in land area and desirability. Mountains and swamps have a way of appearing when this factor is not pre-established.
2. There is no problem in gaining access to any plots. Easements are assured. There are no air rights for any plots.
3. Full plots must be sold or traded. A portion of a plot cannot be sold or traded.
4. Plots cannot be leased.
5. Contacts may be made only by one member of a group talking to one member of another group. When a group desires contact, one representative approaches another group and says, "I would like an appointment." The group contacted then assigns one of their representatives to talk with him. The representatives then retire to designated meeting areas and transact their business only in these areas. Groups are *not* required to grant appointments.
6. A team may be actively negotiating with as many other teams as it chooses at any time providing all meetings are on a one-to-one basis.
7. Members of more than two teams can meet together providing there is only one member from each team at the meeting. For example, it is permissible for five people, each representing a different team to hold a meeting.

Within the framework of these ground rules, groups are free to devise their own plans and to implement those strategies which they believe will be most effective.

Your instructor will give you more information and the materials necessary to start the exercise.

INFORMATION FOR ALL TEAMS

Current ownership of the several plots of ground is as shown on the following map:

A1 Highway Developers Corporation	A2 Orange Investors Corporation	A3 White Home Developers, Incorporated	A4 Highway Developers Corporation
B1 White Home Developers, Incorporated	B2 Blue Manufacturing Company	B3 Orange Investors Corporation	B4 Blue Manufacturing Company
C1 Orange Investors Corporation	C2 Shopping Centers, Incorporated	C3 Highway Developers Corporation	C4 Orange Investors Corporation
D1 Blue Manufacturing Company	D2 Orange Investors Corporation	D3 White Home Developers, Incorporated	D4 Orange Investors Corporation
E1 Blue Manufacturing Company	E2 Shopping Centers, Incorporated	E3 Blue Manufacturing Company	E4 Shopping Centers, Incorporated

SPORTSWEAR, INCORPORATED

INTRODUCTION

Sportswear, Incorporated, is an example of a typical conflict situation found in organizations. In this particular instance, problems of production, shipping, and inventory have reached the point that the manager in charge has called a meeting of those involved. Many of these people hold viewpoints that are in conflict. The manager is under great pressure to achieve some sort of resolution of the situation.

PROCEDURE

Your instructor will give you specific instructions for this exercise. Do not proceed further until you have received these instructions.

Sportswear, Incorporated is a manufacturer of several types of outdoor clothing for men and women, including ski jackets and parkas, special jackets and coats for hunting and fishing, and a line of casual coats and jackets designed to appeal to the high school and college student. The activities of Sportswear are fairly well confined to the western part of the United States, although the company does have one sales representative in the midwestern states.

Although Sportswear has been in business for over forty-five years, it wasn't until the end of World War II that it really began to do well and its line of jackets and coats began to receive popular acceptance. Until the mid-1960's manufacture of coats and jackets was fairly routine. At that time, however, fashion and style became increasingly important in outer wear, especially in ski clothing and casual coats and jackets. Somewhat to its surprise, the company found that it had people on its staff with definite skills in fashion and design, and building on these skills, Sportswear has enjoyed great success and has grown and expanded considerably.

With growth, however, has come a certain amount of difficulty. One of the current problems bothering Jess Robinson, executive vice president, concerns delivery of merchandise to customers. The current situation involves ski jackets, but the same kind of problem has arisen before with other lines.

Because many of the items in the Sportswear line are fashion items, the company is very cautious regarding production and inventory levels for each one. If, for example, quilted ski jackets with a mosaic pattern do not become popular and production on these jackets has been high, Sportswear may find itself in the undesirable position of having a large inventory of these jackets on hand for which there is little market demand. Such inventory would probably have to be sold at a loss. On the other hand, if an item becomes "hot" on the market, Sportswear may find itself unable to meet promptly the demands of its customers for this item, even though production of the items is immediately increased.

Most of the 1300 stores and shops who handle Sportswear products customarily order a few of each item in the line. If an item does become popular, they immediately reorder — often by telephone or wire — to meet their demand. As many of the items are seasonal, speed in filling these orders is imperative. Often, however, a waiting period of four to five weeks is involved before delivery on reorders can be made. During this period pressure for quick delivery becomes intense. Customers call anyone and everyone at Sportswear who they think can help their cause. The nine salesmen of Sportswear, who are paid partially on a commission basis, attempt to have their orders filled as soon as possible and go to great lengths to achieve speedy delivery, even to the point of resubmitting orders with the notation "RUSH" or "URGENT," or when they are in town visiting the factory to attempt to put pressure on the production people to work on their orders first.

The result of such pressure is confusion and even more delay. With duplicate orders on hand, no one knows what the level of demand for an item really is. The production people become incensed at the activities of the salesmen attempting to push their orders through the factory, and customers become irritable and complain because they cannot meet the demands of their customers.

In an attempt to resolve this problem, Jess Robinson has called a meeting of the following individuals: Ross Bennett, production manager; Willis Patten, sales manager; Warren Harte, shipping and inventory control manager; and Douglas Kraft, credit manager.

This exercise concerns these individuals and Mike Hodgson, midwestern sales representative of Sportswear.

Role for Jess Robinson, Executive Vice President

You have called a meeting of several of your people to discuss the problem of delivery on customer reorders and are now on your way to the conference room, where the meeting will be held. You have been tied up on the phone and are a few minutes late, so you expect that everyone will already be there.

The problem, in a nutshell, is that there seems to be no system or priorities for receiving, producing, and shipping reorders — especially on "hot" items. The customer may order a few of several items in the line, find one or two which go over big, order more, and then have to wait four or five weeks for delivery. Because of the seasonal factor, a time lag of four or five weeks can affect total sales significantly.

To compound the problem, your salesmen put pressure on the production people and resubmit the same order several times in an attempt to get their orders filled first. Then, too, customers complain. You have had five calls today from nervous customers concerning their orders.

The easy way to resolve the problem, of course, would be to increase production on all items, but that would involve too large an investment in inventory and too large a risk on those items which didn't sell well.

Something has to be worked out today, for the situation can't continue as it is.

Role for Ross Bennett, Production Manager

You're glad that this meeting has been called because the problem of pressure from salesmen has plagued you for a long time. What they don't realize is that you are six to seven months ahead of them. They're worried about ski jackets now, but you've already started production on the spring line of jackets and fishing stuff.

You're willing to help in any way that you can, but people have to realize that if you really go to work on ski jackets now, the spring line won't be ready on time. You've got to take your instructions for additional production of current stuff from the inventory control people.

One thing you will insist on, though, is that all salesmen are barred from the factory — permanently. As you've told Jess Robinson, things have just gotten out of hand. Why, the salesman from the Midwest was in the factory for several hours today, trying to get his orders pushed through first.

Role for Douglas Kraft, Credit Manager

You're glad that Mr. Robinson has called this meeting, for with the confusion that exists your work is made all the more difficult. One of your main jobs is to see that all incoming orders are checked to determine if the credit status of the customer is O.K. Bad debts have been a problem in the past, but you can control them if you check each order. If a customer's record is not good, you can refuse to ship the order to him or demand full payment before the order leaves the plant.

When the pressure is on, however, you sometimes find that your people are having to go through the process of checking credit several times on what appears to be the same order. And salesmen are not above taking an order right to the factory if they think they can get away with it by by-passing your operation entirely.

Every order must be checked to see that the customer's credit standing is satisfactory.

Role for Warren Harte, Shipping and Inventory Control Manager

Well, perhaps this meeting will result in getting some of the pressure off your department. During the past week you bet that your people have received over two hundred calls wanting to know if a certain order has been shipped yet.

What people don't realize is that you can't just ship orders without a certain amount of processing. You are responsible for control of an inventory valued at $450,000 and you can't run an operation that size without some kind of system. Each order must be checked against paper inventory and physical inventory before it is shipped. If you are low on an item, or completely out, you've got to tell the production people to get to work on it. But you can't do this until the necessary paper work is completed. The duplicate orders you have been receiving lately confuse things terribly.

Your people in shipping are all good people who work hard. Maybe this meeting will be a chance to press for those two new fork-lift trucks they have been wanting. They won't solve the problem, but they should help a great deal in getting orders out once the paper work has been done. You estimate that the new fork-lift trucks will cost about $10,000.

Role for Willis Patten, Sales Manager

Well, you suppose Jess Robinson is going to jump down your throat at this meeting. Every time you get under pressure, everyone blames the Sales Department. They don't realize that sales are the only thing that keep the company going.

You're proud of the sales growth the company has experienced and feel that it is due in large measure to the enthusiasm of your salesmen. Sure, they might get a little out of hand at times, but salesmen who didn't press for their orders wouldn't be worth having. And you can appreciate that your men are paid on commission, too.

People don't realize that repeat orders and customer service are the foundation of the business. Anything and everything should be done to keep the customers happy.

Mike Hodgson, your man who handles midwestern sales, happens to be in town today. You have asked him to attend the meeting because you feel that he can present a picture of what really happens in the field. You're not sure that he knows everyone who will be there.

Role for Mike Hodgson, Midwestern Sales Representative

Will Patten, your boss, has asked you to attend a meeting to discuss the problem of delivery on customer orders. You're not sure who will be there, but as you understand it, he hopes that you will be able to provide a picture of what happens in the field as the result of late delivery to customers.

You will be glad to do that. This problem of late delivery on reorders is especially difficult for you, because you don't get a chance to get back to the factory to push for your orders as often as the other salesmen who are located closer to the home office. And it really burns you up when you have a good customer like, for example, The Campus Shop at the state university which is waiting and waiting for orders to arrive. Then you find that some little clothing store on the West Coast got delivery in two weeks. You realize that everyone can't get their orders at the same time, but something should be done to make sure that the big, steady customers get prompt service. You can tell a little guy that he won't get delivery for a while and he has to take it. A big customer won't. You try to see your big customers about every three weeks and it's embarrassing if their orders haven't come in.

It's more than embarrassing for, if a big customer cancels an order, you may lose a fat commission and the chance to sell your other lines. Right now you have three big orders waiting for delivery and you have spent a good deal of time over in the factory today trying to get them speeded up. You've got to take advantage of your infrequent visits to the home office to do what you can for your customers.

You'll be glad to tell them what it's like in the field!

PART 8

CHANGE IN ORGANIZATIONS

In recent years increasing attention has been paid to the processes of organizational change. Change, planned or unplanned, will occur in all organizations. Thus, it is not a question of whether the organization will change but rather a question of when and how the change will occur.

Many writers in both academic circles and the popular press assert that changes occur ever more rapidly in our society. This implies that organization change will also become more frequent, and interest is increasing in the management of change. The management of change includes the process of anticipating changes in the organization's internal and external environments and effecting a smooth adaptation to those changes. Management must recognize that while most resources need to be devoted to current activities, a portion must be directed toward planning for the future. Structure and management control systems should encourage the development of new ideas. Management of the innovative organization anticipates changes in the environment rather than waiting for such changes to occur and then reacting to them. Paradoxically, organizations that are very successful often hesitate to initiate change since they perceive little to gain and much to lose by tampering with processes that have proved successful.

Consider the many different environmental conditions that each organization faces and how changes in those conditions may require corresponding organizational change. Every business firm faces a competitive environment, composed of other firms in the same industry, as well as firms in industries that produce substitute products. Changes in the activities of competitors can clearly require change in a firm. The general economic environment faced by the firm and industry is also in a process of constant change, while the sociopolitical environment often creates the need for change with the addition of new statutes or legal limitations on the conduct of business. The characteristics of customers or clients must also be considered as they change over time. As the nature of the work force changes, so too will many of the structural aspects of the organization, and of course changes in technology may require substantial change in the processes of the enterprise.

Increasingly, planning for change is becoming an important task for the individual manager. Although planning for total organizational change is a job for top-level management, as a first- or mid-level manager, you will find it necessary to effect and manage change within your own group. Some of the necessity for change will come from other parts of the organization, but the nature of your task and the nature of the people you supervise will also change over time and will require that you respond to those changes.

The first reading in this chapter, "Planned Organizational Change," by Larry Short, presents a model for orderly change. You will note references to a person called a *change agent.* The change agent is typically an outside consultant trained in the behavioral sciences, who assists the organization in its change process. The outside change agent is desirable and perhaps even necessary when contemplating substantial organizational change, but the individual manager must also try to develop skills that will allow him or her to function as a change agent within his or her own section of the organization. The model presented by Short will help you become aware of the forces acting upon the organization and different methods of effecting change. It will also give you a framework for the implementation of change.

Paul Lawrence, in "How to Deal with Resistance to Change," points out that much resistance stems from social factors rather than from dislike of technical changes per se. He also dramatizes the problem of the self-fulfilling prophecy. That is, if management assumes that there will be resistance, they will tend to select an implementation strategy that will *cause* resistance! Lawrence then describes some of the most common mistakes of management in directing change. It is important for each of us to guard against the most common errors. Avoiding problems is generally easier than solving problems.

Finally, in "Planning and Implementing Change," Hersey and Blanchard discuss the relationship between performance and development. They argue that emphasizing only immediate output is a mistake because that emphasis neglects development for the future.

The concept of force field analysis is introduced by the authors as a technique for developing strategies for change. After you read the force field description, you should analyze the potential for change in your own work situation. How might you aid the process by using the "unfreezing-changing-refreezing" model presented in this article?

Change is a part of our personal life as well as our professional life, and we can either manage the forces of change or be managed by them. The choice is ours.

PLANNED ORGANIZATIONAL CHANGE

Larry E. Short

The rapidity of new developments in our modern society necessitates that change become a way of life for most large organizations.[1] Although change within an organization can be either planned or unplanned, management is primarily concerned with the accomplishment of planned change which will be purposeful and beneficial to the organization. *Planned organizational change* can be defined as any planned program that results in significant alterations of the behavior of individuals or groups within the organization in a direction desired by management. Typically, planned organizational change programs are directed toward increasing some element of organizational effectiveness.

The study of planned organizational change is a relatively new field, and behavioral scientists from several disciplines have combined their efforts in its development. Jeremiah J. O'Connell notes:

Psychologists, social psychologists and sociologists laid the theoretical foundation some years ago, beginning with developments in knowledge about the dynamics of change in individuals (learning models, attitude change models and group dynamics) and moving to improved knowledge about group dynamics. An eagerness among some social scientists not only to understand human phenomena but to influence human affairs moved some of these practitioners more deeply into the area of organizational change.[2]

These developments in the dynamics of individual and group behavior have greatly aided organizational theorists in recent work on change in hierarchical systems.

The field of planned change in hierarchical systems typically involves the study of elements such as the change agent, the change process, strategies of planned change, and the introduction of planned change into an organization. This article presents a simple conceptual model for planned organizational change and examines the behavioral, technological, and structural approaches to applied organizational change with particular emphasis on the latter.[3] A summary of some of the elementary concepts of planned change in hierarchical systems is presented to facilitate the integration of the various elements of applied organizational change into an overall conceptual model.

Warren G. Bennis defines planned change as ". . . a deliberate and collaborative process involving a change agent and client system."[4] The change agent calls upon his knowledge of the behav-

From *MSU Business Topics,* Autumn 1973, pp. 53–61. Reprinted by permission of the publisher, Division of Research, Graduate School of Business Administration, Michigan State University.

ioral sciences in affecting organizational change. Bennis postulates that the process of organizational change pivots on interpersonal and group relationships and the implications of these for change in the technology, structure, and task of the organization.[5]

The basic planning premises of the change agent are influenced by the change agent's perception of his actual or expected role in the organization, his personal value orientation or focus, and his familiarity with and propensity to use various intervention strategies. Bennis views the change agent as participator in a variety of collaborative roles in the organization, for example, as researcher, trainer, consultant, and counselor. The intervention strategies used by the people-oriented change agents employ a number of behaviorally oriented techniques (for example, sensitivity training, managerial grid, and so forth) to obtain a set of normative goals. Concepts such as values, norms, interpersonal relationships, group problem solving, and organizational climate play an integral part in the selection and implementation of intervention strategies.[6]

O'Connell views the planning premises of a change agent with a slightly different perspective. Role, focus, and intervention strategies are not restricted to a behavioral orientation, but may fall somewhere on a continuum from one extreme to another. The role of the change agent may fall along a unilateral-collaborative continuum, that is, the change agent may view his role as boss with absolute authority and responsibility for making and implementing decisions or as a partnership collaborating jointly with other employees in deciding on solutions to problems. The focus may fall along a continuum of human-economic values. On one end of the continuum is the desire to maximize human benefits within present financial constraints and on the other end is the desire to maximize economic returns within present human resource constraints. Intervention strategies may be visualized on a continuum ranging from the changing of behavioral patterns of people to the changing of external forces which constitute individual role demands.[7] The change agent will select an appropriate position on each planning premise continuum which will accomplish the planned change program required of his particular organization.

An organization can usefully be viewed as a multivariate system consisting of four interacting variables: *task, structure, technology* and *human element.* Planned organizational change programs can be directed toward three of the interacting organizational variables. Since the basic task of the organization (that is, manufacturing, transportation, education, and so forth) is assumed as given, change programs are not usually developed to modify organizational *task.* Therefore, the change agent can select intervention strategies designed to change either the *structure* of the organization, the *technology* of the organization, or the *human element* operating within the organization. According to Harold J. Leavitt, *structure* refers to the systems of communication, systems of authority (or other roles), and systems of workflow; *technology* refers to the technical tools and problem solving inventions like work measurement, computers, and so forth; and *human element* refers to the people in the organization. (Harold J. Leavitt notes some uncertainty about the line between structure and technology.) Specific intervention strategies can be developed and directed toward the modification of any one or all of these variables.[8]

Larry G. Greiner, through a comprehensive survey of studies on organizational change, identifies methods most frequently used by managers to introduce planned changes in an organization. He categorizes these methods under three alternative uses of power and suggests that the actual introduction of change in an organization can be conceptualized along a "power distribution" continuum. At one extreme of the continuum are those methods which rely on unilateral authority to accomplish change. Such methods include a "one way" announcement of change, replacement of key individuals, or modification of the structure of organizational relationships. Toward the middle of the continuum are the shared power methods which include utilization of group decisions or group problem solving. Finally, at the opposite extreme of the continuum are the delegated power methods which include such tactics as data presentation and discussion and sensitivity training. Greiner concludes that the method used to introduce change into the organization must appropriately "fit" the elements of people, organization, and task for the particular organization.[9]

Kurt Lewin postulates that the overall process of change (regardless of how it is introduced or at what it is directed) must follow a general pattern. All successful change programs must progress through three distinct stages: unfreezing, changing, and refreezing.[10] The unfreezing stage of the change program requires the "thawing out" of preconditioned behavioral and attitudinal patterns. The unfreezing process must create a need within the employee to reject old behavioral patterns and a desire to adopt new ones. The changing stage introduces the actual change program into the organization and develops new operational patterns. Employees are taught new patterns of behavior and are given experience in practicing the new behavioral patterns. The refreezing stage "firms-up" new behavioral and attitudinal patterns in order that organizational or social forces which now exist will not counteract the planned change program. Special organizational forces often must be established to refreeze employees into the new behavioral patterns.

Figure 1 provides a representation of a conceptual model for planned organizational change showing the overall relationships of the general elements previously discussed. As shown in Figure 1, the forces instigating change and the change agent's perception of his role and focus influence his selection of intervention strategies. To ensure that the particular intervention strategy selected to accomplish a planned change program is successful, the change agent must carefully develop the program to accommodate all stages of the process of change and appropriately introduce the change program into the organization. The actual organizational change that takes place will contribute to organization effectiveness and affect the total environment and influence any subsequent change efforts.

INTERVENTION STRATEGIES

Selection of an appropriate intervention strategy is critical to the success of the organizational planned change program. The intervention strategies available to a change agent for designing a program of planned change in a hierarchical system consist of strategies intended to alter the technology of the system, the human element in the organization, or the structural relationships within the organization. These intervention strategies are titled the technological, behavioral, and structural approaches respectively.

Technological Approach

The technological approach to planned change utilizes technical and scientific knowledge to bring about a desired change and thereby improve organizational efficiency. Typically, change programs are directed at specific organizational tasks or the interaction of man with these tasks and emphasize the methodological study of these variables. The scientific management movement has greatly facilitated the development and maturation of a rather extensive body of knowledge directed specifically at technological innovations in organizations.

The technological approach to planned change is involved with the extensive study of at least three basic areas in the organization: machine improvement, man-job relationships, and job-job coordination. First, new or improved machines are sought to ease the burden of man and increase his personal productivity. Benefits of utilizing new or better machines to accomplish higher productivity are readily evident everywhere in a modern industrialized society. Replacement of animal power with machine power, the utilization of high speed, special purpose hand tools, and the utilization of automatic data processing equipment are only a few of the many examples one may point to in proving the effectiveness of this approach in improving organizational efficiency. The basic concept of either replacing man with machines or providing man with mechanical or electronic tools to make his job easier and faster has greatly increased the individual productivity of man.

The second approach to technological change involves the comprehensive study of the actual work of man and the physical environment in which he works in an effort to increase the individual efficiency of a man on a given job. This approach is often accomplished through utilizing such techniques as motion and time study, methods analysis, and so forth. Industrial engineers have classified the basic divisions of work into fundamental motions and developed rather elaborate general principles of motion economy. Utilizing this knowledge, body motions are studied with the objective of eliminating or reducing ineffective movements and facilitating and speeding up effective movements. Utilization and sophistication of these techniques by disciples of the scientific management movement have resulted in tremendous improvements in man-job efficiency.

The third approach to technological change concerns the study of the rela-

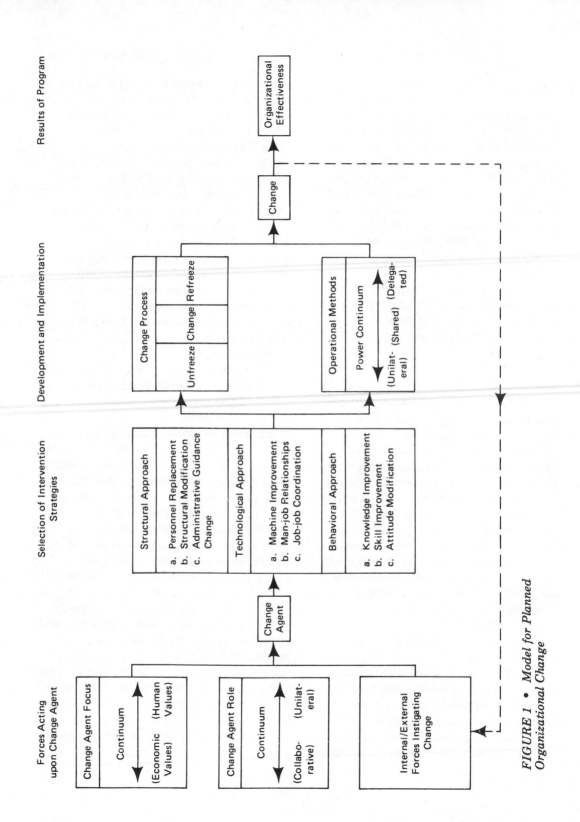

Forces Acting
upon Change Agent

Selection of Intervention
Strategies

Development and Implementation

Results of Program

Change Agent Focus

Continuum

(Economic
Values)

(Human
Values)

Change Agent Role

Continuum

(Collabo-
rative)

(Unilat-
eral)

Internal/External
Forces Instigating
Change

Change Agent

Structural Approach

a. Personnel Replacement
b. Structural Modification
c. Administrative Guidance
   Change

Technological Approach

a. Machine Improvement
b. Man-job Relationships
c. Job-job Coordination

Behavioral Approach

a. Knowledge Improvement
b. Skill Improvement
c. Attitude Modification

Change Process

Unfreeze Change Refreeze

Operational Methods

Power Continuum

(Unilat-
eral)

(Shared)

(Delega-
ted)

Change

Organizational
Effectiveness

FIGURE 1 • Model for Planned
Organizational Change

tionships of the various jobs in an organization through the utilization of such techniques as operation analysis, flow process analysis, plant location, and others. The modern day assembly line is an excellent example of the efficiencies that can be accomplished through the careful study of the relationships of various jobs and the utilization of this information to improve overall coordination.

Only recently have some of the techniques utilized in the technological approaches to planned change come under attack as being counterproductive. This does not imply that the techniques are no longer useful, only that the utilization of certain of these techniques may have reached a point of diminishing return in our present society. For example, the Hawthorne Studies revealed that the social environment of the organization often must be considered when technological innovations are considered. More recently, organizations have turned to job enrichment programs to reconstitute man-job and job-job relationships into more meaningful (although sometimes, but not always, less efficient) operations.[11] In addition, a relatively new field of ergonomics is opening which emphasizes interaction between the worker, his job, and his environment.[12]

To summarize, the technological approach to organizational planned change utilizes advances in science and technology to increase the efficiency of the individual worker. The human element in the organization has typically been considered as an inanimate resource to be used up in the productive process. Recently we have begun modifying our basic concepts of technological

efficiencies to accommodate the vital nature of modern man.

Behavioral Approach

The behavioral approach to planned change attempts to change man himself through training and developmental activities. Since human abilities can be categorized into three broad classifications (knowledge, skills, and attitudes) the behavioral approach to planned change is directed toward the modification of these specific abilities.

Organizational programs designed to improve the knowledge or increase the skill level of employees have generally proven quite successful. The significant industrial achievements of the United States during World War II in changing from a depression economy to a highly productive war economy was partially a result of the ability to develop a highly trained workforce in a relatively short period of time. Individuals who had never worked in an industrial setting were quickly transformed into riveters, machine operators, and so forth, through the methodological application of training programs such as Job Instruction Training. Generally, training programs designed to improve knowledge or increase skills of employees have been successful.

Education specialists may argue that actual behavior modification can best be accomplished through the internalization of change. That is, once the attitudinal elements of the individual are modified, the individual's behavioral patterns will also be modified. For example, an argument concerning the implementation of programs to accomplish equality of opportunity in an organization may go as follows:

When racial prejudice is eliminated, the problem of racial discrimination will disappear. A change program which focuses on eliminating overt acts of discrimination is incorrectly directed at the results of the problem (discrimination) rather than its underlying cause (prejudice). Therefore, planned change programs intended to eliminate racial discrimination in an organization must be designed to produce a change in an employee's attitude toward racial prejudice. Once the affective element is modified, the individual will exhibit behavioral patterns which exclude overt acts of discrimination.

However, training programs intended to modify employee attitudes have not been as successful as training programs designed to change employee knowledge and skills. Employee attitudes are not only extremely difficult to change, but attitudes often affect the application of newly learned skills and knowledge to the job. Although there has been some success in modifying employee attitudes through the utilization of such techniques as role playing, simulation, sensitivity training, and so forth, considerable research into the effectiveness of such training suggests that the direct modification of employee attitudes remains as one of the more difficult tasks to accomplish in organizational planned change programs.[13]

The behavioral approaches to planned change attempt to modify the knowledge, skills, or attitudes of man through some formal training or developmental process. Although training and development programs have been successful in increasing employee knowledge and skills, attitudinal modification change programs have not proven completely successful.

Structural Approach

The structural approach to planned change introduces change through the manipulation of organization structural elements such as revised organization charts, new policies and procedures, and others. Since the structural elements in a hierarchical organization actually established the complex system of man-man relationships, organizational and individual expectations, and individual and group role sets and status, the structural approach to planned change attempts to bring about change by modifying this system of roles, relationships, and expectations within the organization.

Organizational theorists have only recently recognized the utility of the structural approach in accomplishing organizational change. While in the past, structure was often considered as only a static element to be optimized, more recently we have recognized that the modification of roles, relationships, and expectations within an organization can greatly assist management in altering behavioral patterns within the organization in a direction which contributes to organizational effectiveness.

A review of the literature in the field of organizational change reveals numerous studies supporting both the behavioral and technological approaches to planned change. However, fewer studies have been made which support the effectiveness of the structural approach in accomplishing a desired change. This does not imply that the structural approach to planned change is a relatively new and untested field, it merely suggests that the organization structure has only recently been recognized as a dynamic element subject to extensive study and continual modification.

The roles, relationships, and expectations within the on-going organization can be altered in at least three different ways: *personnel replacement, structural modification,* and *administrative guidance changes.* Although few studies specifically examine the effectiveness of the structural approach to planned change, the results of three studies, which have investigated the structural approach to planned change, have been well documented and will be presented to support the utility of this approach.

Personnel Replacement

The personnel replacement approach to planned change focuses on replacing key personnel in the organization while leaving the present organization and administrative structure intact. The replacement of key personnel modifies the role demands of personnel reporting to the replacement thereby bringing about a change in organizational relationships.

A study by Robert H. Guest in 1961 reported the changes that took place in an automobile assembly plant with the replacement of the top man in the plant. Before the implementation of this structural change, the plant was in serious trouble. Performance of the plant was poor and expressions of hostility and discouragement were heard at all levels of the organization. The plant manager was replaced and virtually all other organizational variables remained constant. There was not wholesale replacement of other key managers nor did the new plant manager "toughen" company policies. The replacement of this key

person in the assembly plant resulted in a more efficient operation and the expressions of hostility and discouragement practically disappeared.[14]

Although managers have known intuitively that replacement of key personnel in organizations can significantly alter the operations of an organization,[15] few scientific studies have been made of the effectiveness of the personnel replacement approach to organizational change. Guest's study provides us the opportunity to examine a situation in which an organization was changed in a desired direction through primarily changing only one key man. All other variables had remained virtually unchanged. This suggests that the mere replacement of one "good" executive with another "good" executive (for example, executive rotation) may be an appropriate method of continually upgrading the organization, as well as a beneficial method of upgrading executives.

Structural Modification

The structural modification approach to planned structural change reconstitutes role demands in an organization through the redefinition of organizational relationships. The modification of the organization structure may be accomplished through such tactics as decentralization or centralization, elimination or addition of staff elements, broadening or narrowing spans of control, relocating decision making authority, redefining communication channels, and so forth. Structural modification presumes that current personnel and administrative guidance in the organization are adequate, but that the current structural arrangement of the organization is detrimental to goal accomplishment.

O'Connell reported on a study in 1968 which examined a structural modification of a large multioffice insurance company. The company had problems of climbing expenses and lagging premium growth. The firm undertook a program of decentralization which encompassed a new marketing strategy to place the best resources in the most promising markets. Crucial to the change program was the transformation of a staff position (assistant manager) in the branch offices to a first line supervisory position. The study pinpointed that the modification of the organization structure to include a first line supervisor in each branch office to perform more personal supervision was critical to the success of the planned change program. The change program generally obtained the changes desired. Performance indices showed relative success in improving business results. Control of expenses generally improved and net new premiums increased.[16]

Modification of the organization structure in the past has typically been for the purposes of discovering the optimal arrangement of structural elements which will accomplish highest productivity. It is possible that optimality of organization structure may not be a static arrangement of organization elements but a flexible arrangement that can be continually modified to accommodate external changes in the environment and initiate internal changes in the organization. The basic concept of the matrix organization, which establishes a flexible organization whereby different structural arrangements can be temporarily set up to handle particular problems, is an example of formalizing this approach to planned change.[17] The intuitive practical manager has recognized the need for flexibility in organizations and has often postulated a practice of continual structural change, just to maintain organizational flexibility.

Administrative Guidance Changes

The administrative guidance change approach to planned structural change assumes that present personnel and organization structure are capable of implementing a given change once it is introduced into the system. New administrative guidance (such as policies, procedures, budgets, and so forth) is developed and implemented to reconstitute role demands in order to bring about a desired change. However, since inertia is greater in an organizational system when personnel and organization design changes are not made, administrative guidance changes are sometimes less likely to bring about an intended change. Adequate enforcement machinery is required to insure that the new role demands will be carried out by present employees.

Don Hellriegel and the author in 1971 reported on a study of the federal government's efforts to accomplish equality of opportunity through policy and procedure changes. Three different policy based planned change programs were implemented to accomplish equality of opportunity. The first program (1883–1940) relied upon the good intentions of federal officials in carrying out the provisions of a merit system to insure racial equality. This effort resulted in widespread, overt, racial discrimination in federal employment. The second program (1940–1961) enacted specific policies prohibiting discrimination in federal employment and established administrative procedures to investigate acts of overt discrimination. This program resulted in significant accomplishments in the employment but not advancement of minority employees. The third program (1961–1971), which required affirmative action by local officials to insure equality of opportunity, resulted in significant accomplishments in both employment and advancement of minority employees. It appears that as the enforcement procedures increased in these administrative guidance change programs, the effectiveness of the change program increased.[18]

Management must carefully establish adequate enforcement processes in administrative guidance change programs to insure that permanent shifts occur in organizational expectations. Some administrative changes, such as budget changes, automatically incorporate an enforcement process into the change program. However, in many other administrative guidance change programs (for example, new policies and procedures), the reinforcement of new organizational roles, relationships, and expectations become the most problematic phase of the change effort. Union grievance channels, as well as the judicial system, are packed with cases exemplifying lower level management's disregard for established organizational policies and procedures.[19]

The structural approach to planned change emphasizes modification of roles, relationships, and expectations to bring about changes in an organization. Although managers have utilized the techniques of personnel replacement, structural modification, and administrative guidance change to accomplish change

for many years, the primary objective of this approach in the past often has been to find the most optimal arrangement of organization variables. I suggest that these three approaches to structural change may be considered as additional techniques available to a change agent in assisting him to move the organization in a desired direction. In a dynamic environment there may be no permanently optimal structural arrangement. Therefore, the intelligent use of the personnel replacement, structural modification and/or administrative guidance approaches to planned change may be beneficial to assist management in the alteration of the behavior of individuals or groups within the organization in a direction desired by management. Needless to say, additional research is needed to study the various structural approaches to planned change and their influence on organizational effectiveness before a determination can be made that the structural approach is truly a valuable and versatile tool that can be used to accomplish organization change.

SUMMARY

A program of planned organizational change is affected by a number of factors. First, the basic planning premises of the change agent, which are influenced by the change agent's personal focus and organizational role, will guide the entire change program. Next, the intervention strategies utilized in the planned change program must be carefully selected to fit the role and focus of the change agent and be appropriately introduced into the organization to provide the greatest opportunity for success. Lastly, the actual change program must be designed to insure that the program progresses through all stages of the change process. The program must include appropriate emphasis on the unfreezing of old behavioral patterns, the relearning of new patterns, and the refreezing of these new patterns into the everyday working environment.

Three different intervention strategies are available to the change agent to assist him in accomplishing organizational change. The technological approach to planned change utilizes scientific and technological advancements to bring about economic efficiencies. The behavioral approach to planned change utilizes behavioral science knowledge to adapt or improve man himself. The structural approach to planned change attempts to bring about organizational efficiencies through modification of roles, relationships, and expectations within the organization. Although substantial research has been conducted which documents the success of technological and behavioral approaches to planned change in improving organizational performance, little rigorous research has been conducted which supports the use of structural approaches in planned change programs. A much deeper understanding by organization theorists is needed in the various structural approaches to planned change to assist in distinguishing between the proper and improper uses of structural change.

REFERENCES

1. WILLIAM F. GLUECK, "Organization Changes in Business and Government," *Academy of Management,* December 1969, p. 489.
2. JEREMIAH J. O'CONNELL, *Managing Organizational Innovation* (Homewood, Illinois: Richard D. Irwin, Inc., 1968), p. 1.
3. My concern for the structural approach to planned change is not a result of the preponderance of empirical research supporting the effectiveness of this approach, but rather the lack of such evidence and my own personal belief of its usefulness.
4. WARREN G. BENNIS, KENNETH D. BENNE, and ROBERT CHIN, *The Planning of Change,* 2d ed. (New York: Holt, Rinehart and Winston, Inc., 1969), p. 139.
5. Ibid., pp. 141–42.
6. Ibid., p. 142.
7. O'CONNELL, *Managing Organizational Innovation,* p. 10.
8. HAROLD J. LEAVITT, "Applied Organizational Change in Industry: Structural, Technical, and Human Approaches," *Organizational Change and Development,* ed., GENE W. DALTON, PAUL R. LAWRENCE, and LARRY E. GREINER (Homewood, Illinois: Richard D. Irwin, Inc., 1970), pp. 198–212.
9. LARRY E. GREINER and LOUIS B. BARNES, "Organization Change and Development," pp. 3–12.
10. KURT LEWIN, "Frontier in Group Dynamics: Concept, Method and Reality in Social Science; Social Equilibrium and Social Change," *Human Relations,* June 1947, pp. 5–41.
11. An example of this type of program is described by ROBERT N. FORD, "Job Enrichment Lessons from AT&T," *Harvard Business Review,* January-February 1973, pp. 96–106.
12. "Ergonomics — New Angle on Employee Health and Safety," *Management Review,* December 1967, pp. 47–50.
13. A good review of the effectiveness of sensitivity training is presented by ROBERT J. HOUSE, "T-Group Education and Leadership Effectiveness: A Review of the Empiric Literature and Critical Evaluation," *Personnel Psychology,*

Spring 1967.

14. ROBERT H. GUEST, *Organizational Change, The Effects of Successful Leadership* (Homewood, Illinois: Richard D. Irwin, 1962).

15. Some popular writers even suggest changing key executives in an organization on a regular basis. Note ROBERT TOWNSEND, *Up the Organization* (Greenwich, Conn: Fawcett Publications, Inc., 1970).

16. O'CONNELL, *Managing Innovation,* pp. 119–144.

17. JOHN F. MEE, "Matrix Organization," *Systems Organizations, Analysis, Management: A Book of Readings,* ed., DAVID L. CLELAND and WILLIAM R. KING (New York: McGraw-Hill Book Company,

1969), pp. 23–25, provides a brief but comprehensive description of matrix organization.

18. DON HELLRIEGEL and LARRY SHORT, "Equal Employment Opportunity in the Federal Government: A Comparative Analysis," *Public Administrative Review,* November-December 1972, pp. 851–58.

19. An interesting example of the magnitude of problems that may be encountered through inadequate reinforcement of organizational expectations is reported by CLARENCE C. WALTON and FREDERICK W. CLEVELAND, JR., *Corporations on Trial: The Electric Cases* (Belmont, California: Wadsworth Publishing Company, Inc., 1964).

HOW TO DEAL WITH RESISTANCE TO CHANGE

Paul R. Lawrence

One of the most baffling and recalcitrant of the problems which business executives face is employee resistance to change. Such resistance may take a number of forms — persistent reduction in output, increase in the number of "quits" and requests for transfer, chronic quarrels, sullen hostility, wildcat or slowdown strikes, and, of course, the expression of a lot of pseudological reasons why the change will not work. Even the more petty forms of this resistance can be troublesome.

All too often when executives encounter resistance to change, they "explain" it by quoting the cliché that "people resist change" and never look further. Yet changes must continually occur in industry. This applies with particular force to the all-important "little" changes that constantly take place — changes in work methods, in routine office procedures, in the location of a machine or a desk, in personnel assignments and job titles. No one of these changes makes the headlines, but in total they account for much of our increase in productivity. They are not the spectacular once-in-a-lifetime technological revolutions that involve mass layoffs or the obsolescence of traditional skills, but they are vital to business progress.

Does it follow, therefore, that business management is forever saddled with the onerous job of "forcing" change down the throats of resistant people? My answer is *no*. It is the thesis of this article that people do *not* resist technical change as such and that most of the resistance which does occur is unnecessary. I shall discuss these points, among others:

1. A solution which has become increasingly popular for dealing with resistance to change is to get the people involved to "participate" in making the change. But as a practical matter "participation" as a device is not a good way for management to think about the problem. In fact, it may lead to trouble.
2. The key to the problem is to understand the true nature of resistance. Actually, what employees resist is usually not technical change but social change — the change in their human relationships that generally accompanies technical change.
3. Resistance is usually created because of certain blind spots and attitudes which staff specialists have as a result of their preoccupation with the technical aspects of new ideas.
4. Management can take concrete steps to deal constructively with these staff attitudes. The steps include emphasizing new standards of performance for staff specialists and encouraging them to think in different ways, as well as making use of the fact that signs of resistance can serve as a practical warning signal in directing and timing technological changes.
5. Top executives can also make their own efforts more effective at meetings of staff and operating groups where change is being discussed. They can do

this by shifting their attention from the facts of schedules, technical details, work assignments, and so forth, to what the discussion of these items indicates about developing resistances and receptiveness to change.

Let us begin by taking a look at some recent research into the nature of resistance to change. There are two studies in particular that I should like to discuss. They highlight contrasting ways of interpreting resistance to change and of coping with it in day-to-day administration.

IS PARTICIPATION ENOUGH?

The first study was conducted by Lester Coch and John R. P. French, Jr., in a clothing factory.[1] It deserves special comment because, it seems to me, it is the most systematic study of the phenomenon of resistance to change that has been made in a factory setting. To describe it briefly:

The two researchers worked with four different groups of factory operators who were being paid on a modified piece-rate basis. For each of these four groups a minor change in the work procedure was installed by a different method, and the results were carefully recorded to see what, if any, problems of resistance occurred. The four experimental groups were roughly matched with respect to efficiency ratings and degree of cohesiveness; in each group the proposed change modified the established work procedure about the same degree.

The work change was introduced to the first group by what the researchers called a "no-participation" method. This small group of operators was called into a room where some staff people told

---

[1]See Lester Coch and John R. P. French, Jr., "Overcoming Resistance to Change," *Human Relations,* Vol. I, No. 4, 1948, p. 512.

the members that there was a need for a minor methods change in their work procedures. The staff people then explained the change to the operators in detail, and gave them the reasons for the change. The operators were then sent back to the job with instructions to work in accordance with the new method.

The second group of operators was introduced to the work change by a "participation-through-representation" method — a variation of the approach used with the third and fourth groups, which turned out to be of little significance.

The third and fourth groups of operators were both introduced to the work change on a "total-participation" basis. All the operators in these groups met with the staff men concerned. The staff men dramatically demonstrated the need for cost reduction. A general agreement was reached that some savings could be effected. The groups then discussed how existing work methods could be improved and unnecessary operations eliminated. When the new work methods were agreed on, all the operators were trained in the new methods, and all were observed by the time-study men for purposes of establishing a new piece rate on the job.

Research Findings

The researchers reported a marked contrast between the results achieved by the different methods of introducing this change.

No-Participation Group. The most striking difference was between Group #1, the no-participation group, and Groups #3 and #4, the total-participation groups. The output of Group #1 dropped immediately to about two-thirds of its previous output rate. The output rate stayed at about this level throughout the period of 30 days after the change was introduced. The re-

searchers further reported:

> Resistance developed almost immediately after the change occurred. Marked expressions of aggression against management occurred, such as conflict with the methods engineer, ... hostility toward the supervisor, deliberate restriction of production, and lack of cooperation with the supervisor. There were 17% quits in the first 40 days. Grievances were filed about piece rates; but when the rate was checked, it was found to be a little "loose."

Total-Participation Groups. In contrast with this record, Groups #3 and #4 showed a smaller initial drop in output and a very rapid recovery not only to the previous production rate but to a rate that exceeded the previous rate. In these groups there were no signs of hostility toward the staff people or toward the supervisors, and there were no quits during the experimental period.

Appraisal of Results

Without going into all the researcher's decisions based on these experiments, it can be fairly stated that they concluded that resistance to methods changes could be overcome by *getting the people involved in the change to participate in making it.*

This was a very useful study, but the results are likely to leave the manager of a factory still bothered by the question, "Where do we go from here?" The trouble centers around that word "participation." It is not a new word. It is seen often in management journals, heard often in management discussions. In fact, the idea that it is a good thing to get employee participation in making changes has become almost axiomatic in management circles.

But participation is not something

that can be conjured up or created arti-
ficially. You obviously cannot buy it as
you would buy a typewriter. You cannot
hire industrial engineers and accountants and other staff people who have
the ability "to get participation" built
into them. It is doubtful how helpful it
would be to call in a group of supervisors and staff men and exhort
them, "Get in there and start
participation."

Participation is a feeling on the part
of people, not just the mechanical act of
being called in to take part in discussions. Common sense would suggest
that people are more likely to respond to
the way they are customarily treated —
say, as people whose opinions are respected because they themselves are respected for their own worth — rather
than by the stratagem of being called to
a meeting or asked some carefully calculated questions. In fact, many supervisors and staff men have had some unhappy experiences with executives who
have read about participation and have
picked it up as a new psychological gim-
mick for getting other people to think
they "want" to do as they are told — as
a sure way to put the sugar coating on a
bitter pill.

So there is still the problem of how
to get this thing called participation.
And, as a matter of fact, the question
remains whether participation was the
determining factor in the Coch and
French experiment or whether there was
something of deeper significance underlying it.

RESISTANCE TO WHAT?

Now let us take a look at a second series
of research findings about resistance to
change. Recently, while making some
research observations in a factory manufacturing electronic products, a colleague and I had an opportunity to
observe a number of incidents that for
us threw new light on this matter of
resistance to change.[2] One incident was
particularly illuminating:

We were observing the work of one
of the industrial engineers and a production operator who had been assigned to
work with the engineer on assembling
and testing an experimental product
that the engineer was developing. The
engineer and the operator were in
almost constant daily contact in their
work. It was a common occurrence for
the engineer to suggest an idea for some
modification in a part of the new product; he would then discuss his idea with
the operator and ask her to try out the
change to see how it worked. It was also
a common occurrence for the operator to
get an idea as she assembled parts and
to pass this idea on to the engineer, who
would then consider it and, on occasion,
ask the operator to try out the idea and
see if it proved useful.

A typical exchange between these
two people might run somewhat as follows:

Engineer: "I got to thinking last night
about that difficulty we've been having
on assembling the x part in the last few
days. It occurred to me that we might
get around that trouble if we washed

---

[2]For a complete report of the study, see Harriet O. Ronken and Paul R. Lawrence,
Administering Changes: A Case Study of Human Relations in a Factory (Boston,
Division of Research, Harvard Business School, 1952).

the part in a cleaning solution just prior to assembling it."

Operator: "Well, that sounds to me like it's worth trying."

Engineer: "I'll get you some of the right kind of cleaning solution, and why don't you try doing that with about 50 parts and keep track of what happens."

Operator: "Sure, I'll keep track of it and let you know how it works."

With this episode in mind, let us take a look at a second episode involving the same production operator. One day we noticed another engineer approaching the production operator. We knew that this particular engineer had had no previous contact with the production operator. He had been asked to take a look at one specific problem on the new product because of his special technical qualifications. He had decided to make a change in one of the parts of the product to eliminate the problem, and he had prepared some of these parts using his new method. Here is what happened.

> He walked up to the production operator with the new parts in his hand and indicated to her by a gesture that he wanted her to try assembling some units using his new part. The operator picked up one of the parts and proceeded to assemble it. We noticed that she did not handle the part with her usual care. After she had assembled the product, she tested it and it failed to pass inspection. She turned to the new engineer and, with a triumphant air, said, "It doesn't work."
>
> The new engineer indicated that she should try another part. She did so, and again it did not work. She then proceeded to assemble units using all of the new parts that were available. She handled each of them in an unusually rough manner. None of them worked. Again she turned to the engineer and said that the new parts did not work.
>
> The engineer left, and later the

operator, with evident satisfaction, commented to the original industrial engineer that the new engineer's idea was just no good.

Social Change

What can we learn from these episodes? To begin, it will be useful for our purposes to think of change as having both a technical and a social aspect. The *technical* aspect of the change is the making of a measurable modification in the physical routines of the job. The *social* aspect of the change refers to the way those affected by it think it will alter their established relationships in the organization.

We can clarify this distinction by referring to the two foregoing episodes. In both of them, the technical aspects of the changes introduced were virtually identical: the operator was asked to use a slightly changed part in assembling the finished product. By contrast, the social aspects of the changes were quite different.

In the first episode, the interaction between the industrial engineer and the operator tended to sustain the give-and-take kind of relationship that these two people were accustomed to. The operator was used to being treated as a person with some valuable skills and knowledge and some sense of responsibility about her work; when the engineer approached her with his idea, she felt she was being dealt with in the usual way. But, in the second episode, the new engineer was introducing not only a technical change but also a change in the operator's customary way of relating herself to others in the organization. By his brusque manner and by his lack of any explanation, he led the operator to fear that her usual work relationships were being changed. And she just did not like the new way she was being treated.

The results of these two episodes were quite different also. In the first episode there were no symptoms of resistance to change, a very good chance that the experimental change would determine fairly whether a cleaning solution would improve product quality, and a willingness on the part of the operator to accept future changes when the industrial engineer suggested them. In the second episode, however, there were signs of resistance to change (the operator's careless handling of parts and her satisfaction in their failure to work), failure to prove whether the modified part was an improvement or not, and indications that the operator would resist any further changes by the engineer. We might summarize the two contrasting patterns of human behavior in the two episodes in graphic form; see Exhibit 1.

It is apparent from these two patterns that the variable that determines the result is the *social* aspect of the change. In other words, the operator did not resist the technical change as such but rather the accompanying change in her human relationships.

Confirmation

This conclusion is based on more than one case. Many other cases in our research project substantiate it. Furthermore, we can find confirmation in the research experience of Coch and French, even though they came out with a different interpretation.

Coch and French tell us in their report that the procedure used with Group #1, the no-participation group, was the usual one in the factory for introducing work changes. And yet they also tell us something about the customary treatment of the operators in their work life. For example, the company's labor relations policies are progressive, the company and the supervisors place a high value on fair and open dealings with the employees, and the employees are encouraged to take up their problems and grievances with management. Also, the

	Change		
	Technical aspect	**Social aspect**	**Results**
Episode 1	Clean part prior to assembly	Sustaining the customary work relationship of operator	1. No resistance 2. Useful technical result 3. Readiness for more change
Episode 2	Use new part in assembly	Threatening the customary work relationship of operator	1. Signs of resistance 2. No useful technical result 3. Lack of readiness for more change

EXHIBIT 1 • Two Contrasting Patterns of Human Behavior

operators are accustomed to measuring the success and failure of themselves as operators against the company's standard output figures.

Now compare these *customary* work relationships with the way the Group #1 operators were treated when they were introduced to this particular work change. There is quite a difference. When the management called them into the room for indoctrination, they were treated as if they had no useful knowledge of their own jobs. In effect, they were told that they were not the skilled and efficient operators they had thought they were, that they were doing the job inefficiently, and that some "outsider" (the staff expert) would now tell them how to do it right. How could they construe this experience *except* as a threatening change in their usual working relationship? It is the story of the second episode in our research case all over again. The results were also the same, with signs of resistance, persistently low output, and so on.

Now consider experimental Groups #3 and #4, the total-participation groups. Coch and French referred to management's approach in their case as a "new" method of introducing change, but from the point of view of the *operators* it must not have seemed new at all. It was simply a continuation of the way they were ordinarily dealt with in the course of their regular work. And what happened? The results — reception to change, technical improvement, better performance — were much like those reported in the first episode between the operator and the industrial engineer.

So the research data of Coch and French tend to confirm the conclusion that the nature and size of the technical aspect of the change does not determine the presence or absence of resistance nearly so much as does the social aspect of the change.

ROOTS OF TROUBLE

The significance of these research findings, from management's point of view, is that executives and staff experts need, not expertness in using the devices of participation, but a real understanding, in depth and detail, of the specific social arrangements that will be sustained or threatened by the change or by the way in which it is introduced.

These observations check with everyday management experience in industry. When we stop to think about it, we know that many changes occur in our factories without a bit of resistance. We know that people who are working closely with one another continually swap ideas about short cuts and minor changes in procedure that are adopted so easily and naturally that we seldom notice them or even think of them as change. The point is that because these people work so closely with one another, they intuitively understand and take account of the existing social arrangements for work and so feel no threat to themselves in such everyday changes.

By contrast, management actions leading to what we commonly label "change" are usually initiated outside the small work group by staff people. These are the changes that we notice and the ones that most frequently bring on symptoms of resistance. By the very nature of their work, most of our staff specialists in industry do not have the intimate contact with operating groups that allows them to acquire an intuitive understanding of the complex social arrangements which their ideas may affect. Neither do our staff specialists always have the day-to-day dealings with operating people that lead them to develop a natural respect for the knowledge and skill of these people. As a result, all too often the staff men behave in a way that threatens and disrupts the established social relationships. And the tragedy is that so many of these upsets are inadvertent and unnecessary.

Yet industry must have its specialists — not only many kinds of engineering specialists (product, process, maintenance, quality, and safety engineers) but also cost accountants, production schedulers, purchasing agents, and personnel men. Must top management therefore reconcile itself to continual resistance to change, or can it take constructive action to meet the problem?

I believe that our research in various factory situations indicates why resistance to change occurs and what management can do about it. Let us take the "why" factors first.

Self-Preoccupation

All too frequently we see staff specialists who bring to their work certain blind spots that get them into trouble when they initiate change with operating people. One such blind spot is "self-preoccupation." The staff man gets so engrossed in the technology of the change he is interested in promoting that he becomes wholly oblivious to different kinds of things that may be bothering people. Here are two examples:

- In one situation the staff people introduced, with the best of intentions, a technological change which inadvertently deprived a number of skilled operators of much of the satisfaction that they were finding in their work. Among other things, the change meant that, whereas formerly the output of each operator had been placed beside his work position where it could be viewed and appreciated by him and by others, it was now being carried away immediately from the work position. The workmen did not like this.

  The sad part of it was that there was no compelling cost or technical reason why the output could not be placed beside the work position as it had been formerly. But the staff people who had introduced the change were so literal-minded about their ideas that when they heard complaints on the changes from the operators, they could not comprehend what the trouble was. Instead, they began repeating all the logical arguments why the change made sense from a cost standpoint. The final result here was a chronic restriction of output and persistent hostility on the part of the operators.

- An industrial engineer undertook to introduce some methods changes in one department with the notion firmly in mind that this assignment presented him with an opportunity to "prove" to higher management the value of his function. He became so preoccupied with his personal desire to make a name for his particular techniques that he failed to pay any attention to some fairly obvious and practical considerations which the operating people were calling to his attention but which did not show up in his time-study techniques. As could be expected, resistance quickly developed to all his ideas, and the only "name" that he finally won for his techniques was a black one.

Obviously, in both of these situations the staff specialists involved did not take into account the social aspects of the change they were introducing. For different reasons they got so preoccupied with the technical aspects of the change that they literally could not see or understand what all the fuss was about.

We may sometimes wish that the validity of the technical aspect of the change were the sole determinant of its acceptability. But the fact remains that the social aspect is what determines the presence or absence of resistance. Just as ignoring this fact is the sure way to trouble, so taking advantage of it can lead to positive results. We must not forget that these same social arrangements that at times seem so bothersome are essential for the performance of work. Without a network of established social relationships a factory would be populated with a collection of people who had no idea of how to work with one another in an organized fashion. By working *with* this network instead of *against* it, management's staff representatives can give new technological ideas a better chance of acceptance.

Operators' Know-How Overlooked

Another blind spot of many staff specialists is to the strengths as well as to the weaknesses of firsthand production experience. They do not recognize that the production foreman and the production operator are in their own way specialists themselves — specialists in actual experience with production problems. This point should be obvious, but it is amazing how many staff specialists fail to appreciate the fact that even though they themselves may have a superior knowledge of the technology of the production process involved, the foreman or the operators may have a

more practical understanding of how to get daily production out of a group of men and machines.

The experience of the operating people frequently equips them to be of real help to staff specialists on at least two counts: (1) The operating people are often able to spot practical production difficulties in the ideas of the specialists — and iron out those difficulties before it is too late. (2) The operating people are often able to take advantage of their intimate acquaintance with the existing social arrangements for getting work done. If given a chance, they can use this kind of knowledge to help detect those parts of the change that will have undesirable social consequences. The staff experts can then go to work on ways to avoid the trouble area without materially affecting the technical worth of the change.

Further, some staff specialists have yet to learn the truth that, even after the plans for a change have been carefully made, it takes *time* to put the change successfully into production use. Time is necessary even though there may be no resistance to the change itself. The operators must develop the skill needed to use new methods and new equipment efficiently; there are always bugs to be taken out of a new method or piece of equipment even with the best of engineering. When a staff man begins to lose his patience with the amount of time that these steps take, the people he is working with will begin to feel that he is pushing them; *this* amounts to a change in their customary work relationships, and resistance will start building up where there was none before.

The situation is aggravated if the

staff man mistakenly accuses the operators of resisting the idea of change, for there are few things that irritate people more than to be blamed for resisting change when actually they are doing their best to learn a difficult new procedure.

MANAGEMENT ACTION

Many of the problems of resistance to change arise around certain kinds of *attitudes* that staff men are liable to develop about their jobs and their own ideas for introducing change. Fortunately, management can influence these attitudes and thus deal with the problems at their source.

Broadening Staff Interests

It is fairly common for a staff man to work so hard on one of his ideas for change that he comes to identify himself with it. This is fine for the organization when he is working on the idea by himself or with his immediate colleagues; the idea becomes "his baby," and the company benefits from his complete devotion to his work.

But when he goes to some group of operating people to introduce a change, his very identification with his ideas tends to make him unreceptive to any suggestions for modification. He just does not feel like letting anyone else tamper with his pet ideas. It is easy to see, of course, how this attitude is interpreted by operating people as a lack of respect for their suggestions.

This problem of the staff man's extreme identification with his work is one which, to some extent, can only be cured by time. But here are four suggestions for speeding up the process:

1. The manager can often, with wise timing, encourage the staff man's interest in a different project that is just starting.
2. The manager can also, by his "coaching" as well as by example, prod the staff man to develop a healthier respect for the contributions he can receive from operating people; success in this area would, of course, virtually solve the problem.
3. It also helps if the staff man can be guided to recognize that the satisfaction he derives from being productive and creative is the same satisfaction he denies the operating people by his behavior toward them. Experience shows that staff people can sometimes be stimulated by the thought of finding satisfaction in sharing with others in the organization the pleasures of being creative.
4. Sometimes, too, the staff man can be led to see that winning acceptance of his ideas through better understanding and handling of human beings is just as challenging and rewarding as giving birth to an idea.

Using Understandable Terms

One of the problems that must be overcome arises from the fact that the typical staff man is likely to have the attitude that the reasons why he is recommending any given change may be so complicated and specialized that it is impossible to explain them to operating people. It may be true that the operating people would find it next to impossible to understand some of the staff man's analytical techniques, but this does not keep them from coming to the conclusion that the staff specialist is trying to razzle-dazzle them with tricky figures and formulas — insulting their intelligence — if he does not strive to his utmost to translate his ideas into terms understandable to them. The following case illustrates the importance of this point:

> A staff specialist was temporarily successful in "selling" a change based on a complicated mathematical formula to a foreman who really did not understand it. The whole thing backfired, however, when the foreman tried to sell it to his operating people. They asked him a couple of sharp questions that he could not answer. His embarrassment about this led him to resent and resist the change so much that eventually the whole proposition fell through. This was unfortunate in terms not only of human relations but also of technological progress in the plant.

There are some very good reasons, both technical and social, why the staff man should be interested in working with the operating people until his recommendations make "sense." (This does not mean that the operating people need to understand the recommendations in quite the same way or in the same detail that the staff man does, but that they should be able to visualize the recommendations in terms of their job experiences.) Failure of the staff man to provide an adequate explanation is likely to mean that a job the operators had formerly performed with understanding and satisfaction will now be performed without understanding and with less satisfaction.

This loss of satisfaction not only concerns the individual involved but also is significant from the standpoint of the company which is trying to get maximum productivity from the operating people. A person who does not have a feeling of comprehension of what he is doing is denied the opportunity to exercise that uniquely human ability — the ability to use informed and intelligent

judgment on what he does. If the staff man leaves the operating people with a sense of confusion, they will also be left unhappy and less productive.

Top line and staff executives responsible for the operation should make it a point, therefore, to know how the staff man goes about installing a change. They can do this by asking discerning questions when he reports to them, listening closely to reports of employee reaction, and, if they have the opportunity, actually watching the staff man at work. At times they may have to take such drastic action as insisting that the time of installation of a proposed change be postponed until the operators are ready for it. But, for the most part, straightforward discussions with the staff man in terms of what they think of his approach should help him, over a period of time, to learn what is expected of him in his relationships with operating personnel.

New Look at Resistance

Another attitude that gets staff men into trouble is the *expectation* that all the people involved will resist the change. It is curious but true that the staff man who goes into his job with the conviction that people are going to resist any idea he presents with blind stubbornness is likely to find them responding just the way he thinks they will. The process is clear: whenever he treats the people who are supposed to buy his ideas as if they were bullheaded, he changes the way they are used to being treated; and they *will* be bullheaded in resisting *that* change!

I think that the staff man — and management in general — will do better to look at it this way: When resistance *does* appear, it should not be thought of as something to be *overcome*. Instead, it can best be thought of as a useful red flag — a signal that something is going wrong. To use a rough analogy, signs of resistance in a social organization are useful in the same way that pain is useful to the body as a signal that some bodily functions are getting out of adjustment.

The resistance, like the pain, does not tell what is wrong but only that something *is* wrong. And it makes no more sense to try to overcome such resistance than it does to take a pain killer without diagnosing the bodily ailment. Therefore, when resistance appears, it is time to listen carefully to find out what the trouble is. What is needed is not a long harangue on the logics of the new recommendations but a careful exploration of the difficulty.

It may happen that the problem is some technical imperfection in the change that can be readily corrected. More than likely, it will turn out that the change is threatening and upsetting some of the established social arrangements for doing work. Whether the trouble is easy or difficult to correct, management will at least know what it is dealing with.

New Job Definition

Finally, some staff specialists get themselves in trouble because they assume they have the answer in the thought that people will accept a change when they have participated in making it. For example:

> In one plant we visited, an engineer confided to us (obviously because we, as researchers on human relations, were interested in psychological gimmicks!)

that he was going to put across a proposed production layout change of his by inserting in it a rather obvious error, which others could then suggest should be corrected. We attended the meeting where this stunt was performed, and superficially it worked. Somebody caught the error, proposed that it be corrected, and our engineer immediately "bought" the suggestion as a very worthwhile one and made the change. The group then seemed to "buy" his entire layout proposal.

It looked like an effective technique — oh, so easy — until later, when we became better acquainted with the people in the plant. Then we found out that many of the engineer's colleagues considered him a phony and did not trust him. The resistance they put up to his ideas was very subtle, yet even more real and difficult for management to deal with.

Participation will never work so long as it is treated as a device to get somebody else to do what you want him to. Real participation is based on respect. And respect is not acquired by just trying; it is acquired when the staff man faces the reality that he needs the contributions of the operating people.

If the staff man defines his job as not just generating ideas but also getting those ideas into practical operation, he will recognize his real dependence on the contributions of the operating people. He will ask them for ideas and suggestions, not in a backhanded way to get compliance, but in a straightforward way to get some good ideas and avoid some unneccessary mistakes. By this process he will be treating the operating people in such a way that his own behavior will not be perceived as a threat to their customary work relationships. It will be possible to discuss, and accept or reject the ideas on their own merit.

The staff specialist who looks at the process introducing change and at resistance to change in the manner outlined in the preceding pages may not be hailed as a genius, but he can be counted on in installing a steady flow of technical changes that will cut costs and improve quality without upsetting the organization.

ROLE OF THE ADMINISTRATOR

Now what about the way the top executive goes about his *own* job as it involves the introduction of change and problems of resistance?

One of the most important things he can do, of course, is to deal with staff people in much the same way that he wants them to deal with the operators. He must realize that staff people resist social change, too. (This means, among other things, that he should not prescribe particular rules to them on the basis of this article!)

But most important, I think, is the way the administrator conceives of his job in coordinating the work of the different staff and line groups involved in a change. Does he think of his duties *primarily* as checking up, delegating and following through, applying pressure when performance fails to measure up? Or does he think of them *primarily* as facilitating communication and understanding between people with different points of view — for example, between a staff engineering group and a production group who do not see eye to eye on a change they are both involved in? An analysis of management's actual experience — or, at least, that part of it which has been covered by our research — points to the latter as the more effective concept of administration.

I do not mean that the executive should spend his time with the different people concerned discussing the human problems of change as such. He *should* discuss schedules, technical details, work assignments, and so forth. But he should also be watching closely for the messages that are passing back and forth as people discuss these topics. He will find that people — himself as well as others — are always implicitly asking and making answers to questions like: "How will he accept criticism?" "How much can I afford to tell him?" "Does he really get my point?" "Is he playing games?" The answers to such questions determine the degree of candor and the amount of understanding between the people involved.

When the administrator concerns himself with these problems and acts to facilitate understanding, there will be less logrolling and more sense of common purpose, fewer words and better understanding, less anxiety and more acceptance of criticism, less griping and more attention to specific problems — in short, better performance in putting new ideas for technological change into effect.

THE MANAGEMENT OF CHANGE PART THREE: PLANNING AND IMPLEMENTING CHANGE

Paul Hersey and Kenneth H. Blanchard

In evaluating effectiveness, perhaps more than 90 percent of managers in organizations look at measures of output alone. Thus, the effectiveness of a business manager is often determined by net profits, the effectiveness of a college professor may be determined by the number of articles and books he has published, and the effectiveness of an athletic coach may be determined by his won-lost record.

Others feel that it is unrealistic to think only in terms of productivity or output in evaluating effectiveness. According to Rensis Likert,[13]* another set of variables should be taken into consideration in determining effectiveness. These are *intervening variables* which reflect the current condition of the human resources in an organization and are represented in its skills, loyalty, commitment to objectives, motivations, communications, decision-making and capacity for effective interaction. These intervening variables are concerned with building and developing the organization and tend to be long-term considerations. Managers are often promoted, however, on the basis of short-run output variables such as increased production and earnings, without concern for the long-run and organizational development. This creates a dilemma.

ORGANIZATIONAL DILEMMA

One of the major problems in industry today is that there is a shortage of successful managers. Therefore, it is not uncommon for a manager to be promoted in six months or a year if he is a "producer." Let's look at the example of Mr. X, a manager who realizes that the basis on which top management promotes is often short-run output, and therefore attempts to achieve high levels of productivity by over-emphasizing task accomplishment and placing extreme pressure on everyone, even when it is inappropriate.

The immediate or short-run effect of Mr. X's behavior will probably be increased productivity. Yet if his task-oriented style is inappropriate for those involved, and if it continues over a long period, the morale and climate of the organization will deteriorate. Some indications of deterioration resulting from these intervening variables may be turnover, absenteeism, increased accidents, scrap loss and numerous grievances. Not only the number of grievances, but the nature of grievances is important. Are grievances really significant problems or do they reflect pent-up emotions due to anxieties and frustration? Are they settled at the complaint stage between the employee and supervisor or are they pushed up the hierarchy to be settled at higher levels or by arbitration? The organizational dilemma is that in many instances a manager like Mr. X, who places pressure on everyone and produces in the short run, is promoted out of this situation before the disruptive aspects of the intervening variables catch up.

TIME LAG

There tends to be a time lag between declining intervening variables and significant restriction of output by employees under such management climate. Employees tend to feel "things will get better." Thus, when Mr. X. is promoted rapidly, he often stays "one step ahead of the wolf."

The real problem is faced by the next manager, Mr. Y. Although productivity records are high, he has inherited many problems. Merely the introduction of a new manager may be enough to collapse the slowly deteriorating intervening variables. A tremendous drop in morale and motivation leading almost immediately to significant decrease in output can occur. Change by its very nature is frightening; to a group whose intervening variables are declining, it can be devastating.

Regardless of Mr. Y's style, the present expectations of the followers may be so distorted, that much time and patience will be needed to close the now apparent "credibility gap" between the goals of the organization and the personal goals of the group. No matter how effective Mr. Y might be in the long run, his superiors, in reviewing a productivity drop, may give him only a few months to improve performance. But as Likert's studies indicate, rebuilding a group's intervening variables in a small organization may take one to three years, and in a large organization, may extend to seven years.

SHORT AND LONG TERM

It should be made clear that the choice for a manager is not whether to concentrate on output or intervening variables but often a matter of how much emphasis to place on each. The decision is between short- and long-range goals. If the accepted goal is building and developing an organization for the future, then the manager should be evaluated on these terms and not entirely on his present productivity.

While intervening variables do not appear on balance sheets, sales reports or accounting ledgers, we feel that these long-term considerations can be just as important to an organization as short-term output variables. Therefore, although difficult to measure, intervening variables should not be overlooked in determining organizational effectiveness.

In summary, we feel that effectiveness is actually determined by whatever the manager and the organization decide are their goals and objectives, but should consider these factors: output variables, intervening variables, short-range goals and long-range goals.

FORCE FIELD ANALYSIS

Force field analysis, a technique for

diagnosing situations developed by Kurt Lewin, may be useful in looking at the variables involved in determining effectiveness and in developing strategies for changing in particular the condition of the output or intervening variables.[14]

Lewin assumes that in any situation there are both driving and restraining forces which influence any change which may occur. *Driving forces* are those forces affecting a situation which are "pushing" in a particular direction; they tend to initiate a change and keep it going. In terms of improving productivity in a work group, pressure from a supervisor, incentive earnings and competition may be examples of driving forces. *Restraining forces* are forces acting to restrain or decrease the driving forces. Apathy, hostility and poor maintenance of equipment may be examples of restraining forces against increased production. Equilibrium is reached when the sum of the driving forces equals the sum of the restraining forces. In our example, equilibrium represents the present level of productivity as shown in Figure 1.

This equilibrium or present level of productivity can be raised or lowered by changes in the relationship between the driving and restraining forces. For illustrations, let us look again at the dilemma of Mr. Y, the new manager who takes over a work group where productivity is high but Mr. X, his predecessor, drained the human resources (intervening variables). Mr. X had upset the equilibrium by increasing the driving forces (i.e., being autocratic and keeping continual pressure on his men) and thus achieving increases in output in the short run. By doing this though, new restraining forces developed, such

as increased hostility and antagonism, and at the time of his departure the restraining forces were beginning to increase and the results manifested themselves in turnover, absenteeism and other restraining forces which lowered productivity shortly after Mr. Y arrived. Now a new equilibrium at a significantly lowered productivity is faced by the new manager.

Now just assume that Mr. Y decides not to increase the driving forces, but to reduce the restraining forces. He may do this by taking time away from the usual production operation and engaging in problem-solving and training and development. In the short run, output will tend to be lowered still further. However, if commitment to objectives and technical know-how of his group are increased in the long run, they may become new driving forces, and that, along with the elimination of the hostility and apathy which were restraining forces, will now tend to move the bal-

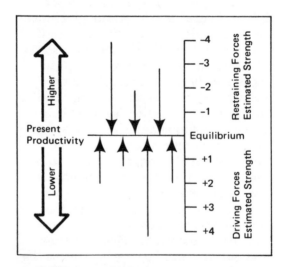

FIGURE 1 • *Driving and Restraining Forces in Equilibrium*

ance to a higher level of output.

A manager, in attempting to implement change, is often in a position where he must consider not only output but also intervening variables, not only short-term but also long-term goals, and a framework which is useful in diagnosing these interrelationships is available through force field analysis.

PROCESS OF CHANGE

In developing a change strategy, another important aspect that must be taken into consideration is the process of change. Kurt Lewin, in his pioneer work in change, identified three phases of the change process.[15] These are unfreezing, changing and refreezing.

UNFREEZING

The aim of unfreezing is to motivate and make the individual or group ready to change. It is a "thawing out" process where the forces acting on an individual are rearranged so now he sees the need for change. According to Edgar H. Schein, some elements that unfreezing situations seem to have in common are: (1) the physical removal of the individual being changed from his accustomed routines, sources of information and social relationships; (2) the undermining and destruction of all social supports; (3) demeaning and humiliating experience to help the individual being changed to see his old self as unworthy and thus to be motivated to change; (4) the consistent linking of reward with willingness to change and of punishment with unwillingness to change.[16]

In brief, unfreezing is the breaking down of the mores, customs, and tradi-

tions of an individual — the old ways of doing things so he is ready to accept new alternatives. In terms of force field analysis, unfreezing may occur when either the driving forces are increased or the restraining forces that are resisting change are reduced.

CHANGING

Once the individual has become motivated to change, he is now ready to be provided with new patterns of behavior. This process is most likely to occur by one of two mechanisms; identification and internalization.[17] *Identification* occurs when one or more models are provided in the environment from whom an individual can learn new behavior patterns by identifying with them and trying to become like them. *Internalization* occurs when an individual is placed in a situation where new behaviors are demanded of him if he is to operate successfully in that situation. He learns these new behavior patterns not only because they are necessary to survive but as a result of new high strength needs induced by coping behavior.

> Internalization is a more common outcome in those influence settings where the direction of change is left more to the individual. The influence which occurs in programs such as Alcoholics Anonymous, in psychotherapy or counseling for hospitalized or incarcerated populations, in religious retreats, in human relations training of the kind pursued by the National Training Laboratories (1953), and in certain kinds of progressive education programs is more likely to occur through internalization or, at least, to lead ultimately to more internalization.[18]

Identification and internalization are not either/or courses of action and effective change is often the result of combining the two into a strategy for change.

Force or compliance is sometimes discussed as another mechanism for inducing change.[19] It occurs when an individual is forced to change by the direct manipulation of rewards and punishment by someone in a power position. In this case, behavior appears to have changed when the change agent is present, but often is dropped when supervision is removed. Thus, rather than discussing force as a mechanism of changing, we would rather think of it as a tool for unfreezing.

REFREEZING

The process by which the newly-acquired behavior comes to be integrated as patterned behavior into the individual's personality and/or ongoing significant emotional relationships is referred to as *refreezing*. As Schein contends, if the new behavior has been internalized while being learned, "this has automatically facilitated refreezing because it has been fitted naturally into the individual's personality. If it has been learned through identification, it will persist only so long as the target's relationship with the original influence model persistspkss new surrogate models are found or social support and reinforcement is obtained for expressions of the new attitudes."[20]

This highlights how important it is for an individual engaged in a change process to be in an environment which is continually reinforcing the desired change. The effect of many a training program has been short-lived when the person returns to an environment that does not reinforce the new patterns or, even worse, is hostile toward them.

What we are concerned about in refreezing is that the new behavior does not get extinguished over time. To insure this not happening, reinforcement (rewards and incenives) must be scheduled in an effective way. There seem to be two main reinforcement schedules: continuous and intermittent.[21] Continuous reinforcement means that the individual being changed is rewarded every time he engages in the desired new pattern. With intermittent reinforcement on the other hand, not every desired response is reinforced. Reinforcement can be either completely random or scheduled according to a prescribed number of responses occurring or a particular interval of time elapsing before reinforcement is given.

With continuous reinforcement, the individual learns the new behavior quickly, but if his environment changes to one of nonreinforcement, extinction (elimination of the behavior) can be expected to take place relatively soon. With intermittent reinforcement, extinction is much slower because the individual has been conditioned to go for periods of time without any reinforcement. Thus for fast learning, a continuous reinforcement schedule should be used. But once the individual has learned the new pattern, a switch to intermittent reinforcement should insure a long lasting change.

CHANGE PROCESS — SOME EXAMPLES

To see the change process in operation, several examples could be cited.

A college basketball coach recruited

for his team Bob Anderson, a 6′ 4″ center from a small town in a rural area. In his district, 6′ 4″ was a good height for a college center. This fact, combined with his deadly turn-around-jump shot, made Anderson the rage of his league and enabled him to average close to 30 points a game.

Recognizing that 6′ 4″ is small for a college center, the coach hoped that he could make Anderson a forward, moving him inside only when they were playing a double pivot. One of the things the coach was concerned about, however, was when Anderson would be used in the pivot, how he could get his jump shot off when he came up against other players ranging in height from 6′ 8″ to 7′. He felt that Anderson would have to learn to shoot a hook shot, which is much harder to block, if he was going to have scoring potential against this kind of competition.

The approach that many coaches use to solve this problem would probably be as follows: The first day of practice when Anderson arrived, the coach would welcome Anderson and then explain the problem to him as he had analyzed it. As a solution he would probably ask Anderson to start to work with the varsity center, Steve Cram, who was 6′ 10″ and had an excellent hook. "Steve can help you start working on that new shot, Bob," the coach would say. Anderson's reaction to this interchange might be one of resentment and he would go over and work with Cram only because of the coach's position power. After all, he might think to himself, "Who does he think he is? I've been averaging close to 30 points a game for three years now and the first day I show up here the coach wants me to learn a new shot." So

he may start to work with Cram reluctantly, concentrating on the hook shot only when the coach is looking but taking his favorite jump shot when he wasn't being observed. Anderson is by no means unfrozen or ready to learn to shoot another way.

ANOTHER APPROACH

Let's look at another approach the coach could have used to solve this problem. Suppose on the first day of practice he sets up a scrimmage between the varsity and freshmen. Before he starts the scrimmage he gets big Steve Cram, the varsity center, aside and tells him, "Steve, we have this new freshman named Anderson who has real potential to be a fine ball player. What I'd like you to do today though, is not to worry about scoring or rebounding, just make sure every time Anderson goes up for a shot you make him eat it. I want him to see that he will have to learn to shoot some other shots if he is to survive against guys like you."

So when the scrimmage starts, the first time Anderson gets the ball and turns around to shoot Cram leaps up and "stuffs the ball right down his throat." Time after time this occurs. Soon Anderson starts to engage in some coping behavior, trying to fall away from the basket, shooting from the side of his head rather than the front, in an attempt to get his shot off.

After the scrimmage, Anderson comes off the court dejected. The coach says, "What's wrong Bob?" He replies, "I don't know, Coach, I just can't seem to get my shot off against a man as big as Cram. What do you think I should do, Coach?" he asks. "Well, Bob, why don't you go over and start working with Steve on a hook shot. I think you'll find it much harder to block. And with your shooting eye I don't think it will take long for you to learn." How do you think Anderson feels about working with Cram now? He's enthusiastic and ready to learn. Having been placed in a situation where he learns for himself that he has a problem, Anderson is already in the process of unfreezing his past patterns of behavior. Now he's ready for identification. He has had an opportunity to internalize his problem and is ready to work with Steve Cram.

So often the leader who has knowledge of an existing problem forgets that until the people involved recognize the problem as their own, it is going to be much more difficult to produce change in their behavior. Internalization and identification are not either/or alternatives but can be parts of developing specific change strategies appropriate to the situation.

THE MILITARY EXAMPLE

Another example of the change processes in operation can be seen in the military, particularly in the induction phase. There are probably few organizations that have entering their ranks people who are less motivated and committed to the organization than the recruits the military gets. Yet in a few short months, they are able to mold these men into a relatively effective combat team. This is not an accident. Let's look at some of the processes that help accomplish this.

The most dramatic and harsh aspects of the training are the unfreezing phase. All four of the elements that

Schein claims unfreezing situations have in common are present. A specific example follows.

1. The recruits are *physically removed from their accustomed routines, sources of information and social relationships* in the isolation of a place such as Parris Island.

   During this first week of training at Parris Island, the recruit is . . . hermetically sealed in a hostile environment, required to rise at 4:55 a.m., do exhausting exercises, attend classes on strange subjects, drill for hours in the hot sun, eat meals in silence and stand at rigid attention the rest of the time; he has no television, no radio, no candy, no coke, no beer, no telephone — and can write letters only during one hour of free time a day.[22]

2. *The undermining and destruction of social supports* is one of the DI's (Drill Instructor) tasks. "Using their voices and the threat of extra PT (physical training), the DI . . . must shock the recruit out of the emotional stability of home, pool hall, street corner, girl friend or school."[23]

3. *Demeaning and humiliating experiences* are commonplace during the first two weeks of the training as the DI's help the recruits *see themselves as unworthy and thus motivated to change* into what they want a Marine to be. "It's a total shock . . . Carrying full seabags, 80 terrified privates are herded into their 'barn,' a barracks floor with 40 double-decker bunks. Sixteen hours a day, for two weeks, they will do nothing right."[24]

4. *Throughout the training there is consistent linking of reward with willingness to change and punishment with unwillingness to change.*

   Rebels or laggards are sent to the Motivation Platoon to get "squared away." A day at Motivation combines constant harassment and PT (physical training), ending the day with the infiltration course. This hot, 225-yard ordeal of crawling, jumping and screaming through ditches and obstacles is climaxed by recruits dragging two 30-pound ammo boxes 60 yards in mud and water. If he falters he starts again. At the end, the privates are lined up and asked if they are ready to go back to their home platoons . . . almost all go back for good.[25]

While the recruits go through a severe unfreezing process, they quickly move to the changing phase, first identifying with the DI and then emulating informal leaders, as they develop. "Toward the end of the third week a break occurs. What one DI calls 'that five per cent — the slow fat, dumb or difficult' have been dropped. The remaining recruits have emerged from their first-week vacuum with one passionate desire — to stay with their platoon at all costs."[26]

Internalization takes place when the recruits through their forced interactions develop different high strength needs. "Fear of the DI gives way to respect, and survival evolves into achievement toward the end of training." "I learned I had more guts than I imagined" is a typical comment.[27]

Since the group tends to stay together throughout the entire program, it serves as a positive reinforcer which can help refreeze the new behavior.

IMPACT OF CHANGE ON TOTAL SYSTEM

The focus in [this three-part] article has been on the management of human resources and as a result we have spent little time on how technical change can have an impact on the total system. And yet, the importance of combining the social and technical into a unified

social systems concept is stressed by Robert Guest.

On his part the social scientist often makes the error of concentrating on human motivation and group behavior without fully accounting for the technical environment which circumscribes, even determines, the roles which the actors play. Motivation, group structure, interaction processes, authority — none of these abstractions of behavior take place in a technological vacuum.[28]

A dramatic example of the consequences of introducing technical change and ignoring its consequences on the social system is the case of the introduction of the steel axe to a group of Australian aborigines.[29]

This tribe remained considerably isolated, both geographically and socially, from the influence of Western cultures. In fact, their only contact was an Anglican mission established in the adjacent territory.

The polished stone axe was a traditionally basic part of the tribe's technology. Used by men, women and children, the stone axe was vital to the subsistence economy. But more than that, it was actually a key to the smooth running of the social system; it defined interpersonal relationships and was a symbol of masculinity and male superiority. "Only an adult male could make and own a stone axe; a woman or a child had to ask his permission to obtain one."[30]

The Anglican mission in an effort to help improve the situation of the aborigines introduced the steel axe, a product of European technology. It was given indiscriminately to men, women and children. Because the tool was more efficient than the stone axe, it was readily accepted but it produced severe repercussions unforeseen by the missionaries or the tribe. As Stephan R. Cain reports:

> The adult male was unable to make the steel axe and no longer had to make the stone axe. Consequently, his exclusive axe-making ability was no longer a necessary or desirable skill, and his status as sole possessor and dispenser of a vital element of technology was lost. The most drastic overall result was that traditional values, beliefs, and attitudes were unintentionally undermined.[31]

This example illustrates that an organization is an "open social system," that is, all aspects of an organization may have an impact on other parts or the organization itself. Thus a proposed change in one part of an organization must be carefully assessed in terms of its likely impact on the rest of the organization.

REFERENCES

13. LIKERT, RENSIS, *New Patterns of Management*, McGraw-Hill, New York, 1961, p. 7.
14. LEWIN, KURT, "Frontiers in Group Dynamics: Concept, Method and Reality in Social Science; Social Equilibria and Social Change," *Human Relations*, Vol. 1, No. 1, June, 1947, pp. 5–41.
15. Ibid
16. SCHEIN, EDGAR H., "Management Development as a Process of Influence" in DAVID R. HAMPTON, *Behavioral Concepts in Management*, Dickinson Publishing Co., Belmont, Cal., 1968, p. 110. Reprinted from the *Industrial Management Review*, Vol. II, No. 2, May, 1961, pp. 59–77.
17. The mechanisms are taken from H. C. KELMAN "Compliance, Identification and Internalization: Three Processes of Attitude Change," *Conflict Resolution*, 1958, II, pp. 51–60.
18. SCHEIN, op. cit., p. 112.
19. KELMAN discussed compliance as a third mechanism for attitude change.
20. SCHEIN, op cit., p. 112.
21. See C. B. FERSTER and B. F. SKINNER, *Schedules of Reinforcement*, Appleton-Century-Crofts, New York, 1957.
22. "Marine Machine," *Look Magazine*, Aug. 12, 1969.
23. Ibid.
24. Ibid.
25. Ibid.
26. Ibid.
27. Ibid.
28. GUEST, op. cit. p. 4.
29. SHARP, LAURISTON, "Steel Axes for Stone Age Australians," in *Human Problems in Technological Change*, ed. EDWARD H. SPICER, Russell Sage Foundation, New York, 1952, pp. 69–94.
30. CAIN, STEPHEN R., "Anthropology and Change," taken from *Growth and Change*, Vol. 1, No. 3, July, 1970, University of Kentucky.
31. Ibid.

DICK SPENCER

CASE 1

After the usual banter when old friends meet for cocktails, the conversation between a couple of University professors and Dick Spencer, a former student who was now a successful businessman, turned to Dick's life as a vice-president of a large manufacturing firm.

"I've made a lot of mistakes, most of which I could live with, but this one series of incidents was so frustrating that I could have cried at the time," Dick said in response to a question. "I really have to laugh at how ridiculous it is now, but at the time I blew my cork."

Spencer was plant manager of Modrow Company, a Canadian branch of the Tri-American Corporation. Tri-American was a major producer of primary aluminum with integrated operations ranging from the mining of bauxite through the processing to fabrication of aluminum into a variety of products. The company also made and sold refractories and industrial chemicals. The

parent company had wholly-owned subsidiaries in five separate United States locations and had foreign affiliates in 15 different countries.

Tri-American mined bauxite in the Jamaican West Indies and shipped the raw material by commercial vessels to two plants in Louisiana where it was processed into alumina. The alumina was then shipped to reduction plants in one of three locations for conversion into primary aluminum. Most of the primary aluminum was then moved to the companies' fabricating plants for further processing. Fabricated aluminum items included sheet, flat, coil, and corrugated products; siding; and roofing.

Tri-American employed approximately 22,000 employees in the total organization. The company was governed by a board of directors which included the chairman, vice-chairman, president, and twelve vice-presidents. However, each of the subsidiaries and branches functioned as independent units. The board set general policy, which was then interpreted and applied by the various plant managers. In a sense, the various plants competed with one another as though they were independent companies. This decentralization in organizational structure increased the freedom and authority of the plant managers, but increased the pressure for profitability.

The Modrow branch was located in a border town in Canada. The total work force in Modrow was 1,000. This Canadian subsidiary was primarily a fabricating unit. Its main products were foil and building products such as roofing

This case was developed and prepared by Professor Margaret E. Fenn, Graduate School of Business Administration, University of Washington. Reprinted by permission.

and siding. Aluminum products were gaining in importance in architectural plans, and increased sales were predicted for this branch. Its location and its stable work force were the most important advantages it possessed.

In anticipation of estimated increases in building product sales, Modrow had recently completed a modernization and expansion project. At the same time, their research and art departments combined talents in developing a series of twelve new patterns of siding which were being introduced to the market. Modernization and pattern development had been costly undertakings, but the expected return on investment made the project feasible. However, the plant manager, who was a Tri-American vice-president, had instituted a campaign to cut expenses wherever possible. In his introductory notice of the campaign, he emphasized that cost reduction would be the personal aim of every employee at Modrow.

Salesman: The plant manager of Modrow, Dick Spencer, was an American who had been transferred to this Canadian branch two years previously, after the start of the modernization plan. Dick had been with the Tri-American Company for 14 years, and his progress within the organization was considered spectacular by those who knew him well. Dick had received a Master's degree in Business Administration from a well-known university at the age of 22. Upon graduation he had accepted a job as salesman for Tri-American. During his first year as a salesman, he succeeded in landing a single, large contract which put him near the top of the sales-volume leaders. In discussing his phenomenal rise in the

sales volume, several of his fellow salesmen concluded that his looks, charm, and ability on the golf course contributed as much to his success as his knowledge of the business or his ability to sell the products.

The second year of his sales career, he continued to set a fast pace. Although his record set difficult goals for the other salesmen, he was considered a "regular guy" by them, and both he and they seemed to enjoy the few occasions when they socialized. However, by the end of the second year of constant travelling and selling, Dick began to experience some doubt about his future.

His constant involvement in business affairs disrupted his marital life, and his wife divorced him during the second year with Tri-American. Dick resented her action at first, but gradually seemed to recognize that his career at present depended on his freedom to travel unencumbered. During that second year, he ranged far and wide in his sales territory, and succesfully closed several large contracts. None of them was as large as his first year's major sale, but in total volume he again was well up near the top of salesmen for the year. Dick's name became well known in the corporate headquarters, and he was spoken of as "the boy to watch."

Dick had met the president of Tri-American during his first year as a salesman at a company conference. After three days of golfing and socializing they developed a relaxed camaraderie considered unusual by those who observed the developing friendship. Although their contacts were infrequent after the conference, their easy relationship seemed to blossom the few times they did meet. Dick's friends kidded him about his ability to make use of his new friendship to promote himself in the company, but Dick brushed aside their jibes and insisted that he'd make it on his own abilities, not someone's coattail.

By the time he was 25, Dick began to suspect that he did not look forward to a life as a salesman for the rest of his career. He talked about his unrest with his friends, and they suggested that he groom himself for sales manager. "You won't make the kind of money you're making from commissions," he was told, "but you will have a foot in the door from an administrative standpoint, and you won't have to travel quite as much as you do now." Dick took their suggestions lightly, and continued to sell the product, but was aware that he felt dissatisfied and did not seem to get the satisfaction out of his job that he had once enjoyed.

By the end of his third year with the company Dick was convinced that he wanted a change in direction. As usual, he and the president spent quite a bit of time on the golf course during the annual company sales conference. After their match one day, the president kidded Dick about his game. The conversation drifted back to business, and the president, who seemed to be in a jovial mood, started to kid Dick about his sales ability. In a joking way, he implied that anyone could sell a product as good as Tri-American's, but that it took real "guts and know-how" to make the products. The conversation drifted to other things, but this remark struck with Dick.

Sometime later, Dick approached the president formally with a request for a transfer out of the sales division. The president was surprised and hesitant about this change in career direction for Dick. He recognized the superior sales ability that Dick seemed to possess, but was unsure that Dick was willing or able to assume responsibilities in any other division of the organization. Dick sensed the hesitancy, but continued to push his request. He later remarked that it seemed that the initial hesitancy of the president convinced Dick that he needed an opportunity to prove himself in a field other than sales.

Trouble Shooter: Dick was finally transferred back to the home office of the organization and indoctrinated into productive and administrative roles in the company as a special assistant to the senior vice-president of production. As a special assistant, Dick was assigned several trouble-shooting jobs. He acquitted himself well in this role, but in the process succeeded in gaining a reputation as a ruthless head hunter among the branches where he had performed a series of amputations. His reputation as an amiable, genial, easy-going guy from the sales department was the antithesis of the reputation of a cold, calculating head hunter which he earned in his trouble-shooting role. The vice-president, who was Dick's boss, was aware of the reputation which Dick had earned but was pleased with the results that were obtained. The faltering departments that Dick had worked in seemed to bloom with new life and energy after Dick's recommended amputations. As a result, the vice-president began to sing Dick's praises, and the president began to accept Dick in his new role in the company.

Management Responsibility: About

three years after Dick's switch from sales, he was given an assignment as assistant plant manager of an English branch of the company. Dick, who had remarried, moved his wife and family to London, and they attempted to adapt to their new routine. The plant manager was English, as were most of the other employees. Dick and his family were accepted with reservations into the community life as well as into the plant life. The difference between British and American philosophy and performance within the plant was marked for Dick who was imbued with modern managerial concepts and methods. Dick's directives from headquarters were to update and upgrade performance in this branch. However, his power and authority were less than those of his superior, so he constantly found himself in the position of having to soft pedal or withhold suggestions that he would have liked to make, or innovations that he would have liked to introduce. After a frustrating year and a half, Dick was suddenly made plant manager of an old British company which had just been purchased by Tri-American. He left his first English assignment with mixed feelings and moved from London to Birmingham.

As the new plant manager, Dick operated much as he had in his troubleshooting job for the first couple of years of his change from sales to administration. Training and reeducation programs were instituted for all supervisors and managers who survived the initial purge. Methods were studied and simplified or redesigned whenever possible, and new attention was directed toward production which better met the needs of the sales organization. A strong controller helped to straighten out the profit picture through stringent cost control; and, by the end of the third year, the company showed a small profit for the first time in many years. Because he felt that this battle was won, Dick requested transfer back to the United States. This request was partially granted when nine months later he was awarded a junior vice-president title, and was made manager of a subsidiary Canadian plant, Modrow.

Modrow Manager: Prior to Dick's appointment as plant manager at Modrow, extensive plans for plant expansion and improvement had been approved and started. Although he had not been in on the original discussions and plans, he inherited all the problems that accompany large-scale changes in any organization. Construction was slower in completion than originally planned, equipment arrived before the building was finished, employees were upset about the extent of change expected in their work routines with the installation of additional machinery and, in general, morale was at a low ebb.

Various versions of Dick's former activities had preceded him, and on his arrival he was viewed with dubious eyes. The first few months after his arrival were spent in a frenzy of catching up. This entailed constant conferences and meetings, volumes of reading of past reports, becoming acquainted with the civic leaders of the area, and a plethora of dispatches to and from the home office. Costs continued to climb unabated.

By the end of his first year at Modrow, the building program had been completed, although behind schedule, the new equipment had been installed, and some revamping of cost procedures had been incorporated. The financial picture at this time showed a substantial loss, but since it had been budgeted as a loss, this was not surprising. All managers of the various divisions had worked closely with their supervisors and accountants in planning the budget for the following year, and Dick began to emphasize his personal interest in cost reduction.

As he worked through his first year as plant manager, Dick developed the habit of strolling around the organization. He was apt to leave his office and appear anywhere on the plant floor, in the design offices, at the desk of a purchasing agent or accountant, in the plant cafeteria rather than the executive dining room, or wherever there was activity concerned with Modrow. During his strolls he looked, listened, and became acquainted. If he observed activities which he wanted to talk about, or heard remarks that gave him clues to future action, he did not reveal these at the time. Rather he had a nod, a wave, a smile, for the people near him, but a mental note to talk to his supervisors, managers, and foremen in the future. At first his presence disturbed those who noted him coming and going, but after several exposures to him without any noticeable effect, the workers came to accept his presence and continue their usual activities. Supervisors, managers, and foremen, however, did not feel as comfortable when they saw him in the area.

Their feelings were aptly expressed by the manager of the siding department one day when he was talking to one of his foremen: "I wish to hell he'd stay up in the front office where he belongs. Whoever heard of a plant manager who had time to wander around the plant all the time? Why doesn't he tend to his paper work and let us tend to our business?"

"Don't let him get you down," joked the foreman. "Nothing ever comes of his visits. Maybe he's just lonesome and looking for a friend. You know how these Americans are."

"Well, you may feel that nothing ever comes of his visits, but I don't. I've been called into his office three separate times within the last two months. The heat must really be on from the head office. You know these conferences we have every month where he reviews our financial progress, our building progress, our design progress, etc.? Well, we're not really progressing as fast as we should be. If you ask me we're in for continuing trouble."

In recalling his first year at Modrow, Dick had felt constantly pressured and badgered. He always sensed that the Canadians he worked with resented his presence since he was brought in over the heads of the operating staff. At the same time he felt this subtle resistance from his Canadian work force, he believed that the president and his friends in the home office were constantly on the alert, waiting for Dick to prove himself or fall flat on his face. Because of the constant pressures and demands of the work, he had literally dumped his family into a new community and had withdrawn into the plant. In the process, he built up a wall of resistance toward the demands of his wife and children who, in turn, felt as though he was abandoning them.

During the course of the conversation with his University friends, he began to recall a series of incidents that probably had resulted from the conflicting pressures. When describing some of these incidents, he continued to emphasize the fact that his attempt to be relaxed and casual had backfired. Laughingly, Dick said, "As you know, both human relations and accounting were my weakest subjects during the Master's program, and yet they are two fields I felt I needed the most at Modrow at this time." He described some of the cost procedures that he would have liked to incorporate. However, without the support and knowledge furnished by his former controller, he busied himself with details that were unneccessary. One day, as he describes it, he overheard a conversation between two of the accounting staff members with whom he had been working very closely. One of them commented to the other, "For a guy who's a vice-president, he sure spends a lot of time breathing down our necks. Why doesn't he simply tell us the kind of systems he would like to try, and let us do the experimenting and work out the budget?" Without commenting on the conversation he overheard, Dick then described himself as attempting to spend less time and be less directive in the accounting department.

Another incident he described which apparently had real meaning for him was one in which he had called a staff conference with his top-level managers. They had been going "hammer and tongs" for better than an hour in his private office, and in the process of heated conversation had loosened ties, taken off coats, and really rolled up their sleeves. Dick himself had slipped out of his shoes. In the midst of this,

his secretary reminded him of an appointment with public officials. Dick had rapidly finished up his conference with his managers, straightened his tie, donned his coat, and had wandered out into the main office in his stocking feet.

Dick fully described several incidents when he had disappointed, frustrated, or confused his wife and family by forgetting birthdays, appointments, dinner engagements, etc. He seemed to be describing a pattern of behavior which resulted from continuing pressure and frustration. He was setting the scene to describe his baffling and humiliating position in the siding department. In looking back and recalling his activities during this first year, Dick commented on the fact that his frequent wanderings throughout the plant had resulted in a nodding acquaintance with the workers, but probably had also resulted in foremen and supervisors spending more time getting ready for his visits and reading meaning into them afterwards than attending to their specific duties. His attempts to know in detail the accounting procedures being used required long hours of concentration and detailed conversations with the accounting staff, which were time-consuming and very frustrating for him, as well as for them. His lack of attention to his family life resulted in continued pressure from both wife and family.

The Siding Department Incident: Siding was the product which had been budgeted as a large profit item of Modrow. Aluminum siding was gaining in popularity among both architects and builders, because of its possibilities in both decorative and practical uses. Panel sheets of siding were shipped in standard sizes on order; large sheets of the coated siding were cut to specifications in the trim department, packed, and shipped. The trim shop was located near the loading platforms, and Dick often cut through the trim shop on his wanderings through the plant. On one of his frequent trips through the area, he suddenly became aware of the fact that several workers responsible for the disposal function were spending countless hours at high-speed saws cutting scraps into specified lengths to fit into scrap barrels. The narrow bands of scrap which resulted from the trim process varied in length from 7 to 27 feet and had to be reduced in size to fit into the disposal barrels. Dick, in his concentration on cost reduction, picked up one of the thin strips, bent it several times and fitted in into the barrel. He tried this with another piece, and it bent very easily. After assuring himself that bending was possible, he walked over to a worker at the saw and asked why he was using the saw when material could easily be bent and fitted into the barrels, resulting in saving time and equipment. The worker's response was, "We've never done it that way, sir. We've always cut it."

Following his plan of not commenting or discussing matters on the floor, but distressed by the reply, Dick returned to his office and asked the manager of the siding department if he could speak to the foreman of the scrap division. The manager said, "Of course, I'll send him up to you in just a minute."

After a short time, the foreman, very agitated at being called to the plant manager's office, appeared. Dick began questioning him about the scrap disposal process and received the stan-

dard answer: "We've always done it that way." Dick then proceeded to review cost-cutting objectives. He talked about the pliability of the strips of scrap. He called for a few pieces of scrap to demonstrate the ease with which it could be bent, and ended what he thought was a satisfactory conversation by requesting the foreman to order heavy duty gloves for his workers and use the bending process for a trial period of two weeks to check the cost saving possible.

The foreman listened throughout most of this hour's conference, offered several reasons why it wouldn't work, raised some questions about the record-keeping process for cost purposes, and finally left the office with the forced agreement to try the suggested new method of bending, rather than cutting, for disposal. Although he was immersed in many other problems, his request was forcibly brought home one day as he cut through the scrap area. The workers were using power saws to cut scraps. He called the manager of the siding department and questioned him about the process. The manager explained that each foreman was responsible for his own processes, and since Dick had already talked to the foreman, perhaps he had better talk to him again. When the foreman arrived, Dick began to question him. He received a series of excuses, and some explanations of the kinds of problems they were meeting by attempting to bend the scrap material. "I don't care what the problems are," Dick nearly shouted, "when I request a cost-reduction program instituted, I want to see it carried through."

Dick was furious. When the foreman left, he phoned the maintenance department and ordered the removal of the power saws from the scrap area immediately. A short time later the foreman of the scrap department knocked on Dick's door reporting his astonishment at having maintenance men step into his area and physically remove the saws. Dick reminded the foreman of his request for a trial at cost reduction to no avail, and ended the conversation by saying that the power saws were gone and would not be returned, and the foreman had damned well better learn to get along without them. After a stormy exit by the foreman, Dick congratulated himself on having solved a problem and turned his attention to other matters.

A few days later Dick cut through the trim department and literally stopped to stare. As he described it, he was completely nonplussed to discover gloved workmen using hand shears to cut each piece of scrap.

SAVEMORE FOOD STORE 5116

CASE 2

The Savemore Corporation is a chain of four hundred retail supermarkets located primarily in the Northeastern section of the United States. Store 5116 employs over fifty persons, all of whom live within suburban Portage, New York, where the store is located.

Wally Shultz served as general manager of store 5116 for six years. Last April he was transferred to another store in the chain. At that time the employees were told by the district manager, Mr. Finnie, that Wally Shultz was being promoted to manage a larger store in another township.

Most of the employees seemed unhappy to lose their old manager. Nearly everyone agreed with the opinion that Shultz was a "good guy to work for." As examples of his desirability as a boss the employees told how Wally had frequently helped the arthritic Negro porter with his floor mopping, how he had shut the store five minutes early each night so that certain employees might catch their busses, of a Christmas party held each year for employees at his own expense, and his general willingness to pitch in. All employees had been on a first-name basis with the manager. About half of them had begun work with the Savemore Corporation when the Portage store was opened.

Wally Shultz was replaced by Clark Raymond. Raymond, about twenty-five

This case was developed and prepared by Professor John W. Hennessey, Jr., Amos Tuck School of Business, Dartmouth College. Reprinted by permission. At the time of this case, the author, a college student, was employed for the summer as a checker and stockboy in store 5116.

years old, was a graduate of an Ivy League college and had been with Savemore a little over one year. After completion of his six-month training program, he served as manager of one of the chain's smaller stores before being advanced to store 5116. In introducing Raymond to the employees, Mr. Finnie stressed his rapid advancement and the profit increase that occurred while Raymond had charge of his last store.

I began my employment in store 5116 early in June. Mr. Raymond was the first person I met in the store, and he impressed me as being more intelligent and efficient than the managers I had worked for in previous summers at other stores. After a brief conversation concerning our respective colleges, he assigned me to a cash register, and I began my duties as a checker and bagger.

In the course of the next month I began to sense that relationships between Raymond and his employees were somewhat strained. This attitude was particularly evident among the older employees of the store, who had worked in store 5116 since its opening. As we all ate our sandwiches together in the cage (an area about twenty feet square in the cellar fenced in by chicken wire, to be used during coffee breaks and lunch hours), I began to question some of the older employees as to why they disliked Mr. Raymond. Laura Morgan, a fellow checker about forty years of age and the mother of two grade-school boys, gave the most specific answers. Her complaints were:

1. Raymond had fired the arthritic Negro porter on the grounds that a porter who "can't mop is no good to the company."
2. Raymond had not employed new help to make up for normal attrition. Because of this, everybody's work load was much heavier than it ever had been before.
3. The new manager made everyone call him "mister . . . he's unfriendly."
4. Raymond didn't pitch in. Wally Shultz had, according to Laura, helped people when they were behind in their work. She said that Shultz had helped her bag on rushed Friday nights when a long line waited at her checkout booth, but "Raymond wouldn't lift a finger if you were dying."
5. Employees were no longer let out early to catch busses. Because of the relative infrequency of this means of transportation, some employees now arrived home up to an hour later.
6. "Young Mr. Know-it-all with his fancy degree . . . takes all the fun out of this place."

Other employees had similar complaints. Gloria, another checker, claimed that, ". . . he sends the company nurse to your home every time you call in sick." Margo, a meat wrapper, remarked "everyone knows how he's having an affair with that new bookkeeper he hired to replace Carol when she quit." Pops Devery, head checker who had been with the chain for over ten years, was perhaps the most vehement of the group. He expressed his views in the following manner: "That new guy's a real louse . . . got a mean streak a mile long. Always trying to cut corners. First it's not enough help, then no overtime, and now, come Saturday mornings, we have to use boxes[1] for the orders 'til the truck

---

[1]The truck from the company warehouse bringing merchandise for sale and store supplies normally arrived at ten o'clock Saturday mornings. Frequently, the stock of large paper bags would be temporarily depleted. It was then necessary to pack orders in cardboard cartons until the truck was unloaded.

arrives. If it wasn't just a year 'til retirement, I'd leave. Things just aren't what they used to be when Wally was around." The last statement was repeated in different forms by many of the other employees. Hearing all this praise of Wally, I was rather surprised when Mr. Finnie dropped the comment to me one morning that Wally had been demoted for inefficiency, and that no one at store 5116 had been told this. It was important that Mr. Shultz save face, Mr. Finnie told me.

A few days later, on Saturday of the busy weekend preceding the July 4 holiday, store 5116 again ran out of paper bags. However, the delivery truck did not arrive at ten o'clock, and by 10:30 the supply of cardboard cartons was also low. Mr. Raymond put in a hurried call to the warehouse. The men there did not know the whereabouts of the truck but promised to get an emergency supply of bags to us around noon. By eleven o'clock, there were no more containers of any type available, and Mr. Raymond reluctantly locked the doors to all further customers. The twenty checkers and packers remained in their respective booths, chatting among themselves. After a few minutes, Mr. Raymond requested that they all retire to the cellar cage because he had a few words for them. As soon as the group was seated on the wooden benches in the chicken wire enclosed area, Mr. Raymond began to speak, his back to the cellar stairs. In what appeared to be an angered tone, he began, "I'm out for myself first, Savemore second, the customer third, and you last. The inefficiency in this store has amazed me from the moment I arrived here. . . ."

At about this time I noticed Mr.

Finnie, the district manager, standing at the head of the cellar stairs. It was not surprising to see him at this time because he usually made three or four unannounced visits to the store each week as part of his regular supervisory procedure. Mr. Raymond, his back turned, had not observed Finnie's entrance.

Mr. Raymond continued, "Contrary to what seems to be the opinion of many of you, the Savemore Corporation is not running a social club here. We're in business for just one thing . . . to make money. One way that we lose money is by closing the store on Saturday morning at eleven o'clock. Another way that we lose money is by using a 60-pound paper bag to do the job of a 20-pound bag. A 60-pound bag costs us over 2 cents apiece; a 20-pound bag costs less than a penny. So when you sell a couple of quarts of milk or a loaf of bread, don't use the big bags. Why do you think we have four different sizes anyway? There's no great intelligence or effort required to pick the right size. So do it. This store wouldn't be closed right now if you'd used your common sense. We started out this week with enough bags to last 'til Monday . . . and they would have lasted 'til Monday if you'd only used your brains. This kind of thing doesn't look good for the store, and it doesn't look good for me. Some of you have been bagging for over five years . . . and you ought'a be able to do it right by now. . ." Mr. Raymond paused and then said, "I trust I've made myself clear on this point."

The cage was silent for a moment, and then Pops Devery, the head checker, spoke up: "Just one thing, Mistuh Raymond. Things were running pretty well before you came around. When Wally was here we never ran out'a bags. The customers never complained about overloaded bags or the bottoms falling out before you got here. What're you gonna tell somebody when they ask for a couple of extra bags to use in garbage cans? What're you gonna tell somebody when they want their groceries in a bag, and not a box? You gonna tell them the manager's too damn cheap to give 'em bags? Is that what you're gonna tell 'em? No sir, things were never like this when Wally Shultz was around. We never had to apologize for a cheap manager who didn't order enough then. What'ta you got to say to that, Mis-tuh Raymond?"

Mr. Raymond, his tone more emphatic, began again. "I've got just one thing to say to that, Mr. Devery, and that's this: store 5116 never did much better than break even when Shultz was

in charge here. I've shown a profit better than the best he ever hit in six years every week since I've been here. You can check that fact in the book upstairs any time you want. If you don't like the way I'm running things around here, there's nobody begging you to stay . . ."

At this point, Pops Devery interrupted and, looking up the stairs at the district manager, asked "What about that, Mr. Finnie? You've been around here as long as I have. You told us how Wally got promoted 'cause he was such a good boss. Supposin' you tell this young fellar here what a good manager is really like? How about that, Mr. Finnie?"

A rather surprised Mr. Raymond turned around to look up the stairs at Mr. Finnie. The manager of store 5116 and his checkers and packers waited for Mr. Finnie's answer.

FORCE FIELD ANALYSIS

INTRODUCTION

In one of the readings in this section, a diagnostic technique for situations involving change was described. Force field analysis, as developed by Kurt Lewin, has proved to be a very useful managerial tool for those involved in implementing change. In this exercise you will get some practice in using this technique in a change situation in which you are currently involved.

PROCEDURE

1. Review the reading noted above so that you are familiar with the concept of force field analysis.
2. Select a change situation *in which you are personally involved.*
3. Apply the force field technique to this situation.

 Specifically, on forms similar to those shown in Figures 1 and 2, do the following:

a. Describe the situation *as it now exists* — in a few words.
b. Describe the situation *as you would like it to be* — in a few words.
c. Identify those forces in the situation that are *driving forces* — forces that are pushing toward the situation as you would like it to be.
d. Identify those forces in the situation that are *restraining forces* — forces that are pushing against the situation as you would like it to be.

 Depending upon the complexity of the situation, a great many forces could be present. Be certain that you identify all of the significant driving and restraining forces that are present in the situation.

 Be very specific in the way that you identify the forces. The more exact and detailed you can be, the easier it will be to work with these forces later on. If you find you have a few very large forces — "the employees are resisting change" — this is a good indication that you have not been specific enough in your analysis. Which employees are resisting? Specifically, what are they doing that is resisting? What specific actions are being taken, etc.?

e. After you have identified the driving and the restraining forces, indicate the *strength* of each force — strong, medium, or weak.

Recognize that this is a value judgment on your part, but it will help to put the forces in perspective.

f. Next, rate the forces in terms of your ability to influence or control them. Again, use the strong, medium, or weak designations. This is a very important step, as it will give you some indication of the more useful places to direct your resources.

g. Develop a specific action plan(s) for each of the forces with which you want to deal.

h. Discussion — your instructor will give you specific directions for this part of the exercise.

FORCE FIELD ANALYSIS

Current situation: Situation as you would like it to be:

Driving Forces   **Restraining Forces**

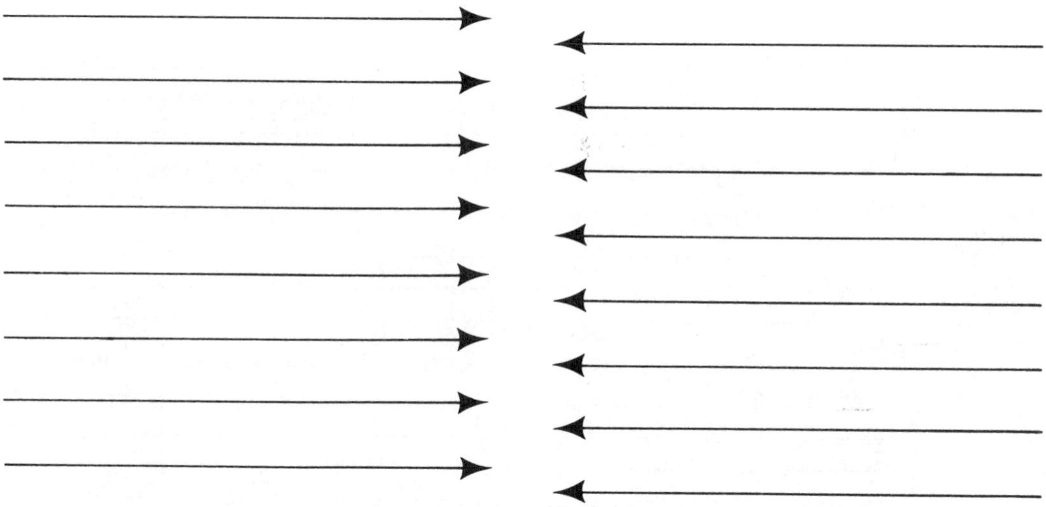

FIGURE 1

Force Field Analysis

Action Plan

Force   (brief description)

_____

_____

_____

Action(s) intended	Date of initiation	Date of completion

Force (brief description)

_____

_____

_____

Action(s) intended	Date of initiation	Date of completion

Force (brief description)

_____

_____

_____

Action(s) intended	Date of initiation	Date of completion

FIGURE 2

EXERCISE 2

ANALYZING CHANGE
IN ORGANIZATIONS

INTRODUCTION

Change is necessary — yet change is resisted. In this exercise you will be asked to describe some change in an organization of your choice. You will also be asked to determine the reasons for the change and the types of resistance encountered.

The necessity for change is often based on technical factors, while resistance to change is often social in character.

Specific reasons for change may include:

1. Need for increased efficiency
2. Changes in the economic picture (positive as well as negative)
3. Growth (or desire for growth)
4. New technology (machiner, processes, reporting systems, etc.)
5. Appointment of a new boss
6. New markets or clients
7. Legal changes, new regulations

Reasons for resistance to change are often based on:

1. Fear of economic loss; e.g., more work for same pay, loss of overtime, etc.
2. Change in perceived security; e.g., possible layoffs, difficulty in learning new routines, etc.
3. Conditions of work; e.g., change in hours, procedures, etc.
4. Job satisfaction; e.g., less challenge, closer supervision, reduction in authority, etc.
5. Social dynamics; e.g., loss of status, group pressure to resist change, requirement to change workmates, etc.
6. Irritation with the way change was handled; e.g., misunderstanding of reasons for change, change made too quickly, not being asked for opinion, etc.
7. Cultural beliefs; e.g., change not consistent with tradition, deep distrust of management, etc.

PROCEDURE

Interview a manager about an organizational change he or she has knowledge of. Review the readings in this part of the text before conducting the interview. Take notes as he or she describes the change and the conditions that precipitated it and the manner in which the change was accepted or resisted. If possible, also interview a worker who participated in the change and elicit his or her description of the change. Then, using the categories above, determine the reasons for the change and the reasons for the resistance. Prepare a report containing your findings, along with recommendations for methods management might have used for avoiding resistance. If no resistance occurred, specify the actions of management and workers that made smooth change possible.